What's on the enclosed CD?

- More than 90 minutes of expert-led video instructi[on]
- Step-by-step training from proven experts
- Simulation exercises which reinforce certification objectives
- Test prep tools to help you prepare for taking the certification exam
- Electronic version of this Study Guide

D0793605

Follow along step-by-step as expert instructors teach you professional skills for job proficiency and the objectives necessary to pass certification exams.

Network Security Issues

| PREV | Windows 2000 Networking Setup | NEXT |

NWLink	Network Connections Control
TCP/IP	TCP/IP Configuration
NetBEUI	DNS & WINS
Bridging Media Types	Advanced TCP/IP Options

GLOSSARY INTERACT

Learn it by doing it

- Real-world scenarios demonstrate best practices
- Animated graphics provide detailed technical instructions
- Expert instructors show you how to do it and why

Special Online Discounts for Osborne Customers!

Because you purchased an Osborne Study Guide, you are entitled to incredible savings on our full line of LearnKey Online training courses.

Save up to 60% on Online Training! Visit www.learnkey.com/osborne Today!

1.800.865.0165 • learnkey.com/osborne

LearnKey

CompTIA A+®
Certification Study Guide,
Seventh Edition

(Exams 220-701 & 220-702)

Jane Holcombe
Charles Holcombe

New York Chicago San Francisco Lisbon London Madrid
Mexico City Milan New Delhi San Juan Seoul Singapore Sydney Toronto

The McGraw·Hill Companies

Library of Congress Cataloging-in-Publication Data

Holcombe, Jane.
   CompTIA A+ : certification study guide : (exams 220-701 & 220-702) /
Jane Holcombe, Charles Holcombe.—7th ed.
       p.   cm.
   ISBN 978-0-07-170145-7 (alk. paper)
   1. Electronic data processing personnel—Certification.
2. Computers—Examinations—Study guides.   3. Computing Technology Industry
Association—Examinations—Study guides.   I. Holcombe, Charles.   II.
Title.   III. Title: CompTIA A plus certification study guide.
   QA76.3.A174   2010
   004—dc22   2010014537

McGraw-Hill books are available at special quantity discounts to use as premiums and sales promotions, or for use in corporate training programs. To contact a representative, please e-mail us at bulksales@mcgraw-hill.com.

CompTIA A+® Certification Study Guide, Seventh Edition
(Exams 220-701 & 220-702)

3456789   DOC DOC   15432

ISBN: Book p/n 978-0-07-170144-0 and CD p/n 978-0-07-170147-1
of set 978-0-07-170145-7
MHID: Book p/n 0-07-170144-3 and CD p/n 0-07-170147-8
of set 0-07-170145-1

Sponsoring Editor Timothy Green	**Acquisitions Coordinator** Meghan Riley	**Proofreader** Susie Elkind	**Composition** Glyph International
Editorial Supervisor Patty Mon	**Technical Editor** Christopher Crayton	**Indexer** Karin Arrigoni	**Illustration** Glyph International
Project Editor LeeAnn Pickrell	**Copy Editor** LeeAnn Pickrell	**Production Supervisor** Jean Bodeaux	**Art Director, Cover** Jeff Weeks

CompTIA Authorized Quality Curriculum

The logo of the CompTIA Authorized Quality Curriculum (CAQC) program and the status of this or other training material as "Authorized" under the CompTIA Authorized Quality Curriculum program signifies that, in CompTIA's opinion, such training material covers the content of CompTIA's related certification exam.

The contents of this training material were created for the CompTIA A+® exams covering CompTIA certification objectives that were current as of March 2010.

CompTIA has not reviewed or approved the accuracy of the contents of this training material and specifically disclaims any warranties of merchantability or fitness for a particular purpose.

CompTIA makes no guarantee concerning the success of persons using any such "Authorized" or other training material in order to prepare for any CompTIA certification exam.

How to Become CompTIA Certified

This training material can help you prepare for and pass a related CompTIA certification exam or exams. In order to achieve CompTIA certification, you must register for and pass a CompTIA certification exam or exams.

In order to become CompTIA certified, you must:

1. Select a certification exam provider. For more information please visit http://www.comptia.org/certifications/testprep/testingcenters.aspx.

2. Register for and schedule a time to take the CompTIA certification exam(s) at a convenient location.

3. Read and sign the Candidate Agreement, which you will receive at the time of the exam(s). You can find the text of the Candidate Agreement at http://www.comptia.org/certifications/policies/agreement.aspx.

4. Take and pass the CompTIA certification exam(s).

For more information about CompTIA's certifications, such as its industry acceptance, benefits, or program news, please visit www.comptia.org/.

CompTIA is a not-for-profit information technology (IT) trade association. CompTIA's certifications are designed by subject-matter experts from across the IT industry. Each CompTIA certification is vendor-neutral, covers multiple technologies, and requires demonstration of skills and knowledge widely sought after by the IT industry.

To contact CompTIA with any questions or comments, please call (1) (630) 678-8300 or email questions@comptia.org.

Jane Holcombe (CompTIA A+, CompTIA Network +, CompTIA CTT+, and Microsoft MCSE) pioneered in the field of PC support training. In 1983, she installed a LAN for her employer, and, commencing in 1984, she was an independent trainer, consultant, and course content author, creating and presenting courses on PC operating systems taught nationwide. She co-authored a set of networking courses for the consulting staff of a large network vendor. In the early 1990s, she worked with both Novell and Microsoft server operating systems, finally focusing on the Microsoft operating systems and achieving early MCSE certification, recertifying for new versions of Windows. Since 2001 she has been the lead author, in collaboration with her husband, of numerous books and book chapters.

Charles Holcombe was a programmer of early computers in both the nuclear and aerospace fields. In his 15 years at Control Data Corporation, he was successively a programmer, technical sales analyst, salesman, and sales manager in the field marketing organization. At corporate headquarters, he ran the Executive Seminar program, served as corporate liaison to the worldwide university community, and was market development manager for Plato, Control Data's computer-based education system.

For the past 30 years, he has been an independent trainer and consultant, authoring and delivering training courses in many disciplines. He is a skilled writer and editor of books and online publications, and he collaborates with his wife, Jane, on many writing projects.

Together, Chuck and Jane Holcombe are a writing team who have authored the MCSE *Guide to Designing a Microsoft Windows 2000 Network Infrastructure* (Course Technology) and both the *A+ Certification Press Lab Manual* and the *MCSE Certification Press Windows 2000 Professional Lab Manual* (McGraw-Hill Professional). They authored two editions of the *Survey of Operating Systems*, the first book in the Michael Meyer's Computer Skills series, and contributed chapters to *The Michael Meyers' Guide to Managing and Troubleshooting PCs, The Michael Meyer's All-in-One A+ Certification Exam Guide, Fifth Edition,* and *Windows 2000 Administration* (McGraw-Hill Professional). They wrote several chapters for the Peter Norton *Introduction to Operating Systems, Sixth Edition* (McGraw-Hill), and rewrote and greatly expanded the *CompTIA A+® Certification Study Guide, Sixth Edition*.

About the Technical Editor

Christopher A. Crayton (MCSE, MCP+I, CompTIA A+, and CompTIA Network+) is an author, technical editor, technical consultant, security consultant, and trainer. Formerly a computer and networking instructor at Keiser College (2001 Teacher of the Year), Chris has also worked as network administrator for Protocol and as a computer and network specialist at Eastman Kodak Headquarters. Chris has authored several print and online books on topics ranging from CompTIA A+ and CompTIA Security+ to Microsoft Windows Vista. Chris has provided technical edits and reviews for many publishers, including McGraw-Hill, Pearson Education, Charles River Media, Cengage Learning, Wiley, O'Reilly, Syngress, and Apress.

About LearnKey

LearnKey provides self-paced learning content and multimedia delivery solutions to enhance personal skills and business productivity. LearnKey claims the largest library of rich streaming-media training content that engages learners in dynamic media-rich instruction complete with video clips, audio, full motion graphics, and animated illustrations. LearnKey can be found on the Web at **www.LearnKey.com**.

CONTENTS AT A GLANCE

1   Personal Computer Components—Motherboards and Processors   1

2   Personal Computer Components—Memory, Storage, and Adapters ...   41

3   Power Supplies, Cooling Systems, and Input/Output   83

4   Installing and Upgrading PC Components   133

5   Troubleshooting, Repair, and Maintenance of PCs   187

6   Installing, Configuring, and Optimizing Laptops   255

7   Troubleshooting and Preventive Maintenance for Laptops   295

8   Operating System Fundamentals   327

9   Installing, Configuring, and Upgrading Operating Systems   371

10   Disk and File Management   415

11   Troubleshooting and Preventive Maintenance for Windows   467

12   Using and Supporting Printers   525

13   Network Basics   575

14   Installing a Small Office/Home Office (SOHO) Network   625

15   Troubleshooting Networks   665

16   Computer Security Fundamentals   701

17   Implementing and Troubleshooting Security   749

18   Operational Procedures   803

A   About the CD   847

     Glossary   851

     Index   909

CONTENTS

Acknowledgments .... *xxv*

Preface .... *xxvii*

Introduction .... *xxxi*

I   Personal Computer Components—
       Motherboards and Processors ....   **I**

Motherboards   3

    Form Factors   4

    Motherboard Components   6

    Chipset   16

    Firmware   16

    Exercise 1-1:   Viewing System Settings in CMOS   19

Processor/CPU   19

    Purposes and Characteristics   20

    CPU Technologies   20

    Manufacturers and Models   25

    Exercise 1-2:   Identifying Your Processor   26

The PC Case   27

    Purpose and Features   28

    Case Form Factors   28

    Case Categories   29

    Case Sizes   29

    ✓   Two-Minute Drill   30

    Q&A   Self Test   33

    Self Test Answers   37

2   Personal Computer Components—
       Memory, Storage, and Adapters **41**

Mass Storage Devices and Backup Media   42

    Magnetic Mass Storage   42

Optical Disc Drives 46

Solid-State Storage 51

Exercise 2-1: Identify Your Storage Devices 53

Hot-Swappable Drives 54

RAID Arrays 54

Removable Storage 56

Backup Media 56

Memory 57

Functional Overview of RAM and ROM Usage 58

RAM Technology 59

Operational Characteristics 64

Exercise 2-2: Calculating the Memory Bank Size 65

Adapter Cards 67

Video Adapter Cards 67

Multimedia Adapter Cards 67

I/O Adapter Cards 68

Communication Adapters 69

Riser Card/Daughter Board 70

Exercise 2-3: Viewing Adapter Cards

in Device Manager 72

✓ Two-Minute Drill 73

Q&A Self Test 75

Self Test Answers 79

**3 Power Supplies, Cooling Systems,
and Input/Output** **83**

Power Supplies 84

Electrical Terminology 85

Voltage 85

Wattage 86

Exercise 3-1: Check Out the Wattage on

PCs and Other Devices 87

Fan 87

AC Adapters 87

Form Factors 87

Cooling Systems 90

CPU and Case Fans 90

Heat Sinks …………………………………………… 90

Thermal Compounds ……………………………… 90

Liquid Cooling Systems ………………………… 91

Case Design …………………………………………… 91

Exercise 3-2: Check Out Your Cooling System ………… 91

Video Adapters and Displays ……………………………………… 92

Video Adapters ……………………………………… 92

Displays ……………………………………………… 96

Display Connectors ………………………………… 99

Display Settings …………………………………… 104

Exercise 3-3: Modifying Display Settings ……………… 105

Input/Output ……………………………………………… 107

Input Devices ……………………………………… 107

Multimedia …………………………………………… 109

Biometric Devices ………………………………… 111

KVM Switches ……………………………………… 111

I/O Interfaces ……………………………………… 112

Classic Multimedia Connectors ………………… 119

Classic Connectors ………………………………… 120

Cables ………………………………………………… 122

✓ Two-Minute Drill ………………………………… 124

Q&A Self Test ………………………………………… 126

Self Test Answers ………………………………… 130

4 Installing and Upgrading PC Components …………… **133**

Motherboards and Onboard Components ………………………… 134

Selecting a Motherboard, CPU, and
Memory Combination …………………………… 135

Replacing a Motherboard ………………………… 135

Installing a Motherboard ………………………… 136

Exercise 4-1: Removing an Old Motherboard …………… 137

Exercise 4-2: Properly Handling and
Installing a Motherboard ………………………… 137

Upgrading a CPU …………………………………… 138

Exercise 4-3: Removing a PGA Processor
from a ZIF Socket ………………………………… 138

Optimizing a System with RAM ………………… 139

Installing and Removing Memory   139
Exercise 4-4:   Installing and Removing a
DIMM or RIMM Module   141
Configuring and Optimizing a Motherboard   142
Exercise 4-5:   Backing Up the BIOS Settings   143
Replacing or Upgrading BIOS   147
Power Supplies   149
Selecting a Power Supply   149
Removing a Power Supply/Installing a Power Supply   149
Exercise 4-6:   Replacing a Power Supply   149
Cooling Systems   150
Common Sense First   150
Selecting an Appropriate Cooling System   151
Installing and Configuring a Cooling System   152
Removing a Cooling System   152
Adapter Cards   153
Selecting an Appropriate Adapter Card   154
Installing and Configuring an Adapter Card   154
Exercise 4-7:   Installing an Adapter Card   154
Removing an Adapter Card   155
Storage Devices   155
Optimizing a PC with Storage Devices   155
Selecting an Appropriate Internal Storage Device   156
Installing Drives on PATA Channels   156
Exercise 4-8:   Choosing a Master   158
Optical Drives   159
Solid-State Storage   160
Installing Drives on SATA Channels   161
Exercise 4-9:   Installing a SATA Drive   161
RAID Arrays   162
Internal Floppy Disk Drives   163
Installing and Configuring SCSI Devices   164
Removing an Internal Storage Device   166
Exercise 4-10:   Removing a Drive   167
Installing and Removing an External Storage Device   167
Preparing a Hard Disk for Use   168

I/O Devices 170
    Selecting an I/O Device 170
    Installing and Removing an I/O Device 170
    Displays 173
    ✓ Two-Minute Drill 176
Q&A Self Test 179
    Self Test Answers 183

5   Troubleshooting, Repair, and Maintenance of PCs 187

Troubleshooting Theory and Techniques 188
    Preparation 188
    Troubleshooting Theory 189
    Exercise 5-1: Troubleshooting with Device Manager 192
    Training 195
Troubleshooting Software Problems 196
    The Quick Fixes: Rebooting, Uninstalling,
       and Reinstalling 196
    Pinpointing the Problem Application 196
    Minimum Requirements 196
    Updates 197
Troubleshooting PC Component Problems 197
    Procedures 197
    Physical Symptoms 198
    POST Audio and Visual Errors 198
    Motherboards 199
    Exercise 5-2: Replacing the CMOS Battery 200
    CPUs 202
    System Resources 203
    I/O Ports and Cards 203
    Storage Devices 209
    Exercise 5-3: Troubleshooting a Drive Failure 210
    Video 217
    Power Supplies 220
    Cooling Systems 222
    Memory 223
    Input Devices 223
    Adapter Cards 224

Troubleshooting Tools 225
    Software Tools 225
        Exercise 5-4: Installing an Inventory Tool 226
        The Hardware Toolkit 227
Preventive Maintenance Techniques 233
    Visual and Audio Inspection 233
    Driver and Firmware Updates 234
    Ensuring a Proper Environment 234
    Providing Good Power 234
    Maintenance and Cleaning of Computer Components 236
        Exercise 5-5: Cleaning a Mouse 238
        Thermally Sensitive Devices 239
    ✓ Two-Minute Drill 242
    Q&A Self Test 245
        Self Test Answers 249

6 Installing, Configuring, and Optimizing Laptops **255**

Introduction to Laptops 256
    Laptops, Notebooks, and Netbooks 257
    Handhelds 258
Installing and Upgrading Laptops 258
    Opening Up a Laptop 258
    Disassembly and Reassembly Processes 259
    Refer to Manufacturer's Documentation 259
    Laptop Replacement Parts 260
    Plastics 260
    Motherboard 261
    CPU 261
    Memory 262
        Exercise 6-1: Installing SODIMM Memory 263
    Fans 264
    Installing Storage Devices 265
    Peripherals 265
    External Expansion Slots 269
    Internal Expansion Slots 272
    Communication Connections 274
    Power and Electrical Input Devices 276
    I/O Devices 278

Power Management 281

    System Management Mode 282

    Configuring Power Management in Windows 283

  ✓ Two-Minute Drill 286

Q&A Self Test 288

    Self Test Answers 292

7 Troubleshooting and Preventive
Maintenance for Laptops **295**

Troubleshooting Laptops 296

    Power Problems 297

    Exercise 7-1: Using a Multimeter to Test
    an AC Adapter 302

    Other Startup Problems 303

    Video Problems 304

    Input Devices 307

    Wireless Problems 311

Preventive Maintenance for Laptops 313

    Transporting and Shipping a Laptop 313

    Cooling Issues 314

    Hardware and Video Cleaning Materials 314

  ✓ Two-Minute Drill 316

Q&A Self Test 318

    Self Test Answers 322

8 Operating System Fundamentals **327**

Introduction to Windows Operating Systems 328

    The Purpose of Operating Systems 329

    Windows Versions, Editions, and Updates 329

    Exercise 8-1: Viewing the Windows Information 333

    32-Bit vs. 64-Bit Windows Operating Systems 333

    Minimum System Requirements 335

    System Limits 336

    Application and Hardware Compatibility 336

    Exercise 8-2: Running Upgrade Advisor 338

    Running Older Applications 339

    Upgrade Paths 341

The Windows User Interface 343

    The Windows Desktop 343

    The Microsoft Management Console (MMC) 355

    Task Manager 356

    Exercise 8-3:   Viewing Running Programs

    in Task Manager 356

    The Registry 357

   ✓ Two-Minute Drill 361

 Q&A Self Test 363

    Self Test Answers 367

9   **Installing, Configuring, and Upgrading
Operating Systems** **371**

Installing Windows 372

    Prepare to Install Windows 372

    Installation Startup and Source Locations 376

    Attended Windows Installation 378

    Unattended Installation 383

    Upgrading Windows 385

    Running an Upgrade 389

Configuring Windows 390

    Network Configuration 391

    Registration and Activation 393

    Updating Windows 395

    Install Additional Applications and

      Windows Components 397

    Installing New Devices 397

    Virtual Memory 400

    Exercise 9-1:   Viewing the Virtual Memory Settings 402

    Power Management 402

   ✓ Two-Minute Drill 405

 Q&A Self Test 407

    Self Test Answers 411

10   Disk and File Management **415**

Disk Management 416
   Disk Storage Types 416
   Exercise 10-1: Viewing the Disk Storage Type 418
   Partitioning Basic Disks 419
Understanding Windows Startup 425
   Windows Startup Phases 425
   The BOOT.INI File and System Startup Settings 430
   Exercise 10-2: Viewing the Contents of BCD
      in Windows Vista or Windows 7 431
File Management 434
   File Systems 434
   Files 439
   Text File Editors 445
   Organizing Files Using Folders 446
   Exercise 10-3: Managing Files and Folders 447
   Exercise 10-4: Managing Directories and
      Files at the Command Prompt 451
   Windows Utilities 452
   Command-Line Utilities 453
   Exercise 10-5: Using the DEFRAG command 453
   Backing Up Data 456
 ✓ Two-Minute Drill 458
Q&A Self Test 460
   Self Test Answers 464

11   Troubleshooting and Preventive
   Maintenance for Windows **467**

Diagnosing and Repairing Operating System Failures 469
   Using the Advanced Options Menu 469
   Exercise 11-1: Working in Safe Mode 476
   System Restore 476
   Recovery Options 479
Operational Problems and Symptoms 484
   OS Instability Problems 484
   Troubleshooting Applications 486
   Common Error Messages 487

Using Diagnostic Utilities and Tools 494

    Documentation Resources 494

    System Information (MSINFO32.EXE) 495

    Device Manager 495

    Exercise 11-2: Getting to Know Device Manager 496

    Task Manager 496

    Task Scheduler 498

    System Configuration Utility (MSCONFIG) 498

    Monitoring Performance 499

    System File Checker (SFC) 500

    Remote Desktop 501

    Remote Assistance 504

    DirectX Diagnostic Tool 506

Performing Preventive Maintenance and Optimization 507

    Defragment Hard Drive Volumes 507

    Tweak Preferences and Display Settings 508

    Modify Indexing Settings 509

    Modify User Account Control 510

    Turn on Automatic Updates 511

    Software Updates 511

    Scheduled Backups 512

    Test Restore 512

    Configure System Restore 512

    ✓ Two-Minute Drill 514

    Q&A Self Test 517

    Self Test Answers 521

12 Using and Supporting Printers **525**

Printer Basics 526

    Printer Types and Technologies 526

    Paper-Feeding Technologies 533

    Printer Components 533

    Printer Interfaces 537

Installing and Configuring Printers 540

    Installing a Printer 540

    Exercise 12-1: Installing a Non–Plug and Play Printer 542

    Installing IP Printing Support 543

Testing a Printer for Compatibility 543
Installing an All-in-One 544
Configuring a Printer 544
Upgrades 548
Optimizing Printer Performance 548
Deleting a Printer 549
Troubleshooting Printer Problems 550
Paper Feed Problems 550
Print Quality 552
Printer Error Messages 556
Exercise 12-2: Adding Paper to an Upright
Friction-Feed Tray 557
Windows Print Spooler Problems 559
Exercise 12-3: Restarting the Print Spooler Service 560
Preventive Maintenance for Printers 560
Maintenance Kits and Page Counts 561
Cleaning a Printer 561
Ensuring a Suitable Environment 563
Use Recommended Consumables 563
✓ Two-Minute Drill 565
Q&A Self Test 567
Self Test Answers 571

13 Network Basics **575**

Network Performance and Classifications 576
Geographic Network Classifications and Technologies 577
Exercise 13-1: Testing Broadband Speeds 586
Bandwidth and Latency 587
Network Software 588
Network Roles 588
Network Operating System (NOS) 589
Network Client 590
TCP/IP 590
Network Addressing 592
Exercise 13-2: Viewing the Physical and
IP Addresses of a NIC 599
Common Ports 601

Network Hardware 602
    Network Adapters 602
    Transmission Medium 603
    Connecting LANs 606
    Exercise 13-3: Identifying Network Hardware 608
Internet Concepts 608
    Internet Service Providers 608
    Internet Services and Protocols 609
    ✓ Two-Minute Drill 613
    Q&A Self Test 617
    Self Test Answers 621

**14 Installing a Small Office/Home Office
      (SOHO) Network** **625**

Installing and Configuring Networks 626
    Installing a NIC 626
    Connecting a Wired NIC to a Network 627
    Exercise 14-1: Connecting an Ethernet Cable 629
    Creating a Wi-Fi Network 630
    Exercise 14-2: Configuring a WAP 638
    IP Configuration 640
    Exercise 14-3: Manually Configuring
      IP Settings in Windows XP 641
    Exercise 14-4: Manually Configuring
      IP Settings in Windows Vista 642
    Configuring a WAN Connection 644
    Configuring Bluetooth 646
    Installing Basic VoIP 647
Installing and Configuring Web Browsers 649
    Browser Add-ons 650
    Internet Explorer 650
    Firefox 651
    Configure Proxy Settings 652
    ✓ Two-Minute Drill 655
    Q&A Self Test 658
    Self Test Answers 662

15 Troubleshooting Networks **665**

Tools for Network Troubleshooting 666

    Status Indicators 666

    Command Prompt Utilities for Network Troubleshooting 667

    Cable Testers 668

Troubleshooting Common Network Problems 669

    Resolving Insufficient Bandwidth 669

    Troubleshooting Modem Problems 671

    Troubleshooting Network Connectivity Problems 672

    Exercise 15-1: Using TRACERT 680

    Exercise 15-2: Using NSLOOKUP to
        Troubleshoot DNS 685

Preventive Maintenance for Networks 688

    Maintaining Equipment 689

    Securing and Protecting Network Cabling 690

  ✓ Two-Minute Drill 692

Q&A Self Test 694

    Self Test Answers 698

16 Computer Security Fundamentals **701**

Security Threats 702

    Computer Hardware Theft 703

    Identity Theft 703

    Fraud 703

    Disasters, Big and Small 703

    Malicious Software Attacks 704

    Grayware 707

    Methods for Gaining Access and Obtaining Information 708

    Exposure to Inappropriate or Distasteful Content 710

    Invasion of Privacy 710

    Cookies—the Good and the Bad 710

    Social Engineering 712

    Exercise 16-1: What Is Your Phishing IQ? 713

Defense Against Threats 715

    Security Policies 715

    Controlling Access to Computers and Networks 716

    Protecting Data 725

Exercise 16-2: Viewing Folder Permissions in Windows ... 729

Firewalls 730

Equipment Disposal 735

Recovery 735

✓ Two-Minute Drill 737

Q&A Self Test 740

Self Test Answers 744

17 Implementing and Troubleshooting Security **749**

Implementing Authentication and Data Security 750

Implementing Authentication Security 750

Implementing Data Security 754

Exercise 17-1: Creating a Share and Modifying

Share Permissions in Windows Vista/7 758

Implementing a Defense Against Malicious Software 766

Self Education 766

Protecting Windows Files and Programs 766

User Account Control 766

Software Firewalls 768

Exercise 17-2: Configuring the Windows

Firewall in Windows Vista 770

Antivirus 772

Phishing Filter 772

Antispyware/Anti-Adware/Pop-Up Blocker 773

Implementing Security Programs 775

Identifying Malware Symptoms 775

Removing Malware 775

Preventive Maintenance for Security 776

Securing a Wireless Network 778

Wireless Access Point/Wireless Router Configuration 778

Wireless Client Configuration 781

Troubleshooting Security 783

BIOS Password Problems 783

Biometrics 784

Forgotten Windows Password 785

No Permissions on FAT32 785

Encryption Issues 786

Software Firewall Issues 787

Wireless Access Point Problems 788

✓ Two-Minute Drill 790

Q&A Self Test 794

Self Test Answers 798

18 Operational Procedures **803**

Workplace Safety and Safe Equipment Handling 804

Cable Management 804

Using Appropriate Repair Tools 805

Moving Equipment 805

Hot Components 806

Electrical Safety 806

Electrostatic Discharge (ESD) 807

Exercise 18-1: ESD-Proofing Your Workspace 809

Electromagnetic Interference (EMI) 810

Power Supplies 810

Inverters 811

Display Devices 812

Printers 812

Compressed Air 814

Disposing of Computing Waste 814

Manufacturers' Recycling Programs 814

Material Safety Data Sheets (MSDS) 815

Batteries 815

Toner Cartridges 815

Display Devices 816

Chemical Solvents and Cans 816

Exercise 18-2: Researching Recycling Centers 817

Communicating with Customers and Colleagues 818

Human Interaction Basics 818

Communication Goals 819

Keys to Effective Communications 821

Active Communication 823

Professionalism 828

✓ Two-Minute Drill 834

Q&A Self Test 838

Self Test Answers 842

A **About the CD** **847**

System Requirements 848
LearnKey Online Training 848
Installing and Running MasterExam and MasterSim 848
    MasterExam 849
    MasterSim 849
Electronic Book 849
CertCam Video Training 849
Help 850
Removing Installation(s) 850
Technical Support 850
    LearnKey Technical Support 850

Glossary **851**

Index **909**

We dedicate this book to Jazzy and Yoda, our "best friends" and an excuse to take several breaks a day through the long days of writing this book. Dogs have to have their walks! They also tried to provide voiceover (barkover) for the CertCam exercise videos.

ACKNOWLEDGMENTS

We thank the many dedicated people at McGraw-Hill Professional who have been so helpful to us, demonstrating that writing a book is truly a team effort. A special thank you goes to Timothy Green, senior acquisitions editor, who convinced us to take on the enormous task of creating this updated seventh edition of the best-selling *CompTIA A+ Certification Study Guide*. He has consistently been creative, responsive, energetic, and dedicated to making this the best book of its kind available. Meghan Riley, acquisitions coordinator, has been very supportive and almost serenely patient with us through extended deadlines. Both of them have smoothed the way for us and deserve great credit for the success of this book.

We also want to thank Christopher A. Crayton, an extraordinary technical editor who must not get much sleep, because he often turned around a chapter in a day. And we know he is a busy man!

Once again, we have the pleasure of working with LeeAnn Pickrell, project editor, who made extremely helpful suggestions in the final edit of the book and whose friendship and dedication to high quality we much appreciate.

Many other people at McGraw-Hill have contributed to the creation of this book. Although we can't list all of their names, they know who they are, and we want them to know that we truly appreciate their outstanding efforts.

This book's primary objective is to help you prepare for and pass the required CompTIA A+ exams so you can begin to reap the career benefits of certification. We believe that the only way to do this is to help you increase your knowledge and build your skills. After completing this book, you should feel confident that you have thoroughly reviewed all of the objectives that CompTIA has established for the exams.

In This Book

We have organized this book around the objectives of the two CompTIA A+ 2009 exams required for certification: the CompTIA A+ Essentials Exam 220-701 and the CompTIA Practical Application Exam 220-702. These objectives divide into domains. The Exam Readiness Checklist at the end of the Introduction lists the domains and each objective, along with the page number where you can find the discussion for each objective in the book.

On the CD

The included CD-ROM has additional tools for helping you prepare for the exams. For more information on the CD-ROM, please see Appendix, "About the CD," at the back of this book.

Exam Readiness Checklist

At the end of the Introduction, you will find an Exam Readiness Checklist. This table is constructed to allow you to cross-reference the official exam objectives with the objectives as they are presented and covered in this book. The checklist also allows you to gauge your level of expertise on each objective at the outset of your studies. This should let you check your progress and make sure you spend the time you need on more difficult or unfamiliar sections. We provide references for the objective exactly as the vendor presents it, the section of the study guide that covers that objective, and a chapter and page reference.

In Every Chapter

We've created a set of chapter components that call your attention to important items, reinforce important points, and provide helpful exam-taking hints. Look at what you'll find in every chapter:

- Every chapter begins with the **Certification Objectives**—what you need to know in order to pass the section on the exam dealing with the chapter topic. The Certification Objective headings identify the objectives within the chapter, so you'll always know an objective when you see it!

- **Exam Watch** notes call attention to information about, and potential pitfalls in, the exam. These helpful hints reinforce your learning and exam preparation.

- **Certification Exercises** are interspersed throughout the chapters. These are step-by-step exercises that mirror vendor-recommended labs. They help you master skills that are likely to be an area of focus on the exam. Don't just read through the exercises; they are hands-on practice that you should be comfortable completing. Learning by doing is an effective way to increase your competency with a product.

- **On the Job** notes describe the issues that come up most often in real-world settings. They provide a valuable perspective on certification- and product-related topics. They often go beyond certification objectives to point out common mistakes and address questions that have arisen from on-the-job discussions and experience.

- **Scenario & Solution** sections lay out problems and solutions in a quick-read format.

SCENARIO & SOLUTION

What are the most common bus architectures in use today?	PCI and PCIe
What drive interface standard is replacing PATA for hard drives?	SATA

- The **Certification Summary** is a succinct review of the chapter and a restatement of salient points regarding the exam.

✓   ■ The **Two-Minute Drill** at the end of every chapter is a checklist of the main points covered. You can use it for last-minute review.

Q&A   ■ The **Self Test** offers questions similar to those found on the certification exams. You can find the answers to these questions, as well as explanations of the answers, at the end of each chapter. By taking the Self Test after completing each chapter, you'll reinforce what you've learned from that chapter, while also becoming familiar with the structure of the exam questions.

Some Pointers

Once you've finished reading this book, set aside some time to do a thorough review. You might want to return to the book several times and make use of all the methods it offers for reviewing the material:

1. *Reread all the Two-Minute Drills*, or have someone quiz you. You also can use the drills as a way to do a quick cram before the exam.

2. *Review all the Scenario & Solutions* for quick problem solving.

3. *Retake the Self Tests*. Taking the tests right after you've read the chapter is a good idea, because it helps reinforce what you've just learned. However, going back later and answering all the questions in the book in one sitting is even better. Pretend you're taking the exam.

4. *Complete the exercises*. Did you do the exercises when you read through each chapter? If not, do them! These exercises cover exam topics, and there's no better way to get to know this material than by practicing.

e x a m

ⓦ a t c h *You should mark your answers to questions on a separate piece of paper when you go through this book for the first time so you may go back and retake the Self Tests as you review for the exam.*

CompTIA A+ Certification

We designed this book to help you pass the CompTIA A+ certification exams. When we wrote this book, CompTIA had posted the objectives for the exams on its Website: **www.comptia.org**. We wrote this book to give you a complete and incisive review of all the important topics the exams target. The information contained here will provide you with the required foundation of knowledge that will not only allow you to succeed in passing the CompTIA A+ certification exams, but will also make you a better CompTIA A+ Certified Technician.

Since the inception of the CompTIA A+ exams, CompTIA periodically revises them to bring them up-to-date in the rapidly changing world of computers. We have extensively revised and expanded this seventh edition of the *CompTIA A+ Certification Study Guide* with much new material to match the 2009 revisions to the CompTIA A+ examinations.

How to Take an A+ Certification Exam

This section discusses the importance of your CompTIA A+ certification and prepares you for taking the actual examinations. It gives you a few pointers on methods for preparing for the exam, including how to study and register, what to expect, and what to do on exam day.

Importance of CompTIA A+ Certification

The Computing Technology Industry Association (CompTIA) created the A+ certification to provide technicians with an industry-recognized and valued credential. Due to its acceptance as an industry-wide credential, it offers technicians an edge in a highly competitive computer job market. Additionally, it lets others know your achievement level and that you have the ability to do the job right. Prospective employers may use the CompTIA A+ certification as a condition of employment or as a means to a bonus or job promotion.

Earning CompTIA A+ certification means that you have the knowledge and the technical skills necessary to be a successful entry-level IT professional in today's environment. The recently revised exam objectives test your knowledge and skills in all the areas that today's computing environment requires. More than 5000 CompTIA A+ certified professionals and employers participated in validating the revised exam's objectives. Although the tests cover a broad range of computer software and hardware, they are not vendor specific.

With the 2009 exams, CompTIA returned to offering only two exams—both required to achieve your CompTIA A+ certification. The first exam is the *CompTIA A+ Essentials Exam 220-701*, which tests core knowledge of hardware and operating systems as well as communications skills and professionalism. The second required exam is the *CompTIA A+ Practical Application Exam 220-702*. This exam measures the hands-on skills required for an entry-level IT professional to install, configure, upgrade, and maintain PC workstations, the Windows OS, and SOHO networks.

Those candidates who previously achieved their CompTIA A+ certification with the 2006 exams may update their certification by taking a single bridge exam. Learn more about the bridge exam at **www.comptia.org**.

Computerized Testing

As with Microsoft, Novell, Lotus, and various other company tests, the most practical way to administer tests on a global level is through Prometric or Pearson VUE testing centers, which provide proctored testing services for many companies, including CompTIA. In addition to administering the tests, Prometric and Pearson VUE also score the exam and provide statistical feedback on each section of the exam to the companies and organizations that use their services.

Typically, CompTIA develops several hundred questions for a new exam. Subject-matter experts review the questions for technical accuracy and then present them in the form of a beta test. The beta test consists of many more questions than the actual test and helps provide statistical feedback to CompTIA to check the performance of each question.

Given the outcomes of the beta examination, CompTIA test designers discard questions according to how well or badly the examinees performed on them. If most of the test-takers answer a question correctly, they discard it as being too easy. Likewise, they also discard questions that are too difficult. After analyzing the data from the beta test, CompTIA has a good idea of which questions to include in the question pool to use on the actual exam.

Test Structure

CompTIA announced that the new test will be a standard, multiple-choice exam. Most questions will have only a single correct answer, while others will have multiple correct answers, in which case, the question will include a note such as "select TWO." You should visit the CompTIA Website to check on the status of the exam before you take it. The CompTIA Web site is **www.comptia.org**. While there, take the practice exams posted at the site.

Remember, unanswered questions count against you. Assuming you have time left when you finish the other questions, you can return to the marked questions for further evaluation.

The standard test also marks the questions that are incomplete with a letter "I" once you've finished all the questions. You'll see the whole list of questions after you finish the last question. This screen allows you to go back and finish incomplete items, finish unmarked items, and go to particular question numbers that you may want to review again.

e x a m
w a t c h

An interesting and useful characteristic of the standard test is that questions may be marked and returned to later. This helps you manage your time while taking the test so you don't spend too much time on any one question.

Question Types

The A+ exams consist entirely of multiple-choice questions, but the computer may present the test questions on the examination in a number of ways, as discussed here. We provide this information primarily for reference. CompTIA states that the current exam is multiple-choice based.

True/False

Everyone is familiar with True/False-type questions, but due to the inherent 50 percent chance of guessing the right answer, you will not see any of these on the A+ exam. Sample questions on CompTIA's Website did not include any True/False-type questions.

Multiple Choice

A+ exam questions are of the multiple-choice variety. Below each question is a list of four or five possible answers. Use the available radio buttons to select the correct answer from the given choices. Some questions will have more than one correct answer, in which case, the number of correct answers required is clearly stated.

Graphical Questions

There are two types of graphical questions. The first type incorporates a graphical element to the question in the form of an exhibit to provide a visual representation of the problem or present the question itself. These questions are easy to identify because they refer to the exhibit in the question and there is an Exhibit button at the bottom of the question window. An example of a graphical question might be to identify a component on a drawing of a motherboard. This is done in the A+ multiple-choice format by having callouts labeled A, B, C, or D point to the selections.

The second type of graphical question is a hotspot. It actually incorporates graphics as part of the answer. These types of questions ask the examinee to click a location or graphical element to answer the question. Instead of selecting A, B, C, or D as your answer, you simply click the portion of the motherboard drawing where the component exists.

Free Response Questions

A test can present another type of question that requires a *free response*, or type-in answer. This is a fill-in-the-blank-type question where a list of possible choices is not given. You will not see this type of question on the A+ exams.

Study Strategies

There are appropriate ways to study for the different types of questions you will see on CompTIA A+ certification exams. The amount of study time needed to pass the exam will vary with the candidate's level of experience. Someone with several years experience might only need a quick review of materials and terms when preparing for the exam.

Others may need several hours to identify weaknesses in their knowledge and skill level and work on those areas to bring them up to par. If you know that you are weak in an area, work on it until you feel comfortable talking about it. You don't want to be surprised with a question knowing it was your weak area.

Knowledge-Based Questions

Knowledge-based questions require that you memorize facts. The questions may not cover material that you use on a daily basis, but they do cover material that CompTIA thinks an IT professional should be able to answer. Here are some keys to memorize facts:

- **Repetition** The more times you expose your brain to a fact, the more it sinks in and your ability to remember it increases.
- **Association** Connecting facts within a logical framework makes them easier to remember.
- **Motor association** Remembering something is easier if you write it down or perform another physical act, like clicking the practice test answers.

Performance-Based Questions

Although the majority of the questions on the CompTIA A+ exams are knowledge-based, some questions are performance-based scenario questions. In other words, they actually measure the candidate's ability to apply his knowledge in a given scenario.

The first step in preparing for these scenario-type questions is to absorb as many facts relating to the exam content areas as you can. Of course, actual hands-on experience will greatly help you in this area. For example, it really helps in knowing how to install a video adapter if you have actually done the procedure at least once. Some of the questions will place you in a scenario and ask for the best solution to the problem at hand. It is in these scenarios that having a good knowledge level and some experience will help you.

The second step is to familiarize yourself with the format of the questions you are likely to see on the exam. The questions in this study guide are a good step in that direction. The more you are familiar with the types of questions the exam may ask, the better prepared you will be on the day of the test.

The Exam Makeup

To receive the A+ certification, you must pass both the CompTIA A+ Essentials Exam and the Practical Application Exam. For up-to-date information about the number of questions on each exam and the passing scores, check the CompTIA site at **www.comptia.org** or call the CompTIA Certification office nearest you.

The CompTIA A+ Essentials Exam 220-701

The CompTIA A+ Essentials Exam 220-701 consists of six domains (categories). CompTIA represents the relative importance of each domain within the body of knowledge required for an entry-level IT professional taking this exam.

1.0 Hardware	27%
2.0 Troubleshooting, Repair, and Maintenance	20%
3.0 Operating Systems and Software	20%
4.0 Networking	15%
5.0 Security	8%
6.0 Operational Procedures	10%

The CompTIA A+ Practical Application Exam 220-702

The CompTIA A+ Practical Application Exam 220-702 consists of four domains (categories). CompTIA represents the relative importance of each domain within the body of knowledge required for an entry-level IT professional taking this exam.

1.0 Hardware	38%
2.0 Operating Systems	34%
3.0 Networking	15%
4.0 Security	13%

Signing Up

After all your hard work preparing for the exam, signing up will be a very easy process. Prometric or Pearson VUE operators in each country can schedule tests at authorized test centers. You can register for an exam online at **www.2test.com** or **www.vue.com/comptia** or by calling the Prometric or Pearson VUE Test Center nearest you. You should keep a few things in mind when you call:

1. If you call during a busy period, you might be in for a bit of a wait. Their busiest days tend to be Mondays, so avoid scheduling a test on Monday if possible.

2. Make sure you have your social security number handy. The test center needs this number as a unique identifier for their records.

3. You may pay by credit card, which is usually the easiest payment method. If your employer is a member of CompTIA, you may be able to get a discount, or even obtain a voucher from your employer that will pay for the exam. Check with your employer before you dish out the money. Alternatively, some CompTIA members, such as Total Seminars (**www.totalsem.com**) sell discounted vouchers bundled with practice exams.

4. You may take one or both of the exams on the same day. However, if you take just one exam, you have only 90 calendar days to complete the second exam. If more than 90 days elapse between tests, you must retake the first exam.

Taking the Test

The best method of preparing for the exam is to create a study schedule and stick to it. Although teachers have probably told you time and time again not to cram for tests, some information just doesn't quite stick in your memory. It's this type of information you want to look at right before you take the exam so it remains fresh in your mind. Most testing centers provide you with a writing utensil and some scratch paper that you can utilize after the exam starts. You can brush up on good study techniques from any quality study book from the library, but some things to remember when preparing and taking the test are:

- Get a good night's sleep. Don't stay up all night cramming for this one. If you don't know the material by the time you go to sleep, your head won't be clear enough to remember it in the morning.

- The test center needs two forms of identification, one of which must have your picture on it (for example, your driver's license). Social security cards and credit cards are also acceptable forms of identification.

- Arrive at the test center a few minutes early. You don't need to feel rushed right before taking an exam.

- Don't spend too much time on one question. If you think you're spending too much time on it, just mark it and return to it later if you have time.

- If you don't know the answer to a question, think about it logically. Look at the answers and eliminate the ones that you know can't possibly be the answer. This may leave you with only two possible answers. Give it your best guess if you have to, but you can resolve most of the answers to the questions by process of elimination. Remember, unanswered questions count as incorrect whether you know the answer to them or not.

- No books, calculators, laptop computers, or any other reference materials are allowed inside the testing center. The tests are computer based and do not require pens, pencils, or paper, although, as mentioned previously, some test centers provide scratch paper to aid you while taking the exam.

After the Test

As soon as you complete the test, your results will show up in the form of a bar graph on the screen. As long as your score is greater than the required score, you pass! The testing center will print and emboss a hard copy of the report to indicate that it's an official report. Don't lose this copy; it's the only hard copy of the report made. The testing center sends the results electronically to CompTIA.

The printed report will also indicate how well you did in each section. You will be able to see the percentage of questions you got right in each section, but you will not be able to tell which questions you got wrong.

After you pass the Essentials and one other exam, you will receive an A+ certificate by mail within a few weeks. You are then authorized to use the A+ logo on your business cards, as long as you stay within the guidelines specified by CompTIA. Please check the CompTIA Website for a more comprehensive and up-to-date listing and explanation of CompTIA A+ benefits.

If you don't pass the exam, don't fret. Examine the areas where you didn't do so well, and work on those areas for the next time you register to take the test.

Once you pass your exams and earn the title of CompTIA A+ Certified Technician, your value and status in the IT industry increases. CompTIA A+ certification carries an important proof of skills and knowledge level that is valued by customers, employers, and professionals in the computer industry.

Exam Readiness Checklists

The following two tables—one for the Essentials Exam and one for the Practical Application Exam—describe the A+ objectives and where you will find them in this book. The tables show each objective with a mapping to the coverage in the Study Guide. There are also three check boxes labeled Beginner, Intermediate, and Expert. Use these to rate your beginning knowledge of each objective. This assessment will help guide you to the areas in which you need to spend more time studying for the exam.

CompTIA A+ Exam 701: Essentials

Exam Readiness Checklist				Beginner	Intermediate	Expert
Official Objective	**Study Guide Coverage**	**Ch #**	**Pg #**			
701: 1.0 Hardware						
1.1 Categorize storage devices and backup media.	Mass Storage Devices and Backup Media	2	42			
1.2 Explain motherboard components, types, and features.	Motherboards	1	3			
1.2 Explain motherboard components, types, and features.	RAID Arrays	2	54			
1.2 Explain motherboard components, types, and features.	Input/Output	3	107			
1.3 Classify power supply types and characteristics.	Power Supplies	3	84			
1.4 Explain the purpose and characteristics of CPUs and their features.	Processor/CPU	1	19			
1.5 Explain cooling methods and devices.	Cooling Systems	3	90			
1.6 Compare and contrast memory types, characteristics, and their purpose.	Memory	2	57			
1.7 Distinguish between the different display devices and their characteristics.	Video Adapter and Displays	3	92			
1.8 Install and configure peripherals and input devices.	I/O Devices	4	170			
1.9 Summarize the function and types of adapter cards.	Adapter Cards	2	67			
1.9 Summarize the function and types of adapter cards.	Input/Output	3	107			
1.10 Install configure, and optimize laptop components and features.	Introduction to Laptops	6	256			
1.11 Install and configure printers.	Printer Basics	12	526			

Exam Readiness Checklist

Official Objective	Study Guide Coverage	Ch #	Pg #	Beginner	Intermediate	Expert
701: 2.0 Troubleshooting, Repair, and Maintenance						
2.1 Given a scenario, explain the troubleshooting theory.	Troubleshooting Theory and Techniques	5	188			
2.2 Given a scenario, explain and interpret common hardware and operating system symptoms and their causes.	Troubleshooting PC Component Problems	5	197			
2.2 Given a scenario, explain and interpret common hardware and operating system symptoms and their causes.	Diagnosing and Repairing Operating System Failures	11	469			
2.2 Given a scenario, explain and interpret common hardware and operating system symptoms and their causes.	Troubleshooting Printer Problems	12	550			
2.3 Given a scenario, determine the troubleshooting methods and tools for printers.	Troubleshooting Printer Problems	12	550			
2.4 Given a scenario, explain and interpret common laptop issues and determine the appropriate basic troubleshooting method.	Troubleshooting Laptops	7	296			
2.5 Given a scenario, integrate common preventative maintenance techniques.	Preventative Maintenance Techniques	5	233			
2.5 Given a scenario, integrate common preventative maintenance techniques.	Performing Preventative Maintenance and Optimization	11	507			
701: 3.0 Operating Systems and Software						
3.1 Compare and contrast the different Windows Operating Systems and their features.	Introduction to Windows Operating Systems	8	328			
3.2 Given a scenario, demonstrate proper use of user interfaces.	The Windows User Interface	8	343			
3.2 Given a scenario, demonstrate proper use of user interfaces.	Operational Problems and Symptoms	11	484			
3.3 Explain the process and steps to install and configure the Windows OS.	Power Management	6	281			

Exam Readiness Checklist

Official Objective	Study Guide Coverage	Ch #	Pg #	Beginner	Intermediate	Expert
3.3 Explain the process and steps to install and configure the Windows OS.	Installing Windows	9	372			
3.3 Explain the process and steps to install and configure the Windows OS.	File Management	10	434			
3.4 Explain the basics of boot sequences, methods, and startup utilities	Motherboards and Onboard Components	4	134			
3.4 Explain the basics of boot sequences, methods, and startup utilities.	Understanding Windows Startup	10	425			
3.4 Explain the basics of boot sequences, methods, and startup utilities.	Diagnosing and Repairing Operating System Failures	11	469			
701: 4.0 Networking						
4.1 Summarize the basics of networking fundamentals, including technologies, devices, and protocols.	Network Performance and Classifications	13	576			
4.2 Categorize network cables and connectors and their implementations.	Network Hardware	13	602			
4.3 Compare and contrast the different network types.	Network Performance and Classifications	13	576			
701: 5.0 Security						
5.1 Explain the basic principles of security concepts and technologies.	Security Threats	16	702			
5.2 Summarize the following security features: wireless encryption, malicious software protection, BIOS security, password management/password complexity, locking workstations, and biometrics.	Security Threats	16	702			
701: 6.0 Operational Procedure						
6.1 Outline the purpose of appropriate safety and environmental procedures and, given a scenario, apply them.	Workplace Safety and Safe Equipment Handling	18	804			
6.2 Given a scenario, demonstrate the appropriate use of communication skills and professionalism in the workplace.	Communicating with Customers and Colleagues	18	818			

CompTIA A+ Exam 702: Practical Application

Exam Readiness Checklist					Beginner	Intermediate	Expert
Official Objective	**Study Guide Coverage**	**Ch #**	**Pg #**				
702: 1.0 Hardware							
1.1 Given a scenario, install, configure, and maintain personal computer components.	Motherboards and Onboard Components	4	134				
1.2 Given a scenario, detect problems, troubleshoot, and repair/replace personal computer components.	Troubleshooting PC Component Problems	5	197				
1.3 Given a scenario, install, configure, detect problems, troubleshoot, and repair/replace laptop components.	Introduction to Laptops	6	256				
1.3 Given a scenario, install, configure, detect problems, troubleshoot, and repair/replace laptop components.	Troubleshooting Laptops	7	296				
1.4 Given a scenario, select and use appropriate tools.	Troubleshooting Tools	5	225				
1.5 Given a scenario, detect and resolve common printer issues.	Troubleshooting Printer Problems	12	550				
702: 2.0 Operating Systems Microsoft Windows 2000, Windows XP Professional, XP Home, XP Media Center, Windows Vista Home, Home Premium, Business, and Ultimate							
2.1 Select the appropriate commands and options to troubleshoot and resolve problems.	File Management	10	434				
2.1 Select the appropriate commands and options to troubleshoot and resolve problems.	Operational Problems and Symptoms	11	484				
2.2 Differentiate between Windows Operating System directory structures (Windows 2000, XP, and Vista).	File Management	10	434				
2.3 Given a scenario, select and use system utilities/tools and evaluate the results.	Disk Management	10	416				

Exam Readiness Checklist

Official Objective	Study Guide Coverage	Ch #	Pg #	Beginner	Intermediate	Expert
2.3 Given a scenario, select and use system utilities/tools and evaluate the results.	Diagnosing and Repairing Operating System Failures	11	469			
2.4 Evaluate and resolve common issues.	Diagnosing and Repairing Operating System Failures	11	469			
2.4 Evaluate and resolve common issues.	Troubleshooting Printer Problems	12	550			
702: 3.0 Networking						
3.1 Troubleshoot client-side connectivity issues using appropriate tools.	Tools for Network Troubleshooting	15	666			
3.2 Install and configure a small office/home office (SOHO) network.	Installing and Configuring Networks	14	626			
702: 4.0 Security						
4.1 Given a scenario, prevent, troubleshoot, and remove viruses and malware.	Implementing Authentication and Data Security	17	750			
4.2 Implement security and troubleshoot common issues.	Security Threats	16	702			
4.2 Implement security and troubleshoot common issues.	Implementing Authentication and Data Security	17	750			

1

Personal Computer Components— Motherboards and Processors

CERTIFICATION OBJECTIVES

❑   **701: 1.2**   Explain motherboard components, types, and features

❑   **701: 1.4**   Explain the purpose and characteristics of CPUs and their features

✓   Two-Minute Drill

Q&A   Self Test

This chapter, along with Chapters 2 and 3, introduces you to basic computer concepts, including categorizing, explaining, classifying, and identifying common components. Consider the contents of these first three chapters to be the basic technical knowledge a computer professional working with PCs needs. Familiarity with the components, as well as a good working knowledge of their function, will allow you to work comfortably with most types of computers, in spite of different layouts or new component designs. Once you have a good feeling for how the parts of a computer system work together, you will be on the road to becoming a PC technical professional. This knowledge will aid in all the technical tasks ahead of you and in passing your CompTIA A+ 2009 exams. This chapter's coverage is not intended to be comprehensive, merely a place to begin. Later chapters will give you an opportunity to learn skills for installing and troubleshooting these components.

CERTIFICATION OBJECTIVE

■ **701: 1.2** *Explain motherboard components, types, and features*

The motherboard is the real estate on which a PC is built; all PC components are directly or indirectly connected to this large printed circuit board. This chapter introduces all of the topics of the CompTIA A+ Essentials (2009 Edition) Exam objective 701: 1.2, including form factors, memory slots, processor sockets, bus architecture, bus slots, PATA, SATA, eSATA, chipsets, and BIOS/CMOS. In later chapters, we will revisit many topics with a different spin, as we look at installing, maintaining, upgrading, and troubleshooting PCs. For instance, we introduce the topic of RAID in this chapter, as it involves a BIOS setting, but we will further explore it in Chapter 2.

on the job *Safety first! Throughout this book, we will ask you to install and remove components on a PC system. Therefore, you must thoroughly understand two areas before opening the cover of a computer: electrostatic discharge (ESD), which can kill your computer, and high voltage (inside the power supply and any CRT-type display), which can kill you. To make sure you know the complete power protection and safety procedures, read Chapter 18 first.*

Motherboards

The basic computer system that sits on your desktop may look like Figure 1-1, but it is an extremely complicated piece of equipment that includes a vast array of technologies in its components. As a computer technician, you do not really need to be overly concerned about the actual inner workings of these components, but understanding what they do will be helpful. We will begin with the motherboard, the foundation of every PC. Each internal and external PC component connects, directly or indirectly, to the *motherboard*. The motherboard, also referred to as the *mainboard*, the *system board*, or the *planar board*, is made of fiberglass, typically brown or green, and with a meshwork of copper lines. Power, data, and control signals, also called *traces*, travel to all connected components through these electronic circuits. A group of these wires assigned to a set of functions is collectively called a *bus*. In this section, we focus on types of motherboards, their typical integrated components, and the differences between the motherboard's communication busses and the types of systems they allow you to use.

on the job *If you work with experienced PC technicians, read trade publications, or visit technical Websites, you'll probably see the term* mobo *used in place of motherboard.*

FIGURE I-I

A typical PC

Form Factors

A motherboard *form factor* defines the type and location of components on the motherboard, the power supply that will work with it, and the corresponding PC case that will accommodate both. There are several motherboard form factors, each with different layouts, components, and specifications. A motherboard will use only certain CPUs and types of memory, based on the type of CPU and memory sockets installed. Therefore, if you decide to build a computer from components, you must ensure that the motherboard, power supply, CPU, memory, and case will all work together. Personal computer motherboards have evolved over the past quarter century, and continue to do so. Although motherboards can vary from manufacturer to manufacturer, Intel Corporation, a major manufacturer, has developed several form factors over the years, including the early AT (not discussed here) and NLX form factors, and the later ATX and BTX form factors. Each of these has size variations, such as the smaller microATX and microBTX form factors. We will discuss their sizes, typical components, and prevalence next.

NLX

One step up from the AT form factor of the 1980s, *New Low-profile eXtended (NLX)* was an Intel standard for motherboards targeted to the low-end consumer market. It was an attempt to answer the need for motherboards with more components built in, including both sound and video, while also saving space and fitting into a smaller case. One method they used to save space was a bus slot called a riser slot, which accepted a card that created an expansion bus perpendicular to the motherboard. This *riser card,* in turn, accepted expansion cards that were oriented horizontal to the motherboard. These motherboards became obsolete very quickly, in part because they used a very old expansion bus, the *industry standard architecture (ISA)* bus, which had some severe limitations that later bus designs overcame.

ATX and MicroATX

The *Advanced Technology eXtended (ATX)* motherboard standard was released by Intel Corporation in 1996 and is the most commonly used form in PCs. The ATX motherboard measures approximately 12" wide by 9.6" from front to back, which keeps it from interfering with the drive bays, as was a problem with the AT motherboards. The processor socket is located near the power supply, so it will not interfere with full-length expansion boards. Finally, the hard- and floppy-drive connectors are located near the drive bays (see Figure 1-2).

FIGURE 1-2   An ATX motherboard with the CPU located in the back next to the power supply

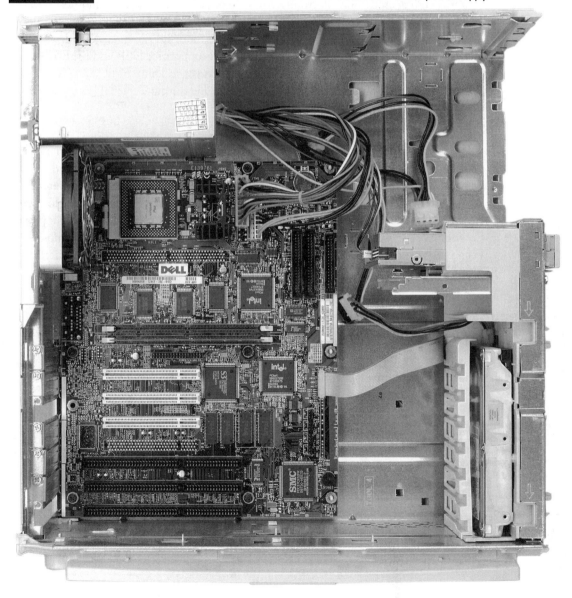

When first introduced, the ATX motherboard included integrated parallel and serial ports (I/O ports) and a mini-DIN-6 keyboard connector. ATX boards also have built-in multimedia support accessed through a game port, as well as mini–audio ports for speaker, line-in, and microphone. Manufacturers have modified the ATX standard to support newer technologies, such as USB, IEEE 1394, PCI, and PCIe. A rear panel provides access to the onboard I/O ports.

Depending on the manufacturer and the intended market, an ATX motherboard will contain up to six memory slots for the latest RAM types, support for BIOS-controlled power management, Intel or AMD CPU sockets, both PATA and SATA drive controllers (described later in this chapter), and support for USB and IEEE 1394.

The MicroATX motherboard is a scaled down version, at 9.6" by 9.6". The lightweight ATX motherboard is the Flex ATX, measuring 9" by 7.5" or smaller.

BTX

Introduced in 2003 by Intel Corporation, the *Balanced Technology eXtended (BTX)* motherboard form factor is the successor to the ATX standard. This standard is a major departure from ATX and offers improved cooling efficiency and a quieter computer through careful placement of the components for better airflow. However, by 2006 manufacturers suspended production of this form factor due to the improved cooling of individual components and BTX's incompatibility with newer chipsets and processors. BTX boards came in three sizes: BTX (or standard BTX), MicroBTX, and PicoBTX. Table 1-1 gives a comparison of these three sizes.

Motherboard Components

The components built into a motherboard include sockets for various PC components, including the CPU and memory; and built-in components such as video and sound adapters, hard drive controllers (PATA and SATA), support for various port types (parallel, serial, USB, and IEEE 1394), and the chipset.

TABLE 1-1	Form Factor	Approximate Size
Motherboard Size Comparison	ATX	12" × 9.6"
	MicroATX	9.6" × 9.6"
	FlexATX	9" × 7.5"
	BTX	12.8" × 10.5"
	MicroBTX	Up to 10.4" × 10.5"
	PicoBTX	8.0" × 10.5"

SCENARIO & SOLUTION

How does the BTX motherboard form factor differ from ATX?	The BTX design provides better cooling through the positioning of components on the motherboard and quieter operation because it does not require as much fan power.
What other computer components must be matched to a motherboard.	The power supply, CPU, memory, and case must match the motherboard.
Which motherboard form is typically the largest?	The standard BTX motherboard is the largest motherboard form factor.

Memory Slots

The motherboard has slots or sockets for system memory. Depending on the vintage and the manufacturer of a motherboard, special sockets accept one of the various types of DRAM or SDRAM memory sticks (also called *modules*). These sticks are *Single Inline Memory Module (SIMM)*, *Dual Inline Memory Module (DIMM)*, and *RAMBUS Inline Memory Module (RIMM)*. SIMM is the oldest technology, and you will not see these sockets in new PCs. The current standards are DIMM and RIMM. Both of these physical memory slot types move data 64-bits or 128-bits at a time. DIMM sockets are the most common, and for desktop or tower PCs, they may have 168 pins, 184 pins, or 240 pins. RIMM sockets for nonportable PCs have 184 pins. DIMM and RIMM sockets for portable computers are yet another story. Laptop motherboards have special sockets to accommodate smaller memory sticks, such as SODIMM or SORIMM. Learn more about memory for laptops in Chapter 6.

The number of slots depends on the manufacturer's design, but typical motherboards have up to four slots for one type of memory stick. For instance, we have an ATX motherboard in one of our office computers with six memory slots—four DIMM slots for DDR2 memory sticks and two DIMM slots for DDR3 memory sticks. The slots look similar, but the DIMM slots for DDR2 have 184 pins, whereas the DIMM slots for DDR3 have 240 pins. Learn about RAM technologies in Chapter 2, and learn about installing RAM in Chapter 4.

on the
Üob

Read a good (motherboard) book. How do you find out about using memory slots on a specific motherboard? You read the motherboard user guide. If you cannot find one for your computer, find the manufacturer's name and the model of the motherboard (or computer system) and query your favorite Internet search engine. You will often find the right book in PDF format.

Processor/CPU Sockets

The two major CPU manufacturers, Intel and AMD, each offer, at any given time, only a few current processor lines, but numerous, even hundreds, of processor models within each line. One of the many differences among the individual processor models is how the processor attaches to the motherboard, which is referred to as the *socket*. Every motherboard contains at least one CPU socket, and the location varies from one motherboard standard to another. A common CPU socket type is a *zero insertion force (ZIF)* socket, which is square, has a retention lever that holds the CPU securely when it is closed, and makes it easy to put a CPU in the socket when it is open.

For many years both manufacturers used some variation of pin grid array (PGA) CPU packaging, meaning that the processor has a square array of pins (numbered in the many hundreds) that insert into a matching socket on the motherboard. One variation is *PGA2*, which is used with Intel Pentium processors, and later the SPGA, or *staggered pin grid array*, came along, in which the pin rows are staggered to allow for a higher pin density than PGA. More recent Intel and AMD processors use the *land-grid array (LGA)* socket. A LGA processor has pads, rather than pins. These pads on the processor come in contact with pins in the socket on the motherboard and permit a higher density than possible with PGA. In many cases, with both PGA and LGA processors, a number that indicates the number of pins or pads in the array follows the word "socket." For instance, some Intel LGA processors have 1155 pads and are called "Socket 1155." Read the motherboard and CPU documentation very carefully to be sure the CPU and socket match, because there are many versions of PGA and LGA sockets. Learn how to install a processor on a motherboard in Chapter 4.

External Cache Memory

The motherboard may have sockets for external cache memory used by the CPU. See the discussion of cache memory later in this chapter in "Processor/CPU."

Bus Architecture

The term *bus* refers to pathways that power, data, or control signals use to travel from one component to another in the computer. Standards determine how the wires are used in the various bus designs. There are many types of busses, including the *processor bus*, used by data traveling into and out of the processor. The address and data busses are both part of the processor bus. Another type of bus is the *memory bus*, which is located on the motherboard and used by the processor to access memory. In addition, each PC has an *expansion bus* of one or more types. The most common types of expansion bus architectures are PCI, PCIe, and AGP, and we discuss these next. Less common types are AMR, ACR, and CNR, which we discuss in Chapter 2.

Expansion Bus Types and Slots

The bus standards for *input/output (I/O)* devices in PCs have evolved along with the PC over the last quarter century. Input refers to bringing data into a computer for processing, whereas output refers to information that comes out of a computer. Examples of common input devices include the keyboard and any pointing device (mouse, trackball, pen, etc.). Data can also be input from devices that also take output, such as storage devices and network cards. The most common output devices are the display, sound card, and printer. Less common I/O devices include bar code readers, biometric devices, touch screens, and KVM switches—all discussed in Chapter 3. The following bus types are those that you can expect to see in PCs today.

on the
Üob

The terms bus, system bus, *and* expansion bus *are interchangeable. A bus refers to either a system bus or an expansion bus attached to the CPU.*

PCI   *Peripheral component interconnect (PCI)* is an expansion bus architecture that was released in 1993 but was replaced by newer bus types. The PCI bus transfers data in parallel over a data bus that is either 32- or 64-bits wide. Over the years several variants of the PCI standard have been developed, and data transfer speeds vary, depending on the variant and the bus width. The original 32-bit PCI bus ran at 33.33 MHz (megahertz) with a transfer rate of up to 133 megabytes per second (MBps). PCI is a local bus, meaning that it moves data at speeds nearer the processor speeds.

The variants on the original PCI bus include PCI 2.2, PCI 2.3, PCI 3.0, PCI-X, Mini PCI, Cardbus, Compact PCI, and PC/104-Plus. These substandards vary in signaling speed, voltage requirements, and data transfer speed. Mini PCI and Cardbus brought PCI to laptops, requiring entirely different connectors to save space. Read more on these two busses in Chapter 6.

PCI slots are 3⅜ " long and are typically white. PCI cards and slots are not compatible with those of other bus architectures. Although initially developed for video cards, PCI cards are also available for networking, SCSI controllers, and a large variety of peripherals.

PCIe   *Peripheral component interconnect express (PCIe)* differs from PCI in that it uses serial communications rather than parallel communications as well as different bus connectors. Also called *PCI Express* and *PCI-E*, it has, for the most part, replaced

PCI and is incompatible with PCI adapter cards. Although PCIe programming is similar to PCI, the newer standard is not a true bus that transfers data in parallel, but a group of serial channels. The PCIe connector's naming scheme describes the number of serial channels each handles, with the designations x1, x4, and x16 indicating one, four, and sixteen channels, respectively. On the motherboard, a PCIe x1 connector is approximately 1½" long, whereas PCIe x4 is about 2" long, and PCIe x16 is close to 4" long. Figure 1-3 shows a black PCIe x16 connector at the top, and three white PCI connectors below it on the motherboard.

The PCIe transfer rate depends on which version of the standard the bus installation supports. For instance, PCEe 1.0 supports data transfers at 250 MBps per channel,

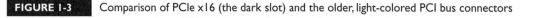

| **FIGURE 1-3** | Comparison of PCIe x16 (the dark slot) and the older, light-colored PCI bus connectors |

with a maximum of 16 channels. Therefore, the maximum transfer rate for 16-channel PCIe 1.0 is 4 GB per second. PCIe 2.0, released in late 2007, adds a signaling mode that doubles the rate to 500 MBps per channel. At this writing, we are looking forward to the 2010 release of PCIe 3.0, expected to support a signaling mode of 1 GBps per channel.

exam
ⓦatch

For the A+ exams, you don't need to know the full specifications of standards, such as PCI and PCIe, but you should understand the basics of each standard. For instance, know that PCI and PCIe are both expansion bus interfaces; remember that PCIe is the newer of the standards and is serial versus PCI, which was parallel. Be sure you can identify their physical differences on a motherboard.

AGP   AGP *(accelerated graphics port)* is a local bus designed for video only. Because this architecture provides a direct link between the processor and the video card, and gives the graphics adapter direct access to main memory, it is a "port" rather than a bus. It runs at the speed of the processor's memory bus. AGP is available in 32-bit and 64-bit versions. Figure 1-4 shows a motherboard with a dark AGP connector above two white PCI connectors.

There is normally only one AGP slot on a motherboard, and it looks very similar to a PCI slot, but it is not compatible with PCI cards. To use AGP, the system's chipset and motherboard must support it. The AGP architecture also includes an AGP controller, which is typically a small, green chip on the motherboard. AGP cards typically run four to eight times faster than PCI and are rated as 2X, 4X, or 8X. A 64-bit 8X AGP transfers data to the display at up to 2GB per second. Fast cards can run in slow AGP slots; however, they will only run at the speed of the AGP port. AGP Pro is a name given to various modified AGP cards with performance enhancements targeted to the very high-performance market. PCIe has, for the most part, replaced AGP.

ATA Drive Interface Standards

The preceding I/O bus architectures are for attaching video and other expansion cards to the computer. Next, we will look at the types of connectors you will find on a motherboard for installing hard drives and optical drives. The standards for

FIGURE 1-4 An AGP connector (the dark one) above two white PCI connectors

the interface behind these connectors all are descendents of the original *Advanced Technology Attachment (ATA)* standard, developed nearly two decades ago. They include a parallel interface, PATA, and a newer serial interface, SATA. The drive and the interface must comply with the same ATA standard in order to benefit from the features of that version. In Chapter 2, we will discuss SCSI, another interface standard for drives and other devices, which is not usually built into the motherboard. We will clarify where the terms IDE and EIDE fit into this picture, define the PATA and SATA interfaces, and then look at other drive interface technologies that are part of the ATA standards.

IDE and EIDE   Since the early years of PCs, the terms *Integrated Drive Electronics (IDE)* and, later, *Enhanced IDE (EIDE)* have been used to describe any drive that has the controller circuitry mounted on the drive itself—true of virtually every hard drive and optical drive. Strictly speaking, this is separate from the ATA interface that connects to one of these drives.

PATA   The first ATA standards defined an interface in which the data signals travelled over a parallel bus. Originally simply called ATA (when it wasn't called IDE or EIDE), this interface is now called *Parallel ATA (PATA)* to distinguish it from the Serial ATA standard introduced in 2003. Versions of the ATA standards were named successively ATA-1, ATA-2, and so forth. Important milestones in the evolution of ATA include ATA-4, which added support for non-hard disks, such as optical drives, tape drives, and some special large-capacity floppy drives via a protocol that allows the ATA interface to carry commands from these devices. This protocol is known as the *ATA Packet Interface (ATAPI)*. In Figure 1-5, you will notice a large ribbon cable on the right. It is connected to (and partially obscuring) the connector labeled IDE 2. In this computer, this cable connects to a DVD drive using the ATAPI standard.

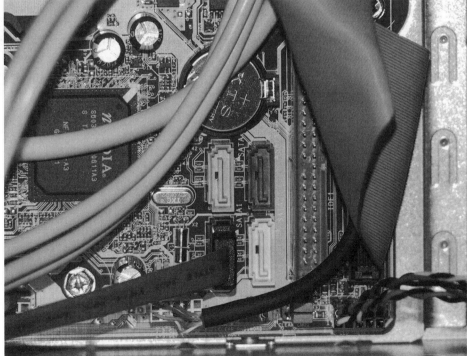

FIGURE 1-5

A connector labeled IDE 1 is the long, vertically oriented connector on the right (partially hidden by a ribbon cable), next to four SATA connectors.

When you open a PC and see wide ribbon cables, they usually connect EIDE drives to the PATA interface. Following one of these ribbon cables from a hard or optical drive to the motherboard leads to a connector labeled "EIDE controller 01" or "EIDE controller 02." Never mind that EIDE is about the drives and PATA is about the interface for these drives. Even in the latest motherboard, you may see these connectors labeled "IDE 1" and "IDE 2," as Figure 1-5 shows where the long PATA connector on the right, labeled "IDE 1," sits next to four SATA drive interface connectors that replace PATA. We will discuss SATA shortly.

Technicians have long detested the wide ribbon cabling used for these connectors because it blocks airflow, and it can sometimes be difficult to get unwieldy ribbon connectors tucked into a case without crimping them when closing the case. Space-saving rounded cables are available, but we still see mostly ribbon cables. PATA cables cannot be more than 18 inches in length, and PATA does not support *hot swapping*—the ability to replace a drive without powering down, so to replace a drive you must shut down the computer. While EIDE drives may advertise transfer rates above 80 megabytes per second, in reality, the PATA interface limits the speed due to protocol overhead and because PATA shares the PCI bus with all other PCI devices.

---

exam

watch

Are you confused yet? The terms IDE, EIDE, ATA, and PATA are all used interchangeably. IDE and EIDE should refer to the drives, whereas ATA and PATA should refer to the interface. The CompTIA A+ Essentials (2009 Edition) Exam objective

701: 1.2 lists IDE and EIDE under PATA. Remember, PATA is the older, slower, parallel technology for interfaces for hard and optical drives. The newer, faster, serial technology is SATA.

SATA The ATA-7 standards introduced *Serial ATA (SATA)*, a faster serial drive interface that has replaced PATA. Although some converters will allow older drives with PATA connectors to connect through this interface, today's drives are manufactured especially for the SATA interface.

PCs now come with SATA connectors on the motherboard. To the end user, the speed of SATA devices is the most attractive feature, but for the technician, the main advantage of SATA is that it uses thinner cabling. SATA uses slender cables that can be up to 39.4 inches long. Because each SATA device has a direct connection to the SATA controller, it does not have to share a bus with other devices, and therefore it provides greater throughput. Unlike PATA, SATA also supports hot swapping. Even the first two SATA standards, SATA 1.5 Gbps (150 MBps) and SATA 3 Gbps (300 MBps), far exceeded the PATA speeds. The SATA 3.0 standard, or SATA 6 Gbps, was released in May 2009.

eSATA   *External Serial ATA* is an extension of the SATA standard for external SATA devices. Its speed (triple that of USB 2.0 and IEEE 1394) positions it to compete with these other external I/O standards. Internal eSATA connectors are included in some newer motherboards, in which case, cabling is required to connect them to an eSATA port on the PC case. Use eSATA adapter cards to add eSATA to motherboards without built-in support. Because it provides the full SATA speed to external devices, expect eSATA to replace FireWire and USB devices that run at much slower speeds.

Miscellaneous ATA Technologies   Hard drive capacities have increased exponentially since the early PCs, and the various generations of the ATA standards were created to support the growing capacities, as well as the need for increased speeds in moving larger and larger amounts of data. Early on, when computer BIOSs limited drive capacities by defining the geometry of a drive in terms of the number of cylinders (tracks), read/write heads, and sectors (sections within a track), ATA provided a way around those limits using methods to hide the geometry of the drives from the BIOS. One method, called *sector translation*, required that the drive circuitry translate between the computer BIOSs logical view of the hard drive and the actual physical geometry. Both the BIOS and hard drive system must support an additional method, *logical block address (LBA)*, that allows for up to 8.3GB capacity. More recent ATA standards support the huge drives we have today.

In any PC, a hard drive is potentially a bottleneck because it depends on moving parts. Therefore, various schemes have been developed for speeding up the flow of data to and from a hard drive, as well as the actual writing and reading from the hard drive platters. Several methods for speeding up the movement of data between a hard drive system and memory come under the heading of *Ultra DMA (UDMA)*, which uses direct memory accessing (DMA). DMA is explained in Chapter 5. These methods were used with hard drive PATA interfaces and were referred to as *modes*. One of the last modes was Ultra DMA mode 5, introduced with ATA-6, which boosted the data transfer rate to 100 MBps, giving it the popular name of ATA/100. The last of the parallel ATA modes was Ultra DMA mode 6, known as ATA-7 or ATA/133 for the speed (133 MBps), and it was introduced at the same time as SATA, which supports speeds of 150 MBps or 300 MBps, depending on the type of SATA.

SCENARIO & SOLUTION	
What are the most common bus architectures in use today?	PCI and PCIe
What drive interface standard replaced PATA for hard drives?	SATA
What standard, also used by other expansion cards, is replacing AGP for video?	PCIe

Chipset

A critical component of the motherboard is the *chipset*. When technicians talk about the chipset, they are usually referring to one or more chips designed to work hand in glove with the CPU. One part of this chipset, referred to as the *Northbridge*, controls communications between the CPU and system RAM on motherboards designed for Intel CPUs. In this case, the Northbridge may also be referred to as a *memory controller chip (MCC)*. The Northbridge supports communication between the CPU and the video card on motherboards designed for AMD CPUs that have a memory controller built in. Another portion of the chipset, the *Southbridge*, manages communications between the CPU and such I/O busses as USB, IDE, PS2, SATA, and others. Chipset manufacturers include Intel, AMD, VIA Technologies, and NVIDIA Corporation, among many others.

Firmware

Firmware refers to software instructions, usually stored on ROM chips. Most PC components, such as video adapters, hard drives, network adapters, and printers contain firmware. Because these instructions must always be available, they are not reprogrammed every time the computer is started.

BIOS

One type of computer firmware is the *basic input/output system (BIOS)*. The BIOS is responsible for informing the processor of the devices present and how to communicate with them. Whenever the processor makes a request of a component, the BIOS steps in and translates the request into instructions that the component can understand.

Older computers contained a true read-only BIOS that was not alterable. This meant that one could not add new types of components to the computer since the BIOS would not know how to communicate with them. Because this seriously limited users' ability to install a new type of device not recognized by the older BIOS, *flash BIOS* was introduced. Now you can electronically upgrade (or flash) the BIOS so that it can recognize and communicate with a new device type.

Usually you can obtain the flash program from the Website of the motherboard manufacturer. The upgrade process typically requires you to copy the flash program to either a Windows program or a bootable device and follow the detailed instructions included in the download to flash the BIOS.

Further, modern motherboards include a great many more devices and capabilities than older motherboards—often more than can be adequately supported by BIOS-based programs. Therefore, when you purchase a motherboard, you will also have a driver disc. You will learn about installing and configuring motherboards and using the driver disc in Chapter 4. Companies such as Phoenix Technologies and AMI specialize in manufacturing BIOSs for PC manufacturers, and many PC and/or motherboard manufacturers make their own BIOSs.

on the
ⓘ o b   *It is very important that you follow the directions given by the manufacturer when performing a flash upgrade. If done incorrectly, the system can become inoperable and require a replacement BIOS chip from the manufacturer.*

CMOS

Another important type of firmware is *complementary metal-oxide semiconductor (CMOS)*. The CMOS chip retains settings such as the time, keyboard settings, and boot sequence. (We describe these settings in more detail in Chapter 4.) CMOS also stores interrupt request line (IRQ) and input/output (I/O) resources that the BIOS uses when communicating with the computer's devices. The CMOS chip is able to keep these settings in the absence of computer power because of a small battery, which usually lasts from two to ten years.

on the
ⓘ o b   *If the system repeatedly loses track of time when turned off, you probably need to replace the battery. This is usually a simple process, requiring opening the case and exchanging the old battery for a new one.*

You can view and modify the computer's BIOS settings by entering the computer's Setup program during bootup. When booting up the computer, watch the screen for instructions such as "Press CTRL-S to access Startup Configuration" or "Press DELETE to enter Setup." You will only have about three seconds to enter the appropriate key combination from the time such a message first displays. You can configure the length of this delay in the CMOS settings, discussed in more detail in Chapter 4, where you will learn about a variety of system settings.

Chapter 4 also describes how to use BIOS-related settings for configuring special hard drive configurations of multiple hard drives called RAID sets. Many motherboard BIOSs support RAID levels 0, 1, and 5, which Chapter 5 will define and describe.

on the
()ob   *Interestingly, the term CMOS settings is a bit of a misnomer. When people talk about the computer's CMOS, or its settings, they are usually referring to the things just described, but CMOS is really simply a type of physical chip. CMOS chips do a variety of things other than retaining BIOS settings. In fact, many processors are actually CMOS chips.*

BIOS and CMOS Roles in the Boot Process

When the computer is started (booted up), the BIOS runs a *power-on self-test (POST)*. During the POST, the BIOS checks for the presence and function of each component it is programmed to manage. It first checks the processor, then the RAM, and then system-critical devices such as the floppy drive (if present), hard drive, keyboard, and monitor. It then tests noncritical components such as CD-ROM drives and the sound card.

Next, the BIOS retrieves the resource settings from the CMOS and assigns them to the appropriate devices. Then, it processes the remaining BIOS settings, such as the time or keyboard status (for example, whether the keyboard number lock should be on or off). Finally, it searches for an operating system and hands control of the system over to it. The BIOS settings are no longer required at this point, but the BIOS continues to work, translating communications between the processor and other components.

on the
()ob   *The BIOS contains basic 16-bit drivers for accessing the needed hardware during bootup, such as the keyboard, floppy disk, hard disk, or any other device needed. Drivers loaded with the operating system (32-bit or 64-bit) give access to more advanced features of the basic components, as well as additional components.*

EXERCISE 1-1

Viewing System Settings in CMOS

1. Restart your computer, and remain at the keyboard.

2. As the computer starts up, watch for a screen message telling you to press a specific key or key combination in order to enter Setup.

3. Press the key or key combination indicated.

4. Spend time viewing the settings, but *do not* make any changes.

5. When you have finished, use the indicated key combination to exit without saving any changes.

CERTIFICATION OBJECTIVE

■ **701: 1.4** *Explain the purpose and characteristics of CPUs and their features*

The CompTIA A+ Essentials (2009 Edition) Exam objective 701: 1.4 includes the following subobjectives: Identify CPU types, hyper threading, multi core, on-chip cache, speed, and 32-bit vs. 64-bit. It does not require that you memorize the hundreds, or perhaps thousands, of CPU models you will encounter on the job.

Processor/CPU

A personal computer is more than the sum of its parts. However, the most important part, without which it is not a computer, or even a useful tool, is the *central processing unit (CPU)*, also called the *processor*. But a CPU may not be the only processor in a PC. Other components may include a processor for performing the intense work of the component. The most common example of this is the *graphics processing unit (GPU)* found on modern video adapters, used to render the graphics images for the display. This saves the CPU for other system-wide functions and improves system performance. The following is an overview of CPUs, their purposes and characteristics, manufacturers and models, and technologies. You can apply it to both GPUs and CPUs.

Purposes and Characteristics

In a PC, the central processing unit (CPU) is the primary control device for the entire computer system. The CPU is simply a chip containing a set of components that manages all the activities and does much of the "heavy lifting" in a computer system. The CPU interfaces, or is connected, to all of the components such as memory, storage, and input/output (I/O) through busses. The CPU performs a number of individual or discrete functions that must work in harmony in order for the system to function.

Additionally, the CPU is responsible for managing the activities of the entire system. The CPU takes direction from internal commands stored within the CPU, as well as external commands that come from the operating system and other programs. Figure 1-6 shows a very simplified view of the functions internal to the CPU. It is important to note that these functions occur in all CPUs regardless of manufacturer.

CPU Technologies

There are a number of technologies employed in a CPU, based on both standards and proprietary designs, which are constantly changing. The following describes common CPU technologies.

Control Unit

The *control unit* shown in Figure 1-6 is primarily responsible for directing all the activities of the computer. It also manages interactions between the other components in the computer system. In addition, the control unit contains both hardwired instructions and programmed instructions called microcode. See the explanation later in this chapter on microcode.

Busses

Notice in Figure 1-6 that there are several pathways among components in the CPU. These are busses, used for special purposes such as moving data from internal memory to the control unit. The *internal bus* of the CPU is usually much faster than the external busses. Other busses connect the CPU to the external devices. The *front side bus* connects the processor to system memory and the video adapter. These busses do not usually connect directly to external busses, such as PCI, except through a device called a *controller*.

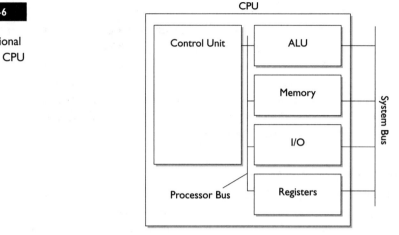

FIGURE 1-6

Simple functional diagram of a CPU

Although certain Intel CPU models have long contained a 36-bit front side or address bus, computer manufacturers generally did not use the additional wires in the address bus to address memory. Therefore, many computers that included these processors supported only 32-bit addressing and could use only up to 4GB of system RAM memory. As the need for more memory grew, so did the address bus. Some implementations used the 36-bit address bus, allowing up to 64GB of addressable memory, and a processor with a 64-bit address bus will address up to one terabyte (1TB) of memory. This also depends on motherboard support, as well as an operating system and application programs that can handle the 64-bit processing. Learn about 32-bit and 64-bit operating systems in Chapter 8.

ALU

The *arithmetic logic unit (ALU)* is responsible for all logical and mathematical operations in the system. The ALU receives instructions from the control unit. The ALU can take information from memory, perform computations and comparisons, and then store the results in memory locations as directed by the control unit. An additional type of ALU, called a *floating-point unit (FPU)* or *math coprocessor*, is frequently used to perform specialized functions such as division and large decimal number operations. Most modern microprocessors include an FPU processor as part of the microprocessor. This includes both those used as the central processor on PC motherboards, and the GPUs used on modern video adapters.

Registers

The ALU and control unit communicate with each other and perform operations in memory locations called *registers*. A register is a location, internal to the micropro-cessor, used as a scratch pad for calculations. There are two types of registers used in modern systems: dedicated registers and general-purpose registers. Dedicated registers are usually for specific functions such as maintaining status or system-controlled counting operations. General-purpose registers are for multiple purposes, typically when mathematical and comparison operations occur.

Memory

Computer memory provides the primary storage for a computer system. The CPU will typically have internal memory (embedded in the CPU) used for operations, and external memory, which is located on the motherboard. The important consideration about memory is that the control unit is responsible for controlling usage of all memory. You will find a more detailed discussion about memory in Chapter 2.

Cache

Cache memory in a computer is usually a relatively small amount of expensive, very fast memory used to compensate for speed differences between two components. The cache memory you hear about the most is between the CPU and the main memory. A CPU moves data to and from memory faster than the system RAM can respond. You might think that the solution is to install fast RAM as system RAM, but this would make a PC too expensive. Therefore, main system memory is most often a type of RAM known as DRAM, and cache memory is the faster and more expensive SRAM. Only a relatively small amount of memory is required for cache as compared to system memory. You will learn more about these types of RAM in Chapter 2.

Cache memory runs faster than typical RAM, and the small programs in a com-ponent called the *cache controller* have the intelligence to "guess" which instructions the processor is likely to need and retrieve those instructions from RAM or the hard drive in advance. Cache memory can also hold preprocessed data, such as out-of-order processing or data used by a game or an applications program. Typical applica-tions may require frequent processing of the same instructions. For example, a game may have repeatedly called video instructions processed by the video adapter's GPU. Newer processors can even create a "decision tree" of possible future instructions and store these in the cache, allowing rapid access to information or instructions by the CPU. Even when generating the tree, some instructions are preprocessed and stored in case the specific branch of logic is followed, and those instructions do not have to be reprocessed again. Intel has this down to an art, and the processors are generally correct in the tree they create.

Internal cache memory, more commonly called *L1 cache* or *Level 1 cache*, resides within the processor itself. This is one example of "on-chip cache" referenced in the CompTIA A+ Essentials (2009 Edition) Exam objective 701: 1.4. *External cache memory*, called *L2 cache* or *Level 2 cache*, resides external to a CPU's core. At one time, external cache memory was only on the motherboard, but today's processors usually have L2 cache installed on the same chip as the processor, but electronically separated from the inner workings of the process. This is another example of "on-chip cache." Beginning with the Itanium CPU, Intel offered a new level of external cache memory residing on the motherboard called *L3* cache *(Level 3 cache)*. It measures in megabytes, whereas L1 and L2 cache most often measure in kilobytes. The use of cache memory with CPUs has greatly increased system performance.

Hyper Threading

A *thread*, or thread of execution, is a portion of a program that can run separately from other portions of the program. A thread can also run concurrently with other threads. *Hyper threading*, also known as *simultaneous multithreading (SMT)*, is a CPU technology that allows two threads to execute at the same time within a single execution core. This is considered partially parallel execution. Intel introduced hyper threading in the Pentium 4 Xeon CPU, referring to it as Hyper-Threading Technology (HT Technology).

Multi-core CPUs

The most visible change in CPUs in recent years has been the introduction of CPUs with more than one core on the same chip. The first of these were *dual-core* CPUs containing two CPU cores. Quad-core CPUs are commonly available, and manufacturers offer six-core, and more. At least one manufacturer has announced a 64-core CPU.

What is the attraction of these multi-core CPUs? Server computers have long been available with multiple CPUs, so why not simply install two or more single-core CPUs on the same motherboard? The answer to both questions is that two cores on the same chip can communicate and cooperate much faster than two single-core processors. A dual-core CPU can simultaneously process two threads in true parallel execution, and each core has its own L1 cache; triple-core CPUs can simultaneously process three threads, and so on.

CPU Clock Speed

The *clock speed* of a CPU is the speed at which it can potentially execute instructions. Older CPUs measured this in millions of cycles per second, or megahertz (MHz); more recent CPUs have become so fast that they are measured in billions of cycles per second, or gigahertz (GHz). A CPU of a certain type and model may be available in a range of clock speeds. All other features being equal, the CPU with the faster clock speed will be more expensive.

However, when comparing different models of CPUs, the faster clock speed alone will not determine the fastest CPU. Manufacturers use many technologies to speed up CPUs. For example, the number of clock cycles required for completing the same operation can vary among CPU models. To the end user, the perceived speed of a PC, or lack of it, may involve other aspects of the computer's total design, such as the cache size, the amount and speed of the RAM, the speed of the busses, and the speed of the hard drive. Some experts give the "actual" speed of a CPU as the speed determined by the manufacturer through testing each CPU. This speed then becomes part of the rating for that CPU. There are software tools for measuring the speed of the CPU while performing certain operations. This could be considered the "real" speed.

exam ⓦatch *The CompTIA A+ Essentials (2009 Edition) Exam objective 701: 1.42 lists "Speed (real vs. actual)" as a subobjective. Since "real" and "actual" are synonyms, it is difficult to determine the distinction between them.*

Overclocking

Overclocking is the practice of forcing a CPU or other computer component to run at a higher clock rate than the manufacturer intended. PC hobbyists and gamers often overclock their systems to get more performance out of CPUs, video cards, chipsets, and RAM. The downside to this practice is that overclocking produces more heat and can cause damage to the motherboard, CPU, and other chips, which may explode and/or burst into flames.

Microcode

Microcode (also called a *microprogram*) is one of many low-level instructions built into the CPU's control unit. An example of an instruction might be the command to fetch information from memory. People often call microcode "hardwired" because you cannot change it.

VRM

A *voltage regulator module*, or VRM, is a chip or tiny circuit card used to condition the power to the CPU and reduce it from the 5 volts of the motherboard to the lower voltage (3.3 volts or less) of the CPU. Modern CPUs in PCs inform the motherboard of the voltage they require and, therefore, may not require a VRM.

Manufacturers and Models

There are many CPU manufacturers, but the prevailing ones in the personal computer market today are *Intel Corporation* and *Advanced Micro Devices, Inc. (AMD)*. Intel received a huge boost when IBM selected their 8088 processor for the original IBM-PC in 1981. For over a decade, AMD produced "clones" of Intel CPUs under a licensing agreement granted to them at a time when Intel's manufacturing capacity could not keep up with the demand for CPUs. Since 1995, AMD has designed and produced their own CPUs. Both companies manufacture more than CPUs, but their competition in the CPU market gets more attention in the trade and business press since AMD emerged as Intel's major competitor. The following discussion includes a sampling of CPU models from both manufacturers and avoids mention of CPU models designed specifically for the laptop market. Learn about those CPUs in Chapter 6.

Intel

Over time, Intel Corporation has released a number of CPU models ranging from the Intel 8086 in 1978 to the latest generation of processors, which come with a variety of model names. Some of these model names carry on the Intel Pentium, Celeron, Xeon, Itanium, and Atom brands. Intel recently changed their branding. Previously, in addition to their CPU brands, they also promoted groups of chips under brand names. For instance, the Centrino brand formerly identified a platform of multiple chips, including the CPU, chipset, and wireless network chips, sold together for use in laptops. With the recent changes, the Centrino brand will only apply to Intel's wireless network chips. As for CPU branding, the word "Core" is now used in the flagship brand, and Intel is moving away from such terms as "Solo," "Core 2 Duo," and "Core 2 Quad." The newer identifiers for the Core brands are Core i3, Core i5, and Core i7. Further, the old brand names (Pentium, Celeron, and Atom) will be assigned to lower performance CPUs. Of course, all this is subject to change.

What is important for a tech to understand is that each of the CPU brands includes many—even dozens—of individual models, and the various models are categorized by the purposes for which they were designed, such as desktop, server, workstation, notebooks, and Internet devices. Additionally, an entire category of CPUs are designed for the embedded and communication devices markets.

exam
ⓦatch

Any computer professional should understand the differences among the CPU models. However, the CompTIA A+ Essentials (2009 Edition) Exam 701, as well as CompTIA Practical Application

(2009 Edition) Exam 702 covered by this Study Guide, do not include specific CPU models or the manufacturers, only the CPU technologies.

AMD

Advanced Micro Devices, Inc. (AMD), is Intel's greatest competitor in the CPU arena. They manufacture a large variety of products based on integrated circuits. Like Intel, they categorize their CPUs by the purposes for which they were designed, such as desktop, server, workstation, notebooks, and embedded devices. They also stay competitive with Intel by offering each brand in a variety of multi-core configurations. The AMD Opteron CPU brand is targeted for use in servers, whereas the FireStream brand is intended for use in graphics workstations. The Turion, Athlon, and Sempron brands are found on CPU models designed for laptops, and other Athlon and Sempron CPU models are targeted to desktop computers. As with Intel, this is all subject to change, but look for more simplification in the product lines from both manufacturers, even as they continue to bring out dozens of CPU models each year.

EXERCISE 1-2

Identifying Your Processor

CertCam

1. Right-click the My Computer/Computer icon.
2. Select Properties.
3. Read the information in the General tab to determine your processor type.

SCENARIO & SOLUTION	
Briefly describe hyper threading.	Hyper threading is a CPU technology that allows two threads to execute at the same time within a single execution core.
Define CPU-based microcode.	Microcode is one of many low-level instructions built into the CPU's control unit. An example of an instruction might be the command to fetch information from memory.
Which companies are the two major manufacturers of CPUs?	The two major manufacturers of CPUs are Intel Corporation and Advanced Micro Devices, Inc., better known as AMD.

The PC Case

The typical PC user only knows his or her computer by its most visible components—the display (also called the *monitor*), the keyboard, the mouse, and the box that houses the main system, called the *case*. When purchased separately, a typical PC case includes the power supply, cooling system, a slot behind each expansion card position, slot covers over the expansion slots, available external I/O port connectors, and a selection of cables. Figure 1-7 shows the back view of a PC case.

A PC case from the back showing a panel of ports and expansion slots

Computer case knowledge is not included in the CompTIA A+ 2009 exam objectives for the 220-701 and 220-702 exams. It is included in this book as useful on-the-job information.

Just as you should not judge a book by its cover, you should not judge a computer by its case. A simple case may hide a very powerful computer, and a well-designed case, built with heavier than usual materials, insulation, and quieter fans, can provide noise reduction, a valuable feature to many of us. Within the computer gaming community, creating highly personalized cases, a practice called case *modding* (modifying), is very popular. These cases may have internal lighting, colorful cable covers, and transparent sides. The components in them may even be liquid cooled. We won't go into these fancy variants because the A+ exams won't test you on case modding. There are many computer case manufacturers.

Purpose and Features

The purpose of a PC case is to hold all the basic components, to protect those components from dust and dirt, to cool the components, and to provide noise reduction. This last is not a high priority with most common cases, but cases are available that provide noise dampening using heavier materials, insulation, quieter power supplies, and quieter cooling fans.

A case typically comes with a power supply, cable management systems, and mounting locations for the motherboard, drives, and other internal components. A case will also provide connectors on the outside for USB, IEEE 1394, and multimedia ports. (Learn more about the standards for USB and IEEE 1394 in Chapter 3.) A high-quality case comes with premium features such as a large capacity, quiet power supply; easy-to-remove exterior body panels; and easy-to-use hard drive bays with features such as shock absorption. Similarly, better models will have features that make the job of installing a motherboard easier, such as a removable tray to hold it.

Case Form Factors

PC cases come in form factors to match motherboard form factors, such as ATX, microATX, microBTX, and NLX. A case form factor must take into consideration the location of the motherboard-based components so you can access them. For instance, the case needs to have exterior openings for the adapter cards and port connectors that are built into the motherboard. It must also position drive bays so they will not interfere with any motherboard components. A case also accommodates the standard power supply formats, described in Chapter 3. A case, motherboard, and power supply must be matched, or the motherboard and power supply may not even fit in the case.

Case Categories

Most PC cases fall into one of two categories: tower and desktop. A tower is designed to stand on a desk or floor with its largest dimension oriented vertically. A desktop case is designed to sit on a desk with its largest dimension oriented horizontally. In a tower, the motherboard is normally mounted vertically, and in a desktop, the motherboard is mounted horizontally.

Case Sizes

Case sizes are not standardized, nor are the names manufacturers give the various sizes. Quality and features vary, so bigger is not always better. When quality is comparable, then, as size and features expand, so will the prices for PC cases. Common names used to describe case sizes include (from largest to smallest) full-tower, mid-tower, mini-tower, desktop, and low-profile. Mini-tower is the case size of most brand-name PCs.

CERTIFICATION SUMMARY

Common computer components include the processor, memory, storage devices, and input and output devices. All of these devices have specific functions, and your familiarity with them will help you to determine when to upgrade or replace a component.

This chapter described general characteristics of motherboards, installed motherboard components and form factors, and CPU technologies. You must use a motherboard that supports the selected CPU and RAM. Motherboards have many integrated functions. This chapter introduced many of the technologies on which you may be tested on the A+ exams. A good knowledge of these concepts is also important when you are repairing or upgrading a computer system. Chapters 2 and 3 will continue with an explanation of other important PC components.

✓ TWO-MINUTE DRILL

Here are some of the key points covered in Chapter 1.

Motherboards

❑ All components, including external peripherals, connect directly or indirectly to the motherboard.

❑ A motherboard form factor defines the type and location of the components on the motherboard, the power supply that will work with that motherboard, and the PC case the components will fit into.

❑ A motherboard will use only certain CPUs and types of memory, based on the CPU and memory sockets installed on the motherboard.

❑ NLX is a very old form factor that became obsolete very quickly.

❑ ATX remains the standard for motherboards, in spite of the introduction of the BTX standard in 2003 by Intel Corporation. The few manufacturers that supported BTX no longer do so.

❑ Both the ATX and BTX form factors come in a variety of sizes, including the standard ATX (12" × 9.6") and BTX (12.8" × 10.5"), the smaller MicroATX (9.6" × 9.6"), MicroBTX (up to 10.4" × 10.5"), and smallest FlexATX (9" × 7.5") and PicoBTX (8.0" × 10.5").

❑ Motherboard components include sockets for various PC components, including the CPU and memory; built-in components such as video and sound adapters; hard drive controllers (PATA and SATA); support for various port types; and the chipset.

❑ Memory sockets can include DIMM or RIMM on motherboards for desktop systems, and SODIMM or SORIMM on laptop motherboards.

❑ Every motherboard contains at least one CPU socket, and the location varies, based on the form factor.

❑ A motherboard may have sockets for external cache memory used by the CPU.

❑ The most common types of bus architectures are PCI (now obsolete), PCIe, and AGP.

❑ PCI, PCIe, and AGP bus architectures are "local" because they connect more directly with the processor.

❏ The long-reigning drive interface standards based on the EIDE/PATA technology gave way to SATA interface for internal mass storage and eSATA for external devices.

❏ The chipset is now one to three separate chips on the motherboard that handle very low-level functions relating to the interactions between the CPU and other components.

❏ The basic input/output system, or BIOS, is firmware that informs the processor of the hardware that is present and contains low-level software routines for communicating with and controlling the hardware.

❏ The CMOS chip is non-volatile RAM, supported by a battery. CMOS stores basic hardware configuration settings (BIOS settings), such as those for drives, keyboards, boot sequence, and resources used by a particular component.

Processor/CPU

❏ The CPU chip is the primary control device for a PC. A GPU is a processor on a video adapter, dedicated to the rendering of display images.

❏ The CPU connects to all of the components, such as memory, storage, and input/output through communications channels called busses.

❏ CPU (and GPU) components include the control unit, busses, the arithmetic logic unit (ALU), memory, controllers, and cache memory.

❏ Hyper threading is a technology that allows a CPU to execute two threads at the same time.

❏ A multi-core processor contains two or more processing cores and can process multiple threads simultaneously, performing true parallel execution.

❏ Intel Corporation and AMD (Advanced Micro Devices, Inc.) are the two top manufacturers of PC CPUs.

❏ Intel has many models under a variety of brand names, such as Pentium, Celeron, Xeon, Itanium, Atom, Centrino, and Core. This last is the latest brand of the newest technology, whereas the older brand names identify lower-end products.

❏ AMD CPU lines include the old K5 and K6 lines, followed by the Athlon, Opteron, Turion, Sempron, Duron, and FireStream.

The PC Case

❑ The computer case is the container that houses and protects the PC motherboard, power supply, and other components.

❑ A computer case is constructed of metal, plastic, and even acrylic.

❑ Cases come in a variety of sizes that are not standardized. They include full-tower, mid-tower, mini-tower, desktop, and low-profile.

❑ A case fits a certain motherboard form factor and comes with a power supply and cabling.

SELF TEST

The following questions will help you measure your understanding of the material presented in this chapter. Read all of the choices carefully because there might be more than one correct answer. Choose all correct answers for each question.

Motherboards

1. Which of the following statements is true?

   A. The motherboard must always be in a horizontal position.

   B. Each internal and external PC component connects to the motherboard, directly or indirectly.

   C. The "lines" on the motherboard provide cooling.

   D. A system board is an unusual motherboard variant.

2. Which of the following describes a motherboard form factor?

   A. The size and color of a motherboard

   B. The processor the motherboard supports

   C. The type and location of components and the power supply that will work with the motherboard, plus the dimensions of the motherboard

   D. Mid-tower

3. The variants of which motherboard form factor continue to be widely used, in spite of a newer standard from Intel that manufacturers rejected?

   A. AT

   B. NLX

   C. BTX

   D. ATX

4. How many memory slots does a typical motherboard have?

   A. Four to six

   B. Three to eight

   C. One to six

   D. None

5. Which statement defines Northbridge?

   A. A chipset component that controls communications between the CPU, the PCI AGP, and PCIe busses, and RAM

   B. A chipset component that controls communications between the CPU and I/O busses

   C. A component that saves configuration settings

   D. The system setup program itself

6. Which statement most accurately describes the relationship between the computer's BIOS and CMOS?

   A. The CMOS uses information stored in the BIOS to set computer configurations, such as the boot sequence, keyboard status, and hard drive settings.

   B. The BIOS configuration settings are stored on the battery-supported CMOS chip so they are not lost when you turn off the computer.

   C. The CMOS uses information stored in the BIOS to communicate with the computer's components.

   D. They perform the same functions, but the BIOS is found only in newer computers.

7. Which of the following describes a difference between PCI and PCIe?

   A. PCIe is only used for graphics adapters; PCI is used by a variety of adapters.

   B. PCI uses parallel data communications; PCIe uses serial communications.

   C. PCIe uses parallel data communications; PCI uses serial communications.

   D. PCIe is used by a variety of adapters; PCI is only used by video adapters.

8. This type of bus connector is only used by video adapters, and it is being phased out in favor of PCIe.

   A. PCI

   B. NIC

   C. AGP

   D. USB

Processor/CPU

9. Which of the following most accurately describes a function of the CPU's cache memory?

   A. To store instructions used by currently running applications

   B. To provide temporary storage of data that is required to complete a task

   C. To anticipate the CPU's data requests and make that data available for fast retrieval

   D. To store a device's most basic operating instructions

10. Where would you find a GPU in a PC?

    A. On the motherboard in place of the CPU

    B. On the SATA controller

    C. On the video adapter

    D. In the chipset

11. What component in a CPU is responsible for all logical and mathematical operations?

    A. ALU

    B. Processor

    C. Control unit

    D. Bus

12. What CPU component contains microcode?

    A. ALU

    B. Processor

    C. Control unit

    D. Bus

13. What type of memory is very fast and too expensive to use as system RAM, but is used as cache memory?

    A. DIMM

    B. RIMM

    C. DRAM

    D. SRAM

14. What is the external data bus width of all Pentium-class processors?

    A. 32-bit.

    B. 36-bit.

    C. 64-bit.

    D. Each Pentium processor has a different data bus width.

15. Which Intel CPU initiated the fifth generation and began an entire dynasty of Intel processors?

    A. Athlon

    B. Opteron

    C. Pentium

    D. Celeron

16. The Intel CPU technology that allows two threads to execute at the same time within a single execution core is

A. Hyper threading

B. Throttling

C. Overclocking

D. Microcode

The PC Case

17. What is the purpose of a PC case?

A. To block all air flow to the motherboard

B. To house the monitor and keyboard

C. To hold, protect, and cool the basic PC components

D. To process data

18. Which of the following features varies among cases and depends on heavier materials, insulation, and quieter fans?

A. IEEE 1394

B. Easy-to-remove exterior body panels

C. Easy-to-use hard drive bays

D. Noise reduction

19. Which statement is true?

A. A case, motherboard, and power supply must match, or the motherboard or power supply will not fit in the case.

B. Any power supply will fit into any case.

C. Any motherboard will fit into any case.

D. The position of drive bays is not a consideration because the motherboard is flat.

20. Which is the case size of most brand-name PCs?

A. Full-tower

B. Mid-tower

C. Mini-tower

D. Low-profile

SELF TEST ANSWERS

Motherboards

1. ☑ **B.** Each internal and external PC component connects to the motherboard, directly or indirectly. This statement is true.
    ☒ **A** is not true because the motherboard can be oriented in whatever position the case requires. **C** is not true because the lines on the motherboard do not provide cooling but carry signals and are part of various busses installed on the motherboard. **D** is not true; system board is simply another name for motherboard.

2. ☑ **C.** A motherboard form factor is the type and location of components and the power supply that will work with the motherboard, plus the dimensions of the motherboard. This statement is true.
    ☒ **A** is not correct because, while size may be part of a form factor, color has nothing to do with the form factor. **B** is incorrect because the processor the motherboard supports is not, by itself, a description of a form factor. **D** is incorrect because mid-tower is a case size, not a motherboard form factor.

3. ☑ **D.** ATX. This form factor has had a long run with motherboard manufacturers, even after the introduction of the BTX form factor.
    ☒ **A** is incorrect because AT is a very old form factor that had too many problems with cooling and the location of components interfering with drive bays. **B,** NLX, is incorrect for the same reasons as AT. **C,** BTX, is incorrect because it is the newest form factor discussed in this chapter, but it has not yet truly replaced the ATX form factor.

4. ☑ **C.** One to six. This is the range of memory slots in a typical motherboard.
    ☒ **A, B,** and **D** are all incorrect because they do not give the correct range of memory slots found on a typical motherboard.

5. ☑ **A.** A chipset component that controls communications among the CPU, the PCI AGP, and PCIe busses, and RAM is the correct answer.
    ☒ **B** is incorrect because it describes the Southbridge (a chipset component that controls communications between the CPU and I/O busses). **C** is incorrect because it describes CMOS memory. **D,** the system setup program itself, is incorrect because this program is found in the system BIOS.

6. ☑ **B.** The BIOS configuration settings are stored on the battery-supported CMOS chip so they are not lost when you turn the computer off—this is the correct answer.
    ☒ **A** is incorrect because it is the CMOS, not the BIOS, that stores computer configurations. **C,** that CMOS uses information stored in the BIOS to communicate with the computer's components, is incorrect because this is the opposite of the actual relationship between the BIOS and CMOS. **D** is incorrect. The CMOS and BIOS do not perform the same functions, and both are found in all PCs, old and new.

7. ☑ **B.** PCI uses parallel data communications; PCIe uses serial communications.

   ☒ **A** and **D** are both incorrect because both PCIe and PCI are used by a variety of expansion cards. **C** is incorrect because the very opposite is true. PCIe uses serial data communications, and PCI uses parallel data communications.

8. ☑ **C.** AGP is correct because this video-only bus connector is being replaced by PCIe.

   ☒ **A** is incorrect because, although PCI is also being phased out and replaced by PCIe, it is not only for video adapters. **B,** NIC, is incorrect because this stands for a type of expansion card, a network interface card, not a bus connector. **D,** USB, is incorrect because this is a peripheral bus, not a bus connector on the motherboard in which an expansion card is installed.

Processor/CPU

9. ☑ **C.** A function of a CPU's cache is to anticipate the processor's data requests and make that data available for fast retrieval.

   ☒ **A,** to store instructions used by currently running applications, and **B,** to provide temporary storage of data that is required to complete a task, are incorrect because these are both functions of RAM memory. **D,** to store a device's most basic operating instructions, is incorrect because this is a function of a device's ROM memory.

10. ☑ **C.** The GPU is located on the video adapter.

    ☒ **A** is incorrect because the GPU does not replace the PC's CPU. **B** is incorrect because the GPU has the processing necessary to produce graphics, not for the SATA controller. **D** is incorrect because a GPU is not part of the motherboard chipset.

11. ☑ **A.** The ALU is the CPU component that is responsible for all logical and mathematical operations.

    ☒ **B,** processor, is incorrect because this is just a synonym for CPU. **C,** control unit is incorrect because this is the component responsible for directing activities in the computer and managing interactions between the other components and the CPU. **D,** bus, is incorrect because a bus is just a pathway among components in the CPU.

12. ☑ **C.** The control unit is correct because it contains microcode.

    ☒ **A,** ALU, is incorrect because it does not contain microcode but receives instructions from the control unit. **B,** processor, is incorrect because this is just another name for CPU. **D,** bus, is incorrect because this is just a group of wires used to carry signals.

13. ☑ **D.** SRAM is correct. Static RAM is fast and expensive. It is used as cache memory because relatively small amounts are required.

    ☒ **A,** DIMM, and **B,** RIMM, are both incorrect because they are each a type of slot and a type of packaging for sticks of DRAM. **C,** DRAM, is incorrect because it is dynamic RAM, which is much slower and cheaper than SRAM.

14. ☑ **C.** All Pentium-class processors have a 64-bit external data bus. This means that 64-bits can enter or leave the processor at a time.
☒ **A,** 32-bit, is incorrect because whereas older processors have 32-bit data buses, all Pentiums have 64-bit external data buses. Pentiums, however, do have a 32-bit register (internal bus). **B,** 36-bit, is incorrect. No Intel CPU has a 36-bit data bus, although some Pentium-class processors have a 36-bit memory address bus. **D** is incorrect. Although Pentium CPUs do differ in memory address bus width, they all have the same data bus width: 64-bits.

15. ☑ **C.** Pentium. This CPU marked the beginning of the fifth generation of Intel CPU and spanned several more generations before the name "Pentium" was dropped from CPU model names.
☒ **A,** Athlon, and **B,** Opteron, are both incorrect because they are AMD CPUs.
D, Celeron, is incorrect because it is a consumer-level version CPU line and was not the first fifth-generation CPU.

16. ☑ **A.** Hyper threading is the CPU technology that allows two threads to execute at the same time within a single execution core.
☒ **B** is incorrect because throttling is the CPU technology that causes the CPU to lower its speed in order to reduce its temperature. **C,** overclocking, is incorrect because this is the practice of forcing a CPU or other computer component to run at a higher clock rate than the manufacturer intended. **D,** microcode, is incorrect because it is the name for the low-level instructions built into a CPU.

The PC Case

17. ☑ **C.** The purpose of a PC case is to hold, protect, and cool the basic PC components.
☒ **A** is incorrect because the design of a case will allow for proper airflow over the motherboard. **B** is incorrect because the monitor and keyboard are located outside the typical case. **D** is incorrect because processing data is the function of the CPU, one of the components located on the motherboard within a case.

18. ☑ **D.** Noise reduction is a feature that depends on heavier materials, insulation, and quieter fans.
☒ **A,** IEEE 1394, is incorrect because it is not a feature of PC cases, although cases will often have exterior ports that connect to circuitry supporting these features on the motherboard.
B is incorrect because easy-to-remove exterior body panels do not rely on heavier materials, insulation, and quieter fans. **C** is incorrect because easy-to-use hard drive bays do not depend on the items listed.

19. ☑ **A.** A case, motherboard, and power supply must match, or the motherboard or power supply will not fit in the case.

☒ **B** and **C** are both incorrect because each case is designed to fit certain power supplies and motherboards. **D** is incorrect because even though the motherboard itself is flat, the components on the motherboard take up varying amounts of vertical space, and therefore, the position of drive bays is a consideration.

20. ☑ **C.** Mini-tower is the case size on most brand-name PCs.

☒ **A,** full-tower, is incorrect because this very large case is uncommon in the consumer PC market. **B,** mid-tower, is incorrect because it is also uncommon in the consumer PC market. **D,** low-profile, is incorrect; although this is a consumer-oriented case size, it is for low-end systems such as those used in medical environments.

2

Personal Computer Components— Memory, Storage, and Adapters

CERTIFICATION OBJECTIVES

- ❏ **701:1.1** Categorize storage devices and backup media

- ❏ **701:1.2** Explain motherboard components, types, and features

- ❏ **701:1.6** Compare and contrast memory types, characteristics, and their purpose

- ❏ **701:1.9** Summarize the function and types of adapter cards

- ✓ Two-Minute Drill

- Q&A Self Test

Thical T is chapter is a continuation of the survey of PC concepts and components begun in Chapter 1, which provided the purposes and technologies of PC motherboards, CPUs, and cases. In this chapter, you will continue along the same vein, and explore PC storage devices, memory, and adapter cards.

CERTIFICATION OBJECTIVES

- **701: 1.1** *Categorize storage devices and backup media*

- **701: 1.2** *Explain motherboard components, types, and features*

This section introduces all of the topics of the CompTIA A+ Essentials (2009 Edition) Exam objective 701: 1.1, including floppy disk drives (FDD), hard disk drives (HDD), optical drives, and removable storage. While objective 701: 1.2 was well-detailed in Chapter 1, one small subobjective involving storage devices was saved for this chapter. Therefore, learn about the three levels of RAID arrays (0, 1, and 5) in this section.

Mass Storage Devices and Backup Media

In computing, the function of a *mass storage device* is to hold, or store, a large amount of information, even when the computer's power is off. Unlike information in RAM, files kept on a mass storage device remain there unless the user or the computer's operating system removes or alters them. Many types of mass storage devices are available, including those that store data on magnetic media, devices that use optical technologies, and devices based on solid-state technology. Note that this list includes both removable and fixed (nonremovable) devices. Further, certain of these, depending mostly on their interfaces, are hot-swappable devices, and many can be considered backup media. Let's explore all these dimensions.

Magnetic Mass Storage

Magnetic mass storage devices used with computers are those that store digital data on magnetized media, such as floppy disks, the metal platters in hard disk drives, and magnetic tape media used in tape drives. Unlike RAM memory, which is erased when power to the device is turned off, this type of storage is nonvolatile. Read/write heads are used to create magnetic patterns on the media. Following are descriptions of three types of devices that can save data onto magnetic media: floppy disk drives, hard disk drives, and tape drives. Note that the terminology differs slightly: magnetic media are called "disks," whereas optical media are called "discs." Don't let it confuse you; they are both devices that spin and write and read data.

Floppy Disk Drives

A 3.5-inch *floppy disk drive*, also referred to as a *FDD*, reads data from a removable floppy disk and provides a now-primitive method for transferring data from one machine to another. A *floppy disk* contains a thin internal plastic disk, capable of receiving magnetic charges contained in the disk's thin magnetic coating. A hard plastic and metal protective casing, part of which retracts to reveal the storage medium inside, surrounds the disk. The back of the disk has a coin-sized metal circle that the drive can grasp to spin the disk. Inserting a floppy disk into a computer's floppy disk drive causes the drive to spin the internal disk and retract the protective cover. An articulated arm moves the drive's two *read/write heads* back and forth along the exposed area, reading data from and writing data to the disk. Each head reads and writes to one side of the disk.

Floppy drives have all but disappeared from PCs. Most new consumer models do not have built-in floppy drives. If you need one, consider buying an inexpensive external USB floppy drive, like that pictured in Figure 2-1.

A 3.5-inch floppy disk can hold 1.44 MB (high density) or 2.88 MB (extra high density) of information. The most commonly used such disk is the 1.44 MB capacity disk. Floppy drives are limited in the types of disks they can access. A 1.44 MB drive can access either a 1.44 MB or the old format called "double density," which had a capacity of only 720 KB per disk. A 2.88 MB floppy drive can read all three 3.5-inch disk densities.

FIGURE 2-1

An external floppy disk drive with its USB interface

Hard Disk Drives

A *hard disk drive*, also referred to in documentation as *HDD*, stores data in a similar fashion to a floppy drive, but it typically is not removable and has a different physical structure (see Figure 2-2). A hard drive consists of one or more hard platters, stacked on top of, but not touching, one another. The stack of platters attaches through its center to a rotating pole, called a *spindle*. Each side of each platter can hold data and has its own read/write head. The read/write heads all move as a single unit back and forth across the stack.

Hard drives are available in a wide range of capacities and can hold much more data than floppy disks. Most new hard drives now have a capacity between several hundred gigabytes and several terabytes.

Most desktop PCs have a single hard disk drive inside the computer case in a drive bay without external access. Figure 2-3 shows a hard disk system designed for internal installation.

All other things being equal, an internal hard drive system is less expensive than an external hard drive system. The need to provide both an individual case and a power supply for an external hard drive accounts for the cost difference. An exception to the latter is a USB hard drive, which may get its power from the PC through the USB connection. Figure 2-4 shows two external hard drives. The large one has a capacity of 300 GB and connects to a PC using either USB or IEEE 1394. This drive requires more power than a USB port can supply, so it has an internal

FIGURE 2-2

The internal structure of a hard disk

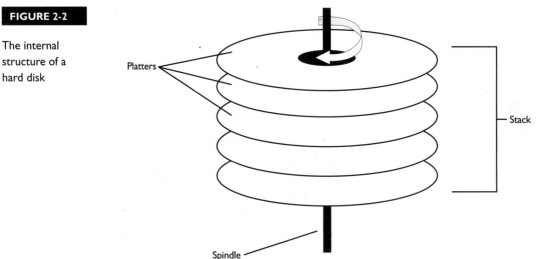

Platters

Stack

Spindle

An internal hard
drive system

Two external
hard drives

power supply with a cable for connecting to an external power source. The smaller drive does not require separate power, as it uses the USB connection for both power and I/O. It has a capacity of 8 GB and measures 2" by 2.5".

Tape Drives

A *tape drive* is a mass storage device primarily used for backing up data from computers. It uses special removable magnetic data tape cartridges. People often choose tape drives for archiving data and backups because the media is relatively inexpensive and long lasting. Because data must be stored sequentially on tape, the access time for restoring individual files is slow. However, newer tape drives can write data to tape at transfer rates that compare well to hard drive speeds.

Although tape drives are available in the consumer market, they most often back up large server systems, where specialized equipment can be used to combine tape drives with auto-loaders that select tapes for use and store filled tapes in tape libraries. High-end tapes can store hundreds of gigabytes per tape. Normally, tape drives read and write just one tape size and format, such as the venerable *Digital Linear Tape (DLT)* technology. Developed in the 1980s, this technology has been improved upon over the years as the *Super DLT (SDLT)* technology, and variations of this standard are still in use today. Both DLT and SDLT are one-half inch (12.7 mm) wide and contained within a cartridge that you insert into a tape drive without touching the tape itself. These data tapes are guaranteed to store data reliably for up to 80 years, under specified conditions.

In the last couple of years, the capacities of hard drives have expanded so much that many people use them as back-up devices. At this writing, multiterabyte hard drives are inexpensive and easily available. They have replaced tape drives for most consumers, but tape storage for data backups is still very common in private business and government.

Optical Disc Drives

Optical disc drives have come a long way since the 1980s. There are now three general categories of *optical drives* and the media (discs) they use—CD, DVD, and a high-definition (HD) optical drive technology called Blu-ray. In addition, although some drives can only read one or two of these disc types, other drives can both read and write to one, two, or all three of these disc types. Are you confused yet? When it comes to understanding these drives, it is best to start with the discs they use, and then look at the drives.

A typical optical disc of any type is, well, disk-shaped and made of polycarbonate. The standard disc is approximately 4.75 inches (12 cm) in diameter, but there are minidiscs that measure about 3.125 inches (8 cm). The surface is smooth and shiny with one labeled side and one plain side (there are exceptions to this single-sided form). The data, music, or video is stored on the disc using microscopic depressed and raised areas called *pits* and *lands,* respectively, that are covered by a protective transparent layer. A laser beam reads the data from the disc. Optical storage offers an interim step between the portability of a floppy disk and the capacity of a hard drive. You can access data much faster from an optical disc than you can from a floppy disk, but more slowly than from a hard drive. Optical disc capacity is hundreds of times greater than a floppy disk, but generally much smaller than commonly available hard disks.

Now that you know what they have in common, we will drop the phrase "optical disc" and talk about these discs using the common terms—CD, DVD, and Blu-ray.

CD-ROM, CD-R, CD-RW

The *compact discs (CD)* sold at retail stores that contain music (audio CDs) or software (data CDs) are *Compact Disc–Read-Only Memory (CD-ROM)* discs, meaning they are only readable; you cannot change the contents. There are other CD media and drive types, a few differences in capacities, and, as the technology has matured, various speeds.

CD Drives and Media   CD music players can usually only play music discs. A CD drive in a computer that can play music CDs and read data CDs, but cannot write to a CD, is a *CD-ROM drive.* The next level up includes CD drives that can write to, as well as read from, CDs. A *CD-Record (CD-R)* drive can write once to each specially designed blank CD-R disc. There are two types of CD-R discs. One type holds 650 MB of data or 74 minutes of audio, whereas the other holds 700 MB of data or 80 minutes of audio. The oldest CD-R drives only support the first format, whereas the next-generation CD-R drives support both formats. All but the earliest CD-R drives are multisession, meaning you can add data to a CD-R disc until you run out of space, but you cannot rewrite to occupied space on the disc. CD-R drives can read CD-ROMs and CDs created on a CD-R drive.

A newer technology has made CD-R drives obsolete. That is *CD-Re-writable (CD-RW)* drives, which can write either to CD-R discs (once only) or to specially designed CD-RW discs. What distinguishes CD-RW drives from CD-R drives is that these newer drives can write more than once to the same portion of disc, overwriting old data. This is not possible with CD-R drives.

CD-ROM, CD-R, and CD-RW drives can play or read from all three types of discs, although the very old CD-ROM drives can have problems reading some newer CD discs.

CD Drive Speeds   The first CD drives transferred (read) data at 150 KBps, a speed now called *1x*. CD drives are now rated at speeds that are multiples of this speed and have progressed up through 72x, which is 10,800 KBps. The appropriate name, such as CD-ROM, CD-R, and CD-RW, will describe a CD drive, and it may be followed by the speed rating, which may be a single number, in the case of a CD-ROM or, in the case of a CD-RW, will be three numbers such as 52x24x16x. In this case, the drive is rated at 52x for reads, 24x for writes, and 16x for rewrites.

DVD Drives and Media

Originally created for video storage in 1995, *digital video discs* have evolved into *digital versatile discs (DVDs)* used extensively on PCs for all types of data storage. Following are the various types of DVD drives and media.

DVD discs are the same physical size as CD discs but have a higher storage capacity and several other differences. Whereas CDs only store data on a single side, DVDs come in both a conventional *single-sided (SS) DVD* and a *dual-sided (DS) DVD* variant that stores data on both sides, requiring the DVD be turned over to read the second side.

In addition, the format on each side may be *single-layer (SL)* or *dual-layer (DL)*. Although the SL format is similar to the CD format in that there is only a single layer of pits, the DL format uses two pitted layers on each data side, with each layer having a different reflectivity index. The DVD package label shows the various combined features as *DVD-5, DVD-9, DVD-10,* and *DVD-18*. Therefore, when purchasing DVD discs, understanding the labeling is very important so you know the capacity of the discs you're buying. Table 2-1 shows DVD capacities based on the number of data sides and the number of layers per side.

	DVD Type	Capacity
TABLE 2-1 DVD Capacities	DVD-5 (12 cm, SS/SL)	4.7 GB of data, or over two hours of video
	DVD-9 (12 cm, SS/DL)	8.54 GB of data, or over four hours of video
	DVD-10 (12 cm, DS/SL)	9.4 GB of data, or over four and a half hours of video
	DVD-18 (12 cm, DS/DL)	17.08 GB of data, or over eight hours of video

Regardless of the actual format, we use the term "DVD." However, the original DVD encoding format for video, used for movies, is called *DVD-Video*. DVD music discs sold at retail stores are *DVD-Audio* discs. An encoding format designed for data is *DVD-RAM*. Most discs that are not, strictly speaking, DVD-Video or DVD-RAM are all lumped together as *DVD-Data discs,* even if they contain video.

When it comes to selecting DVD data discs based on the ability to write to them, you have a selection equivalent to CD discs. The DVD discs sold at retail containing video or software are *DVD-ROM* discs, meaning they are only readable; you cannot change the contents. DVD-ROM has a maximum capacity of 15.9 GB of data. Logically, DVD drives that cannot write to, but can only read from, DVDs are labeled *DVD-ROM drives*.

There are six standards of recordable DVD media. The use of the "minus" (–) or "plus" (+) has special significance. The minus, used in the first DVD recordable format and written as *DVD-R* and *DVD-RW,* indicates an older standard than those with the plus. DVD-R and DVD-RW are generally compatible with older players. DVD-R and *DVD+R* media are writable much like CD-Rs. DVD-RAM, DVD-RW, and DVD+RW are writable and rewritable much like CD-RW. When shopping for a DVD drive, or a PC that includes a DVD drive, you will see the previously described types combined as DVD+R/RW, DVD-R/RW, and simply DVD-RAM. Drives may also be labeled with the combined + and –, showing that all types of DVD discs can be used.

DVD Drive Speeds   DVD drive speeds are expressed in terms similar to those of CD drives, although the spin speed of a 1x DVD drive is three times that of a CD 1x. In fact, a 1x DVD drive transfers data at 1352.54 KB/second, which is faster than a 9x CD drive. When looking at advertisements for DVD drives or PCs that include DVD drives, you will see the combined drive types, as listed in the preceding section, followed by a combination of drive speeds, depending on the drive's operating modes. For instance: "DVD+R/RW 40x24x40x" indicates the three speeds of this drive for reading, writing, and rewriting because each drive has a different potential speed for each type of operation.

However, you need to read the manufacturer's documentation to know the order. As a general rule on DVD drives, reads are fastest, writes may be as fast or a bit slower than reads, and rewrites are the slowest. Table 2-2 shows the read/write transfer rates of a selection of DVD drive speeds along with the equivalent CD drive speeds. Notice that DVD drives leave CD drives behind at the DVD 8x speed.

on the ! Job

Because CDs and DVDs have no protective covering, handling them with care is important. Scratches, dust, or other material on the CD surface can prevent data from reading correctly. Because data is located on the bottom side of the CD, always lay the CD label-side down.

TABLE 2-2

DVD Drive
Speeds and Data
Transfer Rates
Compared to CD
Drive Speeds

Drive Speed	Data Transfer Rate, MB/second	Equivalent CD Transfer Rate
1x	1.35	9x
6x	8.1	54x
8x	10.8	NA
10x	13.5	NA
12x	16.2	NA
16x	21.6	NA
18x	24.3	NA
20x	27	NA
22x	29.7	NA
24x	32.4	NA

Blu-ray

The introduction of high-definition television (HDTV) to the consumer market in the late 1990s created the need for a standard for recording high-definition content. The response to this demand included two competing high-definition optical disc formatting standards: the *HD-DVD* standard, supported by Toshiba, and the *Blu-ray Disc* standard, developed by the Blu-ray Disc Association (originally named Blu-ray Disc Founders). Just a few of the member companies of this organization are Sony Corporation, 20th Century Fox, Dell, Hewlett Packard, Hitachi, Pioneer, Sharp, and TDK. Sony Corporation is the name most frequently attached to this standard. Like the Betamax versus VHS standards competition of decades ago, this competition was important to both the manufacturers and the early-adopter consumers. Those manufacturers and consumers who bought into Betamax were out in the cold when VHS became the winning video tape standard; history repeated itself in the HD-DVD versus Blu-ray wars.

The battles were fought in the marketplace and won by Blu-ray Disc, with the war officially ending in February 2008. Going forward, mass production of optical discs and drives for high-definition video will only use the winning Blu-ray standard. Further, the standard avoids using the term "DVD" for Blu-ray Disc products, preferring to simply use "Blu-ray Disc" or "BD." Following the CD and DVD precedence, different types of Blu-ray Discs are BD-ROM and BD-R, with a third designation, BD-RE that describes the rewritable Blu-ray Disc. Blu-ray Discs are the same physical size as CD and DVD discs but have a much higher storage capacity. And like the

TABLE 2-3	Feature	Blu-ray	DVD
	Disc diameter	12 cm	12 cm
Comparison of Blu-ray and DVD Features	Data transfer rate	36 Mbps (1x)	11.08 Mbps (1x)
	Video/audio data transfer rate	54 Mbps (1.5x)	10.08 Mbps (<1x)
	Maximum video resolution	1920×1080 (1080p)	720×480/720×576 (480i/576i)
	Maximum video bit rate	40 Mbps	9.8 Mbps

CD and DVD technologies, the new Blu-ray Disc drives can read from and write to the older CD and DVD discs.

Blu-ray drives use a blue-violet laser to read the discs, compared to the standard DVD, which uses a red laser. The blue laser, combined with a special lens, allows for a more focused laser, which results in higher density data storage.

Blu-ray Discs hold 25 GB or 50 GB, with capacities of 100 GB and 200 GB having been announced. Movie titles available in Blu-ray format were on the 25 GB discs until November 2007, when the first title appeared on 50 GB discs. Blu-ray Disc isn't just for video. Like DVD, Blu-ray can be used to store any type of data. Table 2-3 compares selected features of Blu-ray versus DVD.

Solid-State Storage

Up to now, the storage devices we have looked at use magnetic or optical technologies and media. However, a growing category of storage devices uses integrated circuits, rather than one of these other technologies. Generically called *solid-state storage* or *solid-state drives (SSDs)*, this technology has no moving parts and uses large-capacity, *nonvolatile memory*, commonly called *flash memory*. Nonvolatile means it does not require power to keep the stored data intact. Although these devices do not yet compare to hard drives in their storage capacity, there are many uses for these very lightweight devices. These devices have many names, some generic and some trademarked. SSDs come in a range of form factors. There are external SSDs and internal SSDs. There are 1 inch, 1.8 inch, 2.5 inch, 3.5 inch, and other sizes to match hard disks for ease of installation, with a variety of interfaces and several storage technologies used. There are SSDs designed to withstand harsh usage, such as internal SSDs installed in *embedded systems*—special-purpose computers designed for certain tasks and installed within a device. Embedded systems exist within mobile phones, sophisticated network devices, home appliances, GPSs, climate control systems, automobiles, and just about every device you encounter from day-to-day.

On rare occasions, nontechnical PC users embrace a new computer device as quickly as the cognoscenti do. One such device is the external SSD called a *thumb drive*, *flash drive*, or *jump drive*. This type of drive is very lightweight and small—it really is about the size of a (flattened) thumb—and most often has a USB interface (explained later in this chapter) and can theoretically hold several hundred gigabytes of data. Thumb drives use a type of memory that can be written to and erased in large blocks, much like other storage devices. When plugged into your computer, it appears as an ordinary drive with a drive letter assigned to it (see Figure 2-5).

Flash memory often describes other removable solid-state memory storage cards, commonly used in a variety of devices, such as in digital cameras to store photos. A prolific photographer will carry several of these devices, swapping out full cards for empty ones. Although many cameras come with software and cables for transferring the photos from the camera's memory card to a computer and/or printer, another method does not require either cable or software. In this method, you remove the card from the camera and insert it into a special slot on the PC or printer. Whether the card is in a camera or inserted directly into the computer's card reader, it is treated like a drive.

Several flash memory card form factors use various sold-state technologies with trademarked names. These include *CompactFlash (CF)*, SmartMedia, MMC, Memory Stick, and the newer smaller forms, such as RS-MMC, miniSD, microDS, and Intelligent Stick. Figure 2-6 shows a CompactFlash card.

FIGURE 2-5

A USB flash drive

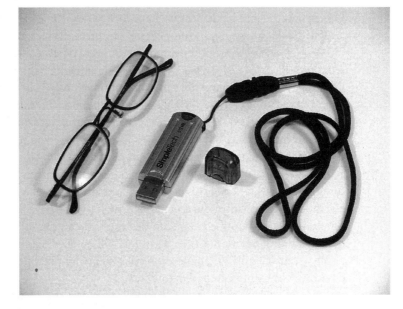

A 128 MB
CompactFlash
card

This computer is
ready to read a
variety of solid-
state storage
devices.

Consider just one of these forms, the *Secure Digital (SD) Card*. Its features go beyond securing against illegal copying, which is implied in its name. SD Cards are high capacity yet tiny, at 32 mm × 24 mm × 2.1 mm, and they support high-speed data transfer. SD cards are in portable devices, such as digital video recorders, digital cameras, handheld computers, audio players, and cell phones.

Figure 2-7 shows the front panel of a PC with a variety of flash memory slots. If these aren't built into your PC, and you require some or all of them, you can buy bus cards or external devices to add these interfaces to your PC.

EXERCISE 2-1

Identify Your Storage Devices

1. Open Computer (Vista) or My Computer (Windows 2000 or XP). This will show you all the attached disk drives.

2. Is there a drive labeled "Floppy Disk Drive (A:)" or "Floppy (A:)"? Don't be surprised if your computer does not have a floppy drive.

3. Identify the other drive or drives displayed in the Computer or My Computer folder.

Hot-Swappable Drives

Hot-swappable drives can be connected or disconnected without shutting down the system. Some hard drive systems are hot swappable, depending, in large part, on the interface. Until USB and FireWire were developed, hot-swappable drives were specially designed drive systems used on servers—often with their own separate case containing two or more drives and using the SCSI interface. They were expensive, but the cost was offset by the ability to keep a server up and running after a single drive died. You may wonder what happened to the data and programs held on the drive while all this occurred. The answer is that these hard drive systems were not just hot-swappable, but they also were RAID arrays, which are discussed in the following section of this chapter, "RAID Arrays."

Hard drives with USB or FireWire interfaces are almost always hot-swappable, as is nearly any USB or FireWire device. This doesn't mean you can "pull the plug," so to speak, any old time. In order to avoid losing data, you need to ensure the disk is not in use before disconnecting it. Close any applications or windows that may be using the drive, and then take the steps necessary, depending on your operating system. In Windows XP and Windows Vista, use the Safely Remove Hardware applet found in the status area on the right end of the taskbar.

RAID Arrays

RAID, which stands for *redundant array of independent (or inexpensive) disks*, is a group of schemes designed to provide either better performance or improved data reliability through redundancy. Often (but not always) using specialized hardware called a *RAID controller*, RAID can also be achieved using specialized software, but it always requires multiple disk drives configured to work together to use one of the RAID schemes. This set of disks is collectively called a *RAID array*. The drives should be of equal size, or space will be wasted. Each RAID scheme is identified by the word "RAID" followed by a number.

For instance, *RAID 0* defines a striped set without parity. It gives improved drive read and write speeds. The separate physical drives in the array are seen by the operating system as a single hard drive, and each time data must be written to the drive array, the controller writes a portion of the data to each drive in the drive array. This is called a *stripe*. RAID 0 also uses the total disk space in the array for storage, without any protection of the data from drive failure. If one of the drives in a RAID 0 array fails, all the data is lost.

RAID 1, also called *mirroring*, provides fault tolerance because all the data is written identically to the two drives in the *mirrored set*. If one of the drives should fail, the data still exists on the surviving drive. You may experience some improved performance on reads with RAID 1, depending on the operating system.

RAID 5, also called *striping with distributed parity* or *striping with interleaved parity*, requires at least three physical drives. This is one of several RAID schemes that employ parity. As data is written to the striped set, it is written in blocks on each drive. In each stripe, the block written on one of the drives (different with each write) is not the actual data, but the result of an algorithm performed on the data contained in the other blocks in the stripe. A single drive in a RAID 5 striped set can fail without a loss of data, because until the drive is replaced, the blocks in each stripe on the surviving drives is either the data itself (if the parity block was on the failed drive) or a parity block. Therefore, the surviving data blocks and parity block in each set can be used to reconstruct the data. Once the missing drive is replaced, the RAID controller will rebuild the data as it existed on the failed drive, using the existing data and parity blocks.

on the **!** Job

In most organizations, RAID is valued for the protection of data through redundancy, available with RAID levels 1 and 5. Therefore, expect to encounter these types of RAID on the job, especially on servers. Outside IT departments, gamers are very savvy about RAID, but they lean toward RAID level 0, which gives performance gains without redundancy protection.

RAID isn't just for expensive server systems anymore. Built-in drive controllers on modern motherboards are often called RAID controllers because they include the ability to support one or more levels of RAID. Similarly, when you shop for a separate drive controller to install in a PC, you will find many that include RAID support.

RAID that is created using specialized RAID controllers is invisible to the operating system. This is a good thing, because managing a RAID array is a job that should be hidden from your operating system, and a RAID controller will do that for you. Many operating systems support software RAID, only requiring the correct number of drives, not a special RAID controller.

What is possible is not always advisable. That is true of software RAID. RAID controllers are now much less expensive and widely available. One may exist in your own desktop computer. Therefore, if you want to install a RAID array in a computer, use a hardware RAID controller and configure it per the controller's documentation. Normally, configuring a RAID controller is much like configuring system BIOS settings, with the addition of a utility for configuring the desired RAID level. Doing software

RAID is interesting, and something many of us did more as a lab exercise years ago when it was cheaper to simply install multiple hard drives and use software RAID just for the experience of working with RAID than to purchase an expensive RAID controller. That was then, and things are much different now.

exam

ⓦatch

Although there are many RAID levels, only RAID 0, 1, and 5 are listed under CompTIA A+ Essentials

(2009 Edition) Exam objective 701: 1.2, so be sure you understand these three RAID levels.

Removable Storage

Many storage devices include removable media, meaning the drive stays in place while the media (disk, disc, or tape) is removed and replaced with another disk, disc, or tape). Traditionally, *removable storage* includes floppy disks, all types of optical discs, and tape. In the last several years, solid-state media has also grown as a very popular type of removable media.

Removable hard disk drives, primarily but not exclusively external devices, are the exception to the rule that the media is removed, not the drive. Removable hard drives come in two types. The most common for everyday users are external hard drives, which usually have their own power supplies, come with their own case, and require an interface cable such as USB, FireWire, or eSATA. Another type of removable hard disk drive is merely an internal hard drive, installed into a special carrier that in turn plugs into a companion cage installed in a PC.

Backup Media

At one time, serious data backup was only done by professional IT staff on corporate servers. PCs have become commonplace, not just in corporations and small businesses, but also in homes, and the amount of business and personal data stored on those PCs is huge. Aside from business data, many of us keep financial documents, family photos, and other valuable documents on our PC hard drives. When you consider the software and multimedia files stored on these systems, we all need to back up our data to avoid disasters.

Today, the average consumer has many options to select for their backups, and *backup media* can be any writable mass storage device—removable or fixed in place.

SCENARIO & SOLUTION	
What type of drive is required to play the latest standard for high-definition video?	Blu-ray Disc drives
You have been asked to recommend a computer to be a file and print server for a small business. What drive configuration should you recommend to the small business owner to add data redundancy to the system?	RAID level 1; mirroring should be considered to give the server redundancy.
You sometimes use the lab computers at school to write your papers and need a very small, inexpensive, portable device to take back and forth. The files you expect to save are not terribly large, even with a few graphics files added. What type of device should you consider?	A solid-state drive, commonly known as a thumb drive, would fit the criteria.

Hard drive manufacturers offer a large variety of external drives, with a variety of interfaces, such as USB, FireWire, and the most popular new interface: eSATA. You can also choose from a huge selection of backup software, from that included with your operating system to individual programs or software bundled with new external hard drives. Internet-based backup storage is available from many sources—even from security software vendors.

CERTIFICATION OBJECTIVE

■ **701: 1.6** *Compare and contrast memory types, characteristics, and their purpose*

This section introduces all of the topics of the CompTIA A+ Essentials (2009 Edition) Exam objective 701: 1.6, including types of RAM, parity versus nonparity, ECC versus non-ECC, single-sided versus double-sided, single channel versus dual channel, and the various speeds of RAM found in PCs today.

Memory

Memory, a computer's temporary working space, is one of the most important, but perhaps least understood, computer components. Computer novices often use the word "memory" when they mean hard drive storage space. Hard drive space is "permanent" storage, in which the data consists of magnetized spots within the surface of the recording medium within the hard drive, and it remains there after you turn the power off. Memory consists of computer chips in which the data resides, but only for as long as the computer remains powered on.

Furthermore, computers use several types of memory, each with a different function and different physical form. Typically, when people discuss memory, they are referring to *random access memory*, or RAM, so called because data stored in RAM is accessible in any (random) order. Most of the memory in a PC is RAM. However, some very important memory is read-only memory, or ROM. Chapter 1 describes the various types of RAM memory slots found on motherboards and also describes one important example of ROM found in all PCs—the BIOS. In this section, you will first explore the relationship between the CPU and the main RAM in a PC. Then you will learn about RAM technologies.

Functional Overview of RAM and ROM Usage

When a user makes a request, the CPU intercepts it and organizes the request into component-specific tasks. Many of these tasks must occur in a specific order, with each component reporting its results back to the processor before it can complete the next task. The processor uses RAM to store these results until they can be compiled into the final result(s).

RAM also stores instructions about currently running applications. For example, when you start a computer game, a large set of the game's instructions (including how it works, how the screen should look, and which sounds must be generated) is loaded into memory. The processor can retrieve these instructions much faster from RAM than it can from the hard drive, where the game normally resides until you start to use it. Within certain limits, the more information stored in memory, the faster the computer will run. In fact, one of the most common computer upgrades is to increase the amount of RAM. The computer continually reads, changes, and removes the information in RAM. It is also *volatile*, meaning that it cannot work without a steady supply of power, so when you turn your computer off, the information in RAM is lost.

Although *read-only memory*, or ROM, has an important function, it is rarely changed or upgraded, so it typically warrants less attention by most computer users. Unlike RAM, ROM is read-only, meaning the processor can read the instructions it contains, but cannot store new information in ROM. As described in Chapter 1, firmware is stored on ROM chips. ROM on peripheral devices maintains the device's basic operating instructions. A PC's system ROM stores the system's basic operating instructions, low-level device drivers, the power-on self-test (POST) program, and the system setup program. Modern ROMs used for system and device BIOS are often *flash ROM*, a ROM technology that can be reprogrammed using special software.

---

e x a m
watch

The CompTIA A+ exams may include such terms as PROM, EPROM, and EEPROM, which stand for programmable ROM, erasable programmable ROM, and electrically erasable programmable ROM, respectively. These are all erasable and, with the exception of PROM, reprogrammable ROM chip technology. They all predated Flash ROM.

RAM Technology

Not all RAM is the same. Over time, RAM technology has improved, changed form, and been used for specialized components. Manufacturers of RAM include Micron Technology, Inc., Crucial Technology (a spinoff from Micron), Kingston, and OCZ Technology. We discuss the most common types of RAM here.

SRAM

Static RAM (SRAM) (pronounced "ess-ram") was the first type of RAM available. SRAM can be accessed within approximately 10 nanoseconds (ns), meaning it takes only about 10 ns for the processor to receive requested information from SRAM. Although SRAM is very fast, compared with DRAM, it is also very expensive. For this reason, PC manufacturers typically use SRAM only for system cache. As you learned in Chapter 1, cache memory stores frequently accessed instructions or data for the CPU's use.

DRAM

Dynamic RAM (DRAM) (pronounced "dee-ram") was developed to combat the restrictive expense of SRAM. Although DRAM chips provide much slower access than SRAM chips, they are still much faster than accessing data from a hard drive. They can store several megabytes of data on a single chip (or hundreds of megabytes, and even gigabytes, when they are packaged together on a "stick"). Every "cell" in a DRAM chip contains one transistor and one capacitor to store a single bit of information. This design makes it necessary for the DRAM chip to receive a constant power refresh from the computer to prevent the capacitors from losing their charge. This constant refresh makes DRAM slower than SRAM and causes a DRAM chip to draw more power from the computer than a SRAM chip does. Because of its low cost and high capacity, manufacturers use DRAM as "main" memory in the computer. The term "DRAM" typically describes any type of memory that uses the technology just described. However, the first DRAM chips were very slow (~80–90 ns), so faster variants have been developed.

The list of DRAM technologies is quite large and continues to grow. We will limit the discussion to RDRAM, SDRAM, and the major implementations of DDR SDRAM.

RDRAM The Pentium 4 had a much faster front-side bus than previous processors, requiring faster RAM. One answer to this need was *Rambus Dynamic RAM (RDRAM)*, which gets its name from the company that developed it—Rambus, Inc. RDRAM used a special Rambus channel with a data transfer rate of 800 MHz, which was doubled by a dual-channel architecture, resulting in a 1.6 GHz data transfer and effectively a 128-bit bus. The RDRAM memory controller chips (MCCs), or Northbridge, achieved this by alternating between two memory modules (hence the "dual" in dual-channel). Previous DRAM modules used single-channel architecture in which the MCC did not alternate between memory modules and, therefore, the speed was tied to the memory refresh rate. Don't look for RDRAM in computers manufactured after 2003, the year Intel stopped making motherboards that supported RDRAM.

SDRAM *Synchronous Dynamic RAM*, or *SDRAM*, runs at the speed of the system clock, or at a speed that is a multiple of the system clock. DRAM is the dominant RAM technology in PCs today, and there are many different sticks of DRAM, in its many physical variations, such as DDR1, DDR2, and DDR3. SDRAM is used only in systems that support it and that have the appropriate slots for the SDRAM sticks.

DDR1 SDRAM People often call any version of *double-data rate (DDR) SDRAM* simply "DDR RAM." The first version, now called DDR1, doubled the speed at which standard SDRAM processed data. That means DDR1 was roughly twice as fast as standard RAM.

The JEDEC Solid State Technology Association (once known as the Joint Electron Device Engineering Council (JEDEC)) defines the standards for DDR SDRAM. There are two sets of standards involved here—one for the module (the "stick") and another for the chips that populate the module. The module specifications include PC1600, PC2100, PC2700, and PC3200. This new labeling refers to the total bandwidth of the memory, as opposed to the old standard, which listed the speed rating (in MHz) of the SDRAM memory—in that case, PC66, PC100, and PC133. The numeric value in the PC66, PC100, and PC133 refers to the MHz speed at which the memory operates, which should match the computer's clock speed.

Each stick or module specification pairs the stick with chips of a certain chip specification. Table 2-4 shows the DDR chip specifications, I/O clock speed, and the DDR module specification (the PC speed rating), as well as the bandwidths achieved with standard stick/chip combinations. Notice the easy translation between the PC speed rating and the bandwidth of the module. For example, a PC-3200 DDR SDRAM module populated with DDR-400 chips operates at 3.2 GBps (gigabytes per second).

A stick of DDR memory is a 184-pin DIMM module with a notch on one end so it can only fit into the appropriate DIMM socket on a motherboard. It requires only a 2.5 V power supply compared to SDRAM's 3.3 V requirement.

DDR2 SDRAM   *Double-data-rate two (DDR2) SDRAM* replaced the original DDR standards, now referred to as *DDR1*. DDR2 can handle faster clock rates than DDR1, beginning at 400 MHz. This is mainly due to the adoption of an RDRAM-style dual-channel architecture in which the memory controller chip (MCC) that manages memory for the CPU switches between two 64-bit-wide memory modules, effectively doubling the speed of the memory. To take advantage of the dual-channel architecture, DDR2 SDRAM sticks must be installed in pairs.

TABLE 2-4 JEDEC Speed Standards for DDR1 SDRAM Chip and Module Combinations	Chip Specification	Chip I/O Clock Speed	DDR Module Specification	Bandwidth
	DDR-200	100 MHz	PC-1600	1.6 GBps
	DDR-266	133 MHz	PC-2100	2.133 GBps
	DDR-333	166 MHz	PC-2700	2.667 GBps
	DDR-400	200 MHz	PC-3200	3.2 GBps
	DDR-433	217 MHz	PC3500	3.5 GBps
	DDR-466	233 MHz	PC3700	3.7 GBps
	DDR-500	250 MHz	PC4000	4.0 GBps
	DDR-550	275 MHz	PC4400	4.4 GBps
	DDR-600	300 MHz	PC4800	4.8 GBps

TABLE 2-5

JEDEC Speed
Standards for
DDR2 SDRAM
Chip and Module
Combinations

Chip Specification	Chip Operating Speed	I/O Clock Speed	DDR2 Module Specification
DDR2-400	100 MHz	200 MHz	PC2-3200
DDR2-533	133 MHz	266 MHz	PC2-4200
DDR2-667	166 MHz	333 MHz	PC2-5300
DDR2-800	200 MHz	400 MHz	PC2-6400
DDR2-1000	250 MHz	500 MHz	PC2-8000
DDR2-1066	266 MHz	533 MHz	PC2-8500

As with DDR1, there are specifications for the chips, as well as for the modules. Table 2-5 shows the JEDEC Speed Standards for DDR2 SDRAM chip and module combinations.

DDR2 sticks are only compatible with motherboards that use a special 240-pin DIMM socket. The DDR2 DIMM stick notches are different from those in a DDR1 DIMM. A DDR2 DIMM only requires 1.8 V compared to 2.5 V for DDR1. Manufacturers of motherboards and processors were slow to switch to support for DDR2, mainly due to problems with excessive heat. Once manufacturers solved the problems, they brought out compatible motherboards, chip sets, and CPUs for DDR2.

DDR3 SDRAM   First appearing on new motherboards in 2007, *DDR3 SDRAM* chips use far less power than the previous SDRAM chips—1.5 V versus DDR2's 1.8 V—while providing almost twice the bandwidth, thanks to several technology improvements on the chips and modules. As with DDR2, the DDR3 DIMMs have 240 pins and they are the same size. However, they are electrically incompatible and come with a different key notch to prevent the wrong modules from being inserted into DDR3 sockets. DDR3 modules can take advantage of dual-channel architecture, and you will often see a pair of modules sold as a dual-channel kit. And it gets better—memory controller chips (MCCs) that support a triple-channel architecture (switching between three modules) are available, and DDR3 memory modules are sold in a set of three as a triple-channel set. DDR3 SODIMMS for laptops have 204 pins. DDR3 SDRAM is quickly replacing DDR2 SDRAM.

As with DDR1 and DDR2, there are specifications for the chips, as well as for the modules. Table 2-6 shows the JEDEC speed standards for the DDR3 SDRAM chip and module combinations.

TABLE 2-6	DDR3 Chip Specification	Chip Operating Speed	I/O Clock Speed	DDR2 Module Specification
Some JEDEC Speed Standards for DDR3 SDRAM Chip and Module Combinations	DDR3-800	100 MHz	400 MHz	PC3-6400
	DDR3-1066	133 MHz	533 MHz	PC3-8500
	DDR3-1333	166 MHz	667 MHz	PC3-10600
	DDR3-1600	200 MHz	800 MHz	PC3-12800

e x a m

ⓦ a t c h

The CompTIA A+ Acronyms, listed at the end of both sets of exam objectives, includes many useful acronyms that you should be sure to understand. However, several of the listed acronyms are for outdated technologies. For instance, **FPM is an acronym for fast page mode, a memory technology that is faster than the original DRAM, but far behind the curve when compared to the newer RAM technologies just discussed.**

VRAM

Video RAM (VRAM) is a specialized type of memory used only with video adapters. The video adapter is one of the computer's busiest components, so to keep up with certain applications' video requirements, many adapters have an on-board graphics processing unit (GPU) and special video RAM. The adapter can process requests independent of the CPU, and then store its results in the VRAM until the CPU retrieves it. VRAM is fast, and the computer can simultaneously read from it and write to it. The result is better and faster video performance. Because VRAM includes more circuitry than regular DRAM, VRAM modules are slightly larger. The term "video RAM" refers to both a specific type of memory and a generic term for all RAM used by the video adapter (much like the term "DRAM," which is often used to denote all types of dynamic memory). In the generic sense, SGRAM, or synchronous graphics RAM, was a relatively inexpensive early type of VRAM. Faster versions of video memory include WRAM, which employs a technique for using video RAM to perform Windows-specific functions to speed up the OS. In Chapter 3, you will learn about other techniques for improving video performance.

SCENARIO & SOLUTION

Which type of memory is responsible for...?	Solution
Storing low-level drivers and programs, as well as the system setup program?	System ROM
Providing temporary storage for application files?	RAM
Storing frequently accessed instructions or data for the CPU's use?	Cache

Operational Characteristics

Among the operational characteristics of DRAM modules, regardless of the type, are memory banks, error-checking methods, single-sided versus double-sided, and single channel versus dual channel.

Memory Banks

The *bit width* of a memory module is very important; the term refers to how much information the processor can access from or write to memory in a single cycle. The phrase *memory bank* does not refer to the slots used to connect the RAM modules to the motherboard, but rather to a match between the processor's data bus width and the appropriate RAM module's bit width. If you are using a CPU with a 64-bit data bus on a more recent motherboard, one 64-bit SDRAM DIMM makes a full bank. In the not-so-distant past, memory modules had smaller bit widths and it took multiples of two or more to create a single memory bank. Therefore, if you are working with an older motherboard with RDRAM RIMM sockets, four 16-bit RIMMs, two 32-bit RIMMs, or one 64-bit RIMM make a full bank.

Modern SDRAM comes in modules that are 64-bits wide, and modern CPUs have a data bus width of 64-bits. Therefore, a single SDRAM DIMM module would be the correct width for most CPUs.

When dealing with processors from the Pentium family, it is not difficult to determine how much memory you need to create a full bank because they all have a 64-bit data bus. However, you might have to work with older processors and older types of RAM. Use the formula in Exercise 2-2 to calculate the number of memory modules you need to install in your computer.

EXERCISE 2-2

Calculating the Memory Bank Size

1. Determine the data bus width of the processor in your computer by locating the specifications published by the manufacturer.

2. Determine the bit width of the memory module. DIMMs are 64-bit, and older RIMMs are 16-bit and 32-bit, whereas the newest RIMMS are 64-bit.

3. Divide the processor's data bus width (Step 1) by the memory's bit width (Step 2). The number you get is the number of memory modules you must install to create one full bank.

Memory Error Checking

Earlier you learned that RAM memory is volatile, so you should realize that memory can be error-prone. The fact is that modern memory modules are very reliable, but there are methods and technologies that you can build into RAM modules to check for errors. We'll look at two of these methods: parity and error-correcting code (ECC).

Parity   In one type of memory error checking, called *parity*, every 8-bit byte of data is accompanied by a ninth bit (the parity bit), which is used to determine the presence of errors in the data. There are two types of parity: odd and even.

In *odd parity*, the parity bit is used to ensure that the total number of 1s in the data stream is odd. For example, suppose a byte consists of the following data: 11010010. The number of 1s in this data is 4, an even number. The ninth bit will then be a 1 to ensure that the total number of 1s is odd: 110100101.

Even parity is the opposite of odd parity; it ensures that the total number of 1s is even. For example, suppose a byte consists of the following data: 11001011. The ninth bit would then be a 1 to ensure that the total number of 1s is 6, an even number.

Parity is not failure-proof. Suppose the preceding data stream contained two errors: 101100101. If the computer was using odd parity, the error would slip through (try it; count the 1s). However, creating parity is quick and does not inhibit memory access time the way a more sophisticated error-checking routine would.

A DIMM is 64-bits wide, but a parity-checking DIMM has 8 extra bits (1 parity bit for every 8-data-bit byte). Therefore, a DIMM with parity is 64 + 8 = 72-bits wide. Although parity is not often used in memory modules, there is an easy way to determine if a memory module is using parity—it will have an odd number of chips.

e x a m

Memory parity versus nonparity is a subobjective of CompTIA A+ Essentials (2009 Edition) Exam objective 701: 1.6, so be sure you understand the concepts involved.

A nonparity memory module will have an even number of chips. This is true even if the module only has two or three chips total.

If your system supports parity, you must use parity memory modules. You cannot use memory with parity if your system does not support it. The motherboard manual will define the memory requirements.

on the

❶ o b

Be aware that the majority of today's computer systems do not support memory that uses parity. Other computing devices use parity, however. One example of parity use is in some special drive arrays, called RAID 5, mostly found in servers. Therefore, understanding the basics of parity is useful.

ECC   *Error-correcting code (ECC)* is a more sophisticated method of error checking than parity, although it also adds an extra bit per byte to a stick of RAM. Software in the system memory controller chip uses the extra bits to both detect and correct errors. Several algorithms are used in ECC.

Single-Sided vs. Double-Sided

The DIMM and RIMM modules discussed in this chapter come in both single-sided and double-sided versions. Single-sided modules have chips mounted on just one side of the memory circuit card, whereas double-sided modules have chips mounted on both sides. Most memory sticks are single-sided because there are incompatibility problems—mainly involving space—with the double-sided modules and motherboards.

CERTIFICATION OBJECTIVE

■ **701: 1.9**   *Summarize the function and types of adapter cards*

This section introduces all of the topics of the CompTIA A+ Essentials (2009 Edition) Exam objective 701: 1.9, including the various types of adapter cards: video, multimedia, I/O (input/output), and communications.

Adapter Cards

The traditional definition of an *adapter card* or *expansion board* is a printed circuit board installed into a PC's expansion bus to add functionality. An adapter card is actually a controller containing the sophisticated circuitry of an entire device, and many such devices do not fit the traditional description. Many devices are external, connecting to a computer via a USB, FireWire, or eSATA port. Examples of common adapter cards include those for controlling video, multimedia, I/O interfaces, networking, and modem communications. As you read about these types of devices, keep in mind that PC motherboards contain more and more of these functions so they no longer need an adapter card added to the system. The functions, however, remain as described in the following sections that describe each of the most common adapter cards.

o n   t h e   J o b   *Although also simply called an "adapter," this usage is confusing, because it also applies to a plug-like device that contains a simple circuit for changing one set of signals to another, like a serial-to-USB adapter.*

Video Adapter Cards

A *video adapter* card controls the output to the display device. This function may be built into the motherboard of a PC or provided through an adapter card installed into the PCI expansion bus, an AGP connector, or a PCIe connector. Learn more about video adapters in Chapter 3.

Multimedia Adapter Cards

In the early 1990s, the term "multimedia PC" was used to describe a PC with a stereo sound card and a CD-ROM drive. Today this is less than the minimum configuration for the most basic consumer PC from a major manufacturer. Today's multimedia PC brings not just music and photos to the user, but also support for sophisticated games and integration with home electronics. A savvy user may connect a PC to digital cameras (still and video), television, PDAs, and much more. Microsoft has special versions of Windows, *Microsoft Windows XP Media Center* and *Microsoft Windows Vista Home Premium*, which include Windows Media Center and are aimed at this more advanced multimedia PC and the consumers who desire these features.

PC manufacturers have created multimedia PCs to meet this need. They often have the words "Media Center" in their product name or description. Multimedia capabilities in PCs can now include enhancements to allow users to store and edit media data such as photos, music, and videos, and to watch and record TV thanks to a tuner integrated into the PC.

The PC now includes these multimedia capabilities through specialized components, either installed on separate adapter cards or integrated into the motherboard with appropriate connectors on the front or back of the case. The following sections give an overview of sound cards, TV tuner cards, and capture cards.

Sound Cards

A modern sound card processes multiple sound formats, including a variety of recorded sound formats, and computer-generated MIDI (musical instrument digital interface) sound. Even the most basic sound card includes support and ports for a joystick, a MIDI musical device, a microphone, and at least two speakers (a pair of stereo speakers, plugged into one port). Sound cards come in a full range of prices, based on the quality of the components and the number of features. For instance, many sound cards support five speakers, including a woofer, to give realistic sound. Some cards support high-quality recording.

Capture Cards

A *capture card* is a category of adapter card that accepts and records video signals to a PC's hard drive. One type of capture card, called a *TV tuner card*, brings a TV signal into a computer, usually for the purpose of recording TV programs onto a hard drive—turning your computer into a digital video recorder (DVR). There are some capture cards that are used to simply capture video from a VHS tape or other video format. Other capture cards are used for editing video files, regardless of how they were obtained.

I/O Adapter Cards

An important characteristic of any peripheral is how it communicates. PCs have evolved, and, with the invention of more and more input/output devices, manufacturers have continued to integrate these new capabilities into the motherboard. There was a time when mouse, serial, and parallel I/O cards had to be added to the expansion bus because these basic I/O standards were not integrated. Today, serial and parallel interfaces are built into the motherboard, but due to decreased use of these interfaces, they are often disabled and do not have external connectors. They will eventually disappear from ordinary PCs. While your PC has various I/O technologies built in, you may still wish to add an adapter card to give you additional ports. We'll describe these I/O technologies, including serial, parallel, USB, IEEE 1394, and SCSI in Chapter 3.

Communication Adapters

We have used the term "communications" many times in this and the preceding chapter, mostly in talking about communications between components within the PC. Now we will talk about the communications devices that connect a PC to a network, whether it is a local area network (LAN) or the Internet. Once again, the motherboards of most PCs now have these functions built in, and it is not usually necessary to add an adapter card to a computer for communications.

Network Communications

There are few PC users who do not require network communications. On the job, a typical desktop PC is connected to a LAN, which in turn may be connected to a larger private network and, ultimately, to the Internet. At home, you may connect two or more PCs via a LAN connection to share a DSL or cable modem Internet connection. The network adapter in the PC may be an Ethernet wired network adapter or a wireless adapter, depending on whether you wish to connect to a wired Ethernet LAN or a wireless LAN.

Most desktop PCs come standard with an Ethernet network adapter installed, either on the motherboard or as an expansion adapter. Laptop computers now usually come with both an Ethernet adapter and a wireless adapter. If you need wireless to your desktop PC, you will need to add it as an internal bus adapter card or as an external USB network adapter. We will save the larger discussion of networking for Chapters 13 and 14.

Modem Communication Adapters

A *modem*, so named for its combined functions of **mod**ulator/**dem**odulator, allows computers to communicate with one another over existing phone lines, a type of communication called *dial-up*. An internal modem may be built into the motherboard, or it may be an adapter card in the expansion bus. An external modem connects to a port on the computer, either serial or USB. Whether internal or external, a modem connects to a regular telephone wall jack using the same connector as a phone.

SCENARIO & SOLUTION

What feature should be in a sound card if you wish to create computer-generated music?	MIDI
What type of device would you install in a PC if you wanted to record TV programs onto a hard drive?	TV tuner card
What term is most properly used for a communications device that allows a computer to make a dial-up connection?	Modem

This type of modem is an *analog modem* as opposed to the data communication devices used to connect to a cable network or to phone lines for DSL service. "Modem" is actually a misnomer for the devices used on cable or DSL networks because the signals involved are all digital, and, therefore, there is no need to modulate or demodulate the signal. However, because they are physically placed between the computer and the network, much like a modem is, manufacturers use the term "modem."

Riser Card/Daughter Board

There are two types of riser cards. The first type, also called a *daughter card*, is a specially designed circuit board that connects directly into a motherboard and adds no additional functionality on its own. Rather, it extends the expansion bus and allows you to add expansion cards in a different physical orientation. The riser card is installed perpendicular to the case and may include several expansion slots. An expansion card inserted into a riser card is on the same plane as the motherboard. Riser cards are available for the standard bus architectures, such as AGP, PCI, and PCIe. Ironically, you will find riser cards both in the largest network servers and in the smallest of low-profile desktop computer cases.

In the case of network servers, the use of a riser card allows the addition of more cards than the standard motherboard allows. Otherwise, the additional expansion boards would increase the size of the motherboards beyond the size of even the large cases used for servers.

At the other extreme are the scaled-down low-profile computers, which cannot accommodate most expansion cards because their case height is so low. These riser cards allow one or more expansion cards to be installed and do not require a full-height case.

The second type of riser card is a small expansion card containing multiple functions. The two standards for this type of riser card are AMR and CNR. Both of these standards add multiple functions at low cost.

AMR

The *Audio Modem Riser (AMR)*, introduced in the late 1990s, allows for the creation of lower-cost sound and modem solutions. The AMR card plugs directly into a special slot on the motherboard and utilizes the CPU to perform modem functions, using up to 20 percent of the available processor power for this purpose. The advantage of this is the elimination of separate modem and sound cards without tying up a PCI slot in newer computers. The AMR card connects directly to a telephone line and audio output devices. One of the shortcomings of AMR was that it was not plug and play.

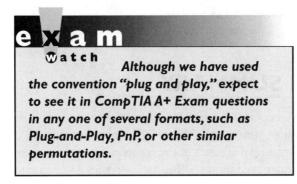

Although we have used the convention "plug and play," expect to see it in CompTIA A+ Exam questions in any one of several formats, such as Plug-and-Play, PnP, or other similar permutations.

ACR

Advanced Communications Riser (ACR) is a standard introduced in 2000 by AMD, 3Com, and others to supersede AMR. It uses one PCI slot and provides accelerated audio and modem functions as well as networking, and it supports multiple Ethernet NICs. With ACR, one telephone jack could be used for both modem and telephone jacks. The ACR PCI slot is blue, and the pin orientation is the reverse of the standard PCI slot.

on the Job *ACR is not listed in the CompTIA A+ Essentials (2009 Edition) Exam objective 701: 1.2, but we discuss it here because it is a newer standard that replaces AMR. On the job, you are more likely to encounter ACR than AMR.*

CNR

The first *Communication Network Riser (CNR)* card was introduced in 2000. Similar to the AMR except that it does support plug and play, CNR also supports LAN in addition to audio, modem, and multimedia systems. The CNR card plugs directly into the motherboard, thus eliminating the need for separate cards for each capability and reducing the cost of expansion cards.

CertCam

EXERCISE 2-3

Viewing Adapter Cards in Device Manager

1. Open Control Panel | Device Manager.

2. In the list of devices in the Device Manager window, note those for adapters named in the previous section. This list will include, but not be limited to, display adapters, network adapters, and various controllers.

3. Close the Device Manager window.

CERTIFICATION SUMMARY

Identifying personal computer components and their functions is the first step in becoming a computer professional. While PC component technologies are ever-changing, understanding the basics of the components and their functions today will help you to understand newer technologies as they are introduced. This chapter described the important features of storage, memory, and adapter cards, as required by three objectives of the CompTIA A+ Essentials (2009 Edition) Exam 701. They include objective 1.1, 1.6, and 1.9.

✓ TWO-MINUTE DRILL

Here are some of the key points covered in Chapter 2.

Mass Storage Devices and Backup Media

❑ A mass storage device holds large amounts of information, even when the power is off.

❑ Mass storage devices come in three general categories: magnetic, optical, and solid-state storage.

❑ Floppy disk drives, hard disk drives, and tape drives are examples of magnetic mass storage devices that store digital data on magnetized media.

❑ Optical drives include CD, DVD, and Blu-ray drives, each of which has a variety of capacities and speeds.

❑ Solid-state storage, or solid-state drives (SSDs), have no moving parts and use large-capacity, nonvolatile memory, commonly called flash memory.

❑ Hot-swappable drives can be connected or disconnected without shutting down the system. Some hard drive systems are hot-swappable, depending, in large part, on the interface.

❑ Hard drives with USB or FireWire interfaces are almost always hot-swappable, as is nearly any USB or FireWire device.

❑ RAID, which stands for redundant array of independent (or inexpensive) disks, is a group of schemes designed to provide either better performance or improved data reliability through redundancy.

❑ RAID 0 defines a striped set without parity. It gives improved drive read and write speeds.

❑ RAID 1, also called mirroring, provides fault tolerance because all the data is written identically to the two drives in the mirrored set.

❑ RAID 5, also called striping with distributed parity or striping with interleave parity, requires at least three physical drives.

❑ Many storage devices include removable media, meaning that the driver stays in place, while the media (disk, disc, or tape) is removed and replaced with another (disk, disc, or tape).

❑ Although you can use any writable storage device for data backups, tape drives are designed exclusively for this purpose.

Memory

❑ *Memory*, a computer's temporary working space, is one of the most important, but perhaps least understood, computer components. SRAM is very fast and very expensive and is used for L2 cache in most systems.

❑ Most of the memory in a PC is RAM, or random access memory.

❑ DRAM is slower than SRAM. It is less expensive, has a higher capacity, and is the main memory in the computer.

❑ DRAM technologies include RDRAM, SDRAM, DDR1 SDRAM, DDR2 SDRAM, and DDR3 SDRAM.

❑ Specialized RAM for video adapters is called VRAM.

❑ You must install DIMMs and RIMMs in full memory banks so their total bit width matches the width of the processor's data bus.

❑ Most memory modules do not perform error checking. Some older memory modules use an error-checking method called parity, and others may use a more complex method called ECC.

❑ DIMM and RIMM modules come in both single-sided and double-sided versions.

Adapter Cards

❑ An adapter card is a printed circuit board that installs into a PC's expansion bus to add functionality.

❑ The need for adapter cards has diminished as PC motherboards contain more functions.

❑ Numerous types of adapter cards are available, including (but not limited to) those for video, multimedia, I/O, and communications.

❑ Riser cards come in two types: 1) a card used to expand a computer's bus and allow other cards to be inserted into the riser card—usually in a different orientation in order to fit into a small computer case, and 2) a small expansion card, such as an AMR or CNR card, containing multiple functions.

SELF TEST

The following questions will help you measure your understanding of the material presented in this chapter. Read all of the choices carefully because there might be more than one correct answer. Choose all correct answers for each question.

Mass Storage Devices and Backup Media

1. This is a component in a hard drive system that reads and writes data.
    A. Spindle
    B. Head
    C. Platter
    D. Cable

2. Name the rotating shaft to which a hard drive's platters attach.
    A. Head
    B. Cable
    C. Pin
    D. Spindle

3. Which of the following is *not* an example of a magnetic mass storage device?
    A. FDD
    B. DVD drive
    C. HDD
    D. Tape Drive

4. Name two common interfaces for external hard drives.
    A. IDE and SATA
    B. Serial and parallel
    C. USB and IEEE 1394
    D. Coaxial and twisted pair

5. This DVD type stores 17.08 GB of data, or over eight hours of video.
    A. DVD-18
    B. DVD-9
    C. DVD-10
    D. DVD-5

6. This type of optical mass storage device was developed to read and write high-definition video.
   A. DVD-18
   B. CD-RW
   C. Blu-ray Disc
   D. DVD-RW

7. This type of mass storage device, once found in nearly every PC, is now rarely installed in a new PC.
   A. Tape drive
   B. Floppy disc drive
   C. Hard disk drive
   D. Optical disc drive

8. This feature indicates that a drive can be connected or disconnected without shutting down the system.
   A. External
   B. RAID
   C. USB
   D. Hot-swappable

9. This magnetic mass storage device type stores data sequentially and has been primarily used as backup storage for servers.
   A. FDD
   B. Tape drive
   C. Optical drive
   D. HDD

10. This is a group of standards defining several schemes for using multiple identical hard drives, working together in an array with the goal of achieving either better performance or redundancy.
    A. RAID
    B. eSATA
    C. USB
    D. Serial

Memory

11. This type of memory is volatile, used as temporary workspace by the CPU, and loses its contents every time a computer is powered down.
    - A. ROM
    - B. RAM
    - C. CMOS
    - D. Solid state

12. Cache memory uses which type of RAM chip because of its speed?
    - A. DRAM
    - B. VRAM
    - C. DIMM
    - D. SRAM

13. RDRAM can use only this type of slot on a motherboard.
    - A. RIMM
    - B. SIMM
    - C. DIMM
    - D. DRAM

14. This type of RAM module uses a special 240-pin DIMM socket and requires far less power than the previous modules, while providing almost twice the bandwidth.
    - A. DDR1 SDRAM
    - B. DDR2 SDRAM
    - C. DDR3 SDRAM
    - D. VRAM

15. This specialized type of RAM memory chip is designed for use on video adapters.
    - A. SRAM
    - B. SDRAM
    - C. DRAM
    - D. VRAM

16. This type of SDRAM module has memory chips mounted on both sides.
    - A. Single-sided
    - B. Double-sided
    - C. ECC
    - D. Dual channel

17. This chip manages the main memory on a motherboard.
    A. CMOS
    B. VRAM
    C. MCC
    D. DDR3

Adapter Cards

18. Which of the following is not an I/O technology?
    A. Serial
    B. USB
    C. IEEE 1394
    D. P1

19. Name a common communications adapter card used to connect PCs to a LAN or to take advantage of a DSL or cable modem Internet connection.
    A. Network adapter
    B. Modem
    C. USB
    D. Serial

20. This category of adapter card accepts and records video signals to a PC's hard drive.
    A. Network adapter
    B. Modem
    C. Capture card
    D. Video adapter

SELF TEST ANSWERS

Mass Storage Devices and Backup Media

1. ☑ **B.** The head is the component in a hard drive system that reads and writes data. There is one head for each platter side.
   ☒ **A,** spindle, is incorrect because this rotating pole holds the platters in a hard drive. **C,** platter, is incorrect because this component holds the data. **D,** cable, is incorrect because a cable connects a device to a computer but does not read data from a hard drive.

2. ☑ **D.** The spindle is the rotating shaft to which a hard drive's platters are attached.
   ☒ **A,** head, is incorrect because this component reads and writes data. **B,** cable, is incorrect because a cable connects a device to a computer and is not a rotating shaft. **C,** pin, is incorrect because it is a component of a cable plug, not the rotating shaft in a hard drive.

3. ☑ **B,** DVD drive, is *not* an example of a magnetic mass storage device; DVD drives use optical technology.
   ☒ **A,** FDD, **C,** HDD, and **D,** tape drive, are all incorrect because they are all examples of magnetic mass storage devices.

4. ☑ **C.** USB and IEEE 1394 are two common interfaces for external hard drives.
   ☒ **A,** IDE and SATA, is incorrect because these are common interfaces for internal hard drives (Chapter 1), not for external hard drives. **B,** serial and parallel, are not common interfaces for external hard drives. The standard serial interface is not fast enough. Parallel was used at one time, but it has been replaced by newer, faster plug and play interfaces. **D,** coaxial and twisted pair, are types of cables and not interfaces for external hard drives.

5. ☑ **A.** DVD-18 stores 17.08 GB of data, or over eight hours of video.
   ☒ **B,** DVD-9, is incorrect because it only holds 8.54 GB of data, or over four hours of video. **C,** DVD-10, is incorrect because it only holds 9.4 GB of data, or over four and a half hours of video. **D,** DVD-5, is incorrect because it only holds 4.7 GB of data, or over two hours of video.

6. ☑ **C.** Blu-ray Disc was developed to read and write high-definition video.
   ☒ **A,** DVD-18, **B,** CD-RW, and **D,** DVD-RW, are all incorrect because, although they are all optical mass storage devices, none of them can handle high-definition video formats.

7. ☑ **B,** floppy disc drive, is correct because, although it was once standard equipment, you now rarely see this type of drive installed in a new PC.
   ☒ **A,** tape drive, is incorrect because tape drives were never common in PCs. And it is even less likely that you will ever see one in a new PC. **C,** hard disk drive, is incorrect because hard disk drives are almost always installed in every new PC. **D,** optical disc drive, is incorrect because they frequently are installed in new PCs.

8. ☑ **D,** hot-swappable, is correct because it is a feature that indicates that a drive can be connected or disconnected without shutting down the system.

    ☒ **A,** external, is incorrect because while some external drives are also hot-swappable, the term "external" itself does not indicate that a drive has this feature. **B,** RAID, is incorrect because, although drives that are part of a RAID array may be hot-swappable, the term "RAID" itself does not indicate that a drive has this feature. **C,** USB, is incorrect because, although some hot-swappable drives use the USB interface, the term "USB" itself does not indicate that a drive has this feature.

9. ☑ **B,** tape drive, is correct because it is a magnetic mass storage device type that stores data sequentially, and it has been primarily used as backup storage for servers.

    ☒ **A,** FDD, and **D,** HDD, are incorrect because, although both are magnetic mass storage device types, neither has been primarily used as backup storage for servers. **C,** optical drive, is incorrect because it is not a magnetic mass storage device type, and it has never been primarily used as backup storage for servers.

10. ☑ **A,** RAID, is correct because this is the acronym for redundant array of independent (or inexpensive) disks, a group of schemes designed to provide either better performance or improved data reliability through redundancy.

    ☒ **B,** eSATA, is incorrect because this is a standard for an external version of the serial ATA interface. **C,** USB, is incorrect because this is the universal serial bus standard. **D,** serial, is incorrect because this is another interface, not a standard for disk arrays.

Memory

11. ☑ **B.** RAM is the type of volatile memory used by the CPU as workspace.

    ☒ **A,** ROM, is incorrect because this type of memory is not volatile; its contents are not lost every time the PC is powered off. **C,** CMOS, is incorrect because it is special battery-powered support memory that holds basic system configuration information used by the computer as it powers up. **D,** solid state, is incorrect because this is a type of storage device that is nonvolatile and is not used by the processor in the manner described.

12. ☑ **D.** SRAM is the type of RAM used for cache memory because of its speed.

    ☒ **A,** DRAM, is incorrect because this is slower than SRAM. **B,** VRAM, is incorrect because although it is fast, this type of RAM is used on video adapters. **C,** DIMM, is incorrect as it is a RAM connector/slot type, not a type of RAM chip.

13. ☑ **A.** RIMM is the type of slot on a motherboard that can only be used by RDRAM.

    ☒ **B,** SIMM, and **C,** DIMM, are incorrect because these slot types cannot be used by RDRAM. **D,** DRAM, is incorrect because it is a type of RAM chip, not a type of slot.

14. ☑ C. DDR3 SDRAM is the type of RAM module that uses a special 240-pin DIMM socket and requires far less power than the previous modules, while providing almost twice the bandwidth.
☒ A, DDR1 SDRAM, is incorrect because it uses a 184-pin DIMM socket, not a 240-pin DIMM socket. B, DDR2 SDRAM, is incorrect because, although it also uses a (different) 240-pin DIMM socket, it requires more power than the previous RAM module type (DDR1 SDRAM). D, VRAM, is incorrect because it is a chip type that mounts on a video adapter, not on a DIMM module.

15. ☑ D. VRAM is correct, as this type of memory chip is designed for use on video adapters.
☒ A, SRAM, B, SDRAM, and C, DRAM, are all incorrect because none of these memory chip types was designed for use on video adapters.

16. ☑ B, double-sided, is correct because this type of RAM module has memory chips mounted on both sides.
☒ A, single-sided, is incorrect because a single-sided memory module only has chips mounted on one side. C, ECC, is incorrect because this stands for error-correcting code, which is an error detecting and correcting mechanism used by some memory modules. D, dual channel, is incorrect because this refers to a technique for speeding up memory access in which the MCC switches between two memory modules, effectively doubling the memory speed.

17. ☑ C. MCC, or memory controller chip, is correct because this chip controls the main memory on a motherboard.
☒ A, CMOS, is incorrect because the CMOS chip is a special battery-supported chip that retains the system settings. B, VRAM, is incorrect because this is a type of RAM used on video adapters. D, DDR3, is incorrect because this is a type of SDRAM, not a controller chip.

Adapter Cards

18. ☑ D. P1 is not an I/O technology, but a type of power connector.
☒ A, serial, B, USB, and C, IEEE 1394, are incorrect because they are I/O technologies.

19. ☑ A. A network adapter is a common communications adapter card used to connect PCs to a LAN or to take advantage of a DSL or cable modem Internet connection.
☒ B, modem, is incorrect because, although it is a communications adapter card, it is used for a dial-up connection, not for a LAN connection. C, USB, is incorrect because it is an I/O interface, not a communications adapter. D, serial, is incorrect because it is an I/O interface, not a communications adapter, although some external modems can connect to a serial port.

20. ☑ C, capture card, is correct. This type of adapter is used to record video signals to a PC's hard drive.
☒ A, network adapter, is incorrect because this type of adapter is used for network communications. B, modem, is incorrect because it is used for a dial-up connection, not for recording video signals. D, video adapter, is incorrect because it is used to drive a display device, not to capture video signals.

3

Power Supplies, Cooling Systems, and Input/Output

CERTIFICATION OBJECTIVES

❑   **701: 1.2**   Explain motherboard components, types, and features

❑   **701: 1.3**   Classify power supply types and characteristics

❑   **701: 1.5**   Explain cooling methods and devices

❑   **701: 1.7**   Distinguish between the different display devices and their characteristics

❑   **701: 1.9**   Summarize the function and types of adapter cards

✓   Two-Minute Drill

Q&A   Self Test

■ **701: 1.3** *Classify power supply types and characteristics*

This section describes power supply types and characteristics. You will learn about voltage, wattage, capacity, power supply fans, and form factors. We will describe AC adapters, used to supply power to laptops and various external devices, in Chapter 6.

Power Supplies

A *power supply* or *power supply unit (PSU)* is the component that provides power for all other components on the motherboard and internal to the PC case. Every PC has an easily identified power supply; it is typically located inside the computer case at the back, and it is visible from the outside when looking at the back of the PC. You will see the three-prong power socket, a label, and sometimes a tiny switch. Figure 3-1 shows the interior of a PC with a power supply on the upper left. Notice the bundle of cables coming out of the power supply. These supply power to the motherboard and all other internal components. Each component must receive the appropriate type and amount of power it requires, and the power supply itself also has its requirements. Therefore, you should understand some basic electrical terminology and apply it to the functions of power supplies.

FIGURE 3-1

The power supply, shown in the upper left, is usually located in the back of the computer case.

Electrical Terminology

Electricity comes in two forms, *alternating current (AC)* or *direct current (DC)*. In direct current, the flow of electrons is in only one direction and is the kind of current generated by a battery. In alternating current, the flow of electrons reverses periodically and has alternating positive and negative values. It is the kind of electricity that comes from a wall outlet.

Volts is the unit of measurement of the pressure of electrons, or the electromotive force. It is calculated using the formula volts = watts / amps. *Watts* is a unit of measurement of actual delivered power. You calculate it using the formula watts = volts × amps. *Amperes (amps)* is a unit of measurement for electrical current or rate of flow of electrons through a wire. The formula is amps = watts / volts. All these calculations are versions of Ohms Law, which represents the fundamental relationship among current, voltage, and resistance.

Voltage

The power supply is responsible for converting the alternating current (AC) voltage from wall outlets into the direct current (DC) voltage that the computer requires: ±12 VDC, ±5 VDC, or ±3.3 VDC (volts DC).

The PC power supply accomplishes this task through a series of switching transistors, which gives rise to the term *switching mode power supply*. A device, such as a laser printer or a CRT, that requires high voltage has its own *high-voltage power supply (HVPS)*.

Typical North American wall outlets provide about 110–120 VAC (volts AC) at a frequency of 60 Hertz (cycles per second), which is also expressed as ~115 VAC at 60 Hz. The frequency means the number of times per second that alternating current reverses direction. Elsewhere in the world, standard power is 220–240 VAC at 50 Hz. Power supplies manufactured for sale throughout the world will have a switch on the back for selecting the correct input voltage setting. Figure 3-2 shows the back of a power supply with the switch for selecting 115 VAC or 240 VAC. It is the tiny slide switch positioned below the power connector, officially called an *IEC-320 connector*, more commonly called a *voltage selector switch*.

exam
ⓦatch　*Make sure you are familiar with the voltages required by computer components: ±12, ±5, or ±3.3 VDC.*

The back of a
power supply,
with the IEC-320
connector and
the voltage
selection switch

Wattage

How big a power supply do you need? First, we are not talking about physical size,
but the *capacity* or wattage a power supply can handle. Figure 3-3 shows the label on
a power supply. Notice that this is a 300-watt power supply. Notice also that the label
specifies this power supply will run on either 120 VAC or 240 VAC and at either
50/60 Hz, which means it will run in almost any country. Just a few years ago power
supplies ranging from 230 to 250 watts were considered more than adequate for PCs;
today you will find many modestly priced PCs with 300-watt or greater power supplies.
High-end computers use 500- to 1,600-watt power supplies. Therefore, to answer the
question, you need a power supply with a capacity that exceeds the total watts required
by all the internal components, such as the motherboard, memory, drives, and various
adapters.

on the
Job

If a device label does not state the number of watts required, simple math will
give you the answer. All you need is the volts and amps, which you should find
printed on the device somewhere. Once you have these two numbers, multiply
them together (watts = volts × amps) and you will have the wattage of the
device.

The maximum
wattage supported
by a power supply
appears on the
left side of this
label, under the
word "output."

EXERCISE 3-1

Check Out the Wattage on PCs and Other Devices

1. Look at the back of a PC and find the power supply label. Record the wattage information. If wattage is not shown, but the volts and amps are, multiply those two numbers to calculate the wattage.

2. Do the same on other devices that are available to you, such as displays, printers, and scanners.

3. Similarly, check out the wattage on noncomputer devices in the classroom or at home.

Fan

Another function of a power supply is to dissipate the heat it and other PC components generate. Heat buildup can cause computer components (including the power supply) to fail. Therefore, power supplies have a built-in exhaust fan that draws air through the computer case and cools the components inside.

AC Adapters

Another form of power supply is an AC adapter used with portable computers and external peripherals. We describe AC adapters in Chapter 6.

Form Factors

Like motherboards and cases, computer power supplies come in a variety of sizes and configurations. The most commonly used is referred to as the *ATX power supply*, used in most case sizes, except the smallest, which have low-profile power supplies for the low-profile cases, and the largest, which have jumbo-sized power supplies for the full-tower cases.

Power supplies have dedicated cables for supplying power directly to the motherboard and to internally installed peripherals—mainly various drives. The cables for peripherals have *Molex connectors* and *miniconnectors*. The Molex and miniconnectors each have four wires and provide 5 and 12 volts to peripherals. Molex connectors are the most commonly used, whereas floppy drives use the miniconnector. Figure 3-4 shows a power splitter cable with a single Molex connector on one end and miniconnectors

FIGURE 3-4

A power splitter cable with a single Molex connector and two miniconnectors

on the other. The SATA power supply cable replaces the 4-pin peripheral cable and adds support for 3.3 volts for power supplies and peripherals that support this standard.

The form factor of the power supply determines the motherboard it works with and the type of connector used for the motherboard. Most motherboards use 20- or 24-pin connectors, called *P1 power connectors*. If a motherboard requires additional power, a separate cable will connect to the motherboard with a 4-, 6-, or 8-pin connector.

W a t c h *The CompTIA A+ Essentials (2009 Edition) Exam objective 701: 1.3 refers to the ATX power supply as "proprietary."*

ATX

The design of an ATX power supply lets it pair with an ATX motherboard. This form factor has a single 20-pin connector for the motherboard, called the P1 connector. Newer ATX power supplies that follow the *ATX12V* standard will also have an additional connector—with four wires, for 12 V. This is the *P4 12V* connector. You can also use ATX power supplies with BTX motherboards.

ATX power supplies and motherboards work together to provide a feature called *soft power*. Soft power allows software to turn off a computer rather than only using a physical switch. Most PCs have soft power. A computer with soft power enabled has a pair of small wires leading from the physical switch on the case to the motherboard. Usually, a system setting exists that controls just how this feature is used. For safety's sake, you should always consider soft power as being on, because when you have enabled software power, turning the power switch off means that, although the computer appears to be off, the power supply is still supplying ±5 volts to the motherboard. This means you can never trust the on-off switch. Some PCs come equipped with two power switches. One is in the front, and you can consider it the "soft" off switch. The other is on the back of the case, in the power supply itself, and this is the "real" off switch.

on the !Job *A motherboard with soft power is never off, even when the switch on the front of the PC is in the "Off" position. There is always a ±5 V charge to the motherboard from the power supply. The only way to ensure that there is no power is to unplug the power supply from the power source. Always do this before opening a PC case.*

Proprietary Power Supplies

In response to the demands of PC-based servers and gamers, power supply manufacturers have added proprietary features beyond those in the standards. You can find power supplies that offer special support for the newest Intel and AMD CPU requirements and greater efficiency, which saves on power usage and reduces heat output.

Energy Efficiency

Although not directly a power supply issue, energy efficiency in all PC components has become a very important feature and affects the selection of a power supply. We seem to need bigger and bigger power supplies to accommodate the increasing number and types of components we include in our PCs: more memory, larger hard drives, more powerful video adapters, and so on. The good news is that the power requirements have not grown proportionally with the performance improvements of these components, which are more energy efficient and have features that reduce their power consumption during idle times. Learn more about managing these energy-saving features in Chapter 6.

CERTIFICATION OBJECTIVE

■ **701: 1.5** *Explain cooling methods and devices*

In Chapter 1, the sections on motherboards, CPUs, and cases introduced the need for cooling the circuitry inside a PC case and briefly discussed the part fans and design play in keeping your computer cool enough to function. The following information provides a more focused look at the various techniques used for this purpose.

Cooling Systems

The more powerful PCs become, the more heat is generated within the case. Heat is your PC's enemy, and it should be yours, too. An overheated CPU will fail. Rather than allow heat to cause damage, several techniques—both passive and active—are used to maintain an optimum operating temperature. Some components will even slow down so they produce less heat before any damage occurs. Manufacturers have struggled to keep ahead of the heat curve and provide sufficient cooling for the entire system. These methods involve fans, heat sinks, thermal compounds, and even liquid cooling systems.

CPU and Case Fans

Early PCs relied on the design of the PC case and the power supply fan to provide all the cooling for the computer's interior. During this era, the typical PC had vents in the front through which the power supply fan pulled cool air and in the back through which the heated air was exhausted. Today, we usually employ additional methods, but the power supply fan still plays an important part in cooling the PC. It is very common to see a fan mounted directly over the CPU, as shown in Figure 3-1, in which the *CPU fan* is clearly visible in the center of the photo.

One or more case fans may also supplement a power supply fan. A *case fan* is a fan mounted directly on the case, as opposed to a power supply fan, which is inside the power supply. Figure 3-1 also shows a black case fan on the left, just below the power supply. Systems that do not come with a case fan may have mounting brackets for adding one or more case fans.

Heat Sinks

Another device that works to cool hot components is a *heat sink*. This is usually a passive metal object with a flat surface attached to a component, a chip, for instance. The exposed side of a heat sink has an array of fins used to dissipate the heat. Look for the white heat sink that is partially visible at the bottom of Figure 3-1. A combined heat sink and fan may even attach directly to a chip.

Thermal Compounds

A special substance, called *thermal compound*, *thermal paste*, or *heat sink compound*, increases the heat conductivity between a fan or heat sink and a chip. The most common is a white, silicone-based paste, but there are also ceramic-based and metal-based thermal compounds that create a bond between the chip and the fan or heat sink, increasing the flow of heat from the chip.

Liquid Cooling Systems

Many of today's motherboards for sale on the Internet or at large electronics stores feature one or more *liquid cooling systems*. There are various types of systems ranging from sealed liquid cooling systems that transfer heat from several components by conduction to active systems that include actual tiny refrigeration units.

Case Design

The design of each case allows for maximum airflow over the components. Part of this design is the placement of vents, positioned to either bring in fresh air or to exhaust air. If this airflow is disturbed, even with additional openings, the system may overheat. Therefore, be sure that all the expansion slot openings on the back of the PC are covered. The expansion card's bracket covers each one that lines up with an occupied expansion slot. A metal *slot cover* covers an empty slot in order to preserve the correct airflow. Flip back to Figure 1-7 in Chapter 1, which shows the back of a PC with (from top to bottom) the vents for the power supply fan, the vents for a case fan, and the expansion slots (all covered).

EXERCISE 3-2

Check Out Your Cooling System

1. Without opening the computer case, look for vents in the case.
2. If the computer is running, you should hear a fan running in the power supply, and see the vent from the power supply. You may hear another fan running and see a set of vents for that fan.
3. Are there vents that do not appear to have a case fan behind them?
4. Hold your hand by the vents you located and determine if air flow is going into or out of the computer case. Is the power supply fan blowing in or out? If you located a case fan, is it blowing in or out?
5. Make note of your findings and discuss with your classmates or coworkers.

■ **701: 1.7** *Distinguish between the different display devices and their characteristics*

This section introduces all of the topics covered by the CompTIA A+ Essentials (2009 Edition) Exam objective 701: 1.7, including the various types of display devices (projectors, CRTs, and LCDs), LCD technologies, connector types for display devices, and display settings.

Video Adapters and Displays

The quality of the image you see on a PC display depends on both the capabilities and configuration of the two most important video components: the video adapter and the display device. You will learn about these components in this section. How a video adapter and display device connect has become a more complex topic as we transition from the old analog technologies to several new digital technologies that have arrived on the scene in recent years. Finally, you will become familiar with display settings and how they affect output to a display.

Video Adapters

The *video adapter* controls the output from the PC to the display device. Although the video adapter contains all the logic, and does most of the work, the quality of the resulting image depends on the modes supported by both the adapter and the display. If the adapter is capable of higher-quality output than the display, the display limits the result. In this section, we will explore video interface modes, screen resolution and color density, and the computer interfaces used by video adapters.

Video Interface Modes

Very basic video modes are text and graphics. As a PC boots, and before the operating system takes control, the video is in text mode and can only display the limited ASCII character set. Once the operating system is in control, it loads drivers for the video adapter and display, and it uses a graphics mode that can display bitmapped graphics. Today these graphics modes—commonly called video modes—support millions of colors. Several video modes have been introduced since the first IBM PC in 1981. However, we will only discuss the video graphics modes you can expect to encounter in business and homes today.

VGA   *Video graphics array (VGA)* is a video adapter standard introduced with the IBM PS/2 computers in the late 1980s. VGA sends analog signals to the display. The analog signal produces a wide range of colors. VGA is an old technology today because we have gone far beyond it in capabilities, but some software packages still list it as a minimum requirement for installing the software, and the connector used on VGA adapters is in use today on many video adapters that also support more advanced video modes—although newer connectors are also available, often on the same adapter. *VGA mode* most often consists of a combination of 640 × 480 pixels display resolution and 16 colors. VGA can produce around 16 million different colors, but can display only up to 256 different colors at a time. Another term for this color setting is *8-bit high color*.

Beyond VGA   In the past two decades, video standards have advanced nearly as fast as CPU standards. *Super video graphics array (SVGA)* is a term that was first used for any video adapter or monitor that exceeded the VGA standard in resolution and color depth. But improvements to SVGA's early 800 × 600–pixel resolution now include 1024 × 768, 1280 × 1024, 1600 × 1200, and 1680 × 1250. Although SVGA also supports a palette of 16 million colors, the amount of video memory present limits the number of colors simultaneously displayed. This is also true of the newer video standards, which are designed to work with flat panel LCD and other digital display devices, including Digital Visual Interface (DVI), High-Definition Multimedia Interface (HDMI), and DisplayPort.

DVI   Of the three newer video technologies, only *Digital Visual Interface (DVI)* offers downward compatibility with analog displays via its analog mode, *DVI-A*. The digital mode of DVI, *DVI-D*, is partially compatible with HDMI. *DVI-I*, or DVI-Integrated, supports both DVI-D and DVI-A signals and can control both digital and analog displays. The current version of the DVI standard is version 1.4. Depending on the exact implementation of DVI, it supports several screen resolutions and color densities. Common resolutions include 1920 × 1200 WUXGA running at 60 Hz, 1280 × 1024 SXGA running at 85 Hz, and 2560 × 1600 WQXGA running at 60 Hz. There are several connector types to support these modes, detailed later in this chapter.

HDMI   *High-Definition Multimedia Interface (HDMI)* is a recent interface standard for use with DVD/Blu-ray players, digital television (DTV) players, set-top cable or satellite service boxes, camcorders, digital cameras, and other devices. It combines audio and video signals into an uncompressed signal and has a bandwidth of up to

**HDMi versus HDMI: The
CompTIA A+ Essentials (2009 Edition)
Exam objective 701: 1.7 spells it "HDMi,"
but in recent years, most references
to this standard use all caps—HDMI.
You should simply recognize either
representation on the exam.**

5 GB/second. HDMI is integrated into many media center PCs, replacing DVI, and many Home Theater PCs (HTPCs) use this interface. Further, it supports a digital rights management (DRM) feature called *High-Bandwidth Digital Content Protection (HDCP)* to prevent illegal copying of Blu-ray discs. The current version of this specification is 1.4, released in May 2009. The first HDMI version 1.4 devices appeared in the second half of 2009.

DisplayPort *DisplayPort*, a digital display interface standard developed by the Video Electronics Standards Association, is the newest of the standards discussed here. Like HDMI, it supports both video and audio signals and contains HDCP copy protection. It is unique in that it is royalty-free to manufacturers and has some important proponents such as Apple, Hewlett-Packard, AMD, Intel, and Dell. At first, industry experts observed that we did not need this standard after the wide acceptance of HDMI, but that changed after DisplayPort received a huge boost in the fall of 2008 when Apple introduced new MacBooks with DisplayPort replacing DVI. DisplayPort neither supports all the color options supported by HDMI, nor is it electrically compatible with DVI, whereas HDMI is backward compatible with DVI. DisplayPort also includes copy-protection for DVDs in the form of DisplayPort Content Protection (DPCP). At this writing, the current version of DisplayPort is 1.2.

Screen Resolution and Color Density

And so it goes; as fast as new standards are developed and adopted by manufacturers, they are modified and improved upon. Table 3-1 gives a summary of screen resolution and color density typical of the listed video standards. There are additional standards available, particularly those starting with *W*, which apply to wide-screen monitors. Keep in mind the best resolution and color density you will see on your display depends on the capabilities of both the video adapter and display and, increasingly, the aspect ratio of the screen. Wide-screen monitors have different native resolutions, which are expressed in columns and rows, as in 800 columns by 600 rows. We will discuss aspect ratio, refresh rates, and other display features later in this chapter in the section, "Displays."

| TABLE 3-1 | A Selection of Video Standards and their Resolution, Color Palette, and Color Density |

Name	Maximum Graphics Resolution	Number of Colors in Palette	Number of Colors Displayed Simultaneously in Standard Color Density
Video graphics array (VGA)	640 × 480	Over 16 million	16
eXtended Graphics Array, (XGA) an IBM standard	1024 × 768	Over 16 million	256 or 65,536
Extended Video Graphics Array (EVGA), a VESA standard	1024 × 768	Over 16 million	256 or 65,536
Super video graphics array (SVGA)	1600 × 1200	Over 16 million	Over 16 million*
Super XG (A SXGA)	1280 × 1024	Over 16 million	Over 16 million*
Super XGA Plus (SXGA+)	1400 × 1050	Over 16 million	Over 16 million*
Ultra XGA (UXGA)	1600 × 1200	Over 16 million	Over 16 million*
Wide UXGA (WUXGA)	1920 × 1200 (wide screen)	Over 16 million	Over 16 million*
Wide Quad XGA (WQXGA)	2560 × 1600 (wide screen)	Over 16 million	Over 16 million
Wide Quad UXGA (WQUXGA)	3840 × 2400 (wide screen)	Over 16 million	Over 16 million

*The actual number of simultaneous colors depends on the video adapter and the amount of video memory installed.

Computer Interfaces

When purchasing a video adapter, pay attention to the interface between the video adapter and the computer so that you select one you can install into your PC. If the motherboard contains a video adapter, it still accesses one of the standard busses in the computer. Our experience is that many brand-name PCs have a separate video card; in which case, the video adapter installs into one of three types of bus connectors: PCI, PCIe, or AGP. We discussed these bus types in Chapter 1. You will find the current version of the video standards mentioned here available with any of these interfaces.

Multi-Monitor

For some years, people who work with simultaneously open multiple documents or who have large spreadsheet or image requirements have used *multi-monitor* PC configurations that extend the desktop to two or more displays. People in specialized application environments such as CAD, stock day trading, and software development use multiple monitors on one computer. Multi-monitors previously required expensive hardware and special software, but today it is easy to have two or more monitors. These days a "dual-headed" video adapter won't break most budgets, and with the correct drivers, a modern operating system manages the image placement. Today's video adapters, which have large amounts of dedicated RAM available, manage these tasks without taking a big performance hit. Monitors can be CRTs or flat-panel displays, and analog, digital, or both, depending on the video adapter. Laptops have long supported two monitors, but for many years the second monitor was a replacement for the laptop display—something a user attached to a laptop while in the office. Once operating systems supported multiple displays, people caught on to using the desktop monitor, not as a replacement, but as an extension of the desktop.

on the job

*Multi-monitor **is also known as** dual-monitor **(if only two),** multi-display, **and even** multi-head.*

Multiple Video Adapters for One Monitor

The opposing model to multi-monitor is the use of two or more video adapters to drive one display to improve video graphics performance. This is generically called a *multi-GPU solution*, because the graphics processing unit is one of the most important components of the video adapter. Two manufacturers stand out for their proprietary multi-GPU systems: ATI and nvidia. Although each manufacturer has several possible configurations for their multi-GPU solutions, both now offer a direct connection between the video adapters that are working together in a PC. This direct connection bypasses the PCIe bus for communications between the adapters, thus avoiding an additional load on the shared bus.

The ATI solution is commonly called *CrossFire*, and the third-generation products carry the ATI CrossFireX brand name. The nvidia multi-GPU solution is branded *Scalable Link Interface (SLI)*. In addition to specific video adapter models, both manufacturers require motherboards with chipsets that support their solution. Expect to encounter multi-GPU solutions in systems that must render high-performance graphics.

Displays

The function of a PC video *display* device is to produce visual responses to user requests. Often called simply a display or *monitor*, it receives computer output from the video adapter, which controls its functioning. The display technology—which you have already learned about—must match the technology of the video card to which it attaches, so in this section we will explore the two main types of displays, the connectors used to connect a display to the video adapter, and display settings. Until a few years ago, most desktop computers used cathode ray tube (CRT) monitors, but today flat panel displays (FPDs) are inexpensive and universally available. This is true both for computer displays and for televisions.

CRTs

A *cathode ray tube (CRT) monitor* is bulky because of the large cathode ray tube it contains. A CRT uses an electron gun to activate phosphors behind the screen. Each dot on the monitor, called a *pixel,* has the ability to generate red, green, or blue, depending on the signals it receives. This combination of colors results in the display you see on the monitor. CRT monitors are rapidly phasing out in favor of flat panel displays, but there are many still in use. CRTs have extremely high-voltage components inside, so be careful when working on them.

Flat Panel Displays

A *flat panel display (FPD)* is a computer display that uses liquid crystal or plasma technology and is not as bulky as a large picture tube. The screen enclosure can be as thin as one to two inches. Because plasma technology is generally more expensive than liquid crystal technology, which greatly outsells it, we will not discuss it in this book.

LCD Technologies Early *liquid crystal displays (LCDs)* did not have picture quality equal to CRTs, but they have improved so much that they now outsell CRTs, in part because they require much less desk space and power. The first LCD panels, called *passive matrix displays,* consisted of a grid of horizontal and vertical wires. At one end of each wire was a transistor, which received display signals from the computer. When the two transistors (one at the x-axis and one at the y-axis) sent voltage along their wires, the pixel at the intersection of the two wires lit up.

Active matrix displays are newer and use different technology, called *thin-film transistor (TFT)* technology. Active matrix displays contain transistors at each pixel, resulting in more colors, better resolution, a better ability to display moving objects, and the ability to view it at greater angles. However, active matrix displays use more power than passive matrix displays. Modern LCD displays are also called *digital LCD displays* because they accept digital signals, whereas early LCD displays accepted only analog signals and converted them to digital internally.

LCD Display Resolution   An LCD panel has hardwired pixels, with a set of red/blue/green (RGB) dots for each pixel. Therefore, each LCD display has a native resolution beyond which it cannot operate. In addition, if you set an LCD at a lower resolution, the image degrades. For this reason, always set an LCD display at its native resolution, as stated on the box and in the display documentation.

LCD Contrast Ratio   *Contrast ratio,* the difference in value between a display's brightest white and darkest black, is an area in which the early LCD displays could not compete with CRTs. Today, however, even inexpensive LCD displays offer a dynamic contrast ratio of 3,000:1 or a static contrast ration of 800:1 or greater, which is excellent.

Display Aspect Ratio   The *aspect ratio* of a display is the proportion of the width to the height. For instance, a traditional CRT monitor has a width-to-height aspect ratio of 4:3. LCD panels come in the traditional 4:3 aspect ratio as well as in wider formats, of which the most common is 16:9, which allows you to view wide format movies. When viewing a widescreen movie video on a 4:3 display, it shows in a *letterbox,* meaning the image size reduces until the entire width of the image fits on the screen. The remaining portions of the screen are black, creating a box effect. Figure 3-5 shows an LCD display with a 16:9 aspect ratio.

Power Efficiency   An LCD display requires less than half the wattage of a comparably sized CRT. Add to this the power saving features built in to displays, such as the features defined by the *display power-management signaling (DPMS)* standard of the Video Electronics Standards Association (VESA). Rather than needing to turn off a display manually when you leave your desk or are not using the computer, DPMS-compliant displays automatically go into a lower power mode after a preconfigured amount of time without any activity.

FIGURE 3-5

An LCD display with a 16:9 aspect ratio

Projectors

A *projector* takes video output and projects it onto a screen for viewing by a larger audience. Most digital projectors pass the light from a high-intensity bulb through an LCD panel to project an image on a screen. There are also projectors that use *Digital Light Processing (DLP)* chips that yield a larger, brighter image, and small projectors that use LEDs (light emitting diodes) or lasers. DLP projectors are also used in rear-projection televisions.

Digital projectors have been available for years, but they were bulky and expensive. Today the prices of projectors have dropped to the point where they are usable as TVs because they can use video as well as digital sources. Their physical size has dropped as well, and now some tiny digital projectors fit in the palm of a hand and are used with a laptop computer for presentations to small groups. They are available in many video modes, including XGA, SVGA, WXGA, and SXGA, among others. Add to this built-in support in Windows operating systems and the ability to network these devices by name or IP and you have a very popular device.

Touch Screens

A *touch screen* is a video display that allows you to select and maneuver screen objects by touching, tapping, and sliding your finger or a stylus on the screen. Touch-screen technology was developed in the late 1960s, appeared on special-use systems as early as the 1970s, and has continued to be popular for use in kiosk-based computer systems. Touch screens for personal computers have been around almost as long as personal computers, but have never enjoyed a great deal of popularity for general use. In the 1980s, touch screens on personal computers ran a text-based operating system, usually a proprietary version of DOS, requiring special versions of any application programs you wished to use. Today's touch screens are so improved over those of 20 years ago that there is very little resemblance. They are now found on many handheld devices, such as smart phones like the Blackberry and the Apple iPhone, personal digital assistants (PDAs), and GPS navigation systems. Digital electronic reading devices, such as the Sony Reader Daily Edition and the Amazon Kindle, also have touch screens.

Display Connectors

For nearly two decades, technicians only needed to work with one video display connector—the DB-15. Now other options are available that go with newer technologies. Here, you will learn about common display connectors. Figure 3-6

DVI-I Dual Link, S-Video, and DB-15 connectors on a video adapter card

shows the back of a video adapter with three connectors: (from left to right) DVI Dual Link, S-Video, and DB-15. The last is often labeled "VGA." The following sections describe these connectors, as well as composite video, HDMI, and DisplayPort.

DB-15/VGA

The DB-15 connector, used on video adapters for connecting to both traditional CRT monitors and many flat panel displays, has three rows of five pins each, slightly staggered. This connector is also commonly called a *Video Electronics Standards Association (VESA)* connector or VGA connector, named for the standards organization that developed this connector standard, as well as many other PC components. This name does not reflect the ability of the video adapter, but only the fact that the earliest VGA video adapters used it. The connector on the monitor cable is male, whereas the connector on the video adapter (the computer end) is female. A male port or connector has pins, and a female port or connector is a receiver with sockets for the pins of the male connector.

LCD displays use a digital signal. Although video adapters actually store information digitally in video RAM, they have long been able to convert the digital signal to analog for CRT displays. Therefore, LCD displays that connect to these traditional video adapters (as distinguished by the DB-15 connector on the LCD's interface cable) must include the ability to reconvert the analog signal back to digital! We call such a display an *analog LCD display* (in spite of its digital nature).

DVI

Now that LCD displays have a much greater market share than CRTs, you will find displays that do not perform the digital-to-analog conversion or that, alternatively, accept both digital and analog signals—the latter requiring the old conversion. Such a display has a connector that accepts the digital signal. You have to match this type of display with an adapter card with the appropriate connector. In the case of DVI, you will also need to match the pins because several different configurations of DVI connectors look alike until you compare them (Figure 3-7). The typical DVI cable is heavy and requires screws to hold it firmly in place.

As a technician, you must pay close attention to DVI pin compatibility because there are five standard DVI connector configurations, distinguished by the type or types of signals they can transmit. All standard DVI type connectors measure 1" by 3/8" with a variety of pin configurations, including one or two grids of pins and a flat blade off to the side of the pin grid area.

DVI connector pin layouts for DVI-I, DVI-D, and DVI-A

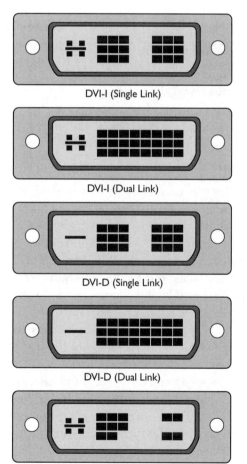

DVI-I (Single Link)

DVI-I (Dual Link)

DVI-D (Single Link)

DVI-D (Dual Link)

DVI-A

DVI-A supports analog signals with four pins positioned around the blade to the side of the main pin grid area. It has two other groupings of pins: the first contains eight pins in a 3 × 3 grid (the ninth position is empty); the second group contains two sets of two pins with space between them.

DVI-D, a digital-only connector, comes in two varieties called Single Link and Dual Link. The DVI-D Single Link connector has two 3 × 3 grids of 9 pins each, whereas the DVI-D Dual Link has a single 24-pin 3 × 8 grid.

DVI-I is interchangeable, supporting either analog or digital signals. It also comes in single-link and dual-link versions. Both versions resemble their DVI-D counterparts with the addition of the four pins around the blade to support analog mode.

Apple briefly used a smaller version of the DVI connector called a Mini-DVI, which they are phasing out. The Mini-DVI connector is about the same width as a standard USB connector, but is twice as thick, containing four rows of eight pins. Yet another miniaturized version, the Micro-DVI connector, is used by ASUS and Apple. This DVI-D-compatible connector is almost the exact size of a USB connector. This connector was also briefly supported by Apple as they moved from DVI to DisplayPort and Mini DisplayPort.

e x a m

ⓦatch *Be sure you recognize the pin compatibility issues with the various types of DVI connectors.*

HDMI

HDMI is backward-compatible with the DVI standard as implemented in PC video adapters and displays. Therefore, a DVI video adapter can control an HDMI monitor, providing an appropriate cable and converter is used. The audio and remote control features of HDMI, however, will not be available. One specially designed cable with an HDMI connector is all you need now between a compatible video device and the TV. Previously, several cables were required.

Four types of HDMI connectors are available. Type A and B were part of the original specification, whereas Type C is defined in the 1.3 version of the specification, and Type D is defined in the 1.4 version. Type A measures 13.9 mm × 4.45 mm (approximately .5" × .18") and has 19 pins. It supports SDTV, EDTV, and HDTV and is electrically compatible with DVI-D Single Link. Type B measures 21.2 mm × 4.45 mm (.8" × .18") and has 29 pins. It includes the same support as Type A, plus it supports very-high-resolution future displays, such as WQUXGA (3840 × 2400). It is electrically compatible with DVI-D Dual Link.

The last two HDMI connectors are miniconnectors designed for use in laptops and other small devices. Type C, defined by the version 1.3 standard, measures just

10.42 mm × 2.42 mm (.4"× .1") with the same 19 pins as a Type A connector but some changes in assignments. The HDMI 1.4 specification introduced the Type D HDMI miniconnector, measuring just 2.8 mm × 6.4 mm (.1" × .25").

DisplayPort

A DisplayPort cable is slimmer than those of its predecessor, and the connectors are much smaller and do not require thumbscrews like those on DVI plugs. Currently, manufacturers that support DisplayPort often include HDMI in the same devices, so you may see both connectors. They come in two sizes: standard and Mini DisplayPort.

Composite Video

The next time you watch television, take a close look at the image. You will notice variations in both brightness and color (unless you are watching a black and white TV!). The traditional transmission system for television video signals, called *composite video*, combines the color and brightness information with the synchronization data into one signal. While television sets have long used separate signals, called *luminance* (brightness) and *chrominance* (color), they receive composite signals and have to separate out the luminance and chrominance information. Errors in separating the two signals from the composite signal result in on-screen problems, especially with complex images.

Component Video Signals

Component video is a video-signaling method in which analog video information is transmitted as two or more discrete signals. Two general types of component video are RGB Video and S-Video. DVI, HDMI, and DisplayPort are replacing these component-signaling interfaces.

RGB Video   *RGB video* is a simple type of component video signal that sends three separate signals: red, green, and blue, using three coaxial cables. Variations on RGB component signaling are based on how the synchronization signal is handled. The SVGA RGB signaling method was widely used for PC displays before DVI and HDMI came along.

S-Video   *Super-Video*, more commonly called *S-Video*, refers to the transmission of a video signal using two signals. These two signals are luminance, represented by "Y," and chrominance, represented by "C." The luminance signal carries the black-and-white portion of video, or brightness. The chrominance signal carries the RGB color information, including saturation and hue. Further, the chrominance signal can be broken into multiple channels for improved speed and more precise color. S-Video ports are round to accommodate a round plug with four pins.

Display Settings

You can adjust a variety of display settings. You will find some of these settings, such as vertical hold, horizontal hold, and refresh rate, only on a CRT display, whereas others, such as resolution, apply to both CRT and LCD displays. Some settings are only available from a special menu built into your display. This menu is independent of your operating system, and you access it through buttons mounted on the monitor, as long as the monitor is powered up, regardless of the presence or absence of a PC. Other settings are accessible from within the Display Settings in Windows.

V-Hold/H-Hold

The *v-hold* setting, also known as *vertical hold*, is a CRT display setting found on the menu built into a CRT. Like CRT televisions, this setting holds the image vertically on the screen. If this setting is only slightly out of adjustment, the screen image will be stationary, but out of position vertically. If this setting is badly out of adjustment, the image will dynamically roll vertically. Similarly, *h-hold*, or *horizontal hold*, is a CRT-only setting that holds the image horizontally.

Vertical Position/Horizontal Position

The built-in menu on an LCD display will have the *vertical position* setting, which adjusts the viewable area of the display vertically, whereas the *horizontal position* setting adjusts the viewable area of the display horizontally.

CRT Refresh Rate

The *refresh rate* of a display is a significant setting for a CRT display. On a CRT, this refers to the *vertical refresh rate*, which is the rate per second at which an image appears on the tube. The video adapter drives this setting. If you are running Windows, you can see the refresh rate of your display under the Advanced Settings in the Display applet. Exercise 3-3 explains how to find this setting. In order to avoid eyestrain, a CRT display should refresh at a rate of 60 Hertz or above. On some CRTs, you may need to reduce the resolution to achieve an adequate refresh rate.

EXERCISE 3-3

Modifying Display Settings

1. Open the Display applet in Windows XP or the Display Setting applet in Windows Vista.

2. Notice the current screen resolution. This will be displayed on the Monitor tab in Windows Vista and on the Settings tab in Windows XP.

3. Click the Advanced or Advanced Settings button.

4. In the resulting dialog, select the Monitor tab.

5. On the Monitor page, notice the screen refresh rate and write down the value. Is it greater than 60 Hertz? If not, first ensure that the box labeled Hide Modes That This Monitor Cannot Display is checked, and then use the drop-down box to select a setting that is 60 Hertz or higher. Click OK on this and subsequent pages to exit the applet.

6. Do the settings work? Is there a noticeable difference?

7. If necessary, return the display to its original settings.

Do not confuse refresh rate with the number of images (*frames*) per second. A traditional movie projector runs at 32 frames per second. A human eye can detect flicker in a movie if it runs at a rate close to or less than 20 frames per second.

on the **Selecting a refresh rate higher than a CRT can support can cause damage**
Job **to the display.**

LCD Response Time

Although you will find a refresh rate setting in Windows for an LCD display, it is still a video adapter setting. On LCD displays, the closest equivalent to a CRT's refresh rate is *response time*, the time in milliseconds (ms) it takes for a single pixel to go from the active (black) to inactive (white) state and back again. This setting is a feature that a manufacturer will list with the other specifications for the model, and it is not adjustable. The response time, now commonly in the single digits, is a best-case scenario under controlled testing. A low number is desirable because the lower the number the faster the response time. If your LCD display occasionally seems to blur moving images, the display has a slow (high number) response time.

e x a m

⍵atch **Understand the display**
settings, particularly those that are
available to you in Windows.

Display Resolution

Display resolution is the displayable number of pixels. A CRT display may easily support several different screen resolutions. If you have a CRT, you can play with this setting, along with others, until you have the most comfortable combination of resolution, color density, and refresh rate. On an LCD display, however, you should keep this setting at the native resolution of the display, which is often the highest available resolution in the Windows Display Settings applet.

Color Quality

The *Color Quality* setting in the Display applet allows you to adjust the number of colors used by the display. Also called *color depth*, this setting may be expressed in terms of 16-bits or 32-bits.

Degauss

CRT monitors have a metal plate—the *shadow mask*—at the front of the tube that focuses electron beams. A shadow mask is vulnerable to external electrical fields, causing color distortion. To counteract this affect, most CRTs have a copper degaussing coil used to create a rapidly oscillating magnetic field, reducing and randomizing the magnetic field on the shadow mask and correcting the color distortion. This process is called *degaussing*. Many CRT monitors and TVs will automatically perform a degauss when powered on. If a monitor does not have an internal degaussing coil, people use an external handheld degaussing device.

Degaussing is also used to erase data on magnetic media. Passing a strong magnetic field across magnetic tape or disks causes the magnetized areas that represent the data to randomize, thus erasing the media.

SCENARIO & SOLUTION

A video adapter will have a connector for one of these three busses.	PCI, AGP, or PCIe
What aspect ratio is desirable on an LCD intended for viewing wide-format videos?	16:9
What three settings will you find in the Display applet?	Resolution, refresh rate, and color quality

■ **701: 1.2**   *Explain motherboard components, types, and features*

■ **701: 1.9**   *Summarize the function and types of adapter cards*

This section brings under one heading the topic "I/O interfaces" from objective 701: 1.2 and the topic "I/O" from objective 701: 1.9. Although Chapter 1 detailed most of the topics from objective 1.2, it just introduced input/output (I/O) devices in the section, "Expansion Bus Types and Slots." Similarly, Chapter 2 simply introduced the concept of I/O adapter cards, leaving the discussion of the I/O technologies for later. This chapter details these topics, relating the various interfaces with their purposes.

Input/Output

This section introduces you to a number of basic peripheral connection concepts, such as input devices, I/O interfaces, cables, and connector types, as well as communication methods. This information will allow you to determine the pros and cons of various I/O interfaces and connection methods.

Although the processor is the central component of a PC, it would not have anything to process without input, and that processing doesn't do any good unless you can get it out of the computer some way. Therefore, it is fair to say that computers are all about input and output—both within the system box and between the system box and a variety of external devices. A display is the most common output device, followed closely by the printer and the sound card. You have already learned about a number of the display interfaces and connectors; printers are detailed in Chapter 12, and sound cards will be discussed in "Classic Multimedia Connectors." How does a network interface card (NIC) fit into all this? It is both an input and output device; you will learn about networks and NICs in Chapter 13. In this section of the chapter, we first examine the most common input devices and then explore the various classic multimedia devices and the interfaces used for I/O peripherals. We will finish with connectors and cables.

Input Devices

An input device sends signals into a computer. The two most common input devices are the keyboard and a pointing device, such as a mouse. Barcode readers are a very common input device in some settings, and multimedia devices for desktop and laptop computers are common. An output device receives data from a computer. Most of the devices detailed here are input devices, with the exception of audio devices.

Keyboards

For the vast majority of PC users, the *keyboard* is their primary input device. There are several types of keyboards, including 84- and 101-key designs. Newer keyboards might include a variety of additional keys for accessing the Internet, using Microsoft Windows, and performing other common functions. Some keyboards even include a pointing device, such as a mouse or touch pad.

There are also several keyboard layouts. The keyset on an ergonomic keyboard's physical form factor (see Figure 3-8) is split in half and each half slants outward to provide a more relaxed, natural hand position. The layout of the keys themselves can also vary, regardless of the form factor. Typical English language keyboards (even ergonomic keyboards) have a QWERTY layout (see Figure 3-9), named after the first six letters on the second row of the keyboard. The Dvorak keyboard has an entirely different key layout (also shown in Figure 3-9) and allows for faster typing speeds. Unfortunately, the Dvorak keyboard has been slow to catch on. Accurately learning and using both layouts is exceptionally difficult, so most people stick to the old QWERTY standby that they learned in school.

Pointing Devices

A *pointing device* is used to manipulate a pointer and other items on the computer display for input. The *mouse* is by far the most popular pointing device. Users learn mouse operations quickly; the movement of a mouse over a surface translates into the movement of the pointer across the screen. Two or more buttons on the mouse

FIGURE 3-8

Ergonomic keyboard with a different structure from a conventional keyboard

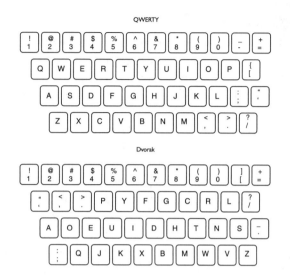

FIGURE 3-9

QWERTY and
Dvorak keyboard
layouts

allow the user to perform various operations such as selecting items and running programs. Another popular pointing device is the trackball, a device that is generally larger than a mouse but remains stationary, so it requires less desk space. The user moves the pointer by rolling a ball mounted in the trackball device. A trackball will also have buttons that you use like the buttons on a mouse.

Bar Code Readers

On nearly every item you buy, every package you ship, and the membership cards you carry, there is a small rectangular image with a unique pattern of black bars and white space. This is a *bar code*, which contains information appropriate to the type of use. On a product, a bar code will contain inventory and pricing information. On your library card, it will identify you as a dues-paying member. A *bar code reader* is a device used to read the bar code. The design of the reader must match the type of code on the item it scans in order to interpret it. The bar code reader uses a laser beam to measure the thicknesses of the lines and spaces. This information is converted to digital data and transferred to a computer. At the grocery store, the computer is in the cash register, which tallies up your total and sends inventory information to a central computer.

Multimedia

A variety of multimedia input devices are available for PCs. The short list includes Web video cameras, digital still cameras, MIDI devices, and microphones.

Cameras

The most common type of camera attached to a PC is a *Web camera,* or *Webcam.* This type of digital video camera broadcasts video images (usually live) over the Internet. While the Webcam as a PC peripheral has not lived up to the predictions of wide-spread adoption a decade ago, it is still an inexpensive and easy-to-use addition to a PC, providing a visual component for meetings and other business communications, as well as entertainment and security functions.

A handheld *digital video camera,* as opposed to Webcam, does not spend its useful life tethered to a computer, but only connects to a computer to transfer its digital video files to the PC for review, editing, and distribution by the user.

A *digital still camera,* most often simply called a *digital camera,* is a camera type that has taken the world by storm, replacing film-based cameras for amateur photographers, as well as for many professional photographers. Like the digital video camera, a digital still camera spends much of its time detached from a PC, connecting only to upload digital photographs to the computer to be reviewed, modified, and printed.

MIDI

The *Musical Instrument Digital Interface (MIDI)* is a standard for connecting electronic musical instruments, such as a synthesizer keyboard, to computers or among themselves. This allows musicians and budding musicians to input their music for mixing and to convert it to musical notation. MIDI has been around almost as long as the PC. A MIDI device also requires an additional piece of equipment in the form of a box connecting the PC and MIDI device.

Newer MIDI devices may have USB connectors and connect to a USB port on a PC, but the classic MIDI device has at least two MIDI ports, each a mini-DIN keyboard connector. These ports are labeled "In" or "Out." There may be more than one "Out" port. On an older PC, look for a special MIDI port on the back of the sound card. The MIDI port is also called the *gameport,* because you can attach a joystick for use with games. The classic MIDI port on the computer side uses a female DB-15 connector that has only two rows of pins, as opposed to the DB-15 connector used for analog video. This type of MIDI cable is coaxial.

Sound Output

Sound is generated and put out via a *sound card.* The typical sound device is a set of speakers or a pair of headphones. Sound cards normally have connectors for both types of devices. The classic connector for these devices is the mini-audio connector, described later in this chapter in "Classic Multimedia Connectors."

Microphones

As a PC input peripheral, a microphone gives a remote meeting attendee a voice at the meeting, and the latest voice recognition programs allow a user to dictate entire documents with a very low error rate. A microphone typically connects to a PC's sound card using a mini-audio connector.

Biometric Devices

Biometric devices provide greater authentication security than simply supplying a user name and password. Using the appropriate biometric device and security software, it identifies the user by some body measurement, such as scanning a fingerprint or the retina of his or her eye.

KVM Switches

The acronym *KVM* stands for *keyboard, video,* and *mouse.* A *KVM switch* is a device that traditionally has been found in server rooms and is used to control multiple computers with one keyboard, mouse, and monitor. A KVM switch is a box to which you connect one local monitor, keyboard, and mouse. Ports on the switch provide a number of keyboard, mouse, and video connectors for cables to each of the computers being controlled. KVM switches are now divided into two broad categories: local KVM and remote KVM.

The *local KVM switch* category is still the norm in server rooms, where it creates a one-to-many connection that allows you to control any one of the servers connected through the switch. Some local KVM switches have USB ports for the shared devices and may share additional types of devices, such as speakers. Other KVM switches reverse this model, connecting two or more sets of keyboards, displays, and mice to one computer. This model is commonly used in a kiosk scenario where the public has access through one set of peripherals, and an administrator has access via another set. In either situation, control is switched through the KVM switch using software and special keyboard commands, so these KVM switches are called *active* or *electronic KVM switches.* An *inactive KVM switch,* the least expensive type of KVM switch, is controlled through a mechanical switch on the box itself. These switches have many limitations and problems; you are unlikely to encounter them, so we will not discuss them.

The *remote KVM switch* category is further divided into two types: local remote KVM and KVM over IP. A *local remote KVM* switch uses either category 5 or USB cabling. A local remote KVM switch using category 5 cabling can be used to control computers over a distance of up to 300 meters, using a proprietary protocol (not IP) and special hardware. A remote KVM switch using USB cabling has a distance limit of up to 5 meters.

A *KVM over IP* switch uses specialized hardware to capture the keyboard, video, and mouse signals, encodes them into IP packets, and sends them over an IP network. They can be used to connect a keyboard, video display, and mouse to a special remote console application that allows the user to control multiple computers across a LAN or WAN. They are also used in one-to-one situations; for example, in hospitals or clinics with a centralized, "paperless" records systems and consoles in the locations where they do not want system units (for a variety of reasons, including sanitary). The console consists of a keyboard, video display, and pointing device—all connected to a KVM device, such as a KVM port extender. There are many possible configurations, but in medical installations, the console may connect to the central system (directly or indirectly) to access and update patient records.

I/O Interfaces

I/O interfaces, connectors, and port types vary among peripheral devices. For example, the straight-pair cable for a printer has a different connector than the straight-pair cable for a monitor. Typically, the term *connector* refers to the plug at the end of a cable, and *port* refers to the location where the cable attaches to the device or computer, sometimes called a *socket*. Even though we refer to connectors and ports, bear in mind the port is also a connector. The following sections contain descriptions of some common I/O interfaces and the connector types related to each.

Interfaces have evolved, but many of the old interfaces, such as serial, parallel, and SCSI, are still with us today, even though we have faster interfaces, such as USB and IEEE 1394 (FireWire).

Serial: RS-232

Although many of the peripheral interfaces described in this book use serial communications, the classic serial port for a PC, the *RS-232 port*, complies with the Recommended Standard-232 (RS-232) in its circuitry, cabling, and connector design. Like all serial communications, RS-232 transfers data serially, one bit at a time. The circuitry behind the physical connector is the *universal asynchronous receiver/transmitter (UART)* chip, which does the parallel-to-serial and serial-to-parallel data conversion required between the parallel bus of the PC and the serial port and its devices.

RS-232 serial communication has a maximum speed of 115 kilobits per second (Kbps). In early PCs, the RS-232 port used a 25-pin male D-Shell connector (or DB-type connector), but because it did not use all the pins, the 9-pin male D-Shell connector with 9 pins in 2 rows (5 in one row and 4 in the other) replaced it. Also called a *DB-9* connector, all D-Shell connectors have this same trapezoidal shape (see Figure 3-10). Although the connector on the computer had only 9 pins, the connector on the device, such as a serial modem, was a female 25-pin *DB-25* D-Shell connector. The serial RS-232 interface was most commonly used for serial devices such as mice and external modems, but has been replaced by faster interfaces with much smaller connectors and cables, mainly USB.

Parallel

In parallel communications, multiple wires simultaneously transmit one bit per wire, in parallel. All other things being equal, this results in faster data transfers for large packets. The parallel interface for peripherals found on PCs in the 1980s was unidirectional, so a computer could send data to a device, such as a printer, but the device could not send information back to the computer. In addition, the transfer rate was 150 kilobytes per second (150 KBps).

In 1991, the IEEE 1284 standard, which supports bidirectional communication and transfer rates of up to 2 MBps, corrected the shortcomings of the old parallel interface. If you buy a parallel cable today, this standard will be prominently displayed on its packaging. Modern parallel interfaces in PCs and parallel devices follow this standard but also support the previous implementations. A PC's built-in parallel port now has several modes of operation, configurable through the system BIOS Settings menu, as described in Chapter 4.

At one time, external drives and other devices used the parallel interface, and it was the "gold standard" for PC printers. Today, most common external peripherals use USB or IEEE 1394, because both achieve faster speeds, both are plug and play,

A female DB-25 connector (top) and two male DB-9 connectors (bottom)

and both use slender cables and small connectors as opposed to bulky parallel cables and connectors.

The parallel port connector is a D-Shell connector with 25 pins or sockets—13 in one row and 12 in the other. Until recently, most computers included one female DB-25 parallel connector. You can see an example of a DB-25 connector in Figure 3-10. On the device end is a 36-pin connector, sometimes referred to as a *Centronics* connector.

SCSI

Manufacturers rarely build a *Small Computer System Interface (SCSI)* into consumer-level PC motherboards, and they are even less likely to do so in the future. Developed by a technical standards organization, the *American National Standards Institute (ANSI)*, and simply referred to as SCSI (pronounced "scuzzy"), this standard has been used for both internal and external hard drive and optical drives, as well as external devices such as printers, modems, scanners, and most other types of peripherals.

SCSI systems differ from non-SCSI systems in several ways. To begin with, SCSI devices are all attached to and controlled by a SCSI controller in a daisy chain, meaning that each SCSI device participates in moving data, as it typically comes with both input and output connectors so another device can be connected to the SCSI bus through the previous device. Figure 3-11 shows several external devices on a SCSI chain. We describe installation and configuration of host adapters and SCSI devices in Chapter 4.

In PCs, the SCSI controller is usually an adapter card, called a *SCSI host adapter,* installed in the expansion bus. This adapter card will typically have a connector

FIGURE 3-11	

Three devices on a SCSI chain

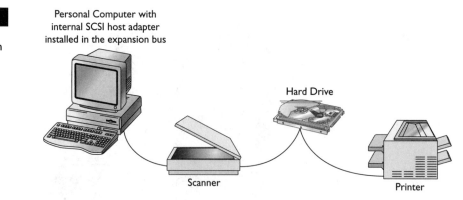

Personal Computer with internal SCSI host adapter installed in the expansion bus

Hard Drive

Scanner

Printer

on the board for connecting an internal SCSI device and a connector on the back of the board for connecting an external SCSI device. For several years, SCSI was popular for high-end devices, such as hard drives, optical drives, and scanners; it was the disk controller of choice for many expensive servers. However, it has had stiff competition from technologies that improve on the old PATA standard (described in Chapter 1), and, more recently, Serial ATA technology (also described in Chapter 1) for drive interfaces is replacing SCSI.

SCSI has several implementations with a variety of speeds. Until recently, SCSI systems all used a parallel interface to the computer. For the traditional parallel SCSI interface, there are four different connectors, including 50-pin Centronics (it resembles the device end of a parallel cable), 50-pin HD D-type, 68-pin HD D-type, and a 25-pin D-Shell identical in appearance to a parallel port. More recently, a serial interface has been used with SCSI—a marriage of SCSI and Serial ATA called *Serial Attached SCSI (SAS)*.

The rapid development of Serial ATA drives means they are replacing SCSI on desktop and laptop computers—to a large extent due to availability and low cost. SCSI is still popular in high-performance workstations and servers and in server RAIDs, although SATA is making inroads there, too.

USB

The *Universal Serial Bus (USB)* interface has become the interface of choice for PCs, making both parallel and serial ports obsolete and even replacing SCSI and IEEE 1394 (discussed next). PCs manufactured in the last several years have at least one USB port (it is rare to have only one), and high-end PCs literally bristle with USB connectors located conveniently on the front, as well as the back, of a desktop PC case, and on the sides and back of a laptop.

USB is an external bus that connects into the PC's PCI bus. With USB, you can theoretically connect up to 127 devices to your computer. There are currently three major versions of the USB standard, version 1, 2, and 3, with some substandards. The low-speed .9, 1.0, and 1.1 versions transmit data up to 1.5 Mbps, whereas the full-speed 1.1 is rated at 12 Mbps. The high-speed 2.0 version transmits data at speeds up to 480 Mbps. You can attach a low-speed device like a mouse to either version, but some devices require, or run best, when attached to a USB port that is up to the 2.0 standard.

The "Super Speed" USB 3.0, or USB3 standard, was introduced in the third quarter of 2008, and, with the usual time-lag for adoption by manufacturers, the first products using this standard were just becoming available as this book was written. USB 3.0 will operate at up to ten times the speed of USB 2.0, although some compatibility problems with devices created for the previous standards are expected. For one thing, it offers new wiring and supports full-duplex and will, therefore, be incompatible with the connectors on the old devices, but you are probably not about to replace the connectors on your old, inexpensive USB devices.

Low-power devices, such as flash drives, receive power through the USB bus, whereas USB devices with greater power needs, such as large external hard drives, printers, and scanners, require separate power supplies that plug into wall sockets.

USB supports plug and play, meaning the computer BIOS and operating system recognize a USB device, and the operating system automatically installs and configures a device driver (if available). Always check the documentation for a USB device, because many require an installed device driver before you can connect the device. USB ports also support *hot swapping,* which means you can attach devices while the computer is running, and they are recognized and used immediately.

If a PC has too few USB ports for the number of USB devices a user wishes to connect, the easiest fix is to purchase an external USB hub and connect it to one of the PC's USB connectors. In fact, you can add other hubs and devices in this way. Although the USB standard allows for daisy chaining of devices, manufacturers do not support this capability because they prefer to use hubs connected directly to the USB controller. There is a limit of five levels of hubs, counting the root hub. Each hub can accommodate several USB devices, possibly creating a lopsided tree. USB supports different speeds on each branch, so devices of varying speeds can be used. Figure 3-12 shows a PC with an internal root hub. Connected to this hub are a USB keyboard and another USB hub. Several devices connect to the first USB hub, including yet another hub, which in turn has several devices connected to it.

FIGURE 3-12

USB hubs can add more USB ports to a PC.

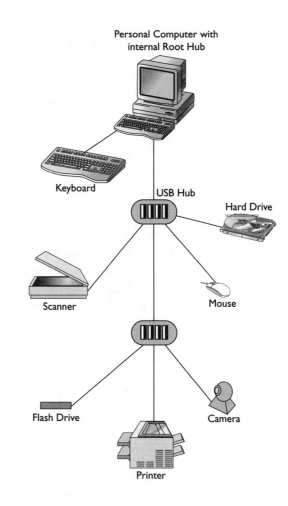

This configuration is common today. In fact, both authors of this book have a similar number of hubs and devices, only with more printers.

A USB port is rectangular and acts as a receiver for a USB type-A connector measuring 1/2" by 1/8" (see Figure 3-13). A plastic device in the port holds the four wires. This, together with a similar plastic device in the connector, polarizes the connectors, which keeps the two from being connected incorrectly. The connector on the device end of a USB cable is a square type-B connector. There are also two variations of mini-USB connectors found on USB digital cameras. All sizes of USB connectors include four wires. Most devices clearly identify USB ports and cable connectors with a fork-shaped symbol.

Two USB ports
and a FireWire
port. Notice the
clear labels.

IEEE 1394/FireWire

The *Institute of Electrical and Electronics Engineers*, or *IEEE*, is an international
nonprofit organization that sets standards as part of its charter. You will encounter
many IEEE standards, represented by "IEEE" followed by a number assigned to that
standard. Like USB, the *IEEE 1394* standard describes an external serial bus that
connects to the internal PCI bus. It is commonly called *FireWire*, which is Apple's
trademarked name, but other manufacturers call it i.link or Lynx. For simplicity,
we will call it FireWire. Today, PC motherboards have FireWire support built in
and often have one or two external FireWire connectors. Like SCSI, each FireWire
device can be used to daisy-chain more devices. A single FireWire port can support
up to 63 daisy-chained devices. Therefore, adding additional ports to the computer
itself is not usually necessary, although you may add them by installing an expansion
card. No single cable in a 1394 port can be longer than 4.5 meters.

The original FireWire standard allowed for faster data transfer than the USB 1.0
standard. Therefore, FireWire was the interface of choice for external devices that
required high-speed data transfers, such as video cameras, hard drives, and DVD
players. After the release and adoption of the USB 2.0 standard, the two bus standards
were close in maximum speed, although FireWire performed better in head-to-head
tests, providing higher sustained speeds than USB, which communicates in bursts.

The original standard, now called *IEEE 1394a*, supports speeds up to 400 Mbps.
In 2003, the IEEE released the *1394b* specification, with cable distances of up to
100 meters and top speeds of 800 Mbps, 1,600 Mbps, and 3.2 Gbps. A significant
limit is that one 1394a device in a chain will cause any 1394b devices to operate
at the lower speed. In addition, although 1394b is generally downward compatible
with 1394a, 3.2 Gbps is only available with special hardware that is not downward
compatible with 1394a devices.

A subsequent standard, *IEEE 1394c-2006*, was published in 2007 and is a major
departure from the old standards in that it uses Category 5e twisted pair cable with
RJ-45 connectors, combining Ethernet and FireWire.

The IEEE 1394d committee formed in 2009 to develop a FireWire standard for single-mode fiber-optic cable, and that is still in process.

A standard 6-pin FireWire port is about 1/2 inch long, with one squared end and one three-sided end, which guarantees the cable connector is connected correctly. As with USB, the wires connect to a plastic device. Alternatively, you will find smaller four-wire ports, especially on laptops. Most devices clearly identify FireWire ports and cable connectors with a Y-shaped symbol (see Figure 3-13).

e x a m
ⓦatch

Be sure you understand the differences between USB and FireWire, are able to describe the ports and connectors, and how multiple devices are normally connected. Also, demonstrate that you understand the differences between RJ-11 and RJ-45 connectors. Remember their uses and the number of wires in each.

Classic Multimedia Connectors

Multimedia encompasses both video and audio. The types and functions of multimedia ports on PCs increase every year, and, as you learned earlier in the "Multimedia" section, video and audio signals are carried in both HDMI and DisplayPort interfaces. Therefore, all that remain to examine are the classic multimedia interfaces that preceded these new technologies and that still appear on many standard PCs. These include MIDI, described previously, and audio connectors. The classic PC comes with a minimum of three color-coded audio ports, or "jacks." Pink identifies a microphone input port, green identifies a speaker output port, and blue is the auxiliary port. Additional audio ports may be present for additional audio channels identified by white for left speaker, red for right speaker, and yellow for composite video. All of these use 1/8" single-pin *mini-audio connectors*, a few generations removed from the larger single-pin RCA phone (as in earphone) connector. Some handheld devices use the 3/32" *sub-mini audio connector*. All of these single-pin plugs come in mono versions and stereo versions. Look for a single black ring around the front end of a mono plug and two black rings around a stereo plug. This applies to all of the plugs described previously.

e x a m
ⓦatch

The CompTIA acronym list for both sets of A+ objectives uses the acronym "SPDIF," but we have shown it below as S/PDIF.

The consumer version of *Sony/Philips Digital Interface (S/PDIF)* uses a single-pin RCA phone jack for transferring digital audio from CD and DVD players to amplifiers and speakers.

Classic Connectors

We have looked at a variety of connectors for video, but there are a few "classic" connectors that we have not mentioned. They include RJ-11, RJ-45, BNC, PS/2, and Mini-DIN.

RJ-11

A *registered jack (RJ)* connector is rectangular in shape and has a locking clip on one side (see Figure 3-14). The number designation of an RJ connector refers to its size rather than to the number of wire connections within it. *RJ-11* connectors contain either two or four wires and usually attach phone cables to modems and to wall-mounted phone jacks.

RJ-45

RJ-45 connectors are slightly larger than RJ-11 connectors and contain eight wires. RJ-45 connectors most commonly attach twisted-pair cables to Ethernet network cards. An RJ-45 port is similar to an RJ-11 port—only wider. Figure 3-15 shows an RJ-45 port, labeled "Ethernet."

 FIGURE 3-14   Two RJ-11 connectors on the left side of a modem card: one for input from the wall jack and the other for attaching to a phone set. A cable with an RJ-11 plug attached is resting on top of the card.

FIGURE 3-15

The RJ-45 port on this PC is labeled "Ethernet." It is just to the right of the bottom two USB ports.

BNC

The acronym *BNC* used for this connector is the subject of some debate. For instance, the CompTIA 2009 Acronym list that accompanies both A+ exam objectives states that it stands for "Bayonet-Neill-Concelman" or "British Naval Connector." What matters is that you can recognize one when you see it. BNC connectors attach coaxial cables to BNC ports. The cable connector is round and has a twist-lock mechanism to keep the cable in place. BNC connectors have a protruding pin that corresponds to a receiver socket in the port. The type of BNC connector formerly used in computer local area networks cannot connect your television to the cable outlet in the wall.

PS/2/Mini-DIN

DIN connectors get their name from Deutsche Industrie Norm, Germany's standards organization. Most (but not all) DIN connectors are round with a circle or semicircle

SCENARIO & SOLUTION

Early PCs frequently used which two ports for peripherals, though newer technology is replacing them?	Serial and parallel
Which two common communications ports are similar in shape, but one is larger?	RJ-11 and RJ-45
Which two external serial bus standards are common on PCs today?	USB and IEEE 1394

of pins. The mini-DIN connector, or more accurately, the *mini-DIN-6* connector, gets its name from the fact that it is smaller than a customary DIN-6 keyboard connector. Mini-DIN connectors most commonly connect *PS/2* style (Personal System/2) mice and keyboards, so people often refer to mini-DIN connectors as PS/2 connectors. Look back at Figure 3-15 to see two mini-DIN connectors at the top of the panel, one for a keyboard and another for a mouse.

Cables

A wide variety of cables physically connect components to each other and to the computer and carry the electronic signals among them. Straight-pair cables consist of one or more metal wires surrounded by a plastic insulating sheath. *Twisted-pair cables* consist of two or more sheathed metal wires twisted around each other along the entire length of the cable to avoid electrical interference, with a plastic covering sheath surrounding them. *Coaxial cables* contain a single copper wire, surrounded by several layers of insulating plastic and a woven wire sheath that provides both physical and electrical protection. Figure 3-16 illustrates some common cable types.

FIGURE 3-16

Common cable types used in computer installations

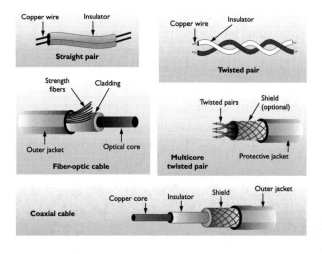

CERTIFICATION SUMMARY

This chapter wraps up the discussion of PC components begun in Chapter 1 and continued in Chapter 2. It described power supplies, cooling systems, display devices, I/O interfaces, cables, and connectors.

Some components, such as power supplies, have more than one function. For instance, because power supplies provide the DC voltages required by various other components, they produce heat. Therefore, each power supply has a fan that dissipates the heat the power supply creates, as well as contributes to cooling the entire system. In most PCs, this is not sufficient, so additional methods are used to keep PCs cool enough for the components to function safely.

Display technologies have changed a great deal. The most recent developments include support for both video and audio through a single interface, connection, and cable. The physical form of the cable and the connectors and ports used with a cable depend on the purpose and design of the interface used and the device or devices that use the cable.

✓ TWO-MINUTE DRILL

Here are some of the key points covered in Chapter 3.

Power Supplies

❑ A power supply provides power for all components on the motherboard and those internal to the PC case.

❑ Volts is the unit of measurement of the pressure of electrons. Watts is a unit of measurement of actual delivered power. Amperes (amps) is a unit of measurement for electrical current or rate of flow of electrons through a wire.

❑ A power supply converts alternating current (AC) voltage into the direct current (DC) voltage required by the computer.

❑ Power supply capacity is measured in watts, with power supplies for desktop computers ranging up to about 1,600 watts.

❑ An AC adapter is a form of power supply used with portable computers and external peripherals.

❑ Power supplies come in form factors to match motherboards and cases.

❑ The power supply fan exhausts heated air out of the case, drawing it in through vents on the front of the case to cool both the power supply and other components.

Cooling Systems

❑ PCs usually require additional cooling systems beyond the power supply fan.

❑ PC cooling systems include well-designed case ventilation, CPU and case fans, heat sinks, thermal compounds, and liquid cooling systems.

Video Adapters and Displays

❑ The video adapter controls the output from the PC to the display device. Display adapters support a variety of display modes and technologies, including VGA, SVGA, DVI, HDMI, and DisplayPort.

❑ A video adapter may be built into the motherboard or may be a separate circuit board that plugs into a PCI, AGP, or PCIe connector.

❑ Multi-monitor systems have two or more displays on a single computer.

❑ The two general PC display types are CRT and flat panel displays (FPDs). Most FPDs use LCD technology and have largely replaced CRT displays.

❑ Projectors take video output and project it onto a screen for viewing by a larger audience. A touch screen is a video display element that allows you to select and maneuver screen objects by touching, tapping, and sliding your finger or stylus on the screen.

❑ Display connectors include DB-15 (VGA), DVI, HDMI, DisplayPort, Composite Video, and Component Video.

❑ Some display settings, such as v-hold/h-hold (for CRTs) and vertical position/ horizontal position (for LCDs) are only available through a menu on the display itself.

❑ Response time is an LCD feature that is not controllable through any menu settings.

❑ Display resolution is a setting that you can control through Windows.

❑ Degaussing is necessary on CRT monitors because of the effect of electrical fields on the shadow mask in the tube.

Input/Output

❑ Displays, printers, and sound cards are the most common output devices. NICs are both input and output devices. Keyboards, pointing devices, barcode readers, and many multimedia devices are input devices. A special category of device, a KVM switch, is used in a variety of scenarios, but the most common is to allow a single person using one keyboard, video display, and pointing device to control many computers.

❑ Common I/O interfaces include serial (RS-232), parallel, SCSI, USB, and IEEE 1394/FireWire.

❑ Classic multimedia interfaces include MIDI and a variety of audio ports using the 1/8" single-pin mini-audio connector.

❑ Classic connectors and ports include RJ-11, RJ-45, BNC, PS/2, and mini-DIN.

❑ Common electronic cables used with PCs include straight-pair, twisted-pair, and coaxial.

SELF TEST

The following questions will help you measure your understanding of the material presented in this chapter. Read all of the choices carefully because there might be more than one correct answer. Choose all correct answers for each question.

Power Supplies

1. Which statement is true?
A. A PC power supply converts wattage to voltage.
B. A PC power supply converts voltage to wattage.
C. A PC power supply converts AC to DC.
D. A PC power supply converts DC to AC.

2. What is the name of the main power connector that goes between an ATX power supply and an ATX motherboard?
A. P3
B. P1
C. P2
D. P4

3. The capacity of a power supply is normally stated in these units.
A. Volts
B. Watts
C. Amperes
D. Ohms

4. What type of current is required by internal PC components?
A. Alternating current (AC)
B. Direct current (DC)
C. IEC-320
D. PSU

5. To determine what capacity you require in a power supply,
A. Add the voltage for all internal components.
B. Add the wattage for all internal components.
C. Add the voltage for all external components.
D. Add the wattage for all external components.

6. This component of a power supply dissipates heat.
   A. Heat sink
   B. P1 connector
   C. Fan
   D. IEC-320

7. What is a common term for a laptop power supply?
   A. PSU
   B. Heat sink
   C. AC adapter
   D. Thermal compound

Cooling Systems

8. Give three locations for PC cooling fans.
   A. Power supply, memory module, and case
   B. Display, power supply, and CPU
   C. Power supply, CPU, and hard drive system
   D. Power supply, CPU, and case

9. This special substance is placed between a CPU and CPU fan to increase heat conductivity.
   A. Liquid cooling
   B. Thermal compound
   C. Metallic foil
   D. Heat sink

10. What type of active cooling system may include a tiny refrigeration unit?
   A. CPU
   B. Case fan
   C. Heat sink
   D. Liquid

Video Adapters and Displays

11. This venerable video interface standard was introduced with the IBM PS/2 computer in the late 1980s.
   A. DisplayPort
   B. HDMI
   C. DVI
   D. VGA

12. Which of the following video interface standards supports both analog and digital signals?

   A. DisplayPort

   B. HDMI

   C. DVI

   D. VGA

13. This video standard supports both digital video and audio and has the thinnest cable and the smallest connectors.

   A. DisplayPort

   B. HDMI

   C. DVI

   D. VGA

14. This type of display uses an electron gun to activate phosphors behind the screen.

   A. CRT

   B. FPD

   C. LCD

   D. Plasma

15. This type of display device takes up less desk space and replaces an older technology that uses more power.

   A. CRT

   B. FPD

   C. ATX

   D. USB

16. Which of the following connectors is *not* used to connect a display to a digital video interface?

   A. DVI

   B. DB-15

   C. HDMI

   D. DisplayPort

17. Which of the following is *not* a DVI connector type?

   A. DVI-A

   B. DVI-B

   C. DVI-I

   D. DVI-D

Input/Output

18. A device with this interface comes with both input and output connectors, so it can connect through a daisy chain to a controlling host adapter.

    A. USB

    B. Serial

    C. Parallel

    D. SCSI

19. This type of external bus interface allows up to 127 devices (theoretically) to be connected.

    A. Parallel

    B. Serial

    C. USB

    D. IEEE 1394

20. If you do not have as many connectors for this interface as you require, you can add more hubs to the existing internal hub in your computer.

    A. Parallel

    B. Serial

    C. USB

    D. IEEE 1394

SELF TEST ANSWERS

Power Supplies

1. ☑ **C.** A PC power supply converts AC to DC.
   ☒ **A,** a PC power supply converts wattage to voltage, is incorrect. **B,** a PC power supply converts voltage to wattage, is incorrect. **D,** a PC power supply converts DC to AC, is incorrect. It does just the opposite.

2. ☑ **B.** P1 is the main power connector used between an ATX power supply and an ATX motherboard.
   ☒ **A,** P3, is incorrect because the chapter mentioned no such connector. **C,** P2, is incorrect because the chapter mentioned no such connector. **D,** P4, is incorrect because this is a four-wire 12 V connector used in addition to the P1 connector.

3. ☑ **B.** The capacity of a power supply is stated in watts.
   ☒ **A,** volts, is incorrect because it is a measurement of electrical potential. **C,** amperes, is incorrect because it is a measurement of electrical current or rate of flow of electrons through a wire. **D,** Ohms, is incorrect because Ohms is a measurement of resistence.

4. ☑ **B.** Direct current (DC) is the type of current required by internal PC components.
   ☒ **A,** alternating current (AC), is incorrect because this is the type of current that is provided through the typical wall outlet. **C,** IEC-320, is incorrect because this is a type of switch found on many power supplies to select the correct power setting. **D,** PSU, is incorrect. This is an acronym for "power supply unit."

5. ☑ **B.** Add the wattage for all internal components to determine what capacity you require in a power supply.
   ☒ **A,** add the voltage for all internal components, is incorrect because this is not the correct measurement required. **C,** add the voltage for all external components, and **D,** add the wattage for all external components, are both incorrect because external components normally have their own power supplies and do not need to draw power from the computer's power supply.

6. ☑ **C.** The Fan is the component in a power supply that dissipates heat.
   ☒ **A,** heat sink, is incorrect because a heat sink is something that draws heat off something and dissipates it in some passive manner, such as via metal fins. **B,** P1 connector, is incorrect because this is a power supply connector, not a part of a power supply that dissipates heat. **D,** IEC-320, is incorrect because this is a type of switch found on many power supplies to select the correct power setting.

7. ☑ **C.** AC adapter is the common term for a laptop power supply.
☒ **A,** PSU, is incorrect because this is an acronym for "power supply unit." **B,** heat sink, is incorrect because heat sinks dissipate heat. **D,** thermal compound, is incorrect because thermal compound is used to increase the heat conductivity among components.

Cooling Systems

8. ☑ **D.** Power supply, CPU, and case are three locations for cooling fans in PCs.
☒ **A,** power supply, memory module, and case, is incorrect because a memory module is not a location for PC cooling fans. **B,** display, power supply, and CPU, is incorrect because the display is external and not a location for cooling fans in PCs. **C,** power supply, CPU, and hard drive system, is incorrect because the hard drive system is not a location for cooling fans in PCs.

9. ☑ **B.** Thermal compound is placed between a CPU and CPU fan to increase the heat conductivity.
☒ **A,** liquid cooling, is incorrect because it describes a method for using liquid in pipes to cool components. **C,** metallic foil, is incorrect because foil is not placed between the CPU and CPU fan. **D,** heat sink, is incorrect because, although a heat sink may be attached to a CPU, either by itself or in combination with a CPU fan, this is not applied between the CPU and CPU fan.

10. ☑ **D.** Liquid is the type of active cooling system that may include a tiny refrigeration unit.
☒ **A,** CPU, is incorrect, as this is an acronym for central processing unit. **B,** case fan, and **C,** heat sink, are incorrect because neither type of cooling device would have a refrigeration unit.

Video Adapters and Displays

11. ☑ **D.** VGA is the video interface standard introduced with the IBM PS/2 computer.
☒ **A, B,** and **C.** DisplayPort, HDMI, and DVI are all incorrect because they are recent standards.

12. ☑ **C.** DVI is the video interface standard that supports both analog and digital signals.
☒ **A,** DisplayPort, and **B,** HDMI, are incorrect because they only support digital signals. **D,** VGA, is incorrect because it is an analog video interface standard.

13. ☑ **A.** DisplayPort supports both digital video and audio and has the thinnest cable and the smallest connectors.
☒ **B,** HDMI, is incorrect because, although it supports both video and audio, it does not have the thinnest cable and smallest connectors. **C,** DVI, is incorrect because it does not support both digital video and audio. **D,** VGA, is incorrect because it only supports analog video.

14. ☑ **A.** CRT is the type of display that uses an electron gun.

☒ **B, C,** and **D** are all incorrect because none of these displays types (FPD, LCD, and Plasma) use electron guns.

15. ☑ **B.** FPD displays take up less desk space and replace an older (CRT) technology that uses more power.

☒ **A,** CRT, is incorrect because it takes up more desk space than an LCD display and uses more power. **C,** ATX, is incorrect because it is a motherboard and power supply form factor, not a type of display. **D,** USB, is incorrect because it is an I/O interface.

16. ☑ **B.** A DB-15 connector is not used to connect a display to a digital video interface.

☒ **A,** DVI, **C,** HDMI, and **D,** DisplayPort, are all incorrect because connectors are all used to connect a display to a digital video interface (of the same name).

17. ☑ **B.** DVI-B is not a DVI connector type.

☒ **A, C,** and **D** are all incorrect because DVI-A, DVI-I, and DVI-D are all DVI connector types.

Input/Output

18. ☑ **D.** SCSI devices come with an input and output connector so that each device can connect through a daisy chain to a controlling host adapter.

☒ **A,** USB, is incorrect because USB devices do not come with input and output connectors (although the original standard did allow for daisy-chaining). **B,** serial, and **C,** parallel, are incorrect because serial and parallel devices do not come with input and output connectors so that each device can connect through a daisy chain to a controlling host adapter.

19. ☑ **C.** USB is a type of external bus interface that allows up to 127 devices (theoretically) to be connected.

☒ **A,** parallel, and **B,** serial, are incorrect because they do not allow up to 127 devices to be connected. **D,** IEEE 1394, is incorrect because it allows only up to 63 devices to be connected.

20. ☑ **C.** A USB interface allows you to connect more hubs to the existing internal hub in your computer.

☒ **A, B,** and **D** are all incorrect. These three I/O interfaces—parallel, serial, and IEEE 1394—do not have internal hubs to which you can connect more hubs.

4

Installing and Upgrading PC Components

CERTIFICATION OBJECTIVES

❑　**701:1.8**　Install and configure peripherals and input devices

❑　**701:3.4**　Explain the basics of boot sequences, methods, and startup utilities

❑　**702:1.1**　Given a scenario, install, configure, and maintain personal computer components

✓　Two-Minute Drill

Q&A　Self Test

This chapter describes and demonstrates how to install and replace common PC components. With a little practice, you will be capable of performing these tasks on most personal computers, in spite of different layouts or new component designs. You will also find tips on how to optimize personal computers, as well as procedures for upgrading common components in them.

You can install many PC components, such as the processor, power supply, and RAM, by simply physically attaching them to the computer. However, some components also require changes to system settings or having operating-system-level drivers installed to become functional.

Many of the components discussed here conform to some type of standard, which means you can replace them with other components made by a different manufacturer that conform to that same standard. You can use the skills discussed here on practically any desktop PC.

CERTIFICATION OBJECTIVES

- **701: 3.4** *Explain the basics of boot sequences, methods, and startup utilities*

- **702: 1.1** *Given a scenario, install, configure, and maintain personal computer components*

The CompTIA A+ Essentials (2009 Edition) Exam objective 701: 1.1 requires that you understand the procedures for adding, removing, and configuring storage devices, motherboards, power supplies, processors, memory, and adapter cards. In addition to installing the hardware components, you should understand how to install device drivers. Also be prepared to describe how to adjust hardware settings. All network-specific installation and configuration issues will be presented in Chapters 14 and 15. A small portion of the motherboards and onboard components topic includes BIOS settings, of which one group of settings allows you to set the disk boot order, which falls under the 701: 3.4 objective.

Motherboards and Onboard Components

Installing, configuring, and maintaining a motherboard requires that you understand the CPU models that will work with the motherboard, as well as the appropriate type of memory compatible with both the CPU and motherboard and the amount of memory they can handle. Therefore, we address these three topics together in this section.

Selecting a Motherboard, CPU, and Memory Combination

In Chapter 1, you learned that there are several motherboard form factors, each with different layouts, components, and specifications. Each motherboard is unique in terms of the memory, processor, and type and number of expansion slots it supports. You cannot tell which components a motherboard supports solely by knowing the form factor of motherboard. Therefore, you must always check the manufacturer's documentation before you select a motherboard and the components you wish to install on it. Any motherboard manual contains a list of installed and supported components, such as chipset, CPUs, and memory. The manual will also be your guide for determining the speed of the motherboard's front side bus (FSB). Motherboards can typically use only one or two processor models and can usually handle only two or three different processor speeds.

Always consult the motherboard manual to determine the type of memory, speed, data width, and maximum amount of memory it will support. A motherboard must support both the technology and the form factor of a memory module. The system must also support the data width of the memory, its method of error correction, and the speed. Today's typical motherboard has some version of the DIMM memory slots, as described in Chapter 1.

exam

ⓦatch *Recall the descriptions of the various memory slots in Chapter 1 and memory sticks in Chapter 2. Be sure you remember that although the various memory sockets may seem similar, they are all keyed differently.*

on the Ⓙob *Whenever you install or replace a computer component that involves opening the case, you must turn the computer's power off and ensure that you follow the electrostatic discharge (ESD) procedures discussed in Chapter 18. All the exercises described in this book assume that you have taken steps to protect yourself, and the computer, from harm.*

Replacing a Motherboard

Replacing a motherboard is not a common occurrence. For one thing, if a motherboard fails while a computer is under warranty, it will be replaced as part of that coverage. Therefore, only if you work for a company that does such warranty work will motherboard replacement be a big part of your job. Second, if a motherboard fails after the warranty period, you will need to decide if a suitable replacement is available and if you will be able to use all your old components. Because most components attach physically to the motherboard, replacing it can be one of the most time-consuming tasks. If you are replacing one motherboard with another of exactly the same brand and version, you should make notes about any BIOS settings and jumper and switch settings (more on jumpers and switches later in "Configuring and Optimizing a Motherboard") for the old motherboard in case you need to change them on the new board. Once you have done this, you are ready for the real work.

on the $\mathbf{\dot{U}}$ o b

When it comes to replacing a motherboard versus building an entirely new system from scratch, doing the latter may be easier, because you can buy all the pieces at once from one source and request their help and guarantee that all the components will play nicely together.

Installing a Motherboard

When installing a motherboard, you should follow the instructions in the motherboard manual. Whether you are installing a new motherboard or replacing one, the motherboard manual is your most important tool. In addition to listing the components supported, the typical motherboard manual includes instructions on installing the motherboard in a case and installing components, such as the CPU, memory, and power supply. The manual will explain how to set appropriate switches on the motherboard and how to attach all the various power and data cables. These include all the drive interface cables, connections to both front and back panel connectors for the various interfaces, such as parallel, serial, USB, FireWire, eSATA, and even video, if the video adapter is on board the motherboard.

on the $\mathbf{\dot{U}}$ o b

Before you open a computer case, be sure to unplug any power cords and turn off the power supply. Then, to prevent damage to the system, equalize the electrical charge between your body and the components inside your computer. If nothing else, touch a grounded portion of your computer's chassis. A better option is to place the computer on a grounded mat, which you touch before working on the PC. You could also wear an antistatic wrist strap. Warning: Do not use an antistatic wrist strap when working with high-voltage devices, such as CRT monitors and laser printers.

EXERCISE 4-1

Removing an Old Motherboard

1. If you haven't done this already, power down and unplug the PC's power cord.

2. Remove all expansion cards and cables from the motherboard.

3. If the drives and/or the drive bays interfere with access to the motherboard, remove them.

4. Remove any screws or fasteners attaching the motherboard to the case, lift the board out of the case, and put it aside. Be sure to carefully save any screws you remove.

The first three steps of Exercise 4-2 describe a recommended procedure for handling a motherboard, which applies to any circuit board. The remainder of Exercise 4-2 includes general steps for installing a motherboard. It assumes that the BIOS, CMOS, CMOS battery, and chipset have come preinstalled on the motherboard (as is customary). Always check the instructions included with the motherboard or other component.

EXERCISE 4-2

Properly Handling and Installing a Motherboard

1. Before unpacking a new motherboard, ensure that you have grounded your body properly. One method is to wear a static safety wrist strap, as described in Chapter 18.

2. Hold the board by its edges and avoid touching any component on it. Always avoid touching module contacts and IC chips.

3. Place the board on a grounded antistatic mat (described in Chapter 18) or on the antistatic bag that came with the board (unless the instructions recommend against this).

4. Install the CPU and memory on the motherboard, per manufacturer's instructions.

5. Follow the manual's instructions for setting any switches on the motherboard and pay attention to instructions for how to attach stand-off screws, which keep the motherboard from touching the metal floor or wall of the case. Now you are ready to install the board.

6. To place the new (or replacement) board in the computer, line it up properly on the chassis screw holes, and fix it into place.

7. Attach the power and drive connectors, as well as connectors to the correct ports on the case (both front panels and back panels).

Upgrading a CPU

Upgrading a CPU is a major undertaking but may not be impossible if you believe that your processor is the only thing holding back performance on your computer. It all depends on the motherboard. With a little research, you may find that all you need to do is change the motherboard's speed, because most motherboards support more than one speed for a particular CPU.

If you find that a new CPU is both necessary and possible, be sure to consult the manufacturer's documentation for your motherboard to determine which processor and speeds it supports. In most cases, you will need to configure the board for the new speed or model using a set of jumpers, but many BIOSs allow you to make such changes through BIOS system setup.

Removing a CPU

How you remove an installed CPU depends on the type of socket. Once again, read any manuals available for your motherboard or computer. You may need to consult the manufacturer for more information. If the socket is a zero insertion force (ZIF) socket, follow the instructions in Exercise 4-3. No doubt the processor will have a heat sink and/or fan attached to it. If possible, remove the processor without removing these attachments. However, if they interfere with the mechanism for releasing the processor, you may need to remove them.

on the
job

The processor will be very hot when you first turn off a PC. You will lose skin if you touch a hot CPU chip, and it will hurt! Always allow at least five minutes for the chip to cool before you remove it.

EXERCISE 4-3

Removing a PGA Processor from a ZIF Socket

1. Lift the socket lever. You might have to move it slightly to the side to clear it from a retaining tab.

2. Pull out the processor. Because this is a ZIF socket, you should encounter no resistance when you remove the CPU.

3. Set the CPU on an antistatic mat or place it in an antistatic bag.

Installing a CPU

The CPU socket on the motherboard will usually have a mechanism to make it easier to install the CPU without damaging pins. The most common method involves a ZIF socket; raise the lever and position the CPU with all pins inserted in the matching socket holes. Then close the lever, which lets the socket contact each of the CPU's pins. In all cases, do not count on these simple instructions alone, but follow those provided in the manuals that come with the motherboard and CPU.

Optimizing a System with RAM

One function of RAM is to provide the processor with faster access to the information it needs. Within limits, the more memory a computer has, the faster it will run. One of the most common and effective computer upgrades is the installation of more system RAM, usually into DIMM sockets. A rare upgrade is to add cache memory. Depending on the vintage and configuration of the motherboard and CPU, special sockets may be available for adding more L2 or L3 cache. Again, check the documentation!

The optimum amount of memory to install is best determined by considering the requirements of the operating system you are installing and how you will use the computer. We will address this in Chapter 9.

Installing and Removing Memory

Installing or removing memory modules is similar for SIMMs, DIMMs, and RIMMs, but you are most likely to work with DIMMs. The following sections describe the specifics of each type of socket. Before you begin, take steps to protect against static electricity damage to the memory modules and motherboard, as described in Chapter 18.

SIMM Modules

As outdated technology, SIMMs are included here mainly because CompTIA still includes this term in the objectives for the 2009 A+ Exams. SIMM sockets were produced in two sizes to accommodate either 30-pin or 72-pin SIMM memory modules.

Thirty-pin SIMMs are 8-bit, meaning that data can be transferred into or out of the module 8 bits at a time. The 72-pin SIMM sockets, which are 32-bits wide, are slightly shorter than DIMM sockets and usually colored white with small metal clips.

To install a SIMM module, line up the module's connector edge with the appropriate-sized slot on the motherboard, keeping the SIMM at a 45-degree angle to the slot. After inserting the SIMM into the slot as far as it will easily go, gently rotate the SIMM upright until it clicks into place. To remove a SIMM, pull outward on the slot's retaining clips. The SIMM should fall to a 45-degree angle. Remove the SIMM.

DIMM and RIMM Modules

Dual Inline Memory Module (DIMM) sockets look similar to SIMM sockets but are longer and often dark in color with plastic clips at each end. DIMM sockets for PCs come in two sizes and three configurations: 184-pin for DDR1 SDRAM and 240-pin for both DDR2 SDRAM and DDR3 SDRAM sticks. They are all keyed differently to fit into slots that support just that type of DDR RAM, and they are not interchangeable. You do not have to install DIMMs in pairs. If a motherboard has two types of memory slots, such as four DIMM slots supporting DDR2 and two DIMM slots supporting DDR3, it is an either/or situation: you can install one or the other type of memory. If you install both, the system will not boot up.

RDRAM RIMM modules have not been manufactured for several years, but if you should encounter an old computer that requires an upgrade, first determine if it is worth the effort. If you decide that it is, you will need to know these basics. RDRAM RIMM sticks for desktops have 184, 232, or 326 pins. The smaller RIMM form factors for laptops are called SORIMMs and have 160 pins. When you install RDRAM, they must be installed in pairs of equal capacity and speed. Because RDRAM has a dual-channel architecture, you cannot leave any RIMM sockets unoccupied, but must install a special terminating stick called a *CRIMM (continuity RIMM)* into the open sockets.

The technique for installing both DIMM and RIMM modules is the same, as shown in Exercise 4-4. Socket keys for DIMM and RIMM modules are different, however, so even if the number of pins is the same, you will not be able to install one in the socket for the other. This is true also of DDR1 DIMM versus DDR2 DIMM versus DDR3 DIMM. As you will see, this technique is slightly different from that used to install a SIMM. The biggest difference is that you hold the DIMM or RIMM module upright and do not position it at an angle for installation. Chapter 6 will detail how to install SODIMM modules.

EXERCISE 4-4

Installing and Removing a DIMM or RIMM Module

1. Align the DIMM or RIMM with the slot, keeping the module upright so the notches in the module line up with the tabs in the slot.
2. Gently press down on the DIMM or RIMM. The retention clips on the side should rotate into the locked position. You might need to guide them into place with your fingers.
3. To remove a DIMM or RIMM, press the retention clips outward, as shown in Figure 4-1, which lifts the module slightly, and then lift the module straight up.

exam
watch

Although both SIMMs and RIMMs are obsolete technology, they are listed in the CompTIA A+ Essentials (2009 Edition) Exam objectives, so be sure you *understand the basic features of SIMMs and RIMMs, as well as the commonly used DIMM modules.*

FIGURE 4-1

Removing
a DIMM

Configuring and Optimizing a Motherboard

Motherboards commonly have jumpers and switches used to configure components. These often enable or disable a feature. A *jumper* is a small connector that slides down on a pair of pins jutting up from a circuit board. There are often a number of pins side by side on the board. A *switch* or *DIP switch* is a very tiny slide that indicates two states. If two or more switches are together, they can both be used to represent binary values of settings. Each possible jumper or switch configuration is interpreted by the system as a setting.

on the *job*

DIP stands for dual inline package, referring to a type of now-obsolete packaging for connecting integrated circuit chips to motherboards. Old timers may recall when the early CPUs, such as the Intel 8088 in the IBM PC, used DIP packaging.

BIOS Settings

The most common way to optimize a motherboard is to modify the BIOS setup configuration, also called the *BIOS settings* or *CMOS settings*. Literally, hundreds of settings are available in different computers; we discuss the most common basic and advanced BIOS settings here. The choices available, and the methods for selecting them, may vary from one BIOS manufacturer to another. The best reference for using the BIOS setup menus is the user manual that came with your PC or the motherboard manual.

To access the computer's BIOS settings, closely watch the computer screen at startup. Following the POST, a message appears indicating the proper key sequence you should use to enter the BIOS settings program. This key combination varies among computers but is typically F2, DELETE, or CTRL-ALT-ESC. In most systems, the message will appear for only three to five seconds, and you must use the indicated key combination within that allotted time.

Note also that BIOS-setting programs differ from each other. Some allow you to use the mouse, and some only the keyboard. Furthermore, the names of the settings might also vary slightly. Use the program's Help feature for information about how to navigate through the program and save or discard your changes. Make notes about the current BIOS settings before you change them, in case you need to change them back. Or, look for a BIOS-settings backup utility in the BIOS menus, sometimes located on a Tools menu. If you are working with a computer that does not have a BIOS-settings backup utility, and the computer has a parallel port with a printer attached, follow the instructions in Exercise 4-5 to print the BIOS settings.

EXERCISE 4-5

Backing Up the BIOS Settings

1. Restart the computer and watch the screen closely for the correct key or keys to press.

2. Enter the BIOS-setting program using the specified key combination.

3. Do not make any changes to the settings.

4. If a printer is connected to the PC's parallel port, ensure it is turned on and is online. Then simply press the PRINT SCREEN key on the keyboard to print the current screen. On some printers, you may need to press a button on the printer to have each page form feed. Although this will not work on all systems, it can provide you with a handy hard copy of the BIOS settings.

5. Repeat this procedure for all the settings screens.

6. Press the correct key or keys to exit Setup without making any changes. This is often the ESC key.

If your BIOS menus do not include a BIOS settings backup program, and the procedure in Exercise 4-5 does not work on your computer, you can purchase a third-party BIOS settings backup program or resort to using pen and paper to write down the settings. You can also use a digital camera to photograph the screens. Figure 4-2 shows a sample BIOS Setup Utility main menu screen.

FIGURE 4-2

The main menu screen for a BIOS Setup Utility

```
          Phoenix - AwardBIOS CMOS Setup Utility

  ► SoftMenu Setup              ►PC Health Status

  ► Standard CMOS Features       Load Fail-Safe Defaults

  ► Advanced BIOS Features       Load Optimized Defaults

  ► Advanced Chipset Features    Set Password

  ► Integrated Peripherals       Save & Exit Setup

  ► Power Management Setup        Exit Without Saving

  ► PnP/PCI Configurations

  Esc : Quit                    ↑ ↓ → ← : Select Item
  F10 : Save & Exit Setup        (NF-CK804-6K61FA1DC-XX)

          Change CPU's Clock & Voltage
```

Parallel Port Settings You can use the BIOS settings to configure the system's parallel port(s). In newer computers, however, most parallel ports support the IEEE-1284 standard, meaning the port is bidirectional and the OS can automatically configure it. You may need to change the BIOS settings to set the parallel port mode in an older PC. For example, many parallel ports run in *unidirectional mode* by default, meaning that peripheral devices attached to the port can receive but cannot send data. The BIOS settings might refer to this mode as "Transfer Only." However, some parallel devices send communication signals back to the computer. These devices require a *bidirectional mode* (also called Standard mode on some machines).

Newer devices take advantage of faster IEEE-1284 bidirectional modes, called ECP or EPP modes. *Enhanced capability port (ECP) mode* allows access to special PC features called DMA channels and is approximately ten times faster than regular bidirectional mode. ECP mode is for printers and scanners. *Enhanced parallel port (EPP) mode* offers the same performance as ECP but is for use with parallel devices other than printers and scanners.

Another BIOS parallel-port setting is enable/disable. You can use this feature to instruct the computer to use or ignore the parallel port. Disabling the port temporarily can be useful when troubleshooting or when the port is in conflict with another component. You might also need to disable the onboard parallel port if it has stopped working. Disabling it will allow you to install an additional (nonintegrated) parallel port.

COM/Serial Port Like the parallel port, you can use the BIOS settings to configure the COM port(s). However, in newer systems, the OS accomplishes this task. As with parallel ports, you can also use the BIOS settings to enable or disable the COM port.

Boot Sequence The *boot sequence* BIOS setting relates to the order in which the BIOS will search devices for an OS. You can normally select from among a variety of possible boot devices, including A: or Floppy, C: or Hard Disk, CD/DVD drive, and even USB device. Figure 4-3 shows a BIOS Setup menu in which the boot order is selected as "First Boot Device," "Second Boot Device," and "Third Boot Device." At one time, having the floppy drive as the first boot device made sense when we often used a bootable floppy for installing, troubleshooting, and maintaining the operating system. None of these reasons are significant today. If the First Boot Device is drive CD/DVD, then, if you leave a bootable optical disc in the drive, the system will boot to that disc. You can change the boot order so the computer looks first on the hard drive. This is particularly helpful in keeping

FIGURE 4-3

BIOS Setup
Utility Advanced
BIOS Features
menu

```
             Phoenix - AwardBIOS CMOS Setup Utility
                    Advanced BIOS Features

   Quick Power on Self Test    Enabled          Item Help
 ► Hard Disk Boot Priority     Press Enter
   First Boot Device           Floppy
   Second Boot Device          Hard Disk
   Third Boot Device           CDROM
   Boot Other Device           Disabled
   Boot Up Floppy Seek         Disabled
   Boot Up NumLock Status      On
   Security Option             Setup
   MPS Version Ctrl For OS     1.4
   OS Select For DRAM > 64MB   Non-OS2
   Delay For HDD (Secs)        0
   Full Screen Logo Show       Enabled



 ↑↓:Move Enter:Select +/-/PU/PD:Value F10:Save ESC:Exit F1:General Help
 F5: Previous Values F6: Fail-Safe Defaults F7: Optimized Defaults
```

boot sector viruses from a floppy disk or bootable optical disc from infecting the computer. For the past several versions, the Windows operating systems have come on bootable DVDs, without requiring booting from a floppy disk first. When installing a new operating system on a brand-new computer, it is important that the boot sequence includes the optical drive. If the system already has an OS on it, before you can upgrade to the new OS, you will need to ensure the boot order places the optical drive before the hard drive.

Floppy Drive In recent years, the floppy drive has disappeared from new computers because, compared to current devices, it is too small and too slow. You may still find it useful to know about the BIOS settings options for configuring and using a floppy drive. You can enable or disable the use of the motherboard's integrated floppy disk controller by selecting the appropriate option. You might want to disable the controller so you can use an expansion controller card instead.

You can also configure the floppy drive controller so a diskette cannot boot the computer. If you don't plan to boot from a floppy, removing the floppy drive from the boot order will speed up the overall boot sequence. If you later find you need to boot from the floppy drive, simply change the BIOS settings accordingly.

Hard Drive Settings You should not have to modify the hard drive settings on a modern PC because hard-drive detection is normally automatic. If your system is having a problem identifying a hard drive, double-check the motherboard manual.

Only in very old systems should you have to manually use the BIOS settings to set the type and capacity (tracks, sectors, and cylinders) of each hard drive installed on the system. Normally, the "type" setting should be set to Auto, instructing the BIOS to read the type and capacity from the drive. If you are having problems, you can also use the Autodetect feature to force the BIOS to search for and identify all hard drives on the system. Use this option when a second drive is added to the system and not automatically detected.

Memory You do not have to configure RAM capacities. Simply install RAM in the computer and the BIOS automatically counts it at startup. However, you can use the BIOS settings to enable or disable the memory's ability to use parity error checking (although you can use this setting only if the RAM supports parity). Warning—if you enable the BIOS parity option but are not using memory that supports parity, the computer will not boot properly.

Date and Time Although changing the time and date settings from within Windows (or from within other operating systems) is simpler, you can use the BIOS settings program to set the computer's *real-time clock (RTC)*, which is actually a chip that keeps track of the time and date. The OS will use the date and time that you set here, as will any applications that are date- or time-aware.

Passwords Although we do not generally recommend using this feature, most BIOS settings programs allow you to set passwords on the computer. This is separate from the password required by your operating system or network. A user password can be set to allow or restrict booting the system. A supervisor password can be set to allow or restrict access to the BIOS-settings program itself or to change user passwords. Some systems (typically newer ones) include both password options; older systems typically include only supervisor-type passwords, required both to boot the system and to enter the BIOS-settings program.

You must be especially careful with supervisor passwords. If you forget the BIOS password, you can't even get into the BIOS setup program to change or disable the password. Fortunately, most systems that have the BIOS password feature include a "clear password" jumper on the motherboard. The user manual or motherboard manual will document this. If you forget the BIOS password, you can open the computer and set the jumper to remove the password. If there is no jumper for clearing the password, you can clear the entire contents of the CMOS by temporarily removing the battery. However, this is a last resort because it will cause you to lose all but the default settings.

on the **job** *Unless you have very high security requirements, do not set either type of password in BIOS settings because this only creates unnecessary inconvenience to the user and to the person supporting the PC. One situation in which such system-level passwords are commonly set is in a computer lab.*

Plug-and-Play BIOS   All modern PC BIOSs are plug and play, and the BIOS-settings program includes some options for configuring it. One option is Plug and Play Operating System. When enabled, this setting informs the BIOS that the OS will configure plug-and-play devices. Another plug-and-play option allows you to enable or disable the BIOS configuration of plug-and-play devices.

Installing Motherboard Drivers

Every motherboard comes with a driver disc for all the onboard components. This disc contains drivers compatible with the latest operating systems. Once the entire system has been assembled and the operating system installed, run this disk to install all the drivers. Until you take this step, you may not be happy with some aspects of the system and may not be able to access all features. For instance, the optimum mode of video display may not be fully supported without the video driver, if the video adapter is on board.

Replacing or Upgrading BIOS

The function of the BIOS is to translate communications among devices in the computer. The BIOS is able to do this because it contains the basic instruction set for those device types. This is required only for certain system devices, such as hard disk drives, floppy disk drives, memory, I/O ports, and so on.

When to Upgrade the BIOS

If you install a device with which the computer seems unable to communicate, you might need to upgrade or replace the existing BIOS. It is important to understand that this is not necessary for a new device, but only for an entirely new device type, and that it requires communications with the computer at a low level even before operating-system-level drivers are installed. You do not need to upgrade the BIOS to use a new mouse or printer.

We think of hard drives as being a single type, but to the BIOS, there are many types of hard drives, and the size of the hard drive makes a difference. For example, you install a new many-gigabyte hard drive that the system will not recognize, and it won't allow you to enter or select that size manually in BIOS Setup. In this case, you must upgrade the BIOS.

You will also want to upgrade to a BIOS version that is appropriate to the operating system you are installing. The general version (Windows XP, Windows Vista, or Windows 7) of the OS is important, but it is also important to know if the OS is a 32-bit or 64-bit version. All the Windows operating systems listed come as one or the other. The specific differences are defined in Chapter 9, but the short lecture is that a 32-bit version of Windows can address up to 4 MB of addresses, whereas a 64-bit Windows version can handle many more. For instance, 64-bit Windows Vista can access from 1 GB of RAM to more than 128 GB of RAM.

Upgrading the BIOS

Most computer BIOSs today are actually Flash BIOS chips that can be electronically upgraded using software from the BIOS manufacturer. The most common way to add support for a new device type is by "flashing" the BIOS. You will need to contact the manufacturer of your computer, or of the BIOS, to obtain the program and instructions for doing this.

In general, you turn off the computer, insert the manufacturer's disc, and restart the computer. The disc contains a program that automatically "flashes" (updates) the BIOS so it can recognize different hardware types or perform different functions than it could before.

Replacing the CMOS Battery

Most motherboards come with a small coin-sized battery, such as a 3-Volt Lithium battery, to support the nonvolatile RAM, called CMOS RAM, where the BIOS settings are stored. This was discussed briefly in Chapter 1. Since this battery supports the date and time tracking, the classic symptom of a failed CMOS battery is a system that does not keep the correct time after being powered down. If that occurs, open the case and remove the battery, much as you would remove a watch battery. Then find a replacement for it that matches the voltage and amperage of the old battery.

Power Supplies

When building a new computer, a power supply may come with the computer case or you can purchase one separately. Power supplies in existing computers do fail from time to time, and you can replace them using the procedure outlined in Exercise 4-6. Whether you are purchasing a power supply for a new system or replacing an old one, you have the same set of concerns when selecting, installing, or removing a power supply.

Selecting a Power Supply

When replacing a power supply, be sure to use one that has sufficient wattage, the correct form factor, and the appropriate power connectors for the motherboard. Do not just check out the number of pins required for the connectors, but the actual pin-outs required. A *pin-out* is a diagram showing the purpose of each wire in a connector.

The ATX (P1) power supply connector for older ATX motherboards is a 1-piece, 20-pin keyed connector. The biggest confusion at this time is among the various 24-pin power supply connectors. Many motherboards for recent multi-core processor models require two connectors, often described as ATX12V 2.0. These connectors include a 24-pin main connector and a 4-pin secondary connector. However, some newer motherboards require EPS12V connectors, which include a 24-pin main connector, an 8-pin secondary connector, and an optional 4-pin tertiary connector.

Removing a Power Supply/Installing a Power Supply

Recall that power supplies can still hold a charge when turned off, especially if you use only the soft power switch. Before removing even a failed power supply, be sure to unplug it from the wall outlet. To avoid the danger of electric shock, do not wear an antistatic wristband while working with power supplies. Exercise 4-6 provides basic steps for removing an old power supply and installing a new one.

EXERCISE 4-6

Replacing a Power Supply

1. Turn off the power and remove the power connector from the wall socket.
2. Remove the power connector(s) from the motherboard, grasping the plastic connector, not the wires.

3. Remove the power connectors from all other components, including hard, floppy, and CD-ROM drives.

4. Using an appropriately sized screwdriver, remove the screws that hold the power supply to the PC case. Do not remove the screws holding the power supply case together!

5. Slide or lift the power supply away from the computer.

6. Reverse these steps to install a new power supply.

Cooling Systems

As a rule, the typical PC comes with a cooling system adequate for the standard components delivered with the PC. Once you start adding hard drives, memory, and additional expansion cards, you should give some thought to supplementing the existing cooling system. How far you go with this depends on just how much you have added to the PC.

An overheated computer will slow down, thanks to new built-in technology that senses the temperature of the motherboard and slows down the processor when the temperature exceeds a certain limit. This reduces the heat the processor puts out. In the extreme, overheating can damage PC components. The other side of this is that modern cooling systems also use heat sensors and will adjust their performance to keep the system cool. New power supply and case fans will change speed to match the temperature.

Common Sense First

Before you consider spending money on a new cooling system, make sure you are not impairing the installed cooling systems. Begin by ensuring that the PC case is closed during operation, that all slot covers are in place, that airflow around the case is not obstructed, and that the computer system is not installed in an unventilated space, such as an enclosed cabinet. Also, check to see if ribbon cables are blocking air flow inside the case. Use plastic ties to secure cables out of the way. Correct these problems before spending money supplementing the cooling system.

Additionally, open the case and give the interior of the PC a good vacuuming before you spend money on upgrading the cooling system. Excessive dust and dirt on components will act as an insulator, keeping the heat from dissipating and causing a computer to overheat, which in turn can cause it to slow down, stop operating, or be permanently damaged. Learn more about vacuuming a PC in Chapter 5.

Selecting an Appropriate Cooling System

When should you consider upgrading the cooling system in your PC? If you are using the PC only for office applications, and you have added several heat-generating components, such as hard drives or adapter cards, then you should consider upgrading the cooling system. If your PC at home or at work needs to operate in an extreme environment, such as in an un-air-conditioned garage, you should do all you can to increase the PC's cooling capabilities. If you are a computer gamer with a highly customized PC, you have no doubt put a great deal of thought into the cooling system. If not, shame on you.

Case Fan

New PCs often come with both a power supply fan and a separate case fan. Perhaps you can simply upgrade the present case fan. Also, check to see if the PC has an empty bay or bracket for a case fan. A case fan is a very inexpensive upgrade, cheaper than a latte and muffin at your favorite coffee shop. The only requirement is a bracket or bay in the case that will accommodate a case fan, and the appropriate power connector.

When shopping for a case fan, you will need the dimensions of the fan bay (usually stated in millimeters), rated voltage, and power input. Features to compare are fan speed in revolutions per minute (RPM), airflow in cubic feet per minute (CFM), and noise level in decibels (dbA). The fan speed and airflow reflect the fan's effectiveness for cooling. The noise level is an important consideration because fans and drives are the only moving parts in a PC and generate the most noise. Look for fans with a noise decibel rating in the 20s or below. Additionally, check out the power connector on new case fans. Many come with a Molex connector that can connect directly to the power supply, and some have a special connector that must connect directly to the motherboard. Figure 4-4 shows a 100 mm–wide case fan with a Molex connector.

A case fan

CPU Fan/Heat Sink

If you are installing a CPU, then you will also need to install a cooling system for the CPU. Today's processors often require a fan/heat sink combination. Often, the cooling system and the CPU are packaged together, making the choice for you. Pay attention to the power connector for the fan, and locate the socket for this connector on the motherboard ahead of time. It is unlikely that you will replace an existing CPU fan and/or heat sink unless the CPU fan has failed. Even then, considering the complexity of it, and the danger of damaging the CPU, it may be easier to replace the entire CPU if the same or similar model is available.

Liquid Cooling Systems

Liquid cooling systems are not just for gamers anymore. Like most technologies, as manufacturers improve liquid cooling systems, more people adopt them, and the prices for the improved systems drop. If you decide to look into this option, do your homework because these systems have several issues. For one, they require special skills to install, and they take up considerable space inside a computer because they require specific tubing, reservoirs, fans, and power supplies to work effectively.

Installing and Configuring a Cooling System

When installing a new cooling system, be sure to read the documentation for the new components as well as for the motherboard, if appropriate. Assemble the components required and follow good practices to avoid damaging the computer or injuring yourself. Turn the computer's power off, disconnect the power cord, and ensure that you follow the electrostatic discharge (ESD) procedures discussed in Chapter 18.

When installing a new case fan, affix the fan to the case in the appropriate bracket or bay, using the screws that came with either the case or the fan itself. Connect the power connector and any required motherboard connectors.

When installing a heat sink and/or fan on a CPU, be sure to apply thermal compound according to the instructions, and carefully connect the heat sink or fan using the clip provided. Plug the fan into the appropriate power socket on the motherboard.

Removing a Cooling System

If a cooling system fails or is inadequate, you will need to remove it from the PC. In that case, turn the computer's power off and ensure that you follow the electrostatic discharge (ESD) procedures. Then reverse the steps for installing the component, unplugging power and motherboard connectors, unscrewing mounting screws, and lifting it out of the case.

SCENARIO & SOLUTION

I would like to build a PC. Is it best to shop for the best price on each component (motherboard, CPU, memory, etc.) from several sources?	No. The best strategy, especially if you are new to this, is to buy all the components from one source and get a guarantee that they will work together.
I read that I might have to upgrade my BIOS before installing the next Windows operating system? Does this mean I have to replace the physical BIOS chip?	You probably will not have to do something this drastic. Most BIOSs today are actually flash BIOS chips that can be electronically upgraded using software from the BIOS manufacturer.
The PC I want to build will be used mostly for running standard office productivity software. Should I consider a water-cooled system?	Generally, a water-cooled system would be overkill in a PC running standard office productivity software, but some new motherboards have built-in sealed (passive) liquid cooling systems.

Adapter Cards

Even with the large number of features built into PCs, technicians need to know how to add new adapter cards to PCs in order to add new functionality. Installing an adapter card is a nontrivial task, requiring that you open up the case and install the card in an available expansion port. For this reason, give careful thought to your decision. What function do you need to add? Must you use an adapter card to add this function, or is this something you can add by purchasing a device with a USB or IEEE-1394 connection? These options are much more desirable than installing an adapter card, if you have a choice. Sometimes, however, an expansion card will provide better bandwidth, as in a network adapter, or performance, as in a video or sound card.

Do you simply need more USB or IEEE-1394 ports? Then, in the case of USB, simply plug one or more USB hubs into your existing USB ports. IEEE-1394 devices usually come with ports that allow the device to participate in a daisy chain. Therefore, if you have an IEEE-1394 connector on the computer, you may simply daisy-chain devices to this port. On the other hand, does your computer not have one of these types of ports, or are the ports it has outdated? Some USB devices refuse to work on older USB ports. In that case, you will need to add a new USB adapter card to upgrade to the new version.

Are you replacing the onboard video adapter with an enhanced video adapter? Are you adding an adapter that will support two monitors, often called dual-headed video adapters? There is no way to avoid installing an adapter to solve these problems.

As new or better technology comes available, you will need experience installing adapters in a PC.

Selecting an Appropriate Adapter Card

When selecting an adapter card, you must first do your homework. First, determine what expansion slots are available (there may not be a slot available) in the PC in which you will install the card. Then, shop for the adapter card that both fits your needs and physically fits in your PC. Adapter cards are available for every purpose, from video adapters, NICs, modems, TV tuner cards, sound cards, storage interfaces, media readers, and all types of I/O interfaces. Many of these functions come integrated into new motherboards, but when they don't, or when they become outdated or you simply want more of them, you can add the functionality via an adapter card. You will also have the choice of buying an internal adapter that plugs into your PC's PCIe expansion bus area, or an external adapter that connects to a USB, eSATA, or FireWire connector on the front or back panel. The following discussion concerns installing, configuring, and removing internal adapter cards.

Installing and Configuring an Adapter Card

Once you have selected the adapter card that meets your needs, you will need to install it in the PC. Exercise 4-7 provides general steps for installing an adapter card. Although installing and configuring many adapter cards is straightforward, you must understand the card's purpose. Before you begin, check the documentation for both the adapter card and the motherboard and note any variations from this general procedure.

EXERCISE 4-7

Installing an Adapter Card

1. Turn off the computer, unplug it, and ensure that you carry out proper ESD procedures, as described in Chapter 18.

2. Remove the slot cover for the appropriate expansion slot, and position the adapter card upright over it (see Figure 4-5).

FIGURE 4-5

Installing an
adapter card

3. Place your thumbs along the top edge of the card and push straight down.
   If necessary, rock the card along its length (never side to side).
4. Secure the card to the case using the existing screw holes.

Removing an Adapter Card

Before removing an adapter card, be sure you have an antistatic bag in which to store
the removed adapter card. Then, to remove it, simply reverse the steps in Exercise 4-7.

Storage Devices

Replacing storage devices is a common task because drives with their moving parts
are one of the most common areas of computer failure. Adding more storage is also
a common upgrade. Fortunately, because most drives are standardized, they can be
recognized by any PC and don't need special configuration.

Optimizing a PC with Storage Devices

Adding more storage to a PC is often a necessity when the user plans to store large
amounts of data files, especially graphic files. As more and more people acquire digital
cameras, their space needs for storing photo collections increases. The general choices
include internal and external storage.

Selecting an Appropriate Internal Storage Device

Internal drives are less expensive than external drives, but require more skill to install. The internal hard drives you are most likely to install in a PC are EIDE drives. These will connect to PATA or SATA drive interfaces on the motherboard. If you are adding an optical drive, it may use the ATAPI standard to connect to the PATA interface, or it may use the SATA connectors on the motherboard.

The computer's BIOS will usually recognize these drives. In the simplest cases, all one needs to do to make a hard drive or a CD-ROM drive functional is to install it physically in the computer. However, drives on the PATA interface have a few configuration issues, as opposed to those on the SATA interface, and SATA offers higher speeds, thinner cables, and support for hot swapping. So, when you have a choice, you should choose SATA over PATA drives. The drives physically look the same until you examine the back of the drives and see the new power and data connectors.

The following sections describe alternative drive installations, including how to configure and install multiple drives in a single system.

Installing Drives on PATA Channels

The typical PC motherboard has two PATA hard-drive controller channels. That is, the motherboard has connectors for two ribbon cables. Each PATA channel supports two drives, so you can install four drives, in total, on the standard two PATA channels. One of the motherboard connectors is the primary connector, and the other is the secondary connector. Unfortunately, manufacturers use several conventions for labeling them on the motherboard, such as primary and secondary (see Figure 4-6), IDE1 and IDE2, or EIDE1 and EIDE2. If only one drive is present, it must connect to the primary channel.

The onboard drive controller of an EIDE hard drive receives commands to the drive and controls the action of the drive itself. The technology incorporated in EIDE and ATA devices allows one controller to take over the function of an additional drive. The controlling drive is the *master drive*, whereas the second drive it controls is the *slave drive*. PATA channels support one master and one slave drive on each channel.

If only one drive is present on a channel, it must be a master drive. The master drive on the first channel is the *primary master*. The slave drive on the first channel is the *primary slave*. Similarly, the master drive on the second channel is the *secondary master*, and the slave drive on the second channel is the *secondary slave*.

FIGURE 4-6

The primary
and secondary
PATA controller
connectors on
the motherboard

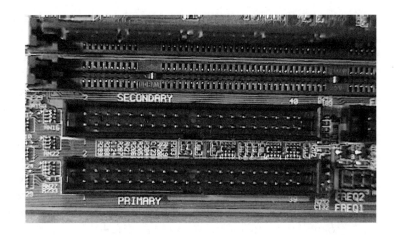

In most cases, a slave drive will work only if a master drive is present. A master can function without a slave drive present. Before you install an EIDE drive on a PATA channel, you will need to configure it for its master or slave role. Do this by setting jumpers on the back of the drive. Most EIDE/PATA drives have a label that shows the master and slave jumper settings. Figure 4-7 shows a drive with two white jumpers over two pairs of pins. This position, according to the drive's label, indicates that it is the master drive. Moving these two jumpers to the two right-most pairs of pins would configure the drive for the slave role.

In many cases, it doesn't matter which is which. That is, there is no real performance difference between master and slave drives. However, as with most computer configurations, there are some exceptions. When using a mixture of old and new

FIGURE 4-7

The back of an
EIDE/PATA drive,
showing two
white jumpers
over two pairs
of pins

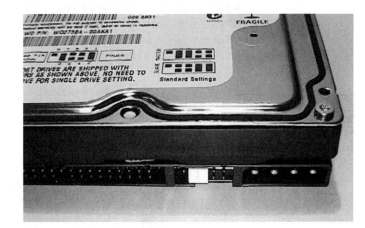

hard drives within the same system, set the newer drive as the master and the older drive as the slave because newer drives can recognize and communicate with older drives, but the reverse isn't true. An older drive's controller will typically be unable to control the newer drive.

It is important to note here that PATA channels can support a mixture of EIDE and ATAPI (optical) drives. How do you determine which drive should be the master and which should be the slave?

When using a hard drive and CD-ROM optical drive together in a master/slave configuration, always set the hard drive as the master and the CD-ROM as the slave, because the CD-ROM's controller is unable to take control of the hard drive. Additionally, some (but not most) older optical drives work only as slaves, and you simply cannot configure them as master drives. To create a master/slave configuration, follow the steps in Exercise 4-8.

PATA uses flat ribbon cables or (rarely) round cables. There are two important differences between the flat ribbon and the round cables—price and cooling. The round cables are currently more expensive, but they are superior to the 2" wide flat cables because they allow better airflow. Both types of PATA cables normally come with three 40-pin connectors—one on either end and one in the middle. One end connects to the PATA channel connector on the motherboard, while the other two connectors plug into the drives. If the system has only one hard drive, attach it to the end of the ribbon cable. The red stripe along the length of the cable represents pin 1. Make sure this stripe aligns with pin 1 on both the hard drive and on the channel connector on the motherboard.

Early PATA cables had just 40 wires, but newer cables have 80 wires, although they still have the same 40-pin connectors. The extra wires ensure better signal quality through grounding that shields against interference.

Some drives have a jumper setting called *cable select*. If this setting is used, the position of the drive on the cable will automatically determine the drive's role. If the drive is on the end of the cable, it is the master drive, and if it is on the middle of the cable, it is the slave drive.

EXERCISE 4-8

Choosing a Master

1. Determine which drive will be the master.

2. Locate the master/slave jumper pins and jumpers using the information on the drive label to determine which jumper settings to use for a master or slave (or cable select) configuration.

3. Use the jumper(s) to set this drive as a master (or cable select).

4. Secure the drive to an available drive bay.

5. Align the red stripe on the cable with pin 1 on the primary channel connector of the motherboard; attach the cable. Then attach the connector on the far end of the cable to the master drive, also ensuring that the red stripe on the cable aligns with pin 1 on the drive.

6. Locate an available Molex connector at the end of a cable coming from the power supply, and connect it to the drive.

7. To install a second drive on the same channel, follow the instructions in the previous steps, but set the drive's jumpers to the slave setting. Figure 4-8 shows the completed installation of two drives on one channel. Notice that both drives connect to the same ribbon cable.

Optical Drives

Physically installing and removing an internal CD or DVD drive is the same as installing and removing hard and floppy drives, except that the CD or DVD drive must be installed into a bay with a front panel that allows access to the drive for inserting and removing discs. The optical drive also requires the connection of a sound cable to the sound card.

Additionally, a DVD drive may need to connect to a decoder card using separate cables. Normally, the BIOS will automatically recognize the CD or DVD drive. Or it

FIGURE 4-8

The finished installation of two hard drives on the same PATA channel may be necessary to enable the device in the BIOS settings. If the computer doesn't recognize, or can't communicate with, the new drive, you need to load a driver for it. Learn about installing device drivers in Chapter 9.

If you are installing two optical drives (of any type) using a PATA interface with the intention of copying from one to the other, for best performance, make sure the rewritable (RW) drive you plan to copy to is primary on the channel to which it is installed.

Blu-ray drives are presently an option when customizing a new system and will become even more mainstream as time goes on. Therefore, you should be prepared to install and configure Blu-ray drives for the users who need to view or record Blu-ray content. At this writing, read-only Blu-ray drives are available for under $200, but to take advantage of this disc format's massive storage feature, you will need a Blu-ray recorder, which is far more expensive. When selecting a drive, carefully consider the reason for the upgrade. Will it only be used for storing nonvideo data, or will it be used to run Blu-ray movies? You can add a Blu-ray drive for storing nonvideo data to a system without upgrading the video system, but in order to run Blu-ray movies, the video system will need to support HD resolutions stated as 720 pixels, 1080i, or 1080p over a digital connection. Further, it must also support High-Definition Content Protection (HDCP) at the graphics chipset level and display level. Part of this is the requirement that the digital connection between the video adapter and display support be either DisplayPort or HDMI to support the HDCP signal. This extends to an HDCP-compliant graphics driver and disc-playback software.

Finally, before installing an optical drive to support running high-definition video content, be sure you have a multi-core CPU and at least 2 GB of RAM under either Vista or Windows 7, or 1 GB of RAM for a Windows XP PC.

on the job *You can usually install hard drives and other devices on their sides with no impact on operation or performance. Never install a hard drive upside down.*

Solid-State Storage

Solid-state storage is available for nearly every storage need. At the low end of the price scale, thumb drives provide a solution for someone needing ease-of-use and portability when transferring data among computers. Similarly, we use a variety of storage devices in smart phones and cameras, often connecting these devices, or their solid-state cards, to our PCs to transfer data. At the high end, solid-state drives are available for large server systems at a much higher price than comparably sized hard-drive systems, but they offer better reliability and power savings over

FIGURE 4-9

FIGURE 4-9

A SATA data
cable connector
(left) next to
a SATA power
connector (right)

conventional hard drives. Low-end solid-state storage will plug into a PC's bus through a media reader, whereas high-end solid-state storage is more likely to come with the SATA interface.

Installing Drives on SATA Channels

Each SATA device has its own dedicated channel and does not require setting jumpers as is required for devices on a PATA channel. Simply connect one end of the SATA data cable to a SATA channel and connect the other end to the drive's data connector. Additionally, SATA devices may come with two power connectors on the drive. If so, one accepts a standard 4-pin Molex connector from the power supply, while the other accepts a special 15-pin SATA power connector. This is an "either-or" situation. Only connect to one of these power connectors—if both are used the drive will be damaged. Exercise 4-9 provides general instructions for installing an internal SATA drive. Be sure to follow the instructions in the manual for your motherboard and drive when installing a SATA drive. Figure 4-9 shows a SATA data cable alongside a SATA power cable.

EXERCISE 4-9

Installing a SATA Drive

1. Secure the drive to an available drive bay.

2. Locate an available SATA connector on the motherboard or on a SATA expansion card. Plug in one end of the SATA cable (it is keyed so it cannot be installed incorrectly).

FIGURE 4-10

Installed SATA
drive (top)
connected to
SATA channel
on motherboard
(bottom left)

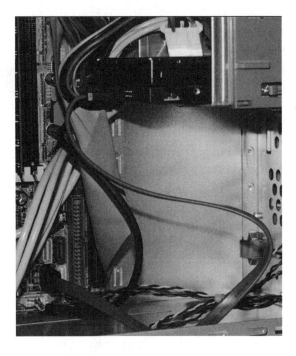

3. Locate an available power connector at the end of a cable coming from the power supply, and connect it to the drive. Figure 4-10 shows an installed SATA drive connected to a SATA channel on the motherboard. Notice the three open SATA channel connectors at the bottom left.

RAID Arrays

Not too many years ago, if you wanted RAID, you had to add a special RAID controller adapter card to your computer. Today, many motherboards come with a RAID controller built in. Therefore, if you need to create a RAID array on a recently manufactured computer, you will probably only need to add the appropriate number of hard drives. If this is not true of the computer you wish to add RAID to, then you will need to purchase an adapter and install it.

The physical installation of a RAID adapter is identical to installation of any other bus adapter. After installing it, you will need to install and connect each drive in the array to the controller, and then start the computer and run the RAID controller setup program.

The setup program will be similar whether the controller was integrated on the motherboard or on a separate controller card. You access it while starting up the machine. In the case of an integrated controller, the RAID setup program may be on the system BIOS Setup menu, normally on an advanced menu. In the case of a separate RAID controller, watch during bootup for a prompt to press a key to enter the RAID setup. From there, you simply follow the menus and select the RAID level you desire.

Internal Floppy Disk Drives

Floppy drives have gone from being a necessity in the early IBM PC to being considered as useless as rotary-dial phones. For this reason, you will rarely see a floppy drive in a new PC, and they vanished from most laptops years ago.

Installing an Internal Floppy Disk Drive

Most modern motherboards still have an integrated floppy drive controller. Therefore, if you desire to add an internally installed floppy drive to a new computer, you just need to obtain a floppy drive and the cabling. Before installing the drive, be sure to turn off the PC and disconnect the power cord.

Internally mounted floppy drives are installed in a fashion similar to hard drives, with one major difference—the floppy drive must be installed into a bay with a front panel that allows access to the drive for inserting and removing floppy disks. Most PC cases still come with this bay. Locate the bay, slide the drive into the drive bay, and fasten it with the retaining screws.

A floppy drive uses a flat ribbon cable that measures 1-5/8 inches wide with 34-pin connectors on both ends. This cable is keyed to only insert one way, with the red edge lined up with pin 1 of the floppy connector on the motherboard and similarly lined up with pin 1 on the drive connector. Attach the floppy drive to the end of the ribbon cable; this drive will be assigned drive letter A.

As it is highly unlikely that you will need to install even one floppy drive in a computer, it is even less likely that you will install a second one. However, in that very unlikely situation, you would need a 34-pin ribbon cable with three connectors, and then the floppy drive connected to the middle connector is assigned the drive letter B.

Once the drive is in place and the ribbon cable connected, locate a power cable coming from the power supply that has a plug that fits the floppy drive. This is usually a 4-pin miniconnector.

Removing a Floppy Disk Drive

To remove a floppy drive, disconnect the power and ribbon cables, unfasten the retaining screws, and then slide the drive out of the bay.

e x a m

ⓦ a t c h   *The red stripe on a ribbon cable indicates pin 1.*

Installing and Configuring SCSI Devices

SCSI systems allow you to attach more devices to the computer than the common EIDE/PATA or SATA systems do, but less than USB or IEEE 1394. By installing a *SCSI host adapter* (also called *a SCSI controller*), you can attach 7, 15, 31 or more additional devices in the computer, depending on the type of SCSI host adapter you are using. SCSI adapters that conform to newer standards, such as SCSI SAS, FC-AL, and SSA can support more than 31 devices. SCSI systems have the disadvantage of being more expensive than EIDE systems and more difficult to configure. When cost and easy installation are factors, EIDE, USB, IEEE 1394, SATA, or eSATA systems are generally preferred.

Devices attach to the SCSI controller in a daisy-chain configuration, described in Chapter 3. Each external SCSI device has two ports: one port receives the cable from the device before it in the chain, and one port attaches the next device in the chain. An internal SCSI device may have only one port that requires a special cable for daisy-chaining other internal devices.

Types of SCSI Systems

Like many other computer standards, SCSI systems have evolved and improved over time. Newer SCSI standards are backward compatible with older standards, so older devices are installable in newer systems.

The T10 SCSI committee of the *InterNational Committee on Information Technology Standards (INCITS)* frequently upgrades the SCSI standard. INCITS (pronounced "insights") is, in turn, accredited by the American National Standards Institute (ANSI). Information on the current standards and revisions of SCSI are available at www.t10.org.

Configuring SCSI

Configuring the SCSI host adapter, and each device on a SCSI chain, requires paying attention to a special address for each called a *SCSI ID*. In addition, each SCSI chain must physically terminate, or the entire chain will not function. The following describes the proper procedures for addressing and terminating SCSI devices so conflicts do not occur. The normal order of steps is to first attach the device to the chain, terminate the SCSI chain, set the SCSI ID, and load the device driver (if applicable).

Addressing SCSI Devices   You must allocate a SCSI ID to each SCSI device in a chain so it can communicate with the controller but not interfere with other SCSI devices in the system. If two devices share an ID, an address conflict will occur. The controller will not be able to distinguish the conflicting devices, and it is likely that neither device will work.

Some SCSI devices are hard-wired to use one of only two or three IDs; others might use any available ID. If the device supports plug and play, the system will automatically assign it an available ID address, whereas other devices require configuring the address manually. On some devices, this configuration is via jumpers on the device, and others depend on a setup program residing on the device's ROM chip. Some SCSI devices that require address assignment through jumpers will indicate, by a label on the device, which setting to use.

The priority of ID addresses is important. The SCSI controller itself usually has ID 7 assigned to it; addresses increase in priority within each octet, and each successive octet has a lower overall priority than the one before it (see Figure 4-11). That is, IDs 8–15 have a lower priority than 0–7. In a 32-bit system, 7 has the highest priority, and 24 has the lowest.

If two SCSI devices try to send data at the same time, permission to transmit will go to the device with the highest-priority ID, and the other device will have to wait. Incidentally, "at the same time" means within 0.24 microseconds!

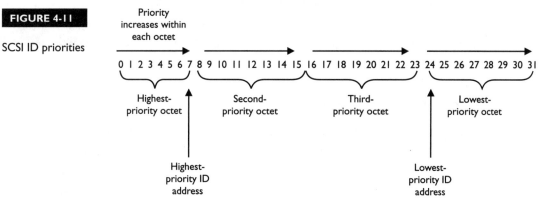

FIGURE 4-11

SCSI ID priorities

SCSI System Termination   Equally important is terminating the SCSI system properly. Improper termination can result in the total or intermittent failure of all devices in the SCSI chain. Special terminators, or *terminating resistors,* must be present to ensure that signals at the end of the chain are absorbed rather than bounced back along the chain. In some cases, the resistor fits into the unused second port on the last SCSI device in the chain. In other cases, the SCSI device will include an onboard terminator, made active by using the appropriate jumper setting.

Whether the SCSI chain is strictly internal or strictly external, the last device and the controller must have terminators. Finally, if the SCSI chain is a mixture of both internal and external devices (which is not recommended), both the last external and last internal devices on the chain are terminated.

SCSI Cabling

SCSI systems employ a variety of cable types. The specific cable type depends on the SCSI type, the device type, and whether the device is internal or external. Furthermore, each cable type might have a different connector. Until recently, SCSI systems all used a parallel interface to the computer.

Although new SCSI specifications no longer support 32-bit systems, you might be required to work on an older one. All 32-bit systems use a 68-pin P-cable and a 68-pin Q-cable or one 110-pin L-cable.

Serial Attached SCSI (SAS) targets the server market, not the desktop PC market. However, like many such technologies, it will probably filter down to the desktop, but it will take time before this happens. Currently, although most new PCs have SATA connectors built in, before a SAS device can be added to a PC, a special SAS host adapter card must be installed.

Connecting an External SCSI Device

Read the documentation for each external device carefully before connecting it, because procedures differ from one manufacturer to another. Most follow the basic steps described previously.

Removing an Internal Storage Device

To remove an internal storage device of any type, check the documentation for the device. Exercise 4-10 provides general steps that will work for all types of internal storage devices.

EXERCISE 4-10

Removing a Drive

1. Remove the power supply and ribbon cables from the back of the drive. Ensure that you grasp the plastic connector, not the wires themselves. If the connector doesn't come out easily, try gently rocking it lengthwise from side to side (never up and down) while you pull it out.

2. Remove the screws that attach the drive to the drive bay. These are usually located on the sides of the drive. Be sure to carefully save any screws you remove.

3. Slide the drive out of the computer.

Installing and Removing an External Storage Device

External storage devices come in many types and sizes. This was not true ten years ago, when external storage was limited to optical drives or conventional hard drives using SCSI or parallel interfaces. These drives were expensive and cumbersome.

Today, the market is practically flooded with inexpensive external storage devices of all types and sizes. In addition, back then external optical drives were popular because they did not come standard in PCs and especially not in laptops. Today, with one or two optical drives standard in new PCs, the demand for external optical drives is down, but the need for external hard drives and solid-state drives has grown, and so have the choices.

Most flash memory drives come with a USB interface, and external hard drives have USB, IEEE-1394, or eSATA interfaces. Newer computers come with eSATA ports for attaching external eSATA devices. An eSATA port connects to the motherboard's SATA bus. If you wish to connect an eSATA device to a computer without SATA support, you will need to add an adapter card.

Traditional external hard disk drives also come in a full range of sizes from the low gigabytes to hundreds of gigabytes and even terabytes. The tiny 2" format drives, like the thumb drives, do not need power supplies; they will draw their power from the USB interface. The more conventionally sized drives require their own power supplies that will need to be plugged into the wall outlet. Besides that one issue, all of these drives are so simple to use that they hardly need instructions. Plug one in and your Windows OS (unless it is very old) will recognize the drive, assign it a drive letter, and include it in the drive list in My Computer. You can browse the contents of the drive and manage data on the drive using the Windows interface.

You do need to take care when removing a USB- or IEEE-1394-connected hard drive. Many people simply unplug their thumb drive when they finish with it, but they risk losing their data or damaging the thumb drive. Windows requires an important step before the drive is disconnected: click the Safely Remove Hardware icon in the tray area of the taskbar, and select the external storage device from the list that pops up. This will notify the operating system that the device is about to be removed so the operating system "stops" the device. If files are open, Windows may issue a message that the device cannot be stopped. Wait until the status message declares that it is safe to remove the device (Windows will turn off the LED on a thumb drive) before unplugging it from the USB or IEEE-1394 port.

Preparing a Hard Disk for Use

Fresh from the factory, a hard disk comes with its disk space divided into concentric tracks, each of which is divided into equal-sized 512-byte sectors. This is the physical format of the disk. The first physical sector on a hard disk is the master boot record (MBR). Within this sector lies a 64-byte partition table, which defines special boundaries on the hard disk, called *partitions*.

The first step in preparing a hard disk for use is to create one or more partitions, the areas of a disk that contain logical drives. The second step is to format the drive. Many hard drives, especially external hard drives, come prepartitioned and preformatted.

Partitioning a Hard Disk Drive

Most operating systems include the partitioning step in a menu-driven process of the installation program, so anyone who can answer a few simple questions can at least succeed in creating a partition on which to install the OS. In addition, each operating system, such as Windows XP and Windows Vista, comes with a partitioning program you can use after installing the operating system on a PC. This program allows you to partition any additional drives you add to the computer. Figure 4-12 shows the Windows Vista Disk Management program, a part of the Computer Management console. A newly installed hard drive shows as Disk 1. The OS has recognized it but has not yet partitioned it; therefore, the space is shown as "unallocated." Right-clicking the rectangle representing the hard drive space brings up a menu with the option to create a new partition.

FIGURE 4-12

The Windows
Vista Disk
Management
program, showing
a newly installed
unpartitioned
hard drive

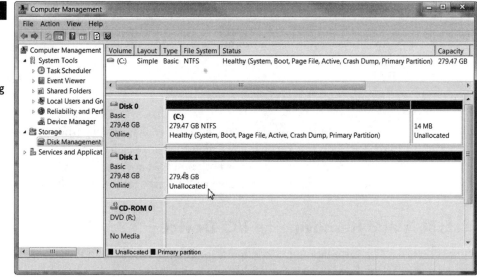

Formatting a Hard Disk Drive

You can format each partition with the logical structure required by a file system.
File systems are described in Chapter 10. This logical format is often simply called
format. Once you have created the partition, use the appropriate utility to format the
drive, which, in most operating systems today, requires selecting the file system. This
is because Windows and other operating systems support more than one file system.
The Partition Wizard in Windows XP creates and formats the new partition, based
on the user's answers to questions the Wizard poses.

A file system is the logical structure on a disk that allows the operating system
to save and retrieve files. Chapter 10 will go into detail on the types of file systems
available in Windows and how to organize files in this logical structure.

CERTIFICATION OBJECTIVE

■ **701: 1.8** *Install and configure peripherals and input devices*

What is a peripheral but an input or output device? According to the language in the
CompTIA 2009 A+ Essentials (2009 Edition) Exam objectives, peripherals and input
devices are separate categories, but are grouped together under this one objective.

I/O Devices

In this section, you will examine input and output devices and how to add, configure, and remove them.

Selecting an I/O Device

Select the input or output device to suit your needs, whether you need a basic input device, such as a keyboard and mouse, or a specialty input device, such as a barcode reader. Sometimes a device is both an input and output device, as is the case with touch screen displays, which we will describe later in this chapter.

Installing and Removing an I/O Device

The installation and configuration required for an I/O device depends largely on the interface. Most input devices use standard interfaces and connectors.

USB

Today, most input devices come with a USB interface and are plug and play. Even some devices that traditionally had a dedicated interface, such as keyboards and mice, now often come with a USB interface. In spite of the variety of devices using USB, installation and removal is simple because of the plug-and-play interface. As always, we remind you to read the manual before installing any device, but the general rule for a USB device is to install the driver before connecting the device.

Keyboards and Mice

Older keyboards and mice come with mini-DIN (also known as PS/2) connectors, whereas newer ones usually come with USB connectors. Most keyboards and mice will work without the need for add-on device drivers. The standard mouse and keyboard drivers installed with the operating system will be sufficient. To access nonstandard keyboard and mouse features, however, you will need to install and configure a device driver and sometimes a special application.

Some input keyboards and mice come with the Bluetooth wireless interface, described in Chapter 6. This short-range *radio frequency (RF)* interface allows devices to communicate over very short distances. Some input devices come with an infrared interface. Bluetooth and infrared require a transceiver device to be attached to the computer. Sometimes they are built into portable computers, but one must be added to desktop PCs and other computers that do not have the built-in Bluetooth or infrared interface. An important difference between using a Bluetooth device versus an infrared device is that, with Bluetooth, you are primarily concerned about keeping the device and receiver within the appropriate distance for the signal. With infrared, line-of-sight is as important as proximity because the infrared signal must not be blocked by anything in its way.

When you buy a Bluetooth keyboard and/or mouse, it will come with a transceiver device to attach to the computer, which, in most cases, connects through a USB port. After installing the Bluetooth transceiver, a Bluetooth keyboard or mouse will function like a more conventional keyboard or mouse.

Biometric devices

As described in Chapter 3, biometric devices are security devices. Therefore, we will save the detailed discussion of these devices for Chapters 16 and 17, and only concern ourselves at this point with the local installation of a fingerprint scanner as a representative biometric device. Read the instructions, and install the scanner as you would any device. Install drivers at the appropriate time, and physically connect the device to the computer. The software that comes with fingerprint scanner requires a fingerprint to compare with the scanned print. This may be stored locally, or it may be stored in a central database. The latter scenario will be discussed in Chapter 17. In the case of a locally stored fingerprint, typically done when using a portable device, you will run a special program after installing the device. This program will take a baseline scan of your fingerprint and store it locally.

Bar Code Readers

There are various types of barcode readers, and you will select the reader that best meets your needs. The most common readers that you will encounter connected to PCs are handheld scanners and stationary scanners, such as those you see in retail stores.

Once you select an appropriate bar code reader, your next concern is the interface. Traditionally, bar code readers used an RS-232 serial interface but expect newer bar code readers to use either a keyboard interface or a USB. Those that use a keyboard interface use a special "Y" connector so a keyboard can also be connected. Read the instructions that come with the device before installing it, but expect to install the drivers before connecting the device, especially in the case of a USB bar code reader.

KVM Switches

Before you install a keyboard, video, and mouse (KVM) switch, you must be sure you have the correct type of switch for your purposes. Then you must read the installation instructions and assemble the cabling, devices, and computers you wish to connect. Memorize the keystrokes required to switch control from one computer to another. Check for the needed drivers. In our experience, these are not necessary because the KVM switch itself captures the keystrokes and changes the focus from computer to computer based on your keyboard commands.

These instructions are for installing an active KVM switch used to control two or more computers. Installing this type of KVM switch is just a bit more complicated than connecting a keyboard, video display, and mouse to a computer. In fact, the first thing you do is connect your keyboard, video display, and mouse to the appropriate connectors on the KVM switch. You will find them grouped together, and there may even be more than one type of connector for the mouse or keyboard or perhaps speaker ports. This grouping of connectors may be labeled "Input"—even though we all know a display is an output device. Once the devices are connected, you can connect the KVM switch to the computers you wish to control. This requires special cables that are usually bundled together with the connectors split out on each end. This bundling ensures that you won't mistakenly connect a cable from one set to two different computers. If you do not have bundled cables, bundle them yourself.

Once all the computers are connected to the KVM switch, power up the switch and then power up each PC. During bootup, the PC should recognize the KVM switch as the keyboard, video, and mouse devices.

Multimedia

Many multimedia devices, such as Webcams, digital camera, and MIDI, often use a USB interface, which usually requires that you install the device driver before attaching the device to a USB port. Microphones only need to be connected to the correct port and do not usually require a special device driver.

Most multimedia devices are fairly simple to connect and use. One exception is a video capture card. These cards are available as bus cards (PCI or PCIe) and as USB devices. However, the bus cards are generally less expensive and have more features than the USB devices. If you decide on a bus card, you will install it like most other adapter cards. Either interface will require a special driver and software. As usual, you will install the drivers for a USB device first and for a bus card after the physical installation. The software that comes with the device may install as part of the driver installation, or you may need to initiate that install. Common software includes Nero for capturing video and burning DVDs, and Beyond TV, which includes *digital video recorder(DVR)* capabilities for recording video to disk. Next, shut down the computer and connect the device to the appropriate TV input, whether cable TV, satellite TV, or broadcast TV. The types of cables you will need depend on the input. Coaxial cable for cable TV, or S-Video, composite, or component cables for other inputs.

Displays

An easy and satisfying PC upgrade is a new video display. In most cases, this will not require replacing the video adapter, since even the most standard video adapter in recently manufactured PCs provide excellent output. Perhaps you have used the same bulky CRT display for several years, keeping it even after upgrading the system unit, because of the high price you paid for it ten years ago. Now may be the time to reclaim lost desk space by upgrading to a new flat panel display. Additionally, many PC tasks are so much easier with two displays. Therefore, you might not be replacing a display, but augmenting it with a second display, so that you can spread your desktop windows across two monitors' real estate.

Selecting an Appropriate Display Device

Where many of us have skimped in the past is on the display, and at the current low prices, purchasing a high-quality flat panel display seems like a no-brainer to upgrade your PC and your user experience. A large FPD display will take up very little desk space. Use the information provided on displays in Chapter 3 to select a new display. Pay attention to the video connector(s) available on your PC.

Installing and Configuring a Display Device

In order to install a CRT monitor or a flat panel display, simply connect the display's cable to the proper connector on the computer and plug in the power cord. Then power up both the display and the computer.

Multi-monitor As for a multi-monitor configuration, most laptops come with the ability to support both the built-in screen and an external display, but a PC normally has a video adapter for just a single display. Therefore, to add a second display (or more) to a PC, you will need to install a video adapter. For better performance, we recommend replacing the PC's single-output video adapter with a multiheaded video adapter. Consult the computer's documentation. If the computer has an inboard video adapter, you may choose simply to add a single-headed bus video adapter, but you must be certain that the computer will support this configuration. We have found installing a dual-headed adapter to be the best solution. Once the adapter and driver are installed, connect to each of the two displays exactly as you would connect to one, with only one power-up after everything has been connected. After powering up, you will need to go into the Windows Display Settings utility and configure one of the monitors to be the main monitor and the other one (or more) to have the desktop extend onto it. If you don't select this second setting, the two monitors will simply display the exact same thing. The main monitor will contain the Taskbar and desktop icons, while the other will contain any windows you wish to place there. Figure 4-13 shows a dual display configuration in the Display Settings dialog box in Windows Vista.

We have used dual displays for years, even using displays of two different sizes when we added an external monitor to a laptop. This was very workable, but we find it much more pleasant to use monitors of identical size and resolution.

Touch Screen   A touch screen will take just a few more steps to connect and install on a PC. First, we are assuming you have a free-standing PC and wish to install a retail touch screen display, rather than convert a conventional display to a touch

FIGURE 4-13	
Configure multi-monitors using the Display Settings dialog box in Windows Vista.	

screen display. Most touch screen monitors will have two interfaces—a standard video connector for the video output to the screen, and either a serial or USB connector for the input from the touch screen component of the monitor. Before you purchase a touch screen, be sure the interfaces will work with the computers to which you will connect them. Connect the cables, power up the display and computer, and then install the device drivers. Some models of touch screen displays require a reboot after installing the drivers. With a conventional display, your job would be done at this point, but with a touch screen display, you still need to calibrate it. Run the calibration program that comes with the display, which will require that you perform several tasks, touching the screen at specific spots, to enable the touch screen interface to line itself up with the images on the screen. After calibration, test the programs you wish to use on this computer. If you are not happy with the results, run the calibration program again. If it still is not satisfactory, you may need to contact the manufacturer to see if an upgrade for the driver is available.

Removing a Display

In order to remove a display, power down the computer and the display, unplug the display from the power outlet, and disconnect the display data cable from the computer.

CERTIFICATION SUMMARY

This chapter led you through the processes required to install, upgrade, and configure PC components. You also learned the important issues for selecting each type of component, because whether you are building a system from scratch or just upgrading one or more components, you need to go through a selection process to ensure that the components will function well together. For this, use the knowledge gained in Chapters 1 and 2 about the basic technologies and features of the components. Then, follow the appropriate step-by-step instructions from the manufacturer for the component you are installing. Never fail to read all the appropriate documentation for both a component and the PC or, specifically, the motherboard.

✓ TWO-MINUTE DRILL

Here are some of the key points covered in Chapter 4.

Motherboards and Onboard Components

❑ Select motherboard, CPU, and memory modules that are compatible with each other by researching the specifications of each.

❑ A motherboard must support both the technology and the form factor of a memory module, such as SIMM, RIMM, or DIMM.

❑ When installing a motherboard, follow the instructions in the motherboard manual.

❑ The ability to upgrade an existing CPU depends on the limits of the motherboard.

❑ One of the most common and most effective PC upgrades is the installation of more RAM.

❑ The BIOS settings program enables you to alter the behavior and configuration of many of the PC's components.

❑ An old BIOS may not be able to recognize a new type of device and may need to be upgraded.

❑ BIOSs today are very rarely replaced. Rather, upgrade the BIOS firmware through a process called BIOS flashing.

Power Supplies

❑ Replace a failed power supply.

❑ Select a power supply that is of the correct form factor for both the motherboard and the case, and select one that has sufficient wattage for the internal components you expect to have.

❑ Older ATX motherboards used a 20-pin ATX (P1) connector to provide power. Some recent motherboards require two ATX12V 2.0 connectors—one is a 24-pin main connector, and the other is a 4-pin secondary connector. Other newer motherboards require EPS12V connectors, which include a 24-pin main connector, an 8-pin secondary connector, and an optional 4-pin tertiary connector.

Cooling Systems

❑ An overheated PC will slow down, stop functioning altogether, or become damaged.

❑ The typical PC comes with a cooling system adequate for the standard components delivered with it.

❑ Supplement the cooling system when adding hard drives, memory, and additional expansion cards or if the PC must function in a hot environment.

Adapter Cards

❑ Select an adapter card that will add the functionality you need and that also fits an available expansion port on the motherboard.

❑ Read the documentation for the adapter card and the motherboard before installing the card.

Storage Devices

❑ EIDE drives come with either a PATA interface or a SATA interface.

❑ Most computers have two PATA channels that can each support two EIDE or ATAPI drives.

❑ Each PATA channel can have one master device, or one master and one slave device, and you must configure each device on a PATA channel for its role on the channel.

❑ Only one SATA device connects to each SATA channel, so there are no configuration issues.

❑ Newer PC BIOSs often support at least one or two types of RAID arrays. Install the correct number of drives for the type of array, and configure the array through BIOS setup.

❑ Most new PCs do not come with floppy drives, and most motherboards have a single channel for floppy drives that can handle up to two floppy drives.

❑ Normally, manufacturers do not build SCSI systems into the typical PC. If you want to add SCSI devices to a PC, you need to install a SCSI bus adapter.

❑ Various external storage devices, such as those with USB or IEEE-1394 connectors, are available today. These devices are truly plug and play, and once one is plugged in, the system recognizes it and assigns it a drive letter.

❑ To remove one of these external devices, use the Safely Remove Hardware icon on the tray area of the Windows taskbar to stop the device, and only after it is stopped, unplug it.

❑ To prepare a hard drive for use, you must first partition it and then format it for a specific file system.

I/O Devices

❑ The installation and configuration of an I/O device depends on the interface. Always read the documentation for the device before installing.

❑ You normally install the drivers for a USB device before connecting the device to a PC.

❑ Keyboards and mice may use the traditional mini-DIN (PS/2) connector or USB.

❑ A Bluetooth or infrared device requires a transceiver on the computer. These are often built in on laptops, but added as a USB device on desktop computers.

❑ A biometric device must be installed as an I/O device and also configured as a security device.

❑ To install a KVM switch for the purpose of controlling two or more computers using one keyboard, video display, and mouse, first connect the keyboard, display, and mouse to the device in the properly marked connectors. Then connect each computer to the appropriate connectors on the switch.

❑ Installing and configuring a display is a fairly simple task, involving connecting the display to the PC and to a power outlet. A touch screen display requires an extra step to calibrate the touch screen with the images on the computer desktop.

SELF TEST

The following questions will help you measure your understanding of the material presented in this chapter. Read all of the choices carefully because there might be more than one correct answer. Choose all correct answers for each question.

Motherboards and Onboard Components

1. How can you determine which CPU and memory modules to use with a certain motherboard?
    A. No problem. All ATX motherboards accept all Intel and AMD CPUs and DIMM memory modules.
    B. Each motherboard is unique; check the documentation.
    C. Check the CPU documentation.
    D. Check the RAM module documentation.

2. Which of the following is true of "Socket 1155?" Select all that apply.
    A. It is a term used to describe all LGA CPU sockets.
    B. It is the socket for DIMM memory modules.
    C. It is the socket for RIMM memory modules.
    D. It describes a LGA CPU socket with 1155 pins.

3. What's a common name for a PGA socket that uses a lever for safely aligning and installing a CPU?
    A. Socket 736
    B. ZIF
    C. Xeon
    D. Athlon

4. If you know a CPU's address bus width, you know ...
    A. The width of a memory bank
    B. The form factor of the CPU
    C. The maximum amount of RAM the CPU can access
    D. The minimum amount of memory that must be installed

5. Which of the following must you do before installing a DIMM module?
    A. Open the retention clips on the socket and tilt the DIMM at a 45-degree angle to the socket.
    B. Open the retention clips on the socket and align the DIMM module with the socket.

   C. Close the retention clips on the socket and tilt the DIMM at a 45-degree angle to the socket.

   D. Close the retention clips on the socket and align the DIMM module without tilting.

6. Which of these events could require flashing the BIOS?

   A. The BIOS does not recognize a new hard drive.

   B. A new mouse does not work.

   C. A new printer does not work.

   D. The monitor goes blank.

7. The BIOS chip in a PC is actually this type of chip, which software can upgrade.

   A. CMOS

   B. Flash BIOS

   C. RDRAM

   D. CPU

Power Supplies

8. Which power supply connector(s) is likely to be used by a new ATX variant motherboard and a Pentium 4 CPU?

   A. ATX (P1)

   B. ATX 5V 2.0: 24-pin main and 4-pin secondary

   C. ATX12V 2.0: 24-pin main and 4-pin secondary

   D. ATX (P2)

9. Select all the items that should be considered when selecting a new power supply.

   A. Wattage

   B. CPU

   C. Form factor

   D. Power connectors

10. What equipment should you never use when working with a power supply?

   A. Screwdriver

   B. Connectors

   C. Motherboard

   D. Antistatic wrist strap

Systems

11. In response to rising temperatures inside a PC, the CPU will take this action.

   A.   Slow down

   B.   Turn off the fan

   C.   Speed up

   D.   Reboot

12. Which of the following could impair the functioning of the installed cooling system? Select all that are correct.

   A.   Keeping the case open during PC operation

   B.   Removing slot covers behind empty expansion slots

   C.   Vacuuming the interior

   D.   Dirt and dust

13. Adding this cooling component is an easy and cheap cooling system upgrade.

   A.   Liquid cooling system

   B.   Fan

   C.   CPU heat sink

   D.   CPU fan

Adapter Cards

14. You have just purchased a new device that requires the latest version of USB, but your USB ports are only at USB 1.1. What is a good solution?

   A.   Buy a new computer.

   B.   Buy a converter for the device so it can use a parallel port.

   C.   Install a USB adapter card with the latest version of the USB standard.

   D.   Exchange the device for one with a parallel interface.

Storage Devices

15. Which one of the following statements about EIDE/PATA hard drive configurations is true?

   A.   Before a master drive will function properly, a secondary drive must be present on the cable.

   B.   The master drive must attach to the ribbon cable using the connector closest to the motherboard.

   C.   The term for any hard drive on the secondary controller is *slave*.

   D.   A slave drive cannot work in the absence of a master drive.

16. You are planning to install a hard drive and an optical drive using the PATA interface in a new system, as the only drives. Which of the following is typically a valid drive configuration for you to use?

    A. Install the hard drive as a primary master and install the optical drive as a secondary master.

    B. Install the optical drive as a primary master and the hard drive as a primary slave.

    C. Install the optical drive as either a primary master or a secondary slave.

    D. Install the optical drive anywhere, as long as the hard drive is a secondary master.

17. What makes the installation and configuration of SATA drives easier than PATA drives?

    A. No need to configure master/slave because it is automatic with SATA.

    B. The SATA cables are much thinner than PATA.

    C. No need to configure master/slave because each drive has its own channel.

    D. SATA drives are physically smaller.

18. Which of the following SCSI IDs has the highest priority on a SCSI chain?

    A. 1

    B. 7

    C. 15

    D. 24

I/O Devices

19. This is a solution for the user who needs to have two documents open and visible on the desktop of a single computer.

    A. Biometric device

    B. Multi-monitor configuration

    C. KVM switch

    D. Multimedia

20. After physically connecting a touch screen and installing necessary device drivers, what important configuration task must you perform?

    A. Record a fingerprint scan.

    B. Calibrate.

    C. Upgrade Windows.

    D. Wash the screen.

SELF TEST ANSWERS

Motherboards and Onboard Components

1. ☑ **B,** each motherboard is unique; check the documentation, is correct.
   ☒ **A** is incorrect because it states that all ATX motherboards accept all Intel and AMD CPUs and DIMM modules. Each motherboard is unique in the components it will support. **C** is incorrect because checking the CPU documentation will not tell you if the motherboard itself will support this CPU. **D,** check the RAM module documentation, is incorrect because this will not tell you if the motherboard itself will support this RAM module.

2. ☑ **D,** Socket 1155 describes a LGA CPU socket with 1155 pins, is correct.
   ☒ **A** is incorrect because each LGA socket style has a unique name. **B** is incorrect because "Socket 1155" is not the socket for DIMM memory, but for a CPU. **C** is incorrect because "Socket 1155" is not the socket for RIMM memory, but for a CPU.

3. ☑ **B.** ZIF (zero insertion force) is the name commonly used for a CPU socket with a lever for safely aligning and installing a CPU.
   ☒ **A,** Socket 736, is incorrect because it would describe a single socket style, not necessarily a ZIF socket. **C,** Xeon, is incorrect because this is the name of an Intel CPU line. **D,** Athlon, is incorrect because this is the name of an AMD CPU line.

4. ☑ **C.** The maximum amount of system RAM the CPU can access is correct. For instance, a 32-bit address bus can address a maximum of 4 GB of system RAM.
   ☒ **A,** the width of a memory bank, is incorrect because the data bus width determines this, not the address bus width. **B,** the form factor of the CPU, is incorrect because the address bus only affects RAM addressing, not the physical form of the CPU. **D,** the minimum amount of memory that must be installed, is incorrect because this is determined by the needs of the operating system and how the computer is to be used.

5. ☑ **B.** To open the retention clips on the socket and align the DIMM module with the socket is correct because DIMM modules will not install at an angle, as SIMM modules did.
   ☒ **A** is incorrect because you must install DIMMs in an upright position. **C,** close the retention clips on the socket and tilt the DIMM at a 45-degree angle to the socket, is incorrect because you cannot insert a module if the clips are closed, and you do not insert a DIMM at an angle to the socket. **D,** close the retention clips on the socket and align the DIMM module without tilting, is incorrect, only because you cannot insert a module if the clips are closed.

6. ☑ **A.** The BIOS not recognizing a new hard drive is an event that could require flashing the BIOS.
   ☒ **B** is incorrect because a nonworking mouse would not require flashing the BIOS. **C** is not correct because you would not flash the BIOS to fix a printer. **D** is not correct because you would not flash the BIOS to fix a monitor that went blank.

7. ☑ **B.** Flash BIOS chips are BIOS chips that software can upgrade.
    ☒ **A** is not correct because CMOS is not a BIOS chip, although a special CMOS chip stores system settings. **C** is incorrect because RDRAM is a type of RAM, not a BIOS chip. **D** is incorrect because a CPU is a processor, not a BIOS chip.

Power Supplies

8. ☑ **C.** ATX12V 2.0: 24-pin main and 4-pin secondary is correct, although new motherboards may also use EPS12V connectors, or connectors that were not in use at the time of this writing.
    ☒ **A,** ATX (P1), is incorrect because this is an old connector used in the early ATX motherboards. **B,** ATX 5V 2.0: 24-pin main and 4-pin secondary, is incorrect as far as the "5V" is concerned. **D,** ATX (P2), is incorrect because the chapter did not mention it as a power supply connector.

9. ☑ **A, C,** and **D.** You should consider wattage, form factor, and power connectors when selecting a new power supply.
    ☒ **B,** CPU, is incorrect because, although its wattage requirements are important, the CPU itself is not an issue when selecting a power supply.

10. ☑ **D.** You should never use an antistatic wrist strap when working with a power supply.
    ☒ **A,** a screwdriver, is incorrect because it may be necessary to remove the screws holding a power supply to the case. **B,** connectors, is incorrect because you must work with the connectors from the power supply to the motherboard and other components. **C,** motherboard, is incorrect because you may need to work with the power supply connectors on the motherboard.

Cooling Systems

11. ☑ **A.** In response to rising temperatures inside a PC, the CPU will slow down.
    ☒ **B,** turn off the fan, is incorrect because this would make the PC even hotter. **C,** speed up, is incorrect because this would create more heat. **D,** reboot, is incorrect because this is not an intended action by the CPU if it senses rising temperatures.

12. ☑ **A, B,** and **D.** **A** and **B,** keeping the case open during PC operations and removing slot covers, disturb the air flow design for the case. **D,** dirt and dust, act as insulation and reduce the cooling ability.
    ☒ **C,** vacuuming the interior, is incorrect because this will remove dirt and dust from components, improving the efficiency of cooling.

13. ☑ **B.** Fan is correct, as this is an easy and cheap cooling system upgrade, as long as there is a place to mount the fan in the case and power is available.
    ☒ **A,** liquid cooling system, is incorrect because this is the most difficult and most expensive cooling system upgrade. **C,** CPU heat sink, is incorrect because it would not be easy, although it may be cheap, unless the CPU is damaged in the process. **D,** CPU fan, is incorrect because it would not be easy, although it may be cheap, unless the CPU is damaged in the process.

Adapter Cards

14. ☑ **C.** Install a USB adapter card with the latest version of the USB standard is correct.
☒ **A** is incorrect because buying a new computer is not necessarily the solution to a single outdated component on a PC. **B,** buy a converter for the device so it can use a parallel port, is incorrect because you do not know that this is even possible with the device, or that the PC has a parallel port. **D,** exchange the device for one with a parallel interface, is incorrect because most devices have a USB interface, not parallel, and many PCs do not have parallel ports.

Storage Devices

15. ☑ **D.** A slave drive cannot work in the absence of a master drive. If a drive is a slave and there is no master present, the slave drive will not be able to communicate.
☒ **A** is incorrect because a master drive can be alone on a PATA channel, and "secondary drive" is not a correct term, although "secondary channel" is a correct term. **B** is incorrect because it states that the master drive must attach to the ribbon cable using the connector closest to the motherboard. The opposite is true. The master drive must be installed at the end of the ribbon cable. **C,** the term for a hard drive on a secondary controller is slave, is also incorrect. The primary controller and the secondary controller can each have a slave drive, as long as a master drive accompanies each.

16. ☑ **A.** Install the hard drive as a primary master and install the optical drive as a secondary master. This is most common, although you could also install the hard drive as a primary master and the optical drive as a primary slave.
☒ **B** and **C** are incorrect because they suggest installing the optical drive as a primary master *and* hard drives cannot be slaves to optical drives. **C** is also incorrect because it suggests installing the optical drive as the secondary slave, but slave drives must be accompanied by a master drive on the same channel. **D** is incorrect because the only hard drive must be a primary master.

17. ☑ **C.** There is no need to configure master/slave, because each drive has its own channel is correct.
☒ **A** is incorrect because there is simply no notion of the master and slave roles with SATA. **B** is incorrect because, although it is true that the SATA cables are thinner, this is not what makes them easy to install and configure. **D** is incorrect because it is not true that the SATA drives are smaller than PATA, and even if it were true, smaller drives would not necessarily be easier to install and configure.

18. ☑ **B.** The SCSI ID with the highest priority on a single SCSI chain is 7.
☒ **A** is incorrect because 1 would come after 7, 6, 5, 4, 3, and 2. **C** is incorrect because 15 would come after 7, 6, 5, 4, 3, 2, and 1. **D** is incorrect because 24 would have the very lowest priority on a 32-bit SCSI system.

I/O Devices

19. ☑ **B.** Multi-monitor configuration is correct. This will give the user more desktop space for viewing two documents at once.

☒ **A,** biometric device, is incorrect because a biometric device is a security device used during login. **C,** KVM switch, is incorrect because this will allow a user to switch between multiple computers, not spread the desktop across two or more monitors. **D,** multimedia, is incorrect because multimedia is about sound, music, videos, etc., not about having more viewable display space.

20. ☑ **B.** Calibrate is correct because this will allow the touch screen interface to line itself up with the images on the screen.

☒ **A,** record a fingerprint scan, is incorrect because a touch screen is not intended to scan fingerprints. **C,** upgrade Windows, is incorrect because screen calibration is the task required by a touch screen display. **D,** wash the screen, is incorrect because, although you will want to do this from time to time for any screen (using the correct method), this is not a configuration task.

5

Troubleshooting, Repair, and Maintenance of PCs

CERTIFICATION OBJECTIVES

❑ **701: 2.1** Given a scenario, explain the troubleshooting theory

❑ **701: 2.2** Given a scenario, explain and interpret common hardware and operating system symptoms and their causes

❑ **702: 1.2** Given a scenario, detect problems, troubleshoot, and repair/replace personal computer components

❑ **702: 1.4** Given a scenario, select and use appropriate tools

❑ **701: 2.5** Given a scenario, integrate common preventative maintenance techniques

✓ Two-Minute Drill

Q&A Self Test

Τhe most common procedures you will perform as a computer technician are troubleshooting and resolving computer problems. The more familiar you are with a computer's components, the easier it will be for you to find the source of a problem and implement a solution. Build your comfort level by studying Chapters 1, 2, 3, and 4 and by gaining experience. In this chapter, you will first learn troubleshooting theory and then you will progress to basic diagnostic procedures and troubleshooting techniques, practice isolating PC component issues, discover the appropriate troubleshooting tools, and become proactive using common preventive maintenance techniques.

CERTIFICATION OBJECTIVE

■ **701: 2.1**   *Given a scenario, explain the troubleshooting theory*

For the A+ exams, CompTIA requires that you understand troubleshooting theory, procedures, and techniques. First, learn the theory, and then learn how to apply the theory using techniques and procedures appropriate to the symptoms and the identified problem area.

Troubleshooting Theory and Techniques

Troubleshooting is the act of discovering the cause of a problem and correcting it. It sounds simple, and if you watch an experienced technician, it may appear to be. However, troubleshooting a PC requires patience, instincts, experience, and a methodical approach. In this section, we will explore a methodical approach to troubleshooting theory and techniques. You will need to acquire the experience on your own, and you will find that your experiences will hone your instincts.

Preparation

When faced with a computer-related problem, resist the urge to jump right in and apply your favorite all-purpose solution. Rather, take time to do the following:

1. Before beginning, verify that you have a recent set of backups of the user's data. If you find there isn't one, perform backups of data (at minimum) and the entire system—providing the system is functional enough for these tasks.

2. Assess a problem systematically, using a strategy of dividing large problems into smaller pieces for individual analysis, and applying the troubleshooting theory described in this chapter.

3. Be prepared to question the obvious. For example, do not even assume that the computer is plugged in, that it is powered on, and that all peripherals are securely connected.

4. Always have a pad and pencil, or a PDA, with which to note your actions, findings, and outcomes. These will be critical to the documentation you create at the end of the entire process.

Troubleshooting Theory

General troubleshooting theory includes the following procedures:

1. Identify the problem.
2. Establish a theory of probable cause.
3. Test the theory to determine actual cause.
4. Establish an action plan to resolve the problem, and then implement the solution.
5. Verify full system functionality and, if applicable, implement preventative measures.
6. Document findings, actions, and outcomes.

e x a m

ⓦ a t c h *For the CompTIA A+ Essentials Exam 220-701, be sure you know the six steps of troubleshooting theory, as stated here.*

Identify the Problem

Even when the problem seems obvious, gather as much information as you can about the computer and its peripherals, applications, operating system, and history. This will help you clearly identify the problem.

Examine the Environment   Ideally, you will be able to go onsite and see the computer "patient" in its working environment so you can gather information from your own observations. Once onsite, you may notice a situation that contributed to the problem or could cause other problems. If you cannot go onsite, you may be able to diagnose and correct software problems remotely, using Remote Assistance or Remote Desktop, methods you will explore in Chapter 11. Otherwise, you must depend solely on the user's observations. Whether onsite or remote, you are looking for the cause of the problem, which is often a result of some change, either in the environment or to the computer directly.

on the *Job*

When troubleshooting a system that is not functioning properly, make it a practice to always perform a visual inspection of all cables and connectors, making sure all connections are proper before you invest any time in troubleshooting.

Question the User: What Has Happened?   The best source for learning what happened leading up to a problem is the person who was using the computer when the problem occurred. Your first question to the user should be, "What happened?" This question will prompt the user to tell you about the problem—for example, "The printer will not work." Ask for a specific description of the events leading up to the failure, and the symptoms the user experienced.

Do other devices work? This will help you isolate the problem. If one or more other devices do not work, you know you are dealing with a more serious, device-independent problem.

Ask about a problem device's history. Did this device ever work? If the user tells you that it is a newly installed device, you have a very different task ahead of you than if the user tells you it has worked fine until just now. The former indicates a flawed installation, whereas the latter points to a possible failure of the device.

If the user mentions an error message, ask for as much detail about the error message as possible. If the user cannot remember, try to re-create the problem. Ask if this error message is new or old, and if the computer's behavior changed after the error. For example, the computer might issue a warning that simply informs the user of some condition. If the error code points to a device, such as an optical drive, ask device-related questions.

The Event logs in Windows save many error messages, so if the user cannot remember the error messages, check the Event logs. Learn more about the Windows Event logs in Chapter 11.

on the *Job*

Sometimes customers are reluctant to give you all the details of the problem because they fear being embarrassed or held responsible. Treat the customer in a respectful manner that encourages trust and openness about what may have occurred. In Chapter 18, you will learn how important good communication skills are and how to apply them every day.

Question the User: What Has Changed? You should also find out about any recent changes to the computer or the surroundings. Ask if a new component or application has been recently installed. If so, has the computer worked at all since the new installation? The answer to this question could lead you to important information about application or device conflicts. For example, if the user tells you the audio has not worked since a particular game was loaded, you can surmise that the two events—the loading of the new game and the audio failure—are related. When troubleshooting, remove the software or other upgrades installed shortly before the problem occurred.

e x a m

ⓦatch *For the exam, be sure you know that you must learn about any expansions or upgrades the customer has tried to make.*

Establish a Theory of Probable Cause

When you have determined the symptoms of a problem, try to replicate the problem and begin an analysis from which you will develop your theory of probable cause. That is, if the user says the printer will not work, have him send another print job to the printer. Watch closely as he performs the task. Take note of any error messages or unusual computer activity that he may not have noticed. Observation will also give you a chance to see the process from beginning to end. Looking over the user's shoulder (so to speak) gives you a different perspective, and you may see the mistake, such as an incorrect printer selection or the absence of an entry in the Number Of Pages To Print field, that caused the problem.

Vendor Documentation As you work to pinpoint the source of the problem, check out any vendor documentation for the software or hardware associated with the problem. This may be in the form of hard copy or information posted on the vendor's Website.

Hardware or Software From your observations and the information you gather from the user, try to pinpoint the cause of the problem. It may be obvious that a device has failed if the device itself will not power up. If the source of the problem is not yet apparent, however, you need to narrow down the search even further by determining whether the problem is hardware or software related. We consider a hardware problem to include the device as well as its device drivers and configuration. Software problems include applications, operating systems, and utilities.

One of the quickest ways to determine if hardware or software is at fault is to use Windows Device Manager, which will indicate any conflicting or "unknown" devices. Just because Device Manager offers no information about the problem does not mean it is not hardware related; it only means Windows has not recognized it. You will work with Device Manager in Chapter 11. For now, Exercise 5-1 shows you how to open Device Manager and look for problem devices, an important task when troubleshooting hardware.

EXERCISE 5-1

CertCam

Troubleshooting with Device Manager

1. Right-click the Computer icon (My Computer in Windows XP) and select Properties.

2. In the System dialog box, select the Device Manager task (on the Hardware tab in Windows XP).

3. In Device Manager's window, you will see the devices on your computer organized under types of hardware, such as Computer, Disk Drives, Display Adapters, DVD/CD-ROM Drives, and Human Interface Devices, as Figure 5-1 shows.

4. If Windows detects a problem with a device, it expands the device type to show the devices. In the case of a device with a configuration problem, you will see an exclamation mark on both the type icon and the device icon. When Windows recognizes a device but does not understand its type, it places the device under a type named Other Devices, and you will see a question mark.

Probable Causes   From your observations and research, compile a list of probable causes, and if any of them has a simple solution, apply those first. If that does not solve the problem, investigate the other items on your list.

Test the Theory to Determine Actual Cause

After establishing a theory of probable cause, test the theory. You may need to do this on a test system, isolated from the rest of the network, or, if that is not an option, simply test the theory on the problem system. Whatever you do, you need to find

FIGURE 5-1

Device Manager,
showing the
types of devices
installed

a way to test your theory in a manner that does not endanger the user's data and
productivity. Does this solution extend beyond a single user's desktop and beyond your
scope of responsibility? If so, you must escalate the problem to another department,
such as network administration. Once you have tested the theory and found it to be
successful, you can move to the next step.

Establish an Action Plan to Resolve the Problem and Implement the Solution

After successfully testing your theory of probable cause, you now move on to the
planning stage. Now you need to think through both the actions you must take and
the possible consequences of those actions. Involve people from all areas affected by
the problem and by the effects of the solution. Business areas can include accounting,
billing, manufacturing, sales, and customer service. You also need to check with all IT
support areas that must take part in the solution. The plan should then include the
steps to take, the order in which to take them, and all testing and follow-up needed.
This will include steps required to minimize any possible bad effects.

Verify Full System Functionality and Implement Preventative Measures

Whether the problem and solution involve a single computer or an entire enterprise, you must always verify full system functionality. If you are dealing with a single desktop, once you have applied the solution, restart the system and the device (if appropriate), and test to be sure everything works. If your solution seems to have negatively affected anything, take additional steps to correct the problem. You may find yourself back in the troubleshooting loop.

Once you have successfully tested a solution, have the user verify and confirm that the problem is solved. This verification should begin exactly as the user's workday begins: with the user restarting the computer and/or logging on and opening each application required in a typical day and then using all peripherals such as printers. Have the user confirm that everything is working.

This is a very important step. Our experience has been that once you touch a user's computer, even though you might solve the problem, she will associate you with the next thing that goes wrong. Then you will receive a call stating that "such and such" has not worked since you were there, even though "such and such" does not relate to any changes you made.

Once everything is working normally and both you and the user have tested for full system functionality, have the user sign off on it to document the satisfactory results. If this last is not an accepted procedure in your organization, you should suggest it because it adds commitment to both sides of this transaction. You are committed to test and confirm a successful solution, and the user is committed to acknowledge the solution worked.

Document Findings, Actions, and Outcomes

Document all findings, actions, and outcomes. Take notes as you work, and once you have resolved the problem, review the notes and add any omissions. Sit down with the user and review what you did. This is your statement to the user that you made certain changes. You should be clear that you made no other changes to the system.

Afterward, these notes, whether informal or formal, such as comments entered into a help desk database, will be useful when you encounter the same or similar problems. It's a good idea to incorporate some of the lessons learned during troubleshooting into training for both end users and support personnel.

SCENARIO & SOLUTION

What should I do as part of the troubleshooting process before making any changes to a computer?	Verify there is a recent set of backups; if a set does not exist, perform a backup of data and the operating system.
Why should I question the user before jumping in with solutions?	To learn what happened and what has changed.
You have found a solution, applied it, and successfully tested it. What is the final step you need to take?	Document the troubleshooting activities and outcomes.

Training

Well-trained personnel are the best defense against problems. Therefore, an important troubleshooting technique is ongoing training for both end users and support personnel. The delivery methods and training materials should suit the environment, as many options are available for high-quality online training, starting with the help programs available in most operating systems and applications, user manuals, installation manuals, and Internet or intranet resources. All personnel involved should know how to access any training resources available. End users can often solve their own problems by checking out the help program or accessing an online training module, cutting down on the number of service calls and associated loss of productivity.

CERTIFICATION OBJECTIVE

- **701: 2.2** *Given a scenario, explain and interpret common hardware and operating system symptoms and their causes*

    The CompTIA A+ Essentials Exam will present scenarios and then require that you be able to explain and interpret common hardware and operating system symptoms and their causes. This section provides an overview of troubleshooting operating system symptoms and causes; however, Chapter 11 will cover this topic in more detail. Later in this chapter, we detail how to interpret common hardware symptoms and their causes.

Troubleshooting Software Problems

Software problems can involve application programs, operating system components, or a combination of both in cases where interaction between an application and the operating system are the cause. Here we look at basic procedures for identifying and solving software problems.

The Quick Fixes: Rebooting, Uninstalling, and Reinstalling

You can use several techniques to troubleshoot software problems. Begin with rebooting the computer, which you may have already done. Restarting the computer releases resources that a device or application needs, but which another device or application is tying up. Restarting the computer also forces the operating system to reestablish the presence of existing devices and clear information out of its memory. If rebooting the computer does not solve the problem, you should then try to narrow the source to a single program and look at minimum requirements, updates, and compatibility. If all of these check out, try uninstalling and reinstalling the software.

Pinpointing the Problem Application

Many applications can use most hardware devices. Therefore, you can narrow the search by trying to access more than one type of device from the suspect application or by using more than one application to access the suspect device.

Suppose, for example, that a user was unable to scan an image using a particular scanning program. Try using a different application to access the scanner. If it works, you can conclude the scanner is physically sound, and turn your attention to software as the problem.

If you have determined the problem is software related, and the problem still occurs after a reboot, turn your attention to the application's configuration. Most applications or utilities include a Preferences, Tools, or Options feature, through which you can configure their operation and the devices they can access.

Minimum Requirements

Check to make sure the computer meets the application's minimum requirements. It is possible the computer simply will not support the application—in which case, you may need to upgrade the hardware or replace the computer in order to use the application.

Updates

Check the application manufacturer's Website for patches and updates. Perhaps this user is experiencing a problem caused by a flaw in the application. Most manufacturers release patches that can remedy discovered problems.

CERTIFICATION OBJECTIVES

■ **701: 2.2** *Given a scenario, explain and interpret common hardware and operating system symptoms and their causes*

■ **702: 1.2** *Given a scenario, detect problems, troubleshoot, and repair/replace personal computer components*

Both the CompTIA A+ Essentials Exam 220-701 and the CompTIA A+ Practical Application Exam 220-702 require that you have important troubleshooting skills. Objective 701: 2.2 requires that you be able to explain and interpret symptoms and causes of hardware and operating system problems, whereas objective 702: 1.2 has a more hands-on approach, requiring that when faced with a scenario you know how to detect problems, troubleshoot, and repair or replace computer components.

Troubleshooting PC Component Problems

This section discusses procedures for troubleshooting common component problems, physical symptoms that can occur with various devices, POST audio and text error codes, and, for certain components, specific symptoms and solutions. For each component problem, we describe scenarios, probable causes, and solutions.

Procedures

When troubleshooting PC components, first do all that you can without opening the PC. If you do not find the source of the problem and a potential solution through nonintrusive methods, then you will have to open the PC. Follow these steps, which will take you from the least intrusive to the most intrusive:

1. Check for proper connections (external device).
2. Check for appropriate components.

3. Check installation: both drivers and settings.

4. Check proper component seatings (internal adapter card, memory, and so on).

5. Simplify the system by removing unneeded peripherals. If the problem goes away, then you must isolate the problem peripheral.

Physical Symptoms

Inspect a computer and its peripherals for physical symptoms. Several symptoms can apply to many components, such as excessive heat, noise, odors, status light indicators, and visible damage to the device itself or cabling. When one of these symptoms occurs, take appropriate action based on the symptom and the device.

Turn off a device giving off excessive heat until you can replace it or otherwise solve the problem. Later in this chapter, we will discuss power supplies and cooling systems—components related to these symptoms. Unusual noises may occur if a device has moving parts, such as a fan or printer. In these cases, a new or different noise usually means a component, such as a fan bearing, is failing. This will reduce the fan's effectiveness and cause an unusual noise.

Many devices, such as printers and network adapters, have one or more *status light indicators*—usually a *light-emitting diode (LED)*—which indicate a problem with the device by changing the color of the light, by blinking or remaining steady, or a combination of both. Look for labels on the device itself defining the function of each light. For example, a network interface card (NIC) may have a light labeled "ACT" for "activity," indicating the card is, indeed, transmitting data. A multispeed NIC might have a different colored light for each of its speeds. These same indicators are often duplicated as icons in the status area (also called the notification area) of the Taskbar on the Windows desktop. The applet associated with the icon will issue alerts when a device malfunctions.

Other physical symptoms include damage to a device, such as an area of melted plastic on a case or cable, a broken cable or connector pin, or a socket device not getting the appropriate signals (often due to a loose connection). Of course, when inspection of a device or cabling shows physical damage, such as a break or the appearance of melted plastic, you need to determine the extent of the damage and the right solution for the problem, such as replacing the device or cable.

POST Audio and Visual Errors

When a computer starts up, the BIOS performs a POST (power-on self-test) to check for the presence and status of existing components. A visual (text) error message on the screen, or a series of beeps, typically indicates errors found during the POST. A single beep or two quick beeps at the end of the POST normally means that no errors were detected and the system should continue booting into the operating system. If you hear any other combination of beeps, or the system does not continue the normal bootup, consult the motherboard manufacturer's documentation. POST text error messages should point you in the right direction for troubleshooting an error at bootup.

Motherboards

A properly configured motherboard will typically perform flawlessly for the useful life of a computer. Things that can change that happy state include power problems, actual component failure, and incorrect changes to the system. A major motherboard failure will prevent the computer from booting properly. However, if the BIOS is able to run a POST, it might report a problem with the motherboard. In either case, consult the motherboard manual and the manufacturer's Website for solutions to the problem.

Locating the Source of a Problem

A faulty motherboard can cause many different symptoms and can even make it appear that a different component is at fault. This is because a motherboard problem might manifest in one particular area, such as a single circuit or port, causing the failure of a single device only. For example, if the video card's expansion slot on the motherboard stops working, it will appear that the display system has a problem. In this case, you are likely to discover the motherboard as the point of failure only after checking all other components in the video system. Later in this chapter, you will learn about a tool called a POST card that you can use to detect a problem with a motherboard or other components. If you do not have access to a POST card, you will need to check for the source of the problem manually. The following sections describe some problem areas and ways to check them.

Physical Motherboard Problems   Physical sources of motherboard problems can include jumper or switch settings, front panel connectors, back panel connectors, sockets, expansion slots, and memory slots.

Motherboards have sets of jumpers or switches. Because these are mechanical elements, they won't change unless someone has opened the system. If you think someone has opened the system, then double-check jumper and switch settings and compare them with the manufacturer's documentation. If you are 100 percent sure that someone made a change that caused the present problems, determine the correct settings and return the jumpers or switches to them. Note the BIOS may support jumper-free settings, meaning settings are BIOS-defined rather than defined by jumpers or switches. In this case, you will need to run the BIOS Setup program to correct the situation.

Another possible physical motherboard problem source is loose, or improperly made, connections. These could include improper insertion of adapter cards into expansion slots, or memory sticks into memory slots, or cables connecting onboard I/O ports to front or back panel connectors.

BIOS/CMOS Problems   Problems associated with the CMOS chip include lost or incorrect BIOS system settings. Lost settings can occur when the CMOS battery begins to lose power. You may discover this problem by a text error message at startup, or by a prompt to enter the correct time and date. A computer that does not maintain the date and time when powered off probably has a failing CMOS battery, which is responsible for maintaining the system clock. Because these batteries only last between two and ten years, you are likely to have to replace a computer's battery before the computer becomes obsolete. To replace the battery properly, follow the steps in Exercise 5-2. Note you cannot follow this procedure in all computers, and you must consult the documentation before doing this.

EXERCISE 5-2

Replacing the CMOS Battery

1. Enter the computer's Setup program and save a copy of the CMOS settings using one of the methods you learned in Chapter 4.

2. Turn off the computer and remove the cover, ensuring you carry out the proper ESD procedures.

3. Locate the CMOS battery on the motherboard.

4. Slide the battery out from under the retaining clip. The clip uses slight tension to hold the battery in place, so you do not need to remove the clip or bend it outward.

5. Note the battery's orientation when installed, and install the new battery the same way.

6. Restart the computer. Enter the system's Setup program again and restore the BIOS settings you recorded in Step 1.

If your system will not support a new device, you may need a BIOS firmware update. Before doing this, be sure to back up the BIOS settings, as Exercise 5-2 described. Then, using the manufacturer's utility, install the BIOS update, either from a local drive or from a source over the Internet. How is it possible to update something that is "read-only?" The answer is that many modern ROMs are not strictly "unwritable"; they can be changed but only by special means. Today, that is normally a special program from the manufacturer that may also require changing a system setting or a dip switch just before performing the procedure so the BIOS accepts the changes. This is why reading the documentation before changing the BIOS is important. Upgrading BIOS is often called *flashing* the BIOS. This applies to system-level BIOS, as well as to the BIOS on an individual adapter.

Be familiar with the system BIOS Setup menu screens and practice navigating through these menus. This means booting the system and selecting the option after the POST that lets you access BIOS system setup. The first thing you should then do is look for the help hints, usually at the bottom or in a sidebar on every screen. Then find out how you can exit without saving any changes. Knowing this is important, because almost everyone who explores these menus gets confused about whether they have inadvertently made a change, and the best way to back out of that situation is to select Exit Without Saving, if it is available. If not, look for two exit methods. For instance, you might use the F10 function key for Save and Exit and the ESC key for Exit. Now you know how to exit without saving.

Although the exact BIOS menu organization varies by manufacturer, the main menu will have the most basic settings, such as system date and time, detected drives, and drive interfaces. An advanced menu will often have the settings for the CPU, the chipset, onboard devices, the expansion bus configuration, and overclocking, an option that boosts CPU performance. You do not need to use overclocking on computers designated for simple office tasks, but people often use it for computers requiring higher performance, such as for gaming and other tasks requiring maximum performance. Other advanced BIOS settings may involve adjusting bus speeds, including the two main components of the systems chipset, the Front Side Bus and the North Bridge. Here, you may also find settings for the PCIe bus and configuration options for USB and other interfaces.

Incorrect BIOS settings can have many permutations because there are BIOS settings for a great variety of system elements, including the hard drives, floppy drive, the boot sequence, keyboard status, and parallel port settings. An incorrect setting will manifest as an error relating to that particular device or function, so pinpointing the CMOS battery as the source of the problem can be difficult. However, when you need to change or update BIOS settings, enter the BIOS Setup menu at startup, make the appropriate change(s), save the new setting(s), and restart the computer.

CPUs

In most cases, CPU problems are fatal, meaning the computer will not boot at all. These problems also closely relate to motherboard problems, such as CPU socket failure. However, you should be aware of some nonfatal error indicators.

If you turn on the computer, and it does not complete the POST or it does nothing at all, and you have eliminated power problems, you might discover the processor has a problem. The solution to a processor problem is to remove the offending component and replace it with a new one. A persistent error indicates a possible problem with the slot or socket that the processor uses to connect to the motherboard. In this case, you need to replace the motherboard. Check the system warranty before taking any action, because the warranty could cover motherboard failure. If you determine the problem is isolated to the CPU, then you will have to replace it, in which case you must replace it with an exact match for the motherboard, including the socket type, speed, number of cores, internal cache, power consumption, and other features. This ensures it matches the Front Side Bus portion of the chipset that includes the memory controller chip (MCC). Use the motherboard documentation or information for the motherboard at the manufacturer's site to determine the exact requirements before purchasing a new CPU.

on the Job

Considering today's low PC prices, if you encounter a CPU or motherboard problem on a computer not covered by a warranty, consider replacing the entire system. First, however, check to see if it is a leased computer, and what the lease agreement says about component failures, service, and replacement.

A computer that has become slower can be a symptom of overheating. The CPU may have reduced its clock speed due to overheating, a practice called *throttling*. A processor that has activated thermal throttling will run slower. Why is the computer overheating? Dust? Blocked vents? Failed cooling fan? Check out these possibilities and remedy any that you find.

Many modern CPUs have 64-bit or better memory bus widths and 64-bit registers, and can run 64-bit operating systems. The 32-bit architecture of the Intel and AMD CPUs is defined by the *Intel x86 Specification*. The newer 64-bit architecture of these CPUs is defined by the *x86-64 Specification*, which was first defined by AMD, with Intel and AMD continuing to cooperate on the 64-bit CPU standard. Intel's Itanium CPU has a different 64-bit architecture that is not compatible with either x86 or x86-64. The point is, expect to see x86, *32-bit*, or similar terms when talking about older CPUs and compatible software, whereas x86-64 or *64-bit* refers to newer CPUs and the operating systems and other programs designed for them.

If a customer wishes to upgrade a computer from a 32-bit operating system to a 64-bit operating system, you will need to confirm the CPU on that computer can support 64-bit processing. Some 64-bit CPUs also support 32-bit applications, so if the customer is currently running a 32-bit OS on such a system, the upgrade to a 64-bit OS is possible. In most cases, the move from a 32-bit OS to a 64-bit OS should include a move to a new computer. Even then, you will need to determine if any 32-bit applications will be required on the new machine and research whether the 64-bit OS and the CPU can support such 32-bit applications.

System Resources

It is time to talk about *system resources*, a finite set of resources controlled by the operating system and critical to the use of all computer components. These resources include memory addresses, I/O addresses, IRQs, and DMA channels. A *memory address* is a logical memory address defined in a processor's address bus that allows the system to access physical RAM or ROM memory locations. A memory address is required by a device that has its own RAM memory or ROM memory and that requires an address on the system bus (subtracting usable addresses from the system RAM) in order to use this memory and make it accessible to the processor. An *I/O address* is an assigned address or range of addresses on a system's address bus that allows the system's processor to recognize a device. An *interrupt request line (IRQ)* is an assigned channel over which a device can send a signal to the processor to get its attention (hence the term "interrupt"). A *direct memory access (DMA) channel* is a system resource that certain devices, such as sound cards and hard drives, can use to move data between the device and system RAM without involving the processor. A specialized chipset component, called the *DMA controller*, manages the use of the DMA channels.

All devices require the use of one or more types of system resources to interact with the processor. Although all devices require I/O ports, the use of other system resources varies from device to device. Configuring a device to use its own unique set of system resources is part of installing a device and its device driver into a system. Today, this assignment is automatic, thanks to plug and play technologies. Only when things go terribly wrong will you need to make changes manually, and this is very rare.

I/O Ports and Cards

Now let's consider troubleshooting common I/O ports and cards, including serial ports, parallel ports, PS/2, sound, USB, IEEE 1394/FireWire, and specialized communications devices, such as NICs and modems.

Serial Ports

As described in Chapter 3, the classic serial port on a PC is an RS-232 port. The USB interface has largely replaced the serial interface that was once the norm on PCs. The serial interface has not disappeared entirely, though.

If a serial port is not functioning, first check the connections and cable. Serial connectors and the interface behind them can be defective. If visual inspection does not show problems, you can test a physical serial port using a loopback plug and special software, as described later in this chapter under "Troubleshooting Tools." Whether you have these tools or not, open Device Manager and confirm that the device is recognized and enabled. If it is not recognized, run the BIOS system setup program and try turning it on.

Another problem area with serial ports involves incorrect configuration. This problem is rare today, thanks to plug and play, but you may encounter it with an older computer or older serial device. To understand configuration issues, knowing the difference between a physical serial connector and a COM port in a PC is important. A physical serial connector (or "serial port") will not work unless it is assigned to a COM *port*, which means assigning it an I/O address range and an interrupt request line (IRQ). COM ports have recognizable names, even at the BIOS level. These names are COM1, COM2, COM3, and COM4 (generically referred to as COM*x*). A serial device, such as an internal modem, requires a COM port, as does any external serial connector before you can use it. Table 5-1 shows the traditional COM port resource assignments with the beginning I/O address and the IRQ. Figure 5-2 shows Device Manager and the Resources tab in the Properties dialog box for COM1. Notice that COM1 has the standard assignments of I/O address range 03F8-03FF and IRQ 4. The COM1 address range includes eight bytes beginning at the I/O base address. This assignment of resources is entirely up to the plug and play process in your computer. You should only attempt to override these settings through this dialog box after researching the problem device and finding that the manufacturer or another reliable source recommends this step.

TABLE 5-1		
The Standard COM Port Assignments		

Port	I/O Base Address	IRQ
COM1	03F8	4
COM2	02F8	3
COM3	03E8	4
COM4	02E8	3

FIGURE 5-2

Device Manager
showing a
working COM1
port with
its resource
assignments

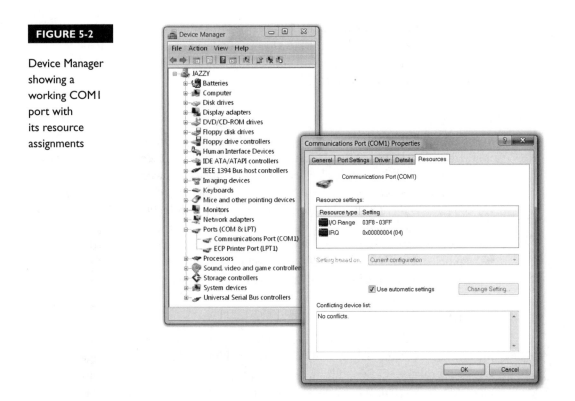

Parallel Ports

If a parallel port is not functioning, first check the connectors and cable, and then open Device Manager and ensure the device is recognized and enabled. When you look for it in Device Manager, you will notice that parallel ports also have names recognized by the system. *LPT* describes any parallel port, whereas *LPT1* and *LPT2* describe the first and second parallel ports on the system. In Figure 5-2, the parallel port is labeled ECP Printer Port (LPT1). If your system has a parallel port, but it is not visible in Device Manager, run the BIOS system setup program and try enabling the device. Like serial ports, parallel ports must have an I/O address and IRQ assignment, normally assigned automatically by the operating system, to operate. The standard assignments for LPT1 are I/O base address 0378 and IRQ 7; the assignments for LTP2 are traditionally I/O base address 0278 and IRQ5. Resource assignments are rarely the issue with a parallel port problem. Rather, you should look at the parallel port mode, as described in Chapter 4. The BIOS Setup program assigns this, so you must check that it is using the correct mode for the device you are connecting to the parallel port. BIOS Setup usually describes these modes as standard parallel (the original, unidirectional mode), bidirectional parallel, *enhanced capability port* (ECP), and *enhanced parallel port* EPP. Most parallel printers require ECP mode, which is usually the default mode. If your device requires a different mode, you will need to change the setting in BIOS Setup.

PS/2

The PS/2 interface is used for input devices, including keyboards and mice. Many motherboards have two of these connectors—one dedicated to keyboard input and the other for mice. Problems with a keyboard or mouse are usually with the device itself, not with the interface, but a physical inspection is always in order. To do that, turn off the computer and unplug the keyboard or mouse. Inspect the cable plug for bent pins. If one is bent, try to straighten it, reconnect the device, restart the computer, and test it. If this does not solve the problem, substitute another keyboard or mouse to determine if the problem is with the device. If the problem is with a keyboard, check for loose or missing keys. Reseat any loose keys, and replace the keyboard if keys are missing.

Sound

Today's PCs, and not just those dedicated to home entertainment systems, have a huge variety of sound output available to them. The most common configuration is stereo speakers—either built in, as with laptops; integrated into the monitor; or separated as external stereo speakers, sometimes including a woofer. So, if a problem appears to be with the sound system, you first need to determine what type of sound output exists, if the correct cables are being used, and if the speakers themselves are powered on—a common issue with external speakers. Then check to see if the problem is with a single program or with all programs, and make sure the program you are using is correctly configured for the sound system.

Today, computers come with multiple sound connectors, so be sure the speakers are connected to the active sound output connector. For instance, video adapters often have sound output built in, as do many motherboards. Installing the drivers for a bus video adapter usually disables the onboard sound output of the motherboard, so when you plug the speakers into the onboard sound connectors, you won't hear anything! Further complicating this is the multiple output and input connectors that come on a single sound card. Make sure you are using the proper connector for the appropriate device. Here we describe common sound card connectors:

■ **Joystick**   This port is traditionally a DB15 connector and is disappearing from video adapters because the devices that use this, mainly joysticks and MIDI devices, have transitioned to USB.

- **Microphone**   This port connects to an external microphone.
- **Line out**   This port connects to an external device, such as a CD player, to send sound output to the device.
- **Line in**   This port is for connecting to an external device, such as a CD player, to send sound input to the computer (and, therefore, out the computer's speakers).
- **Analog/digital out**   You use this connector to output analog sound signals to external center or subwoofer channels on an external speaker system. Alternatively, use it to output digital sound to external digital devices or digital speaker systems.
- **Rear out**   You use this connector for the rear speakers in a surround sound system.

USB

Many common peripherals are now available with a USB interface. We have found this plug and play interface to be the least troublesome of any we have worked with in the past. However, you may encounter problems with these devices. One handy tool for diagnosing problem USB ports and devices is a USB loopback plug and diagnostics software, discussed later in this chapter in "Troubleshooting Tools." The sections that follow describe some common problems you may encounter with USB devices.

USB Device Seems Not to Have Power   Low-power USB devices get their power from the USB system or, more specifically, from the root or external hubs. Other devices require external power and come with their own power supplies that switch on separately from the computer. If this is a new installation, check the documentation and packaging to be sure they did not overlook an external power cord. Check that a self-powered device has power and is turned on. Next, make sure the data cable is securely connected. You should also make sure the device plugs into the proper type of hub. You can plug "low-powered" USB devices into any type of USB hub, but "high-powered" devices (USB 2.1 or greater), which use over 100 milliamps, must only plug into self-powered USB hubs.

USB Keyboard Not Functioning   The BIOS typically controls the keyboard's drivers and resources. When you install a USB keyboard, you must inform the BIOS so it will hand keyboard control over to the USB system. At startup, enter the CMOS settings, ensure the USB keyboard option is turned on, and the BIOS provides a generic driver for USB keyboards. On an older computer, this option may not exist, in which case you might need to upgrade the BIOS in order to use a USB keyboard.

"USB Device Is Unknown" Message, or the Device Is Not Functioning

A message stating that the USB device is unknown, or the device simply does not work, means the computer cannot communicate with the device. First, to make sure the device is properly attached and receiving power, try switching it to another port. Also, check that the device's cable is less than five meters long. Although most USB devices are plug and play, the operating system may still not have the specific device driver, so make sure a driver for this device is loaded.

You should also check that the device is using the proper communications mode. On startup, the USB controller assigns an ID to all devices and asks them which type of data transfer (interrupt, bulk, or continuous) they will use. If a device is set to use the wrong type of transfer mode, it will not work. Finally, check the device by swapping it with a known good one.

---

e x a m

ⓦ a t c h

Some USB devices require installation of the driver before connecting the device to a USB port. This is especially true of USB printers. If you plug in the device before installing the driver, you may not be able to use the device until you uninstall the driver, disconnect the device, reinstall the driver, and reconnect the device. Be sure to read the documentation before installing any device.

None of the USB Devices Will Work

If none of the USB devices works, you could have a problem with the entire system or just with the USB controller. First, make sure your OS is USB-compliant, which is the case for all versions of Windows since Windows 98. Next, make sure the number of devices does not exceed 127 and that no single cable length exceeds five meters. The USB system is also limited to five tiers (or five hubs) in a single chain. Check the cable length and cable connections, especially from the root hub to the first external hubs. A loose connection will prevent all devices attached to the external hub from functioning.

If the problem is not in the USB physical setup, turn your attention to the USB hub. In an older, pre-Windows XP OS, make sure the proper driver has been loaded and that the new device does not have a conflict with another device. You should also check the BIOS for USB support to determine if you can even use USB in this system. You may also want to uninstall the USB hub or controller driver. When you restart the system, the operating system will notify you to reinstall these drivers. This may fix the problem.

IEEE 1394/FireWire

Troubleshoot IEEE 1394/FireWire problems just as you would any interface problem. First, check the connections and cabling, and ensure the peripheral device has power. Also check any status indicator lights. Use Device Manager to make sure the IEEE 1394 Bus host controller is listed and functioning. As with many of the other standard I/O interfaces, a device driver that comes with Windows fully supports IEEE 1394/FireWire. Devices such as hard drives will not need an additional driver, but for other types of devices, check the documentation. If a high-speed device seems to be running slowly, check to see if a slower device is on the same bus. For instance, as described in Chapter 3, one 1394a device in a chain will cause any 1394b device to operate at the lower speed of a 1394a.

NICs and Analog Modems

We will discuss installing and troubleshooting network interface cards (NICs) and analog modems in Chapters 14 and 15. You can begin troubleshooting one of these devices by treating it like any other device. First, check the connections, cables, and the status indicator lights, and open Device Manager to see if the device is recognized. Flip ahead to Chapter 15 for more on troubleshooting to go beyond that.

Storage Devices

The steps you take when troubleshooting problems with storage devices vary based on the type of storage device. We will look at hard disk drives (HDD), floppy disk drives (FDD), optical drives, and solid-state drives (SSDs).

Hard Disk Drives

Many things can go wrong with a hard drive, each of which can result in a number of different symptoms, so it can be difficult to determine the cause of the problem. You should replace a hard drive that begins corrupting data before all the information stored on it is lost. In Chapter 11, you will learn about using specialized utilities to correct data problems on hard drives, including corrupted and fragmented files. We discuss the most common hard drive symptoms and problems in the sections that follow.

The Computer Will Not Boot Properly   When you start a computer, you might receive a POST error message with an error code in the 1700 to 1799 range. You could also get a message stating that there is no hard drive present. Typically, these errors are not fatal, and you can still boot the computer using a special bootable floppy or optical disc.

This type of error means the computer does not recognize, or cannot communicate with, the hard drive. First, restart the computer and go into the CMOS settings. In the BIOS drive configuration, check that it lists the proper hard drive type. If not, enter the appropriate settings, or use the system's hard drive detection option.

If the BIOS settings are correct and the drive still will not work, or if the BIOS cannot detect the hard drive, the system could have a cabling problem. To check on cabling and other physical configurations, perform the steps in Exercise 5-3.

EXERCISE 5-3

Troubleshooting a Drive Failure

1. Reboot the computer, start the BIOS system setup program, and check the settings for the drive and the interface (PATA, SATA, etc.), as appropriate. If you make any changes, restart and check to see if the problem is resolved. If it is not resolved, continue to the next step.

2. Turn off power to the computer and open the case.

3. If the drive connects to a PATA channel, ensure it has the proper master or slave setting. Read the drive manual, or the labels on the drive, to determine whether you make the master or slave setting through jumpers or through the drive's position on the cable (cable select).

4. If the drive connects to a SATA channel, ensure the connections are all secure, including an eSATA connection to the onboard SATA controller.

5. Check to see if the drive connects to a SCSI controller, which may be the source of the problem. In this case, locate another computer with an identical working controller and swap the problem drive into the second computer.

6. Check that data and power cables are securely attached. If the drive has a PATA interface with the conventional ribbon cable, check the hard drive ribbon cable to ensure the red stripe aligns with pin 1 on both ends.

7. If possible, replace the ribbon cable with a known good one, even if it passed your physical inspection.

8. If the cables, jumpers, and BIOS settings all check out, the problem is with the hard drive itself and you must replace it.

The Computer Reports No Operating System Once BIOS finishes the POST, it looks for the presence of an OS on the hard drive. If the BIOS does not find a special OS pointer in the drive's master boot record, it assumes that no OS exists. If you have not yet installed an OS, you must do so at this point. Chapter 9 describes how to install Windows. If an OS exists, but is not accessible, refer to Chapter 11 for steps to take to recover from this situation.

When troubleshooting a disk-booting problem, unplugging all other devices not needed for the boot process and that are using the same interface (PATA or SATA) may be helpful. If the system boots with these devices disconnected, you may be able to isolate the problem. You can reconnect the devices one at a time until you find the problem device.

SATA and eSATA Interface When planning to add a new SATA or eSATA drive to a system, first check that the operating system and motherboard will support it. Windows XP (if fully updated) and newer versions of Windows support SATA and eSATA, but older versions do not. At this writing, Mac OS 9.x and Mac OS X do not support some manufacturers' SATA interfaces. Check the device's documentation.

If you are connecting an external device, the eSATA cables must connect to an eSATA adapter card. You cannot use internal SATA cables to connect a removable eSATA device because the eSATA cables and their connectors are designed for thousands of connection and removal cycles, but the SATA cables and connectors are designed for only about 50 such cycles. Fortunately, the cables are keyed differently, with the I-type eSATA cable plug having a simple narrow oblong connector and the L-type SATA connector having a notch in the female connector and a corresponding key on the cable plug.

e x a m

ⓦ a t c h *Knowing the features of the SATA and eSATA interfaces is important, especially such details as the L-type SATA connector versus the I-type eSATA connector.*

PATA Interface   Although round cables are available for PATA drives, you will normally see the standard wide-ribbon cables. These cables block airflow, contributing to heat build-up within computers. They also get in the way when a technician is working on other components, so any time you have a problem with a PATA-connected drive in a system that you know was opened recently, check that the cables were not accidently loosened or disconnected.

RAID Arrays and Controllers   If a single drive in a raid array fails, you will need to replace the drive with a comparable drive that will work in the array. After that, restart the computer and enter the RAID setup program, which may be part of the BIOS system setup program or, as in the case of a PCIe RAID adapter, may be a similar program from the adapter's BIOS that you can also enter during startup. Once in the RAID setup program, the steps you need to take depend on the level of RAID used.

If a drive in a RAID 0 array fails, you have lost the entire volume, because this type of RAID involves data written across the drives in the array, without any special algorithm for rebuilding the stripes in the array and recovering lost data should a drive fail. Therefore, once you replace a failed drive, run the RAID setup program, and re-create the array combining the drives into what appears to your operating system as a single logical drive. Then you must format the drive and restore your data from your latest backups. Chapter 10 discusses formatting disks and backup of data.

If a drive in a RAID 1 array fails, the system will continue working, writing to the surviving member of the array mirror, but it will no longer mirror the data. This may result in an error message at the time of the failure and at each startup, or you might find a record of a RAID error event in one of the computer's log files. Once you determine that one of the drives in the mirror failed, do a full backup, replace the failed hard drive, and re-create the mirror using the RAID setup program.

Similarly, when a single drive in a RAID 5 array fails, an error message will appear, but the system will continue to write to the array in a stripe across the drives. The system will not be able to create a recovery block on one drive in each stripe, however, so you will have lost your fault tolerance, and reads will be slower, as it re-creates the lost data on each read. Do a backup before replacing the failed drive, and then restart the computer and run the RAID setup utility. The system will then rebuild the array without losing the data on the drive, re-creating the data on the replaced drive by using the data on the remaining drives and the algorithm block, when necessary.

e**x**am

The CompTIA objectives for Exam 220-702 lists "RAID cards" and "eSATA cards" under the topic "storage controllers." Although the actual drive controller circuitry for accessing and writing data to a drive is on the drive itself, a RAID controller does control the use of a group of hard drives in a RAID array. In fact, it is common to use the term "RAID controller." When faced with an exam question that uses the term "storage controller" be prepared to recognize the CompTIA spin on this term, and pick the best answer that matches the scenario.

Solid-state Storage Devices

When supporting solid-state storage, there are concerns for troubleshooting and caring for these devices that are specific to SSDs. One is loss of data from incorrectly removing an external SSD from a computer. We describe this later in this chapter in "External Storage." Other issues are gradually degrading performance, exposure to dirt and grime, and recovering lost data from SSDs.

Performance Degradation   The issue of performance degradation in SSDs was reported in some of the first mass-marketed systems with internal SSDs in place of hard drives—mainly laptops. Although SSDs have much faster random access reads than traditional hard drives, the early drives had issues with random writes and overall performance. So far the high-end SSDs manufactured for use in servers have not displayed this trend. It appears that internal SSDs in consumer-level computers, such as laptops, may be prone to degradation much sooner than their warranty period—a length of time that some manufacturers have kept in mind. If you support a system with an internal SSD, and the user reports that the system seems slow, the internal SSD may be the source of the problem; contact the manufacturer to see if they have a fix. Our research shows that manufacturers have worked to correct this problem in systems developed in the last few years.

Dirt and Grime   Solid-state storage seems indestructible, or at least considerably more stable than conventional hard drives, which are sensitive to being dropped or moved while operating, but with external SSDs, the very portability of these devices makes them vulnerable to dirt, dust, and magnetic interference. People often carry thumb drives on lanyards around their necks, or on key chains, exposing them to a great deal of abuse—including food and beverage spills. Instruct your customers to always keep their solid-state storage devices protected. Thumb drives should always have a protected cap on when not connected to a computer. Each internal SSD has exposed connectors, and you should either install the SSD into a computer or portable device, or keep it in the plastic case in which it came. Cleaning up one of these devices involves carefully removing dirt and debris from the contacts on the device's connectors.

Recovering Lost Data from SSDs   If you are helping someone who lost data on a solid-state storage device, either from deleting the data or from mishandling the device, all may not be lost. Programs are available for recovering files from solid-state devices, such as CompactFlash, SmartMedia, Memory stick, Secure Digital Card, Microdrive, and Multimedia Card. You must be able to access the device from your computer, and many of these utilities run in Windows.

Removable Storage

Removable media, as described in Chapter 2, includes all the storage types in which you can remove the media from the drive. These include optical discs, floppy disks, tape, and solid-state drives. We will discuss optical, floppy, and tape media here.

Optical Drives and Media   CD, DVD, and Blu-ray disc drives and media are functionally similar, so you can use similar methods to troubleshoot them. A common problem with any of these devices is that the computer will report it cannot read the disc. First, check that you inserted the disc the correct way. If the drive is oriented horizontally, the label must be inserted face up so the drive can access the data on the underside of the disc. Next, visually inspect the disc. Scratches or smudges may prevent the computer from reading the disc. Learn how to clean optical discs later in this chapter when we explore maintenance issues in "Maintenance and Cleaning of Computer Components."

To rule out the media as the cause, try more than one disc in the optical drive. When you experience problems reading more than one disc in an optical drive, cleaning the lens may solve the problem. You will explore cleaning optical drives later in this chapter. Sometimes a damaged optical disc will read in one drive, but not in another, although the problem drive reads other discs just fine. If this is true, try making a copy of the disc, and then test the new disc in the original drive.

If the drive is the problem, check Device Manager to ensure the computer recognizes it. Reload the device's driver if necessary, and check its system resources. If the problem persists, check the ribbon cable connection and jumper setting. Try the drive in another computer to confirm or rule it out as the cause of the problem.

Floppy Drives and Disks   The floppy disk, rather than the drive, is the cause of most floppy errors. The easiest way to check this is to eject the disk and insert another. If the problem goes away, the disk, not the drive, is the source of the problem. If you must have the information on a particular disk that is giving you trouble, try gently pulling the metal cover back and letting it snap back into place a few times, and then reinsert the disk in the drive and try to access the data again. Never touch the surface of a floppy disk (under the metal sliding cover), and do not attempt to clean the disk. Do try to use the disk in a different drive, however.

If you try to open the A drive in Windows and receive this message: "Please insert a disk into drive A:" it means the drive cannot detect a floppy disk. The most common reason for this error is simply that there is no disk in the drive. Check to make sure a disk has been inserted. If it has, remove the disk and reinsert it.

A floppy drive light that will not go off indicates an incorrectly attached data cable. Turn the computer off, remove the computer's cover, and reattach the cable the right way. Remember, you must align the red stripe on the cable with pin 1 on both the system board and on the drive.

Ensure the correct floppy drive configuration is present in the BIOS settings. If the computer still does not recognize the floppy drive, try replacing the cable. If that does not fix the problem, replace the drive with a working drive. A cheap and easy solution is to purchase an external floppy drive with a USB interface.

Tape Drives   If a newly installed drive does not work, review the installation procedure and make sure you did not skip a step. Make sure that the adapter card is properly seated and any cable connectors are fully engaged. Check for damage to cables. If the drive is a SCSI tape drive, check to see that it has the correct SCSI configuration and that it is not in conflict with other devices on the chain. If no other devices on the chain work, check for proper termination per the manufacturer's instructions. If other devices work properly, the device itself may be the problem. Most manufacturers recommend cleaning the heads at regular intervals, following instructions you will find in the documentation. Even a new tape drive may need to have the heads cleaned.

Check the tape media to be sure the drive manufacturer certified it. Any other tape could damage the tape drive heads. Only use tapes with the capacity recommended by the manufacturer. Test the drive with a new tape from a different box than the tape used when the problem occurred.

External Storage

External storage devices come in every storage type. A hard drive, floppy drive, or optical drive that has its own case and power supply and connects to a computer via an external cable is external storage. These devices can connect using USB, FireWire, eSATA, and even Ethernet (not discussed here) and still qualify as external storage. There are even external *media readers* (also called *card readers*) for reading a variety of solid-state cards. Of course, all forms of thumb drives are external storage.

Whatever the storage media, when experiencing problems with an external device first check the data cable and connectors between the device and computer as well as the power cable, unless the device is a very low-power USB device that receives its power through the USB cable. Most drives, other than solid state, require more power than is available through USB, so check the power cable. If the cable and its connections are okay, restart the computer and see whether the situation changes. Connect the device to another computer—if it works, the problem is with the interface on the first computer.

Although newer external devices using USB or FireWire are plug and play, you should never disconnect an external storage device from a Windows computer while it is powered up unless you first close all applications that may be using the device. Then use the Safely Remove Hardware applet available as an icon in the notification area on the right of the Taskbar (see Figure 5-3). A single click on this icon opens a list of removable devices. From this list, select the external drive you wish to remove, wait for the Safe to Remove Hardware message to appear (see Figure 5-4), and then disconnect the device.

SCSI Devices

The most common problems with SCSI devices involve incorrect installation or configuration. This is more common than failure of the device itself. If the problem occurs immediately after installation, begin by checking all connections. Then check the two usual suspects: SCSI chain termination and SCSI device ID. Refer back to Chapter 4 if you need help with these two issues.

FIGURE 5-3

The Safely Remove Hardware icon in the Taskbar

The Safe
to Remove
Hardware
message

Video

A computer's video system includes, at minimum, the video adapter, one or more displays, and necessary cable and connectors. It may also include a video capture card or TV tuner, so diagnosing and resolving problems can be a bit tricky. Another difficulty in resolving video problems is that, without a working display, you cannot see the OS or BIOS settings in order to remedy the problem. You must replace failed LCD displays because they are not repairable except by highly trained professionals at great cost. They are so inexpensive today that just replacing them is best. Flat panel displays are now the norm for desktop PCs, and all laptops have this type of display. We will save the discussion of problems specific to flat panel displays until Chapter 7. Following are some common video system symptoms.

Screen Movements Seem Slow

If video appears too slow for the application you are running, recheck the minimum requirements for the application. Then check the amount of memory installed on your video adapter. If the video adapter documentation is not available, open Device Manager, locate the video adapter, and open the Properties dialog box. The Resources tab will show the memory ranges used by the RAM and ROM on the video adapter. Use the Scientific mode of the Windows Calculator program to calculate these quantities. While Device Manager will not indicate which type of memory each address range represents, the larger range or ranges are the RAM installed on the adapter. You may need to add more RAM to the adapter, or you may need to replace the video adapter itself.

During the POST the Computer Issues the Audio Error Code for a Video Problem

This is an indication of a missing display or a faulty video card. First, make sure the display is properly attached to the video card. Next, check the video card function.

Because there is no display, you cannot check the driver settings. If the video adapter is not a motherboard-integrated adapter, and if you have a spare computer, install the adapter in another computer to determine whether it is functioning. If it is not, replace it. Similarly, if the video adapter is integrated, disable it in BIOS Setup and test a known working video adapter in the system. If this adapter works, replace the video adapter.

Complete Lack of Picture

If the display shows nothing at all, and the computer does not issue a beep code, the first thing you should do is move the mouse or press a key on the keyboard. This will reactivate the system if the screen is blank because of a screen saver or a power mode setting that causes it to go blank after a specified period.

If moving the mouse or pressing a key does not solve the problem, check the video system components. Start with the display's connection to the power supply and ensure it is turned on. Check the data cable and verify that none of the pins on the connector are bent, and straighten them if necessary. Also, ensure the brightness is set at an adequate level.

You can determine if the display itself is at fault by swapping it with a known good one. If the new display works in the system, you can assume the original display is the problem. Again, because display costs have decreased so much in the last few years, it is less expensive to simply replace the display with a new one than to have a technician professionally repair it. It seems counterintuitive, and you still have to dispose of the old display appropriately, but that's today's reality. Chapter 18 will describe proper disposal of PCs and their components.

If a problem continues after you have eliminated the display as a cause, check for proper seating of the video card in the expansion slot. AGP cards, especially earlier ones, do not seat easily. Press the card firmly (but not too hard), and listen for an audible click to tell you the card seats properly.

Install a different video card in this computer. Doing so might allow you to view the OS so you can remove a faulty video card configuration, if it exists. Some newer motherboards include an integrated video adapter. If you have an integrated adapter, look for a jumper setting to disable the onboard video and use an adapter card. If this option is not available, you may need to replace the motherboard.

Flickering Display

Flickering may be a symptom of a faulty CRT display. But before you jump to that conclusion, check to see if there is a motor or a fluorescent light very close to the display. Workers often have fluorescent lights in their office cubicles, and many add small fans to cool their workspace. Either of these can cause flickering, which goes away as soon as you remove or turn off the motor or fluorescent light. If possible, look on the other side of the wall partition, where you might find a source of EMI, such as an electrical panel. If you cannot remove the source from the display, move the display away from the source.

An inappropriate refresh rate setting, such as a rate too low for the video system you are using, can cause the display to flicker. On a Windows-based system, you can access the Control Panel's Display icon and choose a different refresh rate. Replace the display with another to see if the problem still exists.

A flickering LCD display is a sign of a failing component within the display—either the backlight or the inverter. Both are reasons to replace the display, but before you go to that expense, perform a small experiment. Test a known good display on the computer. If the test display has the same problem, the video adapter is the cause, but if the test display works just fine, then replace the flickering display.

on the
Job *The standard refresh rate for CRT displays is 75 Hz. Older displays may not work at this rate but may require a refresh rate of 60 Hz. An older display will usually blank out if run at faster speeds.*

Screen Elements Duplicated All Over the Screen

The problem of repeated screen elements is more common in older video systems. They are due to the use of an improper resolution setting for your video system. This setting results in multiple copies of the same image, including the mouse pointer, all over the screen. To solve this problem, go into the Display settings and reduce the resolution setting. This task can be difficult because more than one mouse pointer appears on the screen, making it nearly impossible to work with the mouse. To navigate through the appropriate screens, we suggest using the keyboard.

TV Tuner and Video Capture Cards

Although a TV tuner card and a video capture card are two different devices, some manufacturers may combine them into one device, or they may be separate but work closely together. A TV tuner receives television signals for display on a PC's monitor, and a capture card can save video data to hard disk. When troubleshooting one of these devices, make sure you understand the features and capabilities of the device in question. How does it interface to the computer? The options vary, including all the usual buses and external I/O interfaces. Determine if the problem is with the interface. Check the connection where the TV tuner card receives the TV signal.

If all necessary connections are correct, then troubleshoot the drivers and software. A recent update to the operating system may have created a conflict with the drivers or software. Some TV tuners can receive only analog signals; some can receive only digital signals; and some can receive both. Another type of TV tuner card contains both an analog and a video tuner and can receive both types of signals simultaneously. In the latter scenario, you can watch one while recording the other. Considering all these variations, ensure the user is not expecting the device to do more than it is capable of doing. Then troubleshoot as you would any hardware device.

Power Supplies

Power supplies can experience either total or partial failures, resulting in inconsistent or displaced symptoms. However, to pinpoint the problem, you can identify a few common symptoms of power supply failure; we discuss those symptoms here. When the power supply fails, replace it. Never try to open or repair a power supply because it can hold enough charge to injure you seriously and the time spent on such a repair is more valuable than the replacement cost of a power supply.

When installing a new component in a PC, check the power supply wattage and capacity, the availability and types of connectors, and the output voltage required by the new component to ensure it will have sufficient power and the correct connections.

For the exam, as well as your own safety, remember that, like displays, power supplies can cause serious personal injury. Never open the case of a power supply!

Symptoms Associated with Power Supply Problems

Failed or failing power supplies have many symptoms. Those for a power supply that is failing, but has not stopped working altogether, often appear to be problems with memory or other components.

Memory Errors   Yes, a memory error can be an indication of a failing power supply because the error can be an indication of inadequate power to the RAM sticks. If on each reboot, the memory error identifies a different location in memory, then it is more likely to be a power problem than a memory error. A real memory error would identify the same memory location on each reboot.

Nothing Happens When the Computer Is Turned On   A few things can cause a total lack of activity at system startup. These include a bad processor or memory, but the most likely suspect is the power supply.

When the power supply stops working, so does the computer's fan, which is typically the first thing you hear when you turn on the computer. Therefore, if you do not hear the power supply fan at startup (or any fan or hard-drive noise), you should suspect a power supply problem and turn off the computer immediately. Some power supplies will shut down if the fan is not working.

If only the power supply fan failed, then once the computer is off, try cleaning the fan, using an antistatic vacuum or static-free cloth. Dust, lint, or hair can cause the fan to stop rotating. If cleaning does not resolve the problem, you must replace the entire power supply.

If the problem is not so easily isolated to the power supply fan because the system simply will not turn on, try removing all the power supply connections to internal components and turning the PC back on. The fan on the power supply should run. If it does not, this is a clear indication the power supply has malfunctioned and you must replace it.

If the fan is not at fault, check that the power supply connects properly to an electrical outlet. In addition, check the power selector (on the back of the computer near the power cord connection and the on/off switch) to ensure it has the right setting for your geographic region. North America is 110–120 VAC at 60 Hertz and Europe is 220–240 VAC at 50 Hz.

Also, check that the power cables attach properly to the motherboard and other necessary devices, including the computer's power button. Because you can switch many power supplies to use either 120 or 230 volts, verify that someone did not change the supply to the wrong voltage setting.

e x a m

ⓦ **a t c h**   *If the power supply's fan stops working, you must replace the entire power supply, not just the fan.*

The Computer Reboots Itself, or Some Components Sporadically Stop Working   A computer with a bad power supply may reboot itself without warning. If the power supply provides power to only some devices, the computer will behave irregularly; some devices will seem to work, whereas others will work only part of the time or not at all. Check that all power plugs connect properly.

Cooling Systems

Excessive heat can be a symptom of cooling system failure. Inadequate cooling will cause components to overheat, in which case they might work sometimes but not at other times, and very commonly, an overheated computer will simply shut down or spontaneously reboot. Try cleaning the power supply fan. If this does not solve the problem, replace the power supply or consider adding another case fan, if one will fit in your computer. Many cases come with brackets to add one or more case fans.

Missing Slot Covers

Believe it or not, the removable slot covers at the back of the computer are not there solely to tidy up the appearance of the computer. They keep dust and other foreign objects out of the computer, and if you leave the slot covers off, you run the risk of allowing dust to settle on the PCs internal components, especially the empty expansion slots (which are notoriously difficult to clean). Missing slot covers can also cause the computer to overheat. The design of the computer places the devices that generate the most heat in the fan's "line of fire." Missing slot covers means the cooling air's path through the computer could be changed or impeded, resulting in improper cooling of the components inside.

Noisy Fan

There are more cooling fans inside a computer than the one on the power supply. Today's computers have one (slot) or two (SEC) cooling fans on the CPU. There can also be one or more strategically placed cooling fans inside the case.

When a fan begins to wear out, it usually makes a whining or grinding noise. When this happens, replace the fan, unless it is inside the power supply. In that instance, replace the entire power supply.

CPU Cooling Issues

Considering the reliability of computer circuitry, you do not expect a CPU to fail, but modern CPUs generate a great deal of heat and must be properly installed. Proper installation requires high standards for applying thermal compound and correctly inserting the CPU into the CPU socket on the motherboard and attaching a heat sink and/or a CPU fan. Systems assembled in tightly controlled facilities by experienced technicians who practice excellent quality control methods should not fail due to overheating during normal operation. Normal computer operation usually means the CPU and/or buses are not modified to operate beyond their default system settings, or in an environment with temperature and humidity beyond the manufacturer's specified operating range for the system.

Memory

As with CPUs, physical damage or failure of memory is fatal, meaning when such a problem occurs, the computer will not boot at all. However, you should be aware of some nonfatal error indicators.

If you turn on the computer and it does not even complete the POST or it does nothing at all, and you have eliminated power problems, the main memory might have a problem. The solution to a memory problem is to remove the offending component and replace it with a new one. If the error persists, the memory might be in a damaged slot or socket on the motherboard. In this case, replace the motherboard, or the entire PC.

On a final note: The computer does not report some RAM errors at all. That is, if an entire memory module does not work, the computer might just ignore it and continue to function normally without it. At startup, watch the RAM count on the screen (if BIOS configuration allows this) to ensure the total amount matches the capacity installed in the machine. If this amount comes up significantly short, you probably have to replace a memory module.

e x a m
ⓦ a t c h

Memory failures may not cause a system to appear to malfunction at all. Most modern systems will simply ignore a malfunctioning memory module *and normal operations will continue. The user may note performance loss, however, which is a key symptom of a memory module failure.*

Input Devices

A number of different symptoms are associated with input devices, especially mice, which provide a common source of computer problems. Fortunately, most procedures to resolve such problems are quite simple. Now look at two common mouse-related problems.

The Pointer Does Not Move Smoothly Across the Screen

A common mechanical mouse or trackball problem is irregular movement of the pointer across the screen. Some mice even appear to hit an "invisible wall" on the screen. These symptoms indicate dirty rollers, in the case of a traditional mouse or trackball, or dirt on the lens of an optical mouse or track ball. This problem is very common because, as the mouse moves across a desk or table it picks up debris, which then gets on the internal rollers. You may still need to clean an optical or electronic motion-sensing track ball or mouse, but it is proving to be much more reliable than the older mechanical mouse. Learn how to clean a mouse later in this chapter when we explore preventive maintenance techniques in "Maintenance and Cleaning of Computer Components."

The Pointer Does Not Move on the Screen

The problem could be that the mouse driver is either corrupted or missing altogether. If you suspect a missing driver, you need to load the driver manually from the Setup disk that came with the mouse.

If there is no driver disk, try simply restarting the computer. Most mice are plug and play, so the OS might automatically detect your mouse and load the appropriate driver for it at startup. If you suspect that a mouse driver does exist, but is corrupted, use Device Manager or the Mouse icon in Control Panel to remove the existing driver and reload it. Learn about working with Device Manager in Chapter 11.

on the job *Although PC manufacturers still provide a dedicated Mini-DIN connection for the mouse, USB connectors are very common on pointing devices.*

Adapter Cards

If you must replace or upgrade an adapter card, follow the steps in Exercise 4-7 in Chapter 4. If the adapter card is a video card, ensure the replacement card has the correct interface. Video cards currently come with a choice of interfaces: PCI, AGP,

SCENARIO & SOLUTION	
The computer does not maintain the date and time when powered on. What should I do?	Replace the CMOS battery.
What should I do with a computer that keeps rebooting itself?	Test the power supply. You may need to replace it.
What should I do when the mouse pointer does not move smoothly on the screen?	Clean the mouse or trackball device.

and PCIe. If your computer supports both PCI and AGP (a common configuration, until recently), purchase an AGP card, as it performs better than a PCI card. In newer computers, both PCI and PCIe connectors will be present, and AGP may be present. In this case, PCIe is the best choice.

CERTIFICATION OBJECTIVE

■ **702: 1.4** *Given a scenario, select and use appropriate tools*

Troubleshooting Tools

Troubleshooting tools fall into two categories—software or hardware tools—although you will find that sometimes software and hardware tools work together for trouble-shooting, as in the case of the POST card. The sections that follow describe diagnostic and maintenance tools for both software and hardware.

Software Tools

You will find handy software troubleshooting tools built into the operating system, available through third-party sources, and built into the system BIOS of your PC and the BIOSs of certain components.

Alternate OS Startup Options

One of the most useful tools you can bring with you to a customer's site is knowledge of the operating system's alternate startup options. Additionally, under some circum-stances, a specialized startup (boot) floppy disk, optical disc, or USB thumb drive is handy. Alternate startup options and some boot disks will allow you to start the com-puter in a state with minimal devices and files, so you can locate an offending device, file, or startup program before it causes the computer to halt or crash (see Chapter 11 for details on using these options).

Utilities

We lump various nonapplication programs under the category of utility software. There are several such software tools that you should use, beginning with antivirus and antispyware software. These can be either commercial products or free, and you will learn about them in Chapter 17. Other important software, including the installation software for your operating system and for various applications, also comes into play when you are troubleshooting. Then there are the recovery utilities—some built into Windows and others available through third parties. Chapter 11 introduces the Windows recovery options, as well as diagnostic utilities from a variety of sources—once again, some come with Windows, but the more advanced come from third-party vendors.

Plenty of free utilities are also available over the Internet. One that we have found very helpful when working with users' computers is Belarc Advisor, a program that audits the hardware and software in a computer, alerting you to missing Windows updates and providing licensing information.

EXERCISE 5-4

Installing an Inventory Tool

1. Point your browser to www.belarc.com.

2. On the Belarc Web page, read about Belarc Advisor. Then click the link to the free download.

3. Confirm that your system matches the requirements for installing the software, and then follow the instructions to download and install the program.

4. If prompted to install updates, choose to install them.

5. Once installed and updated, Belarc Advisor will create a profile of your computer that inventories the hardware and software.

6. Take time to review the results.

7. For use on other computers, copy the downloaded program onto an optical disc and keep it in your toolkit.

BIOS and Component Self-Tests

Another available tool is knowledge of how your system BIOS and the BIOSs of various components behave during the POST at bootup, especially in the case of a failure. Earlier in this chapter, in "Troubleshooting PC Component Problems," you learned about error messages produced by the POST when failures with major onboard components occur during startup. Other components, such as PATA or SCSI hard drives, will also issue error codes if they have a serious problem. Watch for these codes whenever starting a computer.

ⓦatch   *If you are upgrading an old PC to a newer operating system, you will most likely need to upgrade the BIOS as well. If you do not upgrade the*   *BIOS, devices may not function properly; the system may lock up for no apparent reason; or the system may not recognize installed devices.*

Hard Drive Software Diagnostics Test

You do not normally think about your hard drive having its own BIOS, but it does, and this BIOS, much like the PC's system BIOS, performs a diagnostics test as the hard drive is powered up. If it discovers a problem, it will display an error message. This should appear immediately after your system POST as a 17*xx* error. In addition, you can obtain hard drive diagnostics utilities from the hard drive manufacturer and from third-party sources. These utilities come in handy when the hard drive does work but is having data error or performance (slowness) issues, and you have exhausted all other avenues.

The Hardware Toolkit

In order to be completely prepared for any onsite computer problem, you would have to equip yourself with every type of cable, connector, battery, or driver that any component might need. Since you cannot do this, you should stick to the basic troubleshooting tools, utilities, and devices described here.

Basic Tools

You may purchase a basic computer technician's toolkit or assemble the components yourself. Figure 5-5 shows some of the tools you should carry with you at all times on the job.

Following is a list of components you should have in your kit:

- An array of Phillips and flathead screwdrivers, as well as varying sizes of nut drivers.

- An *extending extractor*, commonly called a *parts grabber*, is a pen-sized tool that has a plunger at one end. When pressed, the plunger causes small, hooked prongs to extend from the other end of the tool. These are useful for retrieving dropped objects, such as jumpers or screws, from inside a computer. Be very careful not to touch any circuitry when using one of these.

FIGURE 5-5

An assortment of basic tools

- An *extension magnet* is a long-handled tool with a magnet on the end. You use it for the same purpose as a parts grabber; only rather than grabbing an object it attracts small objects that contain iron. This is handy for picking up objects that fall on the floor, but the potential dangers may not be worth the convenience. Never use an extension magnet near a computer, or any peripherals that contain magnetic storage because the magnet can damage data.

- A *flashlight* for illuminating dark places.

- A *small container* for holding extra screws and jumpers (a 35-mm film case works well).

- An *antistatic wrist strap* to use when working on any component except the power supply, monitor, and laser printers (see Chapter 18). Attach the alligator clip to the PC's frame and wrap the wrist strap around your wrist. Use your less-favored wrist for this so the cable does not interfere with your work. Figure 5-6 shows an antistatic wrist strap.

- An *antistatic mat* provides a path to ground for a static charge and is designed for the desktop or floor of a workspace. While this mat will not fit in your toolkit, it is something that should be available at any PC technician's workbench. An antistatic mat (or *grounding mat*) placed on the workbench reduces the risk of electrostatic discharge from components placed on it. An antistatic mat placed on the floor provides the same protection for anyone standing on the mat.

exam
⚲atch *You can expect questions about the dangers of high-voltage devices and antistatic straps on the exam.*

FIGURE 5-6

An antistatic
wrist strap

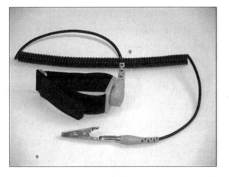

- *Field replaceable units (FRUs)* should be included in your hardware toolkit. An FRU is a component that you can install into a system onsite. This includes such items as memory modules, heat sinks, CMOS batteries, and even spare PSUs, keyboards, and mice.
- A *multimeter* may seem like an advanced tool, but it is indispensable in determining power problems from a power outlet or from the power supply. This handheld device is used to measure the resistance, voltage, and/or current within computer components (see Figure 5-7) using two probes (one negative, one positive) that you touch to power wires in the equipment you are testing. The most common use of a multimeter is to determine if a circuit or cable measures infinite resistance, which means there is a break somewhere in the line. You can also use a multimeter to check that the power supply

FIGURE 5-7

A simple
multimeter

is generating the appropriate voltage or that a motherboard component is receiving the proper current, but other tools are safer and easier to use for this type of testing.

■ A *power supply tester* is a specialized device for testing a power supply unit, and is a bit safer to use than a multimeter for this purpose. A power supply tester comes with connectors compatible with the output connectors on a standard power supply, rather than with the simple probes of a multimeter. An LCD display shows the test results.

■ A *cable tester* will detect if a cable can connect properly end-to-end and determine if a cable has a short. Several types of cable testers are available, such as those for copper Ethernet and phone cables, fiber-optic cable testers, and coaxial cable testers. The most common tester is one used for testing Ethernet cables. We will revisit this topic in Chapter 15.

■ A digital camera will enable you to document the condition of a computer before you begin troubleshooting. One important way we use a digital camera is to document the cabling and connections—both external and internal—before we make any changes, so that we can reconnect all components correctly.

Specialized Diagnostic Toolkits

Various vendors sell comprehensive toolkits for PC hardware and software diagnostic tools. Prices for these toolkits can range from a few dollars to many hundreds of dollars. The differences are in the software and hardware included in the kit and the number of features available.

Diagnostics Software   Some diagnostic kits come with a boot floppy disk or CD disc that will boot any IBM-compatible computer regardless of the operating system. Because they bypass the operating system, these diagnostic programs can probe your hardware for problems by testing ports, drives, busses, CPUs, memory, and other components. Some diagnostic software requires specialized hardware to perform these tests.

In addition to diagnostics, these kits often provide software used for preventive and restorative measures. For instance, a kit may contain software for backing up

CMOS settings and recovering important system information from the hard drive so you can restore the drive after damage to system information. Other software may diagnose and repair other types of damage to disks.

Diagnostics Hardware   The medium-to-high-priced kits will include diagnostics hardware such as loopback plugs and POST cards.

Hardware in a diagnostics kit may include loopback plugs for various common ports. A *loopback plug* is available for any common PC port type and does not connect to a cable, but reroutes the sending pins to the receiving pins. Special software installed on the computer performs a loopback test in which signals are both sent and received. Some come with light-emitting diodes (LEDs) that can show the results of various tests. Others are very simple and depend on running software on the PC to conduct tests and show you the results. Figure 5-8 shows three basic loopback plugs that come with special testing software. These three are for serial ports (both 9 pin and 25 pin) and parallel ports. These plugs are falling out of use, however, since serial and parallel ports are disappearing from PCs.

An example of a loopback plug for a more common port is a USB loopback plug, which looks more like a hub than a plug. Once one of these connects to a USB port, USB diagnostics software (bundled with the loopback plug or downloaded free from

FIGURE 5-8

Three loopback plugs: one 9-pin serial plug, one 25-pin serial plug, and one 25-pin parallel plug

the Internet) can test both the port and the cable used to connect to the port. With a USB loopback plug, you may be able to

- Check if a USB port has power.
- Test the port's ability to send and receive data.
- Detect USB error rates.
- Measure transmission speed.
- Detect retransmitted data.
- Test the port's stability during long periods of transmission.
- Test self-powered USB hubs.
- Check USB cabling.

A *POST card* is an adapter card for checking the POST process. You install it into an expansion slot in a PC, which makes this one of those rare times when you must power up the PC with the case open. When you power up the PC, you watch a small two-character light-emitting diode (LED) on the card. In addition to the LED display, POST cards may also have additional indicator lights. You can interpret the POST card's findings using the manual that comes with the card.

SCENARIO & SOLUTION

When you take your troubleshooting toolkit to a client's site, what two broad categories of tools should it contain?	Both software tools and hardware tools.
You believe a motherboard component has a problem, but swapping out cards has not isolated it, and you do not or cannot remove other components from the motherboard. What should you do?	Consider purchasing a POST card, if you can justify the cost. Alternatively, take the computer to a technician who has one and is experienced in using it. This card will run a variety of tests on the motherboard and isolate the problem.
Digging deeper into your toolkit, you pull out a small device to test the functionality of the USB ports on the PC. What is it?	A USB loopback plug.

Cleaning Products

A variety of cleaning products is available for PCs. The following list includes some of the most common:

- Disposable moistened cleaning wipes
- Antistatic display cleaner
- Canned compressed air
- Antistatic vacuum cleaner
- Nonabrasive liquid cleaning compound, such as isopropyl alcohol

CERTIFICATION OBJECTIVE

- **701: 2.5**   *Given a scenario, integrate common preventative maintenance techniques*

    While preparing for the CompTIA A+ exams, be sure to study and practice preventive maintenance techniques. CompTIA understands that good preventive maintenance will cut down on the time spent solving problems. An important part of preventative maintenance is performing regular data backup procedures. We will explore backup procedures in Chapter 10.

Preventive Maintenance Techniques

The old adage "an ounce of prevention is worth a pound of cure" applies to computers as much it does to anything else. Begin by providing each computer and all peripherals with a well-ventilated location. Then take time to schedule and perform preventive maintenance on the PCs for which you are responsible. This includes regular visual and aural inspections, driver and firmware updates, and component cleaning.

Visual and Audio Inspection

Frequent visual inspections will alert you to problems with cables and connections. This is true of your own personal computer as well as other people's computers. Make yourself consciously look at a computer for connection problems and environmental problems. Things change. You may discover that you have inadvertently piled papers on top of a powered USB hub in a corner of your desk, and it is getting hot. You may find that a computer or peripheral moved, which stretched the data cable or power cables to the point of nearly coming out of the sockets.

An aural inspection involves listening for a noisy fan or hard drive. A squealing fan or hard drive may be a sign of a pending problem. Correct it before you lose the fan or hard drive. Clean and/or replace the fan. Immediately back up a hard drive that makes an unusual noise, and take steps to replace it.

Driver and Firmware Updates

Keep current on driver and firmware updates. When you move from an old computer to one with a newer operating system, or upgrade the operating system on an existing computer, obtain new device drivers from the manufacturers. Also, be sure to install all critical operating system and security updates (more on security in Chapters 16 and 17). Similarly, when you upgrade to a new operating system, you may need to update the firmware, which, as you learned earlier in "BIOS/CMOS Problems," means flashing the system BIOS and sometimes the device BIOSs. We cover driver updates in Chapter 9.

Ensuring a Proper Environment

Extremes of heat, humidity, and dust are damaging to PCs and peripherals. Therefore, the best operating environment for a PC is a climate-controlled room with a filtration system to control these three enemies of electronics. If a PC must operate in a hostile environment that exposes it to extremes of any of these, consider spending money on a PC case that will provide better ventilation and filtration. To find the actual temperature and humidity extremes listed in the user's or technical manual for a PC or component, look under "Operating Environment." A recommended operating environment is in the range of 50 to 90 degrees Fahrenheit (10 to 32 degrees Centigrade) with relative humidity between 50 and 80 percent. A rough guideline: if you are not comfortable, the PC is not either.

Providing Good Power

When you consider a proper environment for computer equipment, you must also think of the power it receives. You should never plug critical equipment into a wall outlet without some provision to protect it from the vagaries of the power grid. While sags in power below the 115 V U.S. standard can cause your computer to reboot or power off, a surge can do significant damage, and a simple power strip offers no protection because it is nothing more than an extension cord with several power outlets.

Surge Protectors

At a minimum, use a surge protector to protect all computer equipment, including modems and phone and cable lines. At first glance, a *surge protector* (also called a *surge suppressor*) may look like an ordinary power strip, but it protects equipment from power fluctuations. Your PC's power supply will also do this for small power fluctuations above the 115 V U.S. standard, but it will eventually fail if it is the first line of defense. Therefore, plug your PC into a surge protector that has a protection rating of more than 800 joules. (A joule is a unit of energy.) Look for a surge protector that carries the Underwriters Laboratories label showing that it complies with UL standard 1449; this is the least expensive power protection device.

Beyond Surge Protectors

Do not just buy the minimum—if you can, buy the best power protection you can afford, which should include protection from power fluctuations, brownouts, voltage sags, and outages. The most common device that protects from power outages and reductions is an *uninterruptible power supply (UPS)*. These are more expensive than simple surge protectors, but they have come down in price as more manufacturers have introduced consumer-level versions of these devices.

In Chapter 3, you learned that for each computer you need a power supply with a capacity that exceeds the total watts required by all the internal components. Similarly, when selecting a UPS you must first determine the power requirements in watts for each device you will connect to the UPS and how much time you would require to save your data when main power fails.

A computer or other device plugged into a UPS is truly isolated from the power source, because during normal operation, it runs directly off the battery through an inverter, rather than switching to the battery only after a loss of power. A UPS is more expensive than a surge protector, but it is excellent power protection.

Once line power to a UPS is off, your computer runs on limited battery power. The limit varies by the capacity of the battery in the UPS and by how much power the computer draws, so unless the power comes back on quickly, you probably have a window of just minutes to save your data and to power down the computer. For this reason, some of these devices include a data cable and software. When installed, and the UPS senses a power outage, the software warns you to shut down. If no one is at the keyboard to respond, it will automatically save open data files, shut down the operating system, and power down the computer before the UPS itself runs out of battery power.

on the
Job

In a real disaster, power can be off for days or weeks, especially for mission-critical systems in certain industries, like banking and hospitals. So expect to encounter backup power generators that can kick in and provide power. Propane or diesel usually powers such generators.

Maintenance and Cleaning of Computer Components

Computer components will last longer and function better with some basic and regular maintenance and cleaning. For example, by regularly cleaning the fans in the power supply and case, you can ensure they properly cool the computer's internal components, preventing system slowdown and potential damage to components.

Internal Components

One of the most common reasons to clean the insides of a computer is to remove dust buildup to protect the system from overheating. Recall that the power supply's fan draws air out of the computer. Outside air comes in through ports and is distributed over the internal components, bringing with it dust. Because dust can cause electrostatic discharge (ESD) and lead to overheated components, cleaning the inside of the computer regularly is important. Pay particular attention to the system board, the bottom of the computer chassis, and all fan inlets and outlets on both the power supply fan and case fans. Of course, make sure you power down the computer before you start cleaning it.

One of the easiest ways to remove dust from the system is to use compressed air to blow the dust out. Compressed air comes in cans roughly the size of spray-paint cans. Typically, liquid Freon in the can compresses the air and forces it out when you depress the can's nozzle. Tilting or turning the can upside down can cause Freon release. Avoid this, because liquid Freon can cause freeze burns on your skin and can damage the computer's components.

Also, be aware of where you are blowing the dust. That is, make sure you are not blowing the dust off one component only to have it settle on another. You can also use compressed air to blow dust out of the keyboard, expansion slots, and ports. Use only canned compressed air, not high-pressure air from a compressor.

Another common method for removing dust from inside a computer is to use an antistatic vacuum cleaner—one that has a conductive path to ground to protect against causing electrostatic discharge damage to a computer during use. This has the advantage of removing dust without allowing the dust to settle elsewhere. It is best to use a handheld vacuum that allows you to get into smaller places and clean the computer without accidentally hitting and damaging other internal components. Take the nozzle out of the computer, and move the vacuum cleaner away before turning it off.

External Components

Finally, you can use a lint-free cloth to wipe off dusty surfaces, such as displays, keyboards, printers, and the outside of the PC case. Antistatic display cleaner is a type of product that contains a gentle cleansing liquid that, when used with a soft cloth, can remove dust and dirt from display screens. Avoid using the newer dust cloths that work by "statically attracting" dust. Remember, static is harmful to the computer. Use a dry lint-free cloth to remove dust from the display screen, and use an antistatic display cleaner to remove grime. Spray a small amount onto a soft cloth, and then wipe dirt from display screens.

For dirt you cannot dust off, use disposable moistened cleaning wipes on optical discs and most plastic, metal, and glass exterior surfaces, such as display screens. A liquid cleaning compound, such as isopropyl alcohol, can come in handy for cleaning gummy residue from the surface of the PC case or from a peripheral. Manufacturer's instructions may also suggest using this for cleaning components inside the PC or other device, but only do this per the manufacturer's instructions.

Input Devices

For input devices, such as keyboards, mice, and trackball devices, schedule frequent cleaning. For the keyboard, this involves vacuuming the crevices between the keys. Simply turning a keyboard upside down over a wastebasket and shaking it will remove a surprising amount of dust and debris, depending on the environment and the habits of the user. You may need to protect a keyboard in a dirty environment, such as an auto repair shop, with a special membrane cover that allows use of the keyboard, but keeps dirt, grease, solvents, and other harmful debris out of it. You can find such covers on the Internet or in computer supply catalogs under the keyboard protector category. For devices that are rarely used, consider using dust covers that remain on the device until needed.

To clean an optical mouse, simply turn the mouse over, locate the tiny lens, and wipe it with a soft static-free cloth. To clean a trackball, simply remove the ball, and wipe the socket with a soft static-free cloth. To clean rollers on a traditional mouse, follow the steps in Exercise 5-5.

EXERCISE 5-5

Cleaning a Mouse

1. Unplug the mouse and turn it upside down.

2. Remove the retaining ring (usually by twisting it counterclockwise).

3. Invert the mouse so the ball drops into your hand.

4. If the ball is dirty or sticky, clean it with warm soapy water and rinse it thoroughly.

5. Locate the rollers inside the mouse (see Figure 5-9). There are typically two long black rollers and one small metallic roller.

6. Use your fingers to remove the "ring" of dust from each roller, taking care not to let any material fall further into the mouse.

7. If the rollers are sticky, or if Step 6 is insufficient to clean the rollers, use a cotton swab dipped in isopropyl alcohol to clean them.

8. When finished, replace the mouse ball and retaining ring, ensuring they are securely in place.

9. Plug the mouse back in. If it is a USB mouse, you can plug it in with the computer running, but you must turn the computer off before you plug in a mouse that uses a serial port or a PS/2 mouse port.

10. With the computer running, test the mouse in Windows.

Storage Devices

Common storage devices also require regular maintenance for better performance. The following sections describe simple tasks for maintaining hard drives, optical drives, and floppy drives.

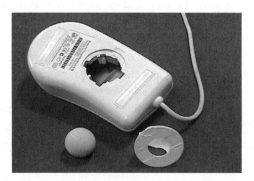

Hard Drives Hard drive maintenance includes running a utility called a *disk defragmenter* (Defrag) or *disk optimizer* to reorganized fragmented files on disk, and Check Disk (CHKDSK) or Scandisk to discover problems with the disk. Run these utilities on a regular basis, perhaps once a week on a drive in which you save many new files and delete old files. Chapter 10 will explain the details of the problems both types of utilities resolve.

Optical Media and Drives You can prevent damage to your optical drives by keeping the discs clean. Commercial optical disc cleaning and repair kits are readily available to restore optical discs. But you can simply wipe any type of optical disc (CD, DVD, or Blu-ray) clean with an antistatic cloth. For more stubborn dirt, use plain water or isopropyl alcohol on the cloth. Ensure the disc is completely dry before inserting it into a drive. The Blu-ray discs (also called "BD") have a hard coating—beyond what you will find on older types of optical discs—that resists scratches.

If a disc is too badly scratched, you may need to replace it, or if it is irreplaceable or too expensive to replace, and you have nothing to lose, consider polishing the disc.

Never clean an optical drive that is working properly, but if you find you must clean a drive, use compressed air to blow dirt out of the drive. If your optical drive has the lens in the disc tray, you will see it when the tray extends. You can carefully clean this type of drive with an antistatic cloth dampened with isopropyl alcohol. Be careful that you do not use too much alcohol and damage the drive. "Dampened" does not mean "dripping."

Be wary of kits for cleaning optical drives, because some of these use a small brush or felt pad to clean the lens of the drive, which can have unintended consequences such as scratching the lens. If you decide to use one of these kits, make sure you follow the directions carefully as improper use may cause more problems than it solves.

Floppy Drive Maintenance You can purchase floppy drive cleaning kits at many computer retail or parts stores. Typically, the kit includes a cleaning solution and what looks like a regular floppy disk. In most cases, you apply the cleaning solution to the disk and insert the disk in the drive. Then the drive cleans the read/write heads as they try to access the disk.

Thermally Sensitive Devices

Many components within a PC are thermally sensitive. These components should only operate within the recommended operating environment, as stated previously in this chapter. Transporting a PC or other thermally sensitive device requires being

SCENARIO & SOLUTION

You have isolated a performance problem to your hard drive, but you would like to run more diagnostics tests to be sure. What programs should you look for?	Look for a hard-drive diagnostics program from the drive's manufacturer, or obtain a third-party hard-drive diagnostics program.
You are visiting a customer whose computer is running slow. The computer is in a fabric store that generates a great deal of dust and fibers. In addition to your basic tools, what should you take along?	Be sure to take a vacuum—an antistatic vacuum, if possible. The slow running may be caused by overheating due to dust and fibers covering the internal components.

aware of the environment. For instance, if you live in a cold climate and bring a new PC home when it is 20° F below zero, be sure to let the PC sit and acclimate before plugging it in and turning it on. If the PC feels cold to the touch when you unpack it, this acclimation time should extended to several hours, because, as it warms up, some condensation will occur on internal components, and the PC needs time to dry out!

In addition, be sure to follow the procedures described earlier in "Maintenance and Cleaning of Computer Components" for cleaning dust and dirt from inside the PC to avoid heat buildup and to allow sufficient airflow around the PC and its peripherals.

Thermally sensitive devices include motherboards, CPUs, adapter cards, memory, and printers.

CERTIFICATION SUMMARY

As a computer technician, you will be required to locate and resolve the source of computer problems. If you have a good knowledge of the functions of the computer's components, you will quickly be able to troubleshoot problems that occur.

However, there are other telltale signs of failed components. For example, you can use POST error codes to determine a problem's cause. Although the troubleshooting procedures differ from component to component, and even for different problems within the same component, many of the procedures involve cleaning the component, ensuring it is properly attached to the computer, or finally, replacing the component.

Understanding troubleshooting theory and taking a structured and disciplined approach will not only help you arrive at a solution but also help you quickly resolve similar problems in the future. If you determine that you have a software problem, check the application's configuration, or try uninstalling and then reinstalling the program. If the problem is hardware related, identify the components that make up the failing subsystem. Starting with the most accessible component, check for power and that the component is properly attached to the computer. Check the device's configuration and the presence of a device driver. Finally, swap suspected bad components with known good ones.

Assemble the right tools for troubleshooting and maintenance before you need them. Take time to perform regular maintenance tasks on computers and peripherals to prevent future problems.

✓ TWO-MINUTE DRILL

Here are some of the key points covered in Chapter 5.

Troubleshooting Theory and Techniques

❑ Perform backups of data and the operating system before making any changes.

❑ Assess a problem systematically, and divide large problems into smaller components to analyze individually.

❑ When troubleshooting, perform the following procedures: identify the problem, establish a theory of probably cause, test the theory to determine actual cause, establish an action plan to resolve the problem, implement the solution, verify full system functionality, and document your findings, actions, and outcomes.

❑ Ongoing user training can prevent many problems and ensure that users know how to respond to common problems.

Troubleshooting Software Problems

❑ The common quick fixes to software problems include rebooting, uninstalling, and reinstalling.

❑ Pinpoint the actual software component that is involved in the problem. Is it the operating system, a single application, or several applications that are affected?

❑ Ensure a computer meets the minimum requirements for an application and all the necessary updates are installed.

Troubleshooting PC Component Problems

❑ Procedures should move from least intrusive to most intrusive, checking proper connections, appropriate components, drivers, and settings, and component seating for internal devices.

❑ Look for symptoms such as excessive heat, noise, odors, and visible damage.

❑ Never open the power supply or try to replace the fan; rather, replace the entire power supply when the fan stops working.

❑ POST error codes, such as 1*xx*, 2*xx*, and 3*xx*, can indicate system board, memory, or keyboard failures, respectively.

❑ Most CPU problems are fatal, which requires replacing the CPU or system. Check your warranty if you suspect a problem with the CPU because it may require replacing the motherboard.

❑ Incorrect CMOS settings can affect a variety of system components. Check and correct these problems by running the system setup and changing the settings.

❑ CMOS batteries last from two to ten years. A computer that does not maintain the date and time when powered off is a symptom of a failed CMOS battery.

❑ Most system board, processor, and memory errors are fatal, meaning the computer cannot properly boot up.

❑ The most common mouse problem is irregular movement, which can be resolved by cleaning the internal rollers of a mechanical mouse or the bottom surface of an optical mouse.

❑ Motherboard errors can be the most difficult to pinpoint and, due to the cost and effort involved in replacement, should be the last device you suspect when a subsystem or the entire computer fails.

❑ Replace a hard drive that begins to develop corrupted data before all the information stored on it is lost.

❑ Most floppy drive problems are with the media (floppy disks) rather than with the hardware. If you find a floppy drive problem that you cannot easily correct, consider replacing it with an external USB floppy drive.

❑ USB device problems may involve power connections for external devices that require external power. Consider using a USB loopback plug to diagnose a stubborn USB problem.

❑ Problems with SCSI devices, beyond failure of the device itself, most often involve termination of the SCSI chain and SCSI device ID.

Troubleshooting Tools

❑ Arm yourself with appropriate troubleshooting tools, including software and hardware tools.

❑ If you must service a large number of PCs, consider investing in a specialized diagnostic toolkit.

❑ Acquire and learn how to use appropriate cleaning products, such as cleaning wipes, antistatic display cleaner, canned compressed air, an antistatic vacuum cleaner, and nonabrasive cleaning compounds, such as isopropyl alcohol.

Preventive Maintenance Techniques

❑ Schedule regular preventive computer maintenance, such as visual and audio inspections, driver and firmware updates, cleaning, and verifying a proper environment.

❑ Schedule regular preventive component maintenance for displays, power devices, and drives. Protect thermally sensitive devices by cleaning regularly and by ensuring proper airflow.

SELF TEST

The following questions will help you measure your understanding of the material presented in this chapter. Read all of the choices carefully because there might be more than one correct answer. Choose all correct answers for each question.

Troubleshooting Theory and Techniques

1. When faced with a large, complicated problem, what strategy should you use?
   A. Call in a high-level service technician.
   B. Divide a large problem into smaller components to analyze individually.
   C. Replace the entire system.
   D. Check the warranty.

2. What should you do before making any changes to a computer?
   A. Turn off the computer.
   B. Use a grounding strap.
   C. Restore the most recent backup.
   D. If no recent backup of data and/or the operating system exists, perform a backup.

3. What are two methods you should employ for identifying a problem?
   A. Examine the environment.
   B. Question the user.
   C. Vacuum the computer.
   D. Read the label on the back of the power supply.

4. You want to narrow down the source of a problem to one of what two broad categories?
   A. Power or data
   B. Operating system or application
   C. Motherboard or component
   D. Hardware or software

5. How do you narrow down the problem to one hardware component?
   A. Remove the data cables.
   B. Run specialized diagnostics.
   C. Swap each suspect component with a known good one.
   D. Restart the computer.

6. After you apply and test a solution, what should you have the user do as part of evaluating the solution? Select all that apply.

A. First, restart the computer and device (if appropriate).

B. First, disconnect the problem component.

C. Test the solution and all commonly used applications.

D. Print out the user manual.

Troubleshooting Software Problems

7. What should you do if you are unsure if a problem is limited to the single application that was in use at the time the problem occurred?

A. Remove and reinstall the application.

B. Upgrade the application.

C. Perform the actions that resulted in the problem from more than one application.

D. Upgrade the driver.

Troubleshooting PC Component Problems

8. The following is a recommended set of troubleshooting procedures. Which two things should you do first?

A. Check for proper component seating (internal adapter card, memory, etc.).

B. Check for proper connections.

C. Check for appropriate components.

D. Check for installation drivers and correct settings.

9. Your video display is blank. Which of the following should you do first?

A. Swap the display with a known good one.

B. Replace the video adapter with a known good one.

C. Check the power and data cables.

D. Check the seating of the video adapter.

10. A customer reports that the computer spontaneously reboots and sometimes will not start at all. Furthermore, even when the computer does start, the fan does not make as much noise as before. What is the likely cause of these problems?

A. The power supply

B. The system board

C. The processor

D. The RAM

11. Your computer consistently loses its date and time setting. Which procedure will you use to solve the problem?

    A. Replace the battery.

    B. Flash the battery using a manufacturer-provided disk.

    C. Use the computer's AC adapter to recharge the battery.

    D. Access the CMOS setting programs at startup and select the low-power option.

12. Which component is typically associated with a 3*xx* BIOS error code?

    A. Motherboard

    B. Keyboard

    C. Processor

    D. RAM

13. Which of the following symptoms is not caused by a RAM error?

    A. The POST cannot be completed.

    B. When you turn on the computer, nothing happens.

    C. The system reports that there is no operating system.

    D. The RAM count at bootup does not match the capacity of the installed RAM.

14. A user reports that the mouse pointer does not move smoothly across the screen. Which of the following is most likely to remedy the problem?

    A. Reinstall the mouse driver.

    B. Ensure that the mouse cable connects securely to the computer.

    C. Replace the mouse with a trackball. Ensure there are no IRQ conflicts between the mouse and another device.

    D. Clean the mouse.

15. Which of the following should you do first when you get this error: "Please insert a disk into drive A:"?

    A. Make sure a floppy disk is in the drive.

    B. Ensure the floppy ribbon cable is attached properly.

    C. Make sure the floppy drive is properly configured in the BIOS settings.

    D. Clean the floppy disk.

16. You have just finished building a computer. You notice that when you turn on the computer, the floppy drive light comes on and will not go off. What should you do?

    A. Insert a different disk into the drive.

    B. Reverse the ribbon cable on the drive.

    C. Swap the drive with another one.

    D. Nothing.

17. You played a game on the computer about an hour ago and closed the game when you were finished. In the meantime, you opened a word processor, sent a print job to the printer, and then closed the application. When you tried to restart the game, nothing happened. Which of the following should you do first?

    A. Obtain a manufacturer's patch for the game.

    B. Troubleshoot the printer.

    C. Restart the computer.

    D. Reinstall the game.

Troubleshooting Tools

18. Which of the following is an advanced hardware diagnostics tool that you insert into an expansion slot?

    A. POST card

    B. Loopback plug

    C. Video adapter

    D. Nut driver

Preventive Maintenance Techniques

19. Which cleaning product blows dirt and dust out of PC components?

    A. Antistatic display cleaner

    B. Canned compressed air

    C. Liquid cleaning compound

    D. Antistatic vacuum cleaner

20. Which of the following power protection devices is an "online" power protection device?

    A. Power strip

    B. Surge protector

    C. SPS

    D. UPS

SELF TEST ANSWERS

Troubleshooting Theory and Techniques

1. ☑ **B.** Divide a large problem into smaller components to analyze individually is the correct answer. The smaller problems will be easier to resolve and eventually you will solve the bigger problem.
   ☒ **A,** call in a high-level service technician, is incorrect. Although this may become necessary, take the steps recommended in this chapter first to save time and money. **C,** replace the entire system, is incorrect because you have not made enough effort yet on the problem to do something so drastic. **D,** check the warranty, is incorrect because you have not yet even narrowed the problem down to the source.

2. ☑ **D.** If no recent backup of data and/or the operating system exists, perform a backup. This is correct because you do not want to risk losing the user's data.
   ☒ **A,** turn off the computer, is incorrect because it is rather irrelevant, although after taking care of the backup, you may want to restart the computer. **B,** use a grounding strap, is incorrect because until you have narrowed down the cause, you do not know if this will be necessary. You must do a backup before you reach this point. **C,** restore the most recent backup, is incorrect because you have no idea if this is even necessary at this point.

3. ☑ **A,** examine the environment, and **B,** question the user, are two methods for identifying a problem.
   ☒ **C** is incorrect because vacuuming the computer seldom helps to identify the problem. **D,** reading the label on the back of the power supply, won't help to identify the problem.

4. ☑ **D.** Hardware or software are the two broad categories of problem sources.
   ☒ **A,** power or data, is incorrect because, although you may have problems in these areas, they are not the two broad categories of problem sources. **B,** operating system or application, is incorrect because these are both types of software, and software is just one of the two broad categories of problem sources. **C,** motherboard or component, is incorrect because these are both types of hardware, and hardware is just one of the two categories of problem sources.

5. ☑ **C.** Swaping each suspect component with a known good one is correct because this will narrow down a hardware problem to one component.
   ☒ **A,** remove the data cables, is incorrect because, although this may be part of removing a component, this alone will not help you narrow down the problem to one component. **B,** run specialized diagnostics, is incorrect because specialized diagnostics lead to general areas, not specific components. **D,** restart the computer, is incorrect because restarting will not indicate one component, although it might cause the problem to disappear.

6. ☑ **A,** first, restart the computer and device (if appropriate), and **C,** test the solution and all commonly used applications, are both correct. The user should perform these steps to confirm the fix works, and to assure herself that the changes you made were not harmful.

☒ **B,** first, disconnect the problem component, is incorrect because without the problem component you cannot evaluate the solution. **D,** print out the user manual, is incorrect because that has little to do with evaluating the solution.

Troubleshooting Software Problems

7. ☑ **C.** Perform the actions that resulted in the problem from more than one application is correct. If the problem only occurs in the one application, then focus on that application.

☒ **A,** remove and reinstall the application, is incorrect because, although this may be a fix for the problem, you must first determine that the problem only occurs with that application before doing something so drastic. **B,** upgrade the application, is incorrect because, although this may be a fix for the problem, you must first narrow it down to the one application. **D,** upgrade the driver, is incorrect because, although this may be a solution, you must first narrow down the cause to specific hardware before upgrading the driver.

Troubleshooting PC Component Problems

8. ☑ The two things you should do first are **B,** check for proper connections, and **C,** check for appropriate components.

☒ **D,** check the installation of drivers and correct settings, should come after checking for proper connections and proper components. **A,** check for proper component seating requires opening up the PC, which you should do last as it is the most intrusive step.

9. ☑ **C.** Check the power and data cables is correct because it is the least intrusive action. If this does not resolve the problem, check the brightness setting, and then continue to **A, D,** and **B,** in that order.

☒ **A,** swap the display with a known good one, is incorrect because this is more trouble than simply checking the cables. **B,** replace the video adapter with a known good one, and **D,** check the seating of the video adapter, are incorrect because these very intrusive actions should wait until you have performed less intrusive actions.

10. ☑ **A.** The power supply is the most likely cause of these symptoms. When a power supply begins to fail, it often manifests in a number of different, sporadic symptoms. If the power supply's fan stops working, the computer will overheat and spontaneously reboot itself. If the components are still excessively hot when the system restarts, the computer may not start at all.

☒ **B,** the system board, **C,** the processor, and **D,** the RAM, are all incorrect. Failure of these components does not cause the specific set of symptoms mentioned in the question. A RAM failure will not cause the computer to reboot (unless all the RAM fails). Although an overheated processor could cause the system to reboot, it would not be associated with the lack of noise from the power supply fan.

11. ☑ **A.** You should replace the battery. When the computer "forgets" the time and date, it is most likely because the CMOS battery, which normally maintains these settings, is getting low on power and you must replace it.
☒ **B** is incorrect because it suggests flashing the battery. This procedure (flashing) applies to the upgrade of a BIOS chip, not a CMOS battery. **C** is incorrect because it suggests recharging the battery with the computer's AC adapter. Although this procedure will work with a portable system battery, you cannot recharge CMOS batteries with an AC adapter. **D** is incorrect because it suggests selecting a "low-power" option in the CMOS settings program. Any low-power setting in the CMOS settings refers to the function of the computer itself, not to the CMOS battery. You cannot adjust the amount of power the CMOS chip draws from its battery.

12. ☑ **B.** The keyboard is typically associated with a 3*xx* BIOS error code. When the computer is started, the BIOS performs a POST, which checks for the presence and function of certain components. If a keyboard error, such as a missing cable or stuck key, is detected, the BIOS typically reports a 3*xx* error code.
☒ **A,** motherboard, and **C,** processor, are incorrect because these errors, if detected by the BIOS, are typically indicated by a 1*xx* error code. **D,** RAM, is incorrect because memory errors are typically associated with 2*xx* error codes.

13. ☑ **C.** The system reports that there is no operating system. The OS resides on the hard drive, and, following the POST, the BIOS looks for the OS, loads it into memory, and gives it control. This message is not associated with a memory error.
☒ **A, B,** and **D** are incorrect because these are all typical symptoms of bad memory. If the memory has totally failed, the BIOS cannot conduct or complete the POST and it is also possible that the BIOS might not even be able to initiate the processor. This problem might make it appear that the computer does absolutely nothing when it is turned on. A bad memory stick may not cause an error, but will not work, and if you watch the memory count during bootup, you may notice the count does not match the installed RAM.

14. ☑ **D.** Cleaning the mouse is most likely to remedy the problem of a mouse pointer that does not move smoothly on the screen.
☒ **A,** reinstalling the mouse driver, is incorrect because if the mouse does not have a proper driver, it will not work at all. Driver problems for any device will cause that device to stop functioning altogether or to work sporadically. **B,** ensuring the mouse cable connects securely to the computer, is also incorrect. If the mouse is not connected to the computer, the mouse will not respond at all. If the mouse connector is loose, the operation of the mouse could be

sporadic, working at some times, and not working at all on other occasions. **C,** replacing the mouse with a trackball, is also incorrect. Although this solution may actually resolve the problem caused by a dirty mouse, it is more extreme than cleaning the mouse.

15. ☑ **A.** Make sure a floppy disk is in the drive. This error indicates the drive did not detect a disk. The most common reason for receiving this error is simply that no disk is inserted or is not inserted all the way.

   ☒ **B,** ensure the floppy ribbon cable is attached properly, and **C,** make sure the floppy drive is properly configured in the BIOS settings, are both incorrect. You should suspect a ribbon cable or BIOS setting problem only if the computer cannot communicate with the floppy drive. **D,** clean the floppy disk, is incorrect because, although this message is used to indicate a problem accessing the disk, you may cause more problems by trying to clean the disk.

16. ☑ **B.** You should reverse the ribbon cable on the drive. A floppy drive light that will not go out is a sure indicator of a reversed ribbon cable in the drive's port. Make sure you align the cable's red stripe with pin 1 on both the floppy drive's port connector and the socket on the motherboard.

   ☒ **A,** insert a different disk into the drive, is incorrect because the floppy light remaining on will occur at startup, with or without a disk present in the drive. **C,** swap the drive with another one, is incorrect because there is probably no need to do so. Reverse the ribbon cable on the drive first. **D** is incorrect because it suggests you should do nothing. However, when the stated condition occurs, the ribbon is backward, and the drive will not work.

17. ☑ **C.** You should restart the computer. In some cases, applications can use computer resources, such as memory or processor time, and will fail to release them, even when the application is closed. By restarting the computer, you will remove the application from memory and cause it to release any system resources.

   ☒ **A,** obtain a manufacturer's patch for the game, and **D,** reinstall the game, are incorrect because you typically use these procedures when an application contains corrupt or improper instructions. Since the game worked originally, this is not likely the case. Furthermore, installing a patch or reinstalling an application is more time-consuming than rebooting the system. **B,** troubleshoot the printer, is incorrect because the printer is also an unlikely suspect in this case. The printer could perhaps cause this problem, but troubleshooting the printer is more time-consuming and less likely to resolve the problem than simply restarting the computer.

Troubleshooting Tools

18. ☑ **A.** POST card is correct. You must install this into an expansion slot. Then, when the computer boots up, it performs advanced diagnostics and displays the results on an LED and through indicator lights.

   ☒ **B** and **D** are incorrect because, although these are examples of hardware tools, neither can be inserted into an expansion slot. **C,** video adapter, is incorrect because this is not a hardware diagnostics tool but a common PC component.

Preventive Maintenance Techniques

19.   ☑   **B.** Canned compressed air is the cleaning product used to blow dirt and dust out of PC components. The drawback to this is that it can also blow dirt and dust into components, and if used improperly, the liquid Freon within the can will spill onto the skin or computer components, causing injury or damage.

☒   **A,** antistatic display cleaner, and **C,** liquid cleaning compound, are both incorrect because these are wet cleaning products you use to wipe off the screen and other surfaces. **D,** antistatic vacuum cleaner, is incorrect because it draws the dust in, rather than blowing it out. This more expensive product is preferred for cleaning out a PC.

20.   ☑   **D.** UPS is correct. This is the only true online power protection device.

☒   **A,** power strip, is incorrect because this provides no power protection whatsoever. **B,** surge protector and **C,** SPS, are incorrect because neither of these alone is an online power protection device in the way that a UPS is, providing full-time power from the battery.

6

Installing, Configuring, and Optimizing Laptops

CERTIFICATION OBJECTIVES

❑   **701:1.10**   Install, configure, and optimize laptop components and features

❑   **701:3.3**   Explain the process and steps to install and configure the Windows OS

❑   **702:1.3**   Given a scenario, install, configure, detect problems, troubleshoot, and repair/replace laptop components

✓   Two-Minute Drill

Q&A   Self Test

Several years ago industry analysts predicted that laptop sales would surpass desktop sales by 2008. That prediction didn't quite hit the mark, because they reached that milestone three years earlier, in 2005, without counting large sales to corporations or direct sales from computer companies. By 2008, laptops accounted for 80 percent of personal computer sales. Why is this? Price and performance. While laptops once commanded premium prices, they now offer higher performance without the high price tags (for the most part), although desktops continue to be a better value in computing power and have larger screens. But you cannot ignore the mobility issue. And mobility is the issue, especially as more and more Wi-Fi hotspots appear in public places, making working away from an office more convenient for certain professions. These trends guarantee that most PC technicians will need to understand laptop-specific technologies.

CERTIFICATION OBJECTIVES

■ **701: 1.10**   *Install, configure, and optimize laptop components and features*

■ **702: 1.3**   *Given a scenario, install, configure, detect problems, troubleshoot, and repair/replace laptop components*

> For CompTIA A+ Exam objective 701: 1.10, be sure you can describe how to install, configure, and optimize laptop components, and demonstrate knowledge of laptop peripherals, expansion slots, ports, connectors, and power and electrical input devices. This list includes technologies that may not be exclusive to portable computers, but which are commonly found in them, such as LCD technologies and such input devices as function keys, built-in pointing devices, and the stylus/digitizer combination. Exam objective 702: 1.3 has some overlap with 701: 1.10, but requires that you delve further into laptop technology and understand how to install, replace, and configure components that require opening the case.

Introduction to Laptops

> A *portable computer* is any type of computer that you can easily transport and that has an all-in-one component layout. In addition to the size difference, portable computers differ from desktop computers in their physical layout and their use of battery power when not plugged into an AC outlet. Portable computers fall into

two broad categories: laptops (by several different names) and handhelds. The 2009 edition of the CompTIA A+ Exams only lists laptops. Therefore, we will focus on laptops, the most common portable computers.

Laptops, Notebooks, and Netbooks

Laptops generally weigh less than 7 pounds, can fit easily into a tote bag or briefcase, and have roughly the same dimensions as a 1- to 2-inch thick stack of magazines. Typically, a laptop opens in the same manner as a briefcase. The top contains the display, and the bottom contains the keyboard and the rest of the computer's internal components. A typical laptop uses a liquid crystal display (LCD) and requires small circuit cards that comply with modified versions of the bus standards found in full-size PCs. People often use the word "laptop" interchangeably with "notebook." Initially, people called most portable computers "laptops" because they could fit on the user's lap, although early laptops were a little heavy to do this comfortably. As technology improved, laptops became smaller and smaller, and the term "notebook" came into use to reflect this smaller size.

As circuitry shrinks, we discover smaller and smaller portable computers and newer terms, such as *ultra-portable* or *mini-notebooks* for laptops that weigh less than 3 pounds and give up features to keep the weight down and maintain the highest battery life. *Netbook* is a recent term for scaled-down laptops in the ultra-portable category, designed mainly for Internet access, and costing about $300 a system. People purchase Netbooks as a second (or even third) computer for traveling, as a teaching aid for schoolchildren, and as a first computer for people in developing countries. Many purchase laptops as full-featured desktop replacements in which performance is more important than battery life. These have large screens and weigh in at over seven pounds. Regardless of the size and type of portable computer, throughout this book, we will use the term "laptop" to encompass all of these types.

on the **!** **(J)o b** *Ironically, a huge increase in the number of Netbooks sold in 2009, combined with these systems' low prices, has created a downward trend in the laptop market share, measured in dollars. For a technician, this still means more laptops out there to support.*

Laptops based on the Intel IBM-compatible platform can run the same operating systems as desktop PCs. Most laptops come with a version of Microsoft Windows installed, but you can also find laptops with Linux installed, or you can install it yourself. Additionally, Apple Computers use an Intel platform for their OS X operating system, although it is not a strictly IBM-compatible platform.

Handhelds

Although the objectives do not specifically list handheld computers for either of the CompTIA A+ 2009 Exams, they merit a mention here. Handheld computers come in a variety of types. The most common type is the *Personal Digital Assistant (PDA)*, a portable computer small enough to fit in your hand and also referred to as a "palmtop" computer. Because it is so small, a PDA does not have the functionality of a laptop or desktop computer. Older models only allow you to perform a small number of personal organizer-related functions, but the number and variety of applications has expanded, especially for those PDAs integrated into cell phones—referred to generically as *smart phones*.

Another type of handheld computer is a single-purpose computer more specialized than a PDA. For example, you may see employees in grocery stores using specialized handheld computers with integrated bar code readers to take inventory counts. This type of device will typically communicate wirelessly with a central inventory database.

Installing and Upgrading Laptops

This section begins with an overview of opening up a laptop and then provides the proper procedure for disassembly and reassembly of a laptop, and finally introduces you to some laptop-specific components and peripherals, describing installation and upgrading procedures where applicable. In all cases, when you consider installing a new component or replacing an old one, you should first check with the manufacturer for any BIOS upgrades. If one is available, install it before you proceed.

Opening Up a Laptop

Before opening a laptop, follow all the safety precautions described in Chapter 18. In addition to unplugging the AC adapter, be sure to remove the battery. To replace some internal laptop components, you may only need to remove an access panel on the bottom. These panels usually have one or two screws to remove. Other components may require that you disassemble the laptop, removing the keyboard, drives, or video adapter, and even the entire display assembly (in the worst case). The keyboard may attach with screws or latches. Let the manufacturer's documentation be your guide.

on the
① o b

Search the Internet for tutorials and videos on how to replace laptop components. These tutorials are often specific to certain models, but they offer lots of useful tips. Use your own judgment and the manufacturer's documentation when doing this type or work.

Disassembly and Reassembly Processes

When you need to open a laptop for any reason, be prepared to follow proper safety procedures, as described in Chapter 18. Also, follow the processes described here when preparing for and performing the disassembly and reassembly of a laptop.

Refer to Manufacturer's Documentation

Before you begin, locate the manufacturer's documentation for the laptop and for any component you are adding or replacing. You may find a service manual for the laptop on the manufacturer's Website that you can use to learn how to access the components you wish to replace and plan the actual steps you will take.

Use Appropriate Hand Tools

After reading the manufacturer's documentation, and before beginning, assemble all the hand tools you expect to use. Please refer to Chapter 5 for a list of tools.

Organize Parts

Have containers ready to temporarily hold the screws and other parts that you will remove (small pill bottles work well), and have antistatic bags handy for any circuit boards you remove. After you reassemble the laptop, you should not have any extra parts except for those that you replaced.

Document and Label Cable and Screw Locations

This most important of these steps is also the one most people would rather skip. For internal component replacements, you will begin by removing screws from the body of the laptop. Before you open the laptop compartment, take photos with a digital camera or make a rough sketch of the exterior portion involved, and label cable and screw locations. You don't have to be an artist to do this—simple lines and shapes, carefully labeled, will suffice. Once you have removed any panels, photograph or sketch the inside, labeling any components and their cables so you will be able to reassemble the laptop after replacing or adding a part.

CompTIA objectives for A+ Essentials Exam 702: 1.3 explicitly lists the topics just discussed for disassembly and reassembly, although they do not mention the use of a digital camera.

Laptop Replacement Parts

Laptop components that distinguish one manufacturer's models from all the others are at least partially proprietary. Then again, some laptop models have widely used components that are fairly generic, such as the CPU, memory, and hard drives. Therefore, if a laptop component fails, a carefully worded query in an Internet search engine should reveal sources for an appropriate replacement part or the name of a company that will replace the part for you. Both interior and exterior replacement parts are available, even plastic exterior components, such as the case, LCD lid, LCD bezels, palm rest, button panels, doors, and compartment covers for some popular laptop models. Always research whether replacing the part is more cost-effective than replacing the entire laptop.

Plastics

The nature of a laptop—its portability—and the tendency of a laptop owner to take for granted that a laptop can survive the rigors of travel means a laptop will typically experience rough treatment during its short lifetime. Although designed for portability, manufacturers do not design most laptops to survive harsh treatment. Those purposely designed for rough treatment, such as the Panasonic Toughbook that can withstand water, dust, temperature extremes, and impact, sell for a premium price that most users cannot justify.

Unless you work for an organization that requires the use of laptops under extreme conditions, you will work on the more vulnerable commonplace laptops, so you need to know what to do in case the plastic that makes up the laptop case falls victim to a mishap that doesn't damage the internals. Cracked laptop case corners can happen. If the laptop is out of warranty, but new enough to be valuable to the owner, you need to research replacing the laptop case or some part of it. You could attempt a repair using epoxy glue for cracks and epoxy putty to fill voids, but if you do this, be very careful not to drip the glue or putty into the interior.

Motherboard

Although laptops run standard PC operating systems and applications, laptop motherboards have different form factors than PCs because of the miniaturization required. A laptop motherboard (also called a *system board*) contains specialized versions of the components you would expect to find in a desktop PC, such as the CPU, chipset, RAM, video adapter (built in), and expansion bus ports.

If you find that a motherboard has failed, and your research and evaluation shows that a replacement is available and cost-effective, be sure the replacement exactly matches the form factor and all electrical and mechanical connections. This type of repair is fraught with failure potential, so you risk going to the expense and trouble of replacing a motherboard but botching the repair. Then you face the expense of the repair plus the cost of replacing the failed laptop.

CPU

Both Intel and AMD have a number of CPUs designed especially for laptops that include mobile computer technologies such as power-saving and heat-reducing features and throttling that lowers the clock speed and input voltage when the CPU is idle. Different models of mobile processors are available, including high-performance models requiring more power that are appropriate for desktop replacement laptops, and CPUs that run at lower voltage and reduced clock speeds to give the best battery life. Many mobile CPUs support Wi-Fi networking. Learn about wireless networking in Chapter 13.

If a laptop CPU fails, or if you wish to replace it in the hopes of obtaining better performance, contact the manufacturer for specifications for a replacement CPU. You may discover the CPU is not replaceable because it is soldered to the motherboard. Manufacturers will not usually sell you a replacement CPU, so if you find the CPU is replaceable, use the specifications to find a compatible CPU. Or, if the CPU is still functioning, you can download a utility program from either the Intel or AMD Websites that will give you the specs of the currently installed CPU. Note the information from the utility, especially the voltage and power draw, and then look for a chip that matches the specs. Powerwise, you want a chip with the same voltage and a power draw that is equal to or less than the one you are replacing.

To replace the CPU, you will need to open up the area inside the case that houses it. Refer to the earlier section "Opening Up a Laptop." No doubt, you will need to remove a heat sink from the installed CPU; set this aside. Once the CPU is exposed, you will need to release it by loosening a screw or other locking mechanism and lift it out. Remove the old thermal compound from the heat sink with isopropyl alcohol and a lint-free rag. When the heat sink is dry, apply a very thin layer of thermal paste to the top of the new CPU. Attach the heat sink to the new CPU and install it into the laptop socket, being sure to lock it in place again. Reassemble the system and start it up, taking care to go into the BIOS setup program to check that it recognizes the CPU.

Memory

Laptop memory modules come in small form factors. The most commonly used is *Small Outline DIMM (SODIMM)*, which is about half the size of a DIMM module. First-generation SODIMM modules had 30 pins, and the next generation had 72 pins. These had a data bus width of 8 bits and 32 bits, respectively, per module. Over the years, SODIMM modules have improved their data width, progressing through form factors with 100, 144, 200, and 204 pins. Notches prevent you from installing a module in the wrong orientation to the SODIMM memory slot. The 200-pin SODIMM in Figure 6-1 measures $2\frac{5}{8}$" wide. To use DDR3 memory, the system must have both a 204-pin SODIMM slot and a chipset that supports DDR3 memory. Table 6-1 shows the data transfer width for each of these form factors.

MicroDIMM, a RAM module designed for subcompact and laptop computers, is half the size of a SODIMM module and allows for higher density storage.

You can add additional RAM to a portable system. Some systems include extra RAM slots within the chassis, which requires either opening the computer's case or removing the compartment cover and inserting the RAM module in an available slot. Exercise 6-1 describes the steps for installing memory in a laptop and for verifying that the system recognizes it.

FIGURE 6-1

A 200-pin
SODIMM module

	Number of Pins per SODIMM Module	Data Bus Width
TABLE 6-1 The Data Bus Width of SODIMM Modules	30	8-bit
	72	32-bit
	100	32-bit
	144	64-bit
	200	64-bit
	204	64-bit

EXERCISE 6-1

Installing SODIMM Memory

For this exercise, you will need a new module of SODIMM memory appropriate for your laptop in an antistatic bag, the user's manual, a spare antistatic bag, and a small nonmagnetic screwdriver for opening the case. If you do not have a new module, simply remove an already installed module and reinstall it. In this case, you will just need an antistatic bag.

1. Turn off the computer and all external devices.

2. Ground yourself using one of the methods described in Chapter 18.

3. Following the instructions in the laptop user manual, open the compartment containing the SODIMM slots.

4. Your laptop may have one or two memory slots. Look for numbers near any open slots and fill the lowest numbered slot first.

5. If you are replacing memory, remove the module or modules you are replacing. To remove a module, press down on the retaining clips located on the sides, lift the edge of the module to a 45-degree angle, and gently pull it out of the slot, being careful to hold it by its edges and not touch the contacts or chips.

6. Place the old module in an antistatic bag. Remove the new module from its antistatic bag, being careful to hold it by its edges and not touch the contacts or chips.

7. Align the notch of the memory module with that of the memory slot and gently insert the module into the slot at a 45-degree angle. Gently rotate the module down flat until the clamps lock it in place (see Figure 6-2).

FIGURE 6-2

Installing a RAM
module in a
portable system

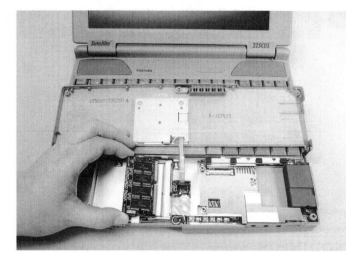

8. Before closing the memory compartment, power up the computer, and, if necessary (according to the user manual), configure it in BIOS setup, although this is not normally required.

9. Perform a normal startup in Windows, and check the System Properties applet in the Control Panel to see if it recognized the new memory.

10. Shut down the computer and close up the memory access panel.

Another way to add more RAM to your portable is to use a memory card of the correct PCMCIA form for your laptop. The choices are PC Card, CardBus PC Card, or ExpressCard, all of which we describe later in the section titled "External Expansion Slots."

No matter how you add memory to your laptop, you may notice the memory count during bootup does not quite add up to the total memory installed, which means your laptop may be using some of your system RAM for the video adapter, which often is the case with integrated video adapters if they do not have their own VRAM. Main RAM memory used in this way is called *shared video memory*.

Fans

Before considering replacing a seemingly failed laptop fan, open the laptop and clean the blades. If the fan still does not work, then attempt to replace the fan.

This process will require the usual search for a suitable fan. Once you locate one and determine the cost is worth the effort, follow the manufacturer's instructions to replace the failed fan, being careful to remove and replace the *heat pipe*, a tubular device that works with the fan to draw heat away from the interior of the laptop. If the installation is successful, you should hear the fan when you power up the laptop.

Installing Storage Devices

For years, laptops came with two mass storage devices: a hard drive and an optical drive. Although the optical drives in laptops are low profile, they are not smaller than those in desktop systems because they must accommodate optical discs. Laptops typically use 2.5" hard drives versus the 3.5" hard drives used in desktop PCs. There are also hard drives that you can install into the PC Card expansion bays. The biggest change in laptop mass storage, however, is large-capacity SSDs replacing hard drives at all price points of the newer ultra-portable models. An SSD drive will typically have a SATA interface, which is the most common interface today. SSDs in laptops are desirable because they are faster than hard drives, lighter, and less vulnerable to damage from impacts or excess motion. While some low-priced Netbooks contain these drives, they are modestly sized at around 32 GB; high-end laptops have SSD drives, such as the 512 GB SSD in Toshiba's Protégé 4600 laptop. These larger drives use newer technology that allows for denser storage and, therefore, higher capacity. One such technology is Secure Digital High Capacity (SDHC) cards.

Replace a hard drive only with another of the same type from the same manufacturer. After you power down the computer, use the same precautions you would use with a PC case before proceeding. Usually, you can remove a small plastic cover on the bottom of the laptop to access the hard drive. Slide the drive out (see Figure 6-3), and then replace it with a new drive and replace the cover.

Peripherals

Laptops can use just about any external peripheral that a PC can use, unless it relies on installing a full-sized expansion card. You can attach a full-sized external display to a laptop and any printer that can use one of your laptop's interfaces, such as USB, FireWire, eSATA, or one of the PCMCIA interfaces discussed in the section, "External Expansion Slots," a little later in this chapter. We now examine peripherals specifically designed for laptops.

Video Adapter

As in a desktop PC, a video adapter controls a laptop's video output, but laptop manufacturers typically integrate the video adapter into the motherboard, or on a separate, scaled-down proprietary card connected to a type of riser card that holds the video adapter just above the motherboard, oriented on the same plane. An integrated card is not upgradeable, and, in most cases, a faulty video adapter requires that you replace the motherboard. You might be able to replace a separate video adapter if you can find a compatible replacement for it that will fit. To replace a video adapter, open the case and locate the component, as discussed earlier in "Disassembly and Reassembly Processes." This is a bit simpler than replacing a CPU, but it is still very delicate. You will remove the old video adapter and replace it with a new one. As when replacing the CPU, after you close up the case, plug it in and restart the system, running system BIOS setup. Of course, if you can even see the POST information and access the BIOS screen, you've won half the battle. The rest will depend on whether the operating system drivers support the adapter or whether you can access all of its functionality.

Display

A laptop has an LCD display screen integrated into the "lid" of the case and connected to the integrated video adapter. In addition to the features discussed in Chapter 3, an LCD screen in a laptop also requires an internal *inverter* to convert the DC current from the power adapter or battery to the AC current the display requires.

Most laptop video adapters can drive two displays—the integrated flat panel display and an external display. You can use the external display as a replacement for the integrated display, display the same desktop on both simultaneously, or use the external display in addition to the built-in display in a multi-monitor configuration, as described in Chapter 3. Use the laptop's function key, marked FN, together with the function key that doubles as the DISPLAY MODE toggle key, to switch the video output among the display modes: laptop display only, external display only, or both displays.

The video display is one of the most expensive laptop components, and one of the most difficult to replace. If you have a failed laptop display and manage to find a suitable replacement, follow the manufacturer's instructions for removing the old display and installing the replacement.

e**x**a**m**

ⓦatch   *The three main compo-nents of the video system in a laptop include the LCD screen, the inverter, and the built-in video adapter.*

Digitizing Tablet

A *digitizing tablet* or *digitizer* is an input device that uses a stylus and position-sensing technology and usually has a tablet area at least the size of a sheet of paper. People primarily use a digitizer to create computerized drawings, so they often call it a *graphics tablet*. A *tablet PC*, a laptop in which the display is overlaid with an integrated digitizer, has two main types. The "convertible" has a screen that swivels to sit on top of the keyboard and conceal it for drawing, whereas the "slate" has no built-in keyboard at all. Although a stylus would seem like the primary input device for this type of computer, an integrated keyboard, if not an integrated pointing device, is standard. These choices allow you to use the mode that fits the current task, such as writing a memo using the keyboard, surfing the Internet using a mouse, and creating drawings using a stylus on the tablet. Replacing a digitizing tablet on a laptop or tablet PC is much like replacing a standard laptop LCD display, with the addition of the overlying grid that senses touch and movement and that has a separate interface from the display to the PC. As described in the discussion of I/O devices in Chapter 4, you will need to run a special calibration program to line up the touch screen inter-face with the underlying LCD display.

Hot-swappable Devices

Most devices today are plug and play, in that the operating system can recognize them, automatically locate and install their drivers, and configure the device and driver. Some, but not all, plug and play devices are hot swappable. *Hot-swappable devices* can be safely installed and removed while a computer is up and running. Hot-swappable devices include most devices that use a USB, FireWire, eSATA, PC Card, CardBus, or ExpressCard interface. You should not remove even hot-swappable devices without regard to open programs and files. Recall the proper procedure, described in Chapter 5, for using the Safely Remove Hardware applet.

Non-Hot-Swappable Devices

Non-hot-swappable devices may still be plug and play, but cannot be removed or installed while the computer is running without damaging the device or the system. Examples of these devices are any cards that you install inside the case of the laptop by opening it up. You must shut down the computer before removing or installing them.

Port Replicators and Docking Stations

The laptop owner who uses a laptop while traveling, but also as a desktop replacement, usually has a "base of operations" office. This office is where the owner will use external devices such as a keyboard, printer, display, and mouse. The user must connect and disconnect these components every time he or she returns to or leaves the office with the laptop.

A *port replicator*, a device that remains on the desktop with external devices connected to its ports, can make this task less time-consuming by providing a single connection to the laptop and permanent connection to these external devices.

A more advanced (and more expensive) alternative to the port replicator is a *docking station*. In addition to the ports normally found on a port replicator, a docking station may include full-size expansion slots and various drives. In the past, port replicators and docking stations were always proprietary—often only fitting one model of laptop. If the manufacturer did not make one of these devices to fit your laptop, you had no options. Now you can easily find an inexpensive "universal" port replicator or docking station that interfaces with a laptop via a USB port. Whether you have a proprietary device that fits your laptop, or one that uses a USB connector, be sure to read the documentation that comes with the docking station or port replicator and follow the instructions for connecting and disconnecting the device.

Media/Accessory Bay

To save space, a laptop may contain a *media bay*, a compartment that holds a single media device that you can switch with another. For instance, you may switch an optical drive, a secondary hard drive, or a floppy drive into and out of a single bay, but you can use only one device in the bay at a time. Figure 6-4 shows a media bay

FIGURE 6-4

A media bay in
a laptop, with two
drives that you
can swap using
this bay

and two drives that you can alternate in the bay. This type of bay, also called an *accessory bay*, is now less common, since so many accessories and drives are available with USB, FireWire, or eSATA interfaces.

Memory Card Reader

A laptop today will often come with a built-in, solid-state card reader. Because these devices have several formats (see Chapter 2), be sure your laptop supports the format you use, such as CompactFlash (CF), miniSD, MMC, Smart Media (SM), and Memory Stick (MS).

External Expansion Slots

Laptops come with specialized small form-factor expansion slots. The most common expansion slots are those based on standards developed by the *Personal Computer Memory Card International Association (PCMCIA)*, an organization that creates standards for laptop computer peripheral devices. All the standards described here support hot swapping, meaning you can connect and disconnect devices while the computer is running. A service called *socket services*, which runs in the laptop's operating system, detects when you have inserted a card. After socket services detects a card, another service, called *card services*, assigns the proper resources to the device.

PC Card/CardBus

At first, people referred to the early standard developed by PCMCIA simply as the "PCMCIA" interface. They also called the credit card–sized cards that fit into this interface, which slid in from slots on the side of a laptop, "PCMCIA cards," but eventually the name changed to *PC Card*. The earliest interfaces and cards used a 16-bit interface. Eventually, PCMCIA modified the standard to use a 32-bit parallel PCI bus, known as *CardBus*. Although the CardBus allows 32-bit burst mode transfers, it still only allows 16-bit memory transfers (for memory devices) and 16-bit I/O transfers for network cards, modems, and other I/O devices.

The cards that fit into the PC Card interface, including both PC Card and CardBus cards, measure 85.6 mm long by 54 mm wide. The three types vary in thickness: *Type I* measures 3.3 mm thick, *Type II* measures 5.0 mm thick, and *Type III* measures 10.5 mm thick. Figure 6-5 shows a Type II PC Card.

The PC Card slots are downward compatible. A Type III card can only fit in a Type III slot, whereas a Type II card can fit in either a Type II or a Type III slot, and a Type I card can fit in all three. They all have 68 pins, fit into the PC Card sockets, and only vary in thickness. The thickness and the circuitry that fits into each size

FIGURE 6-5

A Type II PC Card with a cable to attach to a network

TABLE 6-2

The Kinds of Devices That Use Each Type of PC Card

Type	Device
I	Solid-state memory cards
II	I/O devices: modems and network interface cards
III	Rotating mass storage hard drives

slot dictates the type of device that will use each PC Card type. Table 6-2 lists the PC Card types and the devices that would use each type.

Additionally, there is a physical distinction between the older 16-bit PC Card and a CardBus PC Card. When comparing the two types of cards, look at the area above the connector. On a 16-bit card, this area is smooth, whereas on the newer CardBus PC Card, a gold grounding strip appears that usually has 8 bumps. You can insert a 16-bit PC card into a 16-bit slot or a CardBus slot, but you can only insert the CardBus PC Card into a CardBus slot. You can view the details and driver information for the CardBus adapters in your laptop, as shown in Figure 6-6.

FIGURE 6-6

Device Manager shows the Card-Bus adapters for a laptop.

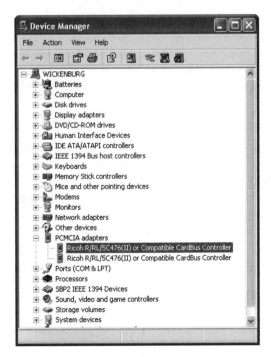

PC Card and CardBus Voltages

PC Cards have different voltages. Some operate at 3.3 V, while others operate at 5.0 V. A PC Card interface that can only operate at 5.0 V will have a key along one edge of the connectors that prevents cards that can only operate at 3.3 V from being inserted into the slots. Some cards, and some PC Card interfaces, can operate at either voltage. All of this voltage variation applies only to the older PC Card interface. The CardBus PC Card interface only operates at 3.3 V.

ExpressCard

Modern laptops use a more recent PCMCIA standard—*ExpressCard,* which comes in two interfaces: the PCIe (PCI Express) interface, at 2.5 gigabits per second, and the USB 2.0 interface, at 480 megabits per second. ExpressCard is incompatible with either PC Card standard. To begin with, the ExpressCard interface does not have actual pins, but instead has 26 contacts in a form referred to as a *beam-on-blade* connector. Although all ExpressCard modules have the same number of contacts (also called "pins"), there are currently two sizes of modules: Both are 75 mm long and 5 mm high, but they vary in width. The form factor known as ExpressCard/34 is 34 mm wide, whereas ExpressCard/54 is 54 mm wide. ExpressCard/34 modules will fit into ExpressCard/54 slots.

ExpressCard supports a variety of device types, including LAN and WAN adapters, FireWire, SATA, SSDs, USB hubs, micro hard drives, and much more. ExpressCard technology is not simply for laptops. The ExpressCard interface is available as standard bus cards for desktops and is built into desktop PCs.

Installing Cards into External Expansion Slots

The various small devices that install in the PC Card, CardBus, or ExpressCard slots are all plug and play, and you can install them without opening up the computer. You simply slide the card into the appropriate slot, pushing it in until it feels firmly seated. Recall that PC Cards and CardBus cards have pin and socket connectors, whereas the ExpressCards have contacts in a beam-on-blade configuration. Once properly installed, the card should not wiggle when gently tapped. When removing one of these cards, look for a small button next to each card that releases it from the socket.

Internal Expansion Slots

Some laptops also have one or more special mini-expansion slots inside the case. The two most common are based on the full-sized PCI and PCIe expansion bus found in a desktop PC. The first is Mini PCI, and the latest is PCIe Mini Card.

These are scaled-down versions of the cards used in desktop PCs and require opening the case to install or remove a card.

Mini PCI

Mini PCI is a standard based on PCI (see Chapter 1). The biggest difference (although there are others) is that Mini PCI is much smaller than PCI—both the card and the slot. Mini PCI has a 32-bit data bus. If a laptop has an installed Mini PCI slot, it is usually accessible via a small removable panel on the bottom of the case. Mini PCI cards also come in three form factors: Type I, Type II, and Type III. Types I and II each have 100 pins in a stacking connector, whereas Type III cards have 124 pins on an edge connector. Each type is further broken down into A and B subtypes, as shown in Table 6-3.

PCIe Mini Card

A newer standard for Mini Cards has replaced the Mini PCI standard on laptop motherboards. That is the *PCIe Mini Card* specification, which provides much faster throughput with a 64-bit data bus. A PCIe Mini Card, at 30 mm by 51 mm, is half the size of a Mini PCI card. Small is good! Manufacturers label their cards that follow this specification with names such as PCI Express Mini and Mini PCI-E. This type of card has a 52-pin edge connector.

TABLE 6-3

Dimensions of the Various Types of Mini PCI Cards

Card Type	Dimensions in mm (depth × length × width)
IA	7.5 × 70 × 45
IB	5.5 × 70 × 45
IIA	17.44 × 70 × 45
IIB	5.5 × 78 × 45
IIIA	2.4 × 59.6 × 50.95
IIIB	2.4 × 59.6 × 44.6

Communication Connections

Portable computers use several communications technologies that differ in the media they use and the effective range of the signal. They may be built into the motherboard; installed in a Mini Card port (Mini PCI or PCIe Mini Card); inserted as a card in a PC Card, CardBus, or ExpressCard slot; or come in the form of an external device connected through a USB, FireWire, or other port.

Wireless Communications

Wireless devices use radio waves or infrared light waves. The major wireless technologies support a range of distances from one meter to many miles. Those wireless devices that communicate over the shortest distances create a personal area network (PAN). Other types of wireless devices have a range in the hundreds of feet and work in a wireless local area network (WLAN). When you need to communicate wirelessly through your laptop over a distance of miles, you need a cellular wireless device.

Infrared   One technology that allows you to create a personal area network for your devices to communicate with your laptop is *infrared (IR)*. These devices use infrared light waves to communicate with each other through infrared transceiver ports. Some laptops and PDAs come with ports that comply with the *Infrared Data Association's (IrDA)* data transmission standards. IrDA is an organization that creates specifications for infrared wireless communication. Microsoft Windows supports plug and play for IrDA infrared devices. IrDA infrared devices support a maximum transmission speed of 4 Mbps. You can add IrDA devices to a system by installing an infrared adapter. They come in a variety of interfaces, but USB is the most common. Any two IrDA-enabled devices can communicate with each other. The drawback to this type of communication is the very short distance supported (one meter) and the fact that it requires line-of-sight, so the ports on the communicating devices must be directly facing one another with nothing in the way.

Bluetooth   *Bluetooth* is another wireless standard. Bluetooth devices use radio waves to communicate with each other. Some laptops come with a Bluetooth adapter built in. If not, you can purchase one—often along with one or more wireless devices that use the Bluetooth standard. A popular peripheral package is a Bluetooth keyboard and mouse bundled with a Bluetooth adapter using a USB interface. Many cell phones have Bluetooth built in for use with wireless headsets and for communicating with a Bluetooth-enabled computer to share the phonebook and other data stored in the phone.

Although one thinks of Bluetooth as mainly a very short distance communications standard, there are actually three classes of Bluetooth, each with its own power requirements, and each with a power-dependent distance. Class 1 Bluetooth devices have a distance limit of about 100 meters, whereas Class 2 devices are limited to about 10 meters, and Class 3 are limited to 1 meter. The class described in this chapter is Class 3. Older Microsoft Windows operating systems do not support the Bluetooth standard; support began with Windows XP.

Wi-Fi   Most new laptops today come with a Wi-Fi radio frequency networking adapter built in. The built-in Wi-Fi adapter will usually have a hidden antenna integrated into the screen lid and a separate switch on the case that enables and disables the adapter. For those laptops without built-in Wi-Fi, a variety of Wi-Fi adapters is available in PC Card, Mini-PCI, CompactFlash (CF), or as an external USB device. We will describe Wi-Fi in more detail in Chapter 13 and talk about configuring a Wi-Fi adapter in Chapter 14.

Cellular WAN   The major cellular telecommunications providers now offer a variety of options for data communications over the cellular networks, but unlike Wi-Fi, they do not usually build cellular adapters into laptops, although several providers bundle their adapter and a contract plan with certain ebooks. Otherwise, if you wish to connect your laptop to the Internet via one of these services, you need to contact a cell provider, sign up for the service, and buy a cellular adapter from that provider. You must be sure the card they offer is of a type (PC Card, CardBus, ExpressCard, etc.) that will work in your laptop. Then install it as you would any device in that format.

Wired Communications

When it comes to wired communications, the choices are the same as those for a desktop PC—dial-up modem and Ethernet. Learn the basics of these networking technologies in Chapter 13 and how to install and configure them in Chapter 14. Most laptops have adapters for both of these built in.

Modem   For those who require a dial-up connection to the Internet, most laptops come with an integrated modem. The only part of the modem visible on the outside of the case is an RJ-11 connector (described in Chapter 3). All you need is a land-based phone line and the services of an ISP. Learn how to configure a dial-up connection in Chapter 14. If the built-in modem fails, you should determine if a replacement modem is available from the manufacturer. You will probably find it is more cost-effective to buy a replacement modem with a USB interface, although this adds the inconvenience of more equipment to pack when traveling and the need to locate the modem and connect it to your laptop.

Ethernet   Most laptops now come with a built-in Ethernet adapter for connecting to a wired network. The only part of a built-in Ethernet adapter visible on the outside of the case is an RJ-45 connector (described in Chapter 3). As with a built-in modem, if your built-in Ethernet adapter fails, you will need to research the replacement options, and you will face the same choice between the higher cost but convenience of an internal replacement versus the lower cost and inconvenience of an external Ethernet adapter.

Power and Electrical Input Devices

Laptops come with two sources of electrical input: an AC adapter for when AC power is available and a built-in battery for when external power is not available. Laptops also have a special power component called the DC controller and a battery to support the CMOS chip.

Laptop Batteries

When not plugged into a wall outlet, a laptop computer gets its power from a special rechargeable battery. The typical laptop today has a *lithium ion (Li-Ion) battery*. You may also run into *Nickel Metal Hydride (NiMH)* batteries in older laptops, or a very old laptop may have a heavy, inefficient, and obsolete *nickel-cadmium (NiCD)* battery. A Li-Ion battery is smaller and lighter than its predecessors and produces more power. These rechargeable batteries have a battery life between recharges in the range of 5 to 8 hours at best. They tend to have only a few years of life, so expect to replace a laptop battery as it approaches two years of age. Replacement batteries can be purchased from the laptop manufacturer or other sources that specialize in laptop parts or batteries. Laptops allow easy access to the battery to change it. In many cases, the battery fits into a compartment on the bottom or on the side of the computer. In this case,

Installing a battery in a compartment on the underside of a laptop

remove the battery compartment's cover, slide the old battery out, and slide the new one in (see Figure 6-7). There may be a release mechanism to let you remove the battery.

The AC adapter recharges the battery, but, if you are not near a wall outlet when the battery's power fades, you will not be able to work until you replace the battery with a fully charged one or until AC power is available again.

Fortunately, most portable systems give you plenty of notice before the battery goes completely dead. Many systems include a power-level meter in the notification area that allows you to see the battery's charge level at all times, whereas others simply give you a visual warning when the battery's power dips below a certain level.

DC Controller

Most laptops include a *DC controller* that monitors and regulates power usage, providing just the correct amount of DC voltage to each internal component. The other features of DC controllers vary by manufacturer, but typically, they provide short-circuit protection, give "low battery" warnings, and can be configured to shut down the computer automatically when the power is low.

AC Adapter

The *AC adapter* (the "brick" or "wall wart") is your laptop's power supply that you plug into an AC power source. Like the power supply in a desktop PC, it converts

FIGURE 6-8

A laptop AC
adapter

AC power to DC power. Figure 6-8 shows an AC adapter for a laptop. If you must replace an external adapter, simply unplug it, and attach a new one that matches the specifications and plug configuration of the adapter it is replacing. Furthermore, since AC adapters have different output voltages, never use one with any laptop other than the one it was made for. Previously, laptop power supplies were *fixed input power supplies* set to accept only one input power voltage. Now, many laptop AC adapters act as *auto-switching power supplies*, detecting the incoming voltage and switching to accept either 120 or 240 VAC.

CMOS Battery

Like a PC, a laptop has a battery on the motherboard that supports the CMOS chip that holds the system's BIOS settings. If a laptop shows signs of a failing CMOS battery—namely losing the date and time when the computer is off and also out of main battery power—you will need to investigate the type and location of battery in the laptop and purchase a replacement. See the information in Chapter 5 on replacing a CMOS battery.

I/O Devices

As with a PC, the primary input devices for a laptop are the keyboard and a pointing device. The primary output device is the display. We will take a closer look at keyboards and other I/O devices designed for portability.

Keyboard

Due to size constraints, the built-in keyboard in a laptop has thinner keys that do not have the vertical travel that those on traditional keyboards do, so they do not give the same tactile feedback. A laptop keyboard has the alphanumeric, ENTER keys, function keys (F1, F2, ... F12), and some of the modifier keys (SHIFT, CTRL, ALT, and CAPS LOCK) in the same orientation to one another as on a full-sized keyboard. But many of the special keys—the directional arrow keys and the INSERT, DELETE, PAGE UP, and PAGE DOWN keys—are in different locations.

A laptop keyboard seldom has the separate numeric keypad that is available on many external keyboards. Rather, the keypad function integrates into the alphanumeric keys, and small numbers on the sides of keys or in a different color on the top of each key indicate what number they are. Each alphanumeric key normally produces two characters—one when pressing the key alone and another when pressing the key with the SHIFT key. Some of these keys have yet a third function, accessed by pressing the FN *(function) key* while pressing the marked keys. This special modifier key enables the alternate functions for a laptop keyboard. Look for special symbols on several laptop keys. For instance, one of the standard function keys may have the symbol of a display screen on it. Pressing the FN key and this key together toggles the video output among the display modes, as described earlier. Another specially marked key on the keyboard is used together with the FN key to enable or disable the speaker.

Laptop keyboards have greatly improved over the last two decades, but for a variety of reasons, users often wish to use an external keyboard. A user who employs the numeric keypad may add an external keyboard or a separate numeric keypad. Some people simply prefer the tactile feel of certain external keyboards, and will add the external keyboard when they are at home. An external keyboard lets you sit farther from the screen.

Like other laptop components, you can replace the built-in laptop keyboard if you can find a suitable replacement. So, if you decide that you must replace a laptop keyboard, and you have determined that it is cost-effective to do so, follow the manufacturer's instructions. Alternatively, you might just decide to use an external keyboard—a very inexpensive alternative since you simply plug it in. The trick is buying a keyboard with the correct connector. Most new laptops have done away with the mini-DIN keyboard connector, and they all now have USB ports—the newer the laptop, the more USB ports it will have. In some portables, plugging in an external keyboard will disable the onboard keyboard, but in others, it stays fully functional with an external keyboard plugged in, or you can manually disable the onboard keyboard per the manufacturer's instructions.

on the job *Anyone who does a great deal of number entry work and feels more comfortable using a more traditional numeric keypad should consider buying a separate one and attaching it to the laptop or desktop PC.*

Pointing Devices

When shopping for a new laptop, you can expect to find a built-in pointing device on all the popular models. After experimenting with a variety of such devices, most manufacturers have settled on the *touchpad* (or *touch pad*), a smooth rectangular panel sitting in front of the keyboard. Moving your finger across the surface of the touchpad moves the pointer on the display, and you use the buttons next to the touchpad as you would use ones on a mouse or trackball. Alternatively, you can tap the touchpad in place of clicking a button.

Other pointing devices you may encounter on laptops are variations of a *pointing stick* (or *point stick*)—a very tiny joystick-type device that usually sits in the center of the keyboard, sometimes between the G, H, and B keys. Barely protruding above the level of the keys, this device usually has a replaceable plastic cap for traction and two buttons located in the front of the keyboard. You operate a pointing stick by pushing it in the direction you want to drive the onscreen pointer. IBM's version of the pointing stick is called *TrackPoint*. Lenovo now owns the IBM laptop and PC business, and you can still see the red-tipped TrackPoint on their laptops. In fact, the entire keyboard on the ThinkPad line is called the TrackPoint keyboard. Many techs use this term generically as *track point*.

Because these devices are small and can be difficult to use, many portable computers allow you to attach a full-sized desktop mouse with a PS 2/mini-DIN connector. In this case, turn off the portable, attach the mouse to the port in the back, and then restart the system. It is not necessary to turn the portable off first if the mouse connects to a USB port. Some portables will automatically disable the onboard pointing device when an external pointing device is connected.

If the installed pointing device, such as a touchpad, fails, replacing it is much like replacing the keyboard because you need to locate a suitable replacement and then open the computer and install it. Consider using an external pointing device if your touchpad fails and the laptop is not still under warranty.

on the job *With the availability of USB devices, it is convenient to add a USB mouse and keyboard to your system, and you can add or remove it as needed. This allows the use of a full-sized keyboard when you are not traveling.*

SCENARIO & SOLUTION

I plug my laptop into a CRT, printer, and keyboard every time I return to the office. Is there an easier way to do this?	Yes. Plug each of these devices into a port replicator and leave them there. To access the devices, simply attach your laptop to the port replicator.
What important step in the disassembly of a laptop will help you the most when you attempt to reassemble it?	Document and label cable and screw locations.
What laptop component allocates just the right amount of DC power to each internal component?	The DC controller.

Speakers

Laptops often come with very small speakers that provide marginally adequate sound. If these speakers fail, you may be able to find suitable replacements, but a better alternative is to plug external speakers into the laptop using either the earphone jack, if that is all that is available, or other audio-out jacks. Replacing internal laptop speakers is nearly as involved as replacing a video adapter, along with all the inherent dangers of opening the laptop. But plugging in external speakers is risk-free, takes only a few seconds, and will improve the sound output. Be sure to test the speakers after replacing or adding them.

CERTIFICATION OBJECTIVE

■ **701: 3.3** *Explain the process and steps to install and configure the Windows OS*

The majority of certification objective 701: 3.3 is detailed in Chapter 9. In this section, we examine a small part of that objective, configuring power management, because power-saving measures are critically important to a laptop user who needs to run on battery for hours at a time.

Power Management

Nearly every component in a modern laptop has some sort of power management feature. Many, like the hard drive, will power down when not in use; CPUs and other circuitry will draw less power when they have less demand for their services.

Displays will power down after a configurable period of time during which there has been no activity from the mouse or keyboard. If a component is not drawing power, it is not creating heat, so power management and cooling go hand-in-hand.

To support the power management features in laptop hardware requires that the system BIOS, the chipset, the operating system, and device drivers be aware of these features and be able to control and manage them. This is called *power management*. Several standards and practices have come together for power management to work at both the hardware and operating system level. They include SMM, APM, and ACPI, described next. You can configure power management through your operating system.

System Management Mode

For over two decades, Intel CPUs have included a group of features called *System Management Mode (SMM)*, and other CPU manufacturers have followed suit. SMM allows a CPU to reduce its speed without losing its place, so to speak, so it does not stop working altogether. In addition, a CPU using SMM mode triggers power savings in other components. System BIOSs and operating systems are upgraded to take advantage of SMM. Intel took the first two steps for involving the BIOS and operating system in power management when they developed two standards, APM and ACPI.

APM

Advanced Power Management (APM) defines four power-usage operating levels: Full On, APM Enabled, APM Standby, and APM Suspend. Details of these operating levels are not important, as they are now a subset of the next standard, ACPI.

ACPI

Advanced Configuration and Power Interface (ACPI) includes all the power-usage levels of APM, plus two more. It also supports the *soft-power* feature described in Chapter 3. ACPI defines how to configure this feature in the BIOS settings. ACPI has seven power-usage levels, called *power states*. These range from G0 Working, a power state in which the computer is fully on and all devices are functional, through several sleeping states to two power off states. The sleeping states include three standby states that involve throttling down components in various combinations and one sleeping state that we call Hibernate, in which the system state and all contents of RAM are saved to disk and then the computer is powered down. The two power off states include G2 Soft Off, which we call the soft power state, and G3 mechanical off, in which the system is completely powered off.

Configuring Power Management in Windows

Getting the most out of your laptop battery depends on how you manage the use of the battery's power. Using the Power Options Control Panel applet in Windows, you can configure the ACPI-compliant settings to minimize the power usage of laptop components.

Using Power-Saving Modes

Imagine you are a business traveler waiting to board a commercial jet. You arrive at the airport and find yourself at the departure gate with 90 minutes to spare. Is this wasted time? No. You open your laptop, complete a report on your trip, and begin to create an expense request. You are not quite finished with it when it is time to board. Rather than completely shutting down your computer, you put it into a sleep mode that will preserve your open files just as they are, slip the machine into your carry-on case, and board the plane. Once settled in your seat, you open your laptop and within seconds you are back where you left off. The actual sleep mode you select, and what it does, depends on the version of Windows you are running. You can also set the *sleep timer,* which maintains the time period for mouse and keyboard inactivity that must pass before the computer goes into power-saving mode. There are many power-saving options available to you in Windows; we will explore just a few of them here and look at more options when we talk about installing and configuring Windows in Chapter 9.

Hibernate   The *Hibernate* sleep mode uses hard drive space to save all the programs and data that are in memory at the time you choose this mode. The computer then completely shuts down, using no power while it is hibernating. Like Standby, Hibernate lets you stop work on your computer but quickly pick up where you left off. It takes slightly longer to go into and out of hibernation. In Windows XP, configure Hibernate mode from the Hibernate tab of the Power Options applet; simply click to place a check in the box next to Enable Hibernate. Now Hibernate will appear at the bottom of the Power Schemes page in place of Standby and as an option under the Power button settings on the Advanced page of the Power Options applet (see Figure 6-9).

Standby/Sleep   Before Windows Vista, you would select *Standby* to save your desktop and all open files in RAM memory in a working state. In this state, the computer appears to be off, and when you wish to resume, you simply press the power button. Your desktop either appears immediately, or after you log on if your computer is configured to require a logon. Standby requires a power source to be available, so when the laptop is running on a battery and the battery runs out of power,

Use the Advanced
tab in Windows
XP to select
power-saving
settings.

any data saved for Standby mode but not saved to disk will be lost. Configure Standby
from the Power Schemes tab in Windows XP Power Options. Once configured, the
system will go into standby after the time-period defined by the sleep timer or when
you select Standby from the Shutdown menu.

Standby underwent a few changes beginning with Windows Vista. Standby is
renamed Sleep, and there is a new sleep state called Hybrid Sleep that combines the
Sleep state with Hibernate, saving contents of memory into RAM as well as to disk.
Hybrid sleep is turned off by default on mobile PCs. You will find these options by
first opening Control Panel, selecting System and Maintenance, and opening the
Power Options applet.

Configuring Low Battery Options

Most laptops will let you know when your battery is low, and Windows allows you to
configure an alarm notification when the battery is low, and when it is critically low.
Windows' default low battery level is 10 percent of remaining battery life, whereas
8 percent remaining battery life is the default critical level. You may change either
or both of these settings, and you may define a warning action for each.

A smart configuration will issue a warning sound for low and for critical and
place the computer into Standby or Hibernate (better choice) when the critical
level is reached.

SCENARIO & SOLUTION

I use my laptop at work, carrying it with me from meeting to meeting in order to take notes. How can I avoid the hassle of waiting for it to power up at the beginning of each meeting?	Select Standby when you power down.
When traveling, I would like to save all my work and the desktop when I shut down, and have the laptop start up with my work state exactly as it was when I stopped. How do I achieve this, plus conserve as much battery life as possible?	Enable Hibernate in the Power Options applet in Control Panel, and then when you are ready, select Hibernate from the Turn Off Computer dialog box.
How do I get my laptop to alert me with an audio alarm when the battery gets to 12 percent battery life?	Open the Power Options applet, select the Alarms tab, and ensure that a checkmark appears in the box under Low Battery Alarm. Position the slider at 12 percent. Click the Alarm Action button and place a checkmark in the Sound Alarm box.

CERTIFICATION SUMMARY

Most PC technicians will need to understand laptop technologies because use of these portable computers is widespread—both in the workplace and in the home. Laptops come in many sizes, from the very lightweight ultra-portables or Netbooks to much heavier desktop replacements.

Although laptops are basically compatible with the Intel/IBM-compatible architecture, they use smaller integrated components that do not conform in either form or size with the standard PC components.

✓ TWO-MINUTE DRILL

Here are some of the key points covered in Chapter 6.

Introduction to Laptops

❑ A portable computer is any type of computer you can easily transport and that has an all-in-one component layout.

❑ A laptop (or notebook or Netbook) computer is a small, easily transported computer that can run the same operating systems as a desktop PC, with an integrated display in a hinged top.

❑ A handheld computer fits in the palm of the hand and runs a specialized operating system and applications.

Installing and Upgrading Laptops

❑ Internal and integrated laptop hardware, such as the display, keyboard, pointing device, motherboard, memory, hard drives, and expansion bus, has special scaled-down form factors, but can use most standard PC peripherals.

❑ Your laptop disassembly and reassembly processes should include consulting the manufacturer's documentation, using appropriate hand tools, organizing parts, and documenting and labeling cable and screw locations.

❑ Although laptop components are at least partially proprietary, you can find replacement parts from the original manufacturer or from other sources. Always research the cost-effectiveness of replacing parts rather than replacing the entire laptop.

❑ The types of parts you can replace in a laptop include just about every component that makes up the laptop.

❑ You add memory to a laptop in the form of SODIMM modules installed into slots inside the case. You can also add it in the form of a PC Card, CardBus, or ExpressCard.

❑ Port replicators and docking stations provide permanent connections for external devices used in the laptop user's office. Universal docking stations and port replicators have USB interfaces and, therefore, connect in the same manner as other USB devices.

❑ Some laptops have a media/accessory bay holding a single device that you can switch with another device that fits in the bay.

❏ Laptops contain specialized expansion slots, such as PC Card, CardBus, ExpressCard, Mini PCI, and PCIe Mini Card.

❏ Laptops often come with built-in communications adapters—including Wi-Fi and Ethernet for LAN connections, IrDA infrared and Bluetooth for short-distance wireless communications, and modems for dial-up connections. You can add a cellular adapter to a laptop.

❏ A laptop comes with two sources of electrical power: a rechargeable battery and an AC adapter.

❏ PC Card, CardBus, or ExpressCard cards can be easily inserted into the proper slot without opening the laptop.

❏ Internal expansion slots in laptops take either Mini PCI cards (in older laptops) or PCIe Mini Cards in newer laptops.

❏ Laptops allow you to change the battery easily.

❏ Most standard peripherals connect to a laptop using the same techniques used for desktop PCs.

❏ You can install and remove hot-swappable devices while a computer is up and running.

❏ Although non-hot-swappable devices may still be plug and play, you cannot remove or install them while the computer is powered on.

Power Management

❏ You can configure laptops that comply with the ACPI power management standards through the operating system to shut down the display, the hard drive, and even the entire system after a period of inactivity and/or when the battery is low.

❏ Hibernate is a Windows sleep state that uses hard drive space to save all the programs and data that are in memory at the time you choose this mode. The computer then completely shuts down and requires no power while it is hibernating.

❏ In Windows XP, Standby is a sleep state that conserves power while saving your desktop in RAM memory in a work state; it requires a minimum amount of power. Beginning in Windows Vista, this mode is called Sleep and there is also a third sleep state that is a hybrid of Standby and Hibernate called Hybrid Sleep.

SELF TEST

The following questions will help you measure your understanding of the material presented in this chapter. Read all of the choices carefully because there might be more than one correct answer. Choose all correct answers for each question.

Introduction to Laptops

1. What are the two broad categories of portable computers?
   A. LCDs
   B. Handhelds
   C. Laptops
   D. PC Cards

2. Some specialized handhelds used for retail inventory counts have this device built in for data collection.
   A. Pager
   B. PDA
   C. Bar code reader
   D. Headphone

3. What built-in component allows laptop use for short periods without an outside power source?
   A. Keyboard
   B. Touchpad
   C. Pointing stick
   D. Battery

Installing and Upgrading Laptops

4. A replacement motherboard must match the form factor of the one being replaced and which of the following?
   A. Weight
   B. Manufacturer
   C. Serial number
   D. Electrical and mechanical connections

5. CPUs for laptops have special power-saving and heat-reducing features, and some have support for which of the following?

A. Wi-Fi

B. Video

C. Audio

D. Ethernet

6. Which is a laptop component used to convert the DC power from the power adapter or battery to the AC power required by the LCD display?

A. Inverter

B. Converter

C. Power switch

D. Generator

7. What is the most common laptop memory module?

A. SORIMM

B. MicroDIMM

C. SODIMM

D. DIMM

8. Which is a common size for a laptop hard drive?

A. 2.5"

B. 5"

C. 3.5"

D. 1"

9. Which of the following allows you to attach nearly any type of desktop component to a portable computer?

A. Port replicator

B. Enhanced port replicator

C. Extended port replicator

D. Docking station

10. Select the two names for a compartment in some laptops that can hold a media device (secondary hard drive, optical drive, floppy drive, etc.) that you can swap with another device.

A. Slot

B. Media bay

C. USB port

D. Accessory bay

11. What organization has produced standards commonly used for laptop expansion slots?
   A. IEEE
   B. Intel
   C. AMD
   D. PCMCIA

12. What two card standards come in types labeled Type I, Type II, and Type III?
   A. PC Card
   B. CardBus
   C. ExpressCard
   D. PCIe Mini Card

13. Which two wireless communications standards are used between a laptop and nearby devices that are within one meter of the computer?
   A. Cellular
   B. Wi-Fi
   C. Bluetooth
   D. Infrared

14. A battery type commonly used in recently built laptops.
   A. Lithium ion
   B. AC adapter
   C. DC controller
   D. Nickel Metal Hydride

15. This group of keys, usually in a separate area of a desktop keyboard, is often integrated into the alphanumeric keys on a laptop keyboard.
   A. Function keys
   B. Directional arrow keys
   C. Numeric keys
   D. Numeric keypad

16. What are two types of built-in pointing devices often found on laptops?
   A. Trackball
   B. Pointing stick
   C. Keyboard
   D. Touchpad

17. Where in Windows can you configure a low battery alarm for a laptop?

A. Power Options in Control Panel

B. System Properties in Control Panel

C. Battery Options in Control Panel

D. BIOS setup

18. What is the name for system memory used by the video adapter and, therefore, unavailable to the operating system?

A. VRAM memory

B. SODIMM memory

C. Shared video memory

D. SRAM memory

19. What is the term that describes a device you can safely install and remove while a computer is up and running?

A. Plug and play

B. Hot-swappable

C. Stoppable

D. Removable

Power Management

20. What is the new power state introduced in Windows Vista that combines Sleep and Hibernate?

A. Standby

B. Standby Hibernate

C. Hybrid Sleep

D. Vista Sleep

SELF TEST ANSWERS

Introduction to Laptops

1. ☑ **B** and **C.** Handhelds and laptops are correct because these are the two main categories of portable computers.

   ☒ **A,** LCDs, is incorrect because LCDs are a type of display screen, not a category of portable computers. **D,** PC Cards, is incorrect because these cards plug into special slots in a laptop and are not a category of portable computers.

2. ☑ **C,** bar code reader, is the type of device built into specialized handheld devices used for retail inventory counts.
   ☒ **A,** pager, **B,** PDA, and **D,** headphone, are incorrect because none of these would be a device on a handheld used for data collection.

3. ☑ **D,** battery, is correct because it provides power to the laptop when not plugged into AC power.
   ☒ **A,** keyboard, **B,** touchpad, and **C,** pointing stick, are all incorrect because, although they may be built into a laptop, they do not make it possible for a laptop to be used for short periods without an outside power source.

Installing and Upgrading Laptops

4. ☑ **D.** Electrical and mechanical connections must be matched when replacing a laptop motherboard.
   ☒ **A,** weight, is incorrect because weight is irrelevant in selecting a replacement motherboard. **B,** manufacturer, is incorrect because replacement motherboards are available from many manufacturers. **C,** serial number, is incorrect because even the exact model motherboard from the same manufacturer will have a unique serial number.

5. ☑ **A** is correct, as some mobile CPUs have support for Wi-Fi.
   ☒ **B,** video, **C,** audio, and **D,** Ethernet, are all incorrect because they are not integrated into CPUs, but included in other components.

6. ☑ **A.** Inverter is correct. This component converts DC power to the AC power required by an LCD panel.
   ☒ **B,** converter, is incorrect because a converter does just the opposite, converting AC power to DC power. **C,** power switch, is incorrect because the power switch simply turns the main power to the laptop on and off. **D,** generator, is incorrect because this is not a component of a laptop. A generator generates power using an engine powered by fuel such as gasoline or diesel.

7. ☑ **C,** SODIMM, is correct because this is the most common memory module. SODIMM is a scaled-down version of the DIMM memory module.

☒   **A,** SORIMM, is incorrect because, although this is a type of memory module for laptops, it is less commonly used. **B,** MicroDIMM, is incorrect because this module is half the size of SODIMM and is used in handheld computers. **D,** DIMM, is incorrect because this is a full-sized memory module for desktop PCs.

8. ☑   **A,** 2.5", is correct because this is the most common size of a laptop hard drive.
    ☒   **B,** 5", is incorrect because this very large size is not used in laptops. **C,** 3.5", is incorrect because this is also a large size that is not used in laptops but is common in desktop PCs. **D,** 1", is incorrect (at this writing) because it is not a size commonly used in laptops, and if it is available at all at this time, it would physically not have sufficient data capacity.

9. ☑   **D.** A docking station allows you to attach nearly any type of desktop component to a portable computer. The docking station can remain on the desk with all the desired devices installed or plugged into it. To access these devices, simply plug the portable into the docking station.
    ☒   **A,** port replicator, and **B,** enhanced port replicator, are incorrect because they do not allow access to the number and variety of devices that a docking station does. **C,** extended port replicator, is incorrect because this is not a real type of portable system component.

10. ☑   **B and D.** Media bay and accessory bay are the correct names for the compartment some laptops have for swapping between one device and another.
    A, slot, is incorrect because that is the socket a circuit card plugs into. **C,** USB port, is incorrect because it is what a USB cable plugs into.

11. ☑   **D.** PCMCIA is correct because the Personal Computer Memory Card International Association has developed the most commonly used laptop expansion slot standards.
    ☒   **A,** IEEE, is incorrect because, although this organization does create standards, they have not produced standards commonly used for laptop expansion slots. **B,** Intel, and **C,** AMD, are incorrect because they are CPU manufacturers, not standards organizations.

12. ☑   **A and B.** PC Card and CardBus are the two card standards that come in types labeled Type I, Type II, and Type III.
    ☒   **C,** ExpressCard, and **D,** PCIe Mini, are incorrect because they are entirely different form factors from the cards that are labeled Type I, Type II, and Type III.

13. ☑   **C and D.** Bluetooth and infrared are two wireless communications standards used between a laptop and nearby devices that are within one meter of the computer.
    ☒   **A,** cellular, is incorrect because this is technology that can be used to connect a laptop to the Internet. **B,** Wi-Fi, is incorrect because this technology connects a laptop to a local area network (LAN).

14. ☑   **A.** Lithium ion is the battery type commonly used in recently built laptops.
    ☒   **B,** AC adapter, is incorrect because this is the laptop's power supply that plugs into an AC power source. **C,** DC controller, is incorrect because this is not a battery type but a laptop component that monitors and regulates power usage. **D,** Nickel Metal Hydride, is incorrect because this type of battery is more common in older laptops.

15. ☑ **D.** Numeric keypad is correct because this group of keys often integrates into the alphanumeric keys in order to save space.

    ☒ **A,** function keys, is incorrect because these are usually in their normal position across the top of the keyboard. **B,** directional arrow keys, is incorrect because these are often (but not always) separate on the laptop keyboard. **C,** numeric keys, is incorrect because these are usually in their normal position in the row immediately below the function keys.

16. ☑ **B and D.** Pointing stick and touchpad are two types of built-in pointing devices often found on laptops.

    ☒ **A,** trackball, is incorrect because, although it is sometimes built into a laptop, the pointing stick and touchpad are used more often. **C,** keyboard, is incorrect because, although this is an input device, it is not a pointing device.

17. ☑ **A.** Power Options in Control Panel is the location where you can configure a low battery alarm for a laptop.

    ☒ **B,** System Properties in Control Panel, is incorrect because you cannot configure a low battery alarm here. **C,** Battery Options, is incorrect because there is no such applet in standard Windows. **D,** BIOS setup, is incorrect because BIOS setup is not in Windows, but at the system level of the computer.

18. ☑ **C.** Shared video memory is the name for system memory used by the video adapter and, therefore, unavailable to the operating system.

    ☒ **A,** VRAM memory, is incorrect because this type of memory is installed on a video adapter (Chapter 2). A video adapter with VRAM installed does not need to use system memory. **B,** SODIMM memory, is incorrect because, although this is the physical memory module used in most laptops, the portion of this memory used by the video adapter is what we are looking for. **D,** SRAM memory, is incorrect because this type of RAM is used only for cache memory.

19. ☑ **B.** Hot-swappable is the term that describes a device that you can safely install and remove while a computer is up and running.

    ☒ **A,** plug and play, is incorrect, although hot-swappable devices are also plug and play. **C,** stoppable, is incorrect because this is not the correct term, although you can stop many devices in Windows. **D,** removable, is incorrect because this term does not fully describe the ability in the question.

Power Management

20. ☑ **C.** Hybrid Sleep is the new power state introduced in Windows Vista.

    ☒ **A,** Standby, is incorrect because this is the name used in previous versions of Windows for the Windows Vista Sleep state. **B,** Standby Hibernate, and **D,** Vista Sleep, are incorrect because these are not names used for power states in Vista.

7

Troubleshooting and Preventive Maintenance for Laptops

CERTIFICATION OBJECTIVES

❑ **701: 2.4** Given a scenario, explain and interpret common laptop issues and determine the appropriate basic troubleshooting method

❑ **702: 1.3** Given a scenario, install, configure, detect programs, troubleshoot, and repair/replace laptop components

✓ Two-Minute Drill

Q&A Self Test

As with desktop computers, the most common procedures computer technicians perform on laptops are troubleshooting and resolving problems. Understanding the technologies of PCs in general, as well as troubleshooting theory, diagnostic techniques, procedures, and use of tools, are all required to work with laptop computers. These were presented in earlier chapters, and Chapter 6 described the components installed in laptops and how to repair or replace many laptop components. In this chapter, you will explore how to detect and troubleshoot problems related to laptops.

CERTIFICATION OBJECTIVES

- **701: 2.4** *Given a scenario, explain and interpret common laptop issues and determine the appropriate basic troubleshooting method*

- **702: 1.3** *Given a scenario, install, configure, detect problems, troubleshoot, and repair/replace laptop components*

CompTIA expects you to understand and apply your knowledge of troubleshooting theory and techniques to laptops. Whereas this chapter incorporates all the objectives of 701:2.4, we detailed most of the objectives for 702:1.3 in Chapter 6 by describing how to replace and repair components. This chapter completes our coverage of the objectives for troubleshooting laptop issues so you can home in on the problem component.

Troubleshooting Laptops

Laptops are much more difficult and costly to repair than desktop PCs. To make matters worse, they are also much more likely to need repairs because they get in harm's way much more often than the typical desktop computer. The busy traveler can easily drop one, bang it into things, and so on, all of which can cause damage. When it comes to troubleshooting laptops, you will use the same skills and procedures you learned in Chapter 5. In addition to the problem areas detailed there, this section examines the laptop-specific problems you may encounter when working with AC adapters and batteries, displays, input devices, and built-in wireless adapters.

Power Problems

Laptops are vulnerable to the same power problems that plague desktop PCs, but they are susceptible to a group of problems unique to laptops involving rechargeable batteries and the external AC power adapters that help put the portability into laptops.

AC Adapter Power Problems

AC adapter problems fall into two areas: damage or failure of the original AC adapter, and damage to the computer due to use of the wrong AC adapter. To understand these problems, we will first consider the requirements for the correct AC adapter in terms of voltage, amperage, and polarity, and then look at power-related problem scenarios.

Never, under any circumstances, casually substitute another AC adapter for the one that came with your laptop unless you are sure it will not harm your computer. The most important features you are looking for are the DC input voltage, amperage, and polarity requirements.

DC input requirements may be in the neighborhood of 19.5 volts and 2.15 amps. Labels on the laptop and the AC adapter show the positive or negative polarity of the laptop power connector, which must be compatible with the polarity of the connector on the AC adapter's plug (see Figure 7-1).

Now look for a label on the AC adapter, and ensure that the output from this device, and the polarity of its connector, match those of the laptop (see Figure 7-2). Connecting an adapter that does not meet the laptop's requirements will damage the laptop. Depending on just which parameter is wrong, you may destroy the laptop's power components or the laptop motherboard and its components.

Some power adapters include an automatic circuit breaker that trips when it detects an input power overload. This breaker works just like the circuit breaker in your home; you need to reset it before it allows power through again. With some

The laptop power connector is labeled for polarity.

AC adapters, you do this simply by unplugging the adapter for a few minutes before reconnecting it. Some laptops have a reset button that you may use. If so, follow the instructions, which may include unplugging the power cord from the laptop and removing the laptop's battery before resetting.

Recall that the AC adapter converts the AC input from the wall outlet to DC current, and the DC controller monitors and regulates the power usage, allocating the correct voltage (typically 5 volts, 12 volts, or 3.3 volts) to the various internal components. Power to the LCD display is handled separately, using an inverter to convert the DC input to the AC power required by the display, as described in Chapter 6. Therefore, if you believe power has failed to the LCD display, but you can hear the fan running in the main system, you will focus on how power gets to the display and troubleshoot the inverter and power connectors between the main system and the display.

Hardware Power Switch Issues

Do not assume that pressing the power button on a laptop (or desktop PC, for that matter) automatically turns it off. One of the many configuration options available through Windows' Power Options is a setting for what occurs when you press the power button. In Windows XP, the choices are Do Nothing, Ask Me What To Do, Standby, and Shut Down. Hibernate replaces Standby if you have enabled Hibernate. Beginning in Windows Vista, the choices are Do Nothing, Sleep, Hibernate, or Shut Down. Imagine how each of these settings might confuse an unwary laptop user. For instance, if the power button puts the laptop into a sleep mode (other than Hibernate), the laptop is not truly powered down and still requires battery power. In some laptops, this situation comes to light when a user complains that the laptop is warm, even when turned off, especially if it is in a carrying case. Ask this user whether he is simply pressing the power off button and what he sees when he does press it. If he sees a message about preparing for Standby or Sleep, then his laptop is not configured to shut down when the power button is pressed.

Someone who is on the go all day, needing to access her laptop quickly between visits to clients, will prefer having the power button configured for a sleep mode. This user must learn that this state still requires power, however, and if she is running the laptop on battery power alone, she should watch the battery level and be sure to plug the laptop in to recharge the battery when it gets low. Learn about the Battery Alarms in the next section.

Battery Problems

Like the average car owner, the typical laptop owner doesn't worry much about the battery until it becomes a problem. On a daily basis, that means watching the battery indicator and recharging the battery when it gets low. To help you keep track of the battery level, turn on and configure the Battery Alarms, as described in Chapter 6. You can set an action for each of these alarms, such as sounding an alarm, displaying a message, putting the computer into a power-saving mode, shutting it down, or having it run a program before shutting down. You can use most of these options together, with the exception of the choice of a sleep mode or shut down.

Another way to track the battery level is by using the Power Meter normally appearing in the System Tray on a laptop. You can turn this feature on or off in the Power Options applet. Power Meter shows the power state. It will show a power plug when the computer is running on AC power and a battery-shaped meter when it is running on battery.

When you believe the laptop has a battery problem, first make sure the battery is inserted properly and is charging. A rechargeable battery has a limited lifetime, beyond which its ability to hold a charge diminishes until it cannot hold a charge at all. In this case, the Power Meter page in Power Options may show a Not Present status, even when a battery is physically present. If a battery fails to fully charge and is about two years old or older, you may need to replace it.

If a newer battery fails, check your warranty or extended warranty, which will cover a laptop battery for a longer period than the standard warranty. You may be entitled to a replacement battery from the manufacturer. If the battery is one that has only two or three connections, you can test it with a multimeter set to read DC volts. A reading much less than the battery rating probably indicates a bad battery. Unfortunately, many laptop batteries have multiple power connectors and no guidance as to which connectors should provide what power, so testing them can be difficult. Sometimes the laptop's manual will indicate the voltages at the various terminals, but not always. If you determine that a battery has failed, replace it as described in Chapter 6.

Power-Related Scenarios

Understanding the basics of AC adapters and batteries will serve you well when faced with symptoms pointing to power problems. The most obvious is when the laptop will not power up. As you learned in Chapter 5, you should always approach troubleshooting systematically, and be sure you observe all the symptoms.

If a laptop will not power up at all when plugged into an AC power source, suspect the AC power adapter. But before you go down that road, first ask, "What has changed since it last successfully started up?" If the hardware has changed, then remove any new hardware devices installed since the laptop last started up normally. This is especially true of memory modules.

If the laptop starts up after removing any new hardware, then check with the manufacturer of the new hardware and/or with the manufacturer of the laptop. The hardware may be incompatible with the laptop.

If no new hardware was added since the last time the laptop started up normally, check out one of the usual suspects: an external display unit. Do you hear normal fan sounds from your laptop? If you are using an external display, keyboard, and mouse with the laptop screen toggled off, the computer may be powering up, but because no image appears on the external display, you may have jumped to the conclusion that the computer failed. Troubleshoot the display by asking these questions:

- Is it simply in a sleep mode?
- Is it turned off?
- Is the contrast or brightness control set too dark?
- Is it connected? Is it powered up?
- Is the display mode switch set to an external display?

If you are using the laptop's integrated display, use similar questions to eliminate it as the problem area.

If you have eliminated new hardware or display problems, continue through the following list of actions until you have either found the source of the problem or resolved it and the computer starts normally:

- Make sure the AC adapter is the one that came with your computer. Using the wrong AC adapter can damage your laptop or other device.
- An AC adapter may (but not always) have an LED indicator light to show that it is receiving power. Check for this light on the adapter as a way to verify it is receiving AC power from the power source.

■ Check that the adapter is securely plugged into the laptop, connected directly to a working power outlet (without an extension cord or other device while troubleshooting), and that the power switch is turned on. Check the power indicator light on the laptop to see that it is receiving power.

■ If the laptop worked when connected directly to a power outlet, but was previously plugged into a power strip or a power protection device, such as a surge protector, SPS, or UPS, troubleshoot that device. Ensure it too is plugged in and the power to this device is turned on. If the circuit breaker in a power strip has tripped, you may need to reset it. After resolving a problem with the device, reconnect the laptop and test again.

■ Make sure power cords show no sign of damage. If there is, replace the cord or the entire device if the cable is not removable.

■ Another way to verify that your AC adapter is or is not working is to swap it with another identical power supply. If the laptop works with the swapped AC adapter, then you have isolated the problem to the AC adapter.

■ Use a multimeter and test the computer end of the AC adapter cable to check the output that the computer is receiving. It should be producing the DC voltage specified on the label or very close to it (see Exercise 7-1 and Figure 7-3).

■ In order to protect itself and the computer, an AC adapter may turn itself off after detecting a power overage. This depends on the AC adapter's design. Check your user manual for how to reset the AC adapter.

■ If you suspect the power outlet is bad, test it simply by plugging in another device, such as a lamp. You may also check it with a multimeter by inserting the probes into the socket and checking the voltage. Typical voltage in the United States is 110–130 VAC (see Figure 7-4).

■ If you have not been able to isolate the problem after performing the preceding checks, disconnect the AC adapter and remove the battery. Wait an entire minute, reinstall the battery, reconnect the AC adapter, and then turn on the power and see if the laptop starts up.

e**x**a**m**

ⓦatch   *Be sure you practice with a multimeter before taking the A+ exams.*

■ If it still fails to start up, disconnect the AC adapter and remove the battery. Leave the battery out but close the compartment door if there is one, reconnect the AC adapter to both the laptop and the power outlet, and try to start the computer again.

A multimeter
testing the power
from the input
line to the AC
adapter

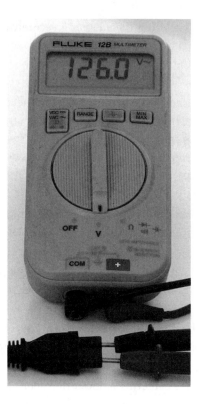

EXERCISE 7-1

Using a Multimeter to Test an AC Adapter

In this exercise, you will verify the DC power output of an AC adapter. For this exercise, you will need a multimeter and an AC adapter with a single plug on the computer end.

1. Unplug the AC adapter from the laptop, but leave it plugged into the wall outlet.

2. Examine the label on the AC adapter and write down the voltage output. Note the polarity and which is positive and negative: the tip of the plug versus the outside of the plug.

3. Set the multimeter to "Volts DC."

FIGURE 7-4

A multimeter
testing the output
of an AC adapter

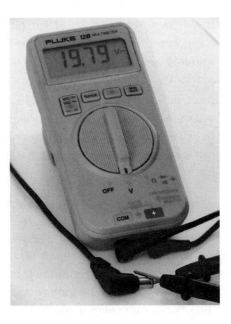

4. Place the positive probe on the positive portion of the plug and the negative probe on the negative portion of the probe (see Figure 7-4).

5. The voltage should be close to that shown in the AC adapter label or just one or two volts more.

Other Startup Problems

A laptop can fail at startup for reasons other than loss of power. Failure can be due to a variety of causes, including both hardware- and software-related. In this section, we will look at hardware errors, limiting our examination of software errors to those errors related to BIOS Setup. Learn about startup problems related to Windows operating systems in Chapter 9.

Laptop Fails at Startup

When a laptop fails at startup, take the following steps:

1. If you have added a new peripheral, remove the peripheral.

2. If you have eliminated power as a problem, remove all unneeded peripherals and add them back one at a time, attempting to restart after each addition.

3. If you cannot isolate the problem, the motherboard or one of its integrated components may be failing. Laptops are not user-serviceable. Check your warranty to see if the suspected component is still under warranty. If you purchased an extended warranty that is still in effect, this is the time to use it.

4. If you do not have a warranty in effect, but have a problem that persists that you cannot solve, check with the manufacturer. The easiest way to do this is to locate its Website and research problems associated with your laptop. You may discover your laptop is part of a recall involving the component that has failed.

on the
job

Although we emphasize that you should have a laptop serviced by the manu-facturer or authorized service center, it is not always practical to do so. If your laptop does not have a warranty, and you feel it is worth the extra effort, check out local or Web-based repair services. Some businesses even specialize in replacement LCD panels for many laptop models. If you choose to go this route, know that there are no guarantees the repair will be worth the cost or it will be successful, especially if you choose to do the repair yourself.

Laptop Fails During POST

If Windows fails to start and a text-mode screen displays, do not panic. The power-on self-test (POST) detected a problem. Simply read the information on the screen and follow any instructions. In the example shown in Figure 7-5, the BIOS hardware monitor found a problem, and the message on the error screen directs you to enter the Power setup menu to see the details. Perhaps the hardware monitor detected a high temperature in the CPU or motherboard, which can indicate a failing cooling fan that is allowing the system to overheat.

on the
job

This scenario can also occur on a desktop PC.

Video Problems

When a laptop LCD display fails, first assure yourself that it is not a power problem (see the preceding section), and then eliminate the simple causes:

■ Move the mouse or press a key on the keyboard to ensure the computer is not simply in a power-saving state that has turned off the monitor.

An error
detected during
the POST

```
BIOS v10.0
Copyright (c) 1984-2006

ACPI BIOS Revision 1205

Intel (R) Pentium 4 3000 MHz
Memory Test: 524288K OK

BIOS Extension V2.0A
Initialize Plug and Play Cards...
PNP Init Completed

Detecting Primary Master ...    MaxDrive 5D090H5
Detecting Primary Slave ...     None
Detecting Secondary Master ... DVD-RW
Detecting Secondary Slave ...  CD-RW

Hardware Monitor found an error. Enter Power setup menu for details

Press F1 to continue, F2 to enter SETUP
```

■ Is the laptop switched to external display only? If you have an external monitor connected, press the FN key while also pressing the function key that doubles as the DISPLAY MODE toggle key, as described in Chapter 6. Sometimes called the "LCD cutoff switch," you press this key combination once and wait a second to see if it makes a difference. If not, press again and wait to see if the display turns on.

Once you have eliminated simple causes, check for the following problems.

Damaged Wiring

The wires for a laptop LCD panel must pass through the hinge of the lid and are subject to a great deal of flexing. Therefore, in some cases, the wiring comes loose at this point. Loose wires can cause a dim or blank display. Manufacturers of conventional laptops have generally solved the wire-through-the-hinge problem, but some Tablet PCs still have issues with this. The hinge on a Tablet PC is more complex than on a standard laptop, because it must allow the lid to both open and rotate into "tablet" position covering the keyboard so the user can hold the PC like a physical clipboard. The manufacturer, or a qualified repair center, must correct these problems.

Temperature Problems

Is the laptop operating in a very hot or very cold room? The liquid crystal material within an LCD panel is sensitive to extremes of hot and cold. If a display that is exposed to temperature extremes goes blank, move the laptop to a heated or air-conditioned room with a moderate temperature and wait an hour before trying it again. If the display appears to work correctly after adjusting the temperature, take steps to avoid the problem in the future.

If you must transport a laptop in extremely cold or extremely hot conditions, do not power it up until you can place it in a room with a moderate temperature and allow it to warm up or cool down.

If you must use a laptop in an inhospitable environment with temperature extremes, consider running it with an external CRT display, which is not as susceptible to problems from temperature extremes as is an LCD display. With the display mode set to external only, you will not have to deal with the display problems. However, prolonged exposure to temperature extremes may permanently damage the laptop display.

Backlight Problems

The backlight in a laptop LCD screen consists of several components. These include Cold Cathode Fluorescent Lighting (CCFL) tubes, positioned at the top, sides, and sometimes behind the screen, and a white diffusion panel behind the LCD that scatters the light evenly. The fluorescent tubes are thinner than a pencil and very fragile. For this reason, if you handle a laptop roughly or drop it, one or more of these tubes can break, causing the display to dim or go totally dark if all the tubes break. Replacing a fluorescent tube is a very difficult task; you also face the task of removing the broken tubes, which may contain mercury or other heavy metal that is equally dangerous to work with. For this reason, we do not recommend that anyone but a highly trained technician take on this task.

Pixilation Problems

Most laptops now use active matrix LCD screens, described in Chapter 3, and therefore have special pixilation problems related to the LCD technology. These screens have three transistors per pixel, one transistor each for red, green, and blue. The transistors turn on and off to create a combination of colors. When a transistor turns off permanently (not by design, but through failure), it shows as a dark spot on the screen called a *dead pixel*. Another, nearly opposite problem is a *lit pixel* (also called a *stuck pixel*). This occurs when a transistor is permanently turned on, causing the pixel to constantly show as red, green, or blue. When pixels contiguous to each other are all in this lit-pixel state, they show as the color derived from their combination.

on the job

Before you decide you have a defective LCD panel, be sure to wipe it clean with a soft, antistatic cloth.

You may have bad or lit pixels on your LCD display without noticing it because the dead pixels are not visible when displaying an image with dark colors in the defective area, and lit pixels may not show when displaying an image showing the colors that result from the dark pixels. A few defective pixels are normal; it is nearly impossible to find an LCD panel without some. It becomes a problem if many bad pixels are located together that cause the image to be distorted or unreadable. To test for dead or lit pixels, you need to configure the desktop with a plain white background, close all windows, and configure the Taskbar so it hides. This will give you a completely empty, white screen. Now examine the screen, looking for areas that are not white. These may appear as the tiniest dot, about the size of a mark made by a fine-point pen on paper. Black dots indicate dead pixels, whereas any other color indicates a lit pixel. You will need to determine if the number you find is acceptable and what, if any, actions you will take.

Video Adapter Problems

The easiest way to test a laptop's integrated video adapter is to plug in an external display and see if it works. Plug it in, power it up, and wait a minute. If nothing appears on the screen, press the FN key and the DISPLAY MODE toggle key. If you have the same problems with the external display, then you have isolated the problem to the video adapter. Check your warranty to see if this problem is covered. If it is covered, then take the steps to have the laptop serviced by the manufacturer or an authorized repair site. If not covered by warranty, you must decide whether the laptop is worth taking it to a repair center at your or your company's expense or whether you want to attempt to replace it. See the discussion on replacing a video adapter in Chapter 6.

Input Devices

If you have problems with an external mouse, refer back to Chapter 5, where we described some common problems and solutions. The specialized laptop input devices, such as touchpads, digitizers, and the integrated keyboard, can have certain problems described here.

Touchpad

Touchpad problems fall into two categories: problems with touchpad functionality and problems with accidental use of the touchpad.

Problems with Touchpad Functionality   Sometimes the touchpad will fail to work, or touchpad control of the pointer will become erratic. In these cases, restart the computer and try again. Rebooting often takes care of the problem. If it occurs frequently, make note of the application software in use at the time. The software may be incompatible with the touchpad driver and the application. Check the laptop manufacturer's Website for any updates to the touchpad driver.

Problems with Accidental Use of the Touchpad   The touchpads on laptops cause problems for some users who cannot seem to avoid unintentionally resting their hands on the touchpad or brushing their hands or fingers over it when using the keyboard. This can cause a variety of problems, depending on what application is open and has the focus at the time. For instance, while the user is typing in a document, the pointer may suddenly jump to another part of the page, and it will insert the typed text where it does not belong. Or it may overwrite or delete text, or applications may open or close without the user intending them to. The result is confusing to the user who is not aware of touching the touchpad.

Check the Mouse applet in Control Panel, which opens the Mouse Properties dialog box. On a laptop with a touchpad, this should include settings to control how the touchpad works. Check for a setting that controls the sensitivity of the touchpad, so it does not respond to light, accidental contact. You may find one such setting under a Tapping tab in a section labeled Typing. Selecting Tap Off When Typing will disable the touchpad when keys are pressed and provides for a configurable delay after the last key is pressed. Manufacturers use different terminology for this, so you will have to look for it and experiment.

If nothing else works, disable the touchpad and attach a more conventional pointing device, such as a mouse or trackball. For the user who travels, this means one more piece of equipment to take along, but it may be well worth the trouble to avoid this annoyance. Check the laptop's documentation to find out how to disable the touchpad; some laptops actually have a switch next to the touchpad to disable it. If you cannot disable the touchpad, just tape a piece of card stock over it as a means of mechanically disabling it.

Keyboard Failure

If a laptop keyboard fails completely, or if some of the keys fail, you may need to replace it. However, some problems that appear to be keyboard-related are actually not. For instance, when pressing a key has an unexpected result, such as displaying the wrong character or multiple characters, first check with the manufacturer to see if this is a problem related to your laptop, because in the past some models had such a problem, and the manufacturer offered a BIOS update. Alternatively, the problem may be that the computer is overheating. Check out the section later in this chapter titled "Cooling Issues."

Keyboard Usage Issues

Laptop keyboards present special problems: first, because some keys have more functions than desktop keyboards, and second, because these functions are squeezed into a smaller space. Problems with laptop keyboards often result from users not remembering that they have turned a certain feature on or off (recall the DISPLAY MODE key problem discussed previously) or have accidentally pressed a combination of keys that enables or disables some function.

When using a laptop for the first time, familiarize yourself with the special function keys. Close all open applications before using any of these key combinations. At the very minimum, be sure to click on an empty area of the desktop so your keystrokes do not affect an open application. We describe a few common keys and their associated problems next. The names provided here are not standard, and keys with similar functions may have different names.

Display Mode Key   We described problems with the DISPLAY MODE key earlier in this chapter. Any time the display is blank, but you can clearly hear the fan and see indicator lights, press the DISPLAY MODE key combination to switch modes and see if this is the cause of the problem. When you first attach an external display, it should be automatically detected and used, but if not, try toggling the DISPLAY MODE key.

Speaker On/Off Key   Another common special key is the SPEAKER ON/OFF key. Some laptop keyboards identify the speaker key by a speaker icon with an "x" over it. This may appear in blue on one of the function keys, such as the F3 key. When the FN key is combined with the SPEAKER ON/OFF key, it toggles the speaker on and off. This feature is handy on a trip when you want to quickly turn off the speaker so you do not bother your fellow travelers. The problem comes in when you either forget that you toggled the speakers off or you accidentally toggled them off. Therefore, if you believe the inboard speakers are not working, first look for the SPEAKER ON/OFF key.

Speaker Volume Key   Similarly, some laptops include a SPEAKER VOLUME key. When the FN key is combined with the SPEAKER VOLUME key and either the up (↑) or right (→) arrow key, the volume will get louder. To lower the volume, press the FN key and the SPEAKER VOLUME key along with either the left (←) or down (↓) arrow key. This changes the speaker volume at the hardware level, bypassing Windows' volume control. Therefore, if you have no sound and using the Windows volume control has no effect, try turning the volume up using the SPEAKER VOLUME key.

Display Brightness Key

The DISPLAY BRIGHTNESS key may appear as a sun icon on one of the function keys. Pressing the FN key and this key plus either the up (↑) or right (→) arrow key will brighten the display. Pressing the FN key and the DISPLAY BRIGHTNESS key plus either the left (←) or down (↓) arrow key will darken the display.

Pay special attention to the problems caused by the laptop's portability features, such as the special FN key combinations that change modes for *the display, speaker, and other components. If these modes have been changed, it may appear to be a more serious problem.*

Digitizer Problems

When using a digitizer, such as one built into a Tablet PC, the user draws or writes on the tablet with the stylus and can even select "ink" of various colors and textures with which to draw. When the user is writing, a handwriting recognition program converts the writing into a text document, but it also saves the handwritten page as a graphic.

Problems with digitizers often involve the use and appearance of the ink while working in various applications. You can often resolve problems common to all applications by updating the digitizer driver. Many, but not all, Tablet PCs use the Wacom driver, as Wacom is the major manufacturer of digitizer tablets—both freestanding and those integrated into Tablet PCs. FinePoint is another digitizer manufacturer.

Digitizer problems associated with only one application, or two or more applications from the same manufacturer, need to be resolved through the application. Sometimes an application update will take care of the problem. A damaged or defective stylus may cause other digitizer problems. Whereas on a handheld computer you can use anything from a pen to your finger to work with a touch screen, on a digitizer you must use a stylus that sends a signal to the digitizer, giving it the position of the stylus on the tablet. The stylus, therefore, must receive power somehow, either by a battery or by an outside source like a USB port.

Further, the stylus used with a digitizer or Tablet PC must be compatible with the digitizer. When replacing a stylus, the general rule is that a Wacom stylus will work with any digitizer or Tablet PC using the Wacom tablet, and similarly the FinePoint stylus will work with FinePoint digitizers and Tablet PCs using the FinePoint digitizer. Therefore, you will need to research the digitizer installed in the Tablet PC you are troubleshooting.

Digitizer tablets are subject to radio frequency interference, which can distort the created image. Some digitizers have additional insulation to block this interference. If you are having problems writing or drawing on a tablet, move it away from any possible sources of interference and try again.

Wireless Problems

Wireless cards in laptops can have many of the same problems as other types of cards. Unless the card is built in and not physically accessible, you should always check that it is connected properly. Beyond the physical connections and complete failure of a wireless adapter, wireless problems specific to laptop computers come in two main categories: antenna problems and interference problems.

Antenna Problems

Many laptops today come with built-in wireless Wi-Fi network adapters, with a built-in antenna usually located in the lid. Most laptops with built-in Wi-Fi have a hardware switch at the side or front to turn off the internal Wi-Fi adapter, or at least the antenna. Accidently turning this switch on or off is easy. Therefore, if a laptop user reports that he suddenly does not have a wireless signal, check the hardware switch. Its label may read "Wi-Fi" or it may have a radiating antenna symbol on the laptop case. Change the switch position, and open the wireless configuration utility. Learn more about troubleshooting wireless networks in Chapter 15.

The built-in antenna may be adequate in many instances, but it lacks the flexibility and power of some add-on external antennas. Therefore, if the problem with a laptop's

SCENARIO & SOLUTION

When I am typing on my laptop, the pointer seems to jump all over the document. How can I prevent this from happening?	This problem is common when a hand or finger contacts a touchpad while typing. If the laptop has a touchpad, try to turn it off, or tape a piece of cardboard over the touchpad and use an external pointing device.
I attached an external display to my laptop, but after I powered it up, no image appeared on the external display, only on the integrated display. What have I done wrong?	Try toggling the DISPLAY MODE key to set the laptop to use the external display.
I upgraded the memory in my laptop with a new SODIMM module. Now the laptop fails to power up at all. What should I do?	Remove the SODIMM module and power up again. If the laptop powers up without the new module, the module may be defective or incompatible.

wireless connection is a weak signal, the solution may be a more powerful antenna to increase the signal range. Attaching an external antenna to a built-in adapter is nearly impossible. Therefore, you may need to disable the built-in Wi-Fi adapter and replace it with an adapter that will solve that weak signal problem. The replacement should then be a USB Wi-Fi card with an antenna at the end of the USB cable. Several manufacturers make such a USB Wi-Fi card and antenna.

Interference Problems

Interference problems are not limited to laptops, and we will look at interference problems common to all computers using wireless networks in Chapter 15. However, using a Bluetooth device with a laptop that also has a Wi-Fi adapter introduces a conflict, because both Bluetooth and some Wi-Fi implementations use the same radio band, 2.4 GHz. You may have to choose which wireless devices you will use, or when you will use them. Because Bluetooth is only for very short distances, it works for keyboards, pointing devices, printers, and headphones. Wi-Fi connects to a local area network and, in many cases, connects through that network to the Internet. You may need to choose between uninterrupted Wi-Fi access or wireless connections between your local devices and the laptop.

Preventive Maintenance for Laptops

In general, laptops and desktop PCs have much in common. Therefore, the preventive maintenance information in Chapter 5 applies to laptops and other portable devices. However, certain issues are either unique to portable computers or more common to them because they use certain technologies not used in most desktop PCs. The following sections cover these issues. Although we discuss laptops specifically, most of these issues also apply to other portable devices.

Transporting and Shipping a Laptop

Portability is the key feature of any laptop. However, moving sensitive equipment is fraught with opportunity for damage. Therefore, when transporting a laptop, always use a proper carrying case or bag to protect it from damage. Select a case that feels comfortable to carry, because a laptop is something that you should normally keep with you whenever you are traveling.

When purchasing a case, try it out in the store with the laptop in it. Look for a case with a wide, padded, adjustable shoulder strap. You will also want adequate compartments for any accessories, such as the AC adapter, an extra battery, a pointing device, and compartments to carry a few optical discs and a flash drive.

People tend to overstuff their laptop bags with books and other equipment. The danger in this practice is that it will put enough pressure on the back of the laptop display to crack the glass on the LCD panel. Therefore, refrain from packing bulky or nonessential items in the laptop case, even if you must use a second carrying case for books and other items.

Never check a laptop as baggage unless you pack it in a case especially designed to protect it while the airline is treating it like, well, baggage. This will not be your typical laptop carrying case, but a metal case with molded foam padding to protect it.

If you must ship a laptop via a package service or the U.S. Postal Service, do not pack it in its carrying case, because this will not be adequate. Nothing beats the original packing material and box. Always save these, because you never know when you may have to ship the laptop for service, in which case manufacturers recommend that you ship it in the original box.

Never leave a laptop in a vehicle for extended periods, especially when the laptop is powered on. Even in mild weather, on a sunny day, the interior temperature can climb into a range that could damage the laptop. The LCD display is especially sensitive to temperature extremes. Extreme cold can also damage the laptop.

Cooling Issues

There are several cooling issues specific to laptops. The fact that a laptop has a great deal of circuitry packed in a very small space makes it more likely to overheat and compounds the problem. All but the LCD display is in the bottom of the laptop case, and this small area contains all the heat-generating equipment. Therefore, you should pay attention to the work environment and consider supplemental cooling when possible.

The Work Environment

When operating a laptop, be sure ventilation around the laptop is adequate. Using your laptop while on the go means you must often improvise a workspace. In fact, you may see travelers who simply unzip the case and run the laptop while it is still nestled in the case. The problem with this practice is that it blocks the air vents, which can cause the laptop to overheat. Ideally, you should never place an operating laptop on soft, conforming surfaces like couches, beds, or even laps.

Another issue, especially for the mobile laptop user, may be air quality. A project manager on a construction site may necessarily expose her laptop to all the dirt and dust of a construction site, whether working out of a pickup truck or an onsite office. Because this cannot be avoided, this user should have the inside of the laptop cleaned frequently, and keep it powered off, closed, and in its case when not in use.

Supplemental Cooling

Supplemental cooling for a laptop can come in the form of a special laptop stand that holds the laptop off the surface of the desk to allow airflow underneath. This alone will help, but these stands also often contain one or more fans. The laptop's USB hub powers some of these, whereas others require 110 VAC power and, therefore, have a power adapter. If you plan to use this device while traveling, look for the lightest one you can find, which means you want to avoid one with an AC adapter. If this device will remain on your office desktop, then weight is no problem, and you should buy the one that you judge will be most effective.

e x a m

ⓌＡＴＣＨ   **Be sure you understand how to protect a laptop during storage, transportation, and shipping.**

Hardware and Video Cleaning Materials

When it comes to cleaning the laptop case and display, treat a laptop just like a desktop PC. Follow the suggestions and instructions in Chapter 5 for materials and techniques to use.

CERTIFICATION SUMMARY

Laptops and other portable computers have much in common with desktop PCs. However, the form factors and technologies that make these computers portable also make them vulnerable to certain problems. When troubleshooting problems with portable computers, a computer technician must apply the same procedures and techniques presented in Chapter 5. In addition, she must also understand the special problems associated with laptops and other portables.

When it comes to preventive maintenance, a similar approach is required. Everything that applies to desktop PCs also applies to portable computers. Portable computers also have certain issues that are either unique or more common to them because they use technologies not used in most desktop PCs. Therefore, the technician must apply these special preventive maintenance and care procedures to portable computers.

✓ # TWO-MINUTE DRILL

Here are some of the key points covered in Chapter 7.

Troubleshooting Laptops

❑ Laptop-specific power problems involve rechargeable batteries and the external AC power adapters that put the portability into laptops.

❑ AC adapter problems fall into two categories: damage or failure of the original AC adapter and damage to the computer due to using the wrong AC adapter.

❑ A battery not properly inserted or charged, an old battery that can no longer hold a charge, or a defective new battery can cause laptop power problems.

❑ Before troubleshooting an AC adapter problem, remove any hardware devices installed since the laptop last powered up normally.

❑ Eliminate the other usual suspects, such as an external display that is in a sleep mode or not powered up, or a blank integrated display that has been switched off accidently via the display toggle keys.

❑ Check with the manufacturer if you are unable to solve the problem. A warranty may cover the problem, or there may be a recall on the laptop that will resolve it.

❑ Like a desktop PC, if a laptop fails at POST, you may have to enter the BIOS Setup program to discover the cause and possibly apply a solution.

❑ A laptop display may appear to have failed because the DISPLAY MODE function key has switched it to external display only. Try pressing the DISPLAY MODE key combination to change the mode.

❑ The wires for a laptop LCD panel must pass through the lid's hinge, and, therefore, the wiring can come loose at this point. Contact the manufacturer or authorized repair center for help with this problem.

❑ The LCD panel in a laptop and other portable devices is vulnerable to temperature extremes, in which case it may go blank. Remove the laptop from exposure to extreme temperatures.

❑ The Cold Cathode Fluorescent Lighting (CCFL) tubes that backlight the LCD screen in a laptop are fragile and can break if the laptop is handled roughly. Rough handling will cause the display to dim or go totally dark.

❏   Most LCD panels (laptop or external) have a few dead or lit pixels. Large numbers of these can distort areas of the screen. If you find this is the case, contact the manufacturer for a replacement LCD panel.

Preventive Maintenance for Laptops

❏   The portability of laptops makes them more vulnerable to damage than desktop computers.

❏   Use a proper carrying case for transporting a laptop.

❏   A laptop should not be shipped as baggage, but if it must be, pack it in an adequate case, preferably a metal case with molded foam padding to protect it.

❏   Save the original carton and packing material in case you need to ship the laptop for repair.

❏   Never leave a laptop in a vehicle for extended periods.

❏   The very compactness of laptops makes them vulnerable to overheating.

❏   Be sure to provide adequate ventilation. If this is not possible, consider buying supplemental cooling in the form of a laptop stand with one or more fans installed.

❏   If you must use the laptop in a dirty, dusty environment, power it off, close it, keep it in its carrying case when not in use, and have it cleaned frequently.

❏   Clean the laptop case and display surfaces as described in Chapter 5.

SELF TEST

The following questions will help you measure your understanding of the material presented in this chapter. Read all of the choices carefully because there might be more than one correct answer. Choose all correct answers for each question.

Troubleshooting Laptops

1. What two components must you check when a laptop experiences power problems?
   A. LCD panel
   B. AC adapter
   C. Power-on self-test
   D. Battery

2. When replacing an AC adapter for a laptop, match these three characteristics.
   A. Voltage, amperage, and polarity
   B. Voltage, amperage, and current
   C. Inverter, converter, and generator
   D. AC, DC, and amps

3. What type of power does a laptop's LCD display require?
   A. DC
   B. Battery
   C. Auto-switching
   D. AC

4. You watch the battery indicator in Windows to determine when this is needed.
   A. Replacement
   B. Recharging
   C. Rebooting
   D. Testing

5. A laptop plugged into an AC power source will not power up. What component should you suspect as the source of the problem, assuming the power source is working?
   A. Battery
   B. LCD panel
   C. AC adapter
   D. Keyboard

6. What is a simple way to test an AC power outlet?

A. Use an inverter.

B. Plug in a converter.

C. Plug a generator into the outlet.

D. Plug a lamp into the outlet.

7. What action will some AC adapters take when they detect a power overage?

A. Turn on

B. Automatically restart

C. Shut down

D. Beep

8. When testing the power output of an AC adapter, what should you set your multimeter to test?

A. Volts DC

B. Volts AC

C. Amps

D. MHz

9. What should you do if your laptop fails to start after you have installed a new memory module?

A. Reboot.

B. Power off, and then power on.

C. Remove the memory module and restart.

D. Update the device driver.

10. What should you do if a laptop fails during the POST?

A. Restart.

B. Return it to the manufacturer.

C. Remove the battery.

D. Read the information on the screen and follow any instructions.

11. A user reports that his laptop remains warm even after he turns it "off" with the power button. What option is configured for his power button in Windows?

A. Shut Down

B. Standby or Sleep

C. Screen Off

D. Hibernate

12. Why would the Power Meter settings in Power Options in Windows show a Not Present status for a laptop's battery, even though the battery is present?
    A. The battery is only half charged.
    B. The battery has failed.
    C. The Power Meter is turned off.
    D. The computer is plugged into an AC outlet.

13. What is a simple cause for a blank display?
    A. Broken fluorescent lamp
    B. Power-saving mode
    C. Damaged wiring
    D. Temperature extremes

14. How do you bring a display screen out of power-saving mode?
    A. Move the mouse or press a key.
    B. Unplug the laptop.
    C. Reset the AC adapter.
    D. Press CTRL-ALT-DELETE.

15. You left your laptop in your car for several hours while visiting Minnesota in the winter. What should you do?
    A. Power it up in the car and run it on battery.
    B. Allow it to warm up before turning it on.
    C. Replace the battery.
    D. Clean the display screen.

16. After you dropped your laptop, you powered it up and the display screen was blank, although you could hear the fan. What may be the problem?
    A. Pixilation problems
    B. Temperature extremes
    C. Failed touchpad
    D. Broken fluorescent tubes

17. What can cause tiny black dots that are always in the same place on the screen, while the rest of the LCD display shows an image correctly?

   A. Lit pixels

   B. Damaged wire

   C. Dead pixels

   D. Backlit pixels

18. Your stylus will no longer write to the digitizer on your Tablet PC. Changing the batteries did not help. What can you use as a replacement for the stylus?

   A. The stylus from a handheld computer

   B. Any digitizer stylus

   C. A stylus from the manufacturer of your digitizer tablet

   D. A ballpoint pen

Preventive Maintenance for Laptops and Portable Devices

19. How should you prepare a laptop to ship via UPS?

   A. Pack it in a laptop case.

   B. Pack it in its original box and packing material.

   C. Remove the LCD panel and pack it in a case.

   D. Clean the LCD panel.

20. What should you do for a laptop that seems to run hot, in addition to having it cleaned and keeping it in a well-ventilated area?

   A. Turn off the display and use an external display.

   B. Purchase a laptop stand.

   C. Close some applications.

   D. Turn down the display's brightness.

SELF TEST ANSWERS

Troubleshooting Laptops

1. ☑ **B and D.** The AC adapter and the battery are the two components you must check when a laptop experiences power problems.

    ☒ **A,** LCD panel, is not correct because you would not check this when troubleshooting a power problem. **C,** power-on self-test, is not correct because if power is off, the self-test will not occur.

2. ☑ **A,** voltage, amperage, and polarity, is correct. These values must match for the AC adapter and the laptop.

    ☒ **B,** voltage, amperage, and current, is not correct. Although voltage and amperage is correct, the third requirement, polarity, is missing. **C,** inverter, converter, and generator, is incorrect because an inverter is a device that converts DC current to AC current; a converter is a device that converts AC current to DC current; and a generator is a device that creates electrical current. **D,** AC, DC, and amps, is incorrect. Only one of these, amps, is one of the characteristics that should match in a laptop and an AC adapter.

3. ☑ **D.** A laptop LCD display requires AC power.

    ☒ **A,** DC, is incorrect, although other laptop components require DC power. **B,** battery, is incorrect because, although the battery may be the source of the laptop's power, it is not the type of power required by the LCD display. **C,** auto-switching, is incorrect because it describes a type of power supply.

4. ☑ **B.** Recharging is correct because this is what you do when the battery indicator in Windows says the battery is low.

    ☒ **A,** replacement, is incorrect because the battery indicator does not explicitly tell you when to replace the battery. **C,** rebooting, is incorrect because the battery indicator does not tell you when to reboot the computer. **D,** testing, is incorrect because the battery indicator does not tell you when to test the battery.

5. ☑ **C.** The AC adapter is the component you should suspect as the source of a problem if a laptop plugged into an AC power source will not power up.

    ☒ **A,** battery, is incorrect because if the laptop is plugged into an AC power source, it does not need the battery to power up. **B,** LCD panel, is incorrect because, although a failed LCD panel will make the laptop appear to be off, the laptop should still power up if it can receive power. **D,** keyboard, is incorrect, because this has nothing to do with the laptop's ability to power up.

6. ☑ **D,** plug a lamp into the outlet, is correct, as this is a simple way to test an AC power outlet.
☒ **A,** use an inverter, is incorrect because this device uses DC power as its input and, therefore, cannot be used to test an AC power outlet. **B,** plug in a converter, is incorrect because although a converter uses AC power as its input, this is not a simple test, as a lamp is more common than a converter. **C,** plug a generator into an outlet, is incorrect because most common generators convert a fuel, such as diesel or gasoline, to AC power. You would not plug one into an AC outlet.

7. ☑ **C.** Shut down is the action some AC adapters take when they detect a power overage.
☒ **A,** turn on, is incorrect because this is not the action of an AC power adapter when a power overage is detected. **B,** automatically restart, is incorrect because this action would not protect the AC adapter or the computer from damage from a power overage. **D,** beep, is incorrect because this, in itself, would not protect the AC adapter or the laptop.

8. ☑ **A,** volts DC, is correct because the AC adapter converts volts AC to volts DC (output).
☒ **B,** volts AC, is incorrect, because the AC adapter converts volts AC to volts DC (output). **C,** amps, is incorrect because, although many multimeters can measure amps, in this case you want to measure volts. **D,** MHz, is incorrect because this is not something most multimeters measure. MHz was mentioned in this book as a measurement of CPU speed.

9. ☑ **C,** remove the memory module and restart, is the correct answer because this component was changed since the computer last successfully powered up.
☒ **A,** reboot, is incorrect because rebooting will not change anything in this case. **B,** power off, and then power on, is incorrect because this would also not change anything. **D,** update the device driver, is incorrect because memory does not require a device driver.

10. ☑ **D,** read the information on the screen and follow any instructions, is the correct answer because the POST may have detected a problem, in which case it will display an error message.
☒ **A,** restart, is incorrect, although you may be instructed to do this by the message on the screen. **B,** return it to the manufacturer, is incorrect because this is a drastic step to take when you have not tried to discover the problem first. **C,** remove the battery, is incorrect because you have no indication that the battery is the problem.

11. ☑ **B.** Standby or Sleep is correct. Standby in Windows XP or Sleep in Windows Vista would put the computer into a sleep mode that would still require a battery and would generate some heat.
☒ **A,** Shut Down, and **D,** Hibernate, are both incorrect because they would power the computer off. **C,** Screen Off, is not an option for configuring the power button in Windows.

12. ☑ **B.** A failed battery will show as Not Present in the Power Meter settings.

☒ **A,** the battery is only half charged, is incorrect because if it had any charge, the battery would show as present. **C,** the power meter is turned off, is incorrect, and **D,** the computer is plugged into an AC outlet, is incorrect.

13. ☑ **B.** Power-saving mode is a simple cause of a blank display. Always check for a simple cause first.

☒ **A,** broken fluorescent lamp, is incorrect because, although a broken lamp can cause a blank display, it is not a simple cause. **C,** damaged wiring, is incorrect for a similar reason. **D,** temperature extremes, is also a possible cause, but not a simple one.

14. ☑ **A,** move the mouse or press a key, is correct because this will bring a display screen out of power-saving mode.

☒ **B,** unplug the laptop, is incorrect because this will not bring the display out of power-saving mode. **C,** reset the AC adapter, is incorrect because this will not bring the display out of power-saving mode. **D,** press CTRL-ALT-DELETE, is incorrect because this will not bring the display out of power-saving mode.

15. ☑ **B,** allow it to warm up before turning it on, is correct because running the laptop in extremely cold temperatures can damage it, especially the display.

☒ **A,** power it up in the car and run it on battery, is incorrect because running the laptop in the extreme cold can damage it. **C,** replace the battery, is incorrect because there is no indication that this is necessary. **D,** clean the display screen, is incorrect because this will not address the problem of temperature extremes.

16. ☑ **D,** broken fluorescent tubes, is correct because the backlight consists of fluorescent tubes.

☒ **A,** pixilation problems, is incorrect because pixilation would not make the screen go blank. **B,** temperature extremes, is incorrect because we did not mention temperature in the question. **C,** failed touchpad, is incorrect because this would not make the screen go blank.

17. ☑ **C.** Dead pixels can cause tiny black dots that are always in the same place on the screen.

☒ **A,** lit pixels, is incorrect because these do not show up as black dots. **B,** damaged wire, is incorrect because symptoms of a damaged wire to the LCD panel include flickering or complete failure. **D,** backlit pixels, is incorrect because pixels, as part of the LCD screen, are always backlit.

18. ☑ **C,** a stylus from the manufacturer of your digitizer table, is correct.

☒ **A,** the stylus from a handheld computer, is incorrect because this type of stylus is a passive device, and a digitizer requires a stylus that uses radio frequency signals to transmit its coordinates on the tablet. **B,** any digitizer stylus, is incorrect because it may not be compatible if not made for the tablet. **D,** a ballpoint pen, is incorrect because, like the stylus from a handheld device, a pen is a passive device, not capable of transmitting the correct radio signals to the digitizer.

Preventive Maintenance for Laptops

19. ☑ **B,** pack it in the original box and packing material, is correct.

☒ **A,** pack it in a laptop case, is incorrect because a laptop case will be inadequate. **C,** remove the LCD panel and pack it in a case, is incorrect because you should never remove the lid. **D,** clean the LCD panel, is incorrect because this in no way prepares the laptop for shipping.

20. ☑ **B,** purchase a laptop stand, is correct because a stand will allow air to circulate underneath the laptop and many stands have one or more fans.

☒ **A,** turn off the display and use an external display, is incorrect because the heat is usually generated in the bottom of the laptop case. **C,** close some applications, is incorrect because this has not proven to have any significant effect on heat generation. **D,** turn down the brightness of the display, is also incorrect because this has also not proven to have any significant effect on heat generation and does not affect the main case of the laptop, which generates the most heat.

8

Operating System Fundamentals

CERTIFICATION OBJECTIVES

❏   **701:3.1**   Compare and contrast the different Windows Operating Systems and their features

❏   **701:3.2**   Given a scenario, demonstrate proper use of user interfaces

✓   Two-Minute Drill

Q&A   Self Test

M

icrosoft Windows, in its many versions, is the most widely used PC operating system for home and business, so technicians should be prepared to work with the Windows desktop operating systems. Like many people, you may have used a computer for much of your life, and you know how to open windows, navigate folders, download files, and run programs. With such proficiency, you may wonder why you need to study the operating system any further. It's because you need a far different set of skills and knowledge to support Windows than you need to simply use it. Prepare yourself to do the support tasks of installing, configuring, optimizing, and troubleshooting an operating system. On the other hand, you do not need to be a systems programmer who understands the OS's programming code. You only need a base of knowledge, a sharp mind, good powers of observation, and patience.

CERTIFICATION OBJECTIVE

■ **701: 3.1** *Compare and contrast the different Windows Operating Systems and their features*

CompTIA exam objective 701: 3.1 requires that you understand the differences among three versions of Windows: Windows 2000, Windows XP (32-bit and 64-bit), and Windows Vista (32-bit and 64-bit). You should be able to recognize the user interface for each of these versions and identify such features as sidebar, Aero, and UAC. Knowing the minimum system requirements for each of these versions, and their system limits and upgrade paths is also important. Although the objectives do not as yet include Windows 7, we include coverage of that version, as well.

Introduction to Windows Operating Systems

In this section, you will learn the purpose of operating systems, the differences among versions of the Windows operating system, the characteristics of 32-bit versus 64-bit Windows OSs, minimum system requirements, system limits, compatibility issues and how to address them, and upgrade paths to certain editions of Windows 2000, Windows XP, Windows Vista, and Windows 7.

The Purpose of Operating Systems

The purpose of an operating system (OS) is to control all of the interactions among the various system components, the human interactions with the computer, and the network operations for the computer system. An OS accomplishes this by building an increasingly complex set of software layers between the lowest level of a computer system (the hardware) and the highest levels (user interactions). From a user perspective, this means the user either points, types, or displays data using a device controlled by the OS.

The OS is responsible for managing the computer's files in an organized manner and allowing the user to manage data files. The OS keeps track of the functions of particular files and brings them into memory as program code or data when needed. Furthermore, the OS is responsible for maintaining file associations so data files launch in the proper applications. The OS is also responsible for managing the computer's disks, keeping track of how each disk is identified, and managing disk space use.

Windows Versions, Editions, and Updates

When speaking of Microsoft Windows, we use the terms "version," "edition," "OEM," "update," and "service pack" in sometimes confusing fashion. We will clarify the differences among these terms.

Version

Each Microsoft Windows *version* is a new level of the venerable operating system, with major changes to the core components of the operating system as well as a distinctive and unifying look to the GUI. The Windows versions included on the CompTIA A+ Essentials 2009 Exams only include Windows 2000 (Figure 8-1), Windows XP (Figure 8-2), and Windows Vista (Figure 8-3).

Edition

Microsoft brings out an entirely new group of products for each version. They call these individual version products *editions*, and not all editions of each version are included in the exam, which is concerned with Windows purchased at retail channels and supported on desktop and laptop PCs. Therefore, Windows 2000

The Windows
2000 desktop

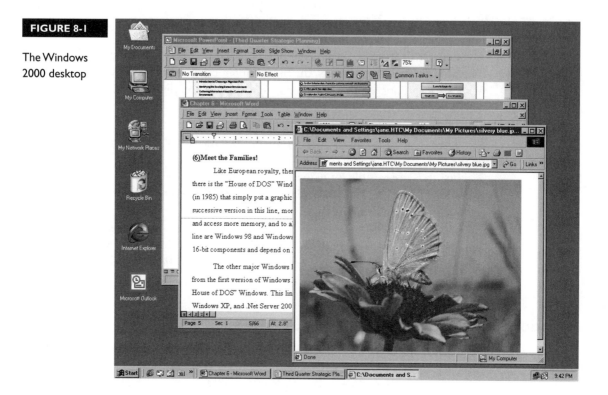

Server edition is not included, nor is Enterprise or Windows Vista Starter Edition. The Windows editions included in the exams are:

Windows 2000 Professional

Windows XP Professional

Windows XP Home

Windows XP MediaCenter

Windows Vista Home Basic

Windows Vista Home Premium

Windows Vista Business

Windows Vista Ultimate

Windows 7 Editions   Windows 7 comes in three retail editions: Windows 7 Home Premium, Windows 7 Professional, and Windows 7 Ultimate. Like Windows Vista, it also comes in an Enterprise edition and two scaled-down versions called Starter and Home Basic. Windows 7 Starter is an OEM version that has many features removed or disabled, including the ability to change the desktop wallpaper or join a Windows domain. Windows 7 Home Basic is destined for emerging markets and is not available in the United States, most of Europe, the Middle East, Australia, New Zealand, and Japan.

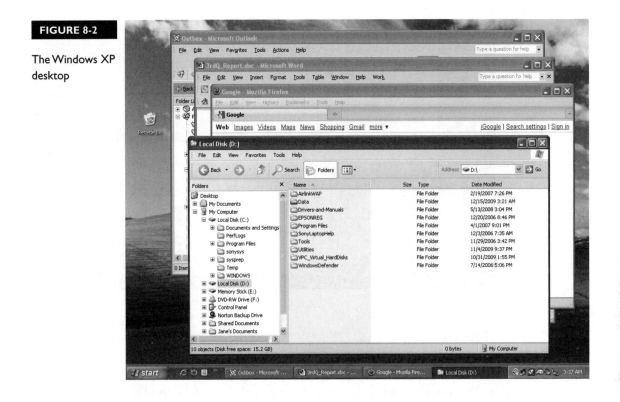

FIGURE 8-2

The Windows XP desktop

Enterprise Edition   Enterprise Edition is currently available in Windows Vista and Windows 7. It includes all the features of that version, plus many features desirable in a large enterprise for mass distribution, security, compliance, productivity, and more. It is not available as a retail product; only customers of the Microsoft Software Assurance plan, a distribution channel for bulk licensing to organizations, can purchase it.

Original Equipment Manufacturer (OEM)

The Windows editions included in the exams are available through retail channels—either the Windows OS purchased alone in retail packaging (sometimes referred to as "full retail") or Windows preinstalled and bundled with a computer and known as "OEM Windows." Microsoft makes OEM Windows available at low prices to manufacturers or system builders with the agreement that they cannot sell it separately from the hardware.

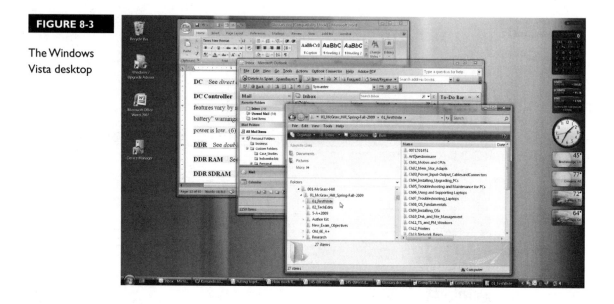

The Windows
Vista desktop

Update

Computer hardware technology does not stand still; therefore, operating systems must change to keep up. Each of the major operating systems is modular, so incremental updates can make some changes to the existing OS version. In Microsoft terminology, an *update* contains one or more software fixes or changes to the operating system. Some updates add abilities to the OS to support new hardware, and some resolve problems discovered with the operating system. More and more, this second type of update is required to fix security problems. A *patch* is a software fix for a single problem.

At one time, these updates, whether for functional or security problems, were issued without a predictable timetable. In recent years, Microsoft has assigned the second Tuesday of each month as the release day for updates. This day is widely called "patch Tuesday."

Service Pack

A *service pack* is a bundle of patches or updates released periodically by a software publisher. Windows service packs are major milestones in the life of a Windows version. For that reason, some devices and applications will require not simply a certain version of Windows, but also a certain service pack. Follow the steps in Exercise 8-1 to view the version, edition, and service pack information for Windows.

EXERCISE 8-1

Viewing the Windows Information

Here is an easy way to determine the version, edition, and service pack level for Windows:

1. Open My Computer or Computer (Vista).
2. Open the Help menu and select About Windows.
3. This will display the About Windows dialog box listing the version information as well as the service pack level, as shown in Figure 8-4.

32-Bit vs. 64-Bit Windows Operating Systems

Operating systems tie closely to the CPUs on which they can run. Therefore, we often use CPU terms to describe an operating system's abilities. For instance, Windows 2000 is a 32-bit operating system. Windows XP, Windows Vista, and

FIGURE 8-4

This About Windows dialog box shows that the version is Windows Vista, the edition is Ultimate, and it includes Service Pack 2.

Windows 7 come in both 32-bit and 64-bit versions. Most of the Windows XP editions are 32-bit except for a special edition, Windows XP Professional x64 Edition.

The biggest difference between the 32-bit and 64-bit versions of Windows is in the address space used by both system RAM and other RAM and ROM in your computer (see Table 8-1). Windows 64-bit does not use the maximum theoretical address space of a 64-bit CPU.

The retail version of Windows Vista Ultimate comes with two DVDs—one with the 32-bit version and the other with the 64-bit version. The license allows you to legally install and use one or the other, but you cannot legally install them on two machines without acquiring a second license. The other retail packages of Windows Vista—Home Basic, Home Premium, or Business—come on a single DVD containing the 32-bit version. If you need the 64-bit version, contact Microsoft and order the 64-bit DVD. You must provide the 25-character product key from the package, and you will need to pay a small shipping and handling fee. This also appears to be true of Windows 7.

A 64-bit operating system requires 64-bit applications, although Microsoft has offered ways to support older applications in each upgrade of Windows, described later in this chapter in "Running Older Applications." To determine if a computer is running 32-bit or 64-bit Windows Vista, open Control Panel and click System and Maintenance, and then click System and look at the System Type field, which will say "32-bit Operating System" or "64-bit Operating System."

TABLE 8-1	Edition	RAM Limit in 32-bit Windows	RAM Limit in 64-bit Windows
Windows Memory Limits	Windows 2000 Professional	4 GB	N/A
	Windows XP Professional	4 GB	128 GB
	Windows Vista Ultimate/Enterprise/Business	4 GB	128 GB
	Windows Vista Home Premium	4 GB	16 GB
	Windows Vista Home Basic	4 GB	8 GB
	Windows 7 Ultimate/Enterprise/Professional	4 GB	192 GB
	Windows 7 Home Premium	4 GB	16 GB
	Windows 7 Home Basic	4 GB	8 GB

Minimum System Requirements

Each revision or version of an OS has specific minimum requirements for the level
of CPU, amount of memory, and amount of free hard disk space. To determine if
it will run on your existing computer, check the *system requirements* listed on the
package and published on the manufacturer's Website.

You can normally count on the system requirements being greater as you move
from one version to another, as from Windows XP to Windows Vista. You must
also consider the issue of the computer platform on which a given OS will run.
A *computer platform* is the hardware architecture, including the CPU, BIOS, and
chipset. Windows runs on the Microsoft/Intel platform, with a range of CPUs (Intel
and AMD), BIOSs, and chipsets compatible with Microsoft OSs. Some call this the
"Wintel" platform. More recently, we make another distinction between the x86,
which refers to Wintel platforms that support 32-bit Windows, and the x64, which
refers to Wintel platforms that support the 64-bit Windows.

TABLE 8-2	Windows System Minimums			
	Windows 2000 Professional	**Windows XP Professional**	**Windows Vista* Home Premium/Business/Ultimate**	**Windows 7**
CPU	133 MHz Pentium (or compatible)	Intel or AMD 300 MHz	800 MHz	1 GHz (32-bit or 64-bit)
RAM	64 MB of RAM	128 MB	512	1 GB (32-bit) or 2 GB (64-bit)
Free Hard Disk Space	650 MB	1.5 GB	15 GB	16 GB (32-bit) or 20 GB (64-bit)
Video Adapter	VGA	Super VGA (800 × 600)	Support for Super VGA graphics	DirectX 9 adapter with WDDM 1.0 or higher driver

Table 8-2 describes the system minimums for four versions of Windows. Additionally, an optical drive is required if you want to install from the Windows CD. But these requirements are modest and far less than you will find in the most minimally configured new desktop PC.

You would be very unhappy trying to work on a PC with a minimal configuration, because the programs most people choose to run on desktop computers have grown in their processor, storage, and memory requirements; you will want many hundreds of GBs of hard drive space for the programs you add and the data you will create with those programs. Therefore, the recommended configuration for Windows Vista Home Premium/Business/Ultimate (32-bit or 64-bit) is 1 GHz 32-bit or 64-bit processor, 1 GB of system memory, a 40 GB hard drive with at least 15 GB free space, a DirectX 9 adapter with 128 MB graphics memory and a GPU that supports Pixel Shader 2.0, and a 32-bits per pixel WDDM driver. Many of the features available with Windows require additional hardware support. For instance, Windows Media Center features need more video RAM and specialized hardware like a TV tuner, and Windows Vista's Windows XP Mode requires an additional 1 GB of RAM and an additional 15 GB of available hard disk space, as well as a processor that supports hardware virtualization.

System Limits

The other end of the spectrum from system requirements is system limits—the maximum amount of a system resource that is usable in Windows. Recall the discussion of system resources in Chapter 5, in which we described those system resources defined in Device Manager: memory addresses, I/O addresses, IRQs, and DMA channels. Within the memory address space, Windows allocates memory for certain uses, such as allocating space for each process and for operational modes. Details of this memory usage are beyond the scope of this book and not within the A+ exam objectives. You should understand that these system resources are finite—Windows limits how much of each resource it can manage. Even if you have a totally maxed-out computer with a powerful CPU, many gigabytes of memory, and lots of hard drive space, you can reach the point in Windows at which you cannot open an additional Window or program because there are simply not enough system resources to handle the task.

Application and Hardware Compatibility

After Microsoft releases a new Windows version, there is a transition time during which many individuals and organizations choose to stay with the old version;

some move to the new version right away; and others make the change gradually. This occurred between Windows 98 and Windows XP, between Windows XP and Windows Vista, and is currently occurring between Windows XP or Vista to Windows 7. Not everyone immediately embraces the new OS and replaces their old OS with the new one. There are many reasons for this:

- **System requirements** Old hardware may be below the system requirements. Therefore, if the old operating system is functioning adequately, individual users, as well as businesses, will not simply reflexively upgrade to the new OS until they have a compelling reason to do so.

- **Hardware compatibility** The compatibility issue has several facets. First, there is hardware compatibility. The BIOS in an older PC may not support critical features of the new OS, and if the manufacturer does not offer a BIOS upgrade, the computer will not support the new OS. Hardware compatibility extends to peripherals when manufacturers do not create new drivers for a new OS.

- **Software compatibility** Some applications are written to take advantage of certain features (or weaknesses) in older versions of Windows. Large organizations have often delayed upgrading to a new OS until they could either find a way to make the critical old applications run in the new OS or find satisfactory replacements that would work in the new OS.

Although the recent versions of Windows test the compatibility of the hardware and (in the case of an upgrade) software early in the installation process, you would be smart to run this test yourself before you start the installation process—even before purchasing the new OS. Microsoft provides a utility for each of its recent upgrades that allows you to test your computer and hardware for compatibility. This program is unique to each version and is called the Readiness Analyzer in Windows 2000 and the Upgrade Advisor beginning with Windows XP. We will focus on the Upgrade Advisor in the newer versions of Windows.

The Upgrade Advisor comes on the Windows XP installation disc, so you can select it from the menu that appears during Autorun. The Windows Vista CD will run the Upgrade Advisor from the Internet. For those who want to run the test before purchasing Windows Vista or Windows 7, you can download Upgrade Advisor from the Internet. Check out the Microsoft Website to locate the Upgrade Advisor for a specific version of Windows.

After testing the hardware and the software, the Upgrade Advisor produces a report providing valuable information and recommendations or tasks that you need to perform before installing the next version of Windows, and it may show tasks to perform after the installation. You may find the tasks needed to make a computer meet the compatibility and minimum system requirements are too expensive to perform on an older computer and decide to postpone your move to the new version until you are ready to replace the old system.

Exercise 8-2 provides the steps for acquiring and running the Windows Vista Upgrade Advisor. Chapter 9 includes details on the practice of upgrading an installed Windows OS with a new Windows OS.

EXERCISE 8-2

Running Upgrade Advisor

You can see if your Windows computer hardware and application software will be compatible with Windows Vista or Windows 7. You will need a broadband Internet connection to successfully complete this exercise.

1. Open your Internet browser and enter the keywords **windows upgrade advisor** into your favorite search engine.

2. From the results, select a link (within the Microsoft.com domain) for the version of the Upgrade Advisor you desire.

3. Download and save the Upgrade Advisor file to the desktop.

4. When the download completes, locate the file on the desktop and double-click it to run the Advisor.

5. When the Upgrade Advisor completes, it will display a task list similar to the one in Figure 8-5. Print this out or save it.

Once, when we ran the Upgrade Advisor, it produced a report that found only one incompatibility—an antivirus program that was only incompatible with the Setup program but was compatible with the new version of Windows. Therefore, it suggested removing the program before installing the OS, and then reinstalling it afterward. The computer in question was a test computer, so we ignored the instructions just to see what the consequences would be. After the upgrade, Windows did not run, and it would not even boot up into Windows's Safe Mode (described in Chapter 11). After several hours of trying to fix the installation, we had to wipe the hard drive clean and start from scratch.

FIGURE 8-5

A portion of the
Windows Vista
Upgrade Advisor
task list

Windows Vista Business Task List

Task list:

Edition	Current System Configuration	
Windows Vista Business	CPU:	Intel(R) Pentium(R) 4 CPU 2.66GHz
	Memory:	1024.00 MB
	Hard Disk Drives:	"C" - 3.75 GB Free (15.00 GB Total)
		"D" - 13.88 GB Free (17.50 GB Total)
		"H" - 53.50 GB Free (149.00 GB Total)

Things you need to do before installing Windows Vista

- Please visit Windows Update to download all the latest critical updates for your system before installing Windows Vista.

Issue Type	Category	Action Required	Explanation
System			
	Hard drive"C:"	Before you install Windows Vista, create additional free hard disk space	You need 15 gigabytes (GB) of free hard disk space to install Windows Vista. Your hard disk currently has 3.75 GB of free space. Do one of the following: - Upgrade your hard disk to increase its capacity. - Remove unwanted files to create additional free hard disk space.

Running Older Applications

Many individuals and organizations use older applications that will not work on newer versions of Windows. The program may fail to install in the new OS, or, if you have upgraded a system to a new version of Windows, an old application may issue an error message, such as "This program requires Windows *x*," where *x* is an older version of Windows. Or, you may not receive such a clear message, but the program may behave erratically. If this program worked in the older version of Windows, you may need to take measures to make it happy in the new version. The official answer to this is to use Compatibility Mode in all versions of Windows discussed in this book or Windows XP Mode in Windows 7. An additional option is available for Windows XP and Windows Vista that is similar to Windows XP Mode.

Compatibility Mode

You enable Compatibility Mode in Windows XP, Windows Vista, or Windows 7 by using the *Program Compatibility Wizard*, also called the Program Compatibility Troubleshooter in Windows 7. Call up this Wizard from the Help and Support Center, and it guides you through the steps to select the application program, the older Windows OS you wish to emulate, and the display settings. The wizard saves the settings it creates in the properties of the application's shortcut or program file. Alternatively, you can manually alter the compatibility settings for any program from the program's properties or from its shortcut. Only use Compatibility Mode for old productivity applications (word processing, spreadsheet, and so on.). Never use Compatibility Mode for antivirus, backup programs, or system programs (such as disk utilities and drivers).

Windows XP Mode and Windows Virtual PC

If Compatibility Mode does not enable an old program to run properly, and if you are running Windows 7 Professional, Enterprise, or Ultimate editions, then you can use Windows XP mode. Windows XP Mode is Microsoft Virtual PC with a fully licensed version of XP installed. Together, they are bundled as "Windows Virtual PC." Virtual XP Mode is not designed for 3D games and other programs with high-end graphics needs, and it may not work with certain hardware, such as TV tuners. Once again, use this for the business productivity program that you need but cannot upgrade to a compatible version. It requires a computer with a CPU that supports virtualization. Go to the Microsoft site and search on **Windows XP Mode**. Then select the result labeled Download Windows XP Mode. Follow the steps, which will include downloading and running a utility to test your computer for compatibility. If your computer passes the compatibility test, follow the instructions to download and install Windows Virtual PC. It is surprising how quickly it installs with a complete version of Windows XP. Windows Virtual PC is a free download for those Vista editions that support it.

Microsoft Virtual PC

Microsoft Virtual PC is a separate product that evolved to Windows Virtual PC. It is still available as a free download from the Microsoft Website, and it installs on Windows XP Professional, Windows XP Tablet, and Windows Vista Business, Enterprise, and Ultimate versions. Additionally, Windows XP must also have

Service Pack 3 installed to support Microsoft Virtual PC. And although Microsoft Virtual PC is free, for these OSs it does not include a fully licensed version of Windows XP, as does Windows Virtual PC. You will have to first install and configure Microsoft Virtual PC and then install a fully licensed version of Windows. We have done this many times in the past in order to test applications and to capture screen shots of Windows installations.

Upgrade Paths

An upgrade of an operating system, also called an "in-place installation," is an installation of a newer operating system directly over an existing installation. An upgrade has the benefit of saving you the trouble of reinstalling all your programs and creating all your preference settings. You would have to do all this after a clean installation, which is an installation on a blank or "clean" hard drive. Upgrades also leave you with a brand-new OS on an old computer, but that is your choice.

You can upgrade the following operating systems directly to Windows 2000 Professional: Windows 95, Windows 98, Windows NT 3.51 Workstation, and Windows NT 4.0 Workstation. You can directly upgrade to Windows XP Professional from Windows 98, Windows Me, Windows NT 4.0 Workstation SP5, and Windows 2000 Professional.

Upgrade paths to Windows Vista from Windows XP are edition-specific, as shown in Table 8-3, in which an "X" indicates in-place installation (upgrade). Blank squares indicate that you must do a clean installation. The upgrade paths for Windows 2000 and Windows XP Professional x64 are not included in this chart because they both require a clean reinstall.

| TABLE 8-3 | Upgrade Paths to Windows Vista |

	Windows Vista Home Basic	Windows Vista Home Premium	Windows Vista Business	Windows Vista Ultimate
Windows XP Professional			X	X
Windows XP Home	X	X	X	X
Windows XP Media Center		X		X
Windows XP Tablet PC			X	X

| TABLE 8-4 | Upgrade Paths to Windows 7 |

	Windows 7 Home Basic	Windows 7 Home Premium	Windows 7 Professional	Windows 7 Enterprise	Windows 7 Ultimate
Windows Vista Business			X	X	X
Windows Vista Enterprise					X
Windows Vista Home Basic	X	X			X
Windows Vista Home Premium		X			X
Windows Vista Ultimate					X

You cannot directly upgrade from Windows XP or older versions to Windows 7. Table 8-4 lists the direct upgrade paths to Windows 7, and, as in Table 8-3, blank fields indicate that you must do a clean install.

SCENARIO & SOLUTION

Which is generally more expensive—Windows purchased as a full retail product or an OEM version purchased preinstalled on a computer?	Windows purchased as a full retail product is more expensive than an OEM version purchased preinstalled on a computer (excluding the cost of the computer).
What is "patch Tuesday?"	Patch Tuesday is the second Tuesday of the month—the day when Microsoft releases regular updates to their products.
Describe the biggest difference between 32-bit Windows and 64-bit Windows.	The biggest difference is in the address space used by both system RAM and other RAM and ROM. A 64-bit Windows OS uses a great deal more address space than the 4 GB of 32-bit Windows, with the actual maximum varying among the versions and editions, but ranging from 8 GB to 192 GB.

CERTIFICATION OBJECTIVE

■ **701: 3.2** *Given a scenario, demonstrate proper use of user interfaces*

This section prepares you for this objective by describing the functions and the ways to use the various user interface components in Windows. It also distinguishes between those utilities you use from the command prompt and run line utilities. You learn that many of the GUI utilities used to administer Windows run in a special graphical console called an MMC. Although you will see some of these utilities in this section, you will have opportunities to work with most of them in the following chapters of this book, where appropriate.

The Windows User Interface

This section provides an overview of the Windows user interface, including both the obvious and the less-obvious GUI components. A less-obvious component in Windows Vista and Windows 7 is Windows Aero, affecting the look of all graphical components. Learn about such objects as the taskbar, Start menu, command prompt, sidebar, Windows Explorer, and so forth. Also learn about a security feature, User Account Control, which you first encounter as an interruption to your work.

The Windows Desktop

Windows provides a *graphical user interface (GUI)* that the user can navigate using a keyboard and mouse or other pointing devices. The Windows GUI uses the desktop metaphor. The main Windows screen, called the "desktop," has containers for your work like when you use a physical desk. Windows organizes these containers, called "folders," in a hierarchical fashion. This organization allows for easy access to the commonly used files and programs, using a mouse or other pointing device for point-and-click operations.

The Windows desktop has a variety of graphical objects in addition to folders, including, but not limited to, the mouse pointer, icons, shortcuts, dialog boxes, windows, buttons, toolbars, menus, and the taskbar. Not all of these appear at the same time, or at least they are not on the desktop at the end of a standard Windows installation. You encounter and use these icons as you navigate in Windows using your keyboard and pointing device.

An *icon* is a tiny graphic image representing applications, folders, disks, menu items, and more. A *shortcut* is an icon that represents a link to any object that an icon can represent. Activating a shortcut (by double-clicking it) is a quick way to access an object, or to start up a program from the desktop, without having to find the actual location of the object on your computer. You can represent a single object, like a program file, by more than one shortcut, and you can place a shortcut on the desktop, taskbar, and other places within the Windows GUI. Shortcut icons are often (but not always) distinguished by a small bent arrow on the lower left, and they have a title below the icon, like the Microsoft Word shortcut icon shown here.

Windows Explorer

Windows has a very important GUI component, *Windows Explorer*—the program EXPLORER.EXE. This program supports the entire Windows GUI. So, as long as the GUI is running, which means as long as you are able to work in Windows, this program is loaded into memory. Once in the Windows GUI, if you call this program, it opens a window called Windows Explorer that you use for browsing your local disks and files. You open Windows Explorer windows every time you open many Start menu shortcuts, such as My Computer/Computer, My Documents/Documents, and so forth. You can also open Windows Explorer from the Accessories menu of All Programs or by entering **explorer** in the Start | Run... dialog box. Paradoxically, entering **explorer** in the Start Search box in Windows Vista or Windows 7 will bring up Internet Explorer, but entering **explorer.exe** will bring up Windows Explorer.

Microsoft makes incremental changes to Windows Explorer in each new version of Windows. For instance, the Search toolbar button in Windows Explorer in Windows XP was replaced by the Search box in Windows Vista and Windows 7. The old Search option did not begin the search until you finished typing in the search string, and then it seemed rather slow. The new Windows Explorer Search box starts searching the contents of the current windows and its folders as you enter the string and displays results as it continues the search.

Windows Aero

Windows Aero is an enhancement to the desktop that Microsoft introduced in Windows Vista and continues in Windows 7. Both versions of Windows support it in all editions except Home Basic, and it requires a compatible graphics adapter. Windows Vista comes with a number of Aero features, which include such visual effects as Glass, which makes the frames of a windows transparent, and Aero Wizards, a standard design for the wizards that walk you through various functions. Aero includes windows animations, such as Windows Flip 3D, that allows you to switch between open Windows by pressing the WINDOWS key and TAB key simultaneously. Windows 7 has added a long list of new features to Aero.

Taskbar and Systray

By default, Windows displays the *taskbar* as a horizontal bar across the bottom of the desktop. You can reposition the taskbar by simply moving the pointer to an "empty" taskbar area and dragging it to a new position, such as at the top of the desktop or vertically positioned at either side. You can also resize the taskbar by dragging just an edge of it until it is the desired size. The taskbar is also (rarely) called the *Start Bar* because it contains the Start button. The Start button has a label in Windows 2000 and Windows XP, but beginning with Windows Vista, it is a simple icon with a Microsoft logo. The Windows XP taskbar, shown in Figure 8-6, and the Windows Vista taskbar, shown in Figure 8-7, are very similar. Each includes (from left to right) a Start button, the Quick Launch toolbar, buttons for currently running programs, and at the far right, the *systray*, also called the *notification area* or *system tray*. Programs and some hardware devices use the systray to display status icons. These icons may represent devices, such as a network adapter, or represent software, such as a battery meter, antivirus program, and so on. Pausing the mouse pointer over one of these icons will cause a rectangular status box to pop up, as shown here.

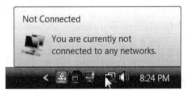

Another type of pop-up box, a message balloon, will pop up over the notification area for events relating to one of the icons, such as when a wireless connection is made or disconnected. The *Quick Launch bar,* just to the right of the Start button, is an optional toolbar you can add to the taskbar using the properties dialog box for the taskbar. You can launch any shortcuts on the Quick Launch bar with a single click without having to first open the Start menu. Configure the taskbar, control the default positioning of windows on the desktop, or open the Task Manager by right-clicking in the empty area of the taskbar and selecting the desired option from

FIGURE 8-6   The Windows XP taskbar

The Windows Vista taskbar

the taskbar menu, as shown here. The choice labeled Properties opens the Properties dialog box for the Start menu.

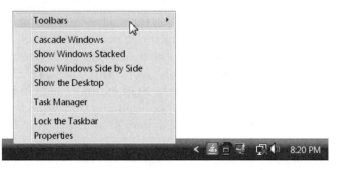

Start Menu

The Start button on the taskbar opens the *Start menu,* which has areas containing shortcuts and submenus. It is the central tool for finding and starting a variety of programs in Windows. The Start menu in Windows 2000, shown here, is a single column list of folders and programs, and by default, the Windows 2000 desktop has a number of shortcuts.

After Windows 2000, Microsoft removed most of the desktop icons, leaving only one shortcut—Recycle Bin—and moved many of the former desktop icons to the Start menu, which now has a two-column format. The right column serves the purpose of the single column in Windows 2000, containing a fairly standard set of icons that you can configure through the Start menu Properties dialog box. An arrow next to an icon indicates that you can expand the item to display the contents or submenus. Windows 2000 contains a Shut Down option at the bottom of the Start menu that will open a dialog box so you can select further options for logging off or shutting down your computer. At the bottom of the Windows XP Start menu is a bar containing two choices: Log Off and Turn Off Computer. The Log Off option will log off the currently logged-on user, replacing the desktop with a logon screen. Selecting Turn Off Computer will open the Turn off Computer dialog box, shown here, which will give you three choices: Standby, Turn Off, or Restart. If you have enabled hibernation, the middle button will read Hibernate.

In Windows Vista, Microsoft moved the Turn Off button (without a label) to the bottom of the Start menu, as shown here. Clicking this button will normally shut down the computer without displaying an additional dialog box. To the right of the Turn Off button is a lock button to lock the computer while leaving it running. We will describe the use of Lock Computer in Chapter 17. To select more options, click the arrow to the right of the Turn Off button. The standard options here are Switch User, Log Off, Lock, Restart, Sleep, and Shut Down.

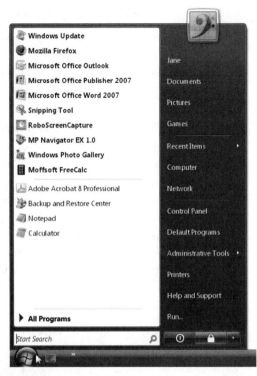

If you downloaded an update to your Windows computer, but did not install it, you will see an indication of this when you attempt to shut down. In Windows XP, the Turn Off

Computer dialog box will display as shown at left, with the Microsoft Security Center icon positioned over the Turn Off button. In Windows Vista, the same icon will display on top of the Turn Off button on the Start menu. In either case, a message will instruct you to click Turn Off to install the updates. If you choose this, do not power off the computer because that will interrupt the update. The computer will turn off automatically after installing the updates.

Pinned Items List

A *pinned items list* is located on the top left of the XP and Vista Start menus. By default, the pinned items list contains shortcuts to Windows Update and programs for browsing the Internet and using e-mail. The shortcuts in the pinned items list remain there unless you choose to remove or change them. To add additional shortcuts to the pinned items list, right-click any shortcut and choose Pin To Start Menu. To remove an item from this list, right-click it and choose Unpin From Start Menu.

Recently Used Programs List

Beginning in the Windows XP, the Start menu has a separator line that marks the end of the pinned items list and the beginning of the *recently used programs list*, which contains shortcuts to recently run programs. You can change the number of items maintained in this list through the Start menu Properties dialog box.

Programs/All Programs

In Windows 2000, the Programs menu item has an icon showing a folder with an overlapping program icon. This indicates that it is a folder containing links to programs and other folders containing programs. Beginning in Windows XP, the All Programs menu item serves the same function but does not have an icon. When you click All Programs in Windows XP, it opens a pop-up menu with a list of programs and program categories, as shown here. Changed in Windows Vista, the list opens on top of the pinned items and recently used programs lists. In all versions, when you install a new application in Windows, it will usually add a folder or program icon to this list.

Personal Folders

The Start menu contains shortcuts to your personal folders. In Windows 2000, the Documents icon on the desktop points to the user's personal data folders. In Windows XP, these titles are My Documents, My Recent Documents, My Pictures, My Music, My Computer, and My Network Places. Microsoft dropped the "My" in Windows Vista. The exact folders displayed will depend on how you have configured the Start menu using the Properties dialog box.

The My Documents/Documents folder contains data files you create. Many applications will, by default, save their data files in this location. In Windows XP, the actual path to the My Documents folder is C:\Documents and Settings\ *username*\My Documents, where *username* is the user name used to log onto the computer. In Windows Vista/7, the path to the Documents folder is C:\Users\ *username*\Documents. The other personal folders are also located in the *username* folder. My Recent Documents/Recent Items contain shortcuts to recent data files, no matter where you saved the files. My Music/Music contains audio files; My Videos/Videos contains video files such as movies; whereas My Pictures/Pictures is the default location for graphic files such as photo files from digital cameras. Some applications with special file types will create their own folders under My Documents/Documents. Each of these icons on the Start menu points to a folder created as part of the user's personal folders, giving the user a ready-made folder structure for organizing data files of many types.

User Account Control (UAC)

While not just a part of the Windows desktop, User Account Control (UAC) directly affects the user experience with the desktop. *User Account Control (UAC) is an effec-tive* but annoying security feature introduced in Windows Vista to prevent unauthorized changes to Windows, a problem that existed for a long time. With UAC enabled, you can expect two scenarios. In the first, a user logged on with a privileged account with administrative rights only has the privileges of a standard account, until the user (or a malicious program) attempts to do something that requires higher privileges. At that point, UAC makes itself known, graying out (dimming) the desktop, displaying the Consent Prompt, with the message, "Windows needs your permission to continue." Further, it asks for your response, "If you started this action, continue," and displays the name of the program that is attempting to run. You must click Continue or Cancel. If you click Continue, the task runs with your administrative privileges, and you return to working with standard privileges in other programs.

In the second scenario, a user logs on with the privileges of a standard user and attempts to do something that requires administrative privileges. In this case, UAC displays the Credentials Prompt requiring the user name and password of an account with administrative privileges. If you provide these, the program or task will run with these elevated privileges, but you will return to the standard user privileges for all other activities. In either case, if you do not respond in a short period of time, UAC will time out, cancel the operation, and return the desktop to you. By default, UAC is turned on in both Windows Vista and Windows 7, although Microsoft made changes to Windows 7 that reduce the number of prompts you will see because they changed the number of Windows programs that require approval to run.

Even with UAC turned off, you will not be allowed to perform all tasks and will see a message such as "The requested operation requires elevation" when you attempt to perform certain functions. We will look at how you respond to this message when we discuss the command prompt commands later in this chapter, and you will learn to configure UAC options in Chapter 17.

The Run Line

Certain Windows utilities are very important for a technician to know, but potentially dangerous in the hands of the ordinary user. Some of these programs are GUI programs that an experienced technician depends on for various administrative tasks. Some of these programs do not have shortcuts within the Windows GUI, whereas others do have shortcuts in the GUI from which you may run them. In either case, technicians find it handy to know the executable name and usually launch these programs from the Start menu's Run box (or Run line). The following are the Run line Utilities you must know for the A+ exams:

CMD	MSCONFIG	NTBACKUP
DXDIAG	MSINFO32	REGEDIT

We describe the CMD command later in this chapter, and you will learn about the NTBACKUP program in Chapter 10. We discuss the remainder of the listed programs in Chapter 11.

Start Search

Beginning with Windows Vista, and continuing in Windows 7, the Start Search box, mentioned earlier in this chapter, is very powerful and useful. Also called Quick Search, it works like the Run line, but that is not all it does; it is much more powerful, searching your entire computer and not just locating files, but when you search on a program, it will actually run it, even if you do not supply its executable name. We have come to use this as a replacement for the Run line. It saves having to discover where a favorite GUI utility is located in Windows Vista or Windows 7. For instance, by default, Microsoft tucked Device Manager away, requiring several mouse clicks to locate it in the GUI and then launch it. Starting it from the Run line is better, but you must carefully type in its executable name, devmgmt.msc. Leave off the extension and you get an error message, but enter **device manager** into Start Search and voila! Device Manager blossoms on your desktop. So, forget the Run line (except for the A+ exams, of course) and use Start Search.

on the *Job* *Start Search isn't the only such Search tool; for a more targeted search of Control Panel applets, use the Control Panel Search box.*

My Computer/Computer

My Computer is a shortcut on the desktop in Windows 2000. It resides on the Start menu in both Windows XP and Windows Vista (as Computer). It opens the My Computer or Computer folder in Windows Explorer, displaying file folders, hard disk drives, and removable storage on the local computer. The actual objects shown depend on the computer's configuration. Clicking the Folders button on the toolbar will change the view from the default view with a task pane on the left and a contents pane on the right to a two-pane view showing a folder hierarchy in the left pane and the contents of the currently selected folder on the right. In the first view, you can select an action from the task pane on the left or open a folder or drive on the right. In Folder view, you can see the entire folder hierarchy on the left while browsing folders in the right pane (see Figure 8-8). Use My Computer/Computer when you need to work with disk folders beyond those available through your other personal folders, for instance, to access folders on a removable drive.

My Network Places/Network

The Start menu icon labeled My Network Places in Windows 2000 and Windows XP, or simply Network beginning in Windows Vista, opens a folder containing shortcuts to network locations on the LAN or the Internet. If the task list is visible, it includes tasks appropriate for working with network locations, such as Add A Network Place, View Network Connections, View Workgroup Computers, and Set Up A Home Or Small Office Network.

FIGURE 8-8

Windows XP My
Computer with
a folder pane on
the left

Administrative Tools

If you configured the Start menu to include the Administrative Tools shortcut, it
gives you a pop-up menu with a selection of utilities. The actual utilities shown
vary among Windows versions, and even among editions of a version. Look for
common tools, such as Services, Event Viewer, and Computer Management, among
others. Performance on the Windows XP Administrative Tools menu calls up a
console containing both *System Monitor* and *Performance Logs and Alerts*. These
replace the Windows 2000 Performance Monitor. We will revisit Administrative
Tools in later chapters.

Control Panel

The Control Panel shortcut opens the *Control Panel* folder, containing numerous
applets you can use to adjust the configuration of many different aspects of the
OS. Windows 2000 has a Settings shortcut on the Start menu. Click this to
select Control Panel and other options for configuring Windows. These other
options are simply links to applets within Control Panel. Beginning in Windows
XP, Microsoft replaced the Settings menu by several shortcuts on the Start

menu, including Control Panel, Printers And Faxes (Windows XP), and Printers (Windows Vista).

Windows XP introduced a new view for Control Panel called Category View. This view displays far fewer icons by lumping them into categories—Appearance And Themes, Network And Internet Connections, and so forth. Some of these icons represent several applets, whereas some, such as Add Or Remove Programs, represent a single applet. The grouping of Control Panel applets continued in Windows Vista, but with a slightly different organization, as shown in Figure 8-9.

Many experienced Windows users prefer the former view, now called Classic View, which lists the individual applets. Suit yourself. Switching between these views using the Classic View link in the task panel in the left pane is easy. Most of the Control Panel applets are common for all installations of Windows, but the presence of some depend on the devices and components installed.

FIGURE 8-9

Windows Vista
Control Panel

Command Prompt

The command prompt in Windows is a place in which you can enter commands in a simple character-mode interface, shown here. If you run a GUI program from the command prompt, it will

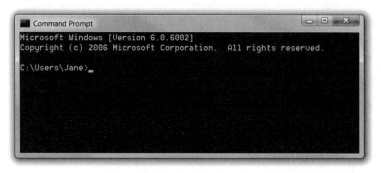

load into a separate Window, but if you run a character-mode program, it will run within the command prompt, displaying any output or messages within the command prompt. You will practice working at the command prompt in Chapter 10. You will find a shortcut to the command prompt at Start | All Programs | Accessories. Our preferred method for opening a command prompt in Windows is to enter the command **cmd** in the Run box on the Start menu. For the A+ exams, you must know the following list of command prompt utilities:

ATTRIB	FORMAT	SFC
CHKDSK	IPCONFIG	TELNET
COPY	PING	TRACERT
DEFRAG	MD/CD/RD	XCOPY
DIR	NET	
EDIT	NSLOOKUP	

When you work at the command prompt, you are still subject to Windows security, and if you attempt to run a command on a Windows Vista or Windows 7 computer and receive the message, "The requested operation requires elevation," you must take some action in order to run the command. One thing you can do is use the Run As Administrator option. To do this for the command prompt, navigate to its shortcut. If you recently ran it, the shortcut will be on your Start menu. Otherwise, it lives in the Accessories folder in All Programs. Right-click the shortcut and select Run As Administrator. The title of the command prompt window will be Administrator: Command Prompt, and anything you run in this window will run with elevated privileges.

The Sidebar

In Windows Vista, Microsoft introduced the *sidebar*, a vertical bar found by default on the right side of the desktop. Here, you will find *gadgets*, mini-programs that show information, such as time and temperature in various locations, stock quotes, and handy tools such as a small yellow notepad or calculator. You choose whether you want the sidebar and the various gadgets you wish to display. The sidebar, shown here, fits nicely on wide displays where you have enough real estate to keep the sidebar visible while working at your normal tasks.

The Microsoft Management Console (MMC)

Beginning with Windows 2000, Microsoft introduced the *Microsoft Management Console (MMC)*, a user interface for Windows administration tools that is flexible and configurable. When you open a Control Panel applet or other administrative tool, it opens a MMC window, but an administrator can build his own custom consoles, consisting of individual snap-ins. To do this, you enter the command **mmc** at the Run line, which opens a blank console window. Using the Add Or Remove Snap-ins option on the File menu, you can select one or more administrative snap-ins to create your custom console. Consoles have a .msc file extension, and you can call up your favorite tool directly from the Run line by entering the correct filename and extension. For instance, to start Computer Management, shown here, from the Run line simply enter the command **compmgmt.msc**. In Windows Vista and Windows 7, start it from the Start Search line by entering **computer management**.

Task Manager

Task Manager is a tool you can use to see what programs, processes, and services are running on your computer. You can also use it to monitor your PC's performance and to close a program that is not responding and that you cannot close from within the program itself. There are many ways to open Task Manager from within the Windows GUI, but our favorite is the less-known option, described in Exercise 8-3, because it works the same in all versions of Windows. You will learn more about using Task Manager in Chapter 11.

EXERCISE 8-3

Viewing Running Programs in Task Manager

Here is an easy way to view which programs are running regardless of the Windows version you are using.

1. From anywhere in Windows, press the CTRL-SHIFT-ESC key combination to open Task Manager.

2. Notice the tabbed pages. At minimum, you should have Applications, Processes, Performance, and Networking (unless your computer does not connect to a network).

3. Note the applications shown on the Applications page.

4. Notice the performance information that appears at the bottom of Task Manager.

5. Explore all the tabs, but be sure not to take any action. When you are done, close Task Manager.

The Registry

The Windows registry, like UAC, is not really a user interface feature, but an important part of the underpinnings of Windows. We discuss it here only because we need to address it before we move on to the next three chapters, in which we refer to it. A basic knowledge of the registry is required of anyone supporting Windows. The Windows *registry* is a database of all Windows configuration settings for both hardware and software. As it starts up, Windows reads information in the registry that tells it what components to load into memory and how to configure them. After startup, the OS writes any changes into the registry and frequently reads additional settings as different programs load into memory. The registry includes settings for

Device drivers

Services

Installed application programs

Operating system components

User preferences

Created when Windows installs, the registry is continually modified as you configure Windows and add applications and devices. If you run the REGEDIT command from the Run line or from Start Search in Windows Vista and Windows 7, it will open Registry Editor, a program that will let you view and directly edit the registry. The best way to change the registry is indirectly, using various tools in the GUI, such as the Control Panel applets. You should directly edit the registry only when you have no other choice and have specific instructions from a very reliable source.

In Registry Editor, you can navigate the registry folders with your mouse in the same way you navigate disk folders. Each folder represents a *registry key*, an object that may contain one or more settings as well as other keys, each of which is a *subkey*

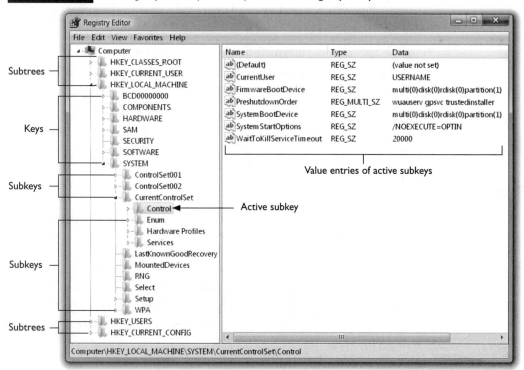

FIGURE 8-10   Use Registry Editor (REGEDIT) to view the registry components.

of its parent key. The top five folders, as seen in Figure 8-10, are *root keys*, often called *subtrees* in Microsoft documentation. Each of these subtrees is the top of a hierarchical structure.

The settings within a key are called *value entries*. When you click the folder for a key, it becomes the active key in Registry Editor. Its folder icon opens, and the contents of the key appear in the right pane, as shown in Figure 8-10. Here is an overview of each subtree and its contents:

- **HKEY_LOCAL_MACHINE**   Information about detected hardware and software, security settings, and the local security accounts database.
- **HKEY_CLASSES_ROOT**   The relationships (associations) between applications and file types. Shown as a root key, it is actually all the information located in HKEY_LOCAL_MACHINE\Software\Classes.

- **HKEY_CURRENT_CONFIG** Configuration information for the current *hardware profile*, which are settings defining the devices, the list of files associated with each device, and configuration settings for each. It also contains a set of changes to the standard configuration in the Software and Systems subkeys under HKEY_LOCAL_MACHINE.
- **HKEY_CURRENT_USER** The user profile for the currently logged-on user, which consists of the NTUSER.DAT file for the user, along with any changes since logon.
- **HKEY_USERS** All user profiles that are loaded in memory, including the profile of the currently logged-on user, the default profile, and profiles for special user accounts for running various services.

Although considered a single entity, the registry is actually stored on disk in a number of binary files. A binary file contains program code, as opposed to a file containing data. The Windows registry files are listed here, along with a description of their contents:

- **SYSTEM** Information used at startup, including a list of device drivers to be loaded, as well as the order of their loading and configuration settings. It also contains various operating system settings including those for the starting and configuring of services.
- **SOFTWARE** Configuration settings for software installed on the computer.
- **SECURITY** The computer's local security policy settings.
- **SAM** The local security accounts database containing local user and group accounts and their passwords.
- **DEFAULT** The user profile used when there is no logged-on user. On a Windows computer that requires an interactive logon, these settings affect the appearance before someone logs on.
- **NTUSER.DAT** The user profile for a single user. Each user who logs onto the computer has a separate NTUSER.DAT file, as well as one located in the DEFAULT USER folder. The NTUSER.DAT file is in the top-level personal folder for each user.

All changes to the registry saved from one session to the next are in these registry file extensions. With the exception of NTUSER.DAT, these registry files do not have file extensions and live in a disk folder named CONFIG. In Windows 2000, the default location of this folder is C:\WINNT\SYSTEM32. In Windows XP, Windows Vista, and Windows 7, this location is C:\WINDOWS\SYSTEM32.

SCENARIO & SOLUTION

The pinned items list on my Start menu contains a program I no longer want in this list. How can I remove it?	Right-click the item and choose Unpin From Start Menu.
I have Windows XP. How can I store my data files in an organized folder structure to make it easy to find the files?	The folder structure for this is already set up in Windows XP. You access these folders through the Start menu shortcuts that begin with "My."
I entered the command **defrag** from the Run line, but the program did not run.	Defrag is a command-line command utility and cannot be run from the Run line.

CERTIFICATION SUMMARY

Before you can install and support computers, you must develop an understanding of the concepts beyond those required to simply use an OS. This begins with understanding the purpose of operating systems, knowing the differences among the major operating systems, and understanding updates, service packs, and revision levels. The versions of Windows studied here have many GUI elements in common, but with each new version, Microsoft has made changes, such as modifications to the Start menu, additions of GUI elements, and the visual enhancements of Aero that were introduced in Windows Vista.

✓ # TWO-MINUTE DRILL

Here are some of the key points covered in Chapter 8.

Introduction to Windows Operating Systems

❑ An OS controls all the interactions among the various system components, human interactions with the computer, and network operations for the computer system.

❑ Microsoft Windows comes in versions, such as Windows 2000, Windows XP, Windows Vista, and Windows 7.

❑ Each Windows version also comes in editions, such as Windows 2000 Professional, Windows XP Professional, Windows Vista Home, Windows Vista Home Premium, Windows Vista Business, or Windows Vista Ultimate.

❑ Windows updates are software fixes to the operating system code to fix problems or enhance security. A patch is a fix for a single problem. A service pack is a bundle of patches or updates released periodically by a software publisher.

❑ Operating systems tie closely to the CPUs on which they run. Therefore, CPU terms such as 32-bit and 64-bit may also describe an OS. Windows XP, Windows Vista, and Windows 7 all have both 32-bit and 64-bit versions.

❑ Each version of an OS has a certain set of system requirements, which include the computer platform, as well as the amount of RAM and disk space.

❑ Each new OS also introduces hardware and software compatibility issues. Windows has features for managing incompatible applications, including Compatibility Mode in Windows XP, Windows Vista, and Windows 7. In addition, Windows 7 has Windows XP Mode, which uses Windows Virtual PC with an instance of a fully licensed Windows XP Professional.

❑ Each edition of Windows at each version level has unique upgrade paths that allow you to upgrade directly, performing an in-place installation, from certain earlier editions of Windows.

The Windows User Interface

❑ The Windows GUI includes important elements, such as the taskbar, Start menu, Windows Explorer, My Computer, Personal folders, Control Panel, command prompt, and My Network Places.

❑ The Start menu has many shortcuts—their placement and names vary somewhat among the Windows versions. There are lists of shortcuts, such as the pinned items, recently used programs, and All Programs. There are shortcuts to personal folders, such as My Documents or Documents, containing user data. There are also shortcuts to various utilities.

❑ Beginning with Windows XP, the GUI for many utilities is a Microsoft Management Console (MMC) window.

❑ The registry is a database of all Windows configuration settings best modified by Control Panel applets, although administrators can use the Registry Editor (REGEDIT) to view the registry and directly edit it.

SELF TEST

The following questions will help you measure your understanding of the material presented in this chapter. Read all of the choices carefully because there might be more than one correct answer. Choose all correct answers for each question.

Introduction to Windows Operating Systems

1. What makes up the layers of an operating system?
   A. Hardware
   B. Software
   C. Memory
   D. Silicon

2. An operating system typically controls what interactions?
   A. Between the system and the human
   B. Between the chair and the keyboard
   C. Between the AC adapter and the wall outlet
   D. Between Windows and Linux

3. Which of the following describes responsibilities of an OS?
   A. Printer cartridges
   B. AC to DC conversion
   C. Disk and file management
   D. Inverters

4. If Windows Vista is a version, what is Windows Vista Ultimate?
   A. OEM Windows
   B. Edition
   C. Patch
   D. Update

5. Which of the following describes the OS code in all but one of the Windows XP editions?
   A. GUI
   B. Multitasking
   C. 64-bit
   D. 32-bit

6. Which of the following best describes system requirements for an OS?
   A. Platform
   B. CPU, amount of RAM, hard disk space, and platform
   C. Form factor
   D. Code size

7. Before you install Windows XP, Windows Vista, or Windows 7, you can use an appropriate version of this program to determine if your computer's hardware and software is compatible with the new OS.
   A. Setup
   B. Backup
   C. Upgrade Advisor
   D. Help | About

The Windows User Interface

8. The Windows GUI uses this metaphor.
   A. Mouse
   B. Desktop
   C. Taskbar
   D. Task list

9. Folders, mouse pointer, icons, shortcuts, dialog boxes, windows, buttons, etc., are all examples of these components of a GUI.
   A. Pixels
   B. Pictures
   C. Graphics
   D. Objects

10. What is the horizontal bar that is usually across the bottom of the Windows screen?
    A. Taskbar
    B. Start menu
    C. Systray
    D. Menu bar

11. What is the central tool for finding and starting programs in Windows?

- A. Taskbar
- B. Start menu
- C. Computer
- D. Menu bar

12. By default, what is the only shortcut displayed on the Windows XP desktop?

- A. Start menu
- B. Recycle Bin
- C. My Programs
- D. My Computer

13. What three buttons usually appear on the Turn off Computer dialog box in Windows XP?

- A. Shut Down, Log Off, Restart
- B. Standby, Shut Down, Restart
- C. Log Off, Turn Off, Restart
- D. Standby, Turn Off, Restart

14. What is the name for the list of items on the upper left of the Start menu beginning in Windows XP?

- A. Recently used programs list
- B. Pinned items list
- C. Quick Launch bar
- D. Task list

15. This enhancement, introduced in Windows Vista, brings to the Windows desktop many new features that affect the entire Windows GUI.

- A. Sidebar
- B. Gadgets
- C. Windows Aero
- D. Systray

16. Which of the following is a feature of Windows Aero that allows you to switch among open windows?

- A. Taskbar
- B. Aero Wizards
- C. Windows Flip 3D
- D. Glass

17. Which of the following is a Run line utility?

    A. DIR

    B. ATTRIB

    C. CHKDSK

    D. MSCONFIG

18. Which of the following is a command prompt utility?

    A. CMD

    B. XCOPY

    C. DXDIAG

    D. MSINFO32

19. Which of the following is a security feature introduced in Windows Vista to prevent unauthorized changes to Windows.

    A. SFC

    B. Windows Aero

    C. UAC

    D. MMC

20. What feature, introduced in Windows XP, allows you to combine your most frequently used administrative tools into a single custom console window?

    A. Windows Aero

    B. Windows Flip 3D

    C. MMC

    D. UAC

SELF TEST ANSWERS

Introduction to Windows Operating Systems

1. ☑ **B.** Software makes up the layers of an operating system.
   ☒ **A,** hardware, is incorrect because the operating system itself is entirely software. **C,** memory, is incorrect because although the OS runs in memory, the layers running in memory are composed of software. **D,** silicon, is incorrect because this is a physical ingredient in computer hardware components, not a part of an operating system.

2. ☑ **A,** between the system and the human, is correct because these interactions are the main reason we have operating systems.
   ☒ **B,** between the chair and the keyboard, is incorrect because the human resides between the chair and keyboard, and the operating system does not control that interface. **C,** between the AC adapter and the wall outlet, is incorrect because all that resides there is a power cord. **D,** between Windows and Linux, is incorrect because this is not an interaction typically controlled by an operating system.

3. ☑ **C.** Disk and file management are responsibilities of an OS.
   ☒ **A,** printer cartridges, is incorrect because they are not responsibilities of an OS. **B,** AC to DC conversion, is incorrect because this is the responsibility of a computer power supply. **D,** inverters, is incorrect because this is not an OS responsibility, but a hardware device.

4. ☑ **B,** edition, is correct because Windows Vista Ultimate is an edition of the Windows Vista version.
   ☒ **A,** OEM Windows, is incorrect because that describes any edition of Windows that is bundled with a computer. **C,** patch, is incorrect because a patch is a software fix for a single problem. **D,** update, is incorrect because an update is software that contains fixes to problems in Windows, often security issues.

5. ☑ **D.** 32-bit describes the OS code in all but one of the Windows XP editions.
   ☒ **A,** GUI, is incorrect because a GUI is a component of any Windows XP edition. **B,** multi-tasking, is incorrect because this describes the OS code of all Windows XP editions. **C,** 64-bit, is incorrect because this describes the OS code in only one edition: Windows XP x64 Edition.

6. ☑ **B.** CPU, amount of RAM, hard disk space, and platform, best describes system requirements for an OS.
   ☒ **A,** platform, is incorrect because this alone does not best describe the system requirements for an OS. **C,** form factor, is incorrect because this describes the dimensions of a hardware device, not the system requirements for an OS. **D,** code size, is incorrect because this just describes the size of the OS code, not the system requirements for the OS.

7. ☑ **C.** Upgrade Advisor is the program that will determine if your computer has hardware and software compatible with Windows XP, Windows Vista, or Windows 7.

☒ **A,** Setup, and **B,** Backup, are incorrect. We have not discussed Setup and Backup as yet, but neither is the program named in this chapter for testing hardware and software compatibility. **D,** Help | About, is incorrect because this is a menu choice in My Computer (and other programs) that will provide version information, not hardware and software compatibility information.

The Windows User Interface

8. ☑ **B.** Desktop is the metaphor used by the Windows GUI.

☒ **A,** mouse, is incorrect because this is not a metaphor for the Windows GUI, but a hardware pointing device used with the Windows GUI. **C,** taskbar, is incorrect because, although this is a Windows GUI component, it is not the metaphor used to describe the Windows GUI. **D,** task list, is incorrect because this is part of the Windows GUI, not a metaphor describing the GUI.

9. ☑ **D.** Objects, such as folders, mouse pointer, icons, shortcuts, dialog boxes, windows, buttons, etc., are components of the Windows GUI.

☒ **A,** pixels, is incorrect because this describes a dot on a display screen, not a component of the OS GUI. **B,** pictures, is incorrect, even though you could call each of the GUI objects a picture. **C,** graphics, is incorrect, even though you could call each of the GUI objects a graphic.

10. ☑ **A,** taskbar, is correct because this horizontal bar is usually across the bottom of the Windows screen.

☒ **B,** Start menu, is incorrect because this is just a small portion on the left end of the taskbar. **C,** systray, is also incorrect because this is just a small portion of the taskbar—located on the far-right end. **D,** menu bar, is incorrect because this is a component of a window, not the horizontal bar that is usually across the bottom of the Windows screen.

11. ☑ **B,** Start menu, is correct because this is the central tool for finding and starting programs in Windows.

☒ **A,** taskbar, is incorrect because this is only the location of the Start menu and the place that displays buttons for open programs. **C,** Computer, is incorrect because this is a shortcut in Windows Vista and Windows 7 that opens to display file folders, hard disk drives, and removable storage on the local computer. **D,** menu bar, is incorrect because this is a component of an open window, not the central tool for finding and starting programs in Windows.

12. ☑ **B.** Recycle Bin is the only shortcut displayed by default on the Windows XP desktop.

☒ **A,** Start menu, is incorrect because this menu is not a desktop shortcut but is located on the taskbar. **C,** My Programs, and **D,** My Computer, are both incorrect because they are not desktop shortcuts (by default) but are located on the Start menu.

13. ☑ **D.** Standby, Turn Off, Restart are the usual three buttons on the Turn Off Computer dialog box in Windows XP.

    ☒ **A,** Shut Down, Log Off, Restart; **B,** Standby, Shut Down, Restart; and **C,** Log Off, Turn Off, Restart, are all incorrect because they are not the usual three buttons in the Turn Off Computer dialog box.

14. ☑ **B.** Pinned items list is the name for the list of items on the upper left of the Windows Start menu.

    ☒ **A,** recently used programs list, is incorrect because this is the list that is below the pinned items list on the Start menu. **C,** Quick Launch bar, is incorrect because this is an optional item on the taskbar, not a list on the Start menu. **D,** task list, is incorrect because this is not the name of the list of items on the upper left of the Windows Start menu.

15. ☑ **C.** Windows Aero is the enhancement to the Windows GUI introduced in Windows Vista.

    ☒ **A,** sidebar, is incorrect. Although this is new in Windows Vista, it does not affect the entire Windows GUI. **B,** gadgets, is also incorrect because a gadget is simply a small program accessed from the sidebar. **D,** systray, is incorrect because it is a portion of the taskbar.

16. ☑ **C.** Windows Flip 3D is a feature of Windows Aero that allows you to switch among open windows.

    ☒ **A,** taskbar, is incorrect. Although you can use the taskbar buttons to switch among open windows, the taskbar is not a feature of Windows Aero. **B,** Aero Wizards, and **D,** Glass, while both features of Windows Aero, do not allow you to switch among windows.

17. ☑ **D.** MSCONFIG is a Run line utility.

    ☒ **A,** DIR, **B,** ATTRIB, and **C,** CHKDSK, are incorrect because these are all command prompt utilities.

18. ☑ **B.** XCOPY is a command prompt utility.

    ☒ **A,** CMD, **C,** DXDIAG, and **D,** MSINFO32, are all incorrect because they are Run line utilities.

19. ☑ **C.** UAC, which stands for User Account Control, is a security feature introduced in Windows Vista.

    ☒ **A,** SFC, is incorrect. It is a Run line utility that is not further defined in this book. **B,** Windows Aero, is incorrect. It is an enhancement to the Windows GUI. **D,** MMC, is incorrect because it is the Microsoft Management Console, a type of GUI window for certain Windows tools.

20. ☑ **C.** MMC, or Microsoft Management Console, allows you to combine your most frequently used administrative tools into a single custom console window.

    ☒ **A,** Windows Aero, is incorrect because it is an overall desktop GUI enhancement feature, and it did not appear until Windows Vista. **B,** Windows Flip 3D, is also incorrect because it is a feature of Windows Aero. **D,** UAC, is incorrect because it is a security feature.

9

Installing, Configuring, and Upgrading Operating Systems

CERTIFICATION OBJECTIVE

❑   **701:3.3**   Explain the process and steps to install and configure the Windows OS

    Two-Minute Drill

Q&A   Self Test

I n this chapter, we will examine the successful installation and configuration of Windows. Whether you are installing from scratch, upgrading, or configuring the system, you must follow certain guidelines and procedures. You will learn basic preparation and installation procedures and post-installation tasks. Configuring Windows involves many components, including network connections, registration and activation, updating, applications and Windows components, devices, power management, and, occasionally, virtual memory.

CERTIFICATION OBJECTIVE

■ **701: 3.3** *Explain the process and steps to install and configure the Windows OS*

The CompTIA exam objective for installing, upgrading, and configuring Windows involves understanding a variety of scenarios for each of these areas. You should have hands-on experience performing a clean installation to a single computer and an understanding of other installation options and types, such as installing from an image, from a recovery CD, and from a factory recovery partition.

Installing Windows

Installing a new operating system is not a one-step process—in fact, it occurs in three stages. In the first stage, you perform necessary tasks to prepare for the installation; in the second stage, you actually install the operating system; and in the third stage, you implement follow-up tasks. In this section, you will learn the necessary tasks for the first two stages when installing Windows.

Prepare to Install Windows

Prepare to install Windows by first ensuring a computer meets the minimum requirements discussed in Chapter 8. You should then verify hardware and software compatibility, understand the basics of disk preparation for installation as well as the choice of file systems (where appropriate), and finally, take steps to migrate data from a previous Windows installation to a new installation.

Verify Hardware and Software Compatibility

As described in Chapter 8, you can run the Upgrade Advisor specific to Windows XP, Windows Vista, or Windows 7 before purchasing the OS in order to determine if your existing computer hardware and software are compatible with the new OS. In addition, the Setup programs for all the versions of Windows covered by the Comp-TIA A+ Essentials (2009) Exams perform a compatibility test of your hardware (clean installation) or hardware and software (upgrade installation). Another source of information is the Windows Marketplace (formerly the Windows Catalog), a searchable list of hardware and software known to work with Windows. You can find this Website at www.windowsmarketplace.com. Once at the Windows Marketplace home page, you can search on specific hardware or software products, or browse through the catalog of hardware and software products known to work with your version of Windows.

Don't forget about the issues of 32-bit versus 64-bit Windows and hardware and software compatibility. Some computer manufacturers only ship 64-bit Windows Vista, and you should expect to see that trend continue with Windows 7, as more applications are released to take advantage of the larger memory space of 64-bit Windows. Both Windows Vista and 7 have better implementations of 64-bit Windows than did Windows XP, which is basically a nonplayer in the 64-bit arena. So, if you are planning to install 64-bit Windows, you should do your homework and ensure that it will work with your computer system and peripherals, especially if you are using an older computer or peripherals.

Disk Preparation

To prepare a hard disk for use, you must first *partition* it and then format it. Partitioning is the act of creating a partition, also called a "volume," which is a portion of a hard disk that can contain both a file system and a logical drive. You first assign a drive letter to a partitioned volume, and then you must format it before it is usable. The formatting process places the logical structure of a file system on the volume. Read more about partitions in Chapter 10 where you will learn how to use the Disk Management console in Windows to perform many tasks, including partitioning.

If you install Windows on an unpartitioned hard disk, the Setup program will automatically prompt you to create a partition. You can do both partitioning and formatting from Setup, and then it will start the actual installation of Windows.

File System Selection

A *file system* is the means an operating system uses to organize information on disks. Windows 2000 and Windows XP support several file systems, including FAT16, e **x** a m

ⓦ a t c h
    *Be sure to remember the
order of tasks for preparing the disk. First,
you must create a partition, and then you
must format the partition. Once you have*
*done this, you can install the operating
system and store data on the partition. The
ability to partition and format the system
partition is built into Windows Setup.*

FAT32, and NTFS. Unless you have a special reason for selecting one of the older file systems, you should choose the NTFS file system during installation. Learn more about file systems in Chapter 10.

User Data Migration

The most valuable files on a PC are not the OS and applications, but the user's data. Therefore, when upgrading the OS or moving the user to a new computer, you must plan for a successful *data migration*. When you do an in-place upgrade, you retain all the user settings and data, so data migration is a nonissue. However, when you do a clean installation on a computer that has an older version of Windows, you often need to ensure that the settings and data from the old installation migrate to the new installation. Or, when you purchase a new computer with a new version of Windows, you face migrating settings and data files from an older computer. Windows XP, Windows Vista, and Windows 7 all have ways of handling this for you.

Migration programs from Microsoft and other vendors make the migration of data from one PC to another easier, as required when you must move data from an old computer to a new computer. Microsoft provides the Files and Settings Transfer Wizard in Windows XP and Windows Easy Transfer (WET) Wizard for Windows Vista and Windows 7. Both wizards bring over your data and place it in the correct locations on your hard drive to fulfill the basic task of data migration. They go further by also migrating the settings for Windows and certain Windows applications, including desktop preferences and preferences for Internet Explorer and all Microsoft applications installed on both the old and the new computers. The wizards do not install any applications on the new PC, however, so you must install your applications on the new PC before migrating the data and settings from the old PC.

Windows XP Files and Settings Transfer Wizard   You must run the *Windows XP Files and Settings Transfer Wizard* on both the old and new computer. You start it from Start | All Programs | Accessories | System Tools on a Windows XP computer, or from the main menu of the Windows XP CD on an old computer running Windows 2000 or Windows XP. Choose the local computer's role in the transfer. When the wizard runs on any version of Windows other than Windows XP, the only role available is that of Old Computer.

When you select Old Computer, the wizard collects files and settings and places them in the location you define. This location can be any local hard drive, flash drive, or network share. You can specify a floppy disk, but the data is normally too large for a single floppy disk, and many newer PCs do not come with a floppy drive. Another rarely used option is a direct cable attached to serial ports, but serial ports are disappearing from new PCs as well.

Once you have collected the data, run the wizard on the new computer, point to the data's location, and the wizard will complete the transfer. This replacement process greatly simplifies the time it once took to move your data and configure a new PC with your preferences.

Windows Vista Windows Easy Transfer   *Windows Easy Transfer (WET)* is the Vista utility to use when doing a single transfer to a new Windows Vista computer from one running Windows XP or Windows Vista. It is not practical to use this utility for multiple computers, because it only works on a one-to-one basis with each old and new pair. You can run the WET wizard, shown in Figure 9-1, on the

FIGURE 9-1

Windows Easy Transfer

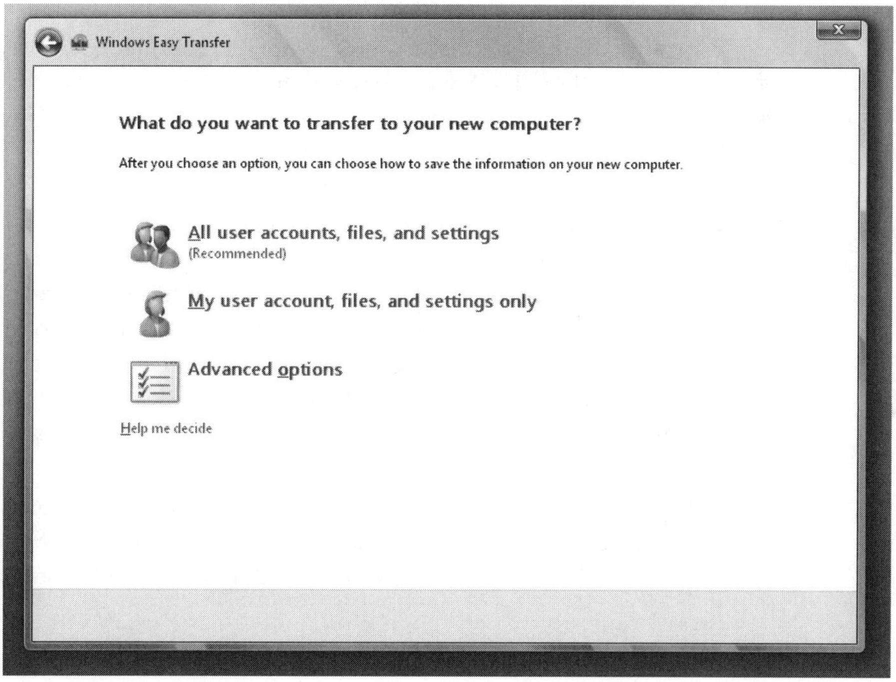

Windows Easy Transfer

What do you want to transfer to your new computer?

After you choose an option, you can choose how to save the information on your new computer.

All user accounts, files, and settings
(Recommended)

My user account, files, and settings only

Advanced options

Help me decide

old Windows XP computer, collecting the settings and files and transferring them directly to the new Windows Vista computer over a network. Or you can transfer them first to an external drive or a writable CD or DVD, and then take the drive or media to the new computer where you run the wizard to complete the transfer.

User State Migration   When you need to migrate data from many computers, or if you need to perform what Microsoft calls a "wipe-and-load migration" from and to the same computer, use the *User State Migration Tool (USMT)*. This tool has been available in succeeding versions for Windows XP, Vista, and Windows 7. It takes longer to prepare, but it results in an automated process that occurs in two stages. The first stage collects files and settings, and the second stage installs the files and settings on the target computer. As with WET, you can use a variety of media locations.

Installation Startup and Source Locations

The most common method for starting Windows Setup for the standard retail version (full or upgrade) is to boot up from the disk or disc media, as we will detail next. Then you will learn about installing over a network, from a recovery CD or DVD, and from a factory recovery partition.

Boot Media

When installing Windows on a new computer that does not have an OS on the hard drive, you will need to boot into the Setup program. How you do this depends on the computer, but your choices include optical drive, floppy drive (not an option in Windows Vista or Windows 7), or USB device.

Optical Drive   The Windows CDs and DVDs are bootable, and if your computer has an optical drive and you have configured the BIOS to boot from that drive, the Setup program should boot. The system BIOS setting, usually described as "boot order" or "boot sequence" and discussed in Chapter 4, is controlled through a PC's BIOS-based setup program. Although we don't recommend modifying the system settings on your computer, if you want to boot from the installation CD and you cannot, you will need to configure the PC's system settings so you can boot from a CD.

Floppy Drive   In the unlikely event that you cannot configure a PC to boot from a CD, Windows 2000 and Windows XP allow you to boot into Setup from a floppy. Of course, this requires a floppy drive, and new PCs don't normally come with floppy drives, but we'll suspend reality for a bit and talk about booting from a floppy. Windows 2000 shipped with four setup boot disks, plus the CD. Windows XP only shipped with a CD and without any boot disks. Therefore, if you must boot Windows XP Setup from floppies, you must create a set of six (yes, six!) Windows XP Setup boot disks using a program downloaded from Microsoft's Website. Then, you insert the first floppy into the drive and start the computer. You will change floppy disks when prompted until all the basic files to support Windows Setup are loaded into memory and the system reboots and requests the Windows CD. Then, the installation proceeds as it would have from that point if you had booted from CD.

USB Device   You can boot into Setup from an external USB drive of any type that can hold the setup boot files, such as a floppy or optical drive, if the BIOS settings support this.

Network Installation

You can also install Windows over a network from a server. A network installation can involve an image installation, an attended installation, or an unattended installation. Any of these network installation methods requires quite a bit of prep work. Here, we will describe the steps required for either an attended or unattended network installation. Later, we will address an over-the-network image installation.

To prepare for an attended or unattended network installation, first, copy the Windows source files into a shared folder on the server; second, configure the client computer to boot up and connect to the server; and third, start the Setup program itself. The actual steps for doing this are extensive, often requiring trained personnel and testing of the procedure.

e x a m

ⓦatch   *The CompTIA A+ Essentials Exam only requires that you understand the differences among the various installation methods. You do not need in-depth hands-on experience with the unattended or drive-imaging methods.*

Installing from a Recovery CD/DVD

Many manufacturers ship computers with OEM Windows installed (whatever version), but most of them do not ship an OEM Windows disc with the computer. They may ship what they call a recovery disc, or they give you the option of creating a recovery disc yourself from a utility installed with Windows. In this case, don't skip creating this disc. However you acquire it, be sure to keep it in a safe place. Without the OEM

Windows disc, the recovery disc is your only source of your legally licensed Windows. If you need to reinstall Windows from a recovery disc, all you need to do is boot up the disc and the recovery program will run. The sad part is that it returns your computer to the state it was in the day you unpacked it and first turned it on. It wipes out all your installed programs and data, and you will have to reinstall the programs and then restore your data from backups. Sometimes installing from a recovery CD is your only option, but not always. In "Diagnosing and Repairing Operating System Failures" in Chapter 11, we will look at how to diagnose operating system failures and how to recover from certain types of failures without reinstalling Windows.

Installing from a Factory Recovery Partition

If a manufacturer does not ship a recovery disc with a Windows computer, or include a utility for creating this disc, they may offer another option, which is a factory recovery partition containing an image of the drive partition on which Windows is installed. The recovery partition itself is hidden and only accessible by a method the manufacturer provides for restoring the system to its fresh-from-the-factory state. Check the manufacturer's documentation long before you need to resort to installing from a factory recovery partition. In many cases, you enter the factory recovery partition utility by pressing a function key as the system starts up. If you install a new version of Windows on a computer with a recovery partition, the new OS may overwrite a critical part of the Windows partition containing information for calling up the recovery program, so check with the manufacturer before upgrading.

Attended Windows Installation

There are two main installation methods: attended and unattended. Installing Windows requires inputting certain unique information for each computer. During an *attended installation* of Windows, also called a "manual installation," you must pay attention throughout the entire process to provide information and to respond to messages.

The Windows Setup Wizard guides you through every step of the process. The on-screen directions are correct and clear, and you will need to make very few decisions. If you are in doubt about a setting, pressing ENTER will likely perform the correct action by selecting a default setting.

Overall, the installation process takes about an hour, and you spend most of that time watching the screen. Feel free to walk away as the installation is taking place, because, if it needs input, the installation program will stop and wait until you click the correct buttons.

on the
job

If you are not available to respond to a prompt on the screen during installation, it will only delay completion. Microsoft has improved the Windows installation process with each version of Windows, and it requires input mainly at the very beginning and at the very end of the process.

The following description is of a clean install, meaning the partitioning and formatting of the hard disk will occur during the installation. You would perform this type of installation on a new computer, or on an old computer when you want a complete new start. A clean install avoids the potential problems of upgrading, which we will describe later in "Upgrading Windows."

Gathering Information

Before you begin an attended installation from a retail version of Windows, gather the specific information you need, which depends on whether you are installing a PC at home or in a business network. Either way, gather the appropriate information, including the following:

- The Product ID code from the envelope or jewel case of the Windows CD
- A 15-character (or less) name, unique on your network, for your computer
- The name of the workgroup or domain the computer will join
- A password for the Administrator account on your computer
- The necessary network configuration information—ask your network administrator

In addition, gather any device driver disks or discs for the computer and its installed peripherals. You may need to download device drivers from manufacturers' Websites. Having these on hand before you start the installation is helpful. Windows may have appropriate drivers for all your devices, but if it does not, it may prompt you to provide them. You can do that during installation or let Windows install minimal generic drivers during Setup, and wait until after the final reboot at the end to install the correct drivers according to the manufacturers' instructions.

The Installation

Begin the attended Windows installation by inserting the Windows distribution CD or DVD and booting the computer. Beyond that, there are some differences in how Setup runs for the various versions of Windows. All the versions examine your hardware configuration early on. Before Windows Vista, the early portion of

Windows Setup ran in character mode until it had copied files to your computer to support the GUI mode portion of Setup. These screens for older Windows versions looked like the one shown here for Windows XP Professional Setup. Notice that you can choose to continue the setup, or repair a Windows XP installation. All versions of Windows that we are studying here include an option to repair an existing installation.

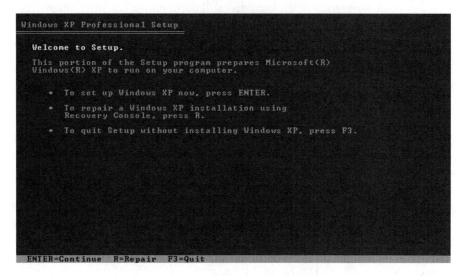

```
Windows XP Professional Setup
───────────────────────────────────────────

  Welcome to Setup.

  This portion of the Setup program prepares Microsoft(R)
  Windows(R) XP to run on your computer.

    ●  To set up Windows XP now, press ENTER.

    ●  To repair a Windows XP installation using
       Recovery Console, press R.

    ●  To quit Setup without installing Windows XP, press F3.




  ENTER=Continue   R=Repair   F3=Quit
```

Windows Vista and Windows 7 Setup screens are nearly identical. They both begin by briefly showing a black character mode screen, then the entire Setup program runs in GUI mode, showing a progress screen with a check-off list of the tasks Setup is performing. These include copying Windows files, expanding Windows files, installing features, installing updates, and completing installation. New with Windows Vista and included with Windows 7 is a screen to select the language and other *regional settings*, such as date, time, and currency formats, and keyboard or input method. See Figure 9-2. Previously, Windows installed in English, and if you wanted a different language for the user interface, you had to add a language pack on top of English. Beginning with Windows Vista, the language component is separate from the rest of the OS code, a feature called the *Multilingual User Interface (MUI)*, which allows you to install a language other than English. You can also install multiple languages without first installing English. Except for the logo and color, this screen is identical in Windows Vista and Windows 7, as are many others.

In all versions, when prompted, enter your product key. This is mandatory. You cannot proceed without doing this. Windows will use the product key when

Select a language on this Windows 7 Setup page.

activating after Setup completes. When the End User License Agreement (EULA) appears, read it and follow the instructions to acknowledge acceptance of the agreement and to continue. This is mandatory, as it is your agreement to comply with your license to use Windows that allows you to install Windows on one computer for each license that you own.

Windows Setup will display a list of existing partitions and unpartitioned space. Select the location where you want to install the OS, partitioning the space if necessary. If you create a new partition, you will need to format it. Windows XP and earlier versions will give you the option of choosing FAT or NTFS file systems, in which case you should select Format The Partition Using the NTFS File System. Windows Vista and Windows 7 will default to formatting a new partition with the NTFS file system.

Setup copies files to the location you indicated or to the newly formatted partition. Unless you specify another location, Setup creates a folder named Windows in C:\, into which it installs the OS, creating appropriate subfolders below it. After it finishes copying the base set of files to this location, your computer reboots. At this point in

Windows XP Setup, graphical mode begins. On the left of the screen, Setup tracks the progress, showing completed and uncompleted tasks (see Figure 9-3).

At that same point in Windows Vista Setup, it briefly displays a text-mode screen while it is restarting, but you are soon back to a GUI that looks a bit more like Windows Vista and is usually at a higher screen resolution than before the restart. All versions of Windows Setup will restart several times as they install components and update Windows. Follow the instructions, accepting the defaults when you are unsure.

If Setup detects a network card, the network components will install and configure with default settings. All versions will give you a chance to personalize Windows by user name and password, computer name, information for connecting to a Windows Domain (if applicable), and options for date, time, and time zone. Figure 9-4 shows the Windows Vista Setup screen in which you create a user name, select a picture to represent that user, and create a password and password hint.

After Setup is complete, your job is not finished. You will now need to configure Windows to personalize it for the user. We'll talk more about that topic after we look at unattended installations and upgrading Windows.

FIGURE 9-3

The graphical mode of Windows XP Setup

A Windows Vista Setup screen where you choose a user name and picture

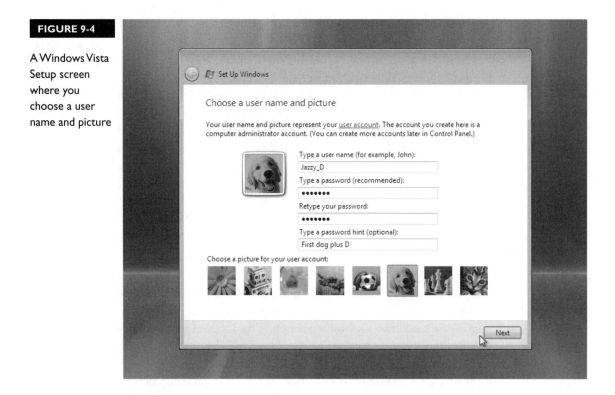

Unattended Installation

An *unattended installation* is one in which the installation process is automated. There are two general types of unattended installations:

- A scripted installation using *answer files* and *Uniqueness Database Files (UDFs)*, which provide the data normally provided by a user during an attended installation
- An image installation, using either Microsoft software tools or a third-party tool

Scripted Installation

A scripted installation uses scripts that someone has prepared ahead of time. Organizations with large numbers of desktop computers needing identical applications and desktop configurations use this. This type of installation normally requires trained people who plan and implement the installation using a variety of automation methods including scripts and access to the Windows source files on a *distribution server*. A typical scripted installation scenario involves placing the Windows source files from the distribution disc onto a file share on a server, which is then called a *distribution share*. This assumes sufficient licenses for the number of installations from these source files. Then, each desktop computer boots up, either from the local hard drive or from another source, and runs a script that connects to the distribution server to begin the installation. Although we place scripted installations under unattended installations here, the amount of interaction required ranges from none to as much as is required for an attended installation. In fact, certain software on the server side, such as Microsoft's Systems Management Server (SMS) can, with proper configuration of each client computer, push an installation down from the server with no one sitting at each desktop. This can include an automated installation of user applications on top of the newly installed Windows OS.

Drive Imaging

In organizations that want to install the same OS and all the same application software on many desktop PCs, drive imaging is often used. A *drive image* is an exact duplicate of an entire hard drive's contents, including the OS and all installed software, applied to one or more identically configured computers. This is a little tricky since each Windows installation must have a unique license and a unique computer name. Tools are available for creating drive images that solve this problem. Before Windows Vista, Microsoft had tools for preparing a computer for imaging, but it did not have imaging software. Since then, Microsoft has created a complete set of tools for preparing the image, creating the image, and distributing the image. Next, we will briefly describe working with the Microsoft tools prior to Windows Vista, and then we will provide an overview of how to do this with newer Microsoft tools.

Imaging with Older Microsoft Tools   Before Windows Vista, the Microsoft tools to perform the various functions for preparing, creating, and distributing an image used a variety of utilities that did not interact well together. A third-party program had to perform the actual imaging. Automation and customization depended on creating scripts, which required considerable knowledge and experience. The entire process was very expensive and time-consuming, so to be cost-effective, only when an organization needed to roll out the images to a large number of desktops was this done.

Imaging with Newer Microsoft Tools   Microsoft has developed an entire suite of tools for deploying Windows to large numbers of desktop computers.

These tools and sets of recommended procedures cover the planning, building (of the images), and deployment phases. Even an overview of these tools would take a great deal of time and space, and the CompTIA exam only requires that you understand the basics of image installations. Therefore, we will simply list and briefly describe the tools for the build and deployment phases. The acronym *BDD* in some of the following tools stands for "Business Desktop Deployment."

- **BDD Workbench**   A technician uses this tool to create and manage both the distribution share and the various images. Plus, this tool will configure several deployment sources, including a single server, a deployment share, a DVD ISO image, or a directory that contains all the files needed for a customized deployment from a server running Microsoft's SMS Server software.
- **Windows System Image Manager**   This tool allows a technician to create the components for automating custom installs using custom scripts.
- **ImageX**   Use this tool to create the disk images.
- **Microsoft Windows Preinstallation Environment (Windows PE)**   PE is a bootable environment that gives operating system support during three types of operations: installing Windows, troubleshooting, and recovery.
- **User State Migration Tool (USMT)**   Technicians use this tool for migrating files and settings to many desktop computers. It does not migrate programs, however, just data files, operating system settings, and settings from Microsoft applications.

Microsoft is not the only source for such tools: many third-party vendors offer an array of imaging and deployment tools. Learn more about all of these tools by searching on Google.

Upgrading Windows

In this section, we will look at why you would upgrade Windows rather than do a clean install, what tasks you should perform before an upgrade, and how to run an upgrade.

Why Upgrade?

An upgrade installation of Windows involves installing the new version of Windows directly on top of an existing installation. During an upgrade, Windows reads all the previous settings from the old registry, adapts them for the new registry, and transfers all hardware and software configuration information, thus saving you the trouble of reinstalling applications and reconfiguring your desktop the way you like it. Although you can upgrade Windows with the full retail disc of the latest version of Windows, you can also buy a special Upgrade version of Windows that is much less expensive. The drawback to this version is that it will only install on a computer with a previous legally licensed version of Windows preinstalled.

Pre-Upgrade Tasks

Before purchasing the Windows OS for an upgrade, check to be sure there is an upgrade path from the installed version to the new one. Then you are ready for the pre-upgrade tasks.

Requirements and Compatibility

When upgrading Windows, pay close attention to compatibility issues, run the Upgrade Advisor, and be ready to resolve any problems you find. For example, if it shows that the new operating system does not have a driver for your network adapter, and you proceed with the upgrade, you will not be able to access the network through the existing adapter. If the Upgrade Advisor found incompatible hardware or software, take steps to resolve these problems before you upgrade.

Resolving Software Incompatibility   If an upgrade is available for an incompatible application program, obtain it and check with the manufacturer. Upgrade the application before upgrading the OS (unless advised otherwise by the manufacturer).

Remove any programs that will not run in the new OS from the computer before upgrading. There are also programs that interfere with the Windows Setup program, but are compatible with the new version after installation. This is often true of antivirus software. The Upgrade Advisor report will list these, in which case follow the instructions under Details in the Upgrade Advisor report. You may need to uninstall the program before the upgrade and reinstall it after the new version of Windows runs successfully.

Resolving Hardware Incompatibility   Before upgrading, remove any program from the computer that will not run in the OS. Go to their Website or phone them. Hardware incompatibility is most often actually due to an incompatible device driver. The manufacturer may have an updated driver that will work. If so, obtain the driver beforehand, and follow the manufacturer's instructions. You may need to wait to upgrade the device driver until after the installation.

If your research shows that a hardware incompatibility cannot be resolved, remove the hardware in question, and replace it with a component that has a driver that works with the new OS.

Backing Up Data

Back up any data from the local hard drive. Installing a new OS should not put your data in danger, but you just never know. Upgrading makes many changes to your computer, replacing critical system files with those of the new OS. If your computer loses power at an inopportune time, it could become unusable. This is a rare but real danger, especially if the computer is very old. Besides, surely you need to back up your hard drive. Backing up can be as simple as copying the contents of your My Documents (Windows 2000/XP) or Documents (Windows Vista/7) folder onto an external hard drive or flash drive, or using the built-in Windows Backup program, NTBACKUP.EXE, to back up files to any nonoptical drive attached to your computer. Learn more about the Windows Backup program in Chapter 10.

Cleaning Up the Hard Drive

Before upgrading your computer to a new version of Windows, clean up the hard drive, especially the C: volume. This cleanup should include removing both unwanted programs and unnecessary files. After you perform these two tasks, use the Windows Drive Defragmenter to optimize the remaining space on the hard drive.

Remove Unwanted Programs   Begin your cleanup by removing all unwanted programs. The programs you should look for are those nifty programs you installed on a whim and now find you either dislike or never use. They are all taking up space on the hard drive. Many (but not all) have an uninstall shortcut on the same menu with the shortcut that launches the program. Select uninstall, and it should remove the program and solve the problem.

For programs that do not have a shortcut to an uninstall program, open Control Panel and find the appropriate program removal tool for your version of Windows. This would be Add/Remove Programs in Windows 2000, Add Or Remove Programs in Windows XP, or Programs And Features in Windows Vista and Windows 7, and scroll through the list looking for programs you are sure you will never use. Be careful not to remove updates for Microsoft Office or Windows. When you complete this task, leave this applet open while you remove unwanted Windows components, as described next.

Remove Unwanted Windows Components   As you prepare to upgrade to a new version of Windows, you should also consider removing unwanted Windows components. To do this, open the applet you used to remove programs. In Windows 2000 or Windows XP, click the Add/Remove Windows Components button on the left. In Windows Vista and Windows 7, select the Turn Windows Features On Or Off task to the left of the Uninstall Or Change a Program page of Programs And Features. In Windows 2000 or Windows XP, this will open the Windows Components Wizard. In Windows Vista or Windows 7, it will open the Windows Features dialog, shown here. Browse through the list and remove any unnecessary components.

Remove Unnecessary Files   It's amazing how fast hard drive space fills up. One way it fills up is with large data files, especially music, video, and picture files. Another, less obvious way that hard drive space fills up is with temporary files, especially temporary Internet files that accumulate on the local hard drive while you are browsing the Internet. Windows has a nifty utility for cleaning up these files—Disk Cleanup. To launch this utility, select Start | All Programs (Programs in Windows 2000) | Accessories | System Tools | Disk Cleanup. It will walk you through the process. In Windows 2000 and Windows XP, you begin by selecting a drive; in Windows Vista, you begin by choosing to clean up those files associated with you, or the files for all users on your computer, and then choose the drive. In all versions, Disk Cleanup then spends a few minutes analyzing your files and calculating the space you can potentially free up. When complete, it will display a list of file types that you can select or deselect. Disk Cleanup will remove all the selected files.

Defragmenting the Hard Drive

Over time, Windows develops a problem on its hard drives called "fragmented files." Fragmentation will slow the system down when reading files into memory. The solution is defragmenting, and you should do it any time you remove programs and/or delete a large number of files. The tool you will use is the Disk Defragmenter utility found in Windows on the same System Tools menu with Disk Cleanup (described in the previous section). In the Disk Defragmenter folder, select a drive volume. Before Windows Vista, you could select Analyze for an analysis showing if the drive(s) needed defragmenting. Beginning in Windows Vista, Disk Defragmenter allows you to defrag one or more volumes immediately or to schedule it for later. The default setting in Vista is to run on a weekly schedule, defragmenting all drives, as shown here.

Running an Upgrade

To start an attended upgrade to Windows, start the existing version of Windows and place the distribution disc into the drive. Wait a minute to see if the Setup program starts on its own. If it does not start, use My Computer or Computer to browse to

FIGURE 9-5

Choose Upgrade in Windows Vista or Windows 7 Setup.

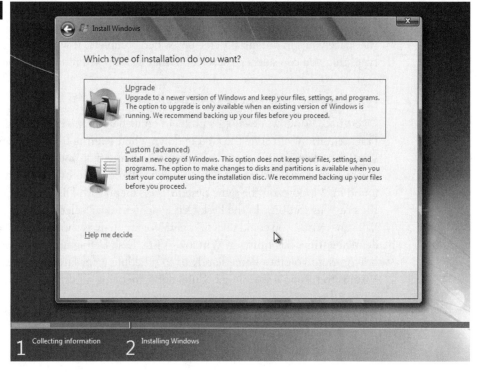

the CD and launch the Setup program. Setup will detect the existing version of Windows. If it is a version that you can directly upgrade, Windows XP Setup will show Upgrade in the Installation Type box, and Windows Vista and Windows 7 will include Upgrade as an active option in the screen shown in Figure 9-5. If the computer cannot be upgraded, this option will be grayed out in these newer Windows Setup programs. Click Next to continue with an upgrade, and Setup will continue in a similar manner to a clean installation, only with fewer interruptions for information, and you will not be prompted to create a new partition for the OS since that would wipe out the installed OS and programs. You will need to provide a product key for any retail version, full or upgrade.

Configuring Windows

After installing Windows, you have a few post-installation and configuration tasks. They include verifying network access (assuming connection to a network), registration, activation, and update installation. You should complete these tasks before moving on to customizing the desktop for yourself or another user, and performing other desktop management tasks such as installing new devices, installing applications, and configuring virtual memory.

Network Configuration

Once you have completed the installation, if the computer is on a network, verify that it can communicate with other computers on the network. If it cannot, you may need to add a device driver for the network adapter and/or configure the network components. Network connectivity is important because this is the best way to download updates to your newly installed operating system—a task you must do as soon as you have Internet access.

Checking Network Connectivity

Use My Network Places (Windows 2000/XP) to determine if you can see any computers on the network besides your own. In Windows 2000, this utility will be on the desktop, and in Windows XP, it is on the Start Menu. In Windows Vista and Windows 7, look for a shortcut named Network on the Start Menu. Only computers with the Server service turned on are visible. This service supports file and print sharing and is turned on by default, so you should see your computer and others on the network.

Adding a Network Adapter Device Driver

If Windows Setup does not recognize your network adapter, it may not install a driver; alternatively, it may recognize the network adapter but may not have the appropriate driver in the source directory. In this case, a prompt to provide a new device driver may appear, but we find it is best to wait until after Setup completes to install new drivers.

If you are installing network drivers or other drivers after the installation, wait until after the final reboot, and then follow the manufacturer's instructions for installing the device driver(s). Learn more about installing and configuring network components in Chapter 14.

Enabling Wake on LAN

Imagine that your computer at your desk at work was powered off, and you are about to give a presentation far from your office when you realize you forgot a file that you need. A feature in many modern network adapters might save you from going back to your desk. Called Wake On LAN, it allows a powered off computer to be powered on when someone connects to it over the network. To enable or disable Wake On LAN, open Device Manager and double-click your network adapter to open its Properties dialog. Click the Advanced tab, and scroll down in the list until you see Wake On LAN (or a similar description), as shown here. If it isn't listed, your network adapter does not support it. If it is there, select it, and enable or disable it using the Value drop down box.

NVIDIA nForce 10/100/1000 Mbps Ethernet Properties

General | Advanced | Driver | Details | Resources | Power Management

The following properties are available for this network adapter. Click the property you want to change on the left, and then select its value on the right.

Property:

- IP Checksum Offload
- Jumbo Packet
- Large Send Offload V1 (IPv4)
- Large Send Offload V2 (IPv4)
- Large Send Offload V2 (IPv6)
- Low Power State Link Speed
- Network Address
- Priority & VLAN
- Speed/duplex settings
- TCP Checksum Offload (IPv4)
- TCP Checksum Offload (IPv6)
- UDP Checksum Offload (IPv4)
- UDP Checksum Offload (IPv6)
- VLAN Id
- WakeOnLAN From PowerOff

Value:

Enabled

OK | Cancel

exam

ⓦ**a t c h**   *The CompTIA A+ Essentials (2009 Edition) Objectives for Exam 220-701 lists Wake On LAN under Power Management, along with Suspend, Sleep Timers, Hibernate, and Standby. Be sure to remember* *that you configure those items through the Power Options applet, and turn on or off Wake On LAN using the Properties dialog box for the network adapter.*

Registration and Activation

During the installation of Windows XP, you are prompted to register Windows and to activate it; Windows Vista and Windows 7 provide a check box to allow activation to occur once installation is complete. Many people confuse registration and activation. These are two separate operations. *Registration* informs the software manufacturer who the owner or user of the product is, and provides contact information such as name, address, company, phone number, e-mail address, and so on, about them. Registration of a Microsoft product is still entirely optional.

Activation, more formally called *Microsoft Product Activation (MPA)*, is a method designed to combat software piracy, meaning that Microsoft wishes to ensure that only a single computer uses each license for Windows. This requirement extends to all versions of Windows since Windows XP. Here you'll learn more about activation.

Mandatory Activation Within 30 Days of Installation

Activation is mandatory, but you may skip this step during installation. You will have 30 days in which to activate Windows, during which time it will work normally. If you don't activate it within that time frame, Windows will automatically disable itself at the end of the 30 days. Don't worry about forgetting, because once installed, Windows XP frequently reminds you to activate it with a balloon message over the tray area of the taskbar. The messages even tell you how many days you have left, as shown here.

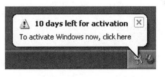

on the **job** *Understanding activation is important because all Microsoft products since Windows XP require it, and Microsoft is not the only software vendor using an activation process. Software purchased with a volume license agreement does not require product activation.*

Activation Mechanics

When you choose to activate, the product ID, generated from the product key code that you entered during installation, combines with a 50-digit value that identifies your key hardware components to create an installation ID code. This code must go to Microsoft, either automatically if you have an Internet connection, or verbally via a phone call to Microsoft, which then gives you a 42-digit product activation code.

on the
Job

If you must activate Windows XP by phone, be sure you are sitting at your computer. Our experience is that you have to do all this in real time, including entering the code, while the representative dictates it to you; you cannot write down the number and use it later. Your experience, however, may be different than ours.

MPA does not scan the contents of the hard disk, search for personal information, or gather information on the make, model, or manufacturer of the computer or its components. Nor does it gather personal information about you as part of the activation process.

Reactivation

Sometimes reactivation is required after major changes to a computer. To understand why, you need to understand how MPA creates the 50-digit value that identifies your hardware. MPA generates this hardware identifier value used during activation, called the "hardware hash," by applying a special mathematical algorithm to values assigned to the following hardware:

Display adapter	Processor type
SCSI adapter	Processor serial number
IDE adapter	Hard disk device
Network adapter MAC address	Hard disk volume serial number
RAM amount range	Optical drive

MPA will occasionally recalculate the hardware hash and compare it to the one created during activation. When it detects a significant difference in the hardware hash, you will be required to *reactivate,* and you may need to contact Microsoft and explain the reason for the reactivation. This is Microsoft's way of ensuring that you did not install the product on another computer.

Adding new hardware will not necessarily require reactivation, but replacing any components in the preceding list, or repartitioning and reformatting a drive, will affect the hardware hash. We have had to reactivate after making a number of changes to a computer and again when we decommissioned a computer and installed the licensed retail version of Windows on a different computer. In both instances, we had to do this over the phone because we had to explain the circumstances to the representative.

Updating Windows

As soon as possible after the installation is completed and network connectivity confirmed, connect to the Windows Update site and update Windows. This task is important for the sake of stability and improved security. Windows Updates have been an important, but often neglected, task for computer users. To provide friendlier ways to update software, Microsoft has provided an automatic update utility and improved their update Web pages.

Windows Update and Microsoft Update

At one time, Microsoft had separate update pages for Windows and Microsoft Office. The *Windows Update Website* only checked for and downloaded updates for Windows and the Microsoft Office Update page only checked for and downloaded updates for Microsoft Office. It does little good to have your OS fully updated but not your Microsoft Office programs.

Now they have combined Windows Update and Microsoft Office Update into one site called Microsoft Update that checks for updates to both Windows and Office. Configure Windows Update to connect to the Microsoft Update site whenever you launch it by opening the Windows Update applet in Control Panel and selecting the Microsoft Update option. Then, when you launch Windows Update from the Start menu in Windows 2000 or Windows XP, it will open Internet Explorer and connect to the Microsoft Update site where you can interactively choose the updates you wish to install. In Windows Vista and Windows 7, when you launch Windows Update, it will open the Windows Update Control Panel applet and check for updates.

Although running Windows Update is handy when you want to update interactively, depend on Automatic Update to reliably keep your computer up-to-date.

Automatic Update

Automatic Update will automatically connect to the Microsoft site and download updates. Soon after installing Windows XP, a message balloon will pop up suggesting that you enable automate updates. If you click this message, the Automatic Updates Setup wizard will run, allowing you to configure the update program.

You do not have to wait to see this message balloon. In Windows XP, simply right-click My Computer (on the Start menu), select Properties, and then click the Automatic Updates tab and select the settings you desire. Windows Vista and Windows 7 install with updates turned on using Microsoft Update (updating both

Windows and Microsoft programs). You can change these settings by opening Windows Update and selecting Change Settings from the Task pane on the left. Then you can configure updates to occur at a regular interval. Figure 9-6 shows the Change Settings page from Windows Vista.

If you have a slow Internet connection (dial-up), you may want to disable Automatic Updates and opt to use Windows Update to manually connect and download the updates at times that will not interfere with your work. If you have a faster connection, you may elect to have the updates downloaded automatically, and review and select those updates you wish to install. Whichever option you choose, keeping Windows up-to-date should reduce the number of viruses that exploit system flaws.

Other Updating Options

In spite of these easy options for updating Windows over the Internet, how you actually obtain updates will depend on the organization (school or business) where

FIGURE 9-6

The Windows
Vista Change
Settings page

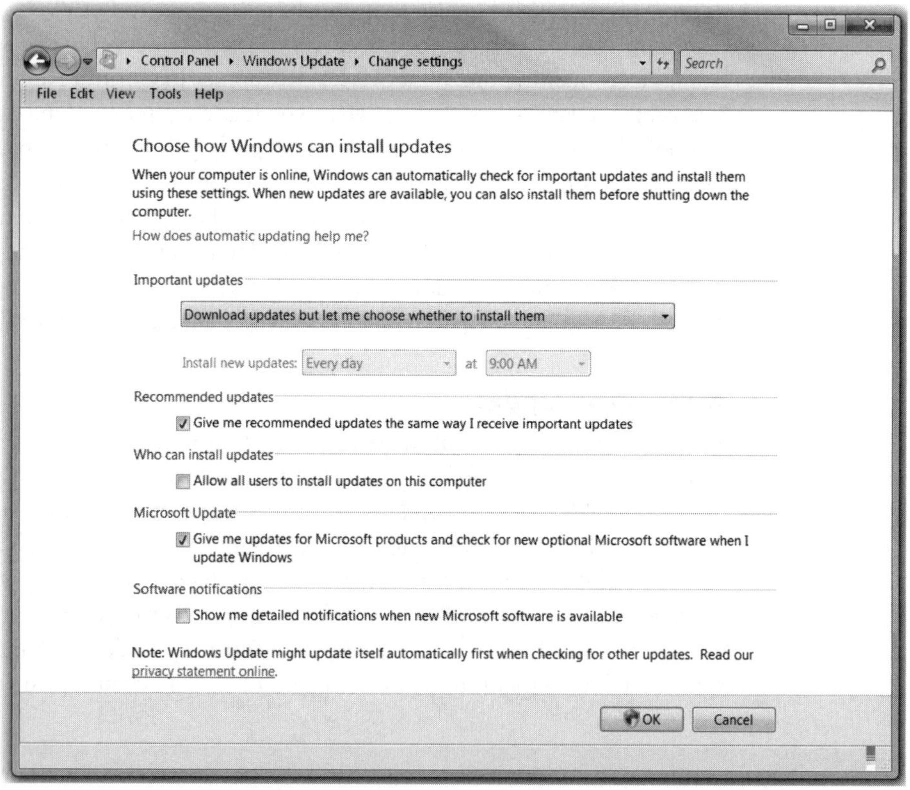

you install Windows. In some organizations, the IT department may distribute updates intended for new installations on optical disc in order to install them before a computer ever connects to a network. Other organizations may make them available on a shared folder on the network.

Updates can bring their own problems. Therefore, many organizations with IT support staff will test all updates before distributing them to the user desktops. For individuals and small organizations, it is too time-consuming to set up a test computer on which to install updates to test them before updating production PCs. Therefore, they rely on the ability to uninstall an update using the Add Or Remove Programs applet in Control Panel in Windows 2000 and Windows XP or the Programs And Features applet in Windows Vista and Windows 7.

Install Additional Applications and Windows Components

After installing Windows and updating it, install and configure any security software, and then install the applications the user requires. For the majority of applications—those that are proven compatible with the new version of Windows—you will simply follow the manufacturer's instructions for installing and configuring the program. Applications will install into a folder named Program Files, located in the root of the disk volume where you installed Windows. In Chapter 10, we will discuss file locations and file management in Windows. After installing each program, be sure to update it and to configure automatic updates for the application, if available. Microsoft knows that sometimes it's absolutely necessary to run a very old, incompatible application in a new version of Windows, so they have provided at least one solution for you. In all versions of Windows studied here, you can run the Compatibility Wizard to configure Compatibility Mode for the application. In Windows 7, Compatibility Mode doesn't work, so instead you can run the application in Windows XP Mode. We described both of these options in Chapter 8.

Installing New Devices

Installing a new plug and play device involves attaching the device and waiting while Windows recognizes the device and installs the appropriate device driver. If Windows does not have a driver, it will prompt you to supply a location (disc drive, hard drive, or network) or connect to the Internet and search. A few devices may require that you run the device installation program before connecting the device; this has been true of printers in the past.

A *device driver* is program code that allows an operating system to control the use of a physical device. Device manufacturers create device drivers for common operating systems and make the drivers available with the device.

Adequate Permissions

In order to install or uninstall device drivers, you must log on as the Administrator or a member of the Administrators group. We discuss user accounts and permissions in Chapter 16. If you attempt to install a device driver while logged on with a nonadministrator account, you will see a message stating that you have insufficient security privileges to install or uninstall a device. However, once installed, an ordinary user may disconnect and reconnect the device without restriction.

Attaching Devices

You can attach most plug and play devices while the computer and the operating system are running. Because most devices today are plug and play, this is almost the rule rather than the exception—but always read the documentation.

Vendor-Supplied Installation Programs

Most devices come with a vendor-supplied installation program. If the documentation tells you to connect or install the device first, do so before installing the software. In this case, the Found New Hardware balloon will appear over the systray, from which you may launch the Add Hardware Wizard, which should then configure the device, often prompting you for information. If the documentation instructs you to install the software first, do so; then, after attaching the device, the Found New Hardware balloon will appear.

Driver Signing

A device driver becomes a part of the operating system with access to the core operating system code. Therefore, a poorly written device driver can cause problems—even system crashes. Drivers have long been a major cause of operating system instability. To prevent this problem, Microsoft works with manufacturers to ensure that driver code is safe to use.

Approved driver files have a *digital signature*, which is encrypted data placed in a file. The all-encompassing term for this is *code signing,* and when applied to device drivers, it is called *driver signing.* Microsoft began signing all of the operating system code starting with Windows 2000.

When you attempt to install a file, Windows looks for a digital signature. If it finds one, it uses a process called *file signature verification* to unencrypt the signature data and use the information to verify that the program code in the file was not modified since the signature was added. If it sees tampering, you will receive a warning and can stop the installation.

This certainly does not mean that all unsigned device drivers are bad. If you trust the source of a device driver, you can let it install on your computer. You will see a warning similar to that shown here. If you trust the source of the driver, select Continue Anyway.

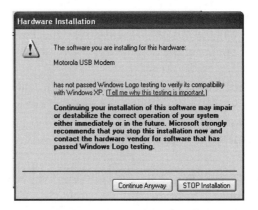

We strongly recommend that if you install an unsigned driver, you first back up all your data. When you install an unsigned driver, Windows will automatically create a restore point before making any changes.

If you suspect a problem with the device driver, restore the operating system to the restore point by opening the System Restore utility from Start | All Programs | Accessories | System Restore and selecting Restore My Computer To An Earlier Time. Click Next, and then select the restore point created at the time you started the device driver installation.

e x a m

⊕ a t c h *Be sure you understand the difference between signed and un-signed drivers.*

Windows will not always allow you to install an unsigned driver. For instance, 64-bit Windows Vista will not load unsigned drivers.

Automated vs. Manual Driver Installation

Most PCs and peripheral devices are fully plug and play, as are the Windows operating systems since Windows 2000. Therefore, when Windows detects a newly installed device, the operating system does an automated search for an appropriate device driver. If it finds one, it installs it and configures the device. You may have to answer a few questions during the configuration process.

The driver it finds during this automated search may be one that came with Windows or one that you preinstalled before installing the device. If Windows cannot find a driver during this automated search, it will prompt you to insert media or browse to the folder containing the driver.

Verifying Driver Installation

After installing a device and its driver and associated utility program, verify the success of the installation. Do this by checking Device Manager and by testing the functionality of the new device.

Device Manager   Immediately after installing a new device, open Device Manager and look for the device you just installed by browsing for it. If the device is in the list, and does not have a yellow circle with an exclamation mark over its icon, the system considers it to be functioning properly.

Functionality   You should also test the functionality of the new device, because sometimes Device Manager does not detect a problem, but when you try to use the device, it does not function properly. This is usually due to a configuration option that does not show up as a problem in Device Manager. An example of this is a network adapter that is functioning okay from Device Manager's point of view but will not allow you to access the network. There are higher-level configuration options for a network adapter that must be correct before it will work. Learn more about configuring network adapters in Chapter 14.

If a device does not work, check the documentation. You may have skipped a configuration step or need to supply more information before it is fully configured.

Virtual Memory

Windows allows you to have several programs open in memory at the same time. Called multitasking, this feature, combined with large program and data files, means that it is possible to run out of physical RAM in which to keep all the open programs. When a Windows computer is running low on memory available for the operating system and any loaded applications, it will use and manage a portion of disk space as if it were RAM.

Virtual memory is the use of a portion of hard disk as memory. Windows uses a special *paging file*, *PAGEFILE.SYS*, to allocate disk space for virtual memory. By default, Windows creates this file in the root of C:. "Swapping" is the act of moving data and code between this file and RAM, and therefore the paging file is also called the "swap file."

Because of virtual memory things do not come to a screeching halt whenever we run out of memory for the operating system and for all the applications we have open. Much of the data and program code not needed in the current application will move into the swap file. The user is generally unaware of this process. When you switch to a program that has code or data in the swap file, you may experience a slight delay while the OS brings it back into memory after moving other data to the virtual memory space on disk.

As a rule, Windows manages virtual memory just fine without intervention. We recommend that, with few exceptions, you should not modify the default settings on your computer. Windows sets the size of the paging file, PAGEFILE.SYS, to 1.5 times the size of the installed physical RAM, which is an optimum setting for most uses of desktop or laptop computers.

There are some exceptions to this size. Sometimes the virtual memory settings need to change to improve performance. As an example, some applications (very few) recommend resizing the paging file (swap file) for better performance. It is also possible that such software would also include resizing in its installation process.

If you must change the page file size, Exercise 9-1 will guide you to the Virtual Memory settings. These settings include the size and location of the page file and the number of page files used. If the present size is less than 1.5 times the size of the installed RAM, select the option for System Managed Size and click Set, followed by OK. The next time you reboot, it will resize the paging file to 1.5 times the size of the physical RAM.

In Exercise 9-1, you will view the Virtual Memory settings on your computer. The default location of the paging file is on drive C:. If you are running out of free disk space on drive C:—and if you have other internal hard drive volumes—consider moving the paging file to another drive that has more free space. You can also have more than one paging file, but this is not normally necessary on a desktop or laptop computer. Never place the paging file on an external hard drive, because it may not be available during startup and this could prevent Windows from launching.

EXERCISE 9-1

Viewing the Virtual Memory Settings

You can easily view the present Virtual Memory settings for your computer.

1. Right-click My Computer, or Computer, and select Properties. If you are running Windows 2000 or Windows XP, skip to Step 3.

2. In Windows Vista or Windows 7, select Advanced System Settings from the task list. This will bring up the System Properties dialog box.

3. In the System Properties dialog box, select the Advanced tab.

4. Under Performance on the Advanced tab page, click Settings.

5. In the Performance Options dialog box, select the Advanced tab.

6. Under Virtual Memory, click Change to view the Virtual Memory settings for all the hard drives on your computer (see Figure 9-7).

7. If you made no changes, click Cancel three times to close the three dialog boxes: Virtual Memory, Performance Options, and System Properties.

Power Management

Another configuration task to consider is power management. In Chapter 6, you learned about the power management features in Windows, how to configure the features that are especially important to a laptop, which are Hibernate and Standby/Sleep, and

SCENARIO & SOLUTION

How do I boot into the Windows Setup program on a computer with an unpartitioned hard disk?	If the computer can boot from the optical drive (as most can), place the Windows distribution disc into the drive, and start the computer.
Windows is prompting me to activate my upgrade of Windows, but I do not want to send personal information to Microsoft. Should I activate Windows?	This is not a problem. Although the activation process is mandatory, it does not send personal information to Microsoft.
I have Windows XP Professional running on my computer and would like to upgrade to Windows 7 Professional, but the retail version is too expensive. What should I do?	Buy the Upgrade version of Windows 7 Professional; it will be much less expensive, and it will install as an upgrade to Windows XP Professional.

FIGURE 9-7

The Virtual
Memory dialog
box

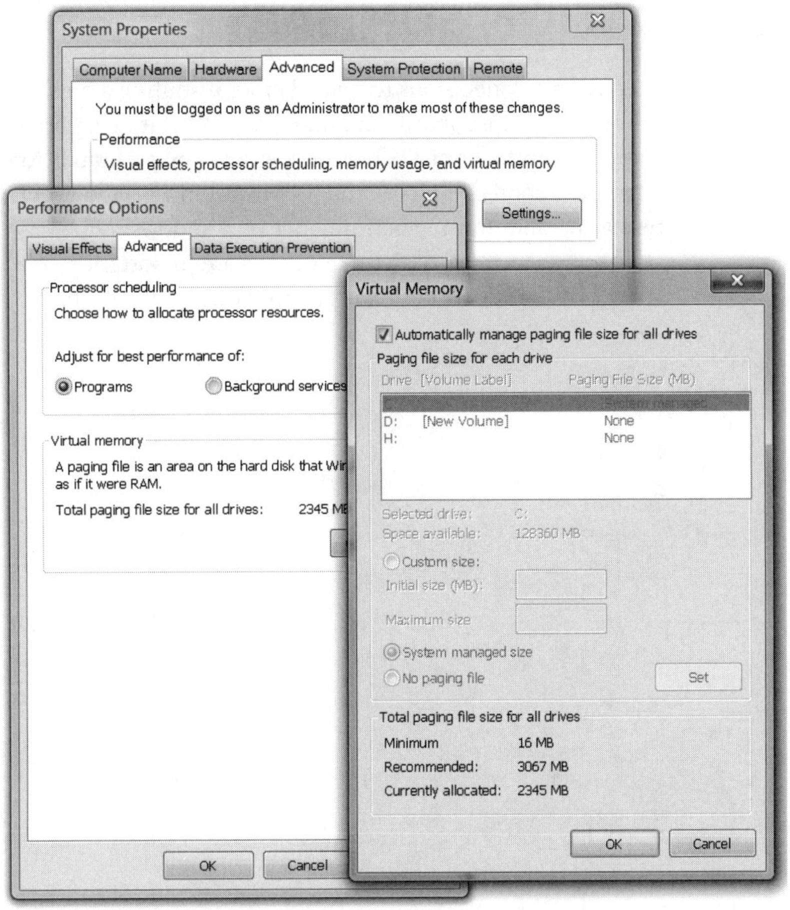

how to set the sleep timers for your settings. Power management is available on all
Windows Computers and is very important for saving power under all circumstances,
not just for laptops. Therefore, after you install a new version of Windows, open the
Power Options applet from Control Panel and explore the options.

CERTIFICATION SUMMARY

You have many decisions to make before installing a new version of Windows. Will this be a clean installation or an upgrade? Will it be an attended or a fully automated unattended installation? What tasks should you perform before installing or upgrading? What tasks should you perform after installing Windows? Finally, what will improve the startup and running performance of Windows?

The answers to all of these questions are important to understand for passing your CompTIA A+ Essentials Exams, and for doing your job.

✓ TWO-MINUTE DRILL

Here are some of the key points covered in Chapter 9.

Installing Windows

❑ Installing Windows involves three stages: preparation, installation, and follow-up tasks.

❑ Preparation tasks include verifying the target computer meets the physical hardware requirements, as well as the hardware and software compatibility requirements.

❑ It is important to plan how to start Setup and the location of the source files.

❑ An attended installation requires the presence of a person who can respond to occasional prompts for information.

❑ Scripts that answer the Setup program's questions automate an unattended installation.

❑ A drive image is an exact duplicate of an entire hard drive's contents, including the OS and all installed software.

❑ An upgrade installs the new version of Windows directly on top of an existing installation, transferring all the settings from the old installation into the new one.

❑ An upgrade version of Windows is less expensive than a full retail version, but will only install into a previous legal installation of Windows.

❑ Before upgrading, test for incompatible software and hardware, and then resolve any incompatibilities.

❑ Before upgrading, back up all data, clean up the hard drive, and then defragment it.

Configuring Windows

❑ After installation, test network connectivity and, if necessary, add and configure a network adapter driver. Enable or disable Wake On LAN through the Properties dialog of the network adapter.

❑ Activating Windows is mandatory, but registration is optional.

❑ As long as you have an Internet connection, you should consider having Windows update automatically. Windows Vista and Windows 7 have Automatic Updates turned on by default.

❑ After completing a Windows installation and performing the most urgent configuration tasks, you should install and configure security programs and then install and configure other applications.

❑ If you must install an old application that is not compatible with the newly installed version of Windows, first attempt to get the program to run by configuring Compatibility Mode. If that does not work, and if you are trying to get a Windows XP application to run in Windows 7, use Windows XP Mode.

❑ Install any device drivers not installed during Setup.

❑ Sometimes the virtual memory settings need to change to improve performance.

❑ Check the Power Options applet to see if you should make any changes to improve power management.

SELF TEST

The following questions will help you measure your understanding of the material presented in this chapter. Read all of the choices carefully, because there might be more than one correct answer. Choose all correct answers for each question.

Installing Windows

1. Which of the following refers to the lowest level of CPU, the minimum amount of RAM, and the free hard disk space needed to install an OS?
   A. Hardware compatibility
   B. Software compatibility
   C. Hardware requirements
   D. Hardware optimizing

2. What is the task order when preparing a new hard drive for a new OS installation?
   A. Format, then partition, then install the OS
   B. Partition, then install OS, then format
   C. Format, then install OS, then partition
   D. Partition, then format, then install OS

3. What is the preferred file system for Windows?
   A. NTFS
   B. FAT16
   C. FAT32
   D. FAT

4. What are the three boot media sources for Windows Setup? Select all that apply.
   A. Floppy disk
   B. SSD
   C. Optical drive
   D. USB device

5. What type of installation requires a person's real-time response to prompts?
   A. Unattended
   B. Image
   C. Scripted
   D. Attended

6. What installation method places an exact copy of a hard drive containing a previously installed operating system and applications (from a reference computer) onto the hard drive of another computer?

   A. Attended

   B. Scripted

   C. Image

   D. Unattended

7. What are the two general types of unattended installations? Select all that apply.

   A. Drive image

   B. Scripted

   C. Upgrade

   D. USMT

8. Which one of the following statements is *not* true?

   A. You can upgrade with a full retail upgrade Windows disc.

   B. You can install the upgrade version of Windows onto an unpartitioned hard drive.

   C. You can upgrade from an upgrade Windows disc.

   D. You can do a clean install from a retail version of Windows.

9. What should you do before an upgrade if you discover incompatible software or hardware?

   A. Nothing. The incompatibility will be resolved during the upgrade.

   B. Buy a special version of Windows for incompatibility problems.

   C. Resolve the incompatibility before beginning the upgrade.

   D. Repartition and format the hard drive.

10. No discs came with my computer purchased with Windows Vista preinstalled. What Windows Vista source can I use to reinstall the OS without spending more money? This is an either-or situation. Select the two best answers.

    A. Windows Vista full retail DVD

    B. Windows Vista Recovery DVD

    C. Factory recovery partition

    D. Windows 7 Upgrade

11. What feature, new in Windows Vista, allows you to install a language other than English as the first language?

    A. USMT

    B. MUI

    C. Aero

    D. Windows PE

12. Which of the following statements is true of the Windows Vista Setup?

    A. It runs entirely in GUI mode.

    B. The first half is character mode.

    C. It looks just like Windows XP Setup.

    D. You must install English as your first language.

Configuring Windows

13. What purpose does Microsoft Product Activation (MPA) serve?

    A. Product compatibility

    B. Prevention of software piracy

    C. Product registration

    D. Disabling the OS

14. What is the most immediate consequence of not completing the activation process for Windows within the required time period?

    A. There is no consequence.

    B. You will not receive updates.

    C. Windows is disabled.

    D. You will not receive e-mails about new products.

15. What task should you do as soon as possible after installation for the sake of stability and improved security?

    A. Upgrade

    B. Activate

    C. Update

    D. Partition

16. What may MPA require if you make too many hardware changes to a Windows computer?

    A. Reinstallation

    B. Removal of Windows

    C. Reactivation

    D. Update

17. What is a simple general test of network connectivity?

    A. Performing Activation

    B. Locating the new computer in My Network Places/Network

    C. Locating the new computer in My Computer/Computer

    D. Adding a network adapter driver

18. To what site does Windows Update connect by default?

   A. The local workgroup

   B. Microsoft Update

   C. Windows Update

   D. Microsoft Office Update

19. What update service does Microsoft offer that will update both your Windows OS and certain Microsoft applications?

   A. Windows Update

   B. USMT

   C. Microsoft Update

   D. MUI

20. What is the term that describes disk space used by the operating system when it runs out of physical memory?

   A. Virtual memory

   B. RAM memory

   C. ROM memory

   D. Flash memory

SELF TEST ANSWERS

Installing Windows

1. ☑ **C.** Hardware requirements are the CPU, minimum amount of RAM, and free hard disk space needed to install an OS.

☒ **A,** hardware compatibility, is incorrect because this refers to the actual make and model of the hardware, not the level of CPU and quantity of RAM and free hard disk space. **B,** software compatibility, is incorrect because it does not refer to the CPU, RAM, and free hard disk space. **D,** hardware optimizing, is incorrect because this does not refer to the level of CPU and quantity of RAM and free hard disk space.

2. ☑ **D,** partition, then format, then install OS, is the correct order for preparing a new hard drive.

☒ **A,** format, then partition, then install OS; **B,** partition, then install OS, then format; and **C,** format, then install OS, then partition are all incorrect because the steps are out of order and actually impossible to complete.

3. ☑ **A.** NTFS is the preferred file system for Windows.

☒ **B,** FAT16, **C,** FAT32, and **D,** FAT, are incorrect because none of them is the preferred file system for Windows.

4. ☑ **A,** floppy disk, **C,** optical drive, and **D,** USB device, are the three boot media sources for Windows Setup.

☒ **B.** SSD is not a boot media source for Windows Setup.

5. ☑ **D.** Attended installation is the type that requires a person's real-time response to prompts.

☒ **A,** unattended installation, is incorrect because this type of installation does not require a person's real-time response to prompts. **B,** image, is incorrect because this method replaces Setup altogether. **C,** scripted, is incorrect because you could use this term to describe an unattended installation.

6. ☑ **C.** Image installation places an exact copy of the operating system and applications (from a reference computer) onto the hard drive of another computer.

☒ **A,** attended installation, is incorrect because this does not place an exact copy of a hard drive onto another computer. **B,** scripted, is incorrect because scripting is just part of an installation, not a method of installation. **D,** unattended, is incorrect because this method may or may not include an image.

7. ☑ **A,** drive image, and **B,** scripted, are the two general types of unattended installations.

☒ **C,** upgrade, is incorrect because you can do this as either an attended or unattended installation. **D,** USMT, is incorrect because this is a tool for migrating user settings and data.

8. ☑ **B.** You can install the upgrade version of Windows onto an unpartitioned hard drive is not true and is, therefore, the correct answer. The upgrade version will only install onto a computer with a previous version of Windows already installed.

☒ **A,** you can upgrade with a full retail upgrade Windows disc, **C,** you can upgrade from a upgrade Windows disc, and **D,** you can do a clean install from a retail version of Windows, are all true and, therefore, are not correct answers.

9. ☑ **C.** Resolve the incompatibility before beginning the upgrade is the correct action to take before an upgrade if you discover incompatible software or hardware.

☒ **A,** nothing, is incorrect because the incompatibility will not be resolved during the upgrade. **B,** buy a special version of Windows for incompatibility problems, is incorrect because there is no such version. **D,** repartition and format the hard drive, is incorrect because this will not solve the problem; it is extreme and will void the ability to install an upgrade.

10. ☑ **B,** Windows Vista Recovery DVD, or **C,** factory recovery partition, are the correct answers, as the manufacturer will normally give you one of these options. If the Recovery DVD did not come with the computer, then you would have had to generate this from a utility on the computer.

☒ **A,** Windows Vista full retail DVD, is incorrect because, although this would work, it requires spending more money. **D,** Windows 7 Upgrade, is incorrect because this would cost money. It will also only work if your Windows Vista is upgradable and is still working.

11. ☑ **B.** MUI, or Multilingual User Interface, allows you to install a language other than English as the first language.

☒ **A,** USMT, is incorrect because this is a tool for migrating files and settings to many desktop computers. **C,** Aero, and **D,** MMC, are incorrect because these are user interfaces.

12. ☑ **A.** It runs entirely in GUI mode is a true statement about the Windows Vista Setup.

☒ **B,** the first half is character mode, **C,** it looks just like Windows XP Setup, and. **D,** you must install English as your first language, are all false.

Configuring Windows

13. ☑ **B,** prevention of software piracy, is correct because this is the purpose of Microsoft Product Activation.

☒ **A,** product compatibility, **C,** product registration, and **D,** disabling the OS, are all incorrect because they are not the purpose of MPA.

14. ☑ **C.** Windows is disabled is the consequence of not completing the activation process for Windows within the required time period.

☒ **A,** no consequence, is incorrect because there is a consequence, and it is answer **C. B,** you will not receive updates, is incorrect because you will receive updates until Windows is disabled when the required period of time is reached. **D,** you will not receive e-mails about new products, is incorrect because this may be a consequence of not registering.

15. ☑ **C,** update, is correct because you should do this task as soon as possible for the sake of stability and security.

    ☒ **A,** upgrade, is incorrect because this is not a task you should do for the sake of stability and improved security. **B,** activate, is incorrect because this is not a task you should do for the sake of stability and improved security. **D,** partition, is incorrect because this is a task for preparing a hard drive for use.

16. ☑ **C,** reactivation, is correct because MPA may require that you reactivate if you make too many hardware changes to a Windows computer.

    ☒ **A,** reinstallation, is incorrect because MPA will not require reinstallation if you make too many hardware changes. **B,** removal of Windows, is incorrect because MPA doesn't care if you remove Windows. **D,** upgrade, is incorrect; MPA will only require reactivation, not upgrading, if you make too many hardware changes.

17. ☑ **B.** Locating the new computer in My Network Places/Network is a simple test of network connectivity.

    ☒ **A,** performing activation, is not a simple test of network connectivity, although you will not be able to activate over the Internet if you do not have network connectivity. **C,** locating the new computer in My Computer/Computer, is not a simple test of network connectivity, although you should be able to browse to the computer through My Computer/Computer. You would not normally use this tool. **D,** adding a network adapter driver, is incorrect because you couldn't perform a simple test of network connectivity if you didn't already have one installed.

18. ☑ **C.** Windows Update is the site to which Windows Update connects by default.

    ☒ **A,** the local workgroup, is incorrect because this is not something Windows Update connects to. **B,** Microsoft Update, is incorrect because this is not where Windows Update connects to by default. It will connect here after you connect to Windows Update and agree to install Microsoft Update. **D,** Microsoft Office Update, is incorrect because this is not where Windows Update connects by default.

19. ☑ **C.** Microsoft Update is the service that will update both your Windows OS and certain Microsoft applications.

    ☒ **A,** Windows Update, is incorrect because it will only update your Windows OS. **B,** USMT, is incorrect because this is not related to updating your software. **D,** MUI, is incorrect because this also is not related to updating your software.

20. ☑ **A.** Virtual memory is the term that describes disk space used by the operating system when it runs out of physical memory.

    ☒ **B,** RAM memory, **C,** ROM memory, and **D,** flash memory, are all incorrect.

10
Disk and File Management

CERTIFICATION OBJECTIVES

❑   **701: 3.3**   Explain the process and steps to install and configure the Windows OS

❑   **701: 3.4**   Explain the basics of boot sequences, methods, and startup utilities

❑   **702: 2.1**   Select the appropriate commands and options to troubleshoot and resolve problems

❑   **702: 2.2**   Differentiate between Windows Operating System directory structures (Windows 2000, XP, and Vista)

❑   **702: 2.3**   Given a scenario, select and use system utilities/tools and evaluate the results

✓   Two-Minute Drill

Q&A   Self Test

T he Windows OSs have changed very little in their file management from version to version. In this chapter, check out Windows disk management theory and practices, file and folder basics, organizing files using folders, creating files, GUI and non-GUI utilities for managing files, and file and disk maintenance.

CERTIFICATION OBJECTIVE

■ **702: 2.3** *Given a scenario, select and use system utilities/tools and evaluate the results*

The 702: 2.3 objective requires that you select and use the appropriate tools for disk management functions—both those performed by certain individual utilities and functions you can perform in the Windows Disk Management console (also called Disk Manager). This section addresses the use of Windows Disk Management and the individual disk management tools—DEFRAG, NTBACKUP, and Check Disk—are described in "File Management" later in this chapter. The utilities listed in objective 702: 2.3 that do not apply to disk and file management are addressed in Chapter 11.

Disk Management

Disk management topics include Windows disk storage types, partitioning, and formatting. PC technicians need to understand how to prepare a disk for use, and, beginning with Windows 2000, this requires understanding storage types and disk partitioning for the storage type you will work with the most in Windows PCs. Finally, learn about drive letter assignments, mount points, and drive paths.

Disk Storage Types

This section discusses how hard disks are prepared for use. Windows 2000 introduced the concept of disk storage types—dynamic and basic—that Microsoft's newer Windows versions continue to use. Basic storage type is the default used with Windows 2000, Windows XP, Windows Vista, and Windows 7. Because you are most likely to use the basic storage type in Windows on desktop computers, we will give only a brief overview and comparison of the basic and dynamic storage types. The remainder of this section dwells on partitioning and managing basic disks.

Dynamic Disks

Dynamic storage is a newer way to allocate disk space and manage hard disks. Support for dynamic storage began with Windows 2000 and continues in newer Microsoft OSs. Using dynamic storage, a *dynamic disk* has space allocated in *volumes*, not partitions, and does not have the limits imposed on basic disks.

- The number of volumes on a dynamic disk is not limited.
- A volume can extend to include available space on any hard disk in the computer.
- Configuration information for a dynamic disk is located on the disk space beyond the first physical sector and is stored outside of any volume on the hard disk.

When you install Windows, the default is the basic disk type. Once the operating system is up and running, you may choose to convert a basic disk to a dynamic disk, but the benefits of dynamic disks really aim at disks on network servers or high-end workstations, not on most desktop computers. In fact, many of the best features of dynamic disks (volume types that support software-level fault tolerance) are not available in Windows 2000 Professional, and only one, disk mirroring, is available in Windows XP, Windows Vista, and Windows 7. Other more advanced features are available only in the Windows Server products.

A dynamic disk that is moved from one Windows computer to another that also supports dynamic disks will have a *Foreign* status in Disk Management until you take steps to add it to Window's configuration. Do this from with Disk Management by right-clicking the disk and clicking Import Foreign Disks. After a few seconds, the volumes on the imported disk will display in Disk Manager and be visible in other GUI elements of Windows. The Foreign status may also display for an existing dynamic disk, in which case it usually indicates damage to the disk—at least to the portion holding the dynamic disk configuration information. In this case, attempt to import the disk, but if that does not solve the problem, you may need to replace it.

Basic Disks

Under the Windows OSs beginning with Windows 2000, *basic disks* are those disks using *basic storage* techniques. Basic disks are prepared and managed in the manner of Microsoft's earlier operating systems, including MS-DOS, Windows 9x, and Windows NT. Such disks use the traditional method for creating partitions, including use of a single partition table per disk that resides in the first physical sector of a hard disk. The partition table occupies a mere 64 bytes of the 512 bytes in the sector. This sector, called the *master boot record (MBR)*, also contains the initial boot program loaded by BIOS during startup. This program, and the partition table, are created or modified in this sector when partitioning a disk.

You can convert a disk from basic to dynamic using Disk Management, but this is something you should not do unless you have very good reasons. Even on Windows Server computers, implementing fault tolerance in the form of disk mirroring and disk striping with parity is most often done at the hardware level and is invisible to the operating system. In these cases, the disks remain basic disks.

Try Exercise 10-1 to view the disk storage type on your computer.

EXERCISE 10-1

Viewing the Disk Storage Type

You can view the disk storage type on your Windows computer by following these steps:

1. Open the Start menu, right-click My Computer/Computer, and select Manage from the context menu. This will open the Computer Management console.

2. In Computer Management, click the Disk Management folder under the Storage node. After a brief delay, the Disk Management snap-in will appear in the right pane of the console.

3. In Disk Management, look for Disk 0. Disk 0 is normally your first internal hard disk drive, and the one from which Windows boots. Just below the words "Disk 0," you will see the storage type (see the Vista Disk Management snap-in in Figure 10-1).

Disk Management will show you important status information for your disks and the volumes they contain. This information displays in the Status field of the volume list (the top pane in Figure 10-1). Status information also displays in the appropriate area of the graphical view, as shown in the bottom pane in Figure 10-1. A status of Healthy indicates that the volume is functioning normally, and you will see other status information, such as Unallocated status on a primary partition,

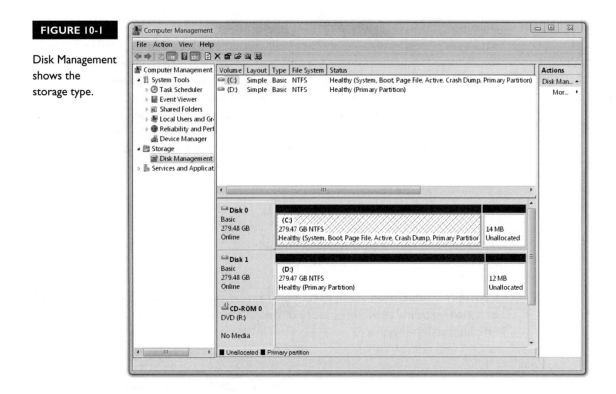

FIGURE 10-1

Disk Management
shows the
storage type.

which means that it has not been formatted, and on an extended partition, which means the partition does not have logical drives assigned. The Active status indicates a partition from which the system can begin the boot process (described later in "Understanding Windows Startup"). The Formatting status only displays during the formatting process, and, of course, Failed is a status we don't like to see; it throws us into troubleshooting mode. A drive status of Offline may appear under special circumstances, like when a disk becomes unavailable, in which case it may be brought back online with a rescan.

Partitioning Basic Disks

Now that you understand Windows storage types, you can continue to the first step in preparing a basic disk—partitioning. Before a new disk drive is able to save data, you must partition and format it. Partitioning a disk means you divide the disk into one or more areas that you can treat as separate logical drives, and each may, therefore, get its own individual drive letter. You must format each logical drive with a file system, and each can have a different file system. This is possible, but not usually practical, unless you have a dual-boot system with operating systems that support two different file systems, as explained in the following discussion.

Normally, you don't want to divide a hard disk into multiple logical drives, so you create a single partition that uses the entire drive. On basic disks, a partition table holds a record of the partition boundaries on a disk, but there are limits to the old type of partition tables that apply to basic disks. A basic disk is compatible with older operating systems, and it can have up to four partitions.

Basic Disk Partition Types

There are two *partition types* used on basic disks in Windows: primary and extended, of which there can be a maximum of four primary partitions, or three primaries and one extended partition (see Figure 10-2).

Primary Partitions   Each *primary partition* can have only one logical drive assigned to it encompassing the entire partition. Because a computer can only boot from a primary partition that is marked as active, a Windows PC with basic disks must have at least one primary partition.

Extended Partitions   An *extended partition* can have one or more logical drives (each with a drive letter). Older operating systems such as MS-DOS, Windows 3.*x*, or Windows 9*x* (including Windows Millennium Edition) could only create two partitions. The extended partition type was, in a real sense, a fix for the limits of these OSs. Because they could not work with more than two entries in the partition table, Microsoft created the extended partition type. An extended partition is divisible into one or more logical drives, each of which has a drive letter assigned. This feature allows these OSs to work with more than two logical drives on a single hard disk system. Furthermore, the older operating systems cannot work with more than one primary partition. If a hard drive has two partitions, under one of these operating systems, one must be primary and the other must be an extended partition.

Things have changed. Although Windows XP computers often came configured with one primary and one extended partition, this was unnecessary, and the second partition should really have been a primary partition because it actually takes longer to access data on a logical drive within an extended partition. This practice has gone away with Windows Vista and Windows 7.

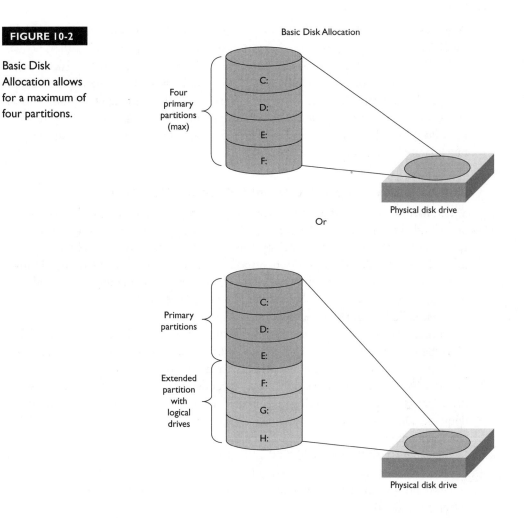

FIGURE 10-2

Basic Disk Allocation allows for a maximum of four partitions.

Basic Disk Allocation

Four primary partitions (max)

C:
D:
E:
F:

Physical disk drive

Or

Primary partitions

C:
D:
E:

Extended partition with logical drives

F:
G:
H:

Physical disk drive

Designating the Active Partition

In order for Windows to boot from a partition, that partition must be a primary partition that is marked as active. This is because the startup procedure common to all PCs looks for an *active partition* on the first physical drive from which to start an OS. Installing Windows on a new unpartitioned hard drive creates a primary active partition.

Partition Size Limits

When you partition a drive, the maximum partition size is the lesser of two values: the maximum partition size supported by the hardware or the maximum partition size supported by the file system. The FAT16 file system has a 4 GB partition size limit in

Windows 2000 and Windows XP, and a 2 GB partition size limit in Windows 9*x* and DOS. The FAT32 file system has a partition size limit of 2 terabytes (2 trillion bytes).

In Windows 2000 and newer OSs, the NTFS file system has a partition size limit of 16 exabytes (an exabyte is one billion billion bytes). Now, this is obviously theoretical, because the hardware limit (mostly a BIOS limit) is smaller, although the exact number is ever increasing. If you are working with a computer that has an old BIOS, you may run into the old 137 GB limit, but modern machines built in the last few years support much larger hard drives.

Logical Drives, Drive Paths, and Mounted Volumes

When it comes to assigning drive letters to primary partitions or logical drives on an extended partition, the 26 letters of the alphabet limit you. In fact, the first two letters, A and B, are reserved for floppy disk drives, so you only have 24 letters for other drives. Windows assigns drive letters automatically in a specific order. During an upgrade installation, it will preserve the drive letter assignments that existed under the previous version of Windows. The drive letter assignments are in a special database called MountMgr, located in the registry.

During a fresh install of Windows, the Setup program will, by default, assign letter C to the first primary partition it detects, marking it as active. It will then assign drive letters (*D, E,* etc.) to the first primary partition on other drives, and then it will assign drive letters to all logical drives in extended partitions. Finally, it will assign drive letters to all the remaining primary partitions. These are also in the MountMgr database. Once assigned, these drive letters are persistent until changed from the Disk Management console.

Beginning with Windows 2000, this limit extends in two ways. First, if you do not have floppy disk drives, you can assign letters A and B to other drives. Second, a pair of new features called *drive paths* and mounted drives allow you to avoid using drive letters in some special cases.

These new features are available on both basic and dynamic disks. A *mounted drive* is a partition (basic disk) or volume (dynamic disk) that is mapped to an empty folder on an NTFS volume. It does not need to have a drive letter assigned at all, but instead can be "connected" to an empty folder on another logical drive. This connection point to a folder is a *mount point;* and the path to the partition or volume is a *drive path*, which requires the NTFS file system on the partition or volume hosting the drive path. A partition or volume can have both a drive letter and one or more drive paths. In My Computer/Computer or Windows Explorer, the mount point is listed along with local folders, but with a drive icon, as shown here where a mount point is labeled "Q1-2006"; the contents of the mounted volume appear in the right-hand pane.

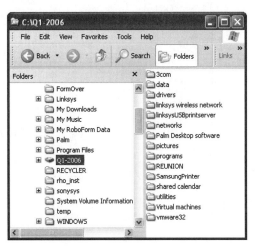

Creating a New Partition

This discussion assumes you are working with the typical computer with a single hard drive installed. If you have two hard drives, we recommend a single partition on each physical drive, but with a single hard drive, we prefer a strategy of dividing the hard disk space into two partitions. This allows the operating system and applications installed into the operating system to "own" the system partition, the partition on which the OS is installed. This also provides a distinct logical drive devoted purely to data, making it easier to back up data.

To that end, we plan for our disk space needs ahead of time, deciding on the portion of the hard disk that should be devoted to the OS and other programs, and the portion that should be devoted to data. Next, during a clean installation of an OS, we create a system partition of the planned size.

Immediately after the installation, we perform the essential post-installation tasks. When these are complete, we create the new partition in the remaining space on the hard drive and then install any necessary applications. This order is important if you install applications from optical disc, which is the most common source. If you choose to change the drive letter of the optical drive, it is best to change it before installing applications, because the setup programs for the applications usually remember the program installation drive as being the former drive letter of the drive.

Any time you want to modify the application using its installation program or the Windows Setup program, it will look for application components at the location

Windows XP
Disk Management
after creating and
formatting a new
partition

where the source files were when first installed. If you change the drive letter of
the optical drive after installing applications from CD, you will have to change the
drive path manually whenever you run an installation program that requires that
remembered location. You can change the drive letter or drive letters from within
Disk Management and then create the new hard drive partition. If you watch Disk
Management carefully during the partitioning process, you will see the status change
from Unallocated to Formatting and finally to Healthy (see Figure 10-3). Close the
Computer Management console when it is complete.

CERTIFICATION OBJECTIVE

■ **701: 3.4** *Explain the basics of boot sequences, methods, and startup utilities*

Coverage of objective 701: 3.4 is split between this section and Chapter 11. Here,
we will address aspects of the Windows startup beginning with a PC's native power-
on self-test and initial startup through all the Windows startup phases. This process
is important to understand to fully support Windows and PCs. In Chapter 11, we
will explore the boot options used for troubleshooting Windows PCs.

Understanding Windows Startup

Windows installs the necessary files to start up the OS. Before you can interpret Windows operating system startup failure symptoms, you must understand the normal Windows startup sequence and learn the role of each boot and system file in this sequence so you can determine at what point Windows startup fails. Then you learn to modify startup options.

Windows Startup Phases

The Windows startup process on a desktop PC has several phases:

- Power-on self-test
- Initial startup
- Boot loader
- Detect and configure hardware
- Kernel loading
- Logon and plug and play device detection

In the first two phases, the hardware "wakes up" and BIOS searches for an operating system. Through the remaining phases, the operating system builds itself, much like a building, from the ground up, with more levels and complexity added at each phase. You will learn about these phases in the order in which they occur.

Power-On Self-Test

The power-on self-test phase is common to all PCs. It starts when you turn on or restart a computer. The CPU loads the BIOS programs from a special read-only memory (ROM) chip. The first of these programs include the power-on self-test (POST). The POST tests system hardware, determines the amount of memory present, verifies that devices required for OS startup are working, and loads configuration settings from CMOS memory into main system memory. During the POST, the BIOS briefly displays information on the screen as it tests memory and devices.

Initial Startup

The initial startup phase is also common to all PCs. In this phase, the BIOS startup program uses CMOS settings to determine what devices can start an OS and the order in which the system will search these devices while attempting to begin the OS startup process. One common order is A:, then a CD drive, then C:, in which case, the system will first look for a bootable floppy disk in drive A:. If one is not there, it will try to boot from a bootable optical disc (if present). If a bootable optical disc is not present, then the startup code will try to boot from the hard disk and load the master boot record (MBR)—the first sector on a hard disk—into memory. The BIOS loads the executable code from the MBR, giving control of the system to this code, which then uses information in the partition table (also in the MBR) to find the boot sector—the first sector of the active partition—which is loaded into memory and called the boot code.

The formatting process places the boot code in the first sector of a partition using any of the Windows file systems. The job of the Windows boot code is to identify the file system on the active partition, find the boot loader file, and load it into memory.

Boot Loader

The boot loader in Windows 2000 and Windows XP is *NTLDR*. During the boot loader phase, NTLDR takes control of the system, switches the CPU to protected mode, starts the file system (the in-memory code that can read and write an NTFS or FAT volume), and reads the BOOT.INI file. In some cases, it then displays the OS Selection menu, but only if more than one operating system is listed, as is the case in a dual-boot configuration.

on the **!** *Up to this point, the CPU is in a very limited mode called "real mode." This*
()ob *was the mode of the early Intel CPUs in the early PCs. Only when the CPU switches to protected mode can it access memory above 1 MB and support both multitasking and virtual memory. Protected mode refers to the fact that each application's memory space is protected from use by other applications.*

If this is a dual-boot computer—one that is capable of booting from two different operating systems—then, if you select Windows 9*x* or DOS from the OS Selection menu, NTLDR loads the boot sector file called BOOTSECT.DOS, and NTLDR is out of the picture for this session. BOOTSECT.DOS contains the boot code for DOS or early Windows versions up through Windows 9*x*. The OS Selection menu may show a choice between two versions of Windows, as seen here.

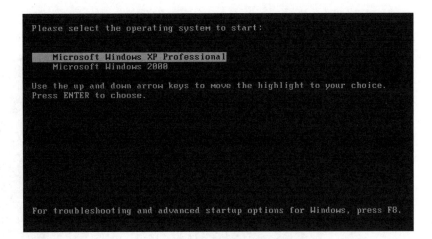

```
Please select the operating system to start:

    Microsoft Windows XP Professional
    Microsoft Windows 2000

Use the up and down arrow keys to move the highlight to your choice.
Press ENTER to choose.




For troubleshooting and advanced startup options for Windows, press F8.
```

When Windows NT, Windows 2000, or Windows XP is selected from the OS Selection menu (either automatically as the default or manually), NTLDR moves to the next phase in the Windows startup process. But before we move to that step, let's look at how the Windows Vista and Windows 7 handle things up to this point.

The boot loader for Windows Vista and Windows 7 is BOOTMGR, which loads the Boot Configuration Database (BCD), an extensible database that replaces the old BOOT.INI file. BCD then loads WINLOAD.EXE, the OS loader boot program. Together, BOOTMGR and WINLOAD.EXE replace the major functions of NTLDR and complete the startup phases for Windows Vista and Windows 7. These two OSs do not need the files NTLDR, BOOT.INI, and NTDETECT.COM, but BOOT.INI and NTDETECT.COM will be present on dual-boot computers that need to start up an older version of Windows requiring these files. Now we will briefly discuss the remaining startup phases.

Detect and Configure Hardware

The detect and configure hardware phase includes a scan of the computer's hardware and creation of a hardware list for later inclusion in the registry.

Kernel Loading

During the kernel loading phase the Windows kernel, NTOSKRNL.EXE (on both old and new Windows systems), loads into memory from the location indicated in either the BOOT.INI file (old Windows versions) or the BCD. During kernel loading, the Windows logo will display, as well as a progress bar, as seen here.

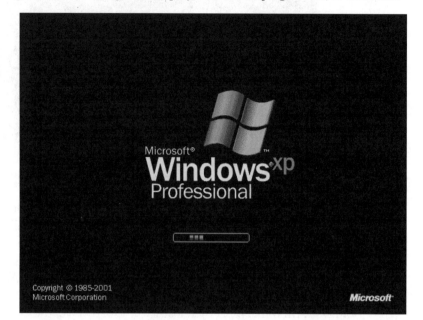

Hardware information passes on to the kernel, and the *hardware abstraction layer (HAL)* file for the system loads into memory, too. The System portion of the registry loads, and the drivers that are configured (through registry settings) to load at startup are now loaded. All of this code is loaded into memory, but not immediately initialized (made active).

Once all startup components are in memory, the kernel takes over the startup process and initializes the components (services and drivers) required for startup. Then the kernel scans the registry for other components that were not required during startup, but are part of the configuration, and it then loads and initializes them. The kernel also starts the session manager, which creates the system environment variables and loads the kernel-mode Windows subsystem code that switches Windows from text mode to graphics mode.

The session manager then starts the user-mode Windows subsystem code (CSRSS.EXE). Just a few of session manager's other tasks include creating the virtual memory paging file (PAGEFILE.SYS) and starting the Windows logon service (WINLOGON.EXE), which leads us to the next phase.

Logon

The key player in this phase is the Windows Logon service, which supports logging on and logging off, and starts the service control manager (SERVICES.EXE) and the local security authority (LSASS.EXE).

At this point, the Log On To Windows message may appear. Depending on how your computer was configured, you may first see the Welcome To Windows screen, requiring that the user press CTRL-ALT-DELETE before the Log On To Windows dialog box or screen appears. A user then enters a user name and password, which the local security authority uses to authenticate the user in the local security accounts database. Figure 10-4 shows just one possible logon screen that you may see in Windows Vista.

on the
ᶔ o b   *The actual screen or dialog box that appears before you log on varies with the configuration of your computer. You may not have to enter a user name and password, or you may only need to select a user name from a list. Learn more about the logon process and its role in security in Chapter 16.*

FIGURE 10-4

Logging on to
Windows

Program Startup   A lot of other things happen during the logon phase. Logon scripts run (if they exist), startup programs for various applications run, and noncritical services start. Windows finds instructions to run these programs and services in many registry locations.

Plug and Play Detection   During the logon phase, Windows performs plug and play detection, using BIOS, hardware, device drivers, and other methods to detect new plug and play devices. If it detects a new device, Windows allocates system resources and installs appropriate device drivers.

The BOOT.INI File and System Startup Settings

The BOOT.INI file holds important information used by NTLDR to locate the operating system and, in the case of a dual-boot configuration, to display the OS Selection menu. In Windows NT, this menu displays by default, even if the system is not dual-boot.

Inside BOOT.INI

For Windows 2000 and Windows XP, the BOOT.INI file indicates where the operating system is located using the now arcane Advanced RISC Computing (ARC) syntax. Here is an example of a BOOT.INI file for a dual-boot installation in which Windows 2000 is booted from the first partition on the hard disk (C:) and Windows XP is booted from the second partition on the hard disk (D:):

```
[boot loader]
timeout=30
default=multi(0)disk(0)rdisk(0)partition(1)\WINDOWS
[operating systems]
multi(0)disk(0)rdisk(0)partition(1)\WINDOWS=
"Windows XP Professional"
/fastdetect
multi(0)disk(0)rdisk(0)partition(2)\WINNT=
"Windows 2000 Professional"
/fastdetect
```

The lines beginning with `multi` provide NTLDR with the location information in a format called an ARC path: `multi(0)disk(0)rdisk(0)partition(1)\WINDOWS`. In brief, this identifies the disk controller, the hard disk on that controller, the partition on that hard disk, and finally, the folder in that partition in which the OS is located.

Following is a more typical BOOT.INI for a Windows XP installation:

```
[boot loader]
timeout=30
default=multi(0)disk(0)rdisk(0)partition(1)\WINDOWS
[operating systems]
multi(0)disk(0)rdisk(0)partition(1)\WINDOWS=
"Windows XP Professional"
/fastdetect
```

The words that appear in quotes on the lines under the `[operating systems]` section are displayed on the OS Selection menu. Anything after the quotes is a switch that affects how Windows starts up. For instance, the /fastdetect switch is the default switch used with Windows 2000 and Windows XP. It causes NTDETECT to skip parallel and serial device enumeration. This is a good thing, now that these two types of ports have all but disappeared from PCs. While many other BOOT.INI switches exist, you should not normally need to manually add any to your desktop installation of Windows.

on the
Job ***Still curious? Learn more about BOOT.INI switches. Point your browser to*** ***www.microsoft.com, and search for the article,*** Available switch options for the Windows XP and the Windows Server 2003 Boot.ini files.

Inside BCD

The Boot Configuration Database is actually a hidden part of the registry, stored in a registry file named BCD, located in C:\BOOT. If you have administrator-level privileges, you can view the contents using the BCDEDIT program, a command prompt utility. The basic information stored in BCD provides locale information, the location of the boot disk and the Windows files, and other information required for the startup process. Exercise 10-2 walks you through the use of this utility.

EXERCISE 10-2

Viewing the Contents of BCD in Windows Vista or Windows 7

1. Right-click on the shortcut for the Command Prompt and select Run As Administrator.
2. In the Command Prompt window, enter the command **bcdedit**.
3. The contents of BCD will display and will resemble Figure 10-5.
4. When you are done, close the Command Prompt window.

FIGURE 10-5

BCDEDIT shows
the contents of
BCD.

```
Administrator: Elevated CMD                                _  □  X
Microsoft Windows [Version 6.0.6002]
Copyright (c) 2006 Microsoft Corporation.  All rights reserved.

C:\Windows\system32>bcdedit

Windows Boot Manager
--------------------
identifier              {bootmgr}
device                  partition=C:
description             Windows Boot Manager
locale                  en-US
inherit                 {globalsettings}
default                 {current}
resumeobject            {ef3228b9-4885-11dd-8bdc-a9a7bf8366e8}
displayorder            {current}
toolsdisplayorder       {memdiag}
timeout                 30
resume                  No

Windows Boot Loader
-------------------
identifier              {current}
device                  partition=C:
path                    \Windows\system32\winload.exe
description             Microsoft Windows Vista
locale                  en-US
inherit                 {bootloadersettings}
osdevice                partition=C:
systemroot              \Windows
resumeobject            {ef3228b9-4885-11dd-8bdc-a9a7bf8366e8}
nx                      OptIn

C:\Windows\system32>_
```

Modifying System Startup

As a rule, you should not edit the BOOT.INI or BCD directly, but as a PC technician,
you may run into a situation in which knowing how to edit this file is important.
In Windows 2000 and Windows XP, you can do this through System Properties |
Advanced. In Windows Vista and Windows 7, open System Properties and select
Advanced System Settings from the task list. In all these versions, the resulting dialog
box is very similar, and from here, you select Startup And Recovery (see Figure 10-6).
The settings that modify the BOOT.INI or BCD are at the top of this dialog box, in
the System Startup section.

FIGURE 10-6

FIGURE 10-6

The Windows
Vista System
Properties and
Startup And
Recovery dialog
boxes look much
as they did in
Windows 2000
and Windows XP.

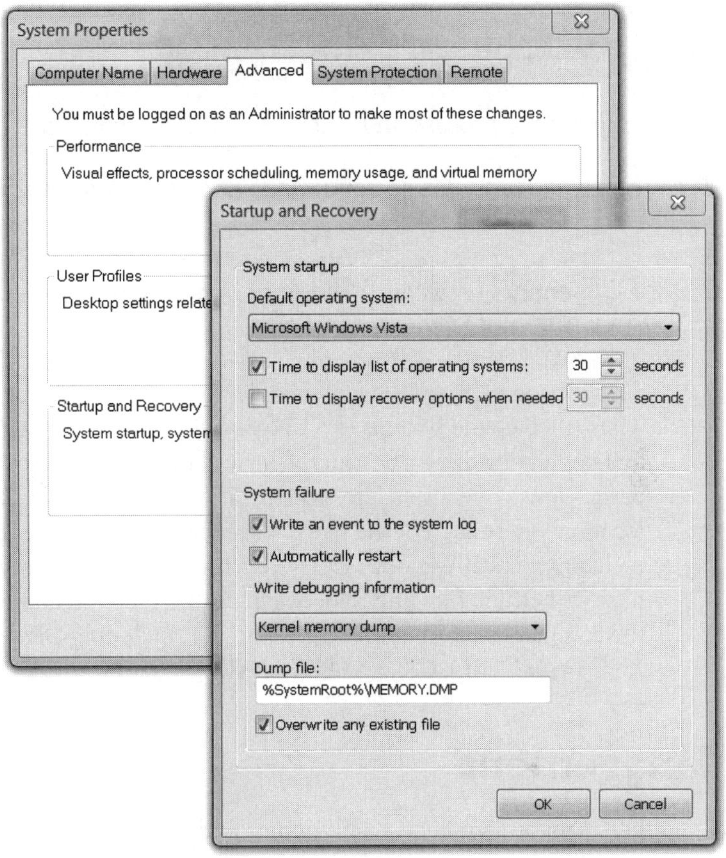

A drop-down list lets you choose the default OS in a dual-boot system and another setting allows you to set the length of time the OS Selection menu displays. The Edit button in Windows XP opens Notepad with the BOOT.INI file loaded in it for editing. We strongly recommend that you do not directly edit the BOOT.INI file (or BCD) without a great deal of preparation and/or expert advice.

on the
①ob

Even though the Edit button will open Notepad with the BOOT.INI file loaded into it in Windows XP, you will not be able to save changes you make unless you remove the read-only attribute from this file.

■ **701: 3.3** *Explain the process and steps to install and configure the Windows OS*

■ **702: 2.1** *Select the appropriate commands and options to troubleshoot and resolve problems*

■ **702: 2.2** *Differentiate between Windows Operating System directory structures (Windows 2000, XP, and Vista)*

> This section explores the few subobjectives of 701: 3.3 not addressed in Chapter 9. These include file systems (FAT32 vs. NTFS), directory structures (creating folders and navigating directory structures), and files (creation, extensions, attributes, and permissions). We also address certification objective 702: 2.2 by defining the default location where each of the listed Windows versions stores certain files and folders, including critical Windows OS system files, fonts, temporary files, application program files, and offline files and folders. Finally, this section addresses the use of several of the commands listed in objective 702: 2.1, including DIR, CHKDSK, EDIT, COPY, XCOPY, MD, RD, CD, and FORMAT.

File Management

File management begins with understanding the underlying file system. Although most file management tasks remain the same across all the file systems supported by Windows, a few features are not available in all these file systems. Next, you will learn about files, text file editors, and organizing files into folders in Windows.

File Systems

Windows NT 2000 and Windows XP fully support three file systems: NTFS, FAT16 (often simply called *FAT* or the FAT file system), and FAT32. All file systems have on-disk components and program code in the operating system. In other words, the operating system must have some code in memory that allows it to manage the on-disk components of the file system.

An operating system installs the on-disk components when it formats a disk with a file system. Since you can only format a disk partition with a single file system at a time, the General tab of a drive's Properties dialog box will show which file system is on a drive.

Windows can use the FAT and NTFS file systems on either disk type—basic or dynamic—and on any partition type. Once you partition a basic disk, you may format it with any of these file systems. This is also true of dynamic disk volumes.

on the
Ⓘob   *Don't confuse disk type with file system. Disk type affects the entire disk underlying the partitions or volumes on the drives. The boundaries of a file system lie within the partition or volume in which it resides.*

FAT 12, FAT 16, and VFAT

The *FAT file system* has been around since the early days of MS-DOS. *FAT12* is for floppy disks and very small hard drives—too small to worry about today. When you format a floppy disk in Windows, it automatically formats it with the FAT12 file system.

FAT16 is the file system used by MS-DOS for hard drives. Windows 95 introduced a modified version of FAT12 and FAT16 called the *virtual file allocation table (VFAT)*. When talking about VFAT in terms of a simple file manager, as we are doing here, technicians usually simply call it the "FAT file system."

FAT File System Components   When Windows formats a disk with the FAT file system, it places the FAT file system's three primary components on the disk. These components are the boot record, the FAT table, and the root directory. They reside at the very beginning of the disk, in an area called the *system area.* The space beyond the system area is the data area, which can hold files and subdirectories.

- ■ **Boot record**   The *boot record* or *boot sector* is the first physical sector on a floppy disk or the first sector on a partition. The boot sector contains information about the OS used to format the disk, and other file system information. It also contains the boot code involved in the boot process, as described earlier.

- ■ **FAT table**   The *file allocation table (FAT)* is the file system component in which the OS creates a table that serves as a map of where files reside on disk.

- ■ **Root directory**   A directory is a place where an operating system stores information about files, including a reference to the FAT table, so it knows where to find the file's contents on disk. The *root directory* is the top-level directory on the FAT file system and the only one created during formatting. The entries in a directory point to files and to the next level of directories.

All space beyond the system area holds files and subdirectories. Let's consider how these components are organized and how Windows uses them.

Using the FAT Table   When Windows formats a disk with the FAT file system, it divides the entire disk space for one volume (A:, C:, and so on) into equal-sized allocation units called clusters. A *cluster* is the minimum disk space that a file can use, even if the file contains only 14 bytes and the cluster size is 32,768 bytes. The FAT table has a single entry for each cluster. The entry is a status code, showing whether a cluster is empty, occupied, or damaged. If the entry shows it as occupied, it also indicates whether the file continues in another cluster by listing the cluster number.

When saving a file to disk, Windows checks the FAT table to find available space and then updates the FAT table entries for the clusters used for the file. When reading a file from disk, it reads the FAT table to determine where all the pieces of the file are located.

FAT32

Windows supports the FAT32 file system, introduced by Microsoft in a special release of Windows 95. This improved version of the FAT file system can format larger hard disk partitions (up to 2 terabytes) and allocates disk space more efficiently. A FAT32-formatted partition will have a FAT table and root directory, but the FAT table holds 32-bit entries, and there are changes in how it positions the root directory. The root directory on FAT16 was a single point of failure, since it can only reside in the system area. The FAT32 file system allows the OS to back up the root directory to the data portion of the disk and to use this backup in case the first copy fails.

FAT Cluster Sizes

The numbers 12, 16, and 32 in the names for the different FAT file systems refer to the size of each entry in the FAT table. On a FAT32-formatted drive, each entry is 32-bits long. The length of the entry limits the number of entries the FAT table can hold and thus the maximum number of clusters that may be used on a disk. The data space on each disk volume divides into the number of clusters the FAT table can handle.

FAT16 Clusters   The FAT16 file system is limited to 65,525 clusters. The size of a cluster must be a power of 2 and less than 65,536 bytes (64 KB). This results in a maximum cluster size of 32,768 bytes (32 KB). Multiplying the maximum number of clusters (65,525) by the maximum cluster size (32,768 bytes) equals 2,147,483,658

(2 GB), which is the maximum partition size supported by Windows 9*x* and older Microsoft OSs. Later versions of Windows have changed these limits slightly and support a maximum cluster size of 65,536 bytes (64 KB). This increases the maximum partition size for a FAT16-formatted disk to 4 GB.

FAT32 Clusters The FAT32 file system still uses the FAT table and root directory, but it uses space more efficiently, so it addresses certain problems with FAT16. For instance, whereas FAT16 creates 32 KB clusters on a 2 GB partition, FAT32 creates 4 KB clusters for partitions up to 8 GB. Because it uses a 32-bit FAT table entry size, FAT32 theoretically supports a partition size of two terabytes (2 TB), but the OS, BIOS, and other hardware limits it to something much smaller than this.

NTFS

Windows 2000, Windows XP, Windows Vista, and Windows 7 support an improved version of a file system introduced in Windows NT. This is NTFS, the NT File System. From its beginnings, NTFS has been a much more advanced file system than any form of the FAT file system.

In contrast to the FAT file system, NTFS has a far more sophisticated structure, using an expandable *master file table (MFT)*. This makes the file system adaptable to future changes. NTFS uses the MFT to store a transaction-based database, with all file accesses treated as transactions, and if a transaction is not complete, NTFS will roll back to the last successful transaction, making the file system more stable.

In another improved feature, NTFS also avoids saving files to damaged portions of a disk, called bad sectors. Windows will not allow you to format a floppy disk with NTFS, because it requires much more space on a disk for its structure than FAT does. This extra space is the file system's overhead. You may format a small hard disk partition with NTFS, but because of the overhead space requirements, the smallest recommended size is 10 MB.

While a USB flash drive normally comes formatted with FAT32 (and readable by your Windows OS), you can format one with NTFS. However, once you do this, you must use the Safely Remove Hardware applet before removing the drive to prevent damaging data on the drive. Although we recommend using this applet for any USB drive, you are more likely to damage data on an NTFS-formatted flash drive if you remove it without using this applet to stop all processes that are accessing the drive.

If you choose FAT32 while installing Windows, and you change your mind later, you can convert the file system to NTFS after the installation using the Disk Management console. This is a safe way to convert without deleting any of your existing data. However, you should still take the precaution of backing up the drive before starting the conversion.

NTFS in its current version offers encryption and indexing features. Encryption allows a user to encrypt a file or folder to protect sensitive data. Once a file or folder is encrypted, only someone logged on with the same user account can access it. The indexing service is part of Windows and speeds up file searches. If this service is on, indexing of any folder that has the index attribute turned on will occur so that future searches of that folder will be faster.

Finally, *NTFS permissions* provide folder and file security, which allows you to apply permissions to any file or folder on an NTFS partition. This difference is one of the most important between NTFS and FAT file systems.

The Properties dialog box of each folder and file on a drive formatted with NTFS will have a Security tab showing the permissions assigned to that folder or file. Learn more about file and folder permissions in Chapter 17.

on the
Ü o b

While Windows uses the term "folder" and shows a folder icon in the GUI, many of the dialog boxes and messages continue to use the old term "directory" for what we now know as a disk folder. People frequently use these two terms interchangeably. In this book, we generally use "folder" when working in the GUI and "directory" when working from the command prompt.

Other File Systems

Although NTFS is the most important file system for anyone supporting Windows PCs, several other file systems exist, and we will briefly examine them. These include CDFS, UDF, and DFS.

CDFS   *Compact Disc File System (CDFS)* is an ISO 9660-compliant file system used by Windows to read CDs, DVDs, and CD-ROMs. While UDF has replaced CDFS, Windows still supports CDFS to use with optical discs that do not support UDF.

UDF   UDF is an acronym with multiple identities. In Chapter 9, it made an appearance as "Uniqueness Database File," a file used in a scripted installation of Windows, and now we have another use for this acronym, Universal Data Format (UDF), a file format used for optical discs. This format is for movie DVDs. Windows Vista was the first Windows version to support writing the UDF format, so prior to Windows Vista, if you wanted to write to disc using UDF format, you needed a third-party program like Roxio. In addition, some versions of Windows could read UDF formatted discs, but could not write to them.

DFS *Distributed File System (DFS)* is a service implemented on Windows Servers that hides the complexity of the network from end users in that it makes files that are distributed across multiple servers appear as if they are in one place. Unless you are managing Microsoft Servers, you will not come in close contact with DFS.

Files

A *file* is information organized as a unit. The author of a file determines just how much information to save in a single file. For instance, the chapter you are reading right now is a single file. We could have chosen to save all of the chapters of this book in a single file, but instead, we chose to save them in individual files because it breaks the information up into more workable "chunks" for us. That's the key to working with information in general—using chunks that you can manage well.

You save a file into a special file on disk called a folder. When you are working in an application, such as a word processor, it will usually have a default folder into which it saves your files, but you can choose to save any file in other folders—you can even create additional folders. You have choices like these when you are working with data files.

As part of managing your files, you'll perform different actions—such as opening, closing, copying, and moving files and folders. File management in the Windows GUI is easy and relatively safe, because you can see exactly what files and folders you have selected for a file management operation.

Naming Conventions

MS-DOS and Windows 3.*x* used the 8.3 naming convention, in which the filename could be a maximum of eight characters long and the file extension was a maximum of three characters long. A *long filename (LFN)* is any file or folder name that breaks the 8.3 file-naming convention. Windows now supports LFNs on all file systems on all media, including hard drives, flash drives, optical discs, and even floppy disks.

The directory entries of the FAT file system were built around the 8.3 naming convention. In fact, the directory entries only had room for 8.3 names. Beginning with Windows 95, the FAT file system directory was modified to save long filenames (with up to 255 characters, including spaces, which were not allowed in 8.3 filenames) as well as the legacy 8.3 filenames.

File Attributes

A file attribute is a component of a file or directory entry that determines how an operating system handles the file or directory. In all the variations of the file systems supported by Windows, the standard file attributes are read-only, archive, system, and hidden. Two other special attributes in all Windows file systems are volume label, which allows you to give a name to the volume, and directory, which identifies an entry as a directory. The operating system modifies these attributes, as do certain programs such as file backup utilities.

The following are explanations of each of the standard file attributes.

Read-Only Attribute　The read-only attribute ensures that the file or folder will not be modified, renamed, or deleted accidentally. In Windows, if you try to delete a read-only file, you will receive a warning message requiring confirmation.

Archive Attribute　By default, Windows turns on the *archive attribute* for all files when they are created or modified. This attribute marks a file as one that needs backing up. Many backup utilities, including Windows Backup, provide the option to back up only files marked with the archive attribute. A backup program can turn off the archive attribute as it backs up a file, allowing the backup program to do subsequent backups that only back up files with the archive attribute turned on, thus backing up only those files created or modified since the last backup.

System Attribute　The OS, or an application, gives certain files the *system attribute* automatically to identify it as a system file. Most system files also get the hidden attribute to keep users from accidentally modifying or deleting them.

Hidden Attribute　A file or folder with the *hidden attribute* turned on will not show in My Computer/Computer or Windows Explorer unless the View settings allow it to be shown. If a folder has the hidden attribute turned on, you cannot view the files within the folder using My Computer/Computer or Windows Explorer, even if those files are not marked as hidden.

Additional Windows File Attributes　The NTFS file system has these original file attributes, just listed, as well as additional file attributes. In fact, NTFS saves a file's actual contents as one or more file attributes. NTFS allows for future expansion of attributes—making this file system more expandable.

The General tab of the Properties dialog box for a file or folder will show two of the traditional attributes: read-only and hidden. On an NTFS file or folder, the Advanced button will display the status of four attributes: archive, index, compress, and encrypt (see Figure 10-7). Index, compress, and encrypt are special NTFS

FIGURE 10-7

The Advanced attributes shown in Windows Vista

file attributes. Use the compress attribute on a folder to compress the contents, and use the encrypt attribute to encrypt the contents of a folder. These two attributes are mutually exclusive. You cannot both compress and encrypt, but you can apply one or the other of these attributes to a file or folder.

File Types

Windows computers use several file types, including, in broad terms, data files and program files. Data files contain the data you create with application programs. Program files (also called "binary files") contain programming code (instructions read by the OS or special interpreters). Program files include those that you can directly run, such as files with the COM or EXE extension (called "executables"), and those that are called up by other programs, such as files with the DLL extension.

Data Files   When it comes to file management, you should only manage data files. Leave management of program files to the operating system. There are a large number of data file types. A short list of the file types and associated extensions includes:

File Type	Associated Extension
Text files	Most often have the TXT extension
Word-processing document files	DOCX extension for Word 2007 DOC extension for versions of Microsoft Word previous to Word 2007 and some other word processors
Graphic files	BMP, DIB, GIF, JPG, TIF, and others
Database files	ACCDB extension for Access 2007 MDB for previous versions
Spreadsheet files	XLSX for Excel 2007 XLS for previous versions
Presentation files	PPTX for PowerPoint 2007 PPT for previous versions
Compressed files	ZIP (zigzag inline package) files
Video files	Several file formats defined by the *Moving Picture Experts Group (MPEG)*, including MPG, MP3, and MP4

System and Program Files   *System files* are program files and some special data files that are part of the OS, and they are very important to the proper operation of Windows. Some are located in the root of drive C:, whereas others are located in the folder in which Windows is installed. The default name for this folder is WINNT in Windows 2000 or WINDOWS in all other versions studied here. This folder, in turn, contains many additional folders containing important operating system files.

In Windows, the default settings for My Computer/Computer will hide the contents of a folder in which system files and other important files are stored. In Windows XP or newer versions, if you try to access one of these folders, a message will appear, informing you that these are hidden files (see the message box). When this occurs, you must take an additional action to view the contents. In Windows 2000, you click a link titled Show Files; in XP, you click the link Show The Contents Of This Folder.

These files are hidden.

This folder contains files that keep your system working properly. You should not modify its contents.

Show the contents of this folder

By default, Windows XP and newer versions hide the contents of both the root folder and the Windows installation folder, whereas Windows 2000 hides only the latter. If you decide to make them visible, do not make manual changes to these folders or their contents. Other changes you make to Windows through Control Panel applets and setup programs will alter the contents of these folders.

Some, but not all, files in these folders have the hidden attribute turned on so that Windows hides them, even when you view the folder contents. But when you are studying or troubleshooting an OS, you may want to change this default so you can see the hidden files. You can change these defaults in My Computer or Windows Explorer if you choose Tools | Folder Options and modify the settings on the View tab. The settings we use when we want to be able to see all files, including operating system files and their extensions, are shown here in Windows Vista. This dialog box is nearly identical to the one in Windows XP.

e x a m

ⓦatch *Hiding the folders in the GUI does not depend on the hidden file attribute. My Computer/Computer or Windows Explorer will hide the contents of a folder without regard to the file attributes.*

Default File Locations   Let's take a brief look at the folder structure created by Windows for data and the program files belonging to the operating system, add-on components, and applications. They include:

- **Documents And Settings**   In Windows 2000 and Windows XP, this folder, located in the root folder of the boot partition, contains the personal folders for all users who log on.

- **Users**   Located in the root folder of the boot partition, this is where Windows Vista and Windows 7 create each user's personal folder.

- **Windows**   This folder, located in the root folder of the boot partition, is where the Windows operating system is stored. Note that you can create a custom installation in which you give the Setup program an alternative location for the operating system files, but we strongly suggest you resist any urge to do this!

- **Program Files**   This folder contains subfolders, where your application programs are typically installed. Under 64-bit Windows, this folder contains 64-bit Windows programs.

- **Program Files (x86)**   In 64-bit Windows, this folder contains 32-bit programs.

- **ProgramData**   Located in the root folder of the boot partition in Windows Vista and Windows 7, this folder contains subdirectories for each installed program, along with each program's settings that apply to all users.

- **Fonts**   Here you will find the various fonts installed on the PC. This folder is a subfolder of the Windows folder and is a special folder.

- **System, System32**   These subfolders of the Windows folder are used to store dynamic link libraries (DLLs) and other necessary support files. Files in the System folder contain 16-bit code, whereas files in the System32 folder contain 32-bit code.

- **SysWOW64**   This subfolder of the Windows folder exists in 64-bit Windows installations and is where the 64-bit support files reside.

- **Temp**   This folder is used to store files temporarily, such as those files used during the installation of new application programs and those temporary files a program creates while it is working. This folder often contains out-of-date files left over from an installation operation.

on the
job

The rule for the Temp folder is that any program writing files to it should delete those files when the program is closed. If a program ends abnormally (you tripped over the power cord or the OS hung up), it can't do this important chore. Therefore, deleting files from the Temp folder that have not been used in over a week is generally safe. In practice, we delete all temporary files dated before the last restart.

Offline Files and Folders   A Windows computer that logs onto a domain will often be configured to save the user profile folders on a server. Therefore, all user data and user preference settings for local applications are saved on the server. If your computer does not always have access to the network, you can configure Windows to save those files to local storage so that when your computer is disconnected from the network, you can continue to work on the files. When the computer is reconnected, the files will be automatically synchronized. The actual location of offline files and folders in Windows 2000 and Windows XP is in a hidden directory named CSC (for client-side cache) located in SystemRoot.

Text File Editors

A type of application called a text editor allows you to create and edit text files using only the simplest of formatting codes (like carriage return, line feed, and end of document codes). A text editor uses only one set of characters, and does not use or understand codes for special character fonts or special paragraph formatting.

As a technician or support person, understanding text editors and knowing how to create and edit text files is helpful. The reason is that the operating system and certain applications use some text files. Although these files may not have the standard filename extension (TXT) used for text files, you can still use a text editor to view and modify them.

One such file is the BOOT.INI file in Windows 2000 and Windows XP. This important system file is actually a text file containing startup instructions for Windows versions beginning with Windows NT and through Windows XP. It is not used beginning with Windows Vista.

Windows comes with two text editors: The first, Notepad, is a Windows application and is the preferred text editor when working in the Windows GUI. The second, Edit, is a DOS application. When you call up Edit in Windows, it is loaded in a text-mode window. Compare the two programs, shown here.

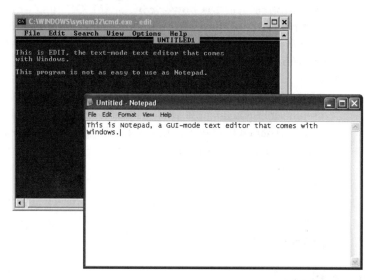

Notepad is a typical Windows GUI application that uses the standard Windows commands and mouse actions. Other applications (WordPad and Microsoft Word) can create and edit text files, but they are primarily word processors, which can create documents with fancy formatting instructions included. To create a text file with a word processor, you must choose to save the file as a text file. Notepad and Edit create only simple text files without the extra formatting.

Organizing Files Using Folders

All information on a computer is stored in files, and typically, you organize those files by separating them into folders containing related files. It's important to understand how to organize files and folders properly so you can easily access key files, and so you know which files you should not touch. And because even the best file organization won't guarantee that you'll always remember the name of that very important file, or even where you saved it, you should practice searching for files.

Any filing system needs a level of organization if it is to be useful. If you use a filing cabinet to hold a number of important documents, most likely you organize those documents into separate file folders and use some sort of alphabetical arrangement of the folders so you can locate the documents quickly when you need them. Imagine what a difficult time you would have finding your tax-related documents if all year you simply threw everything into a large box and then had to sort through each piece of paper to find the few important ones.

In Windows, you do not need to alphabetize your folders; Windows will sort them for you in the GUI. Simply give the folders names that make sense to you. You might simply name a top-level data folder "data." Subfolders below this level should have more meaningful names, perhaps a department name, such as "accounting," or a project or customer name.

As your data files grow in number, you will want to make more folders to organize them more logically. You will soon find that you have created an entire hierarchy of folders. Having them all under one or more top-level folders will make them easier to back up. You can select the top folder and have the backup program back up all subfolders and files.

As you work with Windows, you will develop your own filing system. The only caution is to never save data files in the *root folder* (root directory). Oh yes, the NTFS file system has the notion of the root directory, even though NTFS has a different file system structure on disk. From either the command prompt or the GUI, the folder and file organization looks the same across all the file systems. The root folder is at the top level of any drive, and you should never use it for saving data files. In My Computer/Computer, when you double-click one of the drive icons, it opens to the root folder, showing the top level.

GUI Techniques

If you are already familiar with Windows GUI techniques and tools for file management, you will be tempted to skip this section. But don't! Take the time to check out the drag-and-drop rules and to practice basic file management tasks.

EXERCISE 10-3

CertCam

Managing Files and Folders

In this exercise, you will practice some common file management tasks. First, you will create a folder, and then, you will copy, move, and delete files. Finally, you will open a file from its shortcut and edit it in Notepad.

1. Open the My Documents/Documents folder.
2. Position your cursor over an empty area of the Contents pane (right pane) of the window and then right-click. From the context menu, select New | Folder. Name the folder **data1**. Repeat this step to create a folder named **data2**.

3. Double-click the data1 folder to open it, and then right-click the Contents pane, and select New | Text Document. Name the document **report1.txt**.

4. Drag the file report1.txt from the Contents pane, and drop it on the data2 folder in the Folders pane. This moves the file, so it no longer exists in the data1 folder.

5. Open the data2 folder and confirm that report1 moved to this folder.

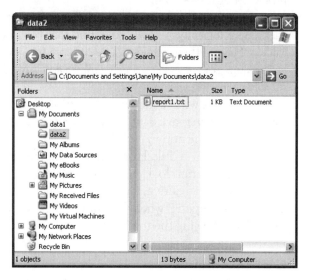

6. Press and hold the right mouse button while dragging the file back to the data1 folder. When you release the mouse button over the data1 folder, a context menu pops up that gives you the choice of copying, moving, or creating a shortcut to the file. Select the option to create a shortcut.

7. Expand the data1 folder and double-click Shortcut To report1.txt. This link is a shortcut to a text file, so double-clicking it causes Notepad to open, because that is the program associated with text files.

8. Now type a few sentences describing what happens when you drag a file from one folder to another folder on the same drive. Then save the file by selecting File | Save. Exit from Notepad.

9. Open the data2 folder and double-click the report1 file. The sentence you typed should be in the file. Exit from Notepad.

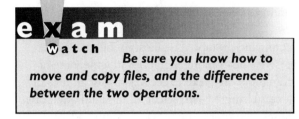

A drag-and-drop operation between folders
on the same drive is a move operation, and a
drag-and-drop operation between folders on
different drives is a copy operation. In both
cases, you are using the primary mouse button
(usually the left button) for the drag operation.
If you drag while holding down the secondary
mouse button (usually the right button), a context menu will pop up with the
options to move, copy, or create a shortcut.

File Management at the Command Prompt

We strongly suggest that under normal circumstances you not do file management
from the command prompt because you can only use text-mode commands that
give you very little feedback, and a minor typo can result in disaster—even with the
friendly warning messages you might receive from Windows.

However, as a support person, you might find yourself working at a special command-line interface—either the Recovery Console or Safe Mode With Command
Prompt, which we will explore in Chapter 11. Use these solely to recover from serious damage to the OS. Therefore, practice working at the command line is valuable.
If you have not worked at the command prompt, learn more about it now, and use
what you learn when you work with the Recovery Console and Safe Mode With
Command Prompt in Chapter 11. Because many programs that you will want to run
from the command prompt require elevated privileges, refer to the instructions in
Chapter 8 for opening the command prompt after turning on Run As Administrator.

on the
Ⓙob   *From a command prompt, you can launch any program that will run in
Windows (depending on your permissions and UAC). If the program is a
character-mode program, it will run within the command-line interface. If
written for text-mode, the program will remain in the Command Prompt
window. If the program is a GUI program, it will launch in a separate window.*

There are two commands for creating and deleting directories at the command
prompt: MD (Make Directory) and RD (Remove Directory). Use the DIR (Directory)
command to view listings of files and directories. Move around the directory hierarchy
at the command prompt using the CD (Change Directory) command. Use two dots
together (..) to indicate the directory immediately above the current directory. You can

use these in many command-line commands. For instance, if you only want to move up one level, type **cd ..** and press ENTER.

You can use wildcards from the command prompt. The most useful one is the asterisk (*). Use the asterisk to represent one or more characters in a filename or extension. For instance, enter the command **dir *.exe** to see a listing of all files in the current directory ending with "exe." Using *.* will select all files and directories.

When you are working at the command prompt, the previous commands and messages remain on the screen until they scroll off. To clear this information from the screen, use the clear screen command (CLS).

When you want to copy files, you need to learn two basic commands. One is COPY, which is a very, very old command that does not understand directories. To use this command on files in different directories, you must enter the path to the directory or directories in the command. It helps to first make either the source directory or the target directory current before using this command. The important switches for the COPY command are /a, /v, and /y.

- ■ **/a** Indicates that you are copying ACSII text files
- ■ **/v** Causes the command to verify each copied file
- ■ **/y** Suppresses the "are you sure" confirmation message from appearing when you are overwriting files of the same name

CompTIA requires that you remember these switches for the A+ 702 Exam.

We have worked with the COPY command since the very early days of DOS, but we rarely ever use it. If we must copy files at a command prompt, we prefer the XCOPY command, which has been around for about 20 years and is still available in a version for the Windows command prompt environment. The XCOPY command is a more advanced command that understands directories. In fact, you can tell XCOPY to copy the contents of a directory simply by giving the directory name. The simple syntax for both of these commands is *command from_source to_destination*.

Exercise 10-4 demonstrates the use of these commands as it walks you through creating and removing a directory. You will also move around the directory structure and copy and delete files.

EXERCISE 10-4

Managing Directories and Files at the Command Prompt

Practice working with directories and files from the command prompt. This exercise requires the folders and files you created in Exercise 10-3.

1. Open the Command Prompt window, type **dir,** and press ENTER. A listing of files and directories within the directory will display. If they scrolled off the screen, type the command again with the pause switch: **dir /p**.

2. Type the clear screen command, **cls**, and press ENTER to clear the screen.

3. In Windows XP, change to the My Documents directory by typing **cd my documents** and pressing ENTER.

4. In Vista or Windows 7, to change to the directory containing the Documents directory, type **cd %homepath%** and press ENTER. To change to the Documents directory itself, type **cd documents** and press ENTER.

5. Create a new directory in the My Documents or Documents directory. At the command prompt, type **md testdata** and press ENTER.

6. Enter the command **dir /ad /p** to confirm that it created the new folder within the current folder. The switch /ad will only display directories; the /p switch will pause the screen.

7. To make the data2 directory current, type **cd data2** and press ENTER.

8. Copy the report1.txt file to the testdata directory. Type **copy report1.txt ..\testdata**.

9. Use the more advanced XCOPY command to copy the contents of the data1 folder into testdata. Type **xcopy ..\data1 ..\testdata** and press ENTER. Figure 10-8 shows Steps 5–9.

10. Change the current directory to the My Documents directory, which is the parent directory of the data1, data2, and testdata directories. To do this, type **cd ..** and press ENTER.

11. Use the DIR command to view the contents of testdata. Type **dir testdata** and press ENTER.

12. To delete the testdata folder, first move into that folder, type **cd testdata** and press ENTER.

13. Now delete all of the files within that folder. Type **del *.*** and press ENTER.

14. Now the testdata directory is empty, but it is the current directory, and you cannot delete the current directory so you must move out of the directory. Type **cd ..** and press ENTER.

15. Now remove the directory. Type **rd testdata** and press ENTER.
16. Confirm that it removed the testdata folder. Type **dir /ad** and press ENTER.
17. Close the Command Prompt window.

Windows Utilities

Windows comes with many utility programs, specialized programs that support people and that technicians use to configure, optimize, and troubleshoot Windows and networks. So far in the book we have introduced you to some of these utilities, such as Device Manager, Disk Defragmenter, and Disk Management, and we even consider the Readiness Analyzer and Upgrade Advisor to be utilities.

In this section, we will look at some of the command-line and GUI utilities that come with Windows. As you continue through the book, you will encounter more of these, where appropriate. Here, you will learn certain command-line utilities used in troubleshooting problems in Windows, and in the chapters on networking (Chapters 13, 14, and 15), you will use utilities for testing network configuration and connectivity.

FIGURE 10-8 Creating a directory and copying files at the command prompt

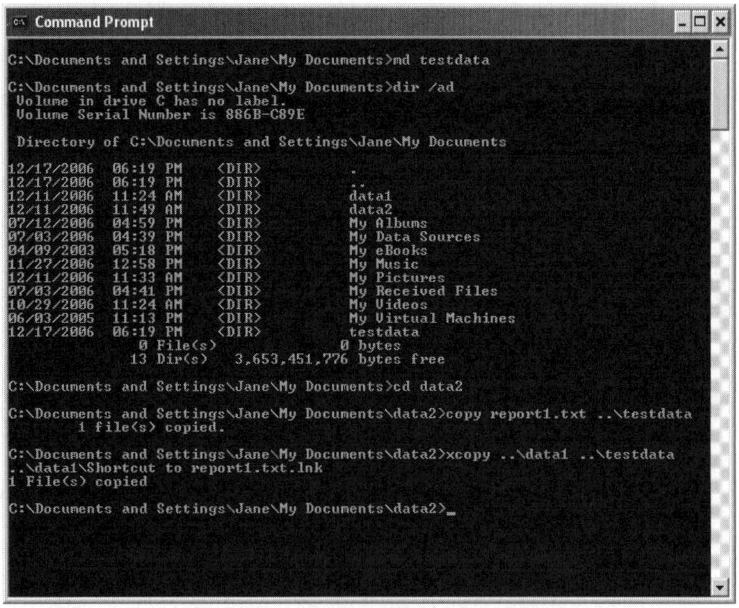

```
Command Prompt
C:\Documents and Settings\Jane\My Documents>md testdata

C:\Documents and Settings\Jane\My Documents>dir /ad
 Volume in drive C has no label.
 Volume Serial Number is 886B-C89E

 Directory of C:\Documents and Settings\Jane\My Documents

12/17/2006  06:19 PM    <DIR>          .
12/17/2006  06:19 PM    <DIR>          ..
12/11/2006  11:24 AM    <DIR>          data1
12/11/2006  11:49 AM    <DIR>          data2
07/12/2006  04:59 PM    <DIR>          My Albums
07/03/2006  04:39 PM    <DIR>          My Data Sources
04/09/2003  05:18 PM    <DIR>          My eBooks
11/27/2006  12:58 PM    <DIR>          My Music
12/11/2006  11:33 AM    <DIR>          My Pictures
07/03/2006  04:41 PM    <DIR>          My Received Files
10/29/2006  11:24 AM    <DIR>          My Videos
06/03/2005  11:13 PM    <DIR>          My Virtual Machines
12/17/2006  06:19 PM    <DIR>          testdata
               0 File(s)              0 bytes
              13 Dir(s)   3,653,451,776 bytes free

C:\Documents and Settings\Jane\My Documents>cd data2

C:\Documents and Settings\Jane\My Documents\data2>copy report1.txt ..\testdata
        1 file(s) copied.

C:\Documents and Settings\Jane\My Documents\data2>xcopy ..\data1 ..\testdata
..\data1\Shortcut to report1.txt.lnk
1 File(s) copied

C:\Documents and Settings\Jane\My Documents\data2>_
```

Command-Line Utilities

You have already learned to use the most common file management utilities at the DOS prompt, but a few more are used for disk management. Some of these commands have strong roots in MS-DOS but have been updated and modified to run from a Windows command prompt. Some may be traditional DOS commands such as DIR, XCOPY, ATTRIB, DEFRAG, and FORMAT. There are also specialized command-line commands, such as the IPCONFIG and PING commands that you will use in Chapter 15 to view the network configuration and to test connectivity, respectively.

One of the handiest commands when you are working at the command prompt is the HELP command, which, when entered alone at the command prompt, gives a list and brief description of commands. A handy trick for a command that sends a great deal of information to the screen, like the HELP command, is to use the pipe (|) symbol, and the MORE filter. Exercise 10-5 will demonstrate the use of the HELP command, the pipe, the MORE filter, and the /? switch that you can use for individual commands. You will also use the DEFRAG command.

EXERCISE 10-5

Using the DEFRAG command

In this exercise, you will run some simple file management and disk maintenance commands from the command prompt.

1. Open the Command Prompt window.
2. Type the HELP command with the MORE filter: **help | more**, and press ENTER to display a list of commands. As you finish reading each page, press SPACEBAR to display a new page. Continue until you are finished. If you wish to end without viewing all the pages, press the CTRL-C key combination.
3. Check out the syntax for the DEFRAG command by using the /? switch. Type **defrag /?** and press ENTER.
4. Now enter the command to run an analysis of drive (volume) C:. To do this, type **defrag c: -a** and press ENTER. This command returns the analysis results much faster than the GUI version of this program (see Figure 10-9).
5. Close the Command Prompt window.

FIGURE 10-9

Run the DEFRAG
command to
quickly analyze
a disk.

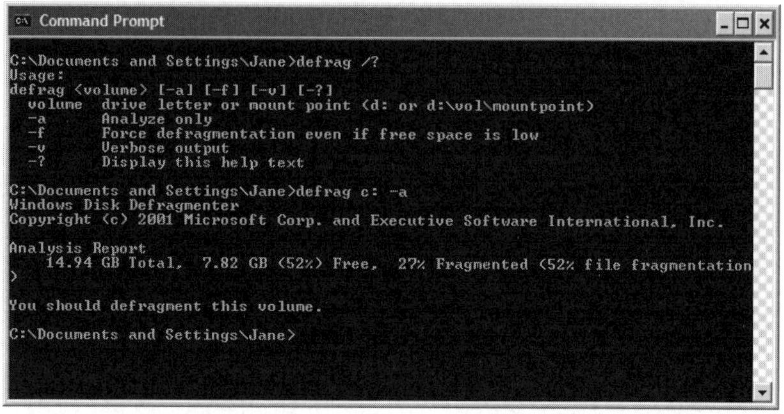

```
C:\Documents and Settings\Jane>defrag /?
Usage:
defrag <volume> [-a] [-f] [-v] [-?]
    volume   drive letter or mount point (d: or d:\vol\mountpoint)
    -a       Analyze only
    -f       Force defragmentation even if free space is low
    -v       Verbose output
    -?       Display this help text

C:\Documents and Settings\Jane>defrag c: -a
Windows Disk Defragmenter
Copyright (c) 2001 Microsoft Corp. and Executive Software International, Inc.

Analysis Report
    14.94 GB Total,  7.82 GB (52%) Free,  27% Fragmented (52% file fragmentation
>

You should defragment this volume.

C:\Documents and Settings\Jane>
```

As you can see, these programs quickly perform a task and then disappear from memory. Other commands, such as EDIT, may start programs called applications, which stay in memory, have a user interface, and allow you to do work such as creating and modifying text or word processing documents, or creating, modifying, and manipulating data with a database.

In addition to these methods of working at the command prompt, Windows also has startup options that allow you to start at a command prompt. Accessing the command prompt in this way is valuable for troubleshooting startup problems. You will have a chance to look at the startup options in Chapter 11.

CHKDSK The CHKDSK command (Check Disk) is the text-mode version of the GUI Error-Checking program you can access from the Tools page of the Properties dialog for a disk. It checks disks for physical and logical errors.

Running CHKDSK without the /f parameter is like running DEFRAG with the −a parameter—it only analyzes the disk. If errors are found, rerun the command with the /f parameter and it will fix disk errors. Use the /r parameter together with the /f parameter and CHKDSK will both fix the disk errors and attempt to recover the data in the bad space by moving it. If the volume is in use (as is always the case with drive C:), you will see a message asking if you would like to schedule the volume to be checked during the next system restart. Press Y and ENTER to schedule this. Be aware that CHKDSK can take as much as an hour to check a very large hard drive.

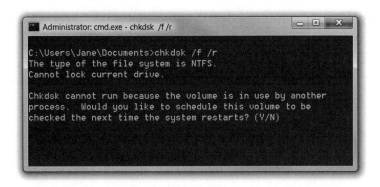

ATTRIB   The ATTRIB command lets you view and manipulate the file attributes read-only, archive, system, and hidden. As a technician, you may encounter a situation in which you need this command.

In one scenario, you may want to modify a file that has the read-only attribute turned on. If this attribute is on, you can open and read the file, and even modify it, but you will not be able to save it with the new changes. The solution is to turn off the attribute, which is something that you would normally do in the GUI by deselecting the read-only attribute in the Properties dialog box of the file. However, you may encounter situations in which you need to do this from a command line.

FORMAT   The FORMAT command will allow you to format a hard drive or floppy disk from a command prompt. Once again, the preferred way is to format from the GUI, where you are less likely to make an error when doing this. The correct GUI tools are the Disk Management console for formatting a hard drive, and My Computer/Computer or Windows Explorer for formatting a floppy disk.

This example shows the command for formatting the D: drive. Notice that it does not proceed until you press Y. Press N to cancel. This command will wipe out the contents of the drive. Using the proper syntax, you can format a hard drive with any of the file systems supported by Windows for the target disk.

Backing Up Data

The data created and stored on computers is far more valuable for individuals and organizations than is the computer hardware and software used to create and store the data. So your backup strategies, the hardware and software used for backup, and the actual habit of backing up are critical to maintaining both data and computers.

In case of the accidental destruction of data, and/or the disks containing the data, having a recent backup on removable media can be the difference between personal or professional disaster and the relatively minor inconvenience of taking the time to restore the data. Therefore, most versions of Windows include backup programs.

Backup in Windows 2000 and Windows XP

The executable name of the backup program that comes with Windows 2000 and Windows XP Professional is NTBACKUP.EXE. In the GUI, this utility is referred to as the Backup Utility and Windows Backup. Running NTBACKUP opens the Backup Or Restore Wizard. You can access it through a shortcut in the System Tools folder or from Start | Run using the executable name NTBACKUP. It will back up to a tape drive, to a local hard disk, or to a network location available as a drive letter (a "mapped" drive).

NTBACKUP is available in Windows 2000 and in Windows XP Professional. By default, it is not included in Windows XP Home. If you find yourself working with Windows XP Home Edition, you may still install Windows Backup if you have the distribution CD. NTBACKUP and its installation program are located under VALUEADD\MSFT\NTBACKUP. Simply launch the installation program located in this directory (it has an MSI extension), and NTBACKUP will install. If your computer came preinstalled with XP Home, and you do not have the distribution CD, search for this folder on your hard drive, because it may be there, along with the other distribution files.

Some excellent third-party backup programs offer additional features and capabilities.

Backup in Windows Vista and Windows 7

Microsoft introduced a new backup program with Windows Vista, the Backup And Restore Center. It is accessible as an applet in Control Panel. From the Backup And Restore Center, you can back up your files and folders to a hard disk, CD, DVD, or network location. You can even schedule backups by clicking the Change Settings link under the Back Up Files button and turning on Automatic Backup. Additionally,

SCENARIO & SOLUTION

What is the function of NTLDR?	It controls the Windows 2000 and Windows XP boot process until the kernel is loaded.
What is the preferred file system for Windows?	NTFS is the preferred Windows file system.
You would like to divide the space of a single basic disk into four logical drives. What partitions would you create?	Create four primary partitions on a basic disk.

you can create a Windows Complete PC Backup And Restore image of the entire computer, saving the image to a hard drive or to DVDs. You can also restore a backup set from this utility.

CERTIFICATION SUMMARY

As a computer support professional, you need to arm yourself with knowledge of operating system disk and file management. Disk management in Windows 2000 and newer versions begins with understanding both basic and dynamic storage types. Technicians working with Windows desktop PCs should focus on creating the primary partitions on basic disks.

Most file management tasks remain the same across all the file systems supported by Windows. NTFS is the preferred file system for Windows, providing more advanced file storage features and file and folder security. You should perform file management from the GUI tools, but a technician should be familiar with command-line file management methods for certain troubleshooting scenarios. Learn about file-naming conventions, file attributes, file types, and text file editors. Organize files into folders, and learn techniques and rules for moving and copying files in the GUI.

Windows comes with a number of utilities, specialized programs used to configure, optimize, and troubleshoot Windows and networks. A technician should be familiar with both GUI tools and command-line tools.

✓ TWO-MINUTE DRILL

Here are some of the key points covered in Chapter 10.

Disk Management

❑ Disk management in Windows begins with the underlying storage type: basic or dynamic.

❑ Dynamic disks have features not available on basic disks; these features are mainly for use on network server computers, not desktop computers, which are the focus of this book and the A+ exams.

❑ Basic disks use the same partition table used by older versions of Windows.

❑ A basic disk can have up to four partitions. Either all four partitions can be primary, or the disk can have a combination of up to three primary and one extended partition. Primary partitions are preferred.

❑ A PC with one or more basic disks must have at least one primary partition in order to boot Windows.

❑ Windows Setup will create a basic disk with a primary, active (bootable) partition and format the partition with a file system.

❑ After installing Windows, use Disk Management to create or modify additional partitions and to format hard drive partitions.

Understanding Windows Startup

❑ The Windows startup phases are power-on self-test, initial startup, boot loader, detect and configure hardware, kernel loading, and logon.

❑ The safest way to modify the startup settings for Windows is through the Startup and Recovery Settings, accessible through the Advanced page of the System Properties dialog box.

File Management

❑ Most file management tasks remain the same across all the file systems available in Windows: FAT12, FAT16, FAT32, and NTFS.

❑ Of these file systems, NTFS is preferred because it works with larger hard drive partitions, is more stable, and offers file and folder security that is not available in the FAT file systems.

❑ Knowing the naming conventions, common file extensions, and file types is important to file management in Windows.

❑ Windows supports the standard file attributes of read-only, archive, system, and hidden. It also supports additional file attributes in NTFS, including index, compress, and encrypt.

❑ Never move program files from their folders in Windows. Most users should manage only data files.

❑ By default, Windows hides system files from view in My Computer/Computer or Windows Explorer. This does not depend on the hidden file attribute, and you can change it through the View page in the Folder Options dialog box.

❑ You can use text file editors to modify certain text files used by Windows and other programs.

❑ Use the Windows GUI to organize data files into folders containing related files.

❑ Do not perform normal file management from the command prompt, but instead, familiarize yourself with command-line file management commands for use in extreme troubleshooting scenarios.

❑ Windows includes a variety of command-line utilities, some for simple file management, but many others as well. Use the HELP command to display a list of command-line utilities.

❑ Command-line disk management utilities include DEFRAG and CHKDSK.

❑ Use the ATTRIB utility to view and modify file attributes.

❑ The FORMAT command will allow you to format a hard disk or floppy disk from the command prompt.

❑ NTBACKUP is a backup utility that comes with Windows 2000 and Windows XP. A new backup program in Windows Vista will back up the entire system or individual files.

SELF TEST

The following questions will help you measure your understanding of the material presented in this chapter. Read all of the choices carefully, because there might be more than one correct answer. Choose all correct answers for each question.

Disk Management

1. Which disk storage type should you use on a typical Windows desktop PC?
   A. Dynamic
   B. Basic
   C. Primary
   D. Extended

2. Which of the following describes a partition from which Windows can boot?
   A. Primary extended
   B. Active extended
   C. Primary active
   D. Simple extended

3. Which is the tool you should use to create a partition after installing Windows?
   A. My Computer
   B. Device Manager
   C. Disk Defragmenter
   D. Disk Management

4. How many logical drives are on a typical primary partition?
   A. 1
   B. 2
   C. 3
   D. Up to 24

5. What is the maximum number of volumes allowed on a dynamic disk?
   A. One
   B. Two
   C. Three
   D. There is no limit.

Understanding Windows Startup

6. This startup phase, common to all PCs, tests system hardware, determines the amount of memory present, verifies that devices required for OS startup are working, and loads configuration settings from CMOS into memory.

   A. Boot loader

   B. POST

   C. Detect and configure hardware

   D. Kernel loading

7. In Windows 2000 and Windows XP, this file holds information used by NTLDR during the boot loader stage to locate the kernel and other operating system files.

   A. BOOTMGR

   B. BCD

   C. NTOSKRNL.EXE

   D. BOOT.INI

8. What is the name of the boot loader in Windows Vista and Windows 7?

   A. BOOTMGR

   B. BCD

   C. NTOSKRNL.EXE

   D. BOOT.INI

9. What is the safest GUI tool for editing the system startup settings for Windows?

   A. Notepad

   B. REGEDIT

   C. System Properties dialog box

   D. Automatic Updates

File Management

10. Which file system supports file and folder security?

   A. FAT12

   B. NTFS

   C. FAT16

   D. FAT32

11. Which file system can you format onto a primary partition? Select only one answer.

A. NTFS

B. FAT16

C. FAT32

D. All three file systems

12. When you format a floppy disk from within Windows, you normally place which file system on the disk?

A. FAT16

B. NTFS

C. FAT12

D. FAT32

13. Which of the following file attributes cannot be changed in a file's Properties dialog box?

A. Read-only

B. Archive

C. System

D. Hidden

14. Which file system supports file compression and encryption?

A. FAT32

B. FAT12

C. FAT16

D. NTFS

15. During Windows installation, you selected FAT32 as your file system, but after learning about NTFS, you would like to change the file system to NTFS. How can you safely do this?

A. It is not possible to do this without losing data.

B. Use the Windows 9*x* FDISK program.

C. Convert from within Disk Management.

D. Use the Convert tool found in System Tools.

16. Which of the following can you use for managing files and folders?

A. Control Panel

B. Notepad

C. My Computer/Computer

D. Disk Management

17. Which of the following best describes the type of files you should not move, delete, edit, or try to manage directly?

A. Text

B. Spreadsheet

C. Program

D. Data

18. What command-line command will list the command-line commands and a brief description of each?

A. DIR

B. HELP

C. PING

D. IPCONFIG

19. What is the correct syntax (command plus switch combination) that will analyze drive C:, looking for file fragmentation, without changing anything on the drive?

A. dir /ad

B. help | more

C. defrag c: –a

D. defrag a:

20. What disk error-checking program can you run from the command prompt to do an analysis of the disk for physical and logical errors?

A. CHKDSK

B. DEFRAG

C. SCANDISK

D. ATTRIB

SELF TEST ANSWERS

Disk Management

1. ☑ **B.** Basic is the disk storage type you should use on a typical Windows desktop PC.
    ☒ **A,** dynamic, is incorrect because this disk type is more suited for a network server. **C,** primary, is incorrect because this is a partition type, not a disk storage type. **D,** extended, is incorrect because this is a partition type, not a disk storage type.

2. ☑ **C.** Primary active describes a partition from which Windows can boot.
    ☒ **A,** primary extended, is incorrect because it describes two different partition types. **B,** active extended, is incorrect because you cannot mark an extended partition as active; only a primary partition can be marked as active. **D,** simple extended, is incorrect because Windows cannot boot from an extended partition (and "simple extended" is not a term that is normally used).

3. ☑ **D.** Disk Management is the tool used for creating a partition after installing Windows.
    ☒ **A,** My Computer, is incorrect because this is not a tool for creating a partition. **B,** Device Manager, is incorrect because this utility is for managing devices. **C,** Disk Defragmenter, is incorrect because this is a tool for defragmenting files on a drive.

4. ☑ **A.** One is the number of logical drives that you can create on a primary partition.
    ☒ **B,** 2, **C,** 3, and **D,** up to 24, are all incorrect because a primary partition can only have one drive letter assigned to it.

5. ☑ **D.** There is no limit on the number of volumes allowed on a dynamic disk.
    ☒ **A,** one, **B,** two, and **C,** three, are all incorrect.

Understanding Windows Startup

6. ☑ **B.** POST is the startup phase, common to all PCs, that tests system hardware, determines the amount of memory present, verifies that devices required for OS startup are working, and loads configuration settings from CMOS into memory.
    ☒ **A,** boot loader, is incorrect because it is not the startup phase described in the question. Boot loader is the third phase in the startup process. **C,** detect and configure hardware, is incorrect because it is not the startup phase described in the question. **D,** kernel loading, is incorrect because it is not the startup phase described in the question.

7. ☑ **D.** BOOT.INI is the file that holds information used by NTLDR during the boot loader state to locate the kernel of the operating system.
    ☒ **A,** BOOTMGR, is incorrect because this file is the boot loader for Windows Vista. **B,** BCD, is incorrect because Windows Vista uses it, not earlier versions. **C,** NTOSKRNL.EXE, is incorrect because this is the kernel of the Windows operating system, which is loaded during the kernel-loading phase of Windows startup.

8. ☑ **A.** BOOTMGR is the name of the boot loader in Windows Vista and Windows 7.
☒ **B,** BCD, is incorrect because this is the Boot Configuration Database, which replaced the BOOT.INI file beginning in Windows Vista. **C,** NTOSKRNL.EXE, is incorrect because this is the kernel of the Windows operating system, which is loaded during the kernel-loading phase of Windows startup. **D,** BOOT.INI, is incorrect because this is a file used by the boot loader in earlier versions of Windows.

9. ☑ **C.** The System Properties dialog box is the safest GUI tool for editing the system startup settings of the BOOT.INI file.
☒ **A,** Notepad, is incorrect because, although this can be used to edit the BOOT.INI file, it is not the safest GUI tool to use for this purpose. **B,** REGEDIT, is incorrect because this is not a tool for editing the BOOT.INI file, but for editing the registry. **D,** Automatic Updates, is incorrect because this is not a tool for editing the BOOT.INI file, but for having updates automatically downloaded to Windows.

File Management

10. ☑ **B.** NTFS is the file system that supports file and folder security.
☒ **A,** FAT12, **C,** FAT16, and **D,** FAT32, are incorrect because none of these file systems support file and folder security.

11. ☑ **D,** all three file systems, is correct because any of these can format a primary partition, as long as it is not too large for the file system.
☒ **A,** NTFS, **B,** FAT16, and **C,** FAT32, are individual file systems, and not the correct answer, even though all of them can be formatted onto a primary partition. However, none of these alone is the full answer, and the question specified that you should select only one answer.

12. ☑ **C.** FAT12 is the file system Windows will apply when it formats a floppy disk.
☒ **A,** FAT16, **B,** NTFS, and **D,** FAT32, are all incorrect.

13. ☑ **C.** System is the file attribute you cannot change in the file's Properties dialog box.
☒ **A,** read-only, **B,** archive, and **D,** hidden, can all be changed in the file's Properties dialog box.

14. ☑ **D.** NTFS supports file compression and encryption.
☒ **A,** FAT32, **B,** FAT12, and **C,** FAT16, are all incorrect because none of these supports compression or encryption.

15. ☑ **C,** convert from within Disk Management, is correct.
☒ **A,** it is not possible to do this without losing data, is incorrect. **B,** use the Windows 9*x* FDISK program, is incorrect because this program does not run under later versions of Windows and does not convert the file system. **D,** use the Convert tool found in System Tools, is incorrect because this tool does not exist in System Tools.

16. ☑ **C.** You can use My Computer/Computer for managing files and folders.

☒ **A,** Control Panel, is incorrect because this is a special folder containing applets for configuring many aspects of the Windows system. **B,** Notepad, is incorrect because this is simply a text file editor. **D,** Disk Management, is incorrect because this tool is for managing disk partitions.

17. ☑ **C.** You should not move, delete, edit, or manage program files in any way.

☒ **A,** text, is incorrect because it is generally acceptable for a user to manage text files, except for those that are created and used by the operating system and stored with the boot files or system files. **B,** spreadsheet, is incorrect because this is a type of data file that the user can manage. **D,** data, is incorrect because the user can and should manage data files.

18. ☑ **B.** HELP is the command that will list the command-line commands and a brief description of each.

☒ **A,** DIR, is incorrect because this command displays a list of files and directories. **C,** PING, and **D,** IPCONFIG, are incorrect because these are commands used to view network configuration and connectivity.

19. ☑ **C.** defrag c: -a is the command that will analyze drive C:, looking for file fragmentation, but without changing anything on the drive.

☒ **A,** dir /ad, is incorrect because this will only display a list of all the directories within the current directory. **B,** help | more, is incorrect because this will display a list of command-line commands with a brief description. **D,** defrag a:, is incorrect because the question asked the syntax for analyzing drive C: and this command would defrag drive A:.

20. ☑ **A.** CHKDSK is the disk error-checking program that you can run from the command prompt to do an analysis of the disk for physical and logical errors.

☒ **B,** DEFRAG, is incorrect because this command analyzes the disk for fragmentation. With the correct switch, DEFRAG will defragment a disk. **C,** SCANDISK, is incorrect because, although this was the Windows 9*x* disk error-checking command, it is no longer in Windows. **D,** ATTRIB, is incorrect because this command displays and manipulates file attributes.

11

Troubleshooting and Preventive Maintenance for Windows

CERTIFICATION OBJECTIVES

❏   **701: 2.2**   Given a scenario, explain and interpret common hardware and operating system symptoms and their causes

❏   **701: 2.5**   Given a scenario, integrate common preventative maintenance techniques

❏   **701: 3.2**   Given a scenario, demonstrate proper use of user interfaces

❏   **701: 3.4**   Explain the basics of boot sequences, methods, and startup utilities

❏   **702: 2.1**   Select the appropriate commands and options to troubleshoot and resolve problems

❏   **702: 2.3**   Given a scenario, select and use system utilities/tools and evaluate the results

❏   **702: 2.4**   Evaluate and resolve common issues

✓   Two-Minute Drill

Q&A   Self Test

Y ou are now familiar with the major functions of the Windows operating systems, understand how to install Windows, and know how to manage files and disks. It is time to learn how to troubleshoot common problems. Your best troubleshooting tool is knowledge. The previous chapters have given you a strong foundation regarding PCs and Windows operating systems. In this chapter, you will learn a set of skills and tools for modifying startup failures, and how to diagnose and solve common operational problems, including instability, Stop errors, application failures, and other problems.

Finally, in order to minimize your risk of problems, and increase your ability to quickly recover from failures, you will learn preventive maintenance for Windows operating systems.

CERTIFICATION OBJECTIVES

- ■ **701: 2.2**   *Given a scenario, explain and interpret common hardware and operating system symptoms and their causes*

- ■ **701: 3.4**   *Explain the basics of boot sequences, methods, and startup utilities*

- ■ **702: 2.3**   *Given a scenario, select and use system utilities/tools and evaluate the results*

- ■ **702: 2.4**   *Evaluate and resolve common issues*

This section begins with Windows boot options, covering the subobjectives of the CompTIA A+ Essentials (2009 Edition) Exam objective 701:3.4 that were not described in Chapter 10. It then details the 701: 2.2 subobjective that includes OS-related symptoms and their causes, and the bluescreen symptom is addressed in both this section and the one that follows. How to resolve Windows start or load problems is also detailed in this section, where you will learn how to use the Advanced Options Menu as well as Windows recovery tools. Several subobjectives of the CompTIA A+ Practical Application (2009 Edition) Exam objective 702: 2.3, including various system utilities and recovery tools, are detailed in all sections of this chapter, as well as the broad set of 702: 2.4 subobjectives. Those 701: 2.2 and 702: 2.4 subobjectives that apply to Windows-specific printing problems are in Chapter 12, however.

Diagnosing and Repairing Operating System Failures

Operating system failures occur for a variety of reasons, but just a few types—startup, device driver, and application failures—account for the majority. In this section, you begin by viewing the Advanced Options Menu, which gives you alternative ways to start Windows when you are troubleshooting. Then, you work with various recovery tools, including System Restore, Recovery Console, Automated System Recovery, and Emergency Repair Process, determining which of these tools are available in Windows 2000, which are available in Windows XP, and which are available in Windows Vista and Windows 7.

Using the Advanced Options Menu

When a Windows computer fails to start normally, the first thing you should do is make sure there are no disks in the floppy or optical drives and restart the computer. If it still fails on restart, use the Advanced Options Menu (Advanced Boot Options in Windows Vista and Windows 7) that gives you several boot methods to use for troubleshooting. For many startup problems, Windows Vista and Windows 7 will automatically open the Advanced Boot Options menu.

If you are having a problem with Windows startup, and this menu has not appeared automatically, access it by restarting the computer and pressing the F8 key. This should take you directly into the menu, but if the OS Selection box appears (as in a dual-boot configuration), simply press F8 again to access the Advanced Options Menu. Figure 11-1 shows the Windows XP version of this menu, whereas Figure 11-2 shows the newer

The Windows
XP Advanced
Options Menu

FIGURE 11-2

The Windows
Vista Advanced
Boot Options
menu

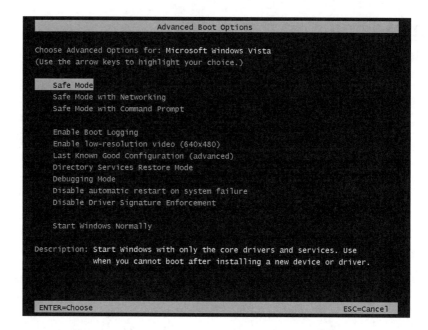

```
                      Advanced Boot Options

Choose Advanced Options for: Microsoft Windows Vista
(Use the arrow keys to highlight your choice.)

      Safe Mode
      Safe Mode with Networking
      Safe Mode with Command Prompt

      Enable Boot Logging
      Enable low-resolution video (640x480)
      Last Known Good Configuration (advanced)
      Directory Services Restore Mode
      Debugging Mode
      Disable automatic restart on system failure
      Disable Driver Signature Enforcement

      Start Windows Normally

Description: Start Windows with only the core drivers and services. Use
             when you cannot boot after installing a new device or driver.


ENTER=Choose                                              ESC=Cancel
```

Windows Vista version. They are nearly identical. There are many options here, including Safe Mode, which allows you to start Windows without some of the components that may be causing the startup failure. Then you can remove, replace, or reconfigure the failed driver or other component.

If Windows will not start normally, but starts just fine in Safe Mode, work in Safe Mode to determine the source of the problem and correct it. In Safe Mode, as in normal mode, you can only access those resources for which you have permissions.

Three Safe Mode variants are available from the Advanced Options Menu. They are Safe Mode, Safe Mode With Networking, and Safe Mode With Command Prompt. Safe Mode does not disable Windows security, so if you must enter a user name and password during a normal startup, you are also required to log on in all three variants of Safe Mode.

Safe Mode

The basic *Safe Mode* starts up without using several drivers and components that Windows normally starts, including the network components. It loads only very basic, non-vendor-specific drivers for mouse, video (VGA.SYS), keyboard, mass storage, and system services, and it displays at a low resolution (see Figure 11-3).

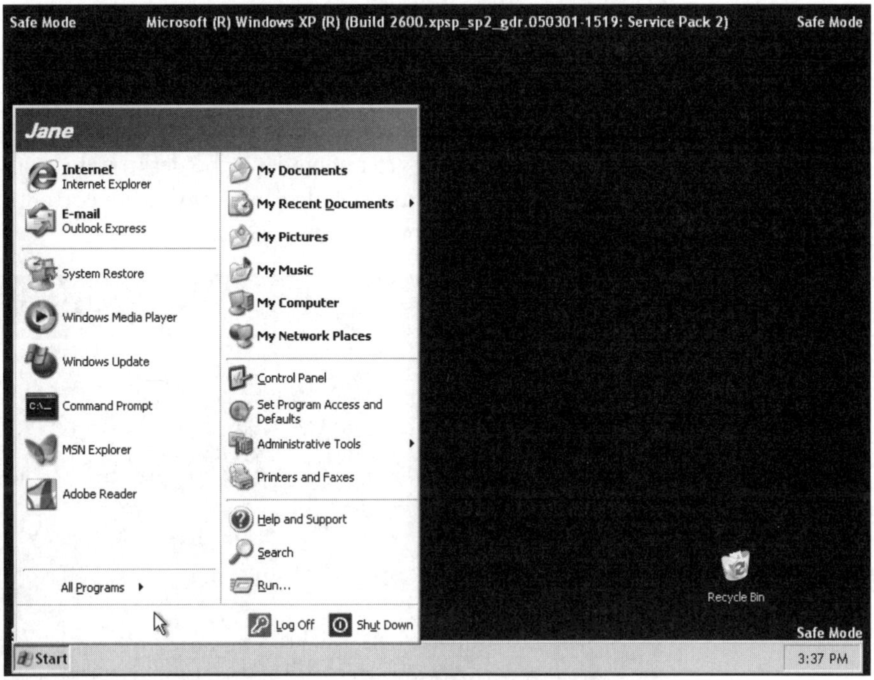

FIGURE 11-3

The Desktop displays at a lower resolution in Safe Mode.

If Windows will not start up normally, but it starts okay in Safe Mode, you know that the problem is with a component that Safe Mode did not start. Networking components do not start in this basic Safe Mode; therefore, once you determine that Windows will start in Safe Mode, a quick test of networking components is to restart and select Safe Mode With Networking.

Safe Mode With Networking

Safe Mode With Networking is identical to basic Safe Mode, except that networking components also start. If Windows fails to start in Safe Mode With Networking after starting in Safe Mode, network drivers or components are the problem. Use Device Manager to disable the network adapter driver (the likely culprit), and then boot up normally. If Windows now works, replace your network driver.

If this problem occurs in Windows XP immediately after upgrading a network driver, use Device Manager in Safe Mode to roll back the updated driver. In Windows 2000, which does not have this option, remove the device driver, and, when an updated driver is available, install it. This applies to other device drivers also—not just to network device drivers.

Safe Mode With Command Prompt

Safe Mode With Command Prompt has no GUI desktop, meaning that the Windows GUI EXPLORER is not running. You have only the command prompt, as shown here, from which to run commands and launch Windows administrative utilities. This mode is a handy option to remember if the desktop does not display at all after a normal startup. The most likely causes of this are corruption of either the EXPLORER.EXE program or the video driver.

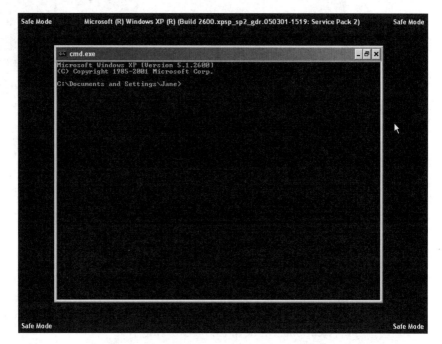

A scenario in which this approach is very valuable is if you had upgraded the video driver in Windows immediately before the last reboot. Restart the computer in Safe Mode With Command Prompt and open Device Manager using its command name, DEVMGMT.MSC, from the command prompt. Then, open the properties for the video adapter and select Roll Back Driver. On a Windows 2000 computer, you do not have the Roll Back Driver option and would, therefore, need to use the Last Known Good Configuration option, explained later in this section.

If you eliminate the video driver as the cause, corruption of the EXPLORER.EXE program may be the problem. Try launching this program from the command prompt. Do not expect the GUI to look like it does when Windows starts normally. If, after starting Explorer from the command prompt, you have a recognizable taskbar at the bottom of the screen and you can open the Start menu, Explorer is not corrupted, and you will need to continue your troubleshooting efforts.

If you believe Explorer is corrupted, you can delete the corrupted version of EXPLORER.EXE and copy an undamaged version. Doing this requires knowing the command prompt commands for navigating the directory structure, as well as knowing the location of the file that you are replacing. The default location of EXPLORER.EXE is C:\Windows. The original compressed file is in the I386 folder of the Windows 2000 or Windows XP CD. From the command prompt, use the EXPAND command to expand it. The actual command line would look like this:

```
EXPAND d:\I386\EXPLORER.EX_  C:\WINDOWS\EXPLORER.EXE
```

If you ruled out the video driver and Explorer as the source of the problem, launch Event Viewer (EVENTVWR.MSC) and search the System and Application logs for recent errors. Learn more about Event Viewer and Computer Management later in this chapter.

on the
job

Launch the Computer Management Console (COMPMGMT.MSC), and you will have several administrative tools in one console.

Enable Boot Logging

When boot logging is enabled, a log of the Windows startup is created in a file named NTBTLOG.TXT and saved in the *systemroot* folder (normally in C:\Windows). Boot logging creates an entry in this file for each component that it loaded into memory. It also lists drivers that were not loaded. An administrator viewing this file can discover what drivers were loaded into memory. Boot logging occurs automatically with each of the three Safe Modes. Enabling boot logging alone from the Advanced Options Menu will turn on boot logging and proceed with a normal startup.

Enable VGA Mode/Enable Low-Resolution Video

The *Enable VGA Mode* (Windows 2000 and Windows XP) or *Enable Low Resolution Video* (Windows Vista and Windows 7) option starts Windows normally, except that the video mode is changed to the lowest resolution (640 × 480), using the currently installed video driver. It does not switch to the basic Windows video driver, as Safe Modes do. Restart your computer, and select this option after making a video configuration change that is not supported by the video adapter and that prevents Windows from displaying properly, thus making it impossible to work in the GUI to change the configuration.

Last Known Good Configuration

A parenthetical phrase, "your most recent settings that worked," appears on the line with the *Last Known Good Configuration* choice in the Advanced Options Menu in Windows before Vista. This phrase says it all. *Last Known Good (LKG)* only lets you restore a group of registry keys containing system settings such as services and drivers. These are the last settings that worked, and you only have a tiny window of opportunity to use LKG—on the first reboot after making a configuration change and *before* logging on. Therefore, the definition of "settings that worked" is those settings used the last time you logged on. Once you log on, Windows deletes the former LKG settings, and the new settings with the changes included become the LKG.

If your computer was configured to start up without presenting you with an actual logon dialog box in which you enter your user name and password, then you are automatically logged on at every restart. In this case, once you have restarted and reached the desktop, it is too late to use the LKG because a logon has occurred.

Directory Services Restore Mode

The *Directory Services Restore Mode* is only available in Windows Servers acting as domain controllers.

Debugging Mode

Debugging Mode is an advanced option used to send debugging information about the Windows startup over a serial cable to another computer running a special program called a debugger.

Disable Automatic Restart On System Failure

This is a setting found on the Startup And Recovery page and accessed through the Advanced page of System Properties. It is located under System Failure and labeled Automatically Restart. If this setting is selected, which is the default for Windows, then Windows will automatically restart when there is a system failure. This is referred to as an auto-restart problem.

The problem that can occur if this setting is on is a situation in which Windows refuses to shut down. In fact, if Windows immediately restarts every time you try to shut down, it is an indication that Windows is failing during the shutdown operation. You may even see the bluescreen during shutdown, followed immediately by a restart.

You can change this setting through the System Properties dialog box, or you can temporarily change it by selecting the Advanced Options Menu option Disable Automatic Restart On System Failure. Using the latter option only changes this setting for one reboot. It will revert on the next reboot.

exam

watch

The CompTIA A+ Practi-cal Application Exam 220-702 objectives include a reference to "Auto-Restart Errors."

Be familiar with the setting described here and the problems that can occur.

Start Windows Normally

Use the *Start Windows Normally* option to start Windows with all its components enabled—a normal, everyday startup. You would use this after using F8 to view the Advanced Options Menu and deciding to continue with a normal startup. It does not restart the computer. It also does not guarantee that Windows will start normally if there is a problem. However, on Vista, when the Advanced Boot Options menu appears automatically during startup when you are not expecting a problem, let it continue. If it continues and seems to start up normally after all, look around to see if there was a problem with a device. For instance, look at the notification area of the taskbar for a failed network adapter. Then work to troubleshoot the failed device.

Reboot

This option restarts the computer with a warm reboot, like Restart Windows from the Windows Shut Down menu. You may then choose to allow Windows to start normally or to open the Advanced Options Menu with the F8 key.

on the

job

In place of the two options, Start Windows Normally and Reboot, Windows 2000 has only one option, Reboot Normally, which behaves like the Windows XP Reboot option.

Return To OS Choices Menu

If the system is configured to dual-boot, the Advanced Options Menu will include the *Return To OS Choices Menu* option. When available, selecting this option will return to the OS Choices menu (OS Loader menu).

EXERCISE 11-1

Working in Safe Mode

It is a good practice to become familiar with Safe Mode before you have a startup problem.

1. Restart your computer. Press F8 after the POST messages.

2. From the Advanced Options Menu, select Safe Mode, and then press ENTER.

3. As Safe Mode loads, notice that the screen lists all the drivers and components as they are loaded and started.

4. What you will see next depends on your computer configuration. You may see the full bluescreen with the message To Begin, Click Your User Name, or you may see a small Welcome To Windows message box displayed against a black background with the build version number at the top of the screen and "Safe Mode" in each corner of the background.

5. In either case, follow the instructions to begin or to log on.

6. A Desktop dialog box will inform you that Windows is running in Safe Mode. Select Yes to proceed with Safe Mode.

7. View the desktop, recalling that the standard video drivers are the only ones installed, and some components are not loaded, so the desktop will not look normal, although it will still have the taskbar and even some desktop icons in place.

8. Explore some of the GUI tools, such as Device Manager (see Figure 11-4) and Control Panel.

9. If time permits, restart your computer and select each of the other Safe Mode configurations.

10. When you have finished working in Safe Mode, use the Start menu to restart Windows normally.

System Restore

If you have ever added the latest software or new device to your Windows computer, only to find that nothing seems to work right after this change, *System Restore* will come to your aid. You must be able to get into the Windows GUI (normal or safe mode) to use this great recovery tool in Windows 2000 or Windows XP. Later versions

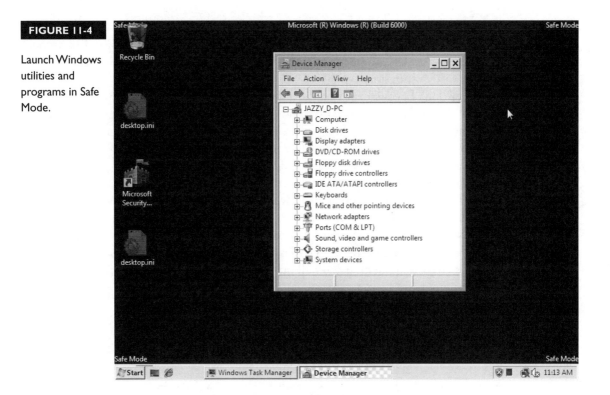

FIGURE 11-4

Launch Windows utilities and programs in Safe Mode.

include this in both the GUI and outside of Windows via the System Recovery Options Menu (described later in this chapter in "Recovery Options").

System Restore creates restore points, which are snapshots of Windows, its configuration, and all installed components. Restore points are created automatically when you add or remove software or install Windows updates, and during the normal shutdown of your computer. You can also choose to force creation of a restore point before making changes. If your computer has nonfatal problems after you have made a change, or if you believe it has been infected with malware, you can use System Restore to roll it back to a restore point.

During the restore process, only settings and programs are changed—no data is lost. Your computer will include all programs and settings as of the restore date and time. This feature is invaluable for overworked administrators and consultants. A simple restore will fix many user-generated problems.

To restore a Windows system to a previous time point, start the System Restore Wizard. Choose Start | All Programs | Accessories | System Tools | System Restore.

In Windows XP, select the first radio button, Restore My Computer To An Earlier Time, and then click Next. In Windows Vista and Windows 7, choose either Recommend Restore or Choose A Different Restore Point. In both cases, click Next and follow the instructions.

You don't have to count on the automatic creation of restore points. You can open System Restore at any time and simply select Create A Restore Point. This is something to consider doing before making changes that might not trigger an automatic restore point, such as directly editing the registry.

System Restore is on by default and uses some of your disk space to save information on restore points. To turn System Restore off or change the disk space usage, open the System Properties applet and select the System Restore tab in Windows XP, or the System Protection tab in Windows Vista or Windows 7. Disabling System Restore is now a common part of cleaning off many virus infections to ensure that a virus isn't hiding in the restore files, but be aware that turning System Restore off, even for a moment, deletes all old restore points. The System Protection tab is shown here.

Recovery Options

There are two sets of recovery tools for the Windows versions this book covers. First is the Recovery Console, available in both Windows 2000 and Windows XP. In Windows Vista and Windows 7, the System Recovery Options menu replaces the Recovery Console.

Windows 2000 and Windows XP Recovery Console

The Recovery Console allows you to recover from an OS failure when all else has failed. It is a totally non-GUI command-line interface. If you have the Windows 2000 or Windows XP Professional CD, you can start the Recovery Console by booting from the CD, running Setup, selecting Repair, and then selecting Recovery Console.

However, if you like to be proactive, you can install the Recovery Console on your hard drive so it is one of your startup options and does not require the Windows CD to run. The steps to do this in Windows 2000 and Windows XP are identical. Log on as an administrator, and insert the Windows 2000 or Windows XP Professional CD-ROM into the drive. If Autorun starts the Setup program, click No. Then open a Windows command prompt by selecting Start | Run and typing **CMD** in the dialog box. At the command prompt, enter the following command:

```
d:\i386\winnt32 /cmdcons
```

where *d* is your CD drive letter.

Just follow the instructions on the screen. If connected to the Internet, allow the Setup program to download updated files. After the Recovery Console installs, at each restart, the OS Selection menu will display with your Windows OS (Windows 2000 Professional or Windows XP) and the Microsoft Windows Recovery Console. It may also show other choices if your computer is dual-boot. When you select the Recovery Console, it will start, and then you will see the Recovery Console command prompt.

The cursor is a small white rectangle sitting to the right of the question mark on the last line. If there is only one installation of Windows on your computer, type **1** at the prompt, and then press ENTER. If you press ENTER before typing in a valid selection, the Recovery Console will cancel and the computer will reboot. Once you have made your selection, a new line appears on the screen prompting you for the administrator password.

Enter the administrator password for that computer and press ENTER. The screen still shows everything that has happened so far, unless something has caused an error message. The screen now looks like this.

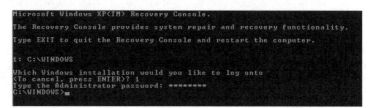

Now what do you do? Use the Recovery Console commands, of course. Recovery Console uses command prompt utilities. To see a list of Recovery Console utilities, simply enter **help** at the prompt. To learn more about an individual command, enter the command name followed by /? Here is a brief description of a few handy commands:

- **DISKPART**   Performs disk partitioning
- **EXIT**   Exits the Recovery Console and restarts your computer
- **FIXBOOT**   Writes a new partition table from the backup Master File Table
- **FIXMBR**   Repairs the Master Boot Record (MBR)
- **HELP**   Displays a Help screen
- **LOGON**   Logs on to a Windows installation
- **SYSTEMROOT**   Sets the current directory to the location of the Windows system files—usually C:\Windows

The files that make up the Recovery Console reside on drive C:, making the Recovery Console unavailable if this partition is badly damaged. The Recovery Console shines in allowing an administrator to restore registry files manually, stop problem services, rebuild partitions (other than the system partition), or use the EXPAND program to extract uncorrupted files from a CD-ROM or floppy disk to replace corrupted files.

You can reconfigure a service so it starts with different settings, format drives on the hard disk, reads and writes on local FAT or NTFS volumes, and copies replacement files from a floppy or CD. The Recovery Console allows you to access the file system, but it is still constrained by the file and folder security of NTFS. Recovery Console is a very advanced tool—definitely not for amateurs!

Windows Vista and Windows 7 System Recovery Options menu

The System Recovery Options menu is available on the Windows Vista or Windows 7 installation disc. If Windows came preinstalled on your computer, the manufacturer may have installed this menu as is, or with some customization, or may have replaced it with their own recovery options. Like the Recovery Console, these tools are useful to you when Windows will not start up normally and you must attempt to recover from an environment outside of Windows. The individual tools on this menu are

- **Startup Repair**   This tool replaces missing or damaged system files, scanning for such problems and attempting to fix them.
- **System Restore**   This tool restores Windows using a restore point from when Windows was working normally.
- **Windows Complete PC Restore**   If you previously created a complete PC Image backup, this tool will let you restore it. This replaces the Automated System Recovery (ASR) that appeared in Windows XP.
- **Windows Memory Diagnostic Tool**   This tool tests the system's RAM (a possible cause for failure to start). If it detects a problem with the RAM, replace the RAM before trying to restart Windows.
- **Command Prompt**   This tool replaces the Recovery Console, by providing a character mode interface where you can use command prompt tools to resolve a problem. See the description of the Recovery Console previously.

To access the System Recovery Options menu, insert the Windows Vista or Windows 7 installation disc and restart the computer, booting from the disc. Choose the language settings, click Next, and click the option Repair Your Computer. Select the OS you want to repair, click Next, and the System Recovery Options menu will display.

Windows XP Automated System Recovery (ASR)

To recover from damage that prevents the operating system from starting up in any way, Windows XP has *Automated System Recovery (ASR)* available from the Backup Utility (NTBACKUP.EXE). ASR replaces the Emergency Repair Disk (ERD) process of Windows NT and Windows 2000, which depended on restoring a special backup of system settings. ASR, in contrast, uses a backup of the entire system partition (where the OS is installed) and, therefore, provides a more holistic repair, restoring the entire operating system to a certain point in time.

Using ASR requires some planning. You must use the Advanced Mode of the Backup Utility (NTBACKUP.EXE) to create an ASR backup set, which includes an ASR diskette to initiate a bootup into the ASR state, and a system partition backup to media such as tape, another local hard disk, or a network location accessed via a drive letter (a mapped drive).

The Welcome page of the Advanced Mode of the Backup Utility contains the option for running the Automated System Recovery Wizard to create an ASR set.

An ASR backup set does not include a backup of other partitions, nor does it allow you to select data folders. Therefore, your Windows XP Professional backup strategy should include occasional creation of an ASR set and frequent backups to save data and changes to the OS since the last ASR set.

Automated System Recovery and the Backup Utility are not included in Windows XP Home Edition. However, you can install the Backup Utility (NTBACKUP.EXE) from the Windows XP Home distribution CD. Some computer manufacturers include a custom system recovery tool for preinstalled OEM Windows, but they may not include a backup utility.

Emergency Repair Process

The *Emergency Repair Process* in Windows 2000 is a carryover from Windows NT. In Windows XP, Automatic System Recovery replaced this awkward, and error-prone, repair process, which, in turn, was replaced by the Windows Complete PC Restore tool in the System Recovery Options menu introduced in Windows Vista.

The Windows 2000 Emergency Repair Process requires an up-to-date *Emergency Repair Disk (ERD)*, or recent emergency repair information stored on the local hard disk. In Windows 2000, clicking a button on the Welcome page of the Windows Backup program (see Figure 11-5) will open an Emergency Repair Disk dialog box that guides you through creating an ERD, including providing an option to also back up the registry to the Repair directory located in *systemroot*.

To perform an emergency repair, you need the Windows 2000 CD and the most recent ERD. If you do not have an ERD, the Emergency Repair Process will look for recent emergency repair information saved to the hard drive.

Boot up to the Setup program. At the Welcome To Setup screen, press R to repair a damaged operating system. On the following screen, select or deselect the desired actions in the box, and then press ENTER to continue.

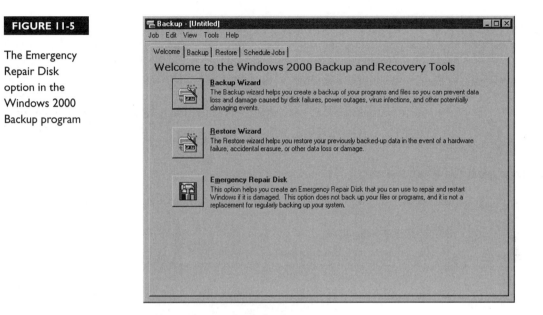

FIGURE 11-5

The Emergency
Repair Disk
option in the
Windows 2000
Backup program

CERTIFICATION OBJECTIVES

■ **701: 2.2**   *Given a scenario, explain and interpret common hardware and operating system symptoms and their causes*

■ **701: 3.2**   *Given a scenario, demonstrate proper use of user interfaces*

■ **702: 2.1**   *Select the appropriate commands and options to troubleshoot and resolve problems*

Both CompTIA exams have objectives requiring knowledge and skill with Windows diagnostic utilities and tools. This section addresses two areas in objective 701: 2.2 that were not previously detailed. They include the often-related issues of resolving system lock-up and other problems associated with applications. Additionally, in this section, we include a discussion of two of the commands listed under both the 701: 3.2 and 702: 2.1 objectives. They are MSCONFIG and CHKDSK, plus the DXDIAG command listed in just 701: 3.2. Other commands, IPCONFIG and SFC, are discussed in the section that follows this one; the troubleshooting commands and options that relate to networks will be included in upcoming Chapters 13, 14, and 15, and we will describe those that relate to security in Chapters 16 and 17.

Operational Problems and Symptoms

Operational problems are those that occur while Windows is running, as opposed to those that occur during startup. These may be instability problems, and they may involve OS components, including drivers, or application components. Regardless of the source of the problem, watching for error messages and familiarizing yourself with common error messages is important.

OS Instability Problems

What does OS instability look like? Instability includes a variety of symptoms such as

- Extreme slowness
- Inability to open programs
- Failure of running programs
- System lock-up
- Complete failure of the OS, resulting in a Stop error on a bluescreen

Let's examine how you would approach an instability problem that results in a bluescreen error. When a system malfunctions due to a fatal error, this results in a text-mode screen with white letters on a blue background. This screen is unofficially called the Blue Screen of Death (BSoD), but it is officially a Stop screen. A message, and multiple numbers that are the contents of the registers and other key memory locations, will display. This information is usually not overly useful to a computer technician, but it can provide a great deal of information to developers and technical support professionals as to the nature of the failure. It is a good idea to capture that information before you contact customer support.

A fatal error is one that could cause too much instability to guarantee the integrity of the system. Therefore, when the operating system detects a fatal error, it will stop and display the Stop screen.

Preparing for Stop Errors

To prepare for a Stop error, you should decide how you want your computer to behave after one occurs. You do this by modifying the System Failure settings on the Startup And Recovery page. You can find these settings by opening the System applet in Control Panel, selecting the Advanced | Advanced System Settings tab, and clicking the Settings button under Startup And Recovery.

- **Write An Event To The System Log** causes Windows to write an event to the System log, which is one of several log files you can view using Event Viewer (found under Administrative Tools). We highly recommend this setting, because it means that even if the computer reboots after a Stop screen, you can read the Stop error information that was on the screen in the System log.

- **Send An Administrative Alert** is a setting that appears in Windows 2000 and Windows XP. It sends an alert message to the administrator that will appear on the administrator's screen the next time he or she logs on. This is a useful setting for alerting a domain administrator if your computer is part of a domain.

- **Automatically Restart** is a setting we recommend, as long as you have also selected the first option, which preserves the Stop error information in the System log file.

- **Write Debugging Information** contains a drop-down list, a text box, and a check box. The drop-down list allows you to control the existence and size of the file containing debugging information. This file, called a dump file, has settings that include None, Small Memory Dump (64 KB), Kernel Memory Dump, and Complete Memory Dump. A complete memory dump contains an image of the contents of memory at the time of the fatal error. You can send this file to Microsoft for evaluation of a problem, but this amount of effort and cost (Microsoft charges for these services) is normally only expended on a critical computer, such as a network server. For a desktop computer, a small memory dump should be adequate, unless a support person advises you otherwise. The text box allows you to specify the location of the dump file. The default is %SystemRoot%\ followed by the dump file name. The variable %SystemRoot% is used by the operating system to point to the folder containing the Windows system files. The final setting is the check box labeled Overwrite Any Existing File. We recommend selecting this option so dump files do not accumulate on your computer's hard drive.

Troubleshooting a Stop Error

If you are present when a Stop error occurs, read the first few lines on the screen for a clue. If the system reboots before you can read this information, you can view it in the System log after the reboot. Open Event Viewer and look in the System log for a Stop error.

For example, say the error message looks something like this: "STOP [several sets of numbers in the form 0x00000000] UNMOUNTABLE_BOOT_VOLUME." If you search www . microsoft.com using just the last part of this message (UNMOUNTABLE_ BOOT_VOLUME), you may find sufficient information to determine the cause and the action to take by examining the values that preceded it. One possible solution offered is to restart Windows using the Recovery Console and to run a command from the command prompt. Now, you see the value of understanding how to work with the Recovery Console.

Troubleshooting Applications

Common problems with applications include the failure of an application to start and problems when running legacy applications in Windows.

Application Fails to Start

Imagine that you have spent days preparing a presentation for work. Your computer is running Windows, and you have several applications open. The presentation consists of a complex Excel spreadsheet, a Word report, and a PowerPoint slide presentation.

In researching a topic for this report, you locate source information in a file on the Internet. The file is in PDF format. You double-click the file, expecting it to load into the Acrobat Reader program. The hourglass appears briefly, but Acrobat does not start up, and no error message appears. You open the Task Manager, which shows current tasks. You expect to see Acrobat listed with a status of Not Responding, but it is not listed. The possible problem is that there is not enough memory to run the additional program. The solution is to close one or more applications and then attempt to open Acrobat. The long-term solution to this problem is to add more RAM to your computer.

An Old Application Will Not Run

Let's say you start an old application in the new version of Windows and it does not run correctly. Maybe the screen doesn't look quite right, or perhaps the program frequently hangs up. To solve this problem, first check for program updates from the manufacturer and install those. If this does not help, try reinstalling the program. If that also does not work, then use the Program Compatibility Wizard for the version of Windows you are running. We described the Program Compatibility Wizard in Chapter 8. After running the Program Compatibility Wizard, test the program to see if there is an improvement. If Compatibility Mode does not solve the problem for a program that ran well under Windows XP, and if you are running Windows 7, you have another option, which is Windows XP Mode, also described in Chapter 8.

Common Error Messages

An IT professional must recognize and interpret common error messages and codes. These range from messages that appear during the early stages of a failed startup, through a variety of operational error messages. Once-fleeting messages that were not available after the fact are now logged in many cases, and a knowledgeable person learns where to find them, as you will see in the sections that follow.

Startup Error Messages

When an OS fails in the early stages of startup, the problem often stems from corruption or loss of essential OS files. If this is the case, you may need to reinstall the OS, but before you take such a drastic step, consider other actions, such as the Recovery Options detailed earlier in this chapter.

NTLDR or NTDETECT.COM Is Missing (Windows 2000 or Windows XP)   If Windows 2000 or Windows XP startup fails, and you see a message that NTLDR or NTDETECT.COM is missing when you boot from your hard disk, simply boot with your Windows startup diskette (also called a "bootable floppy"), and copy the missing file from A:\ to C:\. The startup diskette is very different from the Windows setup boot diskettes that come with Windows 2000 and can be created for Windows XP (described in Chapter 9). If you support computers running either of these operating systems, and if they have floppy drives, we recommend that you create one of these disks for each OS. The Microsoft Support Website has several articles on doing this. Check out "How to create a bootable floppy disk for an NTFS or FAT partition in Windows XP" if you would like to learn more.

On a Windows 2000 computer, the message "NTLDR is missing" may appear when a floppy disk formatted in Windows 2000, and not configured to start Windows, is in a floppy drive during startup. Therefore, when you see this message, be sure to first check that there is no disk in the floppy drive.

NTOSKRNL Is Invalid or Missing   The error message "NTOSKRNL is invalid or missing" does not occur too often, but when it does, this message is usually incorrect and misleading because it is highly unlikely that this file is either invalid or missing.

What is more likely is that NTOSKRNL is not where NTLDR expects it to be. NTLDR finds this location by reading the BOOT.INI file. If a BOOT.INI file is not present, NTLDR attempts to locate this file in the default location for the version of Windows you are using.

In Windows 2000, that location is C:\WINNT32\SYSTEM32, whereas in Windows XP, the default location is C:\WINDOWS\SYSTEM32. If Windows was not installed in the default location, and the BOOT.INI file is damaged or missing, Windows will fail to start and will display the "NTOSKRNL invalid or missing" error.

Similarly, if the BOOT.INI is present but contains incorrect information, NTLDR will look in the wrong location and once again display the error message. If the computer previously started without failure, and if you have a Windows startup disk for the computer, use the disk to start Windows. If Windows starts when using the startup disk, correct the problem by copying the BOOT.INI file to the root of C:. Learn how to create a Windows startup disk later in this chapter.

If Windows does not start properly with the disk, then you have a more serious problem. It may still relate to the BOOT.INI file, but it may involve a change to the disk partitioning. In this case, research the Microsoft site for articles on the BOOT.INI file and how it describes the path to NTOSKRNL.EXE using an ARC path.

Invalid Boot or Invalid System Disk   An error message that reads "Invalid system disk" or "Invalid boot disk" can have several causes. This error message is more likely to occur on a Windows 9*x* computer than on one running newer versions of Windows. But if you see this message on a newer Windows system, here are a few possible causes and their solutions:

- A boot-sector virus may have infected your computer. Learn more about boot-sector viruses at **support.microsoft.com**.
- Third-party hard drive drivers did not copy to the hard disk during Setup. You will need to obtain updated drivers and follow the manufacturer's instructions. This may require reinstalling Windows.
- Specialized security software is preventing access to drive C:. Check the documentation for the security software.

Inaccessible Boot Drive   This error may show as a bluescreen Stop error, in which case the exact wording is "Inaccessible Boot Device." This fatal error has several possible causes and solutions. Here are just a few:

- A boot-sector virus has infected the computer. Learn more about boot-sector viruses at **support.microsoft.com**.

- A resource conflict exists between the two disk controllers. This conflict is most likely to occur after the installation of an additional controller. In that case, remove the new controller and reboot. If Windows starts up normally, then troubleshoot the new controller for a configuration that conflicts with the boot controller.

- The boot volume is corrupt. If you have eliminated other causes, then remove the boot hard drive system and install it in another computer that has a working installation of the same version of Windows. Configure it as an additional drive, boot into the existing operating system, and then run the CHKDSK program on the hard drive to diagnose and fix errors.

Device Has Failed to Start   If you see the message "Device has failed to start," open Device Manager and double-click the device name to open the device's Properties dialog box. On the General tab, look in the Device Status box for an error code. Troubleshoot in accordance with the error code. You may search the Microsoft Website for this error code and find a recommended solution.

If the driver is corrupted, you will need to uninstall the driver and then click the Action menu in Device Manager and select Scan For Hardware Changes to reinstall the driver. Another common solution is to select Update Driver in Device Manager. This will start the Hardware Update Wizard, which will walk you through the update process.

Service Has Failed to Start   If you see the error message "Service has failed to start," open Computer Management, expand the Services And Applications node, and click Services. In the contents pane, scroll down until you see the service that failed to start and right-click it. From the context menu, click Start. It may take several minutes for the service to start. If it starts normally, without any error messages, then do not take any further steps unless the problem recurs. In that case, you will need to research the problem. Do this by searching the Microsoft site on the service name, adding the word "failed" to the search string.

Device Referenced in Registry Not Found   If you see an error message stating that a device referenced in the registry was not found, use the instructions given in the earlier section, "Device Has Failed to Start," to either update the driver or uninstall and reinstall the driver.

Program Referenced in Registry Not Found   If you see an error message stating that a program referenced in the registry was not found, uninstall and reinstall the program.

Viewing Error Messages in Event Viewer

In early versions of Windows, error messages were something fleeting that you could not go back and read again, posing a major problem for PC support personnel relying on the user's memory to describe symptoms and messages. Beginning with Windows NT, error messages are no longer something fleeting that users must write down so you can troubleshoot.

Event logs save most error messages. Become familiar with Event Viewer before a problem occurs, so you will be comfortable using it to research a problem. Use Event Viewer to view logs of system, security, and application events, paying attention to the warning and error logs for messages you can use to solve problems.

Event Logs   Event Viewer has three standard categories of events: system, application, and security. Other event logs may exist, depending on the Windows configuration. For instance, Internet Explorer creates its own event log. You can open Event Viewer from Administrative Tools or by using its filename: **eventvwr.msc** and starting it from the Run line. In Windows Vista or Windows 7, simply enter **event viewer** in the Start Search box. In Windows Vista and Windows 7, the organization of the Event Viewer console has changed quite a bit, displaying Administrative events, which is a selection of events from all the log files that show a status of Warning or Error. This saves scrolling through all the Information events to find an event indicating a problem. To see a view similar to the old view, select the Windows Logs folder in the left pane and select each event log in turn.

- The System log records events involving the Windows system components (drivers, services, and so on). The types of events range from normal events, such as startup and shutdown (called Information events), through warnings of situations that could lead to errors, to actual error events. Even the dreaded "Blue Screen of Death" error messages show up in the System log as Stop errors. The System log, shown here (Windows XP), is the first place to look when a message indicates failure of a component, such as a driver or service. Double-click an event to see the details, including the actual message that appeared on the desktop in the warning. The message itself may lead you to the solution. Each event also has an ID number. Search the Microsoft Website for a solution, using either a portion of the error message or the event ID.

- The Application log shows events involving applications. These applications may be your office suite of applications or Windows components that run in the GUI, such as Windows Explorer or Document Explorer. When a program error occurs, a special program called Dr. Watson starts automatically and records some application events in the Application log. If you see a Dr. Watson error on your screen, you will find the error listed in the Application log.

- Event logs do not record security events by default; therefore, don't be surprised to find an empty Security log. Only after an administrator turns on auditing will security events appear in the Security log, and then it can log several types of events. You can turn on auditing through the Local Security Policy shortcut on the Administrative Tools menu. In the Local Security Setting console, you control auditing through these settings: Security Settings | Local Policies | Audit Policy, shown here for Windows Vista. Once you enable Audit Account Logon Events, the Security log will log each successful and/or failed logon attempt. These events will show in the Security log in Event Viewer as Success Audit or Failure Audit. Other settings that affect Security logging are the three

policies that begin with "Audit" in Local Security Settings under Security
Settings | Local Policies | Security Options.

To learn more about Event Viewer, use the help program from within Event
Viewer.

Working with Event Logs   Windows allows you to manage each log file
separately. If you right-click a log node in Event Viewer, such as Application,
Security, or System, the context menu will give you a list of actions that you can
perform on that log file, including clearing (emptying it of events), saving (in a
separate file to be viewed later), opening a previously saved file, viewing (in a
variety of views), and refreshing (to display updated data). The context menu is
also how you access the Properties dialog for the log file, where you can configure
options such as the maximum size to which each event log may grow, and the
action to take when the event log is full (reaches the maximum size). Figure 11-6
shows the Properties dialog for the System log in Windows Vista. The General tab
is where you configure the local System log, whereas the Subscriptions tab is where
an administrator would configure a special service, called Windows Event Collector
Service, to collect log events from other computers—a very advanced task.

FIGURE 11-6

The Windows
Vista System log
dialog box

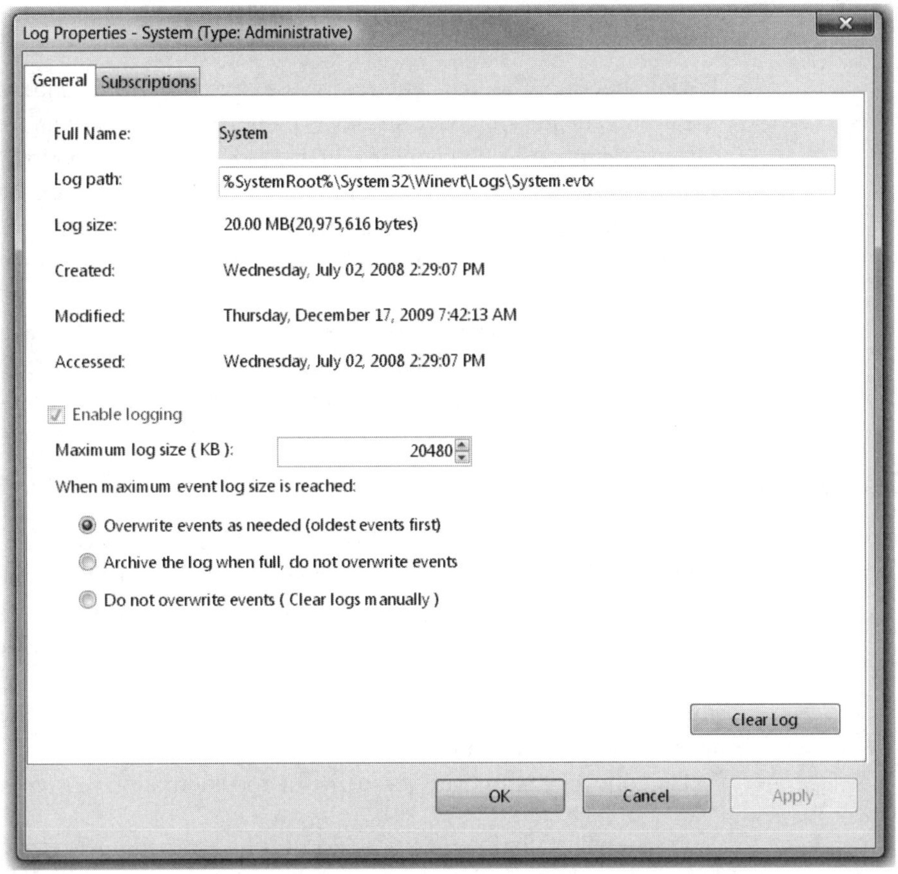

Log Properties - System (Type: Administrative)

General | Subscriptions

Full Name:	System
Log path:	%SystemRoot%\System32\Winevt\Logs\System.evtx
Log size:	20.00 MB(20,975,616 bytes)
Created:	Wednesday, July 02, 2008 2:29:07 PM
Modified:	Thursday, December 17, 2009 7:42:13 AM
Accessed:	Wednesday, July 02, 2008 2:29:07 PM

☑ Enable logging

Maximum log size (KB): 20480

When maximum event log size is reached:

◉ Overwrite events as needed (oldest events first)

◉ Archive the log when full, do not overwrite events

◉ Do not overwrite events (Clear logs manually)

Clear Log

OK | Cancel | Apply

SCENARIO & SOLUTION

What are at least four symptoms of OS instability?	Symptoms include extreme slowness, inability to open programs, failure of running programs, system lock-up, and complete failure of the OS.
An application that ran well in Windows 2000 or XP frequently hangs in Windows Vista. How can I make the program run better in Windows Vista?	Run the Program Compatibility Wizard and configure compatibility settings to create an environment for the old application similar to that provided by the old operating system.
Windows fails to start and the following message displays: "NTLDR is missing." What should I do?	Use a Windows startup disk to boot up the computer. If Windows starts up normally, copy the NTLDR file from the floppy disk to the root of drive C:.

Using Diagnostic Utilities and Tools

Troubleshooting Windows requires the use of a variety of diagnostic utilities and tools, and in this chapter, you have already explored a number of them. For instance, the Advanced Options Menu is an invaluable tool for troubleshooting startup problems; the Recovery Console is a tool for recovering from a total failure; and Automated System Recovery gives you a complete Windows XP operating system backup set, while Windows 2000 relies on the Emergency Repair Process for recovering from a major failure.

In this section, you will explore the documentation resources available to you, learn to create startup disks, and define the value of such tools as Device Manager, Task Manager, System Configuration Utility (MSCONFIG), and System File Checker.

Documentation Resources

An IT professional working with Windows operating systems quickly learns to use all the documentation resources available. The best documentation is from reliable sources—Microsoft, certain third-party vendors, and some other organizations. Regardless of the source of the documentation, there are certain features you should look for. While you will still find paper documentation, the best documentation is up-to-date and searchable, which rules out most paper documentation. This includes a locally installed online manual and Internet-based sources.

The following is an overview of useful documentation resources:

- **User/installation manuals**   Most software comes with some documentation. This can range from a simple "read-me" file to a comprehensive hardcopy or disk-based manual with detailed instructions on installing, using, and troubleshooting the software. Check out the documentation before you have a problem with Windows or an application. Keep the paper-based manuals organized in a handy place.

- **Online Help**   Online Help utilities are very common. Windows and most Windows applications include a Help menu on the main toolbar. Windows Help includes searchable databases with extensive documentation *and the latest ones* will search the local Help data, as well as the Microsoft Website, for answers to your queries. Windows and most Windows applications will bring up context-sensitive Help when you press the F1 key.

- **Internet/Web-based**   Beyond the Help program and the Websites it searches, learn to search manufacturers' sites and to do Internet searches using your favorite search engine, such as Google. There are also certain sites that function as online encyclopedias, such as Wikipedia.

- **Training materials**   Be aware of the training opportunities available to you. You might think that when you are in the middle of troubleshooting, you do not want to participate in training. However, training has taken on new meaning with the sources available both within the Windows Help program and on the Microsoft Website. For instance, Windows Help has Troubleshooters that walk you through troubleshooting common problems. Try this sometime, and you will find yourself receiving training while solving a problem.

- **Subscription support**   In addition to free support options, such as online knowledge bases and newsgroups, Microsoft and other vendors offer for-pay support services, providing varying levels of access to support help based on a range of prices. Microsoft and most other organizations charge for phone support—either a per-incident charge or as part of a support subscription.

System Information (MSINFO32.EXE)

You sit down at a Windows computer you have never touched before. You know little about it, but you need to gather information to troubleshoot a problem. One of the first things you should do is learn as much as you can as quickly as you can. What version, edition, and service pack of Windows is installed? How much memory is installed, what processor, and so on? This information and more is displayed in *System Information*, which you access through the GUI at All Programs | Accessories | System Tools. Then select System Information. A quicker way to do this is by starting it from the Run line using its executable name, *MSINFO32.EXE*.

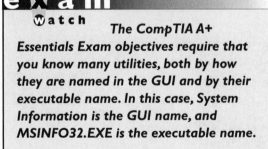

ⓦatch   *The CompTIA A+ Essentials Exam objectives require that you know many utilities, both by how they are named in the GUI and by their executable name. In this case, System Information is the GUI name, and MSINFO32.EXE is the executable name.*

Device Manager

Device Manager is a tool that allows an administrator to view and change device properties, update device drivers, configure device settings, and uninstall devices. Beginning with Windows XP, Device Manager will even allow an administrator to roll back a driver update.

Device Manager can be found through the System applet in Windows XP and Windows 2000 by selecting the Hardware tab and then clicking Device Manager. It is an MMC snap-in and opens up into a separate console window. Device Manager in Windows XP works almost exactly as in Windows 2000, with some small changes in viewing information, and with the addition of the new Roll Back Driver button on the Driver tab of the Properties dialog box. This feature works on device drivers that were updated with new drivers. It is quite handy for those times when you find the new device driver causes new problems.

To access Device Manager in Windows Vista or Windows 7, open the System applet in Control Panel and select Device Manager from the Tasks pane. It is nearly identical to Device Manager in Windows XP.

EXERCISE 11-2

Getting to Know Device Manager

1. Open Device Manager.

2. Use the View menu to experiment with various ways of changing the information display.

3. You have two options for viewing devices and two options for viewing resources, which you can choose from the View menu. You will normally view devices by type, because this approach is simpler and more understandable.

4. When viewing devices by type, you will see a node for each device type, such as Computer, Disk Drives, and so on. Familiarize yourself with Device Manager by opening the nodes.

5. Click the question mark button in the toolbar to open Device Manager Help, and browse through the topics to learn more.

6. Close Device Manager when you are done.

Task Manager

Task Manager is another utility that each successive version of Windows has improved. The current Task Manager does not resemble the simple tool we used to remove unresponsive programs from memory in Windows 9x. Beginning in Windows 2000, Task Manager is a very sophisticated program that allows you to end an unresponsive program and do other tasks.

Knowing how to start Task Manager and how to stop an unresponsive program are important. Our preferred method of opening this tool is with the keyboard shortcut, CTRL-SHIFT-ESC, which starts Task Manager directly. You can also open Task Manager by right-clicking an empty area of the taskbar and selecting Task Manager from the context-sensitive menu that displays.

Task Manager, shown here, has several tabbed pages; the Applications tab is the one from which you view and manage GUI applications. If an application is not responding, and you cannot close the application any other way, open Task Manager, select the nonresponding application, and click End Task.

Select the Processes tab to see the Process list, showing each active process that is currently running in memory. A program runs in memory as one or more processes. A single *process* consists of memory space, program code, data, and the system resources required by the process. Each process has at least one thread, which is the program code executed by the process. An operating system has many active processes at any given time. Add to that the processes for such programs or applications as Windows

Explorer and Microsoft Word, and you have dozens of active processes running in memory at one time performing various functions. A *background process* is one that runs "behind the scenes" and has a low priority, does not require input, and rarely creates output. Many of the processes in the Process list are background processes. Processes are identified in Task Manager by the image name (filename) and *Process ID (PID)*, which is a number dynamically assigned by the operating system as it starts each process. The Processes tab also shows the amount of memory and the CPU usage of the process.

When a programmer creates a program, she gives it a *process priority level*, also called a *base priority level*, which determines the order in which the program code's process or processes are executed in relation to other active processes. There are six levels, listed from the lowest to the highest: Low, Below Normal, Normal, Above Normal, High, and Real Time. A program that has a High priority level has the potential to tie up the processor, and one with a Real Time priority level can cause system crashes. The operating system can adjust these levels to some degree, and you can also temporarily adjust the level of an active process by right-clicking a process and selecting Set Priority. We do not recommend that you do this.

To see the priority level of active processes, first select the Processes tab, and then open View | Select Columns. In the Select Process Page Columns dialog, click to place a check mark in the Base Priority box. This adds the Base Priority column. Most of the processes will have a Base Priority level of Normal, with a few High priorities and perhaps one or two Below Normal.

Task Scheduler

The *Task Scheduler* utility allows you to create tasks that run automatically at times that you configure. Use Task Scheduler to automate daily backups and updates. Launch Task Scheduler from Administrative Tools.

System Configuration Utility (MSCONFIG)

Beginning with Windows XP, and continuing through later versions, Microsoft includes a System Configuration Utility that allows you to modify and test startup configuration settings without having to alter them directly. While you can call this program up from the GUI, the quick way to launch it is from the Run line or from Start Search in Windows Vista and Windows 7 using its executable name, MSCONFIG.EXE.

on the

job

Take time to practice using the System Configuration Utility before you need to use it for troubleshooting.

This utility is great to use when you want to stop a program from launching at startup, but do not want to search all the possible startup locations, including some legacy locations. For instance, Windows 2000 and Windows XP still use some old files designed for Windows 3.x. These files are SYSTEM.INI and WIN.INI, and they still exist for downward compatibility with very old applications, written for early versions of Windows.

The value of MSCONFIG today is that it will let you test what-if scenarios for startup. For instance, you can temporarily disable the startup of one or more programs using MSCONFIG. When you make such changes from within MSCONFIG and then restart the computer, it will start up and reflect the change you made in MSCONFIG. This allows you to test to make sure that making this change would not negatively affect your computer. You can also use MSCONFIG to start Windows with a minimal configuration, much like that used by Safe Mode. Once you have determined what program or service is causing a problem, you can uninstall the program or permanently disable the service so it will not run when the computer boots.

exam

Watch

The CompTIA A+ Essentials Exam objectives list refers to this utility only by its filename, MSCONFIG.EXE. The title bar for this GUI utility clearly shows its full name, System Configuration Utility. In the exam's multiple-choice questions, you are most likely to see it referred to by its filename, but be prepared to recognize it by either of these names. Be sure you understand when to use this utility, and remember both of its names.

Monitoring Performance

Performance monitoring is something that is usually done on network servers, not on Windows desktop computers. Server administrators use performance monitoring to ensure that the quality of service is maintained and as an early warning of potential problems that show up first as performance problems. All Windows server products have performance monitoring tools, and the versions of Windows described in this book have a utility for monitoring performance of many aspects of your computer.

This utility has evolved from one version of Windows to another. In Windows Vista and Windows 7, it is named *Reliability and Performance Monitor*, but it was known as System Monitor in Windows 2000 and Windows XP, which, in turn, replaced the *Performance Monitor* from Windows NT. You can see a "lite" version of this utility on the Performance tab of Task Manager.

System Monitor allows an administrator to gather and view performance data involving memory, disks, the processor, network, and other objects. Each object has one or more counters that you may select for monitoring, and System Monitor displays the data in real time in a report, graph, or histogram (bar chart). Open System Monitor in Windows XP Professional by selecting Start | All Programs | Administrative Tools | Performance. When you first open System Monitor, it displays three commonly used counters, each from a separate object:

- A counter for pages per second of the memory object
- A counter for average disk queue length of the physical disk object
- A counter for the percent of processor time used by the processor object

To learn more about System Monitor, first select the System Monitor node in the Performance console, and then click the Help button (yellow question mark).

The *Performance Logs and Alert* node in the Performance console actually allows you to create alerts and to create log files. An alert is a notification triggered by some system event. An administrator selects the triggering event, such as when the used space on a hard drive reaches a certain percentage of the total space.

System File Checker (SFC)

System files have very privileged access to your computer, and, therefore, malicious software targets them. At one time system files were fair game for such software, but recent versions of Windows come with protections, both at the file system level and through the use of a service that protects system files.

This service, called Windows File Protection (WFP) in Windows 2000 and Windows XP, maintains a file cache of protected files. If a file is somehow damaged, WFP will replace the damaged file with the undamaged file from the cache. WFP will allow digitally signed files to replace existing system files safely. The files it will allow are those distributed through the following:

- Windows service packs
- Hotfix distributions

- Operating system upgrades
- Windows Update
- Windows Device Manager

WFP will overwrite files introduced into Windows in any other way by using files from the cache.

In Windows Vista/7, WFP has been replaced by Windows Resource Protection (WRP), which extends its protection to registry keys.

The System File Checker (SFC) is a handy utility that uses the WFP or WRP service to scan and verify the versions of all protected system files after you restart your computer. The syntax for this program is as follows:

```
sfc [scannow] [scanonce] [scanboot] [revert] [purgecache]
[cachesize=x]
```

When you run SFC with the /scannow parameter, you will see a message box like the one shown here (Windows XP). If SFC finds any files that do not comply, it will replace them with the correct signed file from the cache.

Remote Desktop

Remote Desktop is a network service available in Windows XP Professional, Windows XP Media Center, Windows Vista, and Windows 7. It relies on an underlying Microsoft protocol, *Remote Desktop Protocol (RDP)*. Although it is not strictly a troubleshooting tool, we include it here as both a productivity tool and a means for troubleshooting Windows problems over a network. Remote Desktop allows a remote user to connect to a Windows computer and have total access to the desktop and local resources, including files, printers, and other attached devices. The remote user can see the remote desktop in a window or as a full-screen view. The entire experience is nearly identical to working physically at the computer.

This service is ideal for the user who must work from home but wants access to all the files and programs on his office PC. Remote Desktop can also be a tool for a PC professional requiring access to files and programs on a user's computer for troubleshooting and maintenance. Following is a brief overview of how to set up Remote Desktop.

Preparing the Server Side of Remote Desktop

On the server side (the desktop you wish to connect to and remotely control), enable the Remote Desktop service. To do this in Windows XP, open the Control Panel System applet. In the System Properties dialog box, select the Remote tab. Select Allow Users To Connect Remotely To This Computer and click OK. In Windows Vista or Windows 7, open Control Panel and enter **remote desktop** in the Search box. Then select Allow Remote Access To Your Computer. This opens the System Properties dialog box, displaying the Remote tab, as shown in Figure 11-7. On the bottom half of this page, click the radio button labeled Allow Connections From Computers Running Any Version Of Remote Desktop (Less Secure) or select Allow Connections Only From Computers Running Remote Desktop With Network Level Authentication (More Secure). The second option will only be available if your computer is part of a Microsoft Windows Active Directory domain. Then click OK.

FIGURE 11-7

Turn on Remote Desktop on the server side.

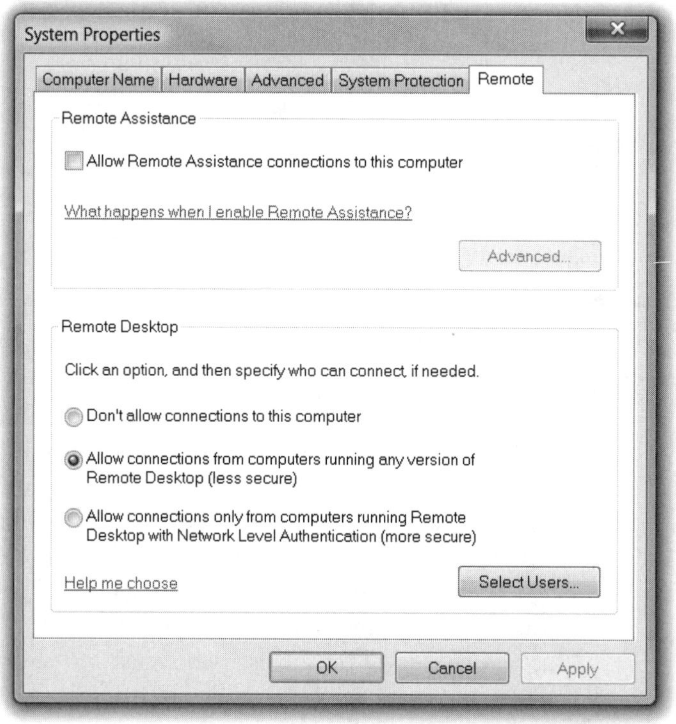

When you make this change, Windows also modifies Windows Firewall to allow Remote Desktop messages to pass through the firewall. Learn more about Windows Firewall in Chapter 17. If you have disabled Windows Firewall and are using a third-party firewall, you will need to check the manufacturer's instructions. In this case, you need to make an exception so the firewall will allow the Remote Desktop messages through. To do this, you need to find how to configure the firewall to allow traffic that is using TCP port 3389. Learn about these types of ports in Chapter 13.

Make a note of the computer name or domain name of this computer, as well as the IP address. You need the computer name if the computer is in a workgroup, and you need the domain name if it is a member of a domain. Even if you are sure you know the computer name or domain name, double-check it now by locating this information in the System applet in Control Panel. Write down the information because you will need it when you are configuring the client (remote) side of Remote Desktop. The reason is that you will need to configure the remote client to log on. That is, if your computer is a member of a domain, you will log on to the domain with your user name and password. If the computer is a member of a workgroup, you will log on to the computer itself. When you have collected this information, close the System applet.

Now find the IP address of the server PC using the IPCONFIG command. If you need help with the command, check out Exercise 13-2 in Chapter 13, and turn to Chapter 15 for more information on this command. Write down the IP address. You will need the IP address and computer or domain name when you configure the Remote Desktop client.

Preparing the Client Side of Remote Desktop

The client side software for Remote Desktop is Remote Desktop Connection. It is installed by default in Windows Vista and Windows 7, but not in previous versions of Windows, in which case you will have to locate and download it from the Microsoft Website (www.microsoft.com). Follow the instructions provided with the download to install Remote Desktop Connection for the client computer.

Once the Remote Desktop Connection software is installed, start the program in Windows XP from Start | All Programs | Accessories | Communications | Remote Desktop Connection, and the Remote Desktop Connection dialog box will display. In Windows Vista and Windows 7, simply enter **remote desktop** in the Start Search box, and the Remote Desktop Connection dialog will display, as shown here. Enter either the IP address or the domain name path (*<server >.<second_level_domain>.<first_level_domain>*) of your office PC in the box labeled Computer. Click the Options button, and on the General tab page, enter the appropriate credentials. Click Connect, and after you are authenticated, a window will open on your desktop containing the desktop of your office computer. You will have access to all programs and files, just as if you were sitting at that computer.

Remote Assistance

Remote Assistance is another service that is available for connecting computers running Windows XP, Windows Vista, or Windows 7. Like Remote Desktop, it relies on the RDP protocol, and the major difference between this and Remote Desktop is that Remote Assistance requires that the user needing assistance send an invitation. A remote assistant cannot connect without this invitation.

There are three requirements for using Remote Assistance:

- Both computers must be running Windows XP or a newer version of Windows.
- Both computers must be connected via a network.
- Windows Messenger must be running for Remote Assistance in Windows XP.

Preparing for Remote Assistance

The computer seeking assistance must have Remote Assistance turned on. Do this in Windows XP by opening the System applet in Control Panel, selecting the Remote tab, and placing a check in the box labeled Allow Remote Assistance Invitations To Be Sent From This Computer. Click OK to close the dialog box.

In Windows Vista, open the System applet in Control Panel and select Advanced System Settings from the Tasks. This opens the System Properties dialog. Select the Remote tab, and click to place a check in the box labeled Allow Remote Assistance Connections To This Computer.

Before requesting remote assistance, check your firewall settings. If you are using Windows Firewall in Windows XP, open the Windows Firewall applet from Control Panel. On the General page, remove the check (if one exists) from the check box labeled Don't Allow Exceptions. Click the Exceptions tab, and on the Exceptions page, scroll through the list of Programs And Services and place a check in the box labeled Remote Assistance. Click OK to close the Windows Firewall dialog box. If you are using the Windows Vista Firewall, the steps are similar for allowing incoming Remote Assistance traffic.

If you are using Windows Vista or Windows 7, open Control Panel and enter the word **allow** in the Search box. This will bring up a list of Control Panel settings containing the word "allow." Locate Windows Firewall, and then select Allow A Program Through Windows Firewall. This will open the Exceptions page of the Windows Firewall Settings dialog box. Click to place a check in the box labeled Remote Assistance. Click OK to close the dialog box. If you have disabled Windows Firewall and are using another personal firewall, you will need to check the manufacturer's instructions.

Requesting Remote Assistance

You request remote assistance by sending an invitation. In Windows XP, you do this by first opening Windows Help And Support, available from the Start menu. Under Ask For Assistance, click Invite A Friend To Connect To Your Computer With Remote Assistance; on the next page, select Invite Someone To Help You. This will open the Remote Assistance page with three choices for contacting your assistant: Windows Messenger, e-mail, or a file. Select one of the first two, and the wizard will guide you through the process of creating and sending the invitation. If you must send an invitation through Web mail, choose to create a file. The wizard will create the file, and then you must attach it to an e-mail message and send it.

To make a request for assistance in Windows Vista or Windows 7, simply enter **remote assistance** in the Start Search box, and the Windows Remote Assistance wizard will open. One big change from Windows XP is that, in addition to requesting assistance, you can offer Remote Assistance help to someone. To request assistance, click the option labeled Invite Someone You Trust To Help You. Then continue through the wizard, choosing to send an e-mail invitation or to create a file that you will manually send to the assistant.

SCENARIO & SOLUTION

My wireless NIC contains no status lights. How can I tell if it is working?	Look in the system tray for an icon for the NIC. Double-click the icon to open a configuration utility, which will show its status.
I have heard experienced technicians talk about network utilities like IPCONFIG and PING, but I cannot find these programs listed anywhere on the Start menu. Where are they?	You will not find these programs on the Start menu because they are command prompt utilities that you must enter from the command prompt. Enter the name of one of these followed by a /? to learn more about it.
I am having trouble understanding the difference between Remote Desktop and Remote Assistance. Which one should I use to help a new user with a Windows problem?	Remote Desktop mainly exists as a means for someone to access her own PC from a remote location, whereas Remote Assistance is a way for a user to invite someone to act as a remote assistant and help solve a problem. Use Remote Assistance to help the new user.

DirectX Diagnostic Tool

The *DirectX Diagnostic Tool (DXDIAG)* is a Run line utility. Launch this program when experiencing video problems, such as the inability to take advantage of DirectX video, sound, and input support required by DirectX applications and evidenced by either poor performance in the inability to display video motion in two dimensions or three dimensions. Start up DXDIAG from the Run line or Start Search (Windows Vista and Windows 7). The utility has been dumbed down a bit in Windows Vista and Windows 7 because those versions do not allow you to run tests of the DirectX systems, just view status information. However, in Windows 2000 and Windows XP, you can run several tests of your multimedia system, including testing both the DirectDraw and Direct3D support for each video adapter and connected display, DirectSound support, Direct Music (synthesizer and any connected sound devices), input and output, and testing network performance for working with interactive DirectPlay applications.

■ **701: 2.5** *Given a scenario, integrate common preventative maintenance techniques*

> This section describes preventative maintenance tasks for the Windows operating systems, covering the subobjectives of the CompTIA A+ Essentials (2009 Edition) Exam objective 701:2.5 that were not described previously in this book. These include techniques for performing software updates, defragmenting hard drive volumes, and modifying a variety of Windows settings for optimal performance.

Performing Preventive Maintenance and Optimization

Preventive maintenance for Windows operating systems includes tasks that either prevent certain problems from occurring or guarantee that you can quickly recover from a problem or disaster with a minimum loss of time or data.

Preventive maintenance tasks include the following: defragmenting hard drives on a regular basis, keeping your operating system and applications updated, backing up the registry before making changes, scheduling OS and data backups, testing your ability to restore backups, and configuring System Restore so it creates restore points without taking up unnecessary space.

Defragment Hard Drive Volumes

A common, and easily corrected, cause of system slowness is fragmented files. Windows writes files in available space beginning near the outside of the disk platters. Over time, as files are deleted, this leaves open space into which new files can be written, but large files may require more space than is available in the first available contiguous open space. The OS then places what will fit into this space, and seeks the next available space.

This practice causes files—especially large ones—to be fragmented, meaning that the various pieces of one file are in several locations on the disk. Reading or writing a fragmented file takes much longer than it does for the same file written into one contiguous space. Therefore, over time, a system will slow down simply because of the large number of fragmented files on a volume.

A simple preventive task is defragmenting the hard drive. You can run Disk Defragmenter as described in Chapter 9. You can also run it from the command-line program, DEFRAG.EXE, or use a third-party defragmenter. Whichever program you use, defrag your hard drive volumes on a regular basis—once a week or once a month.

There are certain tasks you should perform before defragmenting a drive. Because Disk Defragmenter cannot work on the Recycle Bin, consider emptying it before running the program. This will open up more space. It also cannot defrag any open files, so close all other applications before starting Disk Defragmenter. This program also requires 15 percent free space on the drive in which to work as it moves files around. If you start defragmenting when there is insufficient space, it will stop and display an error message. Therefore, before beginning, check on the available disk space on the volume you wish to defrag. You can do this from within the GUI Disk Defragmenter program. Look at the value at the right of the drive to confirm it has more than 15 percent free space before selecting it.

If you find that you do not have enough free space, delete files. Use the Disk Cleanup program to free up adequate space. We described this program in Chapter 9.

Tweak Preferences and Display Settings

An important optimization task is to ensure that Windows desktop preferences and display settings are configured for the best user experience. In organizations where the computers are secured, end users find they can make very few changes to programs and configurations. IT staff normally recognize that users must feel some ownership in their computers, however, and so personalized desktops are usually allowed, within limits. In fact, this ability can be considered both optimization and preventive maintenance, because if the user experience can be made pleasant, then the user will take pride and more interest in learning to work competently in Windows, which always makes the technician's job a bit easier.

Windows has long offered a variety of configurable features for the desktop, such as wallpaper, screen savers, color schemes, and themes that combine all these elements. In Windows Vista, Microsoft introduced more GUI features, such as Aero and Sidebar, both described in Chapter 8.

As you help users to personalize their Windows Vista and Windows 7 desktops, be aware—these features require system resources. For instance, the more gadgets loaded onto a sidebar, the more memory and processor cycles dedicated to tasks that perhaps are not related to the end user's job. Aero features make the entire experience more interesting, but Aero has high system requirements, and some preset power plans in the Power Options applet will limit the Aero features or turn it off altogether. For instance, the preset Power Saver plan will do away with the transparency and window animations as it sacrifices performance for energy savings. You may need to make a compromise and select the Balanced Power plan, but when performance and a great user experience are important and power usage is not an issue, simply select the Higher Performance plan.

Modify Indexing Settings

The Windows Indexing Service, introduced in Windows 2000, runs in the background creating an index of files and their properties. This service shortens the time it takes to search for files and is especially important with the growing size of hard drives and the large amounts of data we store on them. When configuring the Indexing service, you need to balance two opposing needs: quicker file searches versus overall system performance, because this service can slow a system down. Microsoft has worked to make the service more efficient with each subsequent version of Windows, but you will still need to take a look at the indexing settings as a standard maintenance task. When you do, take into consideration how the end user works. Is all his data stored out on a server and virtually none stored locally, or does he store a great number of files locally? If the data files are all saved on a network server, then the indexing service on the server will take care of his search needs, but if the data is stored locally, you will want to ensure that the drive on which the data is stored is indexed.

To tune the Indexing Service in Windows XP, open the Computer Management console, then open the Services And Applications node and right-click the Indexing Service node. Select All Tasks, and then select Tune Performance. In the Indexing Service Usage dialog box, select the description that best matches the frequency of searches on this computer. Click OK to close out of the Indexing Service dialog box. Then move up to the Services node, right-click the Indexing Service, and select Restart. The changes will take effect after the service restarts.

The Indexing Service does not appear as a separate node in Computer Management in Windows Vista or Windows 7. It can be opened from the GUI in several ways; one way is by opening the Performance Information And Tools applet from Control Panel. In the Tasks pane, select Adjust Indexing Options. In the Indexing Options dialog box, shown in Figure 11-8, click the Modify button to add or remove indexing locations. The Advanced button opens Advanced Options, which will let you further modify indexing and rebuild the index catalog.

FIGURE 11-8

The Indexing
Options page in
Windows Vista

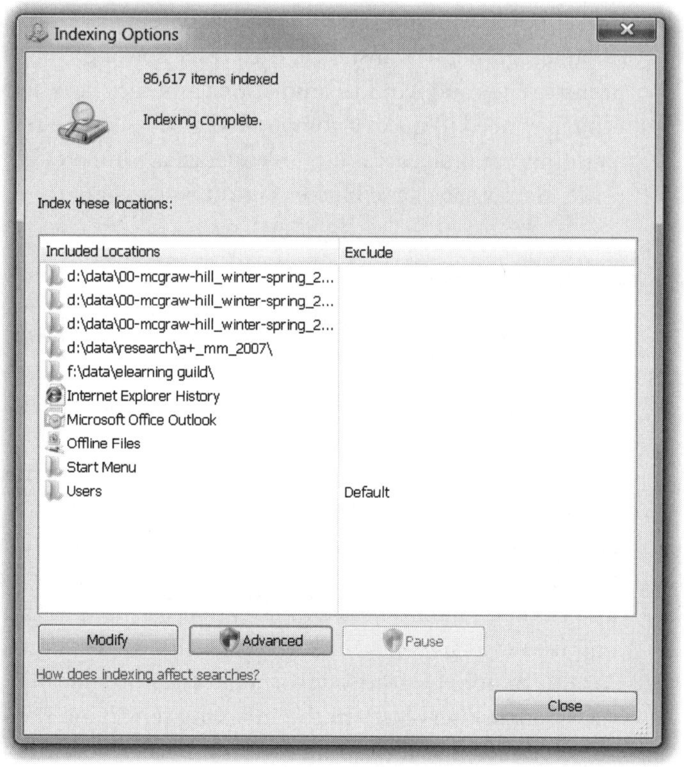

Modify User Account Control

User Account Control (UAC), as described in Chapter 8, is a very important security feature in Windows Vista and Windows 7. Our preference is to keep it turned on, but it can be turned on or off for an individual user through Control Panel | User Accounts, as shown here.

Turn on Automatic Updates

One of the most important preventive maintenance tasks is keeping Windows up-to-date. You learned about Windows Update in Chapters 8 and 9. We recommend using the methods described in "Updating Windows" in Chapter 9.

Software Updates

As discussed in Chapter 9, software updates are also very important. For your Microsoft software, such as Office, you can use either the Microsoft Office Update site or configure Windows Update to update both the operating system and the installed Microsoft applications, as described in "Updating Windows" in Chapter 9.

For non-Microsoft applications, check to see if the application has an automatic update option, and configure it to check for updates automatically. Most applications have this option.

Scheduled Backups

You should perform scheduled backups of your complete system as well as data files using a third-party tool or those included with Windows. The Windows Backup Utility was described in "Backing Up Data" in Chapter 10.

Test Restore

If possible, occasionally test your backups by restoring them. Now, you need to be careful when doing this, because if the backup is even minutes old, and you have made changes to files since the backup, you will end up restoring on top of the changed files and lose your work. Therefore, if possible, test your backups by restoring to another identically configured computer—perhaps one you use for testing or training purposes.

Configure System Restore

System Restore is on by default, but it can also be totally disabled. We recommend that you enable it and tweak the configuration, so it does not take up too much disk space and so it is not monitoring drives that do not require the System Restore

SCENARIO & SOLUTION	
What is the difference between Safe Mode and Safe Mode With Networking?	Safe Mode starts up without using several drivers and components that Windows normally starts, including networking components. Safe Mode With Networking only differs from Safe Mode in that networking components also start.
I often forget to run the Windows Update program to connect to the Microsoft site and update my computer. What is the solution?	Use the Automatic Updates page in System Properties to turn on Automatic Updates.
There are programs starting up in Windows, and I would like to stop them. What is a safe way to do this?	Use the System Configuration Utility (MSCONFIG.EXE) to select the program or programs you do not want to start. Then test your changes by restarting. Once you are satisfied with the results, you can make the changes permanent through this utility.
How can I ensure that System Restore is on?	Open the System Restore page in System Properties, and make sure System Restore is on for drive C: and all other permanently attached hard disk drives.

service. The default setting is for System Restore to reserve up to 12 percent of each drive for saving restore data. This amount can be excessive on very large hard drives. If you have a drive used exclusively for data, turn off System Restore on that drive. Since you normally only use removable hard drives for data, be sure to turn it off for all removable hard drives.

CERTIFICATION SUMMARY

An IT professional must have a foundation of knowledge about Windows in order to troubleshoot common problems. The Advanced Options Menu offers a variety of choices for modifying startup for troubleshooting. The Safe Modes offered on this menu are invaluable in allowing access to a Windows installation that may otherwise fail during startup.

You also need to understand when and how to use Windows system recovery tools and to know which ones are available in the various versions of Windows. You should recognize operational problems by their symptoms, and understand the common causes and solutions to these problems. Such symptoms include instability, system lock-up, and device driver failure. Know how to troubleshoot a failed application and how to configure a legacy application to run in a new version of Windows. Recognize common error messages and codes, and understand how to work with Event Viewer.

Familiarize yourself with the utilities and tools for troubleshooting. Begin with documentation resources available to you for troubleshooting and training yourself in using and supporting Windows and applications. Practice using Device Manager, Task Manager, System Configuration Utility (MSCONFIG), and System File Checker.

Perform preventive maintenance on Windows computers, including defragmenting hard drive volumes, turning on Automatic Updates for both Windows and applications, scheduling backups, testing restore, and configuring System Restore.

✓ TWO-MINUTE DRILL

Here are some of the key points covered in Chapter 11.

Diagnosing and Repairing Operating System Failures

❏ You can access the Windows Advanced Options Menu (Advanced Boot Options in Windows Vista) by pressing F8 as the computer is restarting. It contains many alternative ways to start Windows when you are troubleshooting startup problems.

❏ Select from three Safe Mode options to troubleshoot and solve Windows problems. These are Safe Mode, Safe Mode With Networking, and Safe Mode With Command Prompt.

❏ System Restore creates restore points, which are snapshots of Windows, its configuration, and all installed programs; these are created automatically, and you can manually create a restore point before making changes to your computer.

❏ If your computer has nonfatal problems after you have made a change, you can use System Restore to roll it back to a restore point.

❏ The Recovery Console in Windows XP is a non-GUI command-line interface that allows you to recover from an OS failure when you cannot get into Windows.

❏ Start the Recovery Console from the Windows 2000 or Windows XP CD by running Setup, selecting Repair, and then selecting Recovery Console.

❏ In Windows XP, Automated System Recovery (ASR) allows you to create a backup of the system partition, which will include a bootable disk and backup media. Use this to recover from a complete failure when all other options have failed.

❏ The Emergency Repair Process in Windows 2000 involved the creation of a repair disk or the saving of repair information on the local hard disk. If the OS failed, you would run the Windows Setup program and select the Repair option.

❏ Beginning in Windows Vista, the System Recovery Options menu gives you very powerful recovery tools that you can use to recover or restore Windows after a failure.

Operational Issues and Symptoms

❑ Operational problems are those that occur while Windows is running. They include instability and may involve OS components and applications.

❑ Instability problems include extreme slowness, inability to open programs, failure of running programs, system lock-up, and complete failure of the OS, resulting in a Stop error.

❑ When an application fails to start, but there are no other obvious symptoms, suspect that insufficient memory is the problem.

❑ If an old application will not run, and that application was for an earlier version of Windows, use the Program Compatibility Wizard to modify the environment in which the program runs in Compatibility Mode.

❑ If Compatibility Mode does not enable an XP application to run in Windows 7, use Windows XP mode.

❑ Be familiar with common error messages, such as those that appear at startup. Use Event Viewer to see error messages you missed.

Using Diagnostic Utilities and Tools

❑ Documentation resources for your operating system and other software include quick start guides, installation manual, user manuals, online help, Internet-based sources, and training materials.

❑ Use the System Information Utility (MSINFO32.EXE) to learn quickly about a system you must troubleshoot or support. Become familiar with Device Manager before you need to use it for troubleshooting.

❑ Use Task Manager to stop a program that has stopped responding and cannot be stopped any other way.

❑ Use the System Configuration Utility (MSCONFIG.EXE) to modify startup configuration settings without having to alter the settings directly. You can test startup settings without making them permanent until you are satisfied with the results.

❑ Monitor performance in Windows Vista and Windows 7 using the Reliability And Performance Monitor, an upgrade of the System Monitor in Windows 2000 and Windows XP.

❑ Use System File Checker (SFC) to have the Windows File Protection (WFP) service scan and verify the versions of all protected system files.

❑ In Windows XP or newer, there are two choices for remotely accessing Windows PCs. Use Remote Desktop to connect to a Windows computer and have total access to the desktop and local resources. Use Remote Assistance to remotely access a computer at the explicit invitation of the user, and assist the user in solving a problem with the computer.

❑ Use the DirectX Diagnostic Tool (DXDIAG) to diagnose problems with the Windows DirectX components.

Performing Preventive Maintenance and Optimization

❑ Defragment files on your hard drives on a regular basis to prevent the slowdowns that can result from file fragmentation.

❑ For better performance or user experience, tweak preferences and display settings and modify indexing settings.

❑ Turn on Automatic Updates for both Windows and your applications.

❑ Schedule regular backups of both the OS and data files using either the Backup utility in Windows or a third-party backup program. Test a restore of your data to ensure that it will work when you really need it.

❑ Configure System Restore so it does not take up too much disk space.

SELF TEST

The following questions will help you measure your understanding of the material presented in this chapter. Read all of the choices carefully because there might be more than one correct answer. Choose all correct answers for each question.

Diagnosing and Repairing Operating Systems Failures

1. Where can you access Safe Mode?
   A. Start menu
   B. Advanced Options Menu
   C. Control Panel
   D. Systems Properties

2. In what startup mode should you attempt to start Windows after making a change to the video settings that result in the Windows GUI not displaying properly, making it impossible to work in the GUI?
   A. Software Compatibility Mode
   B. System Restore
   C. Boot logging
   D. Enable VGA Mode/Enable Low-Resolution Video

3. Automated System Recovery (ASR) in Windows XP replaced this recovery option, discontinued after Windows 2000.
   A. Recovery Console
   B. Emergency Repair Process
   C. Startup
   D. System Restore

4. Last Known Good (LKG) only works within a narrow window of opportunity that ends when the following occurs:
   A. A user logs on.
   B. The computer reboots.
   C. The disk is defragmented.
   D. A restore point is created.

5. This Windows XP recovery tool creates a backup of the entire system partition, as well as a boot disk to start the recovery process.

    A. System Restore

    B. Automated System Recovery

    C. Last Known Good

    D. Safe Mode

6. This new recovery option for Windows Vista gives you an entire set of software tools that you can use outside of Windows when Windows fails to start up.

    A. System Recovery Options menu

    B. Windows Memory Diagnostic Tool

    C. Startup Repair

    D. Windows Complete PC Restore

7. What Windows 2000 utility would you use to create an Emergency Repair Disk (ERD)?

    A. MSCONFIG

    B. Burn ERD

    C. System Restore

    D. Windows Backup

Operational Issues and Symptoms

8. If a Windows XP application will not run in Compatibility Mode in Vista, what can you try next?

    A. Compatibility Mode Plus

    B. Dual-boot

    C. Windows XP Mode

    D. A Windows Vista-compliant application

9. How can you control Windows' automatic behavior after a Stop error?

    A. Power off and power up.

    B. Modify System Failure settings.

    C. Open Event Viewer.

    D. Use System Restore.

10. What can cause an application to fail to start without issuing an error message?

    A. A Stop error

    B. Hibernation turned off

    C. Sleep Mode

    D. Insufficient memory

11. What mode can you use to allow a legacy application to run well in Windows?
   A. GUI Mode
   B. Legacy Mode
   C. Compatibility Mode
   D. Virtual Mode

12. Which of the following describes when you would encounter an operational problem?
   A. During Windows Setup
   B. During Windows startup
   C. While Windows is running
   D. During Windows Update

Using Diagnostic Utilities and Tools

13. After receiving an error message in Windows, I searched for the error message using the Help program and the Microsoft Knowledge Base. It failed to find a solution. What should I do now?
   A. Locate the paper documentation for Windows.
   B. Call Microsoft's free 24-hour support line.
   C. Search the Internet using the error message.
   D. Locate the Windows Read Me file.

14. What Run line command opens up a GUI utility with a lot of information about the computer and its Windows installation, including memory, processor, Windows version, and more?
   A. MSINFO32
   B. MSCONFIG
   C. SYSINFO
   D. REGEDIT

15. If you upgrade a device driver in Windows XP (or a newer version) only to find it causes problems, use this feature in Device Manager to return to the old device driver.
   A. Roll Back Driver
   B. Update Driver
   C. Uninstall
   D. Driver Details

16. What GUI tool will you use to stop an application that is not responding to mouse and keyboard commands?

    A. Startup disk

    B. Task Manager

    C. System Configuration Utility

    D. Device Manager

17. What GUI tool will allow you to modify and test Windows startup configuration settings without having to alter them directly? Once you are satisfied, you can use this tool to make the settings permanent.

    A. Device Manager

    B. Safe Mode

    C. Notepad

    D. MSCONFIG

Performing Preventive Maintenance

18. What utility should I run to free up more disk space before using Disk Defragmenter on a drive?

    A. Format

    B. Task Manager

    C. Disk Cleanup

    D. System File Checker

19. Where do you enable or disable UAC?

    A. Control Panel

    B. User Accounts

    C. Computer Management

    D. Services

20. Where does System Restore store its restore points?

    A. In RAM

    B. On the hard disk

    C. On a network share

    D. On removable drives

SELF TEST ANSWERS

Diagnosing and Repairing Operating Systems Failures

1. ☑ **B.** The Advanced Options Menu is the place where you can access Safe Mode. Get to this menu by pressing the F8 key immediately after restarting your computer.
☒ **A,** Start menu, **C,** Control Panel, and **D,** System Properties, are all incorrect because these are all part of the Windows GUI, and the Advanced Options Menu is something you use before you start Windows.

2. ☑ **D.** Enable VGA Mode/Enable Low-Resolution Video is the startup mode you should attempt after making a change to the video settings that result in Windows not displaying properly.
☒ **A,** Software Compatibility Mode, is incorrect because this is not a startup mode, but a mode for running a legacy application. **B,** System Restore, is incorrect because this is not a startup mode, but a tool for restoring the operating system to a previous point in time. **C,** Boot Logging, is incorrect because this startup option will cause the system to create a log of all components as they are loaded and started.

3. ☑ **B.** Emergency Repair Process is the discontinued Windows 2000 recovery option replaced by Automated System Recovery (ASR) in Windows XP.
☒ **A,** Recovery Console, is incorrect because, although this is a recovery option, it existed for Windows 2000 and was also included with Windows XP. **C,** Startup, is incorrect because this is not a recovery option. **D,** System Restore, is incorrect because, although it is a recovery option, it did not exist in Windows 2000 but is part of Windows XP, Windows Vista, and Windows 7.

4. ☑ **A.** A user logon is the event that terminates the window of opportunity for using Last Known Good.
☒ **B,** the computer reboots, is incorrect because you must restart the computer and press F8 to access the Advanced Options Menu from which to select Last Known Good Configuration. **C,** the disk is defragmented, is incorrect. This has no bearing on the use of Last Known Good. **D,** a restore point is created, is incorrect because this has no effect on using Last Known Good.

5. ☑ **B.** Automated System Recovery is the Windows XP recovery tool that creates a backup of the entire system partition, as well as a boot disk to start the recovery process.
☒ **A,** System Restore, is incorrect because this does not create a backup of the entire system partition, nor does it create a boot disk. **C,** Last Known Good, is incorrect because Last Known Good only uses a set of registry keys; it does not back up the entire system partition. **D,** Safe Mode, is incorrect because this is simply a special startup mode, not a backup of the system partition.

6. ☑ **A.** System Recovery Options menu is the new recovery option in Windows Vista that includes an entire set of software tools for recovering Windows.

   ☒ **B,** Windows Memory Diagnostic Tool, **C,** Startup Repair, and **D,** Windows Complete PC Restore, are all incorrect because these are all individual tools available through the System Recovery Options menu.

7. ☑ **D.** Windows Backup is the Windows 2000 utility that you use to create an Emergency Repair Disk (ERD).

   ☒ **A,** MSCONFIG, is incorrect because this utility is for controlling what programs start with Windows. **B,** Burn ERD, is incorrect because there is no such utility. **C,** System Restore, is incorrect because it is used to restore the system to a point in time.

Operational Issues and Symptoms

8. ☑ **C.** Windows XP Mode is correct.

   ☒ **A,** Compatibility Mode Plus, is incorrect because there is no such mode. **B,** dual-boot, is incorrect because, although you could configure the system to dual boot into Windows XP and Windows Vista, this would be rather clumsy and you would try Windows XP Mode first. **D,** a Windows Vista-compliant application, is incorrect because, although this is the ideal, we often do not have a choice and must find a way to use old applications.

9. ☑ **B.** Modify System Failure settings.

   ☒ **A,** power off and power up, is incorrect because this will not change the System Failure settings. **C,** open Event Viewer, is incorrect because this does not control Windows' automatic behavior after a Stop error. **D,** use System Restore, is incorrect because this will not alter Windows' automatic behavior after a Stop error.

10. ☑ **D.** Insufficient memory can cause an application to fail to start without issuing an error message.

    ☒ **A,** a Stop error, is incorrect because, although this will only display the Stop error message, it is not necessarily the cause of the problem described. **B,** hibernation turned off, is incorrect because this is not related to the problem described. **C,** Sleep Mode, is incorrect because this will not cause the problem described.

11. ☑ **C.** You can use Compatibility Mode to allow a legacy application to run well in Windows XP.

    ☒ **A,** GUI Mode, is incorrect because this is not used to allow a legacy application to run well in Windows XP. **B,** Legacy Mode, is incorrect because this is not the mode described. **D,** Virtual Mode, is incorrect because this is not the mode described.

12. ☑ **C.** While Windows is running is correct because this describes when you would encounter an operational problem.

☒ **A,** during Windows Setup, **B,** during Windows startup, and **D,** during Windows Update, are all incorrect because operational problems occur while Windows is running.

Using Diagnostic Utilities and Tools

13. ☑ **C.** Search the Internet using the error message is correct.

☒ **A,** locate the paper documentation for Windows, is incorrect because this is not as searchable as the Microsoft site or the Internet. **B,** call Microsoft's free 24-hour support line, is incorrect because the Microsoft phone support is a service for which it charges. If it is available to the user, that user will either pay per-incident or be part of a paid subscription plan. **D,** locate the Windows Read Me file, is incorrect because it holds very limited information.

14. ☑ **A.** MSINFO32 is the Run line command that opens up the System Information page with information about the computer and its Windows installation.

☒ **B,** MSCONFIG, and **D,** REGEDIT, although both Run line utilities, do not provide the information that MSINFO32 does. **C,** SYSINFO, is not a Run line utility.

15. ☑ **A.** Roll Back Driver is the feature in Windows XP's Device Manager that will allow you to return to an old device driver after upgrading.

☒ **B,** Update Driver, is incorrect because this feature installs an updated driver; it does not remove an updated driver and return to the old driver. **C,** Uninstall, is incorrect because this will completely uninstall the driver for the device. **D,** Driver Details, is incorrect because this will only display information about the driver files.

16. ☑ **B.** Task Manager is the GUI tool used to stop an application that is not responding to mouse and keyboard commands.

☒ **A,** startup disk, is incorrect because this is neither a GUI tool nor the tool to use to stop a nonresponsive application. **C,** System Configuration Utility, and **D,** Device Manager, are incorrect because neither is the correct GUI tool to use to stop a nonresponsive application.

17. ☑ **D.** MSCONFIG is the tool that will allow you to modify and test startup configuration settings without having to alter them directly.

☒ **A,** Device Manager, is incorrect because this GUI tool works solely with device drivers, not with the Windows startup settings. **B,** Safe Mode, is incorrect because this is simply a startup mode that allows you to troubleshoot and make changes using a variety of tools. **C,** Notepad, is incorrect because this is simply a Windows text editor.

Performing Preventive Maintenance

18. ☑ **C.** Disk Cleanup will free up more disk space to be defragmented.

☒ **A,** Format, is incorrect because this will remove all files from the drive. **B,** Task Manager, is incorrect because this utility will not free up more disk space. **D,** System File Checker, is incorrect because it is not the utility to use for freeing up more disk space.

19. ☑ **B.** User Accounts is where you enable or disable UAC (User Account Control).

☒ **A,** Control Panel, is incorrect, although you will find the User Accounts applet here. **C,** Computer Manager, and **D,** Services, are both incorrect.

20. ☑ **B.** System Restore stores its restore points on the hard disk.

☒ **A,** in system RAM, is incorrect because you would not want restore points to be stored in volatile RAM. **C,** on a network share, is incorrect, and **D,** on removable drives, is incorrect.

12

Using and Supporting Printers

CERTIFICATION OBJECTIVES

❑　**701:1.11**　Install and configure printers

❑　**701:2.2**　Given a scenario, explain and interpret common hardware and operating system symptoms and their causes

❑　**701:2.3**　Given a scenario, determine the troubleshooting methods and tools for printers

❑　**702:1.5**　Given a scenario, detect and resolve common printer issues

❑　**702:2.4**　Evaluate and resolve common issue

✓　Two-Minute Drill

Q&A　Self Test

I n this chapter, you will examine printers to understand the types in use and the technologies, components, and consumables involved. You will learn about the typical issues involved with installing and configuring printers, the typical upgrading and optimizing options, and preventive maintenance and troubleshooting.

CERTIFICATION OBJECTIVE

■ *701: 1.11 Install and configure printers*

CompTIA requires that candidates for A+ certification recognize the various types of printers available for use with PCs, and understand the differences among these device types so that you can make purchasing decisions and determine the consumables required for each. This set of objectives also requires that you understand printer drivers, the compatibility issues you may encounter, and how to install a local printer versus a network printer.

Printer Basics

Printers are the most common peripherals used with PCs. Understanding such printer basics as printer types and their related technologies, paper feeding technologies, printer components, and printer interfaces is important to your success on the exams and on the job.

Printer Types and Technologies

Several types of printers are commonly used, including impact, laser, inkjet, solid ink, and thermal.

Impact

Impact printers include daisy wheel, line printer, and dot matrix, among others. Like an old-fashioned typewriter, an impact printer has a roller or platen the paper is pressed against and a print head that strikes an inked ribbon in front of the paper, thus transferring ink to the paper. The impact printing process is often very loud, and the wear-and-tear of the repeated hammering makes these printers prone to mechanical failures. Today, the average office or home user does not use an impact printer, but will almost certainly have an inkjet or laser printer.

Dot Matrix   The dot matrix impact printer is the original type of printer used with PCs. The most common use for dot matrix impact printers today is for printing multiple-page receipts or forms that require an impact to make an impression on the second and third sheet of the form. We often refer to them as "receipt printers," and we see them in use in retail stores and service centers connected to point of sale systems (cash registers).

Dot matrix printers use a matrix of pins to create dots on the paper, thus forming alphanumeric characters and graphic images. Each pin is attached to an actuator, which, when activated, rapidly pushes the pin toward the paper. As the print head (containing the pins) moves across the page, different pins move forward to strike a printer ribbon against the paper, causing ink on the ribbon to adhere to the paper. Because they create printouts one character at a time, dot matrix printers are called character printers.

Dot matrix printers do not provide very good resolution. Text and images appear grainy, and you can usually see each individual printed dot. Furthermore, dot matrix printers are limited in their ability to use color. Most of these printers can only use one printer ribbon color (typically black, although you can substitute another color available for that printer). Although some dot matrix printers can use ribbons with up to four colors and/or up to four printer ribbons, dot matrix printers are not capable of producing as many color combinations as other printer types.

Line Printer   Yet another category of impact printer is the *line printer,* a high-speed printer that prints an entire line at a time at speeds of up to 1,000 lines per minute. The technologies include chain or type bar. This category has been in use for decades in large datacenters that need high-speed printing on multipart forms. The ones extant today are either band printers or line matrix printers.

Daisy Wheel   A daisy wheel printer is a now-extinct category of impact printer with a wheel of fixed characters, much like a typewriter, used to imprint these characters on paper. In the early days of PCs, a daisy wheel printer was the best option for high-quality text printing, but it lost market share in the printer category after the advent of consumer-priced laser printers in the late 1980s and early 1990s.

Laser

Laser printers use a coherent, concentrated light beam (laser) in the printing process. We call this a *laser beam*. They are generally faster than other types of printers, provide the best quality, and have the most complex structure and process. Because of their high quality and speed, these are perhaps the most commonly used printers in business environments, especially for shared network printers. Figure 12-1 shows a typical laser printer. Laser printers are generally the quietest and fastest printers, but they are also the most expensive to operate.

Although some laser printers use slightly different processes, we'll describe a typical order of events that occurs in the laser printing process. Note that these events occur in repeating cycles, so it is not as important to know which step is first or last, as it is the sequence of events. For example, some sources list charging as the first step, whereas others list cleaning as the first step.

FIGURE 12-1

A desktop laser printer with the manual tray open. The toner cartridge is hidden behind the panel above the paper feeder.

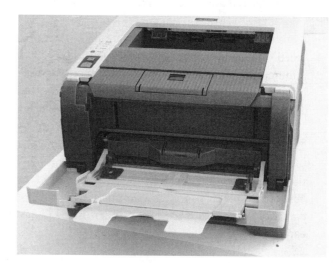

In a laser printer, the *electro-photosensitive drum* is made of metal with an electro-photosensitive coating. The drum is actually more like a slender tube, with a typical circumference of less than an inch; therefore, the printing cycle must repeat several times per printout page. Both the drum and the primary corona wire are often contained within the toner cartridge. When printing a page, the paper starts to move and the drum rotates. All the steps that follow occur repeatedly while the paper is moving and the drum is turning:

1. **Charging** In the *charging* step, the printer's high-voltage power supply (HVPS) conducts electricity to the *primary corona wire*, a wire that stretches across the printer's photosensitive drum, not touching it, but very close to the drum's surface. The charge exists on the wire and in a corona (electrical field) around the length of the wire. The high voltage passes a strong negative charge to the drum.

on the
() o b   ***Some laser printers use charged rollers rather than a corona wire to pass
voltage to the drum.***

2. **Writing** The surface of the electro-photosensitive drum now has a very high negative charge. In the *writing* step, the printer's laser beam moves along the drum, creating a negative of the image that will eventually appear on the printout. Because the drum is photosensitive, each place that the laser beam touches loses most of its charge. By the end of the writing step, the image exists at a low voltage while the rest of the drum remains highly charged. The lamp that generates this laser beam is normally located within the printer body itself, rather than in the toner cartridge.

3. **Developing** In this stage, the "discharged" areas on the drum attract microscopic toner particles through the open cover on the printer's toner cartridge. By the end of this stage, the drum contains a toner-covered image (in the shape of the final printout).

4. **Transferring** During the *transferring* step, the paper moving through the printer passes the drum. The *transfer corona wire*, located within the body of the printer, and very close to the paper, applies a small positive charge to the paper as it passes through. This positive charge "pulls" the negatively charged toner from the drum onto the paper. The only thing holding the toner to the paper at this point is an electrical charge and gravity.

5. **Fusing** As the paper leaves the printer, it enters the fusing stage, passing through a set of *fusing rollers* heated by a *fusing lamp* that presses the toner onto the paper. The hot rollers cause the resin in the toner to melt, or fuse, to the paper, creating a permanent nonsmearing image. The fusing components, called the "fuser assembly," are normally located within the body of the printer rather than in the toner cartridge.

6. **Cleaning** There are two parts to the *cleaning* state. First, when the image on the drum transfers to the paper a *cleaning blade* (normally located within the toner cartridge) removes residual toner, which drops into a small reservoir or returns to the toner cartridge. Next, one or more high-intensity *erasure lamps* (located within the body of the printer) shine on the photosensitive drum, removing any remaining charge on that portion of the drum. The drum continues to rotate, and the process continues.

on the **Job** *Understanding the laser-printing process will help you determine which component is at fault when troubleshooting problems.*

A laser printer is a nonimpact printer, because it does not require any form of physical impact to transfer an image to a printout. Because it creates printouts one page at a time (rather than one character or line at a time), a laser printer is called a "page printer."

Laser printers use very small dots of toner, so they are able to provide excellent resolution. Color laser printers are able to blend colors into practically any shade, typically using four toner cartridges. Therefore, the writing and developing stages take place four times (once for each color—black, cyan, magenta, and yellow) before the image transfers to the paper.

Inkjet

The printers we lump together as *inkjet* printers use several technologies to apply wet ink to paper to create text or graphic printouts. These printers provide much better resolution than dot matrix printers, and many of them create wonderful color output because, unlike dot matrix printers, inkjets can combine basic colors to produce a wide range of colors. Inkjet printers are not nearly as loud as dot matrix printers and are much faster.

exam **Watch** *Technically, we could lump inkjet and bubblejet printers under the heading of "ink dispersion" printers. However, the A+ exam objectives use the term "inkjet" to cover both technologies.*

The two most popular inkjet printer lines are the InkJet, developed by Hewlett-Packard, and the *Bubble Jet*, developed by Canon.

As described here, inkjet and bubblejet printers only differ in how they transfer an image to the paper. Beyond discussing these differences, however, we use the term "inkjet" in this chapter to apply to both types of printers, as well as to others with similar technology.

The ink cartridge print head in an inkjet printer contains a tiny pump that forces ink out of the reservoir, through nozzles, and onto the page. There are many kinds of nozzles that make small droplets measured in picoliters (one millionth of a millionth of a liter); a typical droplet measures 1.5 picoliters.

Bubblejet printers resemble inkjets, but their print heads contain heating elements rather than pumps. When the element is heated, the ink expands and forms a bubble of ink on the nozzle, which, when it becomes large enough, "bursts" onto the paper and creates a dot of color. Although this process sounds messy, bubblejets produce very high-quality printouts. Inkjet and bubblejet printers print a character at a time, so they are character printers, and their print mechanisms do not contact the page, making them nonimpact printers as well.

Inkjet and bubblejet printers are usually inexpensive. The significant operating costs of these printers are the ink cartridges, which can cost between 8 and 25 cents per printed color page. Black and white pages are less expensive. So, although these printers are inexpensive to buy, the cost of the consumables (ink) can be high.

Solid Ink

Two printer types are considered *solid-ink printers,* using solid (rather than liquid) ink. One is dye-sublimation, and the other is a thermal wax transfer printer, normally classified as a thermal printer. We will discuss thermal printers a little later.

The ink in a dye-sublimation printer is in a solid form, embedded into a roll of heat-sensitive plastic film. The roll contains page-size areas of solid ink (or dye)—one for each color (normally cyan, magenta, and yellow) and often black. The film roll (also called a "dye ribbon roll") rolls past a print head that is normally the width of the paper. The print head presses the film against the paper as the paper passes over a roller that acts much like the platen roller in a typewriter or dot matrix printer. The print head contains thousands of heating elements that vaporize the ink so it adheres to the paper.

For each page printed out, the dye-sublimation process requires one pass for each color, causing the colors to mix to the desired shade as they adhere to the paper. Dye-sublimation printers are very expensive, and their use is limited to when high-quality color printing is very important.

Thermal

A *thermal printer* uses heat in the image transfer process. In spite of the use of heat, bubblejets are not considered thermal printers. Thermal printers for PCs fall into two categories: direct thermal printers and thermal wax transfer printers.

In a *direct thermal printer,* a heated print head burns dots into the surface of heat-sensitive paper. Early fax machines used this technology for printing, and direct thermal printers still work as receipt printers in retail businesses.

In thermal wax transfer, printers use a film coated with colored wax that melts onto paper. These printers are similar to dye-sublimation printers but differ in two major ways: the film contains wax rather than dye, and these printers do not require special paper. Thermal wax transfer printers are, therefore, less expensive than most dye-sublimation printers, but the dye-sublimation printers create higher-quality output.

Scanner-Printer-Fax-Copier Combinations

Not many years ago, a printer and a scanner were two separate devices. Today combination devices abound. These *multifunction printers (MFDs)* or *multifunction devices (MFDs)* combine the scanner, printer, and copier in one box, often with a built-in fax as well. Although an all-in-one device can function like a copier or a fax machine—you place an image to copy on the platen and the copied image comes out or a fax is sent over a phone line—there are significant differences between the old and the new. An MFD shines as a PC-connected device that provides all the functionality of a printer as well as a copier and scanner. This means you can send output to the printer, receive digital images from the scanner, or create copies while using up the desk space of just one of these devices. Figure 12-2 shows an all-in-one device combining an inkjet printer, scanner, copier, and fax in one machine.

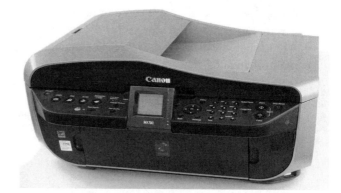

FIGURE 12-2

An all-in-one inkjet printer that combines scanner, printer, fax, and copier in one machine

e x a m

ⓦatch

Be sure you can distinguish
among the four types of printers listed in

CompTIA A+ Essentials Exam objective
701: 1.11: laser, inkjet, thermal, and impact.

Paper-Feeding Technologies

The two most common paper-feeding technologies are friction feed and continuous form feed. A printer using friction feed moves paper by grasping each piece of paper with rollers. All the printer types discussed here can and usually do use friction feed.

Inkjet, bubblejet, and laser printers use friction feed to move paper through the printer. Some, especially laser printers, use more than one set of rollers to keep the page moving smoothly until ejecting it. Friction-fed printers usually have more than paper source available; one tray that can hold a lot of paper, and another that holds a smaller amount of paper. These trays can hold from a few pages up to several reams in the large paper feeders of high-end network printers.

Dot matrix printers are often capable of friction feed, but also offer continuous form feed, which requires sheets of paper attached to each other at perforated joints. Further, continuous form paper has about a half-inch-wide border at each side, attached with perforations that contain holes that accommodate the sprockets on the tractor feed mechanism, thus pulling the paper through the printer. When using continuous form feed, you must disable the friction feed.

Checks, receipts, and other forms, including multiple-part forms, use continuous form feed paper. Because these forms often have specific areas in which the information must print, a necessary step when inserting this paper into the printer is to align the perforation accurately between each form with a guide on the printer.

Printer Components

The actual printer components vary, depending on the printing and paper-feed technology of the printer. However, regardless of the printing technology used, all printers have a certain set of components in common, which include the system board, memory, driver and related software, firmware, and consumables.

System Board

Each printer contains a system board that serves the same purpose as a PC's motherboard. Often referred to simply as a printer board, this circuit board contains a processor, ROM, and RAM. The processor runs the code contained in the ROM, using the RAM memory as workspace for composing the incoming print jobs (in most printers) and storing them while waiting to print them.

Driver

A new printer comes packaged with a disc containing drivers—usually for several operating systems. Like drivers for other devices, a print driver allows you to control a printer through the operating system.

Printer Language

Beyond a driver that physically controls the action of a printer, the computer must also have special software printer language that translates the characters and graphics of your computer-generated document into a form that the printer can compose and print out. Common printer languages include PostScript, Hewlett-Packard Printer Control Language (PCL), Windows GDI, and other vendor-specific printer languages.

Firmware

A printer, like a computer and most devices, has its own firmware code, including BIOS code that contains the low-level instructions for controlling it. Printer BIOS code is accessed by the driver, which is installed into the operating system. Another type of firmware code in printers is an interpreter for at least one printer language.

Consumables

Printer consumables include the printer medium, some components, and paper. The printer medium is a consumable that contains the pigment for the image that a printer creates. The medium comes in a special form for the technology and specific to the model of printer. The most common forms are ink ribbon, ink cartridge, and laser printer toner cartridge. A printer cannot work without consumables, such as paper and ink cartridges. If you are the one responsible for purchasing and storing these products, letting these supplies run out is bad for your career!

Shelf Life   The shelf life of both laser printer toner cartridges and inkjet cartridges are similar, and are usually two years from production date and six months from when you first open the package, or first put it into use. Even printer paper has a shelf life because paper for friction-feed printers must contain a certain range of moisture content in order to feed properly without causing jams. Old paper also may discolor unless it is of very high quality. Used printer consumables can negatively affect the environment and should be disposed of in a manner that is both legal and respectful of the environment. In Chapter 18, you will explore the best methods for disposing of used consumables.

Ink   The most common forms of ink for printers are ink ribbons for dot matrix printers, and *ink cartridges* for inkjet and bubblejet printers. The medium for a dot matrix printer is an inked ribbon—a fabric ribbon embedded with ink. The medium for inkjet printers is ink contained in reservoirs. In the case of inkjet printers, this reservoir is part of a small cartridge that also may contain the print head that sprays the ink on the paper. Bubblejet printers use cartridges with the ink reservoir that also contains the print head required to heat the ink, so it creates the bubbles that burst onto the paper. Figure 12-3 shows an open inkjet printer with the cartridges exposed. You must turn this model on when you change the cartridges because when it is turned off, the cartridges are "parked" out of sight. Lights on each cartridge give the status of the cartridge: steady when there is adequate ink, blinking when ink is low.

If you search the documentation or the manufacturer's Website, you can discover the expected yield of a cartridge. The yield of a typical inkjet cartridge is in the hundreds of pages. One printer shows a black ink cartridge yield of 630 pages of text and 450 pages for graphic printouts that have 5 percent coverage. The same printer shows a color ink yield of 430 pages with 5 percent coverage per color. If your printouts use more ink per page, then the yield will be smaller.

FIGURE 12-3

An open inkjet
printer with the
ink cartridges
exposed

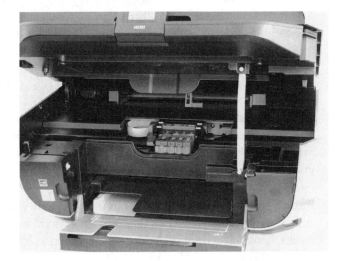

Toner Toner cartridges for a typical noncolor desktop laser printer run around $50 and up, but they last for several thousand pages, making these printers relatively inexpensive per page to use. Color laser cartridges are several hundred dollars a set, but they offer very high quality, and they too print thousands of pages before you need to replace the cartridges.

Toner is the medium for laser printers and is normally available packaged within a *toner cartridge*. The toner consists of fine particles of clay combined with pigment and resin. The cartridges for many laser printers also contain the cylindrical photo-sensitive drum, the cleaning blade, and other components that are also considered consumables, because you normally replace the entire cartridge together with its contents once the toner is gone.

Many companies take used printer cartridges, recondition the drum and other components, refill the toner reservoir with fresh toner, and offer them at significantly lower cost than manufacturer's fresh cartridges. We have had mixed experience with these "refilled" cartridges. Some refilled/reconditioned cartridges have performed as well as the best brand-name new toner cartridges, whereas others have been very poor. Caveat emptor!

The brand-name cartridges from your printer's manufacturer will normally produce the highest quality and demand the highest price. We often buy new cartridges from a company that sells both new and reconditioned cartridges. No matter what vendor we use for our toner cartridges, we always buy from one that takes our old toner cartridges for recycling at no cost to us.

The yield of a laser cartridge for a typical desktop monochrome black laser printer is several thousand pages. Numbers such as 3,000 to 8,000 are common. The yield for a color laser printer generally runs over 1,000 pages per cartridge. For instance, the documentation for one printer estimates the yield for a standard-capacity black toner cartridge at 4,000 pages, whereas the estimate for each of the standard cyan, magenta, yellow, and black (CMYK) cartridges is given at 1,500 pages. The high-capacity color toner cartridges show an expected yield of 4,000 pages.

on the
job

When working with laser printers and handling toner cartridges, avoid breathing in the toner powder. Although the chemical makeup of laser toner may not be harmful, the super-fine powder of laser toner poses a hazard to your lungs.

Paper With the exception of printers that require tractor-feed paper, most printers can use ordinary copier paper for drafts and everyday casual printing. For the best results, however, consult the printer documentation for the type and quality of paper to use.

Printer Interfaces

There are a number of interfaces for connecting a printer to a computer. For example, you can configure a printer so it attaches directly to a computer or indirectly through a network. You can also configure a printer so it is accessible to only one person or to an entire network of people. Printers use the common interfaces described in Chapter 3. Therefore, the following text only surveys usage of each of these interfaces with printers and scanners.

Parallel

For almost two decades after introduction of the IBM PC in 1981, the most common way to attach a printer to a computer was through the computer's parallel port. The parallel interface requires a significant amount of space on the PC case for its 25-pin connector, needs an even larger 36-pin Centronics connector on the printer or other device, and a heavy cable with appropriate connectors on each end. Notice the large parallel port connector on a PC, as well as the small USB connectors (bottom left) that replace it. A Centronics connector on a printer has 36-pins and is about 2" per side, as shown here above a USB connector.

The parallel interface dominated for a long time and was the hands-down favorite over another common, but slower, interface—serial—that shared its long history. While the parallel interface transfers 8 bits at a time (in parallel), it originally only supported one-way communication. For this reason, it was best suited for early printers, sending print data to the printer, but not capable of receiving status data from the printer. The speed of the standard one-way parallel port is 150 Kbps. Today's printers send status data back to the PC, alerting you when you are out of paper or low on ink or toner. This requires two-way communications.

When you buy a new parallel cable, it will be labeled as compliant with the IEEE 1284 standard introduced in the 1990s. This standard defines a parallel interface that is backward-compatible with the original parallel port in the early IBM PCs. It also introduced five modes of operation for unidirectional or bidirectional communications and speed enhancements:

■ **Compatibility mode** Data only travels in one direction—from the PC to the device—in compatibility mode (also called "Centronics mode"). This mode ties up the PC's CPU. Its speed is 150 Kbps.

■ **Nibble mode** Used together with compatibility mode, nibble mode offers limited bidirectional communications. Because this mode depends on software to send each 8-bit byte in two chunks of 4 bits (a "nibble"), nibble mode uses more CPU cycles than compatibility mode. Its top speed is 50 Kbps.

■ **Byte mode** Also called "Enhanced Bidirectional Port mode," byte mode, used together with compatibility mode, supports two-way 8-bit data communications with a device. This configuration can communicate at speeds close to 150 Kbps.

■ **Enhanced Parallel Port (EPP) mode** Enhanced Parallel Port (EPP) mode offers high-speed, bidirectional speeds of between 500 Kbps and 2 Mbps. This speed is possible because the parallel interface hardware does most of the work of data transfer, requiring less CPU involvement. This mode is not for printers but for network adapters, portable hard drives, and other devices that require high transfer speeds, such as data acquisition hardware used to collect data automatically from special sensors and readers used in factories, test laboratories, scientific research, and medical equipment.

■ **Extended Capability Port (ECP) mode** The fastest parallel port mode for use with printers and scanners is Extended Capability Port (ECP) mode. Like EPP, ECP requires hardware that supports its features, and like EPP, ECP supports speeds of 500 Kbps to 2 Mbps and bidirectional communications.

on the
job

On some computers and peripherals, you may encounter parallel port modes that are not part of the IEEE 1284 standard. These come with names such as "Fast Centronics Mode" or "Parallel Port FIFO Mode." They are proprietary and not supported on all parallel devices or computers.

In the past several years, other, faster interfaces have become far more popular than the parallel interface. Where it was once considered a given that a parallel port was standard on a new PC, many new computers today, especially laptops, do not come with a parallel port. This omission goes unnoticed by most people because most new printers and scanners do not come with a parallel interface.

Serial

The serial interface, as described in Chapter 3, was once a common printer interface. But even the original parallel interface was, and is, faster than the traditional RS-232 serial ports. Therefore, even back in the day, parallel was more popular than serial. Serial interface does not natively support plug and play, and printers rarely use a serial interface; in fact, the serial port is disappearing from standard PC configurations.

Universal Serial Bus (USB)

The Universal Serial Bus (USB) is the current dominant printer interface. As its name implies, data travels one bit at a time over the USB interface. However, as described in Chapter 3, USB is fast and requires only a very small connector on each end. The PC end uses a USB type A connector, and the device end of the cable may be either a type A or type B connector, depending on what the device requires. Printers do not always come with a USB cable, and you may need to supply your own.

A USB interface can only provide a small amount of electrical power from the PC, but printers normally require more power than that and, therefore, use an external power supply. To attach a USB device, simply plug it into a USB external or root hub. There is no need to even turn off the computer for this plug and play interface, but be sure to read the instructions first, because for some USB printers, you must install the device driver before plugging in the device.

e x a m

ⓌatchⒽ *Remember that IEEE 1284 is a standard for the parallel interface, and IEEE 1394 is the newer, faster standard known as FireWire.*

IEEE 1394/FireWire

The IEEE 1394 interface is now the second-most-common printer interface after USB. Most low-end printers come with only USB, but many medium- and higher-priced printers offer both interfaces (as well as network interface).

Network Printer vs. Local Printer

A printer connected to your PC for your own use is a local printer. A printer connected directly to the network is a network printer. However, this line blurs because it has long been common to share printers over a network, and there are two ways to connect a printer to a network.

■ Use a true network printer that contains a network interface card (NIC) and that you configure in the same manner as any computer on the network. The printer acts as a print server, accepting print jobs over the network. If the printer is powered on, and online, it is available to network users. The NIC may be an Ethernet NIC or a wireless NIC, or the printer may contain both types. Although this is not a hard-and-fast rule, high-end network printers most often have Ethernet NICs for use in businesses and large installations. The most common wireless printers use Wi-Fi technology, although some may use infrared or Bluetooth. We describe these wireless technologies in Chapter 13.

■ A computer with a network connection can share a local printer attached to that computer's local interface (parallel, USB, FireWire, or other). This computer becomes the print server. In this case, you can only access the printer from the network if the computer attached to it is on and has network access.

Installing and Configuring Printers

The plug and play nature of Windows, as well as of printers and scanners, makes installing and configuring these devices quite easy, even for the ordinary PC user. In this section, explore the issues related to installing and configuring printers.

Installing a Printer

Before installing any printer, you need to unpack it (if new) and test it. The actual steps you take to install it will depend on the individual printer and whether it is plug and play or non–plug and play. Any new printer today is plug and play, but on the job, you may run into some old printers that are not.

Unpacking and Testing a Printer

Follow the manufacturer's instructions to unpack a new printer, removing all the shipping material. Next, plug in the power cable, but do not connect the printer to the computer, and follow the instructions to install toner or ink cartridges and to load paper. You must power up some printers before you can install the cartridges. Follow the manufacturer's instructions for printing a test page directly from the printer. Then move on to installing the printer, as per the next two sections on plug and play printers and non–plug and play printers.

Installing a Plug and Play Printer

Windows includes extensive plug and play support for printers. As with other plug and play devices, if a printer connects to a plug and play interface on the PC (USB, IEEE 1394, or IrDA), Windows automatically detects the printer, installs the driver, and configures it. If the printer uses an infrared interface, this will require turning the printer on and pointing its infrared port at your computer's infrared port. When Windows detects a printer, it briefly displays a Found New Hardware message from the notification area of the taskbar, as shown here. Then it installs the driver and configures the printer, displaying another message after completing these tasks.

Installing a Non–Plug and Play Printer

In the event that you attach a non–plug and play printer, you will have to install it manually. A non–plug and play printer is most likely to be an old printer with a parallel or serial interface. After connecting the printer to a power source and testing it, connect it to the PC, power it up, and install the print driver and associated software. Each of the Windows versions studied here have a slightly different path to opening the folder for working with printers. They are as follows:

- In Windows 2000, you select Start | Settings | Printers.
- In Windows XP, select Start | Printers and Faxes.
- In Windows Vista, select Start | Printers.
- In Windows 7, select Start | Devices and Printers.

For the sake of simplicity, we will refer to the window that opens as the Printers folder across all these versions of Windows, and we will discuss the small differences within the Printers folder.

Once in the Printers folder, in Windows 2000 and Windows XP, you will then select Add Printer, and in Windows Vista and Windows 7, select Add A Printer, which opens the Add Printer Wizard, shown in Figure 12-4.

FIGURE 12-4

Use the Add Printer Wizard to install a non–plug and play printer.

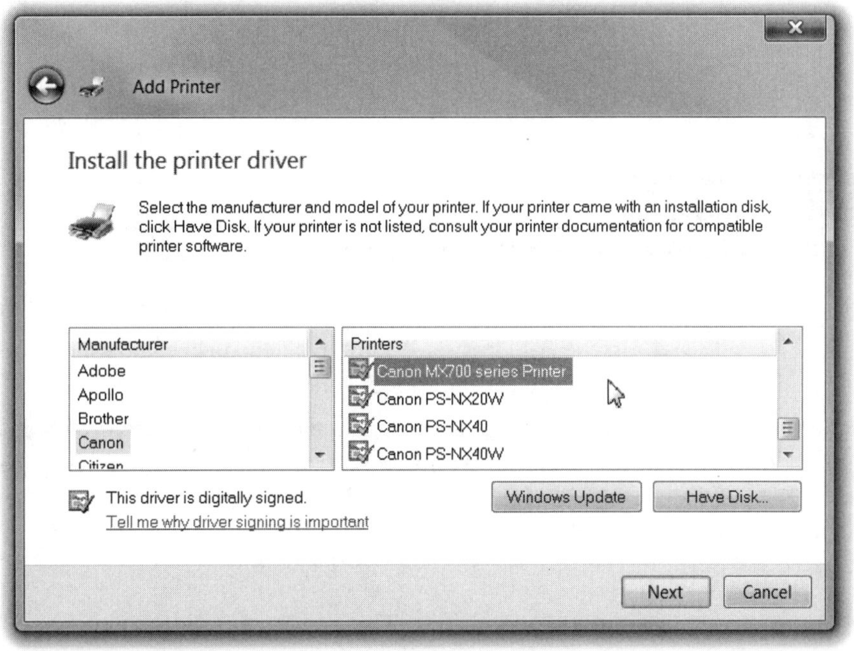

Be prepared to make selections on each page of the wizard. You will need to know the following:

- Is it a local printer or a network printer?
- For a local printer, you will need to know the port it uses.
- For a network printer, you will need to know its location on the network.
- For a local printer and some network printers, to install the printer driver and other software, either select the printer manufacturer and model number from a list provided by the wizard, or provide a disk or a location for the driver files.
- For a network printer, the printer software may automatically install over the network from the print server.
- Give the printer a user-friendly name to better identify it, if you would like.
- For both local and network printer installation, you will be asked if you want to set the printer as the default printer.
- You will be asked if you wish to share the local printer over the network.
- You will be asked if you wish to print a test page to confirm proper printer installation and functions. We recommend you always do this to ensure that you can print from Windows.

If you are prepared with the answers to the questions it asks, the Windows Add Printer Wizard makes installing a non–plug and play printer easy, as demonstrated in Exercise 12-1.

EXERCISE 12-1

Installing a Non–Plug and Play Printer

1. In the Printers folder, select Add A Printer from the Printer Tasks list or bar.
2. In the Add Printer Wizard, read each page and follow the instructions to make a selection from the choices given.
3. Complete each page, using the responses you prepared from the list that precedes this exercise. When prompted, choose to print a test page to confirm that the printer installation is working correctly.

4. Click Finish to close the Add Printer Wizard, and it will copy the files, the installation will finish, and the test page will print out.

5. After successfully installing a printer, the Printers folder will display. Look for the icon for the new printer.

Installing IP Printing Support

You can print to a printer that is only known to you by its IP address if you have the correct software installed in Windows to support this. Previous to Windows Vista, the client software that allowed a computer to print to an "IP printer" was the Line Printer Remote (LPR) client software, also called the LPR Port Monitor. It prints to a server with the Line Printer Daemon (LPD) service installed. Both the LPR and LPD software can be installed on any of the Windows versions studied here. In versions previous to Vista, LPD is known as Print Services for UNIX. In Windows 2000 and Windows XP, you add and enable LPD or LPR through the Add/Remove Programs applet in Control Panel.

Windows Vista and Windows 7 have an improved and preferred alternative to LPR: the Internet Printing Client. This client is installed and enabled by default along with TCP/IP protocols and services (more on networks in Chapters 13, 14, and 15). In Windows Vista and Windows 7, you install and enable the Internet Printing Client in the Windows Features dialog box, accessed by first opening the Programs applet in Control Panel, then locating Programs And Features and selecting the task labeled Turn Windows Features On Or Off. Then open the Print Services node, and select the check box for Internet Printing Client. The LPD Print Service and LPR Port Monitor (the new names for the old services) are also available there, but you will normally use the new client service.

Testing a Printer for Compatibility

The printer test you perform at the end of printer installation in Windows will print a test page and verify the compatibility of your printer and its software with Windows. The Windows printing system eliminates most problems with incompatibility between individual applications and a printer. However, there are the rare instances in which output from an application does not produce the expected results. Therefore, to further test the compatibility of your applications with the new printer, open each application and print a document to the printer.

Installing an All-in-One

When installing an all-in-one device with a scanner, copier, and fax, you will have a few additional tasks. When unpacking a new device, pay extra attention to the setup instructions because the scanner in the all-in-one may have a lock to secure the fragile internal components from damage during shipping. Release this lock once you have the device positioned properly on a clean surface. The installation program on the disc that comes with the device will have all the software for the three types of devices.

The driver for the scanner component will likely conform to a set of standards for scanners and cameras called *TWAIN* (this is not an acronym). In fact, the driver is often called a "TWAIN driver." The software other than the driver should also be TWAIN-compliant. For the scanner, this will include not just the driver and software to manage scanning, but *optical character recognition (OCR)* software. OCR software is important because your computer sees a scanned image as a graphic bitmap image, which is just fine if the image is a photo or other image. When the scanned image is of a printed page, and your intent is to be able to edit the document as such, you will need OCR software to interpret the pattern of dots in the image as alphanumeric characters. This is quite a job, considering all the various fonts and treatments we use in our documents, as shown here.

If the all-in-one includes a fax, then you will need to connect a phone cable to the device's RJ-11 connector and connect this to a phone wall jack. Then follow the manufacturer's instructions for configuring the fax to send and receive fax messages.

Configuring a Printer

Windows has two sets of printer settings: Printer Properties and Printing Preferences.

Printer Properties

Open a printer's Properties dialog box to configure settings for the printer itself, such as single-sided versus double-sided printing, sharing the printer on a Microsoft network, which computer or network port the printer uses, color management, security, and maintenance tasks. Right-click the appropriate printer's icon, and select Properties (in Windows 7, select Printer Properties). This will open a window similar to Figure 12-5. The tabs may vary, depending on the printer's capabilities and Windows' configuration.

FIGURE 12-5

Configure a
printer using
the printer's
Properties dialog
box.

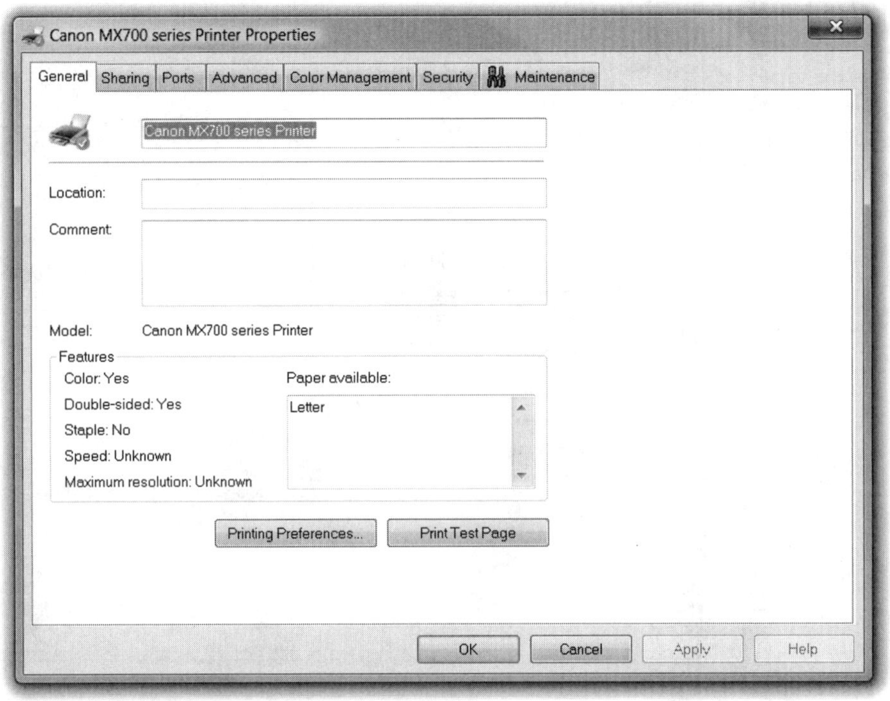

You will be able to control a variety of settings such as resolution, paper type, color use, and print density. You can also print a test page from this dialog box and, in some printers, use one or more cleaning and diagnostic modes for the printer.

Windows includes a print spooler, software that stores the print job in memory or on disk until the printer is ready to print it. This feature is turned on by default, and is especially important when sending several jobs to a printer at once, as is typical with a network printer. The correct spool settings for a printer will avoid potential problems. These settings are found on the Details tab in Windows 2000 and the Advanced tab in Windows XP and later.

Enable spooling by selecting Spool Print Jobs So Program Finishes Printing Faster. The alternative to spooling is to select the Print Directly To The Printer option. If you have enabled spooling, you will be able to decide whether the printer begins printing after the first page is spooled or after the last page is spooled.

You can also select the spool data format. In Windows 2000, find this setting on the Spool Settings page. In Windows XP and later, this setting is contained in a dialog box that opens from the Print Processor button on the Advanced page of the printer's Properties dialog box, as shown in Figure 12-6.

Select the data type from the Print Processor dialog box.

Enhanced Metafile Format (EMF) is a Windows graphic-rendering language. When you use EMF spooling, the printing application builds an EMF file representing the print job, and Windows sends this file to the printer. When the RAW data type is used, Windows translates each print job into printer-specific code. It actually takes Windows longer to do this than to create an EMF file. Windows then sends the resulting RAW file to the printer. The output will look the same with either file format, but not all printers can print EMF print jobs. The printer's installation program will normally select the correct spool data format, and normally you should not select a different format.

Printing Preferences

Another group of options, Printing Preferences, controls how documents are printed, and these settings vary from printer to printer. This dialog is where you select the number of copies, paper orientation, paper source, paper size, paper type, graphic options, output mode (number of pages per side, etc.), print order (front-to-back, back-to-front, etc.), printed overlays, and watermarks. To access printing preferences, right-click a printer in the Printers folder, and select Printing Preferences or access it from the Printing Preferences button in the Properties dialog.

Configuring a Network Printer

When preparing to connect a printer directly to a network via the printer's built-in NIC, first unpack the printer, install ink or toner cartridges, load the paper, connect to a power source, and then connect the appropriate cable to a switch. If the printer has a Wi-Fi NIC, ensure that an appropriate wireless router is configured and within signal range of the printer. Then power up the printer and follow these general steps:

1. *Configure the IP address for the printer's network adapter.* Networks come with network protocols, including TCP/IP built in, and on most networks, you will need to configure an IP address for the printer's NIC. You usually do this through a menu on the printer's control panel, or via special software on a PC directly connected to one of the printer's ports, such as a USB port. The manufacturer's instructions will give you the details on the method, but you may want to talk to a network administrator to discover the correct IP address to assign to the printer's network adapter.

2. *Test the IP address.* Once you have assigned the IP address, test that the printer can be reached over the network. Testing will require going to a computer proven to be connected to the network and running the following command from a command prompt: **ping <*ip_address*>**, where <*ip_address*> is the IP address assigned to the printer. Learn more about IP addresses in Chapter 13.

3. *Prepare each network computer.* Install the printer driver and other utilities on each computer that will print to the printer. After installing the printer, open the Properties page for the printer in Windows and select the Ports tab. Scroll down and check that the port for the network printer is installed. You will need to check the manufacturer's documentation. For instance, the port for the Canon MX700 is not installed automatically; you need to add it, and you need to assign the IP address of the printer to the port on each computer. To add a port, click the Add Port button and scroll down through the Printer Ports list until you see the port for your printer. For instance, the Canon port, shown here, is listed as "Canon BJNP Port." Select the port, and click the New Port button. In the Add Port dialog box, either select IP Address and manually enter the address of the printer, or select Auto Detection, in which case you will need to wait until the printer is detected and the correct IP address appears in the box. Once the IP address is either entered or detected, click the Next button. If you manually entered the address, the wizard will not proceed until it detects the printer on the network. Then follow the instructions to complete the wizard.

Printer Ports

Available port types:

Adobe PDF Port
Canon BJNP Port
Local Port
PDF2U Monitor
Standard TCP/IP Port

New Port Type...   New Port...   Cancel

Upgrades

Printers are somewhat limited in how you can upgrade them, unlike computers that you can upgrade in many ways, such as by adding memory, installing a large selection of new peripherals, upgrading the ROM BIOS, and upgrading the software. We will describe some possible software and hardware upgrades for printers.

Device Driver and Software Upgrades

Like other software, software associated with printers and scanners calls for occasional upgrades, with drivers being the most frequently upgraded. When an updated driver is available for your printer, follow the manufacturer's instructions to install it. If it comes with its own installation program, run it. Alternatively, the instructions may tell you to use the Update Drivers option in Windows XP. To update a printer driver in this fashion, open the printer's Properties, select the Advanced tab, click New Driver, and follow the instructions in the Add Printer Driver Wizard.

Hardware Upgrades

Popular hardware upgrades for printers and scanners are automated document feeders for scanners and larger-capacity paper trays for laser printers. Higher-end devices in both categories are most likely to offer upgrade options, usually offered by the manufacturer.

Another popular hardware upgrade is memory, particularly for laser printers. Adding memory can increase the speed when printing complex documents or graphics. A search of the Internet will turn up many manufacturers of memory upgrades for laser printers.

Firmware Upgrades

Some printers, in particular laser printers, support firmware upgrades. This, of course, depends on the manufacturer releasing firmware upgrades. First, determine the firmware version currently in your printer, and then check on the manufacturer's Website for notices of upgrades. Instructions from the manufacturer will guide you through upgrading the firmware, which you do from your computer.

Optimizing Printer Performance

The average user is happy if a printer is reliable and creates reasonable printouts, but a growing number of users have more discerning tastes and more exacting needs. For them, printers offer a variety of optimizing choices.

Tray Selection

If a printer has multiple trays, there are ways to optimize their use. One is to load plain paper in one tray and special stationery in another. Then instruct users on which tray to select for the types of jobs they send to the printer.

Tray Switching

You should use a different strategy when users send a large volume of printing to a multiple-tray printer using just one kind of paper. With this, you set the printer's preferences for tray switching so it will use the first tray until it is empty and then automatically switch to the second tray.

Deleting a Printer

When you no longer use a printer, delete it from Windows by opening the Printers folder, right-clicking on the printer, and selecting Delete. Respond to the confirmation dialog box ("Are you sure...?"), and the printer will be deleted.

SCENARIO & SOLUTION

We need a printer that will print an image to multipart forms for retail receipts. What should we buy?	Buy an impact printer, such as a dot matrix, which will be able to print to carbon copy forms.
In a laser printer, how does the image get from the drum to the paper?	The transfer corona wire applies a positive charge to the paper. As the paper passes the drum, the negatively charged toner is attracted to the page.
What cleans the photosensitive drum in a laser printer?	A cleaning blade removes residual toner from the drum, and an erasure lamp removes any remaining charge from the drum.
I am trying to install a printer on a parallel port, but when I plug it in, it is not recognized. What can I do?	Use the Add Printer Wizard in Windows to install the printer and configure the port.

CERTIFICATION OBJECTIVES

■ **701: 2.2**   *Given a scenario, explain and interpret common hardware and operating system symptoms and their causes.*

■ **701: 2.3**   *Given a scenario, determine the troubleshooting methods and tools for printers.*

■ **702: 1.5**   *Given a scenario, detect and resolve common printer issues*

■ **702: 2.4**   *Evaluate and resolve common issues*

This chapter includes coverage of the entire 702: 1.5 exam objective, plus it details small portions of objectives 701: 2.2, 701: 2.3, and 702: 2.4 that concern Windows-specific printing problems. For the exam, be prepared to identify symptoms of common printer problems—both hardware and software—and select the correct resolution for a problem.

Troubleshooting Printer Problems

When troubleshooting printers, apply the same troubleshooting theory and procedures used with other computer components and use the same toolkit, as described in Chapter 5. When a printer needs a major repair, first evaluate the cost benefit of the repair. How much would it cost to replace the printer versus to repair it? In this section, learn about common printer problems and their solutions.

on the
Job   *Printers are one of the most commonly accessed network resources and are the cause of a majority of network-related trouble calls.*

Paper Feed Problems

A common printer problem, paper jamming, has a variety of causes. Here are just a few:

■ **Too much paper in a paper tray**   Too much paper can cause more than one page to feed through the printer at a time. The extra page can cause problems with the print process itself and jam within the printer. To avoid this, reduce the amount of paper you place in the tray.

- **Static electricity**   If static builds up within the pages, it can cause the pages to stick together. Use your thumb to "riffle," or quickly separate, the pages before you load them into the paper tray. Riffling allows air between the pages and can reduce "static cling." Remove dust from the printer, as this can also cause static build-up.

- **Moisture in the paper**   Moisture can cause pages to stick together or not feed properly. Keep paper in its packaging until needed to protect it from moisture changes. Store paper in a cool dry place.

- **Worn out friction feed parts**   Worn parts will fail to move the paper smoothly. Check feed rollers for wear. Feed rollers are often rubber or plastic, and you should replace them (depending on the cost of replacing parts versus replacing the printer).

- **The wrong paper**   Use paper that is not too thin, not too thick, and that has a certain range of moisture content to avoid static build-up. Try using a different weight paper. Try feeding from an alternative (straight-through) paper path. Most printers have the option of a more direct paper path that can handle heavier weight paper than the standard path.

- **Paper will not feed from upright paper tray**   If the stack of paper is too small, the friction rollers might not be able to make good contact with the top page. Try putting a larger stack of paper in (without making it too large).

Most paper jams will stop the current print job. If you suspect a paper jam, consult your printer documentation. In general, turn off and open the printer, and carefully remove any paper jammed in the paper path, following the manufacturer's instructions. Some printers include levers that you can release to more easily remove jammed paper. Normally, you will need to gently pull the paper in the direction the paper normally moves through the printer. Pulling in the opposite direction could damage internal components, such as rollers. This is especially true of the fusion roller in a laser printer. Avoid tearing the paper. If it tears, be sure you locate and remove all pieces from the printer.

Inspect for any broken parts in the paper path. If you find any, you will have to investigate repairing or replacing the printer. If necessary, clean the printer, and once you have finished clearing the jam, either resume the print job or send another print job. Most printers will not resume operation until you have completely cleared the jam. Many printers also require you to press the reset or clear button to restart the printer.

Tractor feed has its own problems. These feed mechanisms are notorious for feeding paper incorrectly through the printer. Misalignment of the paper in the printer usually causes the problem. Tractor feeds require special continuous form paper, in which each page of paper attaches to the one before it, much like a roll of paper towels. If the perforations between pages do not line up properly, the text for one page will print across two pages. When this happens, look for a paper advance button on the printer that will incrementally advance the paper until it is properly aligned. If you do not have the documentation for the printer, this task may take trial and error.

Another problem with tractor feeds occurs when the friction-feed mechanism is not disabled. The most obvious symptom of this problem will be torn paper if the tractor pulls faster than the friction feed, or bunched paper if the opposite condition exists.

Print Quality

Print quality problems are very common with all types of printers. In laser printers, print quality problems are most often (but not always) associated with a component in the toner cartridge. When troubleshooting a print quality problem on a laser printer, swapping the toner cartridge often solves many of the problems listed here. Following are several common print quality problems and their suggested solutions.

Blank Pages

If a dot matrix printer produces blank pages, pay attention to the sound coming from the printer. If you cannot hear the pins striking the page, try replacing the print head. If the pins are striking the page but not printing, you have a ribbon problem. Make sure the ribbon lines up with the print head; if it does not, move it into position. You may have to find a way to remove slack from the ribbon, which you can do by removing the ribbon cartridge and manually rewinding the ribbon before reinserting it into the printer. If the ribbon does line up properly, but there is no print or just very faint print, the ribbon has probably worn out, and replacing the ribbon will resolve the problem. If carbon copies printed on a dot matrix printer are blank or dim, consult the documentation to adjust the distance between the print head and the paper.

If an inkjet printer produces blank pages, the likely cause is an ink cartridge. Use the printer software to determine the amount of ink left in an ink cartridge. The printer software may be a separate program that you will start from an icon in the

Windows GUI, or it may be integrated into the Windows Printer Properties dialog box. If the printer software is integrated into the Printer Properties dialog box, it may be in the form of a custom tab or a special button.

A warning that the printer is running low on ink, as shown here, does not necessarily mean that you should immediately replace the cartridge. We go for weeks with this status showing and warnings popping up when we print. We simply tell it to continue. We normally only replace a cartridge if the quality of the printout is not adequate for our purposes, or if the print job will not continue without changing it.

If there is ink, the problem could be clogged nozzles. Follow the printer manufacturer's instructions for cleaning the nozzles in the print head. Software installed with the printer driver usually does this and should be available on the Maintenance tab of the Printer's Properties dialog. If it doesn't, check the documentation for a way to initiate this from the printer's controls. In the extreme, follow the manufacturer's instructions for manually cleaning the print head, perhaps with a lint-free cloth slightly dampened with distilled water.

If a laser printer is producing blank pages, suspect some component of the printing process. For instance, a blank page can result if the image fails to transfer to the paper, which could be a problem with the transfer corona wire. Shut down the printer, disconnect the power cable, open the printer, and inspect the corona wire (consult your manual for its location). You may find dirt or debris (like a staple) shorting out the wire. You may discover that the wire itself is broken, although it would take rough treatment indeed to do this. If the wire is intact, but has debris on it, it could be shorting out. Clean the printer, and then try to print again.

It is rare for a laser cartridge to be the cause of a completely blank page, unless it contains the drum and the drum has failed. If it has, you must replace it. If the drum is part of the cartridge, replace the cartridge. You are more likely to see some of the other problems described next when the cartridge has a problem.

Random Speckles, Smudging, and Smearing

Ribbon ink, cartridge ink, and toner residue can be within the printer itself and transfer onto the paper. If any type of printer produces a page with speckles, smudging, or smearing of the ink or toner, try cleaning the printer. This includes manually cleaning it and/or using the printer software to instruct the printer to perform cleaning and other maintenance tasks. We describe printer cleaning in this chapter in "Preventive Maintenance for Printers."

If a dot matrix printer produces a smudged or smeared printout, check the pins on the print head. Stuck pins can cause printouts to have a smudged appearance as they continue to transfer ink to the page, even when they do not create a character or image. If this is the case, notify the manufacturer, and replace the print head or the entire printer.

If the output from an inkjet printer appears smudged or smeared, the most likely cause is someone touching the printed page before the ink dries. The ink used in inkjet and bubblejet printers must totally dry before it is touched, or it will smear. Most inkjet and bubblejet printers do not use permanent ink, and even after it has dried, these inks may smear if they become wet.

The heat and pressure of the fusion stage in a laser printer creates a smudge-proof permanent printout. Smudged laser printouts are usually the result of a failed fusing stage. Depending on the exact source of the problem, you may need to replace the fusing rollers, the halogen lamp, or the entire fuser assembly.

Repeated Pattern of Speckles or Blotches

A repeated but unintended pattern on a printout is not intended is another indication of ink or toner residue in the printer. Clean the printer, paying attention to the feed rollers in an inkjet and the transfer corona wire in a laser printer. If a repeated pattern is on the printout of a laser printer, suspect the drum. A small nick or flaw in the drum will cause toner to collect there, and it will transfer onto each page in a repetitive pattern. In addition, some drums lose their ability to drop their charge during the cleaning step. The drum has a very small diameter, so this same pattern will repeat several times down the length of the page. In either case, replacing the drum should solve the problem.

Ghost Image from the Previous Page

A ghost image occurs when an image, usually very faint, from a previous page appears on subsequent pages. This problem occurs only in laser printers and indicates a cleaning stage failure. The drum might have lost the ability to drop its charge in the presence of light. Replace the drum to resolve the problem. If the drum is not the cause, it could be either the cleaning blade or the erasure lamps. Because both the cleaning blade and drum are inside the toner cartridge in many laser printers, you can resolve this problem by replacing the toner cartridge. The erasure lamps are always (to our knowledge) in the printer itself, and they are not easy to replace. You will probably have to send the printer back to the manufacturer or to a specialized printer repair shop.

The Wrong Colors

Assuming this is not an application-related setting, one or more color cartridges may be out of ink or toner (color laser printer), causing the incorrect colors. If the nozzles on an inkjet clog, the colors may come out "dirty" or might not appear at all. Follow the manufacturer's instructions for cleaning the nozzles. In any type of color printer, if one cartridge gets low, it will not be able to produce the proper shades. To get the desired results in a printout, you may simply need to replace the cartridges.

Lines

If lines appear in a printout from a dot matrix printer, the print head may have a malfunctioning pin, in which case, replace the print head. In any printer, parallel lines of print can indicate an incompatible driver, a problem you may solve by updating or replacing the driver. This symptom can also be a sign of a malfunction in the printer's electronics, so you need to repair or replace the printer, depending on its value and the cost of repair.

"Garbage"

Garbled output—often called "garbage"—usually indicates a communications problem between the computer and printer. The most common cause of this is an incorrect or corrupted print driver, but first check that the data cable is firmly and properly attached, and then try doing a power cycle (turning the printer off and then back on) because it may have simply experienced a temporary problem. Restarting the computer may also solve the problem.

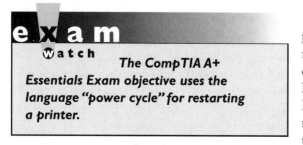

The CompTIA A+ Essentials Exam objective uses the language "power cycle" for restarting a printer.

If there are no connection problems and a power cycle of the printer and computer does not improve the printing, then check that the computer is using the correct printer driver. Look at the printer settings by opening the Printers folder. Ensure that the physical printer matches the printer shown in this dialog box. If the driver is not correct, uninstall it and reinstall the correct driver. If the driver appears to be correct, look at the manufacturer's site for an update and install the update. If the version of the driver is the most current, try reinstalling the driver.

Finally, this problem could be the result of insufficient printer memory. You can test this by trying to print a very small document. If it works, there is a chance that the original document was too large for the printer's memory. You can add more RAM. Check the documentation to find out how to check on the amount of memory, what type of memory to install, and how to install the memory.

Printer Error Messages

Printers generate a variety of error messages. They often come with their own configuration and monitoring utility installed on your computer when you install the printer driver. We'll describe some of the more common error messages that could appear on the computer screen or the printer's console, or both. The OS generates some of these messages. Any time you get a printer error message that you do not understand, check the message or error code number in the manufacturer's documentation. You may need to do a search on the manufacturer's Website, where a more complete list is often available.

Paper Out

A Paper Out message indicates that there is no paper in the printer. If the printer uses a tractor feed, you will need to lift the printer lid, feed the first sheet of the new stack through the paper path, and line up the holes with the feed wheels. As this procedure varies from model to model, consult the manufacturer's documentation.

Adding paper to any printer should only take a few seconds because it does not involve turning off the printer's power. If you are using a tray to feed a friction-feed printer, simply pull out the appropriate paper tray. Fan a stack of fresh paper and insert it into the tray. If there is a lid for the tray, replace that before inserting the tray into the printer. The error message should go away on its own. If you do not close or insert the tray properly, a Tray Open or Close Tray message may appear. If the printer uses an upright friction feed, follow the steps in Exercise 12-2 to add more paper.

Adding Paper to an Upright Friction-Feed Tray

If you have access to a printer with an upright friction-feed tray, you can follow these instructions:

1. Release the tray lever at the back of the printer (if so equipped). Doing this will cause the paper tray to drop away slightly from the friction rollers.
2. Place a small stack of paper in the tray, using the paper guides.
3. Engage the tray lever to bring the paper closer to the feed rollers.
4. The printer might automatically detect the paper and continue the print job. If not, look for and press the Paper Advance button on the printer. This instructs the printer to detect and try to feed the paper.

The Paper Out message could appear even if there is paper in the tray. Over time, the surface of the rollers used to feed the paper may lose their ability to grip and move the paper. This issue occurs especially as the paper becomes low in the tray, and the rollers cannot benefit from the pressure of a full stack of paper to grip and feed the paper. Locate the rollers and clean them, first wipe the dust and grime off, and then use isopropyl alcohol to clean any residue that may make the rollers slippery.

Out of Memory Error

A laser printer composes each page of a print job, using its own memory. Therefore, if an Out of Memory error appears on a printer's display, then the printer does not have enough memory for the print job. For the short term, break up complex print jobs. The more permanent solution is to add more RAM to the printer, as described previously when we discussed the symptom of garbage or "garbled" printing.

I/O Error

An I/O error message can take many forms, including "Cannot communicate with printer" or "There was an error writing to LPT# or USB#." Windows typically reports this message, and it indicates that the computer cannot properly communicate with the printer, clearly identifying it as a connectivity problem. Or is it? Start by ensuring that the printer is on. If it is not, turn it on, and then try to print. Next, make sure the printer data cable firmly and properly attaches to both the printer and the computer and that a proper driver has been loaded. If you suspect the driver is corrupt, remove it, and then reload it. Ensure that the driver uses the correct port by checking the Ports tab in the Properties dialog for the printer.

Incorrect Port Mode

An Incorrect Port Mode error applies to parallel ports. Wording of this message may vary, but it indicates that the parallel port the printer attaches to is using the wrong mode. This message usually appears on the computer screen rather than on the printer's display. Enter the computer's BIOS system setup program, and change the parallel port to the proper mode (unidirectional, bidirectional, or ECP). If the error message does not indicate the correct mode, consult the printer manufacturer's documentation.

No Default Printer Selected

The first printer installed in Windows gets the Default Printer designation. A default printer is the printer that automatically receives a print job when you select the

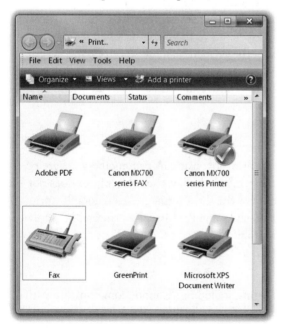

Print command from within a program, but do not specify which printer you want to use. If you install one or more printers after that, the first one will remain the default printer until you change its status. A small solid-color circle containing a white check mark indicates the default printer in the Printers folder, as shown here. Make the printer you use most often the default printer by right-clicking the desired printer. From the context menu, select Set As Default Printer.

If there is no installed printer and you attempt to print, Windows will issue the error message No Default Printer Selected. Once you install at least one printer, this error message is rare, but it is not totally extinct. Corrupted printer drivers and utility files can disable the printer and cause this message to appear, but it will probably appear before or after another message that begins "Rundll has caused an error in…" This message will include a filename and will end with "Rundll will now close." If this occurs, attempt to uninstall the printer software, and then reinstall it. If this occurs immediately after installing a new printer, contact the manufacturer for another copy of the printer software, as the one that came with the printer may be corrupted.

Low Toner or Ink

The Low Toner (or similar) message applies to laser printers, and it appears well before the toner is completely gone as an early warning. The printer should continue to print normally. You can often make the error message go away by removing the toner cartridge and gently rocking the cartridge back and forth. This will resettle and redistribute the toner within the cartridge. Note, however, that this is not a solution to the problem. The reason for the error is to warn you to replace the toner cartridge soon. Most laser printers will not work at all if the toner cartridge is empty.

When you are using an inkjet, the Ink Low (or similar) message will appear on your computer screen or an ink level bar will be displayed. Replace the cartridge.

o n t h e
Ö o b
When an ink cartridge gets low, you should replace rather than refill it. By refilling an old cartridge, you are reusing old, possibly worn-out components.

Windows Print Spooler Problems

Sometimes the Print Spooler service stops, and when it does, nothing prints until it is restarted. This is referred to as a "stalled print spooler." You need to determine if the spooler is stalled, so if a print job has failed to print, or has stopped before completing, first check that the printer is not out of paper, ink, or toner. Check the power cable and status lights. If everything seems to be normal, then you will need to treat it like a print spooler problem. For this, you must have the Manage Documents permission to the printer. Assuming you are logged on as a member of the Administrators group, which is one of the groups automatically assigned this permission, open the Printers folder and double-click the printer. Doing this opens the user interface for the print queue from which you can manage the print jobs the print spooler is holding. Check the status of the print job. If the print job status is Paused, right-click it and select Restart. If this fails, attempt to cancel the print job. Sometimes canceling the first job in the queue will allow the other jobs to print.

If this does not help, then cancel each job in the queue. If you are not able to restart or cancel jobs in the queue, you will need to restart the Print Spooler service. Follow the steps in Exercise 12-3 to restart this service.

EXERCISE 12-3

Restarting the Print Spooler Service

Use the Services node in Computer Management to restart a stalled print spooler:

1. Right-click My Computer or Computer, and select Manage from the context menu.

2. In the Computer Management Console, select Services And Applications, and then double-click Services.

3. In the contents pane, scroll down to Print Spooler.

4. Right-click on Print Spooler and select Restart (see Figure 12-7).

5. If restarting the service fails, then close all open windows and restart. When Windows restarts, the Print Spooler service will restart.

6. Restart the printer.

7. Resend the print jobs to the printer.

Preventive Maintenance for Printers

Because of the frequency with which printers are used, they require almost constant maintenance. Fortunately, the maintenance procedures are usually easy. Consider scheduling regular maintenance, such as cleaning, based on the amount of usage for

FIGURE 12-7

Right-click the Print Spooler service and select Restart.

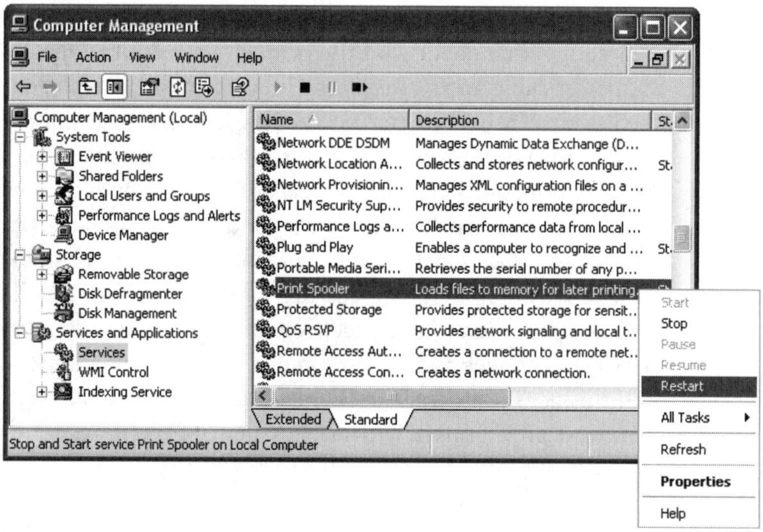

each printer and scanner. Manufacturers may provide a list of other maintenance tasks, such as vacuuming the ozone filter in laser printers, which should occur along with a regular cleaning, but not at the same frequency.

Maintenance Kits and Page Counts

Some printers—mainly professional-quality and high-production laser printers—have "maintenance counts." The printer counts the number of pages printed over the lifetime of the printer, and when this page count reaches a certain number, called the maintenance count (in the hundreds of thousands), a service message will appear on the printer's display. This message indicates that the printer has reached the end of the expected service life for some of its internal components. When this occurs, you must install the manufacturer's maintenance kit of replacement parts, after which you must reset the page count so it can track the expected life of the parts in the new maintenance kit.

If you do not reset the page count, the printer will continue to issue the maintenance warning. Use the manufacturer's instructions for resetting the page count. In the rare instance when you must install a new maintenance kit before the page count reaches the maintenance count, on some models, you must reset the maintenance count to match the page count. Then, when the next page is printed, you will receive the maintenance message and can proceed with the maintenance and reset the page count.

Cleaning a Printer

The best thing you can do to prolong the life of a printer and prevent problems from occurring is to clean it regularly. In all printers, small particles of paper and other debris can be left behind and cause a potentially harmful build-up. As mentioned earlier, this build-up can hold a static charge, which can, in turn, damage components through electrostatic discharge (ESD) or cause pages to stick together.

We do not recommend using any solvents to clean a printer, and never spray a liquid on or into a printer for any reason. Use a very dilute mixture of water and white vinegar to dampen a cloth, and thoroughly ring it out before wiping off the exterior. Do not use liquids inside the printer unless following the advice of the manufacturer.

Before opening up a printer for cleaning, power it down and unplug it. Do not touch the printer's power supply, and allow the fusing roller in a laser printer to cool down before you clean inside.

Removing the build-up will also keep the paper path clear, thus reducing paper jams and ensuring there is no inhibition of moving parts. You can remove dust and particle build-up using compressed air or a vacuum. As you clean the printer, be on the lookout for small corners of paper left behind during the print process or after you cleared a paper jam.

In an inkjet printer, you should look for and remove ink from the inside of the printer. Ink can leak and cause smudges on the paper. As the ink dries, it can cause moving components or paper to stick. Laser printers can accumulate toner. Remove excess toner using a paper towel or cotton swab. But beyond that, only clean laser printer internal components using the manufacturer's instructions. Figure 12-8 shows the interior of a laser printer.

Some manufacturers add a Maintenance tab to the Printer Properties dialog box for tasks such as those shown in Figure 12-9. Notice the four buttons for cleaning various components, plus the buttons for Print Head Alignment and Nozzle Check.

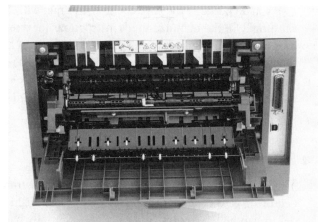

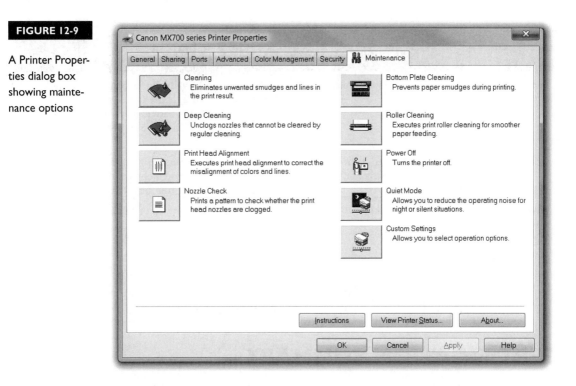

FIGURE 12-9

A Printer Properties dialog box showing maintenance options

You can also prevent paper jams and component wear and tear by using the proper paper for your printer. Read the documentation for the printer to determine the best paper for the results you desire.

Ensuring a Suitable Environment

Prevent a myriad of problems with your printer by providing a suitable environment. Be sure the printer is on a level surface, close to the computer to which it is connected, and convenient for the user. Temperature extremes, dirt, and dust will negatively affect either type of device. Dirt and dust will affect the quality of scanned documents, and, if they infiltrate the case, can cause heat build-up in any device.

Use Recommended Consumables

For the best results, use the manufacturer's recommended consumables. This includes ink and toner cartridges as well as paper for printers. In the case of the major printer manufacturers, their branded ink and toner products may only be

SCENARIO & SOLUTION

The output from my laser printer is smeared. What should I do?	Clean the printer, especially the fusion roller. If this doesn't work, replace the drum. If the drum is in the toner cartridge, replace the toner cartridge. If none of this works, the problem may be with the fuser assembly, which will need replacing.
I am careful not to handle the printouts from my inkjet printer, but they are coming out with smudges. What can I do?	Check the paper path. Something may be contacting the page before the ink has had a chance to dry, or people may be handling the printout before it is dry.
Why do printouts from my color inkjet printer have the wrong colors?	The printer is probably low in one or more colors or has a clogged nozzle.

available at premium prices. To save money, consider third-party sources, but be prepared to buy and test one set of cartridges before ordering quantities.

CERTIFICATION SUMMARY

This chapter explored printer issues for IT professionals. The focus of this chapter was the components, procedures, troubleshooting, and maintenance procedures for common printer types. Dot matrix printers provide the lowest quality, and today they mainly print multiple-part forms. Laser printers, the most expensive, can provide excellent printouts and are the most common type used in offices. For this reason, you are likely to deal with laser printers in businesses more frequently than with other printer types. Inkjet printers are extremely popular as inexpensive desktop color printers.

Before installing a printer, carefully read the manufacturer's instructions. When working with printer problems, apply the troubleshooting procedures learned in Chapter 5, and familiarize yourself with the symptoms and problems common to the printer or scanner. Printers require maintenance to replenish paper and, less frequently, ink or toner. Clean printers regularly to ensure high-quality results, and to avoid many problems that dirt, dust, and grime can create.

✓ TWO-MINUTE DRILL

Here are some of the key points covered in Chapter 12.

Printer Basics

❑ Printers are the most common peripheral used with PCs.

❑ Dot matrix impact printers are usually of low quality, use a ribbon, move paper with friction feed or tractor feed, and most often are used for printing multiple-part forms, such as retail receipts.

❑ Laser printers use laser light technology in the printing process. The stages of the laser printing process are charging, writing, developing, transferring, fusing, and cleaning.

❑ The term "inkjet" refers to printers that use one of several technologies to apply wet ink to paper to create text or graphic printouts. Manufacturers use several names for these printers, including "inkjet," "bubblejet," and others.

❑ Printers that use solid ink usually fall under one of two headings: dye-sublimation and thermal wax.

❑ Thermal printers use heat in the image transfer process.

❑ The two most common paper-feed technologies are friction feed and continuous form feed.

❑ The typical printer has a system board, ROM (containing firmware), and RAM memory, as well as various components related to the specific printing technology and paper-feed mechanism. Additional components include the device driver and related software, and consumables in the form of paper, ink ribbons, ink cartridges, or toner cartridges.

❑ Manufacturers offer multifunction products that include a scanner, printer, copier, and fax integrated within the same case. These are called multifunction printers (MFPs) or multifunction devices (MFDs).

❑ Printer interfaces include parallel, serial, USB, IEEE 1394/FireWire, SCSI, Ethernet, and wireless.

Installing and Configuring Printers

❑ Before installing a printer, be sure to read the manufacturer's instructions.

❑ Installing a printer in Windows is a simple job, especially for plug and play printers. Even non–plug and play printers are easy to install using the Add Printer Wizard.

❑ After installing a printer, perform a test print, and then print from each installed application to ensure compatibility.

❑ Configure a printer through the printer's Properties dialog box and through the Printing Preferences dialog box.

❑ There are a few common upgrades to printers, including device drivers and other software, document feeders, memory, and firmware.

❑ Ways to optimize a printer's performance include tray selection for different stationery and enabling tray switching.

Troubleshooting Printers

❑ The troubleshooting process for printers is identical to that used for computers.

❑ Common printer problems include those involving paper feed and print quality. Printer error messages on your computer screen or the printer display panel will alert you to common problems, such as Paper Out, I/O errors, and Print Spooler problems.

Preventive Maintenance for Printers

❑ Some laser printers track the number of pages printed in a page count and require that critical components be replaced using a maintenance kit. After installing the maintenance kit, you must reset the page count.

❑ Clean each printer according to the manufacturer's recommendations to avoid poor output and other problems.

❑ Provide a suitable environment for each printer to avoid problems that dirt and temperature extremes can cause in these devices.

❑ For the best results, use the recommended consumables in printers. This may require using the media and paper provided by the manufacturer or less expensive substitutes of equal quality from other sources.

SELF TEST

The following questions will help you measure your understanding of the material presented in this chapter. Read all of the choices carefully, because there might be more than one correct answer. Choose all correct answers for each question.

Printer Basics

1. What is a common use for dot matrix printers?
    A. High-quality color images
    B. High-speed network printers
    C. Multiple-part forms
    D. UPC code scanning

2. What type of printer is the most often-used shared network printer in businesses?
    A. Laser
    B. Dot matrix
    C. Thermal
    D. Inkjet

3. In what stage of the laser printing process does a laser beam place an image on the photosensitive drum?
    A. Cleaning
    B. Developing
    C. Charging
    D. Writing

4. Which stage in the laser printing process is responsible for creating a permanent nonsmearing image?
    A. Cleaning
    B. Fusing
    C. Transferring
    D. Writing

5. What name is given to the type of printer that applies wet ink to paper?
    A. Laser
    B. Dot matrix
    C. Thermal
    D. Inkjet

6. What is the unit of measure used to describe the size of droplets created by the nozzles in an inkjet printer?

A. Millimeter

B. Meter

C. Picoliter

D. Liter

7. What are two examples of solid-ink technology?

A. Inkjet and bubblejet

B. Laser jet and dot matrix

C. Dye-sublimation and thermal wax

D. Direct thermal and thermal wax transfer

Installing and Configuring Printers

8. What type of software converts a scanned page of text from graphic format to editable text format?

A. Copy

B. OCR

C. Scanning

D. Graphics editing

9. What Windows GUI tool can you use to install a non–plug and play printer?

A. Add Printer Wizard

B. Device Manager

C. My Computer/Computer

D. Add or Remove Programs

10. What important configuration task must you perform on a network printer before it will be recognized on the network?

A. Install TCP/IP.

B. Assign an IP address.

C. Give it the address of each client.

D. It must be detected by the clients.

11. What is the most common software upgrade for a printer?

    A. Graphics software

    B. Word processing software

    C. Firmware upgrade

    D. New device driver

12. When installing a network printer be sure to configure this setting for the printer's NIC.

    A. Page Setup

    B. Advanced

    C. Printing Preferences

    D. IP address

Troubleshooting Printers

13. What can contribute to static build-up in a printer?

    A. Dust

    B. Ink

    C. Overloaded paper tray

    D. Paper jams

14. What component on an inkjet printer may clog with ink?

    A. Nozzles

    B. Hammers

    C. Friction-feed rollers

    D. Tractor feeder

15. What is a possible source of a problem causing blank pages to print out on a laser printer?

    A. Paper path

    B. Transfer corona wire

    C. Power supply

    D. Paper tray

16. What component in a laser printer could be the source of a repeated pattern of speckles?

    A. Fusion roller

    B. Drum

    C. Toner

    D. Primary corona wire

17. When a ghost image from a previous page occurs on subsequent pages printed on a laser printer, what component is a probable source of the problem?

    A. Fusion roller

    B. Drum

    C. Toner

    D. Primary corona wire

18. Of all the possible solutions for "garbage" printing, these two are the first ones you should try. Select the two correct answers.

    A. Check for loose data cable.

    B. Upgrade driver.

    C. Power cycle the printer and computer.

    D. Uninstall and reinstall driver.

Preventive Maintenance for Printers

19. What should you do after installing a maintenance kit in a laser printer?

    A. Reset the maintenance count.

    B. Reset the page count.

    C. Reset the printer.

    D. Call the manufacturer.

20. What simple maintenance task for printers helps maintain high-quality results?

    A. Memory upgrade

    B. Installing a maintenance kit

    C. Replacing the fuser

    D. Cleaning

SELF TEST ANSWERS

Printer Basics

1. ☑ **C.** Multiple-part form printing is a common use for dot matrix printers.

☒ **A,** high-quality color images, is incorrect because dot matrix printers do not create high-quality color images. **B,** high-speed network printers, is incorrect because dot matrix printers are not high-speed printers. **D,** UPC code scanning, is incorrect because no stand-alone printer can scan.

2. ☑ **A.** The laser printer is the most often-used shared network printer in businesses.

☒ **B,** dot matrix, **C,** thermal, and **D,** inkjet, are all incorrect because these types of printers seldom are shared network printers in businesses.

3. ☑ **D.** Writing is the laser printing stage in which the laser beam places an image on the photosensitive drum.

☒ **A,** cleaning, is incorrect because it is the stage in which the drum is cleaned. **B,** developing, is incorrect because it is the stage in which toner is attracted to the image on the drum. **C,** charging, is incorrect because it is the stage in which a charge is applied to the drum.

4. ☑ **B.** Fusing is the stage in the laser printing process in which the image permanently fuses to the paper.

☒ **A,** cleaning, **C,** transferring, and **D,** writing, are incorrect because none of these is the stage that creates a permanent nonsmearing image.

5. ☑ **D.** Inkjet is the type of printer that applies wet ink to paper.

☒ **A,** laser, is incorrect because in this type of printer dry toner is fused to the paper. **B,** dot matrix, is incorrect because this type of printer uses an ink ribbon. **C,** thermal, is incorrect because this type of printer uses heat to print an image.

6. ☑ **C.** Picoliter is the unit of measure used to describe the size of droplets created by the nozzles in an inkjet printer.

☒ **A,** millimeter, and **B,** meter, are both incorrect because neither one is the unit of measure used for the size of droplets from the nozzles in an inkjet printer, which is a measurement of liquid volume. Both millimeter and meter are units of measure for distance. **D,** liter, although a measure of liquid volume, is far too large a volume for such small drops.

7. ☑ **C.** Dye-sublimation and thermal wax are two examples of solid-ink technology.

☒ **A,** inkjet and bubblejet, is incorrect because these are printers that use liquid ink. **B,** laser jet and dot matrix, is incorrect because laser printers use dry toner, and dot matrix printers use an ink ribbon. **D,** direct thermal and thermal wax transfer, is incorrect because, although thermal wax transfer uses solid-ink technology, direct thermal does not, but instead actually burns an image into paper.

Installing and Configuring Printers

8. ☑ **B.** OCR, or optical character recognition, is the software used to convert a scanned page of text from graphic format to editable text format.
☒ **A,** copy, is incorrect because this is not software that converts a scanned page of text from graphic format to editable text format. **C,** scanning, is incorrect because scanning is not the software that converts a scanned page of text from graphic format to editable text format. **D,** graphics editing, is incorrect because this software does not convert a scanned page of text from graphic format to editable text format.

9. ☑ **A.** The Add Printer Wizard is the Windows GUI tool for installing a non–plug and play printer.
☒ **B,** Device Manager, **C,** My Computer/Computer, and **D,** Add or Remove Programs, are incorrect because none of these is the GUI tool for installing a non–plug and play printer.

10. ☑ **B.** Assign an IP address is the important configuration task you must do on a network printer before it will be recognized on the network.
☒ **A,** install TCP/IP, is incorrect because a network printer comes with TCP/IP installed. **C,** give it the address of each client, is incorrect because the network printer does not need the address of each client; each client needs the address of the network printer. **D,** it must be detected by the clients, is incorrect because the network printer must have an IP address before it can be recognized on the network.

11. ☑ **D.** New device driver is the most common software upgrade for a scanner or printer.
☒ **A,** graphics software, is incorrect because this is not the most common software upgrade for a scanner or printer. **B,** word processing software, is incorrect because this is not the most common software upgrade for a scanner or printer. **C,** firmware upgrade, is incorrect because it is not the most common software upgrade for a scanner or printer.

12. ☑ **D.** IP address is the printer's NIC setting that you must configure for a network printer.
☒ **A,** Page Setup, **B,** Advanced, and **C,** Printing Preferences, are all incorrect because these are not settings for a printer's NIC.

Troubleshooting Printers and Scanners

13. ☑ **A.** Dust can contribute to static build-up in a printer.
☒ **B,** ink, is incorrect because, although ink residue may build up in a printer, it does not appreciably contribute to static buildup. **C,** overloaded paper tray, is incorrect because this is not a cause of static build-up in a printer. **D,** paper jams, is incorrect because, although static build-up in a printer may occasionally cause a paper jam, it is not a primary cause.

14. ☑ **A.** Nozzles in an inkjet printer can become clogged with ink.
☒ **B,** hammers, **C,** friction-feed rollers, and **D,** tractor feeder, are incorrect because these components do not become clogged with ink.

15. ☑ **B.** The transfer corona wire is a possible source of a problem causing blank pages to print on a laser printer.
☒ **A,** paper path, **C,** power supply, and **D,** paper tray, are incorrect because they are not considered possible sources for blank pages printing out on a laser printer.

16. ☑ **B.** The drum could be the source of a repeated patter of speckles on printouts from a laser printer.
☒ **A,** fusion roller, **C,** toner, and **D,** primary corona wire, are incorrect because none of these is a probable source of repeated pattern of speckles on printouts from a laser printer.

17. ☑ **B.** The drum is the probable source of a ghost image printing on subsequent pages from a laser printer.
☒ **A,** fusion roller, **C,** toner, and **D,** primary corona wire, are incorrect because none of these is a probable source of a ghost image.

18. ☑ **A,** check for loose data cable, and **C,** power cycle the printer and computer, are the first two solutions you should try for "garbage" printing because they are simple and easy to try.
☒ **B,** upgrade the driver, and **D,** uninstall and reinstall the driver, are incorrect because they are not as simple and fast to try as the first two.

Preventive Maintenance for Printers and Scanners

19. ☑ **B.** Reset the page count of a laser printer after installing a maintenance kit.
☒ **A,** reset the maintenance count, is incorrect because resetting this count will set the number at which the printer should receive maintenance to zero pages. **C,** reset the printer, is incorrect because this will not turn the page count to zero, and the printer will display a maintenance warning. **D,** call the manufacturer, is incorrect because this step is unnecessary when all you need to do is reset the page count.

20. ☑ **D.** Cleaning is the simple maintenance task for printers that helps maintain high-quality results.
☒ **A,** memory upgrade, is incorrect because this is not a simple maintenance task, and it will not help maintain high-quality results. **B,** installing a maintenance kit, is incorrect because this is not a simple maintenance task. **C,** replacing the fuser, is incorrect because it is not a simple maintenance task but a complex repair task.

13

Network Basics

CERTIFICATION OBJECTIVES

❑   **701:4.1**   Summarize the basics of networking fundamentals, including technologies, devices, and protocols

❑   **701:4.2**   Categorize network cables and connectors, and their implementations

❑   **701:4.3**   Compare and contrast the different network types

✓   Two-Minute Drill

Q&A   Self Test

Computer networks provide users with the ability to share files, printers, resources, and e-mail globally. Networks have become so important that they provide the basis for nearly all business transactions.

Obviously, a discussion of the full spectrum of network details and specifications is too broad in scope to be contained in this book. However, as a computer technician, you should be aware of basic networking concepts so you can troubleshoot minor problems on established networks. This chapter focuses on basic concepts of physical networks; Chapter 14 guides you through simple small office/home office (SOHO) network installation, and Chapter 15 provides the basis for troubleshooting common network problems.

CERTIFICATION OBJECTIVES

- **701: 4.1** *Summarize the basics of networking fundamentals, including technologies, devices, and protocols*

- **701: 4.2** *Categorize network cables and connectors, and their implementations*

- **701: 4.3** *Compare and contrast the different network types*

This chapter is an overview of networking technologies, devices, protocols, hardware, and types, as required by the above objectives, including the appropriate networking technologies and terms.

Network Performance and Classifications

For a computer professional working with PCs, the networked computer is the norm, not the exception. A computer not connected to a network is a *stand-alone computer*, and this has become a nearly extinct species, as more and more PCs network together—even within homes.

To understand networks, you must first be familiar with basic network performance and classifications, which describe networks by speed, geography, and scale, beginning with the smallest networks up to globe-spanning ones.

Geographic Network Classifications and Technologies

We classify networks by geographic area types, and there are specific technologies designed for each of them. Network builders select these technologies for the capabilities that match the distance needs of the network.

Personal Area Network (PAN)

You may have your own *personal area network (PAN)*, if you have devices, such as phones and personal digital assistants (PDAs), that communicate with each other and/or your desktop computer. A PAN may use a wired connection, such as USB or FireWire, or it may communicate wirelessly using one of the standards developed for short-range communications, such as IrDA or Bluetooth.

e x a m

ⓦ a t c h   *Although the term "PAN" is not included in the objectives for the CompTIA A+ Essentials Exams, the wireless technologies used in a PAN are included, so be familiar with them and their distance limit, which is 1 meter for IrDA and 10 meters for Bluetooth (see Chapter 6).*

Local Area Network (LAN)

A *local area network (LAN)* is a network that covers a much larger area than a PAN, such as a building, home, office, or campus. Typically, distances measure in hundreds of meters. A LAN may share resources such as printers, files, or other resources. LANs operate very fast—with speeds measured in megabits or gigabits per second—and have become extremely cost effective. While there are many LAN technologies, the two most widely used in small office/home office (SOHO) network installations are Ethernet, and several standards that fall under the Wi-Fi heading.

Ethernet   Most wired LANs use hardware based on standards developed by the 802.3 subcommittee of the IEEE. *Ethernet* is the word created to describe the earliest of these networks, and we continue to use this term, although there really are many Ethernet standards. These standards define, among other things, how computer data is broken down into small chunks, prepared, and packaged before the Ethernet network interface card (NIC) places it on the Ethernet network. This chunk of data is an Ethernet *frame*. Ethernet standards also define the hardware and medium that control and carry the data signals.

Early implementations of Ethernet are *half-duplex*, meaning that while data can travel in either direction, it can only travel in one direction at a time. Later implementations are capable of *full-duplex* communication, in which the signals travel in both directions simultaneously, but will usually auto-negotiate and automatically use either half- or full-duplex depending on what is in use on the network. Networks today are usually full-duplex, unless a network has very old hardware.

Depending on the exact implementation, Ethernet supports a variety of transmission speeds, media, and distances. All Ethernet standards using copper cabling—either unshielded twisted pair or shielded twisted pair—support a maximum cable length of 100 meters between a NIC and a hub or switch (more on hubs and switches in "Connecting LANs"). The maximum distances for fiber installations vary, depending on the exact fiber-optic cabling in use. Here is a summary of several Ethernet levels and their speeds:

- **10BaseT/Ethernet** For many years the most widely used implementation, 10BaseT transfers data at 10 Mbps over unshielded twisted-pair (UTP) copper cabling in half-duplex mode with a maximum cable length of 100 meters.

- **100BaseT/Fast Ethernet** Using the same cabling as 10BaseT, 100 Base-T or *Fast Ethernet* operates at 100 Mbps and uses different network interface cards, many of which are also capable of the lower Ethernet speeds, auto-detecting the speed of the network and working at whichever speed is in use. Early 100BaseT NICs were half-duplex, but later ones support full-duplex.

- **1000BaseT/Gigabit Ethernet** Supporting data transfer rates of 1 Gbps over UTP, there are several *Gigabit Ethernet* standards, but the most common one is 1000BaseT. It is capable of full-duplex operation using four-pair UTP cable with standard RJ-45 connectors (see the description of cable later in "Transmission Medium").

- **10-Gigabit Ethernet/10 GbE** WANS and very high-end LANs use one of the many standards of 10-Gigabit Ethernet, which operates at speeds of up to 10 Gbps in full-duplex mode over either copper (10GBaseT) or fiber. There are many 10-Gigabit Ethernet fiber standards for both WANs and LANS, and we will only briefly mention two of them here. The 10GBaseSR standard is one of the standards used for fiber-optic LANs, whereas 10GBaseSW is one of the standards used for fiber-optic WANs.

Wireless LAN (WLAN)   *Wireless LAN (WLAN)* communication (local area networking using radio waves) is very popular. The most common wireless LAN implementations are based on the IEEE 802.11 group of standards, also called *Wireless Fidelity (Wi-Fi)*. There are several 802.11 standards, and more have been proposed. These wireless standards use either 2.4 GHz or 5 GHz frequencies to communicate between systems. The range on these systems is relatively short, but they offer the advantage of not requiring cable for network connections.

In many homes and businesses, Wi-Fi networks give users access to the Internet. In these instances, the wireless communications network uses a wireless router connected to a broadband connection, such as a cable modem or DSL modem.

Wi-Fi is now standard on laptops, and many public places, restaurants, and other businesses offer free- or pay-access to Wi-Fi networks that connect to broadband Internet service. These access points are called *hot spots*. In large corporations, users with wireless-enabled laptops and handheld computers can move around the campus and continue to connect to the corporate network.

Here is a brief description of several 802.11 standards and their features:

- **802.11a**   The *802.11a* standard was developed by the IEEE at the same time as the slower 802.11b standard, but the "a" standard was more expensive to implement. Manufacturers, therefore, tended to make 802.11b devices. 802.11a uses the 5 GHz band, which makes 802.11a devices incompatible with 802.11b and the subsequent 802.11g devices. Because 802.11a devices do not provide downward compatibility with existing equipment using the 802.11b or newer 802.11g standards, they are seldom used. An 802.11a network has speeds up to 54 Mbps with a range of up to 150 feet.

- **802.11b**   The *802.11b* standard was the first widely popular version of Wi-Fi, with a speed of 10 Mbps and a range of up to 300 feet. Operating in the 2.4 GHz band, which is also used by other noncomputer devices such as cordless phones and household appliances, these devices are vulnerable to interference if positioned near another device using the same portion of the radio spectrum.

- **802.11g**   *802.11g* replaced 802.11b. With a speed of up to 54 Mbps and a range of up to 300 feet, it also uses the 2.4 GHz radio band. 802.11g devices are normally downward-compatible with 802.11b devices, although the reverse is not true.

- **802.11n**   The *802.11n* standard has speeds of up to 100+ Mbps and a maximum range of up to 600 feet. The standard defines speeds of up to

600 Mbps, which actual implementations do not achieve. *MIMO (multiple input/multiple output)* makes 802.11n speeds possible using multiple antennas to send and receive digital data in simultaneous radio streams that increase performance. Some manufacturers of wireless NICs, signal boosters, and access points manufactured before the release of the full specification used terms such as "802.11pre-n" to describe their equipment.

When considering a wireless network, determining its speed and range can be nebulous at best. In spite of the maximums defined by the standards, many factors affect both speed and range. First, there is the limit of the standard, and then there is the distance between the wireless-enabled computer and the *wireless access point (WAP)*, a network connection device at the core of a wireless network. Finally, there is the issue of interference, which can result from other wireless device signals operating in the same band or from physical barriers to the signals. In Chapter 14, you will learn about installing a WLAN to avoid interference and devices that will extend the range of the signals. You will also learn about the configuration options for wireless networks, including the use of identifiers for the wireless devices, secure encryption settings, and settings for keeping intruders out.

Metropolitan Area Network (MAN)

A *metropolitan area network (MAN)* is a network that covers a metropolitan area, connecting various networks together using a shared, community network, and often providing WAN connections to the Internet. A MAN usually runs over high-speed fiber-optic cable operating in the gigabits-per-second range. SONET is one long-established fiber-optic WAN technology. Although people tend to be less aware of MANs, they nonetheless exist. In fact, a MAN may well be somewhere between you and the Internet.

e x a m

Wide Area Network (WAN)

A *wide area network (WAN)* can cover the largest geographic area. A *WAN connection* is the connection between two networks over a long distance (miles). The generic term for these connected networks is an *internetwork*, if it is a public network. The most famous, and largest, internetwork is the *Internet*. An *intranet* is a private internetwork, generally owned by a single organization. Your Internet connection from home is a WAN connection, even when the network at home consists of a single computer. WANs, which traditionally used phone lines or satellite communications, now also use cellular telecommunications and cable networks.

WAN speeds range from thousands of bits per second up into the billions of bits per second. At the low end today are 56 Kbps analog modems (56,000 bits per second). At the high end of WAN speeds are parts of the Internet backbone, the connecting infrastructure of the Internet.

on the
ⓘob *The speed of your communications on any network is a function of the speed of the slowest part of the pathway between you and the servers you are accessing. The weakest link affects your speed.*

Dial-Up WAN Connections   A *dial-up* network connection uses an analog modem (described in Chapter 2) rather than a network card, and uses regular phone cables instead of network cables. In a dial-up connection, you configure the client computer to dial the remote host computer and configure the host computer to permit dial-up access. Once a dial-up connection is established, the client communicates with the host computer as though it were on the same LAN as that computer. If the host computer is already part of a LAN, and if the host configuration allows it, the client computer can access the network to which the host is connected. Many home PCs still use a modem connection for dial-up Internet access. In this case, the host computer is just a gateway to the Internet. This is the slowest, but cheapest, form of Internet access, and in some areas, it may be all that is available.

Broadband WAN   WAN connections that exceed the speed of a typical dial-up connection come under the heading of broadband WAN. Broadband speeds are available over cellular, ISDN, DSL, cable, and satellite technologies. WAN connections can connect private networks to the Internet, and to each other. Often, these connections are "always on," meaning that you do not have to initiate the connection every time you wish to access resources on the connected network, as you do with dial-up. If you wish to browse the Web, you simply open your Web browser.

- ■ **Cellular**   Cellular Internet data connections, also referred to as wireless WAN (WWAN), vary in speed from less than dial-up speeds of 28.8 Kbps to a range of broadband speeds, depending on the cellular provider and the level of service you have purchased. Because the trend in cellular is to provide faster-than-dial-up speeds, we include it under broadband WAN. In the United States, the move away from the original analog cellular networks to all-digital cellular networks supports this trend to higher speeds. The most common digital cellular networks in the United States are based on two standards: *Code Division Multiple Access (CDMA)*, used by Verizon and Sprint-Nextel, and *Global System for Mobile communications (GSM)*, used by T-Mobile and AT&T. Cell providers add other technologies that speed things up. For instance, both Verizon and Sprint-Nextel have used *Evolution Data Optimized (EVDO)* on their networks in the past. Both CDMA and GMS are 3G digital mobile broadband technologies. The next big technology leap is 4G, with many megabits per second promised. Sprint's Worldwide Interoperability for Microwave Access (WiMax) network is the first, with others following suit in 2010.

- ■ **ISDN**   *Integrated Service Digital Network (ISDN)* was an early international standard for sending voice and data over digital telephone wires. These days, newer technologies such as DSL and cable have largely replaced it. ISDN uses existing telephone circuits or higher-speed conditioned lines to get speeds of either 64 Kbps or 128 Kbps. ISDN lines also have the ability to carry voice and data simultaneously over the circuit. In fact, the most common ISDN service, called Basic Rate Interface (BRI), includes three channels—two 64 Kbps channels, called B-channels, that carry the voice or data communications, and one 16 Kbps D-channel that carries control and signaling information. ISDN connections use an ISDN modem on both ends of the circuit. Figure 13-1 shows an ISDN connection between two networks. This connection uses a conditioned phone line provided by the phone company.

FIGURE 13-1

An ISDN network
connection
between two
computer systems

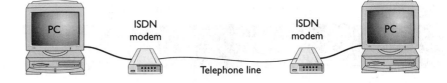

- **DSL** *Digital subscriber line (DSL)* uses existing copper telephone wire for the communications circuit. A DSL modem splits the existing phone line into two bands to accomplish this; voice transmission uses the frequency below 4000 Hz, whereas data transmission uses everything else. Figure 13-2 shows the total bandwidth separating into two channels; one for voice, the other for data. Voice communications operate normally, and the data connection is always on and available. DSL service is available through phone companies, which offer a large variety of DSL services usually identified by a letter preceding "DSL," as in ADSL, CDSL, SDSL, VDSL, and many more. Therefore, when talking about DSL in general, the term "xDSL" is often used. Some services, such as asymmetrical digital subscriber line (ADSL), offer asymmetric service in that the download speed is higher than the upload speed. The top speeds can range from 1.5 Mbps to 9 Mbps for download and between 16 Kbps and 640 Kbps for upload. However, CDSL (consumer DSL) service aims at the casual home user and offers lower speeds than this range. CDSL service is limited to download speeds of up to 1 Mbps and upload speeds of up to 160 Kbps. Other, more expensive services aimed at business offer much higher rates. Symmetric DSL offers matching upload and download speeds. Table 13-1 shows some DSL services and their maximum data transfer speeds. Most of these services are available as second-generation services with higher speeds, indicated with a "2" at the end of the name, as in ADSL2, VDSL2, and HDSL2.

FIGURE 13-2

A DSL connection
showing both data
and voice over
a single phone line

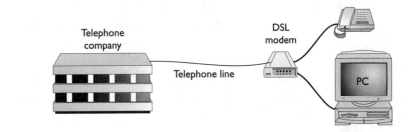

| TABLE 13-1 | DSL Services with Maximum Download and Upload Speeds |

Service	Maximum Speed Download	Maximum Speed Upload	Comments
Asymmetric DSL (ADSL)	1.5–9 Mbps	16–640 Kbps	Different upload and download speeds
Consumer DSL (CDSL)	1 Mbps	16–160 Kbps	Different upload and download speeds. Also called DSL-lite (G.lite)
High-data-rate DSL (HDSL)	1.544 Mbps in North America; 2.048 Mbps elsewhere	1.544 Mbps in North America; 2.048 Mbps elsewhere	Same upload and download speeds
Symmetric DSL (SDSL)	1.544 Mbps in North America; 2.048 Mbps elsewhere	1.544 Mbps in North America; 2.048 Mbps elsewhere	Same upload and download speeds
Very high data-rate DSL (VDSL)	13–52 Mbps	1.5–6.0 Mbps	Different upload and download speeds

■ **Cable**   Cable television service has been around for several decades offering *subscription channel (SC)* television service. Most cable providers have added Internet connection services with promised higher speeds of up to 30 Mbps, which is three times the practical maximum for the typical DSL service. Whereas DSL service is point-to-point from the client to the ISP, a cable client shares the network with their neighboring cable clients. It is like sharing a LAN that, in turn, has an Internet connection. For this reason, speed degrades as more people share the local cable network. You still get impressive speeds with cable, depending on the level of service you buy. Cable networks use coaxial cable to connect a special cable modem to the network. The PC's Ethernet NIC connects to an integrated switch in the cable modem with twisted pair cable.

■ **T-carrier**   Developed by Bell Labs in the 1960s, the T-carrier system multiplexes voice and data signals onto digital transmission lines. Where previously one cable pair carried each telephone conversation, the *multiplexing* of the *T-carrier system* allows a single pair to carry multiple conversations. Over the years, the T-carrier system has evolved, and telephone companies have offered various levels of service over the T-carrier system. For instance, a *T1* circuit provides full-duplex transmissions at 1.544 Mbps, carrying digital voice, data, or video signals. A complete T1 circuit provides point-to-point connections, with a *channel service unit (CSU)* at both ends. On the customer side, a T1 multiplexer or a special LAN bridge, referred to as the *customer premises equipment (CPE)*, connects to the CSU. The CSU receives data from the CPE and encodes it for transmission on the T1 circuit. T1 is just one of several levels of T-carrier services offered by telephone companies over the telephone network.

■ **Satellite** *Satellite communications* systems have come a long way over the last several years. Satellite communications systems initially allowed extensive communications with remote locations, often for military purposes. These systems usually use microwave radio frequencies and require a dish antenna, a receiver, and a transmitter. Early satellite communications systems were very expensive to maintain and operate. Today, a number of companies offer relatively high bandwidth at affordable prices for Internet connections and other applications. Satellite connections are available for both fixed and mobile applications, and these systems offer download speeds of up to 2 Mbps (upload speeds typically range from 40 to 90 Kbps). Satellite providers offer different levels of service. The highest speeds require a larger dish antenna. The authors formerly used a 0.74-meter dish (larger than modern TV dish antennas) with a special digital receiver/transmitter referred to as a modem. This dish and modem combination gives a certain range of speeds, and larger and more expensive dishes provide greater speeds. As with TV satellite service, you must have a place to mount the dish antenna with a clear view of the southern sky. One plan designed for homes and small business has a download speed of 700 Kbps and an upload speed of 128 Kbps. The next higher level of service offers speeds of 1000 Kbps for downloads and 200 Kbps for uploads.

■ **Fiber** In order to compete with cable companies, AT&T, Verizon, and a few other telecommunications companies offer fiber to the home in many areas. Where this is available, subscribers can have the combined services of phone, Internet, and television. The Internet access speeds vary by provider and service level, but look for speeds greater than 100 Mbps.

■ **Permanent virtual circuit (PVC)** A *virtual circuit (VC)* is a communication service provided over a telecommunications network or computer network. A VC logically resembles a circuit passing over a complex routed or switched network, such as the phone company's *frame relay* or *asynchronous transfer* mode (ATM) network. A *permanent virtual circuit (PVC)* is a virtual circuit, created and remaining available, between two endpoints that are normally some form of data terminal equipment (DTE). Telecommunications companies provide PVC service to companies requiring a dedicated circuit between two sites that require always-on communications.

■ **Virtual private network (VPN)**   A *virtual private network (VPN)* is not in itself a WAN connection option, but rather a way to create a simulated WAN-type point-to-point connection across a complex unsecured network. For instance, at one time, if you wanted to connect the computers in a small district office to your employer's private internetwork, you either used a very slow dial-up connection or a fast but expensive physical point-to-point connection. Today, you would connect a single computer or network to the private internetwork over the Internet in a way that keeps your data secure and appears to be a point-to-point connection. You would still need a physical connection to the Internet, preferably a WAN connection, and on top of that you run special software on both ends of the connection that create a VPN. We will revisit the security aspects of VPNs in Chapter 16.

EXERCISE 13-1

Testing Broadband Speeds

Regardless of the broadband service you use, they all vary in the actual speeds they provide from moment to moment. Connect to one of the many broadband speed-testing sites on the Internet and test yours now.

1. Open your favorite search engine and enter a search string. We used **network speed test**.

2. From the results listed in the search engine, select a site (we chose www.internetfrog.com).

3. Follow the instructions for testing your connection. Some sites test as soon as you connect.

4. View the results (see Figure 13-3). Are the results congruent with the service you expect from your broadband connection?

5. Time permitting, try this at another time, or even on another day.

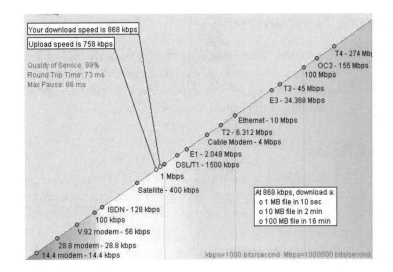

FIGURE 13-3

The speed of
a broadband
Internet
connection
can vary.

Bandwidth and Latency

While the range of a network—the distance over which signals are viable—is one
important defining characteristic of a network, bandwidth is another. *Bandwidth* is
the amount of data that can travel over a network within a given time. It may be
expressed in kilobits per second (Kbps), kilobytes per second (KBps), megabits per
second (Mbps), and even gigabits per second (Gbps); that is, thousands of bits per
second, thousands of bytes per second, millions of bits per second, and billions of bits
per second, respectively.

Another network characteristic related to bandwidth is latency. *Latency* is the
amount of time it takes a packet to travel from one point to another. In some cases,
latency is determined by measuring the time it takes for a packet to make a round
trip between two points. This can be a more important measurement, as it is does
not measure the speed at which the packets travel, but the length of time it takes a
packet to get from point A to point B. It is like measuring the actual time it takes
you to travel by car from Los Angeles to San Francisco. The actual speed you travel
varies by the amount of traffic you encounter and the interchanges you must pass
through. The same is true for a packet on a network.

Network Software

The software on a network is what gives us the network that we know and use. This is the logical network—although it certainly could not exist without the network hardware. In this section, explore the network roles, protocol suites, and network addressing of the logical network.

Network Roles

You can describe a network by the types of roles played by the computers on the network. The two general computer roles in a network are clients, the computers that request services, and servers, the computers that provide services.

Peer-to-Peer Networks

In a *peer-to-peer network*, each computer system in the network may play both roles—client and server. They have equal capabilities and responsibilities; each computer user is responsible for controlling access, sharing resources, and storing data on their computer. In Figure 13-4, each of the computers can share its files, and the computer connected to the printer can share the printer. A typical peer-to-peer network is very small, with users working at each computer. Peer-to-peer networks work best in a very small LAN environment, such as a small business office, with fewer than a dozen computers and users. Microsoft calls a peer-to-peer network a *workgroup*, and each workgroup must have a unique name, as must each computer.

Client/Server-Based Networks

A *client/server-based network* uses dedicated computers called *servers* to store data and provide print services or other capabilities. Servers are generally more powerful computer systems with more capacity than a typical workstation. Client/server-based models also allow for centralized administration and security. These types of

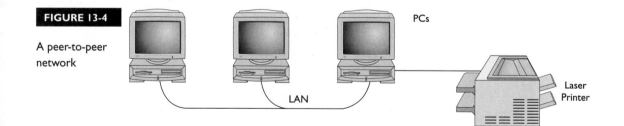

FIGURE 13-4

A peer-to-peer network

PCs

LAN

Laser Printer

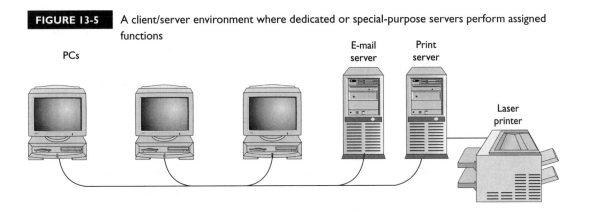

FIGURE 13-5 A client/server environment where dedicated or special-purpose servers perform assigned functions

networks are scalable in that they can grow very large without adding additional administrative complexity to the network. A large private internetwork for a globe-spanning corporation is an example of a client/server-based network. The network administrator can establish a single model for security, access, and file sharing when configuring the network. Although this configuration may remain unchanged as the network grows, the administrator can make changes, if needed, from a central point. Microsoft calls a client/server network a *domain*. The domain must have a unique name, and each client or server computer must have a unique name.

Organizations use client/server environments extensively in situations that need a centralized administration system. Servers can be multipurpose, performing a number of functions, or dedicated, as in the case of a Web or mail server. Figure 13-5 shows a network with servers used for e-mail and printing. Notice in this example that each of the servers is dedicated to the task assigned to it.

on the Job *Although TCP/IP is actually a protocol suite, techs commonly refer to this suite as "the TCP/IP protocol." This is also how the published CompTIA A+ Essentials Exam objectives refer to it. On the job, take your cue from the experienced techs, and use the terms they use for easy communication. Hey, that sounds like a protocol!*

Network Operating System (NOS)

A *network operating system (NOS)* is an operating system that runs on a network server and provides file sharing and access to other resources, account management, authentication, and authorization services. Microsoft Windows Server operating systems, Novell Server operating system, and Linux are examples of network operating systems. The distinction is clouded somewhat by the ability of desktop operating systems, such as Windows 2000, XP, Vista, and Windows 7, to allow file sharing, but these operating systems do not provide the robust services that, coupled with high-performance servers and fast network connections, add up to reliable server operating systems.

Network Client

A *network client* is software that runs on the computers in a network and that receives services from servers. Windows, Mac OS, and Linux, when installed on desktop computers that have a network connection, automatically install a basic network client that can connect to servers and request file and print services. In each case, the automatically installed clients can only connect to a certain type of server. In the case of Windows, it is a Windows server. Novell has client software that comes in versions that install on various operating systems available for accessing Novell servers.

Beyond a basic file and print client, Windows and other OSs usually come with an e-mail client, a browser (Web server client), and other clients, depending on the options you select during installation. You can add other clients. For instance, if you install an office suite such as Microsoft Office 2007, you will have a more advanced e-mail client than the one that comes with the OS. Outlook is the Microsoft e-mail client.

TCP/IP

Every computer network consists of physical and logical components controlled by software. Standards, also often called *protocols,* describe the rules for how hardware and software work and interact together. Ethernet, detailed earlier in this chapter, is a standard for the physical components, such as cabling and network adapters, as well as for the software that controls the hardware, such as the ROM BIOS in the network adapters and device drivers that allow the network adapters to be controlled from the operating system.

However, in most discussions about networks and related documentation, the term "protocol" describes certain software components that work on top of such underlying protocols as Ethernet. These protocols control communication at a higher level, including the addressing and naming of computers on the network, among other tasks. They combine into suites that include a group of protocols built around the same set of rules, with each protocol describing a small portion of the tasks required to prepare, send, and receive network data.

The CompTIA exams require that A+ candidates understand the basics of the *TCP/IP* protocol suite because it is the most common protocol suite used on LANs and WANs, as well as on the Internet. It actually involves several protocols and other software components, and together, we call these a "protocol stack."

In recent years, TCP/IP has largely replaced two other protocol suites for use on most computer networks, namely Microsoft's NetBEUI and Novell's IPX/SPX. You may encounter these in some organizations or hear about them from long-term network techs.

Transmission Control Protocol/Internet Protocol (TCP/IP) is by far the most common protocol suite on both internal LANs and public networks. It is the Internet's protocol suite. TCP/IP requires some configuration, but it is robust, usable on very large networks, and routable (a term that refers to the ability to send data to other networks). At each junction of two networks is a router that uses special router protocols to send each packet on its way toward its destination.

Although the TCP/IP suite has several protocols, the two main ones are the Transmission Control Protocol (TCP) and the Internet Protocol (IP). There are many subprotocols, such as UDP, ARP, ICMP, and more. UDP will be described later in the discussion about common ports; *Address Resolution Protocol (ARP)* is used to resolve an IP address to a MAC address; and ICMP is described in Chapter 15.

TCP/IP allows for cross-platform communication, meaning that computers using different OSs (such as Windows and Linux) can send data back and forth, as long as they are both using TCP/IP. We now briefly describe the two cornerstone protocols of the TCP/IP suite as well as NetBIOS, a leftover from the NetBEUI suite.

Internet Protocol (IP)

Messages sent over a network are broken up into smaller chunks of data, called *packets*. Each packet has information attached to the beginning of the packet, called a *header*. This packet header contains the IP address of the sending computer and that of the destination computer. The *Internet Protocol (IP)* manages this logical addressing of the packet so that routing protocols can route it over the network to its destination. We will describe addressing later in "Network Addressing."

Transmission Control Protocol (TCP)

When preparing to send data over a network, the *Transmission Control Protocol (TCP)* breaks the data into chunks, called datagrams. Each *datagram* contains information to use on the receiving end to reassemble the chunks of data into the original message. TCP places this information—both a byte-count value and a datagram sequence—into the datagram header before giving it to the IP protocol, which encapsulates the datagrams into packets with addressing information.

When receiving data from a network, Transmission Control Protocol (TCP) uses the information in this header to reassemble the data. If TCP is able to reassemble the message, it sends an acknowledgment (ACK) message to the sending address. The sender can then discard datagrams that it saved while waiting for an acknowledgment. If pieces are missing, TCP sends a non-acknowledgment (NAK) message back to the sending address, whereupon TCP resends the missing pieces.

An excellent movie describing how TCP/IP works in an amusing and interesting fashion is available free at www.warriorsofthe.net. It is a 73 MB download and is well worth watching.

NetBIOS

People often confuse NetBEUI with NetBIOS, perhaps because *NetBEUI* was the original protocol suite within which *NetBIOS* was a single protocol. NetBEUI was the default protocol suite on Microsoft networks in the 1980s and 1990s, but TCP/IP has replaced it. NetBIOS is a single protocol for managing names on a network. In a Windows network, you can use NetBIOS names and the NetBIOS protocol with the TCP/IP suite. NetBIOS only requires a computer name and a workgroup name for each computer on the network. NetBIOS naming has limited value in modern networks, and the Internet-style names of the DNS protocol (which requires TCP/IP) have replaced it. Learn more about DNS later in "DNS Server."

Network Addressing

Identifying each computer or device directly connected to a network is important. This is done at two levels—the hardware level, in which the network adapter in each computer or network device has an address, and the logical level, in which a logical address is assigned to each network adapter.

Hardware Addressing

Every NIC, and every device connected to a network, has a unique address, placed in ROM by the manufacturer. This address, usually permanent, is called by many names, including *Media Access Control (MAC) address*, physical address, Ethernet address (on Ethernet devices), and NIC address. For the sake of simplicity, we will use the term "physical address" in this book.

FIGURE 13-6

The physical
address of a NIC,
labeled "MAC,"
and shown on
the NIC

A MAC address is 48-bits long and usually expressed in hexadecimal. You can view the physical address of a NIC several ways. It is usually, but not always, written on a label attached to the NIC. Figure 13-6 shows the label on a wireless USB NIC. The word "MAC" precedes the physical address. The actual address on this NIC is six two-digit hexadecimal numbers, but on this label, there are no separating characters. It is easier to read these numbers if separated by a dash, period, or space, like this: 00-11-50-A4-C7-20.

Locating this address is not always so easy. You can also discover the address of a NIC through Windows. Simply open a command prompt and type the **ipconfig /all** command. The physical address is in the middle of the listing. Notice that it shows six two-digit hexadecimal numbers, each separated by a dash.

This physical address identifies a computer located in a segment of a network. However, you use logical addresses to locate a computer that is beyond the local network segment.

Logical Addressing/IP Addressing

In addition to the hardware address, a computer in a TCP/IP network must have a logical address that identifies both the computer and the network. This address comes under the purview of the IP protocol. The Internet Protocol version 4 (IPv4) and its addressing scheme have been in use for the past three decades. It offers almost 4.3 billion possible IP addresses, but the way in which they were allocated throughout the world reduces that number. The Internet is currently transitioning to Internet Protocol version 6 (IPv6) with a new addressing scheme that provides many more addresses.

An IP address identifies both a computer, a "host" in Internet terms, and the logical network on which the computer resides. This address allows messages to move from one network to another on the Internet. At the connecting point between networks, a special network device called a router uses its routing protocols to determine the route to the destination address, before sending each packet along to the next router closer to the destination network. Each computer and network device that directly attaches to the Internet must have a globally unique IP address. Both versions of IP have this much and more in common. Following are explanations of these addressing schemes to help you distinguish between them.

IPv4 Addresses An IPv4 address is 32-bits long, usually shown as four decimal numbers, 0–255, each separated by a period; for example, 192.168.1.41. Called *dotted decimal notation*, this format is what you see in the user interface. However, the IPv4 protocol works with addresses in binary form, in which the preceding address looks like: 11000000.10101000.00000001.00101001.

IPv4 addresses are routable because an IP address contains within it both the address of the host, called the host ID, and the address of the network on which that host resides, called the network ID (netid). A mask of ones and zeros separates the two parts. When you put one above the other, the ones "cover up" the first part, or network ID, and the zeros "cover up" the remaining part, or host ID. The address portion that falls "under" the ones is the network address, and the address portion that falls "under" the zeros is the host address. In the preceding example, with a mask of 11111111.11111111.11111111.00000000, or 255.255.255.0, the network ID is 11000000.10101000.00000001.00000000, and the host ID is 00101001 (see Figure 13-7). In dotted decimal form, the network ID is 192.168.1.0, and the host ID is 41. Often called a subnet mask, this mask is an important component in a proper IP configuration. After all, the IP address of a host does not make any sense until masked into its two IDs. When you enter the subnet mask into the Windows user interface in the Properties dialog box of the NIC, you will enter it in dotted decimal notation, but we commonly use a shorthand notation when talking about the subnet mask, and you will see this notation in some user interfaces. For instance, a subnet mask of 255.255.255.0 is easily represented as /24. Therefore, using our example

The subnet mask defines the network ID and host ID portions of an IP address.

```
IP address      11000000.10101000.00000001.00101001
Subnet mask     11111111.11111111.11111111.00000000
```

Network ID   Host ID

address from earlier, rather than saying the IP address is 192.168.1.41, with a subnet mask of 255.255.255.0, you can put it together as 192.168.1.4 /24.

The Internet Assigned Numbers Authority (IANA) oversees the allocation of IP addresses for use on the Internet. They did this directly in the early years, and now do it through a group of Regional Internet Registries (RIRs) that allocate the addresses to the largest Internet Service Providers. In the early years of IPv4, they divided the IP address pool up into groupings of addresses, called Class IDs, with five classes, each defined by the value of the first octet of the IP address, as Table 13-2 shows.

So, the organization that received a Class A network ID of 12 actually has more than 16,277,214 host IDs. Obviously, this scheme is a very inefficient way to allocate IP addresses. In fact, they can subnet this Class A network into smaller networks, wasting individual host IDs in the process. Today some organizations have returned all or part of their original allotment, and the large ISPs give out portions of these "classful" networks using subnetting rules called Classless Inter-Domain Routing (CIDR).

IPv6 Addresses   In preparation for the day when ISPs and the Internet routers are fully IPv6 ready, Windows Vista and Windows 7 support both IPv6 and IPv4, as do most new network devices. In fact, some high-speed internetworks already use IPv6. IPv6 has 128-bit addressing, which theoretically supports a huge number of unique addresses—340,282,366,920,938,463,463,374,607,431,768,211,456 to be exact.

TABLE 13-2	Class	First Octet (Network ID)	Address Range	Hosts per Network
IPv4 Class IDs	A	1–126	1.0.0.0–126.255.255.255	16,277,214
	B	128–191	128.0.0.0–191.255.255.255	65,534
	C	192–223	192.0.0.0–223.255.255.255	254
	D	224–239	224.0.0.0–239.255.255.255	N/A because this is a multicast class
	E	240–255	240.0.0.0–255.255.255.255	Reserved

An IPv6 address is shown in groups of hexadecimal numbers separated by colons, such as this: 2002:470:B8F9:1:20C:29FF:FE53:45CA.

When you use the IPCONFIG command in Windows Vista or Windows 7, you will see the configuration for both protocols, but you can also see these details in the GUI. Access this by opening the Network And Sharing Center applet in Control Panel and selecting the task titled Manage Network Connections. Then double-click the connection you wish to view. This opens the Status box for the connection. Notice this dialog box is similar to the one in previous versions of Windows, but with a new button titled Details. Click the Details button to display the Network Connection Details dialog box. Figure 13-8 shows the details for a single network connection as seen in the Windows Vista and Windows 7 Network Connection Details dialog. Notice that this connection has both IPv4 (dotted decimal) and IPv6 (hexadecimal) addresses. Only the IPv4 protocol has addresses for the Default Gateway, DHCP Server, and DNS Server, indicating that this computer is configured for a IPv4 network.

FIGURE 13-8

The Network Connection Details dialog box in Windows Vista

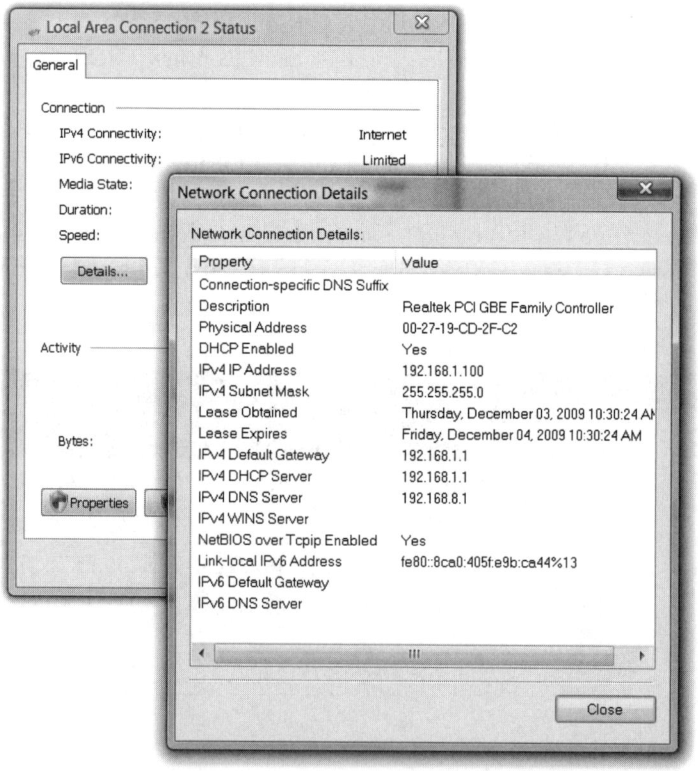

IP Configuration Addresses

When you view the IP configuration for the NIC on your PC, you may be surprised to see other IP addresses besides that of the NIC. These include addresses labeled Default Gateway, DHCP Server, DNS Servers, and (sometimes) Primary WINS Server.

Default Gateway   When your IP protocol has a packet ready to send, it examines the destination IP address and determines if it is on the same IP network (in the earlier example, this is 192.168.1.0) as your computer. If it is, then it can send the packet directly to that computer (host ID 41 in the example). If the destination IP address is on another IP network, then your computer sends it to the IP address identified as the *Default Gateway*. This address is on your network (same IP network ID), and it belongs to a router that will send the packet on to the next router in its journey to its destination. Without a Default Gateway, your computer does not know what to do with packets that have a destination address beyond your IP network.

DNS Server   A DNS client uses the *DNS Server* IP address for name resolution. The *Domain Name Service (DNS)* manages access to Internet domain names, like mcgraw-hill.com. The server-side service maintains a database of domain names and responds to queries from DNS clients (called resolvers) that request resolution of Internet names to IP addresses. A client will do this before sending data over the Internet, when all it knows is the domain name. For instance, if you wish to connect to a McGraw-Hill Web server, you might enter **www.mcgraw-hill.com** in the address bar of your browser. Then, your computer's DNS client (the "resolver") sends a request to a DNS server, asking it to resolve the name to an IP address. Once the DNS server has the answer (which it most likely had to request from another DNS server), it sends a response to your computer. The IP protocol on your computer now attaches the address to the packets your computer sends requesting a Web page.

Primary WINS Server   *Windows Internet Naming Service (WINS)* has a function similar to that of DNS, but it resolves NetBIOS names rather than DNS host names. WINS works in Microsoft networks, but the need for it has diminished over the years. Newer versions of Windows and its client/server environment, Active Directory, can locate computers strictly by DNS name. Sometimes the WINS service is required on a network because of old operating systems or applications that only know how to work with NetBIOS names and depend on querying the WINS service. In that case, the address of the *WINS Server* must be included in the IP configuration.

Assigning IP Addresses to NICs   There are two ways to assign an IP address to a network host: manually and automatically. We will discuss assigning an address manually here and automatically in the next section when we discuss DHCP. When you assign an address manually in Windows, you must open the Properties dialog box for the NIC and enter the exact IP address (obtained from your network administrator), subnet mask, and other configuration information, which includes the addresses for the Default Gateway, DNS Server, and (if necessary) WINS Server. An IP address configured in this manner is a *static address*. This address is not permanent, because an administrator can easily change it, but some documentation uses the term "permanent" rather than "static."

e x a m

ⓦ a t c h   *Be sure you understand how the subnet mask divides the host ID and network ID of an IP address and that you understand the purpose of the following addresses as used in an IP configuration: Default Gateway, DNS Server, WINS Server, and DHCP Server.*

DHCP Server   When you install any non-server version of Windows, the Setup program installs the TCP/IP protocol suite and configures TCP/IP as a DHCP client, meaning it is configured to obtain an IP address automatically. A NIC configured as a DHCP client will send a special request out on the network when Windows starts up.

Now, you would think that a client computer without an IP address would not be able to communicate on the network, but it can in a very limited way. Using a special protocol (BOOTP), the computer sends a very small message that a *Dynamic Host Configuration Protocol (DHCP)* server can read. It cannot communicate with other types of servers until it has an IP address. A properly configured *DHCP Server* will respond by sending the DHCP Client an IP address and subnet mask. This configuration is the minimum it will assign to the client computer. In most cases, the server will provide the other IP configuration addresses, including Default Gateway, DNS Server, and Primary WINS Server. Only Windows networks that require this last address get that one.

A DHCP Server does not permanently assign an IP address to a client. It leases it. "Lease" is the term used, even though no money changes hands in this transaction between a DHCP Client and a DHCP Server. When one-half of the leased time for an IP address (and its associated configuration) has expired, the client tries to contact the DHCP Server in order to renew the lease. As long as the DHCP Server has an adequate number of unassigned IP addresses, it will continue to reassign the same address to the same client each session. In fact, this happens every day for a computer that is turned off at the end of the workday, at which point the DHCP Client will release the IP address, giving up the lease.

Exercise 13-2 will walk you through using a command that will display the physical address, as well as the IP address for your network card. This command is very handy to use because, although you can see the manually configured IP addresses in the properties of a dialog box, you cannot see the automatically configured IP information in this box for a DHCP Client running Windows previous to Windows Vista.

EXERCISE 13-2

CertCam

Viewing the Physical and IP Addresses of a NIC

To view the physical and IP addresses of a NIC, follow these steps:

1. Open a command prompt.

2. In the Command Prompt window, enter the command **ipconfig /all** and press ENTER.

3. The result should look something like Figure 13-9 (Windows XP), only with different addresses.

FIGURE 13-9

Use the IPCONFIG/ALL command to view the physical address and the IP address of a NIC and the other addresses that are part of the IP configuration.

```
Command Prompt                                              _ □ ×
Microsoft Windows XP [Version 5.1.2600]
(C) Copyright 1985-2001 Microsoft Corp.

C:\Documents and Settings\Jane>ipconfig /all

Windows IP Configuration

        Host Name . . . . . . . . . . . . : saguaro
        Primary Dns Suffix  . . . . . . . :
        Node Type . . . . . . . . . . . . : Hybrid
        IP Routing Enabled. . . . . . . . : No
        WINS Proxy Enabled. . . . . . . . : No
        DNS Suffix Search List. . . . . . : localdomain

Ethernet adapter Local Area Connection:

        Connection-specific DNS Suffix  . : localdomain
        Description . . . . . . . . . . . : AMD PCNET Family PCI Ethernet Adapter
        Physical Address. . . . . . . . . : 00-0C-29-09-80-65
        Dhcp Enabled. . . . . . . . . . . : Yes
        Autoconfiguration Enabled . . . . : Yes
        IP Address. . . . . . . . . . . . : 192.168.227.138
        Subnet Mask . . . . . . . . . . . : 255.255.255.0
        Default Gateway . . . . . . . . . : 192.168.227.2
        DHCP Server . . . . . . . . . . . : 192.168.227.254
        DNS Servers . . . . . . . . . . . : 192.168.227.2
        Primary WINS Server . . . . . . . : 192.168.227.2
        Lease Obtained. . . . . . . . . . : Tuesday, January 30, 2007 11:35:49 PM
        Lease Expires . . . . . . . . . . : Wednesday, January 31, 2007 12:05:49 AM

C:\Documents and Settings\Jane>
```

4. The address of the NIC is in the middle, labeled Physical Address. Notice that the physical address is six pairs of hexadecimal numbers separated by hyphens.

5. Three lines below that is the NIC's IP Address.

6. Locate the other addresses discussed in the preceding text, including Default Gateway, DNS Server, DHCP Server (if present), and WINS Server (if present).

7. When you run this command on a Windows Vista or Windows 7 computer, you will also see IPv6 information.

e x a m

watch

All modern network cards support the ability to start up a computer over the network, without relying on a disk-based operating system, using an Intel standard called Preboot eXecution Environment (PXE). Both the computer's BIOS and NIC must support PXE, which includes an extension to DHCP. It can be used to initiate the startup of a computer from a network server to install a new operating system or run diagnostic software, thus allowing an administrator to complete major tasks without physically visiting a computer. The details of using PXE are too advanced for A+, but understand this basic definition of PXE for the A+ exams.

Special IPv4 Addresses   You use public IP addresses on the Internet, each address globally unique. But there are some special IP addresses that are never used for Internet addresses. They are as follows:

- **Loopback addresses**   Although it is generally believed that the address 127.0.0.1 is the IPv4 loopback address, any Class A address with a network ID of 127 is a loopback address, used to test network configurations. If you send a packet to a loopback address, it will not leave your NIC. Sounds like a useless address, but you will use it for testing and troubleshooting in Chapters 14 and 15. Also, note that the IPv6 loopback address is ::1 (0:0:0:0:0:0:0:1).

■ **Private IP addresses**   If an IPv4 network is not directly connected to the Internet or if you wish to conceal the computers on a private network from the Internet, you use private IP addresses. These addresses are used in millions of locations all over the world, and are, therefore, not globally unique because they are never used on the Internet. In Chapter 16, we will describe how you can use these addresses on your private network, yet still access resources on the Internet, thanks to methods that hide your address when you are on the Internet. The private addresses include the following:

   ■ 10.0.0.0 through 10.255.255.255 (1 Class A network)

   ■ 172.16.0.0 through 172.31.255.255 (16 Class B networks)

   ■ 192.168.0.0 through 192.168.255.255 (256 Class C networks)

■ **Automatic private IP address (APIPA)**   If a DHCP client computer fails to receive an address from a DHCP Server, the client will give itself an address with the 169.254 /16 network ID. If a computer uses this range of addresses, it will not be able to communicate with other devices on the network, unless they also have addresses using the same network ID, which means the other computers must also be using an APIPA address. These clients will not have a Default Gateway address and, therefore, will not be able to communicate beyond the local network.

Common Ports

It isn't enough for a packet to simply reach the correct IP address; each packet has additional destination information, called a port, that identifies the exact service it is targeting. For instance, when you want to open a Web page in your browser, the packet requesting access to the Web page includes both the IP address (resolved through DNS) and the port number of the service. In this case, it would be HTTP for many Web pages and HTTPS for a secure Web page where you must enter confidential information. All the services you access on the Internet have port numbers. These include the two services just mentioned, plus FTP, POP3, SMTP, TELNET, SHH, and many more. Each port is also associated with a protocol. The most common protocols for communicating with Internet applications are TCP and UDP. TCP is used for communications that are connection-oriented, which is true of most services you are aware of using, whereas *Universal Datagram Protocol (UDP)* is used for connectionless communications, in which each packet is sent without establishing a connection. Therefore, in Table 13-3, we identify the protocol along with the port number for common TCP/IP services.

TABLE 13-3	Service	Port	Descriptions
Protocol and Port Numbers for Common Internet Services	FTP	TCP 20/21	File transfer
	HTTP	TCP 80	Web pages
	HTTPS	TCP 443	Secure Web pages
	IMAP4	TCP 143	E-mail
	POP3	TCP 110	E-mail
	SMTP	TCP 25	Sending e-mail
	SSH	TCP 22	Secure terminal emulation
	Telnet	TCP 23	Terminal emulation
	TFTP	UDP 69	File transfer

Network Hardware

Network hardware includes many network connection devices that are part of the infrastructure of small networks, as well as large internetworks, and of the largest internetwork—the Internet. The hardware described in this section is limited to the network adapters used in PCs, the medium that connects these adapters to the network, and devices that connect networks to one another.

Network Adapters

While network interface cards were mentioned previously in this chapter, we now focus on this particular type of network hardware device, because each computer on a network must have a connection to the network provided by a *network interface card (NIC)*, also called a network adapter, and some form of network medium that makes the connection between the NIC and the network. NICs are identified by the network technology (Ethernet or Wi-Fi) used, and the type of interface used between the card and the PC, such as the PCI and PCIe interfaces introduced in Chapter 1, the USB or FireWire interfaces defined in Chapter 2, or for a laptop, the PC Card interfaces explored in Chapter 6.

Most NICs come with status indicators—lights on the card itself—and/or as software that displays the status on the notification area of the taskbar. Learn more about these in "Status Indicators" in Chapter 15.

Transmission Medium

The transmission medium for a network carries the signals. These signals may be electrical signals carried over copper-wire cabling, light pulses carried over fiber-optic cabling, or infrared or radio waves transmitted through the atmosphere. In these examples, the copper wire, fiber-optic cable, and atmosphere are the media. When it comes to wired media, one important issue is plenum versus PVC, which we will explore next, and then we'll look at the basics of twisted pair, coaxial, and fiber-optic cabling.

Plenum vs. PVC

Many commonly used network cables use a PVC (polyvinyl chloride) outer sheath to protect the cable. PVC is not fire resistant, and, by code, you cannot use it in overhead or *plenum* areas in offices—those spaces in a building through which air conditioning and heating ducts run. Plenum cable uses a special fire-resistant outer sheath that will not burn as quickly as PVC. Plenum cable frequently costs more, but is required in most areas. Most of the standard cables discussed in this chapter are available in plenum-grade ratings.

Twisted Pair

Twisted-pair cable is the most popular cable type for internal networks. The term "twisted pair" indicates that it contains pairs of wires twisted around each other. These twists help "boost" each wire's signals and make them less susceptible to elec-tromagnetic interference (EMI). The most common type of twisted-pair wiring is unshielded twisted-pair (UTP), which, although it has a plastic sheathing, does not have actual metal shielding.

Twisted-pair cable is also available as shielded twisted-pair (STP), with an extra insulating layer that helps prevent data loss and blocks EMI. However, due to the expense of STP, UTP is more commonly used.

There are several standards for twisted-pair cables, each with a different number of wires, certified speed, and implementation. These standards are often referred to as CAT (short for "category") followed by a number—for example, CAT3 or CAT4. Currently, CAT5 and CAT5e are the most common twisted-pair cable types. Table 13-4 summarizes twisted-pair cable standards. CAT 5e is an enhanced version of CAT5 that was more stringently tested and offers better transmission characteristics than CAT5. CAT6 cable offers even higher bandwidth and improved signal handling characteristics.

	Type	Speed	Common Use
TABLE 13-4	CAT1	1 Mbps	Phone lines
Cable Categories	CAT2	4 Mbps	Token Ring networks
	CAT3	16 Mbps	Ethernet networks
	CAT4	20 Mbps	Token Ring networks
	CAT5	100 Mbps	Ethernet networks
	CAT5e	1 Gbps	Ethernet networks
	CAT6	10 Gbps	Ethernet networks

You can identify a twisted-pair cable by its use of RJ-45 connectors, which look like regular RJ-11 phone connectors but are slightly larger, as they contain eight wires, whereas RJ-11 connectors contain four wires.

on the Job

The oldest cabling you should normally encounter in a business is CAT5, although it is certainly possible to find very old installations of CAT3 cabling, which is not adequate for modern networks running 100 Mbps or faster.

Coaxial Cable

The type of cabling used to connect a cable modem to a cable network is coaxial cable, which consists of a central copper wire surrounded by an insulating layer, which is itself surrounded by a braided metal shield that protects the signals traveling on the central wire from outside interference. A plastic jacket encases all of this. Coaxial cable used for Internet access is usually RG-6 cable with a 75 Ohm rating, whereas the older television-only cable installations used RG-49 cabling with a lesser Ohm rating. Expect an RG-6 cable to connect to the cable wall jack and cable modem with F-type connectors that you must securely screw on.

Fiber-Optic Cable

Until recently, local area networks (LANs) seldom used *fiber-optic cable* ("fiber" for short), but fiber is often used to join separate networks over long distances. Increasingly, however, many new homes, apartments, and businesses have both fiber and copper wiring installed when being built. Also, some phone companies are using fiber to connect to homes and businesses.

Fiber transmits light rather than electrical signals, so it is not susceptible to electromagnetic interference (EMI). It is capable of faster transmission than other types of cable, but it is also the most expensive cable.

A single light wave passing down fiber cabling is a *mode*. Two variants of fiber used in fiber-optic cables are *single-mode fiber (SMF)* and *multi-mode fiber (MMF)*. Single-mode fiber allows only a single light wave to pass down the cable. Multi-mode fiber allows for multiple light waves to pass simultaneously and is usually larger in diameter than single-mode fiber; each wave uses a certain portion of the fiber cable for transmission.

Fiber-optic data transmission requires two cables—one to send and another to receive. Connectors enable fiber-optic cable to connect to transmitters, receivers, or other devices. Over the years, the various standards for connectors have continued to evolve, moving toward smaller connectors. Here are brief descriptions of four types of connectors used with fiber-optic cable:

- **Straight tip (ST)** The *straight tip (ST) connector* is a straight, round connector used to connect fiber to a network device. It has a twist-type coupling.

- **Subscriber connector (SC)** The *subscriber connector (SC)* is a square snap coupling, about 2.5 mm wide, used for cable-to-cable connections or to connect cables to network devices. It latches with a push-pull action similar to audio and video jacks.

- **Lucent connector (LC)** The *Lucent connector (LC)*, also called local connector, has a snap coupling and, at 1.25 mm, is half the size of the SC connector.

- **Mechanical Transfer Registered Jack (MT-RJ)** The *Mechanical Transfer Registered Jack (MT-RJ) connector* resembles an RJ-45 network connector and is less expensive and easier to work with than ST or SC.

Figure 13-10 shows ST and SC connectors.

FIGURE 13-10

The ST and SC connectors used with fiber-optic cable

Connecting LANs

Most LANs now connect to other LANs, or through WAN connections to inter-networks, such as the Internet. A variety of network connection devices connects networks. Each serves a special purpose, and two or more of these functions may be contained in a single box.

Repeater

A *repeater* is a device used to extend the range of a network by taking the signals it receives from one port and regenerating (repeating) those signals to another port. Repeaters are available for various networks. For instance, on an Ethernet network, you would use an Ethernet repeater, and on a Wi-Fi network, you would use a wireless repeater (often called a signal booster) to boost the signal between wireless networks. In both cases, the repeater must be at the appropriate level and speed for the network (Ethernet, Fast Ethernet, Gigabit Ethernet, 802.11b, 802.11g, 802.11n, etc.).

Bridge

A *bridge* is a device used to connect two networks, and it passes traffic between them using the physical address of the destination device. Bridges are specific to the hardware technology in use. For instance, an Ethernet bridge looks at physical Ethernet addresses and forwards Ethernet frames with destination addresses that are not on the local network.

Hub

A *hub* is a device that is the central connecting point of a classic 10BaseT Ethernet LAN. It is little more than a multiport repeater, because it takes a signal received on one port and repeats it on all other ports.

Switch

After the introduction of 100BaseT, the *switch* replaced the classic hub. This is a more intelligent device that takes an incoming signal and sends it only to the destination port. This type of switch is both a bridge and a hub. At one time switches were very expensive, but now small eight-port switches are inexpensive and commonly used—even in very small LANs. As always, each computer or other device in a network attaches to a switch of the type appropriate for the type of LAN. For example, computers using Ethernet cards must connect to an Ethernet switch; wireless devices attach wirelessly to a wireless hub—more often called a wireless access point (WAP). Devices may combine these functions, as in the case of a WAP that includes an Ethernet switch (look for one or more RJ-45 connectors on a WAP).

Router

Connections between networks usually require some form of routing capability. In the case of a connection to the Internet, each computer or device connected to the network requires a TCP/IP address. In order to reach a computer on another network, the originating computer must have a means of sending information to the other computer. To accomplish this, routes are established, and a *router*—a device that sits at the connection between networks—is used to store information about destinations.

Routers use several specialized router protocols to update their list of routes dynamically, such as *routing information protocol (RIP)*, a protocol that dates to the 1980s and is considered obsolete even though it has been updated a few times and is still supported by most routers.

A router is specific to one protocol. The type of router used to connect TCP/IP networks is an *IP router*. An IP router knows the IP addresses of the networks to which it connects, and the addresses of other routers on those networks. At the least, a router knows the next destination to which it can transfer information.

Many routers include bridging circuitry, a hub, and the necessary hardware to connect multiple network technologies together, such as a LAN and a T1 network, or a LAN to any of the other broadband networks. The Internet has thousands of routers managing the connections between the millions of computers and networks connected to it. Figure 13-11 shows a router between a LAN and a WAN.

FIGURE 13-11 A router connecting a LAN to a T1 network

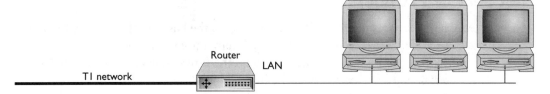

EXERCISE 13-3

Identifying Network Hardware

See what network hardware you can identify in your home, office, or school.

1. If you have a PC in your home and it has a connection to the Internet, locate and identify the network components.

2. If you use a dial-up connection, look for the modem, the telephone cable between the modem and the phone jack on the wall, and the RJ-11 connectors at either end of the telephone cable.

3. If you have a DSL connection, look for the Ethernet cable that runs between your computer and the hub/switch, or modem. Examine the RJ-45 connectors on either end of the cable. The cable may connect to a single box that performs all of these functions.

4. If you have cable Internet service, look for an Ethernet cable between your computer and the cable modem, and then look for a coaxial cable between the modem and the wall connector.

5. At school or work, all you may find is an Ethernet cable connecting your computer to a wall jack that connects to the cable in the walls that connects to the network. Ask the network administrator to describe how you connect to the Internet through the network.

Internet Concepts

In this section, we will explore methods for accessing the Internet and some of the services and protocols that run on a TCP/IP network.

Internet Service Providers

An *Internet service provider (ISP)* is a company in the business of providing Internet access to users. When you connect to the Internet from your home or office, you connect through your ISP. While you are on the Internet, your ISP relays all data transfers to and from locations on the Internet. Traditionally, ISPs were phone companies, but now ISPs include cable companies and organizations that lease phone or cable network usage.

The ISP you select will depend on the type of connection available to you. For instance, a cellular provider will be your ISP if you chose to connect to the Internet via the cellular network, and a cable company will be your ISP if you connect over the cable network. As for DSL, at first local phone companies mainly offered this service, but many other companies now offer DSL using the telephone network, and some telephone companies are now offering Internet access via their fiber-optic networks. Meanwhile, some ISPs specialize in satellite Internet access.

There are also levels of ISPs, with the highest-level ISPs only serving very large corporations and providing Internet access to the ISPs at the next level. The ISP you use from home or a small business may be at the bottom of several layers of ISPs.

In addition to Internet connection services, ISPs now provide a huge number of other services. Some of these services, such as e-mail, are free, but the cost of others, such as hosting Web servers, are based on the complexity of the Web services provided. An e-commerce site in which you sell products and maintain customer lists is an example of a service that would come at additional cost. You also are not limited to purchasing Internet services from your ISP. You now have a huge variety of sources for all of these services.

Internet Services and Protocols

There are a large number of Internet services. You may use many every day if you frequent the Internet. In this section, we will describe a few of these services.

Simple Mail Transfer Protocol (SMTP)

Simple Mail Transfer Protocol (SMTP) transfers e-mail messages between mail servers. Clients also use this protocol to send e-mail to mail servers. When configuring a computer to access Internet e-mail, you will need the address or name of an SMTP server to which your mail client software will send mail.

Post Office Protocol (POP)

Post Office Protocol (POP) is the protocol used to allow client computers to pick up (receive) e-mail from mail servers. The current version is POP3.

Internet Message Access Protocol (IMAP)

Internet Message Access Protocol (IMAP) is a protocol used by e-mail clients for communicating with e-mail servers. This protocol is replacing the POP protocol. IMAP allows users to connect to e-mail servers and not only retrieve e-mail, which removes the messages from the server as they do with the POP protocol, but also manage their stored messages without removing them from the server.

Hypertext Markup Language (HTML)

Hypertext Markup Language (HTML) is the language of Web pages. Web designers use the HTML language to create Web page code, which your Web browser converts into the pages you view on your screen.

Hypertext Transfer Protocol (HTTP)

The World Wide Web (WWW) is the graphical Internet consisting of a vast array of documents located on millions of specialized servers worldwide. The *Hypertext Transfer Protocol (HTTP)* is the information transfer protocol of the Web. Included in HTTP are the commands Web browsers use to request Web pages from Web servers and then display them on the screen of the local computer.

Secure Sockets Layer (SSL)

The *Secure Sockets Layer (SSL)* is a protocol for securing data for transmission by encrypting it. *Encryption* is the transformation of data into a code that no one can read unless they have a software key or password to convert it back to its usable form (decrypt it). When you buy merchandise online, you go to a special page where you enter your personal and credit card information. These Web merchants almost universally use some form of SSL encryption to protect the sensitive data you enter on this page. When you send your personal information over the Internet, it is encrypted, and only the merchant site has the key to decrypt it. As with most computing technologies, there are improvements to SSL, and a newer encryption technology, *Transport Layer Security (TLS)*, is used for secure transmission over the Internet.

Hypertext Transfer Protocol Secure (HTTPS)

Hypertext Transfer Protocol over Secure Sockets Layer (HTTPS) is a protocol that encrypts and decrypts each user page request, as well as the pages downloaded to the user's computer. The next time you are shopping on a Website, notice the address box in your browser. You will see the URL preceded by "HTTP" until you go to pay for your purchases. Then the prefix changes to "HTTPS," because the HTTPS protocol is in use on the page where you will enter your personal information and credit card number.

Telnet

At one time, all access to mainframes or minicomputers was through specialized network equipment called *terminals*. At first, a terminal was not much more than a display, a keyboard, and the minimal circuitry for connecting to the mainframe.

People called it a "dumb terminal." With the growing popularity of PCs in the 1980s, it wasn't unusual to see both a terminal and a PC on a user's desktop, taking up a great deal of space. Eventually, by adding both software and hardware to a PC, the PC could emulate a terminal, and the user would switch it between terminal mode and PC mode.

The *Telnet* utility provides remote terminal emulation for connecting to computers and network devices running responsive server software, and it works without concern for the actual operating system running on either system. The original Telnet client was character-based, and it was a popular tool for network administrators who needed to access and manage certain network equipment, such as the routers used to connect networks.

File Transfer Protocol (FTP)

File Transfer Protocol (FTP) is a protocol for computer-to-computer (called host-to-host) file transfer over a TCP/IP network. The two computers do not need to run the same operating system; they only need to run the FTP service on the server computer and the FTP client utility on the client computer. FTP supports the use of user names and passwords for access by the FTP client to the server. FTP is widely used on the Internet for making files available for download to clients.

Voice over IP (VoIP)

Voice over IP (VoIP) is a set of technologies that allows voice transmission over an IP network—specifically used for placing phone calls over the Internet—rather than using the *public-switched telephone network (PSTN)* or *plain-old telephone service (POTS)*. Both terms describe the worldwide network that carries traditional voice traffic. Several applications allow you to makes calls over the Internet with little or no cost, as compared to regular long-distance phone service. Skype is a very popular VoIP application that uses the peer-to-peer technology used in the Kazaa file-sharing system.

e x a m

🐝 a t c h   *You need to have a general understanding of the Internet services and protocols described here, and you need to know the purpose of an ISP.*

Proxy Server

In many instances, an Internet connection includes a *proxy server*—a network service that handles the requests for Internet services, such as Web pages, files on an FTP server, or mail for a proxy client without exposing that client's IP address to the Internet.

SCENARIO & SOLUTION

My computer is part of a large corporate network. What role is my desktop computer most likely playing in this network?	A large corporate network is a client/server network. A desktop PC in this network has the role of a client.
What is the protocol suite of the Internet?	The protocol suite of the Internet is TCP/IP.
I understand that NetBEUI is very easy to install and use. Why does our corporate internetwork not use it?	A corporate internetwork consists, by definition, of interconnected networks requiring a protocol suite routable between networks. NetBEUI, as a nonroutable protocol, is therefore not used.

There is specific proxy server and client software for each type of service. Most proxy servers combine these services and accept requests for HTTP, FTP, POP3, SMTP, and other types of services. The proxy server will often cache a copy of the requested resource in memory, making it available for subsequent requests from clients without having to go back to the Internet.

CERTIFICATION SUMMARY

IT professionals preparing for the CompTIA A+ exams must understand only the basic concepts of computer networks. More in-depth knowledge is required for other exams, such as the CompTIA Network+, Security+, and Server+ exams. Basic concepts include the geographic classifications of networks into LANs, MANs, and WANs. You must understand LAN technologies, such as Ethernet and Wi-Fi, and the various WAN connection methods, including dial-up and broadband WAN connections like ISDN, cable, DSL, satellite, and cellular. Be able to identify the most common cabling types, connectors, and common network adapters used in PCs.

Understand that TCP/IP is a protocol suite designed for the Internet and now used on most LANs and interconnected networks. Understand network-addressing concepts, including physical addresses assigned to network adapters and logical addresses assigned and used through the network protocols.

Understand the various addresses that are part of an IP configuration and their roles. These include the IP address and subnet mask of the network adapter, Default Gateway, DNS Server, DHCP Server, and WINS Server addresses.

Identify and describe basic Internet concepts, including the role of ISPs and the basic functions of Internet services and protocols, such as SMTP, POP3, IMAP, HTML, HTTP, HTTPS, SSL, FTP, and VoIP.

✓ TWO-MINUTE DRILL

Here are some of the key points covered in Chapter 13.

Network Performance and Classifications

❑ Networks fall into several network classifications, including PAN, LAN, MAN, and WAN.

❑ PAN technologies include the use of standards for wireless transmissions over very short distances. These include infrared (IrDA), limited to about 1 meter, and Bluetooth, which has a range of up to 10 meters.

❑ Common LAN technologies include Ethernet in wired LANs and Wi-Fi in wireless LANs.

❑ Ethernet has several implementations, each with increasing speeds, including 10Base-T at 10 Mbps, 100Base-T at 100 Mbps, 1000Base-T at 1 Gbps over UTP, and 10-GBaseT with speeds up to 10 Gbps. In addition, fiber-optic cable supports fast speeds.

❑ The Wi-Fi standard 802.11a supports speeds up to 54 Gbps using the 5 GHz frequency. Other Wi-Fi standards are more popular. These include 802.11g, which also supports speeds of up to 54 Gbps, but uses the same frequency (2.4 GHz) as its predecessor, 802.11b. 802.11g equipment is usually downward-compatible with the slower and older 802.11b equipment.

❑ The 802.11n Wi-Fi standard provides speeds of up to 100 Mbps and beyond. The standard actually defines speeds of up to 600 Mbps.

❑ Dial-up WAN connections are the slowest and require initiation of the connection every time a user wishes to connect to a remote resource.

❑ Broadband WAN connections, all offering speeds faster than dial-up, include cellular, ISDN, DSL, cable, T-carrier, satellite, and fiber.

Network Software

❑ The roles played by the computer on the network describe the network. The two most general roles are those of clients and servers.

❑ A network in which any computer can be both a client and a server is a peer-to-peer network.

❑ A client/server network is one in which most desktop computer are clients and dedicated computers act as servers.

❑ A network operating system (NOS) is an operating system that runs on a network server and provides file sharing and access to other resources, account management, authentication, and authorization services. Examples of NOSs are Microsoft Windows Server operating systems, Novell Server operating systems, and Linux.

❑ A network client is software that requests services from compatible servers. Windows, Mac OS, and Linux, when installed on desktop computers that have a network connection, automatically install a basic network client.

❑ A protocol suite is a group of related protocols that work together to support the functioning of a network. TCP/IP is the dominant protocol suite.

❑ TCP/IP supports small to large networks and interconnected networks called internetworks. The Internet is the largest internetwork.

❑ Network addressing occurs at both the physical level and the logical level. Every Ethernet network adapter from every Ethernet NIC manufacturer in the world has a unique physical address, also called a MAC address, that is 48-bits long and is usually shown in hexadecimal notation.

❑ Internet Protocol is concerned with logical addresses. An IPv4 address is 32-bits long and is usually shown in dotted decimal notation, as in 192.168.1.41. IPv6 has 128-bit addressing, which theoretically supports a huge number of unique addresses.

❑ An IPv4 address configuration will include a subnet mask, which determines the host ID and network ID portions of an IPv4 address. In addition, the IPv4 configuration may include addresses for a Default Gateway, DNS Server, Primary WINS Server, and DHCP Server.

❑ In addition to an IP address, a packet will also contain a port number identifying the service on the target computer that should receive the packet's contents.

Network Hardware

❑ A network adapter provides the connection to the network medium. Network adapters are available for the various networking technologies, such as Ethernet and Wi-Fi.

❑ Physical transmission media include twisted-pair, fiber-optic, and coaxial cable.

❑ Networking requires various network connection devices. A repeater is a device used to extend the range of a network by taking the signals it receives from one port and regenerating (repeating) those signals to another port.

❑ A bridge is a device used to connect two networks and pass traffic between them based on the physical address of the destination device.

❑ A hub is a device that is the central connecting point of a 10BaseT Ethernet LAN, with all network devices on a LAN connecting to one or more hubs.

❑ More intelligent devices called switches or switching hubs now replace hubs on Ethernet networks. These take an incoming signal and send it only to the destination port.

❑ An IP router sits between networks and routes packets according to their IP addresses.

❑ Many routers combine routing and bridging, and connect multiple network technologies, such as a LAN and a T1 network.

Internet Concepts

❑ An ISP is a company in the business of providing access to the Internet.

❑ There are a large number of Internet protocols and services.

❑ SMTP transfers e-mail messages between mail servers. Clients also use this protocol to send their mail to mail servers.

❑ POP is the protocol used to allow client computers to pick up e-mail from mail servers. The current version is POP3.

❑ IMAP is a protocol used by e-mail clients for communicating with e-mail servers. It is replacing the POP protocol.

❑ HTML is the language of Web pages that your browser converts into the pages you view on your screen.

❑ HTTP is the transfer protocol used to transmit browser-requested Web pages over the Internet to your computer.

❑ SSL is a protocol for securing data for transmission by encrypting it. When you pay for merchandise over the Internet, you connect to a page that uses SSL to encrypt your personal and financial data before sending it to the Web site where it is decrypted.

❑ HTTPS is a protocol that uses SSL to encrypt data and then transports it to the Web site for decryption.

❑ Telnet is a utility that provides remote terminal emulation for connecting to computers and network devices that are running the Telnet server software.

❑ FTP is a file transfer protocol for computer-to-computer transfer of files over a TCP/IP network.

❑ VoIP is a set of technologies that allows voice transmission over an IP network. You use it to place phone calls over the Internet rather than using the public-switched telephone network.

❑ A proxy server is a network service that handles the requests for Internet services, such as Web pages, for a proxy client without exposing the client's IP address to the Internet.

SELF TEST

The following questions will help you measure your understanding of the material presented in this chapter. Read all of the choices carefully because there might be more than one correct answer. Choose all correct answers for each question.

Network Performance and Classifications

1. Which of the following statements is true about a LAN versus a WAN?
   A. A LAN spans a greater distance than a WAN.
   B. A WAN spans a greater distance than a LAN.
   C. A LAN is generally slower than a WAN.
   D. A WAN is used within a home or within a small business.

2. Which of the following is a PAN technology?
   A. Ethernet
   B. Satellite
   C. Bluetooth
   D. 802.11a

3. What is the type of network that connects many private networks in one metropolitan community?
   A. PAN
   B. MAN
   C. WAN
   D. LAN

4. Of the following technologies, which is downward-compatible with 802.11b?
   A. 802.11a
   B. 802.11g
   C. Bluetooth
   D. IrDA

5. Which of the following is usually the slowest WAN connection?
   A. Dial-up
   B. DSL
   C. Cable
   D. Satellite

6. Which of the following WAN technologies uses a network originally created for television transmissions?
   A. DSL
   B. Cellular
   C. Cable
   D. Dial-up

7. Which of the following is a term that describes the amount of time it takes a packet to travel from one point to another?
   A. Bandwidth
   B. KBps
   C. Latency
   D. MBps

Network Software

8. A large corporate internetwork is likely to be this type of network, based on the roles of the connected computers.
   A. Peer-to-peer
   B. Client-to-client
   C. Client/server
   D. Server-to-server

9. What is the protocol suite of the Internet?
   A. TCP/IP
   B. NetBEUI
   C. IPX/SPX
   D. TCP

10. What protocol used on the Internet is concerned with the logical addressing of hosts?
    A. TCP
    B. IP
    C. UDP
    D. ARP

11. What protocol adds the old Microsoft naming system to TCP/IP?

    A. NetBEUI

    B. NetBIOS

    C. DHCP

    D. DNS

12. What divides an IP address into its host ID and network ID components?

    A. Default Gateway

    B. DNS Server

    C. DHCP Server

    D. Subnet mask

13. A NIC has this type of a permanent address assigned to it by the manufacturer.

    A. IP address

    B. Physical address

    C. Host ID

    D. Automatic address

14. A packet with a destination address not on the local network will be sent to the address identified by which label in the IP configuration?

    A. Default Gateway

    B. DNS Server

    C. DHCP Server

    D. Subnet mask

Network Hardware

15. Which of the following attaches to a PC with a bus connector, USB, or other interface, and gives it a connecting point to a network?

    A. WAP

    B. NIC

    C. LAN

    D. PAN

16. Which of the following is not a network medium?

 A. Plenum

 B. Twisted-pair cable

 C. Fiber-optic cable

 D. Atmosphere

17. Which type of cable uses ST, SC, LC, or MT-RJ connectors?

 A. STP

 B. UTP

 C. Fiber-optic

 D. Coaxial

18. Thousands of this type of device exist on the Internet between networks, direct the traffic of the Internet using the destination IP address of each packet, and pass the packets to their destinations along the interconnected networks of the Internet.

 A. Router

 B. Modem

 C. NIC

 D. Hub

Internet Concepts

19. What type of organization provides Internet access to its customers?

 A. Server

 B. Client

 C. ISP

 D. DHCP

20. What Internet service allows users to connect to a mail server and manage their messages, giving them the option to leave the messages they have read on the server?

 A. SMTP

 B. POP

 C. FTP

 D. IMAP

SELF TEST ANSWERS

Network Performance and Classifications

1. ☑ **B.** A WAN spans a greater distance than a LAN.
   ☒ **A,** that a LAN spans a greater distance than a WAN, is not true. **C,** that a LAN is generally slower than a WAN, is not true. **D,** that a WAN is used within a home or a small business, is not true.

2. ☑ **C.** Bluetooth is a personal area network (PAN) technology used to connect devices and computers over very short distances.
   ☒ **A,** Ethernet, **B,** satellite, and **D,** 802.11a, are all incorrect because none of these is a PAN technology. Ethernet is a wired LAN technology; satellite is a WAN technology; and 802.11a is a set of WLAN standards.

3. ☑ **B.** MAN is the type of network that connects many private networks in one community.
   ☒ **A,** PAN, is incorrect because this is a very small personal area network that only connects devices in a very small (usually a few meters) area. **C,** WAN, is incorrect because this type of network connects over long distances. **D,** LAN, is incorrect because this network type is limited to a distance of hundreds of meters that would not span an entire metropolitan community.

4. ☑ **B.** 802.11g is downward-compatible with the slower 802.11b standard because they both use the 2.4 GHz bandwidth.
   ☒ **A,** 802.11a, is incorrect because this Wi-Fi standard operates in the 5 MHz band, which makes it totally incompatible with 802.11b. **C,** Bluetooth, is incorrect because it is a standard for very short distances and is not downward-compatible with 802.11b. **D,** IrDA, is incorrect because this is a standard for very short-range infrared communications, which is totally incompatible with 802.11b.

5. ☑ **A.** Dial-up is usually the slowest WAN connection at an advertised rate of 56 Kbps, but with a top actual rate of about 48 Kbps.
   ☒ **B,** DSL, **C,** cable, and **D,** satellite, are all incorrect because each of these is a broadband service with maximum speeds that go up to several times that of dial-up.

6. ☑ **C.** Cable is the WAN technology that uses a network originally created for television transmissions.
   ☒ **A,** DSL, is incorrect because it uses the telephone network, not a network created for television transmissions. **B,** cellular, is incorrect because it uses the cellular network, originally created for voice transmissions but which has been upgraded to digital and can be used for broadband data transmissions. **D,** dial-up, is incorrect because it uses the telephone network, not a network created for television transmissions.

7. ☑ **C.** Latency is the term for the amount of time it takes a packet to travel from one point to another.

☒ **A,** bandwidth, is incorrect because this is the amount of data that can travel over a network within a given time. **B,** KBps, and **D,** MBps, are incorrect because these terms mean kilobytes per second and megabytes per second, which are used to describe the amount of data that can travel over a network.

Network Software

8. ☑ **C.** Client/server is the type of network found in a large corporate internetwork.

☒ **A,** peer-to-peer, is incorrect because this type of network, where each computer can serve as both client and server, is only used in very small networks of less than a dozen computers. **B,** client-to-client, is incorrect because this is not really a network type. **D,** server-to-server, is incorrect because this is not a network type.

9. ☑ **A.** TCP/IP is the protocol suite of the Internet.

☒ **B,** NetBEUI, and **C,** IPX/SPX, are not the protocol suites of the Internet, although both are protocol suites. **D,** TCP, is incorrect because this is just one of the many protocols in the TCP/IP protocol suite.

10. ☑ **B.** IP is the protocol used on the Internet that is concerned with the logical addressing of hosts.

☒ **A,** TCP, is incorrect because this protocol is not concerned with the logical addressing of hosts. **C,** UDP, is incorrect because this protocol, which we only mentioned and did not describe, is not concerned with the logical addressing of hosts. **D,** ARP, is incorrect because this protocol is not concerned with the logical addressing of hosts.

11. ☑ **B.** NetBIOS is the protocol that adds the old Microsoft naming system to TCP/IP.

☒ **A,** NetBEUI, is incorrect because this is the old Microsoft network protocol suite of which NetBIOS was just a part. **C,** DHCP, is incorrect because this is the protocol used for automatically allocating IP addresses. **D,** DNS, is incorrect because this is the protocol that supports Internet-style names.

12. ☑ **D.** A subnet mask divides an IP address into its host ID and network ID components.

☒ **A,** Default Gateway, is incorrect because this is the name of the router address to which a computer directs packets with destinations beyond the local network. **B,** DNS Server, is incorrect because this is where a network client sends queries to resolve DNS names into IP addresses. **C,** DHCP Server, is incorrect because this is what automatically assigns IP addresses to DHCP Client computers.

13. ☑ **B.** The physical address is the type of permanent address assigned to a NIC by the manufacturer.
☒ **A,** IP address, is incorrect because this is not a permanent address but a logical address not permanently assigned to a NIC. **C,** Host ID, is incorrect because this portion of an IP address identifies the host. **D,** automatic address, is incorrect because this usually refers to an IP address assigned to a PC by a DHCP Server.

14. ☑ **A.** The Default Gateway is the address to which the router sends packets that have addresses not on the local network.
☒ **B,** DNS Server, is incorrect because this server resolves DNS names. **C,** DHCP Server, is incorrect because this server assigns IP addresses automatically. **D,** subnet mask, is incorrect because this is not an address but a mask used to divide an IP address into its host ID and network ID components.

Network Hardware

15. ☑ **B.** A NIC is a device that attaches to a PC with a bus connector, USB, or other interface, and gives it a connecting point to a network.
☒ **A,** WAP, is incorrect because this is a network connecting device. A PC would require a wireless NIC to connect to a WAP. **C,** LAN, is incorrect because this is a type of network that a PC connects to, not a device that connects the PC to the network. **D,** PAN, is incorrect because this is a type of network of devices connecting to each other and to a computer over very short distances.

16. ☑ **A.** Plenum is not a network medium, but rather a characteristic of certain network media (cables), indicating the cable sheath is fire resistant and appropriate to run in plenum space.
☒ **B,** twisted-pair cable, **C,** fiber-optic cable, and **D,** atmosphere, are all network media.

17. ☑ **C.** Fiber-optic cable uses ST, SC, LC, or MT-RJ connectors.
☒ **A,** STP, **B,** UTP, and **D,** coaxial cabling, do not use ST, SC, LC, or MT-RJ connectors.

18. ☑ **A.** A router is the device that exists on the Internet and passes IP packets from many sources to destinations along the Internet.
☒ **B,** modem, is incorrect because it does not pass packets along the Internet, although it is a beginning point for a single computer to send packets. **C,** NIC, is incorrect because this is simply a device for connecting a single computer to a network. **D,** hub, is incorrect because this is an older device used at the heart of a LAN but not an Internet device.

Internet Concepts

19. ☑ **C.** An ISP is an organization that provides Internet access to its customers.

 ☒ **A,** server, is incorrect because this term describes a single computer role, not an organization. **B,** client, is incorrect because this term describes a single computer role, not an organization. **D,** DHCP, is incorrect because this term describes a service for assigning IP addresses, not an organization that provides Internet access to customers.

20. ☑ **D.** IMAP is an Internet service that allows users to connect to a mail server and manage their messages, giving them the option to leave messages they have read on the server.

 ☒ **A,** SMTP, is incorrect because this is a service used to send e-mail, not to pick it up or manage it. **B,** POP, is incorrect because IMAP is replacing this service. POP allows users to connect to a mail server and pick up mail, which is then deleted from the server. **C,** FTP, is incorrect because this service has nothing to do with e-mail but is used for transferring files over the Internet.

14

Installing a Small Office/Home Office (SOHO) Network

CERTIFICATION OBJECTIVES

❑   **702: 3.2**   Install and configure a small office/home office (SOHO) network

❑   **702: 1.1**   Given a scenario, install, configure, and maintain personal computer components

✓   Two-Minute Drill

Q&A   Self Test

I n this chapter, you will learn the tasks required to install and configure client computer access to a LAN or WLAN, focusing on a small network, such as you would find in a small office or home office (SOHO).

■ **702: 3.2**   *Install and configure a small office/home office (SOHO) network*

■ **702: 1.1**   *Given a scenario, install, configure, and maintain personal computer components*

An A+ certification candidate must know how to connect desktop and laptop computers to a LAN, WAN, or WLAN. This requires understanding how to install and configure common network hardware, and how to configure the OS to recognize and work with the hardware. As with all other hardware, vendors occasionally upgrade network hardware drivers, and the technician must understand how to update the network drivers and protocols. A very small subset of Objective 702.1.1 includes working with wired and wireless network cards, while objective 702.3.2 covers a long list of knowledge and skills required to install and configure a small office/home office network, all of which is included in this chapter.

Installing and Configuring Networks

A connection to a LAN requires a network interface card (NIC) for each computer. Therefore, the first step in connecting a computer to a network is to install a NIC appropriate for the type of network—wired or wireless. Once the NIC and driver are installed, you need to configure the NIC with an appropriate IP configuration, along with any other settings appropriate to the type of network.

Installing a NIC

When installing any NIC into a PC or laptop, there are two connections to consider— the connection to the computer and the connection to the network. You must first decide how the NIC will interface with the computer based on the choices available in the computer. NICs are available for all of the expansion bus types for desktop PCs described in Chapter 1. If you need a NIC for a laptop, you will also find NICs for the various laptop expansion slots described in Chapter 6. Similarly, if you need an external NIC, a large selection of USB NICs are available.

Installing an Analog Modem

If you are connecting via dial-up, the modem is, in effect, your NIC. Although modems come installed in most laptops, they are less common in desktop computers. If you need to install a modem in a computer, you will first decide if you want a bus modem or an external modem. At one time an external modem had to use a serial interface, but today they use the USB interface. Installing a bus modem is no different than installing any other bus adapter card. Once you have physically installed either type, start Windows and provide the driver disc if prompted. After that, you will connect the modem to a telephone wall jack, using a phone cable with RJ-11 connectors, which is similar to connecting an Ethernet cable to a NIC, as described in Exercise 14-1. Once you connect it, you are ready to configure the modem, as described later in this chapter in "Configuring Dial-up and Cellular Connections."

Installing a Bus NIC

Because of the array of expansion slots in PCs and laptops, before choosing a NIC to install, you must first determine what expansion bus type or types are available in the computer. Once you have selected and purchased the appropriate NIC for the computer, follow the manufacturer's instructions for installing it. Then, in the case of an Ethernet NIC, connect the network cable (described in Exercise 14-1: "Connecting an Ethernet Cable") and boot the computer.

Installing a USB, FireWire, or PC Card NIC

Before installing a USB, FireWire, or PC Card NIC, check the manufacturer's instructions. In most cases, you will connect the NIC to the USB or FireWire port or PC Card slot and connect the NIC to the network, and then let Windows recognize it. When prompted, provide the disc or location of driver files.

Connecting a Wired NIC to a Network

Connecting a wired Ethernet to a network is a task you will perform many times—whether you are connecting to a simple LAN or to a broadband router. In both cases, you will connect the cable from the PC to a switch, either a simple Ethernet switch or a switch integrated with a broadband router. An Ethernet NIC will need to connect to the LAN using UTP CAT5/5e or better cabling that has RJ-45 connectors and does not exceed the 100 meter distance limit between the computer and the switch for UTP or STP cable. Before connecting the cable, turn off power to the PC and the switch, if applicable. This step may seem a bit extreme and is generally not required, but we have found that some SOHO Ethernet switches include this instruction, which ensures that the switch will properly detect the new connection upon being repowered. Connect one end to the NIC and the other to a wall jack, or directly to a hub (rarely) or switch. In a large organization, a network administrator or technician will tell you where to connect to the LAN, which will probably be to a wall jack with an RJ-45 connector. At home or in a small office, you will normally connect directly to a small switch or to a broadband router with an integrated switch.

Figure 14-1 shows a device that acts as an Ethernet switch, as well as a router to a cable or DSL WAN connection. The cable on the left connects to a cable modem, whereas the center cable connects to the PC. The cord on the right provides power to the device. The manufacturer calls this device a router, although it is a multifunction device, as described in Chapter 13.

FIGURE 14-1

A device that performs the functions of an Ethernet switch and an IP router between WAN and LAN networks.

EXERCISE 14-1

Connecting an Ethernet Cable

You can easily connect an Ethernet cable to an RJ-45 outlet on a PC, switch, or hub.

1. Align the RJ-45 cable connector with the RJ-45 outlet on the computer so the clip on the cable connector lines up with the notch in the center of one side of the outlet.

2. Push the connector into the outlet until you hear the clip click into place. Doing this secures the cable so it makes a good connection and cannot accidentally fall out of the outlet.

3. Use the same technique to connect the cable to an outlet on an Ethernet switch or wall-mounted plate. (See Figure 14-2, in which the cable connector is in front of the outlet on the router.)

4. If this is the first time you have connected an Ethernet cable, practice unplugging it by grasping the connector, pressing on the clip, and gently pulling the connector out. Never force it, or you will break off the clip and then your cable will be not be securely connected. Now plug it back in.

FIGURE 14-2

The clip on the RJ-45 connector must align properly with the RJ-45 outlet.

The next step is to configure the TCP/IP properties of the connection in Windows. Since this configuration is common to both wired Ethernet connections and Wi-Fi connections, we will explore the IP configuration after we examine how to create a Wi-Fi network.

Creating a Wi-Fi Network

Before you install a wireless network, you must consider some special issues for selecting and positioning wireless hardware. These issues include obstacles between the computers and the WLAN, the distances involved, any possible interference, the standards supported by the devices on the Wi-Fi network, and the wireless mode for your WLAN. Then you should take steps to update the firmware on the wireless access point (WAP), if necessary.

Obstacles and Interference

Certain devices emit radio signals that can interfere with Wi-Fi networks. These devices include microwave ovens and cordless telephones that use the 2.4 GHz radio band. WAPs normally support channel selection. Therefore, if you have a 2.4 GHz cordless phone that supports channel selection, configure the phone to use one channel (channel 1, for instance), and the WAP and each wireless NIC to use another channel, like channel 11. In addition, metal furniture and appliances, metal-based UV tint on windows, and metal construction materials within walls can all block or reduce Wi-Fi signals.

on the
job

When a computer or other physical device connects to a network, it is called a node.

Certain businesses and organizations require a professional site survey, a set of procedures to determine the location of obstacles and interference that would disrupt wireless signals. WAP placement is then determined from this site survey. Although a professional site survey is too costly for a small business or home owner, you can use the site survey feature of your wireless NIC to discover which channel nearby wireless networks are using. Then configure the WAP and all the wireless nodes in your WLAN to use a different channel. The name of the site survey feature may simply be Available Network, as shown here, in which a list of wireless networks is shown. Clicking a network in the list reveals the channel in use and other important information.

Distances and Speeds

A huge issue with wireless networks is the signal range of the communicating devices. All of the Wi-Fi standards used give maximum outdoor signal ranges of 75 to 125 meters, but that is for a signal uninterrupted by barriers, such as walls that may contain signal-stopping materials like metal lath. Position a WAP in a central location within easy range of all devices, NICs, and access points.

The farther a wireless NIC is from a WAP, the more the signal degrades and the greater the chance of slowing down the connection speed. Actual ranges for these devices once in place vary greatly. For instance, the documentation for our 802.11g WAP shows that the outdoor range of this device is 40 meters at 54 Mbps and 300 meters at 6 Mbps or less. Indoor range is 15 meters at 54 Mbps and 120 meters at 6 Mbps. Compare that with the ranges for the standards shown in Table 14-1.

In the past, we preferred to use USB NICs attached to a USB cable (Figure 14-3) rather than bus or PC Card NICs that were internal to the computer. The cable gives

TABLE 14-1	IEEE Standard	Operating Frequency	Typical Data Rate	Maximum Data Rate	Indoor Range	Outdoor Range
Summary of Common Wi-Fi Standards	802.11b	2.4 GHz	6.5 Mbps	11 Mbps	~35 meters	~100 meters
	802.11g	2.4 GHz	25 Mbps	54 Mbps	~25 meters	~75 meters
	802.11n	2.4 GHz or 5 GHz	200 Mbps	540 Mbps	~50 meters	~125 meters

FIGURE 14-3

A USB wireless NIC can be positioned for better signal strength.

you more flexibility in positioning the wireless antenna for best signal reception. However, unless you can find a Wi-Fi NIC with a USB 3.0 interface, the 480 Mbps speed of USB 2.0 is slower than the maximum data rate for 802.11n. Alternatively, you can find bus Wi-Fi NICs with antennas attached via a cable to the NIC, allowing you some flexibility for positioning the antenna.

When a wireless network spans buildings, you encounter special problems. For instance, the material in the building's walls may interfere with the signal. Now you need to get creative. For instance, consider a wireless NIC with a directional dish antenna (see Figure 14-4) that you can position in a window and point directly toward the WAP. Another option is a wireless range extender—a device that resembles a WAP but is designed to boost the signals from a WAP and extend its coverage distance.

Another issue is the standard supported by each device. If possible, for each wireless network installation, select NICs and WAPs that comply with the exact same Wi-Fi standard. Even though 802.11g, which is faster than 802.11b, is downward-compatible with the slower standard, even a single 802.11b device on the wireless network will slow down the entire WLAN. Similarly, an 802.11n device is downward-compatible with 802.11a, 802.11b, and 802.11g devices. However, a single, slower non-802.11n device may slow down the entire WLAN.

Additionally, use devices from the same manufacturer, when possible, because some manufacturers build in special proprietary features—support for higher speeds

FIGURE 14-4

A USB wireless
NIC with a
directional dish
antenna

or greater range—that are only available in their device. However, this rule is difficult to enforce in practice, especially when you add a laptop with a built-in wireless NIC to your network.

A *Service Set ID (SSID)* is a network name used to identify a wireless network. Consisting of up to 32 characters, the SSID travels with the messages on the wireless network, and all of the wireless devices on a WLAN must use the same SSID in order to communicate. Therefore, assigning a SSID is part of setting up a wireless network. A WAP comes from the manufacturer with a preconfigured SSID name. You must change this name in the WAP, as well as the default administrator user name and password, so that no one can easily log on to the WAP and change its configuration. Learn how to do this in Exercise 14-2: "Configuring a WAP."

Wireless Modes

The steps required to set up a wireless network depend on the wireless mode you select—ad hoc mode or infrastructure mode. If your goal is to have just two or three

PCs communicate with each other wirelessly, and they do not need connections to other LANs or the Internet, you can consider having these computers communicate directly—without the use of a WAP—in *ad hoc mode*. In this case, each computer will require a wireless NIC, which you must position within range of the others. Then you will configure the wireless cards in each computer to work in ad hoc mode. The wireless nodes communicating together in this mode make up an *Independent Basic Service Set (IBSS)*. This small group of computers is similar to the peer-to-peer model of Microsoft workgroup administrative models.

However, ad hoc is a minimal configuration. Even in a small home network, when you wish to use a Wi-Fi connection to gain access to an Internet connection, you will not use this model. In most cases, the reason for a wireless network is to have access to a wired network or to connect to a broadband connection to the Internet. For this, you will use *infrastructure mode*, which requires a WAP; a WAP acts as a hub for a wireless network.

Many wireless nodes can connect to a single WAP. In fact, the WAP itself may be a multifunction device, acting as a WAP, an Ethernet switch, and an IP router. It, in turn, can connect to a wired Ethernet network, a cable, or a DSL modem. Figure 14-5 shows a WAP. Many manufacturers refer to these as wireless routers. The one pictured is a WAP that you can use to share a broadband connection; it includes a dedicated Ethernet port for connecting to a broadband modem, plus a four-port Ethernet switch.

The wireless nodes (including the WAP) communicating together in infrastructure mode make up a *Basic Service Set (BSS)*.

Ad hoc Setup

If you are setting up two or more computers to communicate wirelessly in ad hoc mode, connect a wireless NIC to each computer. Once the NIC is connected, the Found New Hardware Wizard will run and install the software for your NIC. If prompted for configuration information, select Ad Hoc Mode. The NIC will now communicate peer-to-peer with other ad hoc wireless NICs within range. Although we do not recommend ad hoc mode for most environments, it is very handy in a conference or business meeting for temporarily connecting two wireless laptops together to share files or to print.

Updating the Firmware

Occasionally, manufacturers release firmware updates for their equipment, and WAPs and NICs are not immune to this. These updates can be crucial to the successful operation of your WLAN. Therefore, even if you purchased your wireless equipment

FIGURE 14-5

A wireless access point

yesterday, it is worth taking the time to check out the manufacturer's Website, using the model number and serial number for your devices. Then follow the instructions for updating the firmware on each device. You can update a WAP through its Ethernet port before creating the WLAN, and update wireless NICs through their PC interface, providing the connected PC has access to the Internet through another network. Otherwise, you may have to update the wireless NICs after installing the WLAN.

Infrastructure Setup: WAP

Position a WAP in the center of all the computers that will participate in the wireless network. If there are barriers to the wireless signals, you will need to determine if you can overcome them with the use of an enhanced antenna on the WAP, as shown in Figure 14-6, or a wireless signal booster to reach computers that are beyond the WAP's range. A wireless signal booster physically resembles a WAP.

A wireless access point with an enhanced antenna attached

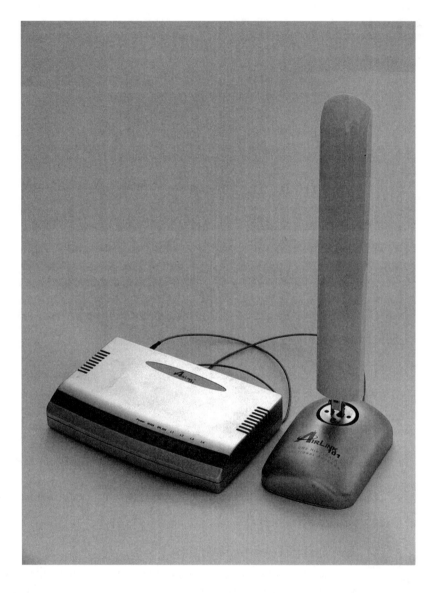

In order to configure a new WAP, you normally connect to it using an Ethernet cable between a computer with an Ethernet NIC and the WAP. Check the documentation that comes with the WAP in case you need to use a special cable. Direct connection via the Ethernet port is only required for initial setup of the WAP. Once it is up and running, you can connect from any computer on the network and modify the configuration.

It only takes a few minutes to set up a WAP physically and then configure it to create your wireless LAN. You will need a WAP and its user manual, a computer with an Ethernet NIC, two Ethernet cables (one may have come with the WAP), and the WAP's IP address, obtained from the user manual. If you are setting this up as a broadband router, you will need the DSL or cable modem. With all the materials assembled, follow these general instructions for connecting and configuring a WAP that is a DSL/cable router, commonly called a wireless router. The actual steps required to configure a WAP may vary from these steps.

These instructions work for most WAPs we have used:

1. Before connecting the WAP, turn off the computer and the DSL or cable modem.

2. Connect one end of an Ethernet cable to the WAN port of the WAP, and connect the other end of the cable to the DSL or cable modem.

3. Take another network cable and connect one end of the cable to your computer's Ethernet NIC and the other end to one of the Ethernet ports on the WAP.

4. Turn power to the modem on, and wait for the lights on the modem to settle down.

5. Turn the WAP's power on by connecting the power cable that came with the WAP, first to the WAP and then to an electrical outlet. If the WAP has a power switch, turn it on now.

6. Turn the computer's power on.

7. Now look at the WAP and verify that the indicator lights for the WAN and WLAN ports light up. Ensure that the indicator light for the LAN port to which the computer connects is lit as well.

Once you have completed these steps, you can test the connection to the WAP, and if all works well, you can configure the WAP settings. Exercise 14-2 will walk you through testing the WAP connection and then using your Web browser to connect and configure the WAP settings.

EXERCISE 14-2

Configuring a WAP

You will need to obtain the IP address for the WAP and then use the PING command to test the connection between the computer and the WAP. Once you determine that the connection works, you can connect and configure the WAP.

1. Open a Command Prompt window in Windows.

2. Test the connection using the PING command. Type **ping** *ip_address_of_WAP*. A successful test will show results similar to those shown in Figure 14-7.

3. Open the browser and enter the address you successfully tested in Step 2.

4. If prompted for a user name and password, use the one provided in the WAP's user manual. At your first opportunity, change this user name as well as the password so no one else familiar with the default settings can connect and change the settings.

5. The next screen should be a setup utility for the WAP. Follow the instructions and provide the type of Internet access (using information from your ISP). Perform other steps appropriate to your type of Internet access, and provide the user name and password required for Internet access so the router can connect to the Internet.

6. Most WAPs, by default, act as DHCP servers, running the DHCP service and giving out private IP addresses to computers on the internal WLAN and LAN (if appropriate). In Chapter 17, you will learn the steps to make a WLAN more secure, but for now, if there is no other DHCP server on your network, leave this as the default. If there is a DHCP server for your LAN, disable DHCP for the LAN (all Ethernet connections), but leave it enabled for the WLAN (all wireless connections).

FIGURE 14-7

A successful test of the Ethernet connection to the WAP

FIGURE 14-8

Change the SSID and other settings, as needed.

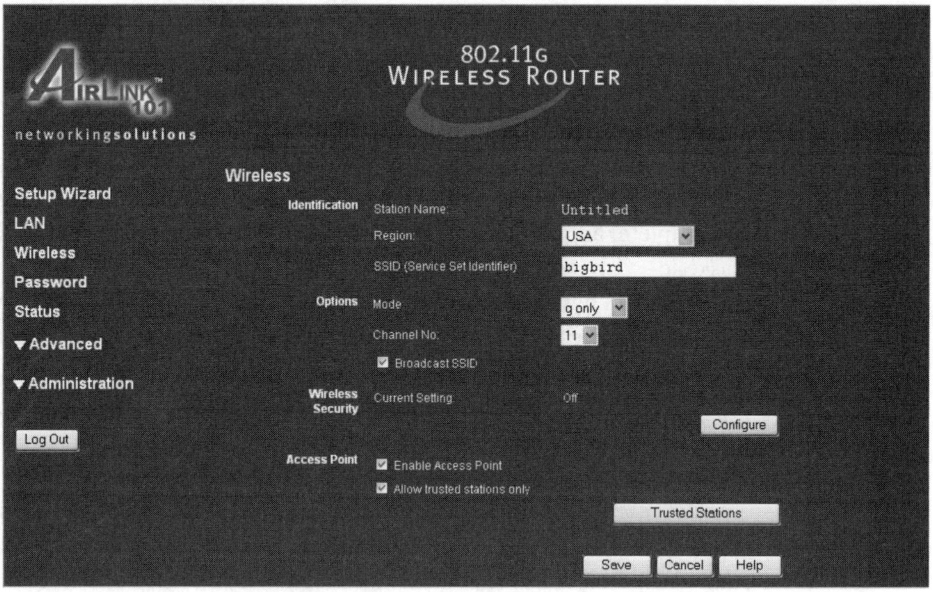

7. A screen will appear in which you can configure other settings for the wireless router. Look for the SSID setting, and change it from the default name to a unique name.

8. Figure 14-8 shows a configuration screen for a WAP with a changed SSID.

9. If all the nodes on the wireless LAN will be using the same 802.11 standard, select that standard for the WAP; otherwise, select a standard that will allow NICs using an older standard to connect.

10. After completing the configuration, save your settings and back up the configuration to a file on your computer (an option in many WAPs or broadband routers), and then log out of the setup program.

Your WAP/router is set up and configured, but not quite ready for use, because you should not use any wireless network without making it more secure. To do this effectively, you will have to configure the WEP or WPA wireless encryption, firewall setting (such as MAC filtering), and disable the SSID broadcast. In Chapter 17, you will learn how to do all these tasks, plus disable DHCP and use static IP addresses. For now, move on to installing and configuring the wireless NICs for this WLAN.

Infrastructure Setup: Wireless NIC

Follow the manufacturer's instructions for installing, connecting, and configuring your wireless NIC. After the NIC is connected, Windows will detect the new hardware, and the Windows Found New Hardware Installation Wizard will display. Select the option Install The Software Automatically and click Next. Follow the instructions to install the NIC, including providing the SSID of your wireless network. Once the installation is complete, an icon for the wireless NIC will appear on the notification area of the taskbar.

Once you have installed the software, you can change the configuration by double-clicking the systray icon for your wireless NIC. This program will let you search for available wireless networks, change the mode in which your wireless NIC is operating, set security settings for encryption of the data transmitted, change channels, and much more.

As shown here, status messages will appear over your notification area when a wireless connection is first established and when a wireless connection fails. These messages only display briefly, so most NICs also change the appearance of the icon, showing perhaps a blue or green icon when the NIC is connected and a red icon, or an icon with an x over it, when the NIC is disconnected. A laptop with an integrated wireless adapter will usually have a hardware switch to enable or disable the wireless connection. Be sure you have this turned on.

IP Configuration

By default, Windows assumes that each network connection will receive an IP address automatically via a DHCP server on your network. This is true of connections made via an Ethernet NIC as well as through a wireless NIC.

You may need to set up a computer on a LAN in which all the computers are assigned static IP addresses. In that case, you will obtain the configuration information from a LAN administrator and then manually enter an IP configuration into Windows. This information should include the IP configuration addresses described in Chapter 13. The list will resemble Table 14-2, although the actual addresses will be unique to your network. Notice that these are private IP addresses. Add the address for a WINS Server only if the computer is part of a routed network that requires WINS.

TABLE 14-2	IP Configuration Setting	Setting Value
Sample IP Configuration Settings	IP address	192.168.227.138
	Subnet mask	255.255.255.0
	Default Gateway	192.168.227.2
	DNS Server	192.168.227.3
	WINS Server (rarely used)	192.168.227.4

If you need to manually configure IP settings, make a list similar to that in Table 14-2, showing the required settings that you received from your network administrator. Then open the IP configuration dialog for your network adapter. Exercise 14-3 describes how to do this in Windows XP, and Exercise 14-4 describes the steps used in Windows Vista and Windows 7.

EXERCISE 14-3

Manually Configuring IP Settings in Windows XP

The following steps will guide you through entering IP configuration settings into Windows XP. The steps are very similar in Windows 2000.

1. Open the Network Connections applet in Control Panel, and then select and right-click the icon for the network connection you wish to configure. Select Properties from the context menu.

2. The resulting dialog box will vary based on the type of connection. The General tab of an Ethernet or wireless connection will have a Connect Using field showing the NIC and the list of protocols and services used by that NIC (called Items), whereas a dial-up or cellular connection will have the list of protocols and services on the Networking tab.

3. Locate the list of items used by the connection, and double-click Internet Protocol (TCP/IP) to open the Properties dialog box. Click the radio button labeled Use The Following IP Address.

4. Enter the IP address, subnet mask, and Default Gateway settings.

5. If you have a DNS Server address, click the radio button labeled Use The Following DNS Server Addresses and enter the Preferred DNS Server. If you have an address for the Alternate Server, enter that address, too.

Test the configuration by pinging the gateway.

```
Command Prompt                                          _ □ ×
Microsoft Windows XP [Version 5.1.2600]
(C) Copyright 1985-2001 Microsoft Corp.

C:\Documents and Settings\Jane>ping 192.168.227.2

Pinging 192.168.227.2 with 32 bytes of data:

Reply from 192.168.227.2: bytes=32 time=40ms TTL=128
Reply from 192.168.227.2: bytes=32 time<1ms TTL=128
Reply from 192.168.227.2: bytes=32 time<1ms TTL=128
Reply from 192.168.227.2: bytes=32 time<1ms TTL=128

Ping statistics for 192.168.227.2:
    Packets: Sent = 4, Received = 4, Lost = 0 (0% loss),
Approximate round trip times in milli-seconds:
    Minimum = 0ms, Maximum = 40ms, Average = 10ms
```

6. Check the numbers you entered, click OK to accept these settings, and then click the Close button in the Properties dialog box.

7. To test your settings, open a Command Prompt window and ping the gateway address to ensure that your computer can communicate on the LAN. If your configuration is correct, and if the gateway router is functioning, you should see four replies. Figure 13-9 shows the results of pinging a gateway address of 192.168.227.2.

EXERCISE 14-4

CertCam

Manually Configuring IP Settings in Windows Vista

The following steps will guide you through entering IP configuration settings into Windows Vista. The steps are very similar in Windows 7.

1. Open the Network And Sharing Center applet in Control Panel, and select Manage Network Connections from the list of Tasks in the left pane to open the Network Connections window.

2. Select and right-click the icon for the network connection you wish to configure. Select Properties from the context menu.

3. Locate the list of items used by the connection and double-click Internet Protocol Version 4 (TCP/IPv4) to open the Properties dialog box. Click the radio button labeled Use The Following IP Address.

4. Enter the IP address, subnet mask, and Default Gateway settings.

FIGURE 14-10

Static IP information in the Windows Vista Internet Protocol Version 4 (TCP/IPv4) Properties dialog.

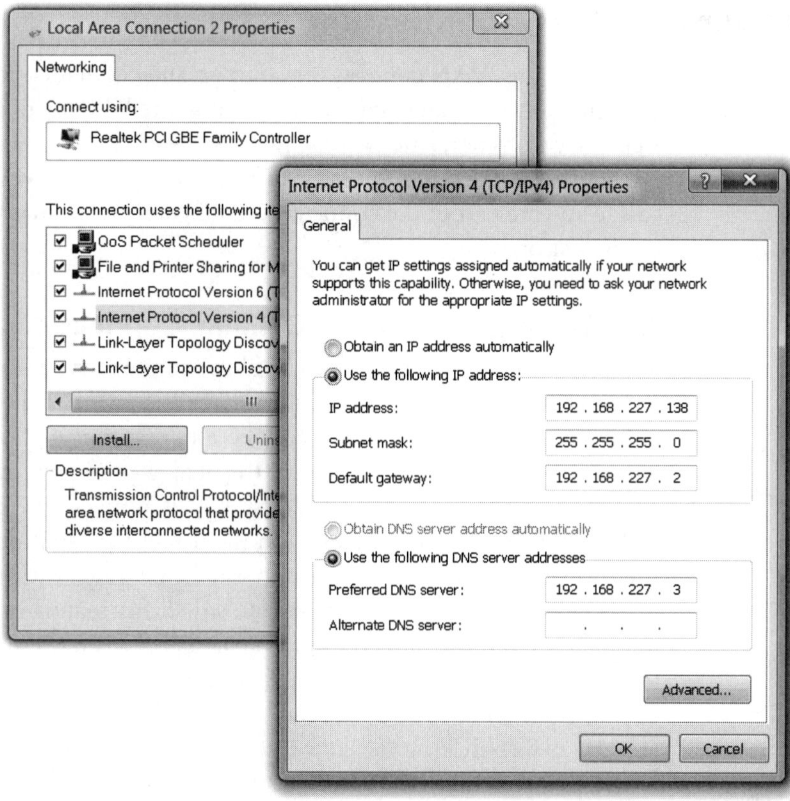

5. If you have a DNS Server address to use, click the radio button labeled Use The Following DNS Server Addresses and enter the Preferred DNS Server. If you have an address for the Alternate Server, enter that address, too.

6. If you have a WINS Server address, click the Advanced button, select the WINS tab, click the Add button, and enter the address. Click Add and click OK to close the Advanced TCP/IP Settings.

7. The Internet Protocol Version 4 (TCP/IPv4) Properties dialog box should resemble Figure 14-10. Check the numbers you entered, click OK to accept these settings, and then click the Close button in the Properties dialog box for the connection.

8. To test your settings, open a Command Prompt window and ping the gateway address to ensure your computer can communicate on the LAN. If your configuration is correct, and if the gateway router is functioning, you should see four replies.

Configuring a WAN Connection

Of the various WAN connections, dial-up and cellular connections have similar configuration steps, and DSL, cable, and satellite WAN configurations have common steps. A VPN is not, strictly speaking, a WAN connection, as it depends on an existing network connection, but because VPNs are used to make WAN connections more secure and are part of the connection configuration for many users, we include VPN configuration here.

Configuring Dial-up and Cellular Connections

The steps to configure dial-up and cellular connections are very similar because, in both cases, the WAN connection device is connected directly to the computer, and it provides a point-to-point connection, requiring a phone number or similar address to connect. First, you install the analog or cellular modem, which creates a connection object in the Windows Network Connections dialog box. In the case of an analog modem, the installation is entirely separate from the configuration of the connection because you do not normally purchase the modem from the dial-up provider. For a dial-up connection, you will either manually enter the connection information into the Properties for the modem, or you will use a configuration utility received from the ISP. In either case, enter the phone number, logon name, and other configuration information. You can view the status of a modem (disabled, enabled, etc.) by double-clicking the connection object in the Network Connections window.

A cellular modem will come directly from your cellular service provider, and you will install and configure it in one operation. When you run the installation disc to install the device driver and other software for the cellular connection, you will be prompted to enter the connection information you received for your connection from the ISP. When you wish to view the configuration of a cellular connection, you will use the cell provider's software, but you will also normally be able to view it through the connection's Properties from the Network Connections windows. In fact, attempting to do this through the Network Connections window may result in an error message similar to this one that came up when we double-clicked the Verizon modem. Clicking the Advanced button opens the Properties dialog where we can view and change the settings.

Configuring DSL, Cable, and Satellite Connections

The configuration of a client computer for DSL, cable, and satellite connections is very similar. Connect a cable between the client's Ethernet NIC and a switch that connects to the broadband router. In many cases, the broadband router will have an integrated switch. Then the broadband router will have a DHCP server enabled, and it will give the client computer an appropriate IP configuration. If DHCP is disabled on the router, then you will need to know the address of the LAN interface of the router versus the WAN interface. Once you know this, you can configure the client's NIC with an IP address with the same NetID, and also provide it with the LAN address of the router as the client's Default Gateway. The final piece of IP configuration is the address of a DNS Server. Your ISP will give you this.

Configuring a VPN Connection

Before you can configure a VPN, you must have the specific configuration information, which you will obtain from whomever is providing the VPN connection. You will need the host name or IP address of the VPN. Then, to configure the VPN connection in Windows XP or Windows Vista, open the Internet Options applet from Control Panel, and select the Connections page. Here is where things differ between these two Windows versions. In Windows XP, click the Add button to open the New Connection Wizard (see Figure 14-11), in which you will select the radio button labeled Connect To A Private Network Through The Internet. Continue through the Wizard, entering the required information.

From the Connections page in Windows Vista, click the Add VPN button, which opens the Create A VPN connection wizard, as shown in Figure 14-12.

The Windows XP New Connection Wizard

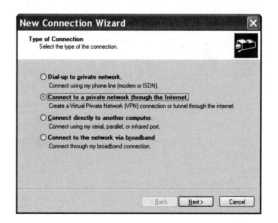

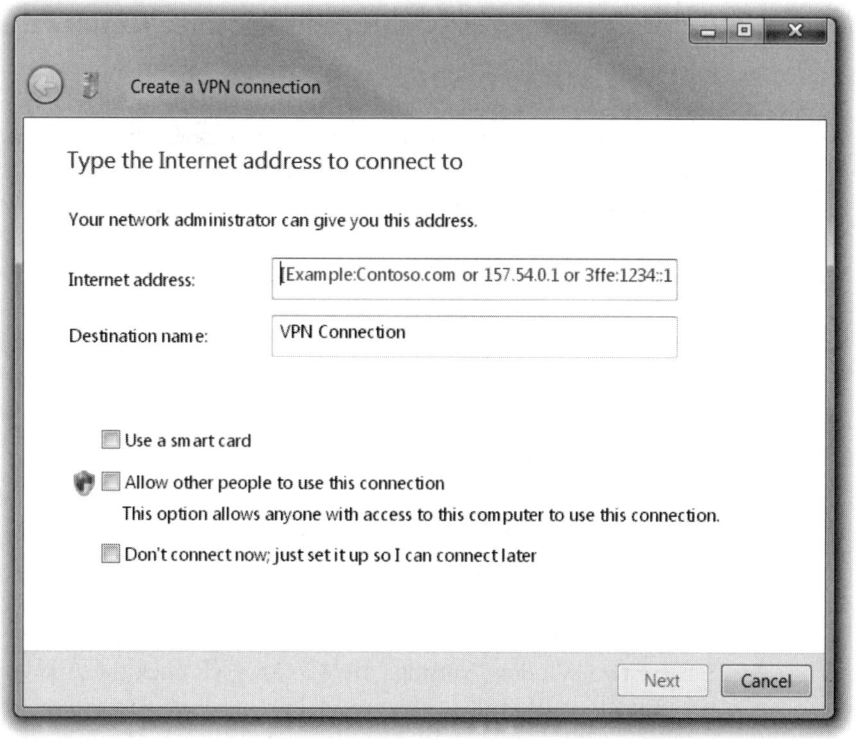

FIGURE 14-12

The Windows
Vista VPN
Connection
Wizard

Create a VPN connection

Type the Internet address to connect to

Your network administrator can give you this address.

Internet address: | [Example:Contoso.com or 157.54.0.1 or 3ffe:1234::1

Destination name: | VPN Connection

☐ Use a smart card

🛡 ☐ Allow other people to use this connection
This option allows anyone with access to this computer to use this connection.

☐ Don't connect now; just set it up so I can connect later

Next   Cancel

Configuring Bluetooth

If your computer does not have Bluetooth, you can purchase and install a Bluetooth transceiver, exactly as you would install any device in your PC, depending on the PC's interface. The one corollary to this is that the Bluetooth driver packaged with the device may be better than the one installed with Windows, especially with Windows XP, in which case, you may be wise to install the driver before installing the Bluetooth transceiver into the computer. Look for the Bluetooth Devices applet in Control Panel, as seen here.

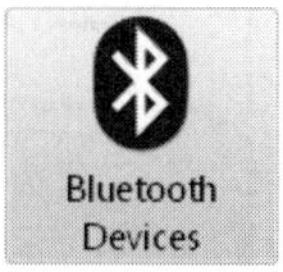

When installing and configuring a Bluetooth device, you should not have version problems, even though there have been two major Bluetooth standards, 1.0 and 2.0, as well as 1.0B, 1.1, 1.2, and 2.1. Each new version has improved discovery and connection, as well as speed, with the latest versions reducing the power consumption of the devices. New devices should be at version 2.1, and each version beginning with 1.2 is backward-compatible. If you are connecting two devices that comply with different versions of the standard, the connection will only support the speed and features of the older version.

The most common Bluetooth device you may need to connect to a PC is a cell phone or smart phone; in which case, you will need to first access the phone's Bluetooth configuration menu and make sure it has a name and is discoverable. If your computer has Bluetooth installed, and it is enabled, then simply turn on the Bluetooth device within range of the PC's Bluetooth transceiver, and then open the Bluetooth Devices applet and click Add (Windows XP) or Add Wireless Device (Windows Vista and Windows 7). Then follow the steps in the wizard, including entering a password and enabling encryption. Bluetooth security is not very strong; therefore, if you keep sensitive information on your phone, never use Bluetooth communications if it is possible for someone who might be able to crack the passkey and encryption to pick up your signals. The very short range of Bluetooth devices is probably the best security they offer.

Installing Basic VoIP

Once a rogue technology used by people trying to avoid telephone company long-distance call charges, Voice over IP (VoIP) has now been embraced by those same telephone companies. If you live in an area where one of these companies offers the service, you can purchase it from them. Look for it under the title of "broadband phone service." Qwest, for instance, offers it in some areas where they can provide connections of at least 1.5 Mbps. We recommend a higher speed.

If you have connected your computer to a broadband router, or connected a modem to a phone line, you have the skills necessary for installing VoIP in your home or small office. If you sign up for this service, the company provides a broadband modem and a broadband phone adapter. You must have the company's broadband Internet service to subscribe to its broadband phone service. The modem, a conventional DSL modem, connects to the wall jack with phone wire and an RJ-11 connector, and you connect the broadband phone adapter via Ethernet cable to an Ethernet port on the broadband modem. You then connect an analog phone to the RJ-11 connector on the broadband phone adapter, which acts as an *Integrated Access Device (IAD)*, a device that converts digital signals from the broadband connection to voice for the analog phone, and the analog voice signals to digital signals for the digital network. A computer is not necessary for this service. The basic broadband phone service costs about $20 a month in some cities.

Similarly, cable providers offer this service in some areas, and it is as easy to install it as it is to install a cable Internet connection because, of course, that is required for the service. On a cable network, the generic name for the device used at the customer site for the analog/digital conversion is Multimedia Terminal Adapter (MTA), and it sits between an analog phone and the cable modem. An MTA is unnecessary if you connect a digital IP telephone set directly to the cable modem. Cisco, among others, manufacturers these phones.

There are many VoIP services, including the very popular Skype, which offers free service between Skype users, but charges for calling outside their network. You will need speakers and a microphone (headset preferred) and a broadband connection, as well as Windows 2000 or newer. A Webcam is optional. Simply point your browser to www.skype.com and download the program. The installation takes several minutes, and after the setup screen closes, the Skype Create Account window opens. Here, you must provide your name, a Skype Name, and a password. Once you complete this information, you log on and the Welcome screen displays over the Skype console window, as shown in Figure 14-13. From the Welcome Screen, you can browse the services offered by Skype, check your microphone, headset, and Webcam, find friends, and import contacts. If all checks out, then close this window and make your first call from the Skype window. The Echo/Sound Test Service is automatically included in your contacts list, so this is a good first call. You hear a recorded voice and then you respond. Skype records your voice and then plays it back to you. You are now ready to use Skype.

These VoIP services are the most basic and generally for only one or two phones. If you need to provide this service for many phones at a single site, you may need to purchase a piece of equipment called a SMB IP PBX, designed for small to medium businesses. A Private Branch Exchange (PBX) is a device with functions that provide services similar to the equipment in the phone company's central office. A SMB IP PBX connects to either one or more standard phone lines, or to a T-1 line or better. Then, you connect an Ethernet cable to this device and to your LAN switch. Finally, you connect special IP phones with Ethernet connections to the network. Further configuration is required for this type of setup—some of it by the phone company and some of it by you following the company's instructions for configuring the PBX. After VoIP is configured and in use, the only charges are for the connections.

FIGURE 14-13 The Skype Welcome Screen

Installing and Configuring Web Browsers

While the World Wide Web (the Web) is just one of the many services that exist on the Internet, it alone is responsible for most of the huge growth in Internet use that began after the Web's introduction in the 1990s. Web technologies changed the look of Internet content from all text to rich and colorful graphics and made it simple to navigate by using a special type of client called a *Web browser*. The two top browsers are Microsoft's Internet Explorer and Mozilla's FireFox. Other browsers, such as Opera (at www.opera.com) and Google's Chrome currently have a very small share of this market. In this section, learn how to configure and install Internet Explorer and Firefox, how to install and manage browser add-ons, and how to configure proxy settings.

The Web browser's ease of use hides the Internet's complexity, because it uses protocols to transfer the contents from a Web page to the user's computer, where the Web browser translates the plain-text language into a rich, colorful document that may contain links to other pages—often at disparate locations on the Internet. We'll describe Internet Explorer and Mozilla Firefox in the next sections, and we will describe security settings for these two Web browsers in Chapter 17.

A related service is a proxy server, also described in the next sections. If this service is available on your network, you may need to configure your computer as a proxy client. Learn more about the relationships among proxy servers and Web browsers and other services.

Browser Add-ons

You can add functionality to a browser by installing add-ons, small programs that are often free and available as downloads, and are also called browser helper objects (BHOs) or plug-ins. For instance, most of us depend on being able to open Adobe PDF files within our browsers. Doing this is possible only if you have installed the Adobe Acrobat add-on. Some add-ons change the browser interface by adding toolbars, such as those from Yahoo and Google. There are add-ons for quickly accessing one or more social networking sites, helping you track the bidding on eBay, keeping up-to-date on the latest news, and much more. Some programs that you install for other purposes, such as security suites, also include browser add-ons. Therefore, when you install programs, watch for options to install a browser toolbar and decide if you really need another add-on to your browser.

View and manage the installed add-ons in Internet Explorer 8 by opening the Tools menu and selecting Manage Add-ons; in Firefox, open the Tools menu and select Add-ons. You can disable or enable add-ons in this dialog. Our favorite add-on is the FireFTP add-on to Firefox, which we use for FTP file transfers with various FTP servers.

Internet Explorer

In August 1995, Microsoft introduced the *Internet Explorer (IE)* Web browser when they launched the Windows 95 operating system. IE was included (or bundled) free with the operating system, and it has been included in each subsequent Windows version. Free updates to newer versions of IE for Windows and Mac OSs are available at the Microsoft Website.

Installing and Upgrading Internet Explorer

Internet Explorer is well-integrated into the OS. You should not need to install IE, but expect to upgrade it as Microsoft releases a new version every few years. If you have Automatic Updates turned on, it will download and install updates to IE automatically. You can also use Windows Update from the Start menu, or go directly to the Microsoft download site at www.microsoft.com/downloads.

If you install a second Web browser, do not uninstall IE. Not only is it not advisable to uninstall IE, some Web pages do not display correctly in other browsers, but look fine in IE. This functionality has to do with Web page content that is running small programs in ActiveX, which run best in IE. ActiveX is a technology developed by Microsoft for making Web pages more interactive by downloading small programs from Websites and running them in an ActiveX-enabled browser—mainly Internet Explorer. These programs include sound files, Java applets, and animation.

Conversely, some Web pages may not display properly in IE but will work fine in other Web browsers, including Mozilla's Firefox. In this scenario, the problem may be one or more Java scripts that are not compatible with IE. In the past, we have run into problems with Web pages not working in Firefox; these problems have disappeared in recent versions of the browser, but could still be a problem with certain Websites.

Configuring Internet Explorer

Configure Internet Explorer through its Tools menu. From here, in IE 8, you can turn on and configure the Pop-up Blocker, turn on and configure a Phishing Filter (learn about phishing in Chapter 16), run Windows Update, diagnose connection problems, and open the Internet Options dialog box, which has pages of settings to further control IE's behavior. You can also manage add-ons such as Adobe PDF Reader, Link Helper, Diagnose Connection Problems, Sun Java Console, and Windows Messenger.

Firefox

Firefox, by Mozilla, is an increasingly popular free Web browser. Some consider it a safer Web browser than Internet Explorer because malicious attacks do not target it as much as they do the Microsoft browser. You still need to have security in place when you use Firefox.

Installing and Upgrading Firefox

To download Firefox, point your browser to www.mozilla.com and follow the instructions for downloading and installing Firefox. The installation process will copy your Favorites from Internet Explorer. You will have an opportunity to select Firefox as your default browser during installation. The default browser is the browser Windows opens when the user clicks a URL.

Configuring Firefox

There are many options for configuring Firefox. You should do the first configuration task as soon as Firefox is installed, and that is to open the Options dialog box from the Tools menu, select Advanced, and then select the Update page. If you have a broadband Internet connection, make sure Firefox is set to check for Firefox updates, installed add-ons, and search engines automatically. If you did not make Firefox your default browser during the installation, and you want to do so later, select Tools | Options, and on the General tab, click the Check Now button under System Defaults. When it detects that Firefox is not your default browser, it will offer to change the setting. Then decide what action you want taken when it discovers updates. Choose between having Firefox ask what you want to do when it discovers an update or having Firefox automatically download and install the update. Find additional settings on the Advanced page. The General tab includes settings for Accessibility, Browsing, and System Defaults.

Use the Options dialog box to configure Firefox further. The Startup options on the Main page allow you to configure the home page—the page that appears when you first open the browser—and the connection settings. The Downloads options let you choose what happens when you are downloading files, including the display of the Downloads window and where the files should be saved.

Also configure the settings for Tabs, Content, Applications, Privacy, and Security.

Configure Proxy Settings

If your network has a proxy server, you can configure your browser to send requests to the proxy server, which will forward and handle all requests. To configure Windows to use a proxy server, open Control Panel's Internet Options applet and click the Connections tab. This tab has two places for configuring a proxy server, depending on how you connect to the Internet.

If you have a dial-up connection, click the Settings button under Dial-up, and then Virtual Private Network settings. Follow the instructions for configuring the proxy server, which will include entering the server's IP address.

If your computer connects to the Internet through a LAN, go to the bottom of the Connection page, and click the LAN Settings button to open the Local Area Network (LAN) Settings dialog. Under Proxy Server, click to place a check in the box labeled Use A Proxy Server For Your LAN. (These setting will not apply to dial-up or VPN connections.) Then enter the IP address in the Address box and the Port number (obtained from your network administrator or from the documentation for the proxy server) in the Port box. Click Advanced if you need to add more addresses and ports for other services. Figure 14-14 shows the Proxy Settings dialog in Windows Vista, which is similar to that in Windows 2000, XP, and 7.

However, Windows only provides options for four types of proxy servers: HTTP, Secure (HTTPS), FTP, and Socks. You should be familiar with all but the last of these terms. Socks is a proxy server protocol. If you have a proxy server for other services not supported by Windows, you will need to install a proxy client provided by the vendor of the server software.

FIGURE 14-14

Proxy Settings for Windows

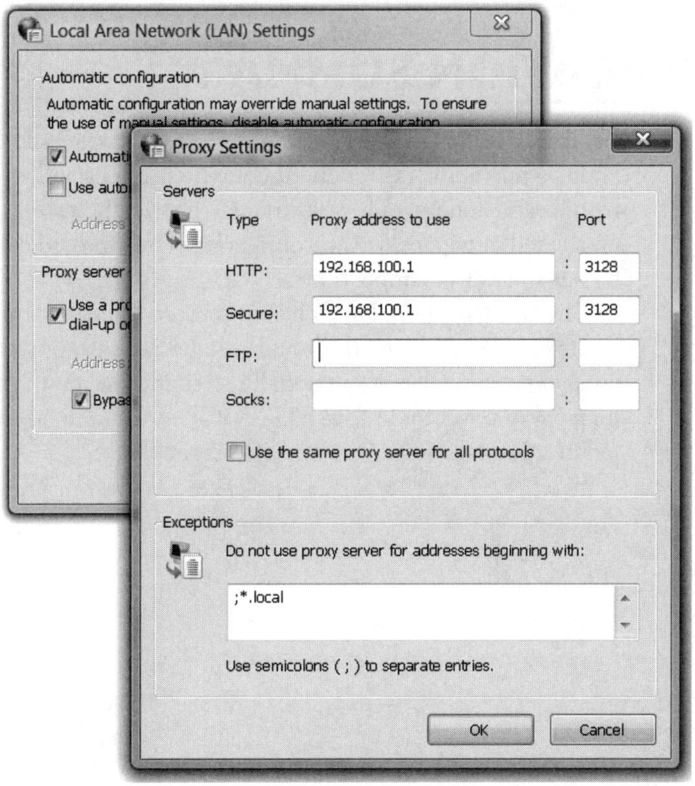

SCENARIO & SOLUTION

I plan to use Mozilla Firefox as my Web browser. Should I uninstall Internet Explorer?	No. Do not uninstall Internet Explorer. You can make Firefox your default browser.
I connect to the Internet via the company LAN, and my LAN administrator has e-mailed me proxy server addresses. Where do I enter these in Windows?	Open Control Panel | Internet Options. On the Connections page, click the LAN Settings button at the bottom. In the Local Area Network Settings dialog, place a check in the box under Proxy Server and enter the settings provided by your administrator.
At home, we have two computers and a broadband Internet connection. We have decided that we want our two computers to connect to the WAN connection via WLAN. Can we use ad hoc mode and save the cost of a wireless router?	No, an ad hoc WLAN cannot connect to another network. Use a wireless router and infrastructure mode to connect these computers to the Internet.

CERTIFICATION SUMMARY

An A+ certification candidate must understand the tasks required to install, configure, and upgrade networks for client computers on a small office/home office network. Installation and upgrade tasks include physically installing all types of NICs, setting up a wired or wireless LAN, configuring IP settings, and configuring both dial-up and broadband WAN connections.

The two most popular Web browsers are Microsoft Internet Explorer and Mozilla Firefox. A PC technician should be familiar with both and know how to install, configure, and update them. Finally, a technician must know how to configure settings for a proxy server for HTTP, FTP, POP3, SMTP, and other types of services using the Connection tab of the Internet Options applet.

✓ TWO-MINUTE DRILL

Here are some of the key points covered in Chapter 14.

Installing and Configuring Networks

❑ Each computer on a network requires a NIC for its physical installation.

❑ Decide how a NIC should interface with your computer (bus, USB, or other interface), and select a NIC for the type of network you require—LAN or WLAN.

❑ For a bus NIC installation, first install the NIC, then, if it is an Ethernet NIC, connect the cable, and lastly, start the computer and install the drivers.

❑ When installing a USB, FireWire, or PC Card NIC, you will connect the NIC to the USB or FireWire port or PC Card slot, connect the NIC to the network, and then start the computer and let Windows recognize the NIC. When prompted, provide a disc or the location of driver files.

❑ When connecting to a wired Ethernet network, use CAT5/5e or better UTP cabling with an RJ-45 connector. Connect one end to the NIC and the other to the wall jack, or directly to a hub or switch.

❑ When creating a Wi-Fi network, check for possible obstacles and interference sources that can block the signal. Signals degrade over distance causing slower data speeds, so verify that the distances between the wireless devices are well within the published signal range for the devices.

❑ A Service Set ID (SSID) is a network name used to identify a wireless network. All of the wireless devices on a WLAN must use the same one.

❑ Ad hoc wireless mode is useful for only a very few computers and cannot connect directly to another network.

❑ To connect a wireless network directly to another network, you need to use a wireless access point (WAP) and infrastructure mode for all nodes on the network.

❑ You normally do the initial setup of a WAP with a directly wired Ethernet connection between a PC and the WAP. Then you use a Web browser to access the configuration program on the WAP. You can make subsequent changes over the wireless network.

❑ Most WAPs run the DHCP service to give out IP addresses on the WLAN. Most can also do the same over their Ethernet port or ports.

❑ Change the default SSID of a WAP to a unique name, change the default user name and password to ones that will not be easily guessed, and set other security options, as appropriate for your WLAN.

❑ Once a NIC connects to the network and the drivers are installed, configure the TCP/IP properties. If your network has a DHCP Server, you can leave these settings at their default and your computer will acquire an IP address automatically from the DHCP Server.

❑ If you do not use a DHCP Server and wish to communicate beyond a single network, you must configure IP settings manually (static IP), including IP address, subnet mask, Default Gateway, DNS Server, and (rarely) WINS Server.

❑ Although there are many types of WAN connections, some of them have common configuration steps. Configuring a dial-up connection is very similar to configuring a cellular WAN connection, whereas the steps for configuring several broadband services are almost identical. They include DSL, cable, and satellite.

❑ Configure a VPN for a secure connection over the Internet to a private network. It requires a VPN server on the private network, but Windows has a wizard that will walk you through the configuration for a VPN.

❑ Although many laptops have Bluetooth capabilities, desktop PCs usually do not. If you need to connect a PC to a Bluetooth device, such as a cell phone or smart phone, you may need to install a Bluetooth transceiver into the PC. Once a PC or laptop has Bluetooth turned on, then use the Bluetooth Devices applet in Windows Control Panel to configure the connection.

❑ There are many VoIP service providers, including telephone companies, cable companies, and even Internet-based services, such as Skype. The configuration and costs will vary based on the type of service.

Installing and Configuring Web Browsers

❑ A Web browser is software that transfers the contents of a Web page to a computer and translates the plain-text language into a rich, colorful document. Microsoft Internet Explorer (IE) and Mozilla Firefox are two common Web browsers for Windows.

❑ IE is installed in Windows by default, and, although you can and should upgrade it as updates and new versions are available, do not try to uninstall it from Windows—even if you install a second browser.

❑ Configure IE through its Tools menu where you can turn on and configure the Pop-up Blocker, turn on and configure a Phishing Filter, manage add-ons, run Windows Update, diagnose connection problems, and open the Internet Options dialog box, which has pages of additional settings.

❑ Mozilla Firefox is an increasingly popular free Web browser that is not as big a target of malicious attacks as is the more prevalent IE. Download Firefox from www.mozilla.com.

❑ Configure Firefox from Tools | Options. Be sure to configure it to update automatically.

❑ A proxy server handles requests for Internet resources, such as Web pages, files on an FTP server, and mail for a proxy client. It does this without directly exposing the proxy client's IP address to the Internet.

❑ You can configure a proxy server in the Internet Options Control Panel applet.

SELF TEST

The following questions will help you measure your understanding of the material presented in this chapter. Read all of the choices carefully because there might be more than one correct answer. Choose all correct answers for each question.

Installing and Configuring Networks

1. What is the first step in connecting a client computer to a LAN?
   A. Finding an ISP
   B. Installing a proxy server
   C. Configuring TCP/IP
   D. Installing a NIC

2. What are the two connections required for every PC NIC?
   A. Computer and network
   B. USB and FireWire
   C. Bus and PC Card
   D. Wi-Fi and Ethernet

3. What type of connector is used on both ends of the cable connecting an analog modem to the wall jack?
   A. RJ-45
   B. USB
   C. RJ-11
   D. FireWire

4. Which Wi-Fi radio band is most likely to experience interference from microwave ovens and cordless telephones?
   A. 5.0 GHz
   B. 5.4 GHz
   C. 2.4 GHz
   D. 2.0 GHz

5. What is the maximum UTP/STP cable distance between an Ethernet NIC and a switch?
   A. 300 meters
   B. 100 meters
   C. 300 feet
   D. 100 feet

6. What secures an RJ-45 connector to an outlet on a PC or switch?

    A. A torx screw

    B. A clip on the connector

    C. A latch on the outlet

    D. A slot cover

7. What term describes a name that identifies a wireless network?

    A. BSS

    B. IBSS

    C. SSID

    D. WAP

8. What radio band do three Wi-Fi standards use?

    A. 2.4 GHz

    B. 4.2 GHz

    C. 5 GHz

    D. 7 GHz

9. What happens as you move a wireless NIC and host computer farther away from a WAP?

    A. Signal increases

    B. Connection speed increases

    C. No change

    D. Connection speed decreases

10. Use this wireless mode if you wish to connect a Wi-Fi network to a wired network.

    A. Infrastructure

    B. Ad hoc

    C. IBSS

    D. SSID

11. Even a new NIC or wireless access point may need this updated if the manufacturer makes certain changes after the device has been released for sale, and you can usually download it from the manufacturer's Website.

    A. Cabling

    B. Password

    C. Firmware

    D. Admin user name

12. Not a WAN connection in itself, this device is used to make a connection over the Internet to a private network more secure and is part of the connection configuration for many users.

A. Bluetooth

B. DSL

C. Cable

D. VPN

13. If this one address is missing from your IP configuration, you will be able to communicate on your LAN but not have access to the Internet.

A. DHCP

B. Default Gateway

C. WINS

D. Subnet mask

14. Which of the following pairs of WAN connections are similar because the WAN connection device is installed in the computer, and it provides a point-to-point connection between the computer and the other end of the WAN connection?

A. Cellular and cable

B. Dial-up and DSL

C. Dial-up and cellular

D. Wi-Fi and satellite

15. If you subscribe to your phone company's VoIP service over DSL, what device is used to make the analog/digital signal conversion between your analog phone and the DSL network?

A. Multimedia Terminal Adapter (MTA)

B. Modem

C. Smart phone

D. Integrated Access Device (IAD)

16. Which of the following acronyms represents an alternative term to describe an add-on to Internet Explorer or Firefox?

A. BHO

B. ARP

C. IMAP

D. ISDN

17. Which wireless mode is appropriate for two computers that only need to communicate with each other peer-to-peer and do not need to connect to the Internet through a Wi-Fi connection?

    A. Ad hoc

    B. Infrastructure

    C. 802.11g

    D. 802.11n

18. Which of the following wireless standards operate at 2.4 GHz or 5 GHz and has a typical data rate of 200 Mbps?

    A. 802.11a

    B. 802.11b

    C. 802.11n

    D. 802.11g

Installing and Configuring Web Browsers

19. What is the recommended action to take when you install Firefox?

    A. Uninstall Internet Explorer.

    B. Disable Internet Explorer.

    C. Leave Internet Explorer installed.

    D. Make Internet Explorer the default browser.

20. What service handles requests for Internet services for a client without exposing the client's IP address to the Internet?

    A. DSL

    B. DHCP

    C. Proxy

    D. WINS

SELF TEST ANSWERS

Installing and Configuring Networks

1. ☑ **D.** Installing a NIC is the first step to connecting a client computer to a LAN.
   ☒ **A,** finding an ISP, is incorrect because it is not necessary to have an ISP in order to connect to a LAN. **B,** installing a proxy server, is incorrect because you would not normally install a proxy server on a client computer, and it is definitely not the first step in connecting a computer to a LAN. **C,** configuring TCP/IP, although an important step, is not the first step in connecting a computer to a LAN.

2. ☑ **A.** A computer and network are the two connections required for every PC NIC.
   ☒ **B,** USB and FireWire, is incorrect because both of these are computer connections, and with each, a connection to a network (wired or wireless) is required. **C,** bus and PC Card, is incorrect because both of these are computer connections, and with each, a connection to a network (wired or wireless) is also required. **D,** Wi-Fi and Ethernet, is incorrect because both of these are network connections, and with each, a connection to a computer is also required.

3. ☑ **C.** RJ-11 is the type of connector used to connect an analog modem to a telephone wall jack.
   ☒ **A,** RJ-45, is incorrect because this connector is used on Ethernet cable. **B,** USB, and **D,** FireWire, are both incorrect because these are not used to connect an analog modem to a telephone wall jack.

4. ☑ **C.** The 2.4 GHz radio band is most likely to experience interference from microwave ovens and cordless telephones.
   ☒ **A,** 5.0 GHz, is incorrect, although it is a Wi-Fi radio band. **B,** 5.4 GHz, and **D,** 2.0 GHz, are both incorrect because neither of these are Wi-Fi radio bands.

5. ☑ **B.** 100 meters is the maximum distance for an Ethernet UTP/STP cable running between a NIC and switch.
   ☒ **A,** 300 meters, **C,** 300 feet, and **D,** 100 feet, are all incorrect distances.

6. ☑ **B.** A clip on the connector is what secures an RJ-45 connector to an outlet on a PC or switch.
   ☒ **A,** a torx screw, is incorrect because this is not used to secure an RJ-45 connector to an outlet on a PC or switch. **C,** a latch on the outlet, is incorrect because, although the outlet has a notch into which the connector clip fits, this is not a latch. **D,** a slot cover, is incorrect because this covers an empty slot in the back of a PC and does not secure an RJ-45 connector to an outlet on a PC or switch.

7. ☑ **C.** SSID, or Service Set ID, is the term that describes a name that identifies a wireless network.
☒ **A,** BSS, or Basic Service Set, is incorrect because this term describes the wireless nodes (including the WAP) communicating together in infrastructure mode. **B,** IBSS, or Independent Basic Service Set, is incorrect because this term describes the wireless nodes communicating together in ad hoc mode. **D,** WAP, or wireless access point, is incorrect because this is a hub for a wireless network.

8. ☑ **A.** 2.4 GHz is the band used by three Wi-Fi wireless standards: 802.11b, 802.11g, and 802.lln (just one of two bands used by this last standard).
☒ **B,** 4.2 GHz, and **D,** 7 GHz, are both incorrect because none of the Wi-Fi wireless standards use these radio bands. **C,** 5 GHz, is incorrect because only two of the Wi-Fi wireless standards use it: 802.11a and 802.11n (just one of two bands used by 802.11n).

9. ☑ **D.** Connection speed decreases as you move a wireless NIC and host computer farther away from a WAP.
☒ **A,** signal increases, is incorrect because the opposite happens as you move a wireless NIC and host computer farther away from a WAP. **B,** connection speed increases, is incorrect because the opposite happens as you move a wireless NIC and host computer farther away from a WAP. **C,** no change, is incorrect because connection speed definitely decreases because the signal degrades as distance increases.

10. ☑ **A.** Infrastructure mode is the wireless mode to use if you wish to connect a Wi-Fi network to a wired network.
☒ **B,** ad hoc mode, is incorrect because it will not allow you to connect a Wi-Fi network to a wired network. **C,** IBSS, and **D,** SSID, are both incorrect because neither of these are wireless modes.

11. ☑ **C.** Firmware may need to be updated on a NIC or wireless access point.
☒ **A,** cabling, **B,** password, and **D,** admin user name, are all incorrect because these are not things that the manufacturer would update.

12. ☑ **D.** VPN is correct.
☒ **A,** Bluetooth, is incorrect because this is a PAN network technology, not something used to make a connection over the Internet to a private network more secure. **B,** DSL, and **C,** cable, are both incorrect because these are WAN connection technologies, not something that would make a connection more secure.

13. ☑ **B.** Default Gateway is the address used to send messages beyond your LAN.
☒ **A,** DHCP, is incorrect because it is not really a single address in the IP configuration. **C,** WINS, is an address in the IP configuration, but it does give access beyond the LAN. **D,** Subnet mask, is actually part of the IP address, and if it is missing, you will not be able to communicate at all.

14. ☑ **C.** Dial-up and cellular WAN connections are similar configurations because, in both cases, the WAN connection device is installed in the computer and it provides a point-to-point connection, requiring a phone number or similar address to connect.

    ☒ **A,** cellular and cable, and **B,** dial-up and DSL, are incorrect because only one of each of these pairs of WAN connections matches the description. **D,** Wi-Fi and satellite, is incorrect because Wi-Fi is not a WAN connection.

15. ☑ **D.** Integrated Access Device (IAD) is the device used to make the analog/digital signal conversions.

    ☒ **A,** Multimedia Terminal Adapter (MTA), is incorrect because this device does the signal conversion between an analog phone and a cable VoIP service. **B,** modem, and **C,** smart phone, are both incorrect because these are not the correct devices.

16. ☑ **A.** BHO, short for browser helper object, is an alternative term to describe an add-on to Internet Explorer or Firefox.

    ☒ **B,** ARP, **C,** IMAP, and **D,** ISDN, are all incorrect.

17. ☑ **A.** Ad hoc is the wireless mode used for peer-to-peer wireless networking.

    ☒ **B,** infrastructure, is incorrect because this mode goes beyond peer-to-peer, allowing many computers to communicate and to also access a network through a connection to the wireless WAP. **C,** 802.11g, and **D,** 802.11n, are both incorrect because these are Wi-Fi standards, not modes, although the modes are part of the standards.

18. ☑ **C.** 802.11n is the wireless standard that operates at 2.4 GHz and 5 GHz and has a typical data rate of 200 Mbps.

    ☒ **A,** 802.11a, **B,** 802.11b, and **D,** 802.11g, are all incorrect because each of them only support a single frequency and none of them comes close to the 200 Mbps typical data rate, even at their theoretical maximum.

Installing and Configuring Web Browsers

19. ☑ **C.** To leave Internet Explorer installed is the recommended action to take when you install Firefox, because some Web pages appear better in Internet Explorer than in Firefox. The opposite is also true.

    ☒ **A,** uninstall Internet Explorer, is incorrect because some Web pages appear better in Internet Explorer than in Firefox. **B,** disable Internet Explorer, is incorrect because some Web pages appear better in Internet Explorer than in Firefox. **D,** make Internet Explorer the default browser, is incorrect because you can set either of these browsers as the default, which only affects which browser opens automatically when the user clicks a URL.

20. ☑ **C.** The proxy service handles requests for Internet services for a client without exposing the client to the Internet.

    ☒ **A,** DSL, is incorrect because this is a type of broadband service. **B,** DHCP, is incorrect because this service allocates IP addresses automatically. **D,** WINS, is incorrect because this is a name service that supports NetBIOS names.

15

Troubleshooting
Networks

CERTIFICATION OBJECTIVE

❏ **702: 3.1** Troubleshoot client-side connectivity issues using appropriate tools

  Two-Minute Drill

Q&A Self Test

Although there are many network problems only a trained network specialist can re-solve, there are also many common and simple network problems that you will be able to resolve without extensive training and experience. You can also run certain tests that will give you important information to pass on to more highly trained network specialists, such as those in a large corporation or at your local ISP.

In this chapter, you will explore the tools and techniques for troubleshooting common network problems. You will also learn about preventive maintenance tasks for networks.

CERTIFICATION OBJECTIVE

- **702: 3.1** *Troubleshoot client-side connectivity issues using appropriate tools*

CompTIA A+ Practical Application exam 220-702 tests your ability to trouble-shoot common network problems. However, in-depth knowledge of networks is not required. Be prepared to identify hardware and software tools for basic network troubleshooting and demonstrate that you understand how they are used. You should practice and review troubleshooting techniques for networks.

Tools for Network Troubleshooting

There are many tools for network troubleshooting. In this section, you will learn about the basic network troubleshooting tools the A+ certification candidate should know how to use. These include status indicators, command-line utilities, and cable testers.

Status Indicators

Status indicators for network hardware include LED lights on the physical device itself and/or software installed along with the driver. With a quick glance at the lights on a device, or at the icons and messages on your computer screen, you will know that the device is powered up, that it is receiving and transmitting data, and (in the case of wireless devices) the strength of the signal. Read the documentation so you understand what these lights mean when troubleshooting.

Most NICs—both Ethernet and Wi-Fi—install with a configuration utility that can be opened from an icon in the taskbar's system tray. A balloon message may appear over the system tray when the status of one of these devices changes. The icon may also change to indicate the device's current status, and you can pause your mouse over one of these icons to display the status of the devices. The status message shown here appeared when we passed a mouse over the status icon for the Local Area Connection. The icon for this connection also had a red "X" over it, so we knew there was a problem.

> Local Area Connection
> A network cable is unplugged.

Command Prompt Utilities for Network Troubleshooting

If you are unable to access another computer on the network, several command prompt utilities will help in pinpointing the source of a problem and arriving at a solution. When the TCP/IP protocol suite installs into Windows, it also installs a variety of command-line tools, such as IPCONFIG, PING, TRACERT, NETSTAT, and NSLOOKUP. These are the handiest and least expensive tools you can use for network troubleshooting or a variety of problems—those both local to and far removed from the computer, such as DNS and DHCP problems.

Each utility provides different information and is most valuable when used appropriately. For instance, you should first view the IP configuration using the *IPCONFIG* utility and verify that the configuration is correct for the network to which you are connected. If you discover any obvious problems when you view the IP configuration, correct them before proceeding. Then, select the tool that will help you diagnose and—in some instances—resolve the problem.

Most of these utilities have many optional parameters you can enter at the command line to change the command's behavior. In this book, we provide the simplest and/or most often used syntax. If you would like to learn more about each command, in Windows, simply open a Command Prompt window and enter the command name followed by a space, a slash, and a question mark, and then press ENTER. For the IPCONFIG command, enter the following: **ipconfig /?**.

A parameter is entered at the command prompt along with the command. Some parameters are data, such as the IP address you enter with the PING command, and other parameters are switches, which alter the behavior of the command, such as the "/?" switch that requests help information about a command. Most command prompt commands will accept either a hyphen (–) or a slash (/) character as part of a switch.

When entering commands at the command prompt, separate the command name, such as "ipconfig," from any parameters with a space. In the case of **ipconfig /?**, the slash and question mark together comprise a parameter and are separated from the command name with a space. Do not insert a space between the slash or hyphen and what follows, such as "?" or "all." If additional parameters must be used, separate each parameter with a space.

Cable Testers

As we stated at the beginning of this chapter, no one expects an A+ candidate to have the knowledge and skills of a network professional, but you should be able to diagnose and correct common network problems. An inexpensive cable testing device, such as the one shown in Figure 15-1, should be included in your hardware toolkit. Notice that there are two separate components: a master unit and a smaller remote terminator. This makes it possible to connect to each end of a cable when those ends are in separate rooms or even on separate floors. To test an Ethernet cable, plug one end into the master unit and the other end into the remote unit. Turn on the master unit and watch the lights on the remote unit. The LEDs on the remote terminator will light up in turn as the master unit sends signals down each pair of wires. If the cable wiring is intact, the LEDs corresponding to each pair will be green. If there is damage to the cable wiring, the LEDs will not light up at all, or may first be green and then turn red. This is true for each pair of wires tested.

FIGURE 15-1

A cable testing tool

Some cable testers will test more than one type of cabling, but in most LANs, being able to test Ethernet cable is very useful and may be all you need.

on the
job

If you use your favorite search engine to query cable tester, you will find a large selection of cable testers. You are sure to find one that fits your budget and needs. Some vendors, such as LANshack (www.lanshack.com), publish free tutorials on working with various types of cables.

Troubleshooting Common Network Problems

To troubleshoot networks, a PC professional must call on all the skills required for hardware and software support, applying a structured approach to determining the problem, applying solutions, and testing. However, keep in mind that if you make all the connections properly, and all the hardware is working properly, the most common problems will involve the TCP/IP configuration of NICs.

Connectivity problems are more obvious because the user simply fails to connect to a computer and usually receives an error message. For the PC technician supporting connectivity problems involving the Internet, there are literally worlds of possible locations for the problems. Learn how to pinpoint the location of a connection problem from the local computer to Internet routers.

Resolving Insufficient Bandwidth

Chapter 13 described bandwidth as the amount of data that can travel over a network at a given time. You must rely on the user's perception of network slowness. Therefore, when a user perceives a network to be slow, increasing the bandwidth will improve its speed. The more data you can send at once, the faster data will move from beginning to end, and the faster the network will run overall. There are two ways to increase bandwidth. One is the low-cost method of reducing the broadcast sources, and the second, more costly, method is a hardware upgrade.

Reducing Sources of Network Broadcasts

Most protocol suites have at least a few subprotocols that rely on network broadcasts. A broadcast is a transmission of packets addressed to all nodes on a network.

Broadcast traffic is, to some extent, unavoidable within a network segment, but too much of it takes up bandwidth needed for other traffic. Although broadcasts do not cross routers, they still persist within the network segments between routers, thus taking up valuable bandwidth. Reduce these sources by searching for the unnecessary protocol suites, and then look within the suites that are necessary and reduce the amount of broadcasting within them.

Why do unnecessary protocols exist on a network? First, more than one protocol suite can be active on a Windows computer, but that is rarely necessary anymore. If you have a TCP/IP network, and you find another protocol suite on a computer, without a good reason to have it, remove it. Likely unnecessary (and outdated) protocol suites are Microsoft's NetBEUI, Novell's IPX/SPX, or Microsoft's NWLink (a version of IPX/SPX).

When it comes to the use of excess protocol suites, the most common offenders are not usually computers, but old print servers, which may have come with several protocol suites enabled. Whether a print server is a separate box or integrated into a network printer, find out how to access the print server configuration. In the case of a separate print server box, you will normally enter the print server's IP address into a Web browser's address box and access it remotely. You will need the administrative user name and password to access it. For a print server integrated into a printer, it all depends on its design. Access its configuration through a Web browser or through a control panel on the printer. In both instances, look for protocols and remove protocol suites that are not required on your network.

Upgrading Network Hardware

Once you have eliminated unnecessary protocol suites and unnecessary broadcasting, if there is still a bandwidth problem, increase the bandwidth by upgrading the network's components. If the network has any Ethernet hubs, replace them with switches. Recall that a hub takes a signal received on one port and repeats it on all other ports. This consumes bandwidth. A switch, on the other hand, is a more intelligent device, which takes an incoming signal and only sends it to the destination port. This saves bandwidth.

If the network already has switches, then consider upgrading to faster equipment. For example, a LAN with Ethernet (10 Mbps) equipment can be upgraded to Fast Ethernet (100 Mbps), and a network that currently has Fast Ethernet equipment can be upgraded to Gigabit Ethernet (1 to 10 Gbps).

Be sure that when you upgrade to increase bandwidth, the upgrade is thorough. That is, all the NICs, switches, and routers must support the new, higher speed. Although the faster equipment is downward-compatible with the slower equipment, the network will only be as fast as its slowest hardware component. Also, on an Ethernet network, do not forget to upgrade the cabling to the grade required for the network speed you want to achieve. So, if you want to achieve Gigabit Ethernet speeds, you need a Gigabit Ethernet NIC, cable, and switch.

Similarly, to upgrade a wireless network, replace slower equipment with newer, faster equipment. Increase signal strength with proper placement of the wireless antenna, and install signal boosters, if necessary.

Troubleshooting Modem Problems

When an analog modem fails, without even attempting to make a connection, first check all the connections, as you would for any network device, then check the modem configuration. If it is a bus or USB modem, plug and play allocates resources, and there should not be any resource conflicts, meaning the OS avoids such conflicts among devices by managing the allocation and use of these resources. The old conflicts were with the COM port, IRQ settings, or I/O addresses. Find out if the person who installed the modem manually configured the modem or any other device and undo these changes, allowing Windows to allocate them without interference.

If a modem actually dials up, but fails to connect, make sure the sound is turned on, and test it again, if necessary. If you hear the dial tone, dialing, and some beeps in response, followed by a dropped connection, suspect that the modem you are using is not compatible with the modem on the other end of the connection. There are actually still some very old 33.6 Kbps modems out there that are no longer supported by ISPs, or old 56 Kbps modems that were manufactured before standards for this speed were established. ISPs that still support dial-up support 56 Kbps modems using the latest set of standards, so if the modem is the right speed, check with the ISP for any special configuration information you may have overlooked.

Open the Control Panel's Phone and Modem Options applet. Here is where you can resolve configuration issues, especially by checking out the Dialing Rules tab. A common configuration issue is getting a modem to dial out through a PBX, which will not give you a dial tone for an outside line until you "request" it, usually by dialing a 9 and waiting for the dial tone. The dialing program you use, whether it is a special utility from an ISP or the Phone and Modem Options applet in Windows, will allow you to program this, along with a short pause, so the modem requests a line before attempting to dial. The Dialing Rules tab is where you enter the phone number and other dialing settings. If you are dialing through a PBX and you neglect to provide the number that gives you an outside line, then, when the modem attempts to dial, it will return a "no dial tone detected" message. The Vista Phone and Modem Options applet is shown in Figure 15-2, and it is very similar across all the versions of Windows listed in the A+ objectives.

FIGURE 15-2

The Windows
Vista Phone and
Modem Options
applet looks
much like the one
in Windows 7 and
in earlier versions
of Windows.

Troubleshooting Network Connectivity Problems

When you suspect that a computer does not have network connectivity, check the network hardware, and use a variety of utilities to determine the cause, as described in the following sections.

Checking Network Hardware

When there is a connectivity problem, first check the hardware. Check the NIC, cables (for a wired network), hub, switch, WAP, and router. Check the NIC by examining the status indicator lights on the NIC, if available. On a bus NIC, the lights are on the card's bracket adjacent to the RJ-45 connector. Status indicator lights typically indicate link (a connection to a network), activity, and speed. Since most NICs (bus or USB) receive power from the PC, any light is a good indication that the NIC's connection to the PC is working (at least the power lines are). Look closer to check the connection. The Link light (usually green), when steady, indicates the connection to the network is live, and it will usually blink when sending or receiving. Multispeed NICs may have a separate Link light for each speed the NIC supports, and the lights may be labeled 100M for 100 Mbps and 1000M for 1000 Mbps (1Gbps). If a Link light is off, there is either no power to the NIC or the connection is broken, which may be caused by a broken connector or cable.

If you see an amber light, especially on an older NIC, this may be a collision light, flashing as collisions are detected on the network. It will usually be on an older NIC because modern Ethernet switches make the need for this light obsolete, since a switch is designed to minimize collisions. If you do see a collision light on an old NIC on an old Ethernet network, then pay attention to it, because if it is blinking so excessively that it almost appears steady, this means there are excessive collisions on the network, and it could indicate that there is more traffic than the network can handle. The solution is to swap out the hub (which allows collisions) for a switch.

In addition, some wireless NICs have five LEDs that indicate signal strength, much like the bars on a cell phone. One lit light indicates a poor connection, and five lit lights indicate an excellent connection.

With many Ethernet and wireless NICs now built into computers, you often do not have physical status lights but must rely on status information provided in Windows. Check the system tray on the taskbar for an icon for the NIC.

If you have determined that a NIC has power, but there is no evidence of a connection (Link lights or status icon), take steps to correct this. In the case of a wired Ethernet NIC, check for a loose or damaged cable and examine the RJ-45 connectors for damage. Follow the cable to the hub or switch.

If the cable appears okay, check that the hub, switch, WAP, and router are functioning. Check for power to each device. These devices also have status lights similar to those of NICs. If all the lights are off, check the power supply. In the case of an Ethernet hub or switch, if it has power, look at the status light for each Ethernet connection on the device. If the light is out for the port to which the computer connects, swap the cable with a known good cable, and recheck the status. Also check the cable standard that is in use. You may still find very old CAT3 cabling in use on a Fast Ethernet network. Upgrade the cabling to, at minimum, CAT5e.

Check for any source of electrical interference affecting the cabling. UTP cabling does not have shielding from interference, relying instead on the twists in the cable pairs to resist electromagnetic interference (EMI). Many things can cause EMI. Heavy power cables running parallel to network cabling can cause interference, especially if there are intermittent loads on the power cable such as when a large electric motor starts and stops. *Radio frequency interference (RFI)* can also affect networks if an RFI generator, such as a poorly shielded electronic device, is located near network cabling. If you find such a situation, take steps to move the cabling or the source of EMI.

If you cannot find any physical problems with the NIC, cabling, hub, switch, or WAP, and cannot find a source of interference, check the status of the NIC in Network Connections.

Figure 15-3 shows the Status dialog from a Windows 7 computer with a connection problem (left) and a Windows Vista computer with no problem indicated. This does not necessarily mean there is absolutely no problem with the NIC on the Vista computer, but when you are first troubleshooting a network problem, accept this opinion at least temporarily, and perform other tests before doing anything drastic, like replacing

FIGURE 15-3

Check the status of the NIC.

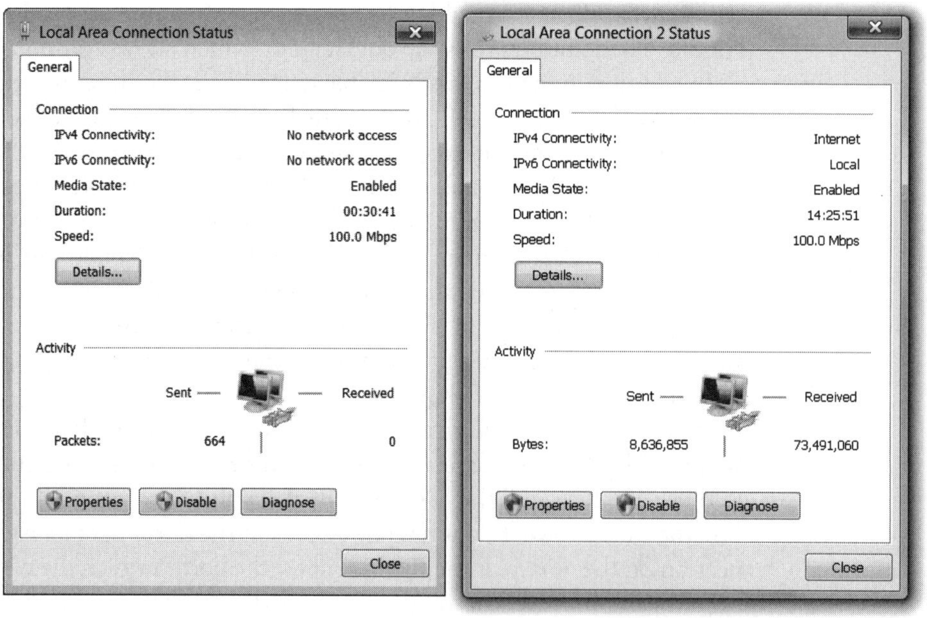

the NIC. In the case of the Windows 7 computer, we eventually found that we had a problem with the device driver. Installing the correct driver solved the problem.

The following section describes how to use IPCONFIG to view the NIC's TCP/IP configuration. If this test indicates that nothing could bind to the NIC, then swap out the NIC with an identical NIC, reboot the computer, and test the replacement. This may solve the problem.

Testing IP Configuration and Connectivity

When a computer has the TCP/IP suite installed, it includes many protocols and many handy little programs that computer professionals quickly learn to use. IPCONFIG and PING are two that you should learn right away, if you have not used them before.

Verifying IP Configuration with IPCONFIG   When you are troubleshooting network connectivity problems on an IP network, after eliminating an obviously disconnected or failed NIC, use the IPCONFIG command to verify the IP configuration. Ensure that the IP address is within the correct range and has the appropriate subnet mask and DNS settings. If you completed Exercise 13-2 in Chapter 13, you already saw what this command can do, but you will now learn how to use the information.

When you open a command prompt and enter **ipconfig /all**, it will display the IP configuration of all network interfaces on the local computer, even those that receive their addresses and configuration through DHCP. In fact, if your NIC is a DHCP client, this is the best way to see the resulting IP configuration quickly in all versions of Windows. Previously, there were no good GUI options for displaying this information in Windows, since the TCP/IP Properties dialog for a DHCP client connection will only show that it is configured to receive an IP address automatically, and it will not show its IP configuration. Windows Vista and Windows 7 display the IP configuration information, regardless of how the NIC received it, in the Network Connections Detail box, as shown in Figure 13-8 in Chapter 13. You can only view this information for one connection at a time, so techs still like to use **ipconfig /all** to see information about all connections at once.

Figure 15-4 shows an example of running the **ipconfig /all** command on a Windows XP computer with a single network adapter.

When the output from the IPCONFIG command shows an IP address other than 0.0.0.0, you know that the IP settings have been successfully bound to your network adapter. "Bound" means that there is a linking relationship, called a "binding," between the network protocol and the adapter. A binding establishes the order in which each network component handles network communications.

FIGURE 15-4

The result of running the ipconfig /all command

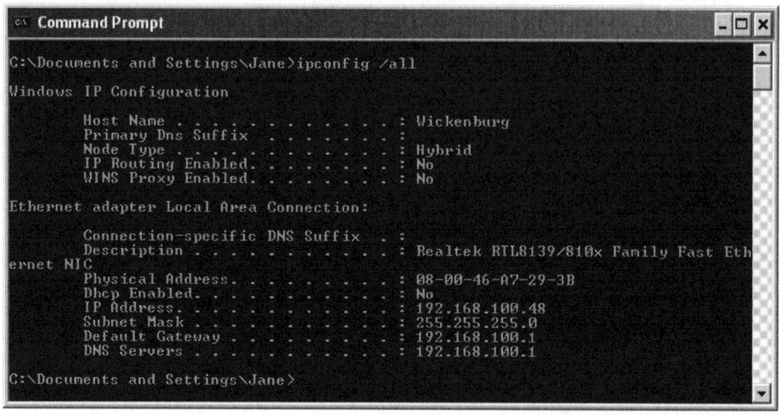

```
cx  Command Prompt                                                      _ □ ×
C:\Documents and Settings\Jane>ipconfig /all
Windows IP Configuration

        Host Name . . . . . . . . . . . . : Wickenburg
        Primary Dns Suffix  . . . . . . . :
        Node Type . . . . . . . . . . . . : Hybrid
        IP Routing Enabled. . . . . . . . : No
        WINS Proxy Enabled. . . . . . . . : No

Ethernet adapter Local Area Connection:

        Connection-specific DNS Suffix  . :
        Description . . . . . . . . . . . : Realtek RTL8139/810x Family Fast Eth
ernet NIC
        Physical Address. . . . . . . . . : 08-00-46-A7-29-3B
        Dhcp Enabled. . . . . . . . . . . : No
        IP Address. . . . . . . . . . . . : 192.168.100.48
        Subnet Mask . . . . . . . . . . . : 255.255.255.0
        Default Gateway . . . . . . . . . : 192.168.100.1
        DNS Servers . . . . . . . . . . . : 192.168.100.1

C:\Documents and Settings\Jane>
```

In addition, when viewing the IP configuration information, verify that each item is correct for the IP network segment on which the NIC is connected. There are three rules to keep in mind when evaluating an IP configuration:

■ The network ID and the subnet mask of each host on an IP segment must match.

■ The Default Gateway address must be the IP address of a router on the same subnet.

■ Each host on an IP segment must have a unique host ID.

Therefore, if there are other hosts on the same subnet, run IPCONFIG on each of them to determine if all the hosts comply with these rules. If not, correct the problem.

Finally, if the computer in question has an IP address that begins with 169.254, this is an Automatic Private IP Address (APIPA)—an address that a DHCP client can assign to itself when it cannot reach a DHCP server. If this is a very small network of just a few computers in which all of the computers use APIPA, this may be okay, but in most cases, consider this address a sign of a failure. If possible, check to see if the DHCP server is available. For a large network, you will need to contact a network administrator.

For a small or home network, the DHCP server may be part of a broadband router. In that case, reset the router. If you wait long enough, the DHCP server should assign an address to the DHCP client computer. If you wish to take control of the process, open a command prompt window on the PC and enter the following command: **ipconfig /release**. Once this command completes, enter this command: **ipconfig /renew**. This command forces the DHCP client to release any IP address it may have and request an IP address. It may take several seconds before you see a response, but it should receive a new address if it is able to reach the DHCP server. The output from the command will make it clear whether the computer receives an address.

Troubleshooting Connection Errors with the PING Command   The *PING* command is useful for testing communications between two hosts. The name of this command is an acronym for *Packet Internet Groper*. We prefer to think (as many do) that it was named after the action of underwater sonar. Instead of bouncing sound waves off surfaces, the PING command uses data packets, sending them to specific IP addresses and requesting a response (hence, the idea of pinging). Then, PING "listens" for a reply.

If you completed Exercise 14-2 or 14-3 in Chapter 14, you know the simplest syntax of the PING command, which is **ping *target-IP-address***. However, you do not always need to know a target's IP address. You can use the *fully qualified domain name (FQDN)*, for instance, www.mcgraw-hill.com, and on a network running Windows computers, you can ping the computer name. Use the PING command to test a new network connection and, for troubleshooting, a connection failure. The following is a suggested order for doing this.

1. Ping the local NIC using the following command: **ping localhost**. The standard hostname *localhost* is given to the loopback network interface. Recall the discussion of loopback in Chapter 13. If the ping results in four responses, move on to the next step. If this fails, troubleshoot the NIC as you would any hardware component. If you have another identical NIC known to work, swap it with the current NIC. If the replacement NIC works, replace the original NIC.

2. Ping the IP address of the Default Gateway. If this does not work, verify that the Gateway address is correct. If there are other computers on the network, compare the IP configuration settings. If the local settings match those of other hosts on the network, ping the Default Gateway address from another computer.

3. Ping the IP address or DNS name of a computer beyond the Default Gateway.

This order confirms, first, that the NIC is working. It also confirms that the address works within your LAN, because the Default Gateway address is on the LAN and has the same network ID as the local NIC. Finally, pinging an address beyond the Gateway confirms at least two things: the router works, and the NIC of the target host is functioning and can respond to ping requests. If you cannot ping any computer beyond the router, the problem may be in the router itself.

PING has several switches, and we will take a look at the two identified in the CompTIA A+ Exam 220-702 Practical Application (2009 Edition) Objectives, –t and –l (the letter *L*). Use the –t command when you want to ping an address repeatedly. The default is to ping an address four times. It will continue until you stop it. Pressing the CTRL-BREAK key (in combination in Windows Vista and Windows 7) will cause it to display statistics and then continue. To stop this command, press the CTRL-C key combination. Figure 15-5 shows the output from this command.

Another default of the PING command is the size (or length) of the data it uses. The default size is 32 bytes, which is not a very heavy load for any connection. Therefore, administrators sometimes test a connection by sending more data. Do this with

Using the PING command with the –t parameter

```
Command Prompt

C:\Users\Jane>ping 192.168.1.1 -t

Pinging 192.168.1.1 with 32 bytes of data:
Reply from 192.168.1.1: bytes=32 time<1ms TTL=64
Reply from 192.168.1.1: bytes=32 time<1ms TTL=64
Reply from 192.168.1.1: bytes=32 time<1ms TTL=64
Reply from 192.168.1.1: bytes=32 time<1ms TTL=64
Reply from 192.168.1.1: bytes=32 time<1ms TTL=64
Reply from 192.168.1.1: bytes=32 time<1ms TTL=64

Ping statistics for 192.168.1.1:
    Packets: Sent = 6, Received = 6, Lost = 0 (0% loss),
Approximate round trip times in milli-seconds:
    Minimum = 0ms, Maximum = 0ms, Average = 0ms
Control-Break
Reply from 192.168.1.1: bytes=32 time<1ms TTL=64
Reply from 192.168.1.1: bytes=32 time<1ms TTL=64
Reply from 192.168.1.1: bytes=32 time<1ms TTL=64

Ping statistics for 192.168.1.1:
    Packets: Sent = 9, Received = 9, Lost = 0 (0% loss),
Approximate round trip times in milli-seconds:
    Minimum = 0ms, Maximum = 0ms, Average = 0ms
Control-C
^C
C:\Users\Jane>
```

the –l switch followed by a space and the size, such as 1024. For instance, type the command **ping –l 1024 192.168.1.1**. A connection that can easily handle the 32-byte size with 0 percent loss of data may now show some data loss.

Now for some technical information about PING and related commands. The PING command uses a subprotocol of IP called the *Internet Control Message Protocol (ICMP)*. This little protocol has a big job in a TCP/IP internetwork. It detects problems that can cause errors. Such problems include congestion and downed routers. When ICMP detects these problems, it notifies other protocols and services in the TCP/IP suite, resulting in routing of packets around the problem area.

PING sends ICMP Echo packets to the target node. An Echo packet contains a request to respond. Once the target node receives the packets, it sends out one response packet for each one that it receives. You see information about the received packets in the lines that begin with "Reply from." Pay attention to the time information on this line. It should be below 200 ms; if the time is greater than 500 ms, there is a connectivity issue between the two hosts. Of course, a little common sense may tell you that it will take a longer time to receive a response from the other side of the world.

on the **job** *Practice working with these command-line tools before your network has a problem. Then you will be more comfortable with the tools and their screen output.*

Using TRACERT to Troubleshoot Slow Communications   You may have situations in which you can connect to a Website or other remote resource, but the connection is very slow. If this connection is critical to business, you will want to

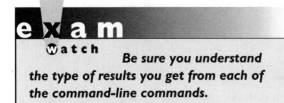

watch *Be sure you understand the type of results you get from each of the command-line commands.*

gather information so a network administrator or ISP can troubleshoot the source of the bottleneck. You can use the *TRACERT* command to gather this information. TRACERT is a command-line utility that traces the route taken by packets to a destination.

When you use TRACERT with the name or IP address of the target host, it will ping each of the intervening routers, from the nearest to the farthest. You will see the delay at each router, and you will be able to determine the location of the bottleneck. You can then provide this information to the people who will troubleshoot it for you.

Understanding *time to live (TTL)* is also important. Each IP packet header has a TTL field that shows how many routers the packet can cross before being discarded. Like PING, TRACERT creates ICMP Echo packets. The packet sent to the first host or router has a TTL of one (1). The TTL of each subsequent packet is increased by one (1). Each router, in turn, decreases the TTL value by one. The computer that sends the TRACERT waits a predetermined amount of time before it increments the TTL value by one for each additional packet. This repeats until the destination is reached. This process has the effect of pinging each router along the way, without needing to know each router's actual IP address.

Consider a scenario in which your connection to the Google Website (www .google.com) is extremely slow. You are working from a small office that has a cable modem connection to the Internet, and you are accustomed to very fast responses when you browse the Web. You have connected in the last few minutes to other Websites without significant delay, so you believe there is a bottleneck between you and Google.

Use TRACERT as described in Exercise 15-1 and report the results to your ISP. TRACERT will reveal the address of the router that is the bottleneck between you and a target host. Normally, the first and last numbered lines in the output represent the source IP address and the target IP address. Every line in between is a router located between your computer and the target. You can verify that the last line is the target by matching the IP address to the one you entered at the command line. If you entered a DNS name at the command line, the IP address will display below the command line.

EXERCISE 15-1

Using TRACERT

In this exercise, we use Google as the target, but you can substitute another domain name or IP address.

1. Open a command prompt.

2. Type **tracert www.google.com.**

3. In Figure 15-6, one of the routers shows a value that is much greater than the others, but it is not greater than 500 ms, so there is a bottleneck relative to the others, but it is not a serious one. If your test shows a router with a much greater value, report this to your ISP or to a network professional in your company, if appropriate.

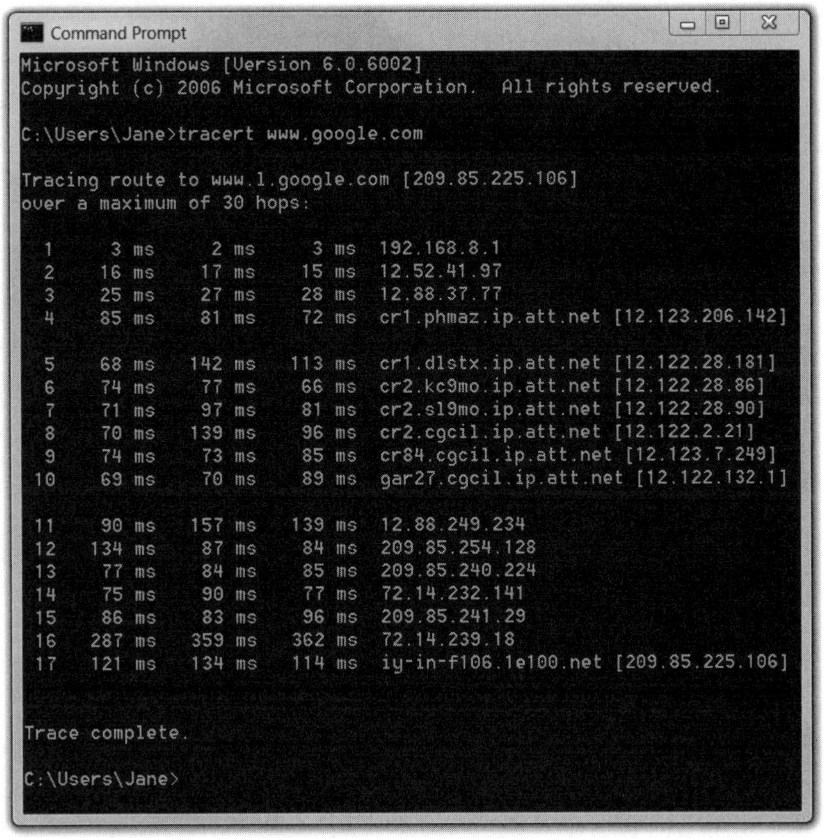

FIGURE 15-6

Using TRACERT
to trace the route
to www.google
.com

```
Command Prompt                                              □  ▣  ⌧

Microsoft Windows [Version 6.0.6002]
Copyright (c) 2006 Microsoft Corporation.  All rights reserved.

C:\Users\Jane>tracert www.google.com

Tracing route to www.l.google.com [209.85.225.106]
over a maximum of 30 hops:

  1     3 ms     2 ms     3 ms  192.168.8.1
  2    16 ms    17 ms    15 ms  12.52.41.97
  3    25 ms    27 ms    28 ms  12.88.37.77
  4    85 ms    81 ms    72 ms  cr1.phmaz.ip.att.net [12.123.206.142]

  5    68 ms   142 ms   113 ms  cr1.dlstx.ip.att.net [12.122.28.181]
  6    74 ms    77 ms    66 ms  cr2.kc9mo.ip.att.net [12.122.28.86]
  7    71 ms    97 ms    81 ms  cr2.sl9mo.ip.att.net [12.122.28.90]
  8    70 ms   139 ms    96 ms  cr2.cgcil.ip.att.net [12.122.2.21]
  9    74 ms    73 ms    85 ms  cr84.cgcil.ip.att.net [12.123.7.249]
 10    69 ms    70 ms    89 ms  gar27.cgcil.ip.att.net [12.122.132.1]

 11    90 ms   157 ms   139 ms  12.88.249.234
 12   134 ms    87 ms    84 ms  209.85.254.128
 13    77 ms    84 ms    85 ms  209.85.240.224
 14    75 ms    90 ms    77 ms  72.14.232.141
 15    86 ms    83 ms    96 ms  209.85.241.29
 16   287 ms   359 ms   362 ms  72.14.239.18
 17   121 ms   134 ms   114 ms  iy-in-f106.1e100.net [209.85.225.106]


Trace complete.

C:\Users\Jane>
```

**Using the NETSTAT Command to Troubleshoot Connection
Errors**   The *NETSTAT* command will give you statistical information about the
TCP/IP protocols and network connections involving your computer, depending
on the switches you use when you enter the command. Although NETSTAT has
many options, there are a few you should remember. For instance, running **netstat**
without any parameters, as shown in Figure 15-7, will show the current connections
by protocol and port number. NETSTAT by itself can show you a connection that is
not working—perhaps because an application has failed. Running **netstat -s** displays
statistics on outgoing and incoming traffic on your computer. If this test shows there
is no traffic in one direction, you may have a bad cable.

FIGURE 15-7

The NETSTAT command shows current connections.

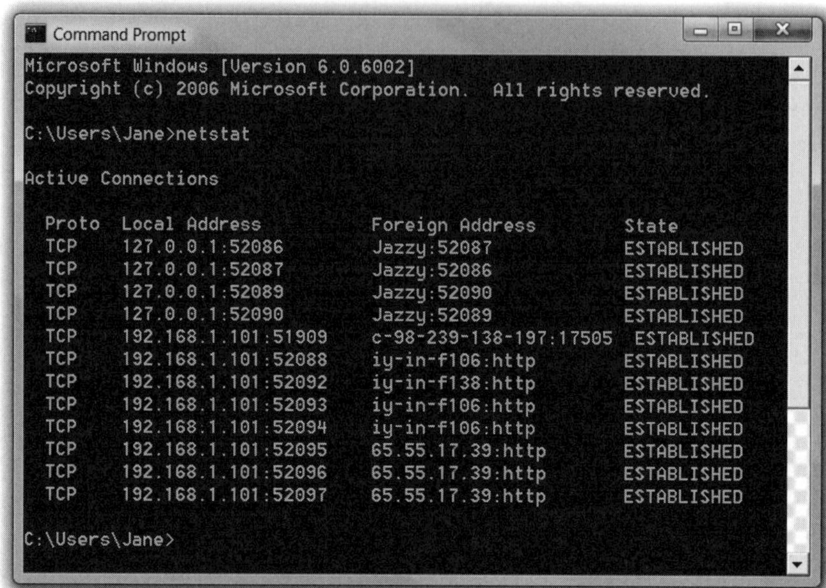

```
Command Prompt
Microsoft Windows [Version 6.0.6002]
Copyright (c) 2006 Microsoft Corporation.  All rights reserved.

C:\Users\Jane>netstat

Active Connections

  Proto  Local Address          Foreign Address        State
  TCP    127.0.0.1:52086        Jazzy:52087            ESTABLISHED
  TCP    127.0.0.1:52087        Jazzy:52086            ESTABLISHED
  TCP    127.0.0.1:52089        Jazzy:52090            ESTABLISHED
  TCP    127.0.0.1:52090        Jazzy:52089            ESTABLISHED
  TCP    192.168.1.101:51909    c-98-239-138-197:17505 ESTABLISHED
  TCP    192.168.1.101:52088    iy-in-f106:http        ESTABLISHED
  TCP    192.168.1.101:52092    iy-in-f138:http        ESTABLISHED
  TCP    192.168.1.101:52093    iy-in-f106:http        ESTABLISHED
  TCP    192.168.1.101:52094    iy-in-f106:http        ESTABLISHED
  TCP    192.168.1.101:52095    65.55.17.39:http       ESTABLISHED
  TCP    192.168.1.101:52096    65.55.17.39:http       ESTABLISHED
  TCP    192.168.1.101:52097    65.55.17.39:http       ESTABLISHED

C:\Users\Jane>
```

Troubleshooting with the NET Command

The Windows NET command is a command prompt utility that can be used to perform a variety of administrative and troubleshooting tasks. We have even used this command to create scripts for automating the creation of user accounts in a Windows domain—an advanced task. You can use the NET command to start and stop network services. To learn more about the NET command, enter **net help** to display a list of subcommands, such as those shown in Figure 15-8. You can then learn more about a single subcommand. For instance, the command for starting network services is **net start** *service*, where *service* is the name of the network service you wish to start. To see a list of the services you can start, enter this command: **net help start**.

Use the NET command with the **use** subcommand to connect to a network *share*. For instance, to connect to a shared folder named DATA on the computer named Wickenburg, enter **net use \\Wickenburg\data**. Use this command if you have determined that you can ping another computer, but are not able to access a shared folder on that computer.

FIGURE 15-8

Viewing the
subcommands
for the NET
command

e x a m

w a t c h   *The 702.3.1 exam objective*
explicitly lists net /?, which is another
way to view information about the NET
command. However, this version is really

a condensed version of net help and gives
you less information. So, remember net /?
for the exam, but use net help on the job.

Troubleshooting DNS Problems

DNS problems show themselves as messages such as "Server not found." These
messages can appear in your Web browser, your e-mail client, or any software that
attempts to connect to a server. How do you know it is a DNS problem? You do
not know this until you eliminate other problems, such as a failed NIC, a broken
connection, a typo, or an incorrect IP configuration. But once you have eliminated
these problems, use the following tests to troubleshoot DNS problems.

Using PING to Troubleshoot DNS Problems   Notice that in the steps provided for using both the PING and TRACERT commands in the previous sections, you can use either the IP address or the DNS name. When you use the DNS name with either of these commands, you are also testing the DNS. For instance, if you open a Command Prompt window and enter the following command: **ping www .mcgraw-hill.com**, before the PING command can send packets to the target, www .mcgraw-hill.com, the DNS client must resolve the DNS name to an IP address. This is exactly what happens when you enter a URL in the address box of a Web browser. The DNS client resolves the name to an IP address before the browser can send a request to view the page.

When pinging a DNS name is successful, you know several things: your DNS client is working, your DNS server is responding and working, and the target DNS name has been found on the Internet. Now, notice that the name we used (www .mcgraw-hill.com) has three parts to it. Reading from right to left, "com" is the *top-level domain (TLD)* name, and mcgraw-hill is the *second-level domain (SLD)* name within the com TLD. Both of these together are usually referred to as a domain name. So what is "www"? The owner of the second-level domain name defines anything to the left of the second-level domain name.

For instance, www.mcgraw-hill.com is listed in DNS servers that are probably under the control of McGraw-Hill or its ISP. The entry points to a server, named "www," where Web pages can be found. So, to the left of the second-level domain name are the names of servers or child domains of McGraw-Hill.com. This allows McGraw-Hill to organize their portion of the DNS name space and help client computers locate resources on these servers.

And what about all those letters, numbers, slashes, and other characters to the right of the TLD? They point to specific documents on the servers. Simple? To the casual observer, yes, because DNS hides the complexity of the organization and the locations of servers and documents. Understanding this much will help you to work with DNS and perform basic troubleshooting.

So, the next time you cannot connect to a Website from your browser, first double-check your spelling. If you entered the URL correctly, then open up a command prompt and ping on the portion of the URL that contains the TLD and SLD. If the PING is not successful, you should immediately ping another domain name, and/or try connecting to another URL through your browser. If you are successful pinging another location, then the problem may be with a router in the path to the first location. Use TRACERT, described earlier, to pinpoint the problem router.

Using NSLOOKUP to Troubleshoot DNS Problems   To further troubleshoot DNS problems, use the *NSLOOKUP* command, which lets you troubleshoot
DNS problems by allowing you to query DNS name servers and see the result of the
queries. In using NSLOOKUP, you are looking for problems such as a DNS server not
responding to clients, DNS servers not resolving names correctly, or other general
name resolution problems.

NSLOOKUP has two modes: *interactive* and *noninteractive*:

- **Interactive mode**   In interactive mode, NSLOOKUP has its own command
  prompt, a greater than sign (>) within the system command prompt. You
  enter this mode by typing **nslookup** without any parameters, or **nslookup**
  followed by a space, a hyphen, and the name of a name server. In the first
  instance, it will use your default name server, as shown here, and in the
  second instance, it will use the name server you specify. While in interactive
  mode, enter commands at the NSLOOKUP prompt, and type **exit** to end
  interactive mode and return to the system command prompt, as shown here.

- **Noninteractive mode**   In noninteractive mode, you enter the NSLOOKUP
  command plus a command parameter for using one or more NSLOOKUP
  subcommands. The response is sent to the screen, and you are returned to the
  command prompt.

  Exercise 15-2 uses noninteractive mode.

EXERCISE 15-2

Using NSLOOKUP to Troubleshoot DNS

Use NSLOOKUP to resolve any Internet domain name to an IP address:

1. Open a Command Prompt window, and enter the following command:
   nslookup mcgraw-hill.com. If the name server is working, the result will
   resemble Figure 15-9.

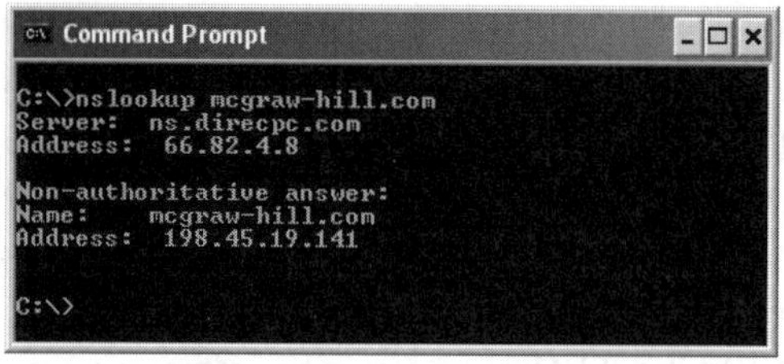

FIGURE 15-9

The NSLOOKUP
command queries
the default name
server.

```
Command Prompt                              _ □ ×

C:\>nslookup mcgraw-hill.com
Server:  ns.direcpc.com
Address:  66.82.4.8

Non-authoritative answer:
Name:    mcgraw-hill.com
Address:  198.45.19.141

C:\>
```

- ■ The Server and Address in the first and second lines of the output are the name and IP address of the DNS server that responded to your request. This will be the name server used by your ISP or your company.

- ■ The second group of lines shows the result of the query. It is called a nonauthoritative answer because the name server queried had to query other name servers to find the name.

2. The results in Figure 15-9 show that DNS name resolution is working. Therefore, if you are unable to connect to a server in this domain, the server may be offline, or a critical link or router between it and the Internet has failed. If you were troubleshooting a connection problem to this domain, you would pass this information on to a network administrator or ISP.

Troubleshooting WINS Problems

The Windows Internet Naming Service (WINS) is nearly extinct because it was mostly a Microsoft naming system, and Microsoft networks now use DNS. However, if you have a network that is using TCP/IP and has older versions of Windows, you will still need WINS.

The most likely scenario for problems with WINS will be a computer running Windows 9x that cannot see a Windows server in Network Neighborhood and cannot connect to it, whereas newer versions of Windows can see that server on the network and can connect to it if their permissions allow. In such a scenario, if you have eliminated TCP/IP configuration problems and hardware problems, then suspect a WINS problem.

If the target host is located on the same IP network, then the Windows 9x computer will use NetBIOS broadcasts rather than contacting a WINS server to resolve the name. In this case, check that the target computer is online and functioning, and that the user on the Windows 9*x* computer is using the correct NetBIOS name. Verify that the problem is not due to two computers having the same NetBIOS name.

If the host the Windows 9*x* computer cannot locate is on a network segment beyond the local router, verify the Windows 9*x* TCP/IP configuration is correct. It may not be a WINS problem, but a configuration problem, if either the Default Gateway address or the WINS address is incorrect. If you have eliminated configuration as the problem, this is the point at which you consult a network administrator who must ensure that the WINS server is online and that it has the target host name and address in its database.

Troubleshooting with Terminal Software

Telnet is character-based terminal software that has a server component that allows a Telnet client to connect. The connected client works in a character-mode environment and can enter commands. Windows XP and earlier have a Telnet client installed. Historically, network devices like routers contained a Telnet server service to which router administrators connected and used cryptic commands to configure the router. In today's SOHO network equipment, the Telnet server has been replaced by a Web server, and a technician connects to the device by entering the IP address of the device in a browser.

However, Telnet still has its uses as an advanced troubleshooting tool. Recall in Chapter 13 that you learned about ports and how a port identifies the exact service targeted at a certain IP address. When you use Telnet, it uses TCP port 23, but you can direct it to use a different port number, say TCP port 25, which is normally used by SMTP. Here is the scenario: Your e-mail client is unable to send messages. You have used the ping command to ping the mail server successfully. Therefore, it is possible that the physical server is up and running on the network, but the SMTP service is not working. If you direct Telnet to connect to the IP address/port for the SMTP server and are unable to connect, then notify the mail server administrator because this can indicate the SMTP service is down.

SCENARIO & SOLUTION

My network has a DHCP server. I need to see if the NIC received an IP address, but when I look at the properties of the Local Area Connection, the IP address is empty. What can I do?	Open a command prompt and enter the following command: **ipconfig /all**. This will display the IP configuration.
I have connected to a certain Website many times, but today the connection to this one Website is very slow. I would like to talk to my ISP about this, but I need more information. How can I tell where the problem is?	Because other Websites do not seem as slow, use the TRACERT command to trace the route to the Website and determine where the bottleneck may be.

Rather than use the cryptic character-based Telnet client, which has the added disadvantage of not being secure, consider downloading a GUI-based terminal client with security features. Secure Shell (SSH) is a terminal client that has replaced Telnet. It can be used to connect to terminal servers that require sophisticated security protocols, which we will describe in more detail in Chapter 16. Many free terminal clients are available—many with "Telnet" in their name—but most of them are some form of SSH. One free terminal client is PuTTY, which is described on the Website as "a free Telnet/SSH client." Learn more about secure connection protocols, including SSH and HTTPS in Chapter 16.

Preventive Maintenance for Networks

It is always better to prevent problems than to spend your time solving them. In this section, you will learn the basic maintenance tasks specific to networks, which include maintaining all the equipment directly attached to the network and the media over which the signals travel. However, the value and usability of a network also depend on proper functioning of the attached computers (clients and servers), as well as other shared devices, such as printers. In previous chapters, you learned preventive maintenance for computers and printers. Preventive maintenance for network devices, such as NICs, hubs, switches, WAPs, and routers, is identical to that for computers and printers.

A network also depends on the maintenance of an appropriate and secure environment for both the equipment and data. Chapters 16 and 17 explore security issues for computers and networks, and Chapter 18 presents safety and environmental issues.

Therefore, although this chapter presents some network-specific maintenance tasks, keep in mind that a computer professional must look beyond the components and software that are specific to a network and approach network maintenance holistically.

Maintaining Equipment

Network equipment, from the NICs in the computers to the bridging and routing devices that connect networks together, all have similar requirements. For instance, they all require sufficient ventilation and cooling systems to maintain the appropriate operating environment.

Reliable Power

All computer and network components must have electrical power. Providing reliable power begins with the power company supplying the power, but your responsibility begins at the meter. Do not assume that the power will always be reliable. Most of us have experienced power outages and can understand how disrupting they are. However, bad power, in the form of surges, spikes, and voltage sags, can do a great deal of damage. Prevent damage and disruption from these events by using uninterruptible power supply (UPS) devices or other protective devices discussed in Chapter 5. Versions of these power protection devices come in a form factor for mounting in equipment racks. Equipment racks are discussed in the following section.

Be aware of the number and location of circuits in the building, and the total power requirements of the equipment you have on each circuit. If you have network equipment unprotected by a UPS, be sure this equipment is not sharing a circuit with a device that has high demands, such as a laser printer or photocopier.

Consider using a dedicated circuit for the most critical equipment. A dedicated circuit has only one, or very few, outlets.

Housing Servers and Network Devices

Servers and network devices such as switches and routers should be in a physically secure room or closet with proper climate controls. The humidity should be at or near 40 percent, and the temperature should be no higher than 70 degrees. Provide adequate spacing around the equipment for proper ventilation. When dealing with more than a few servers plus network equipment, use rack-mounted servers that fit into the specially designed equipment racks for holding servers and other devices, such as UPSs, routers, and switches. These take up less space and, unlike tables and desks, allow more air to flow around the equipment.

Dedicate the room or closet to the equipment. Do not make this a multipurpose room for storage or office space because that is inviting disaster, especially if the space is readily accessible by people who have no professional reason to be in contact with the servers or network equipment. The unintended consequences of such an arrangement can damage the equipment.

on the
! o b
As a new technician you may find yourself in a new and growing company. Take a professional approach to organizing and protecting the networking equipment from the beginning. This will make the changes required to accommodate a larger network easier.

Securing and Protecting Network Cabling

Regardless of the size of the network, keep network cabling neat and labeled. In the equipment room or closet, use patch panels. A patch panel is a rack-mounted panel containing multiple network ports. Cables running from various locations in the building connect to ports on the back of the patch panel. Then shorter cables, called patch cables, connect each port to switches and routers in the closet or equipment room. This keeps cables organized and even allows for labeling the ports. This will help prevent damaged cables and confusion when troubleshooting a cable run.

e x a m
w a t c h *Know how to secure and protect network cabling for CompTIA A+ Essentials Exam 702.*

Horizontal runs of cabling often must run through suspended ceilings. Resist the urge to simply lay the cabling on the top of the ceiling tiles. This arrangement may be okay for a very small number of cables, but it only takes a few cables to make a tangle. Further, running additional cables into this space can be very difficult. Therefore, bundle cables together and run them through channels where possible. If the budget allows, specialized cable management systems are worth the investment. Use cable trays for running cables in the ceiling. A cable tray is a lightweight bridge-like structure for containing the cables in a building.

CERTIFICATION SUMMARY

This chapter explored the tools and techniques for troubleshooting networks and preventive maintenance for networks. The tools discussed included physical and software status indicators, command prompt utilities, and cable testers. In this chapter, you learned strategies for using these commands to analyze network problems.

A problem that may appear to be caused by insufficient bandwidth may actually be caused by inefficient use of bandwidth, and you solve this by removing unnecessary protocol suites from computers and network devices, such as print servers.

Analyze network connectivity problems based on error messages or other symptoms. If you see no obvious source for the problem, check the hardware, beginning with the NIC, cables, hubs, switches, WAPs, and routers. Check for any source of EMI. If you detect no physical source of a problem, check the IP configuration of the NIC and correct any errors you find.

Use command prompt utilities to reveal the IP configuration, test connectivity, locate a bottleneck on the Internet, reveal statistics about the TCP/IP protocols and network connections involving the local computer, and detect DNS and WINS problems.

Most preventive maintenance for network devices is identical to that for computers. There are some special considerations for the servers, network devices, and the cabling, for which preventive maintenance begins with providing a proper and secure environment and carefully organizing the cabling and the cable runs through ceilings and walls. Restrict access to network-specific devices to protect them from people with no professional reason to be in contact with the servers or network equipment.

✓ TWO-MINUTE DRILL

Here are some of the key points covered in Chapter 15.

Tools for Network Troubleshooting

❑ Status indicators for network hardware include LED lights on physical devices and/or status information from software installed along with the driver.

❑ A quick glance at indicator lights on a device, or icons and messages on the computer screen, reveals valuable information.

❑ The typical NIC installs with a configuration utility that you can open from an icon in the system tray of the taskbar. A change in status, or pausing your mouse over this icon, will cause a message to appear over the system tray.

❑ A group of command prompt utilities installs with the TCP/IP protocol suite. Among them are IPCONFIG, PING, TRACERT, NETSTAT, and NSLOOKUP.

❑ Use the /? switch with any command prompt utility to learn about the variety of subcommands and parameters that alter the behavior of the utility.

❑ A cable tester connects to the ends of a cable and sends a signal down the cable in order to detect breaks in the cable.

Troubleshooting Common Network Problems

❑ One way to increase network bandwidth is to remove unnecessary protocol suites from the network. Check computers for unneeded protocol suites and other network devices, such as print servers, which may come with several protocols enabled.

❑ A more costly method of increasing network bandwidth is to upgrade hardware. Begin by replacing hubs with switches, and then consider changing all the network hardware (NICs, switches, cabling, etc.) to hardware capable of higher speeds than the existing equipment.

❑ If you eliminate physical connection as the source of a modem problem, check out the configuration and dialing properties.

❑ When troubleshooting network connectivity problems, physically check the local network hardware. Next, check the status of the NIC driver in the Properties dialog for the NIC.

❑ Use the IPCONFIG command to check the IP configuration.

❑ Use the PING command to test for connectivity to another host.

❑ Find a network bottleneck on a routed network (like the Internet) using the TRACERT command.

❑ Use the NETSTAT command to view statistics about connections to the local computer.

❑ Troubleshoot DNS problems with PING and NSLOOKUP.

❑ WINS problems involve NetBIOS names within Microsoft networks. Check for duplication of NetBIOS names or problems with the WINS server.

Preventive Maintenance for Networks

❑ Preventive maintenance for network devices, such as NICs, hubs, switches, WAPs, and routers, is identical to what we described in previous chapters for computers and printers.

❑ Do not overload circuits, and provide reliable power using power protection devices, as described in Chapter 5. Consider using a dedicated circuit for the most critical equipment.

❑ Locate servers and network devices in a dedicated space, such as a room or closet. Make sure the environment in this space is appropriate, and restrict access to the equipment.

❑ Secure, protect, and organize network cabling by using patch panels in the closet or room housing the network devices and by using cable management systems, such as cable trays for horizontal runs through ceilings.

SELF TEST

The following questions will help you measure your understanding of the material presented in this chapter. Read all of the choices carefully because there might be more than one correct answer. Choose all correct answers for each question.

Tools for Network Troubleshooting

1. Which of the following items can be either one or more lights on a physical device or a message in software?
   A. Wi-Fi NIC
   B. Ethernet NIC
   C. Command-line utility
   D. Status indicator

2. In what form will you find the handiest and least expensive network troubleshooting tools for problems that are local to the computer as well as those far removed from the computer and its LAN?
   A. Status indicators
   B. Command prompt utilities
   C. Ethernet NIC
   D. Cable tester

3. Which of the following is a command prompt utility you would use to view the IP configuration of a local NIC?
   A. NETSTAT
   B. PING
   C. IPCONFIG
   D. NSLOOKUP

4. What tool would you use if you suspected that a cable was bad?
   A. Cable ping
   B. Cable tester
   C. Status indicator
   D. LED

Troubleshooting Common Network Problems

5. When you see a blinking green LED (labeled "Link"), what does it usually mean?

   A. 1000 Mbps connection

   B. 100 Mbps connection

   C. Network activity

   D. Broken cable

6. What should you look for first on a network that seems to have a bandwidth problem?

   A. Unnecessary protocol suites

   B. Unnecessary servers

   C. Unnecessary network printers

   D. Unnecessary print servers

7. Where should you enter the setting to configure your modem to dial out through a PBX system?

   A. Network and Sharing Center

   B. Phone and Modem Options | Dialing Rules

   C. Phone and Modem Options | Advanced

   D. Network Connection Properties

8. How can you quickly view the IP configuration information for all the network connections in your computer?

   A. Open Network Connections Detail

   B. Run **netstat**

   C. Run **ipconfig /renew**

   D. Run **ipconfig /all**

9. Which of the following devices reduces network traffic within an Ethernet LAN?

   A. Hub

   B. Switch

   C. Router

   D. NIC

10. How would you check the signal strength received by a wireless NIC? Select all that apply.

   A. Check indicator lights on the wireless NIC.

   B. Check indicator lights on the WAP.

   C. Open the NIC's program from the system tray.

   D. Run IPCONFIG.

11. What is the result of mixing 802.11b and 802.11n equipment on the same wireless LAN?

    A. Network speed will be at the 802.11n level.

    B. Network speed will be mixed.

    C. Nothing—the two do not work together.

    D. Network speed will be at the 802.11b level.

12. What is the result of mixing Ethernet and Fast Ethernet hardware?

    A. Transmissions at 100 Mbps

    B. Transmissions at 10 Mbps

    C. Transmissions at 1 Gbps

    D. Transmissions at 10 Gbps

13. The distance between a WAP and one group of wireless hosts causes the signal to degrade so badly that the transmissions are too slow and users are complaining. What can you do?

    A. Install a signal booster.

    B. Upgrade all the wireless devices to a faster speed.

    C. Install an Ethernet network.

    D. Install a router.

14. Which type of server automatically assigns IP addresses to hosts?

    A. DHCP

    B. WINS

    C. DNS

    D. APIPA

15. What command can you use to force a DHCP client to request an IP address assignment?

    A. ping localhost

    B. ipconfig /renew

    C. ipconfig /all

    D. tracert

16. A user complains that an Internet connection to a Website she needs to access for her work is extremely slow. Which of the following commands will you use first to analyze the problem?

    A. NETSTAT

    B. IPCONFIG

    C. TRACERT

    D. NSLOOKUP

17. Which two command prompt utilities can you use when troubleshooting a possible DNS problem?

   A. NETSTAT

   B. PING

   C. TRACERT

   D. NSLOOKUP

18. How do you stop the output from a PING command in which you used the –t switch?

   A. Type **exit**.

   B. Press the CTRL-C key combination.

   C. Type **pause**.

   D. Press the CTRL-BREAK key combination.

Preventive Maintenance for Networks

19. Which of the following is the preferred environment for network equipment and servers in a law office?

   A. A broom closet

   B. A reception desk

   C. A dedicated, climate-controlled room

   D. A conference room

20. You need to run a group of wires through a suspended ceiling. What should you use to keep the wires organized within the ceiling area?

   A. An equipment rack

   B. A UPS

   C. Cable wraps

   D. Cable trays

SELF TEST ANSWERS

Tools for Network Troubleshooting

1. ☑ **D.** A status indicator can be either one or more lights on a physical device or a message in software.

   ☒ **A,** Wi-Fi NIC, and **B,** Ethernet NIC, are both incorrect because, although both can have status indicators, neither is itself a status indicator. **C,** command-line utility, is incorrect because a command-line utility is not one or more lights on a physical device or a message in software, but a program.

2. ☑ **B.** Command prompt utilities are the handiest and least expensive network troubleshooting tools for problems that are local to the computer as well as those far removed from the computer and its LAN.

   ☒ **A,** status indicators, is incorrect because, although these are handy for detecting problems local to the computer (NIC) or its local connection, they are not useful for problems far removed from the computer. **C,** Ethernet NIC, is incorrect because this is a network device, not a troubleshooting tool. **D,** cable tester, is incorrect because, although this is a good troubleshooting tool for local problems, it is not the handiest or least expensive compared to the command prompt utilities.

3. ☑ **C.** Use IPCONFIG to view the IP configuration of a local NIC.

   ☒ **A,** NETSTAT, is incorrect because this displays network statistics but does not display the IP configuration. **B,** PING, is incorrect because this tests a connection between two hosts but does not display the IP configuration of a local NIC. **D,** NSLOOKUP, is incorrect because this tests for DNS problems and does not display the IP configuration.

4. ☑ **B.** You would use a cable tester if you suspected that a cable was bad.

   ☒ **A,** cable ping, is incorrect because such a tool was not even mentioned and may not exist. **C,** status indicator, and **D,** LED, are incorrect because neither is a tool you would use if you suspected that a cable was bad, although they would supply the clue that such a problem exists.

Troubleshooting Common Network Problems

5. ☑ **C.** Network activity is usually indicated by a blinking green LED.

   ☒ **A,** 1000 Mbps connection, and **B,** 100 Mbps connection, are incorrect, although a multispeed NIC may have a separate Link light for each speed. **D,** broken cable, is incorrect and would probably result in the Link light being off.

6. ☑ **A.** Unnecessary protocol suites are what you should look for on a network that seems to have a bandwidth problem.

   ☒ **B,** unnecessary servers, **C,** unnecessary network printers, and **D,** unnecessary print servers, are all incorrect because none of these contribute to bandwidth as much as unnecessary protocol suites.

7. ☑ **B.** Phone and Modem Options | Dialing Rules is the correct place to enter the setting to configure your modem to dial out through a PBX system.

☒ **A,** Network and Sharing Center, **C,** Phone and Modem Options | Advanced, and **D,** Network Connection Properties, are all incorrect locations for entering this information.

8. ☑ **D.** Run **ipconfig /all** to quickly see the IP configuration information for all the network connections in a computer.

☒ **A,** Open Network Connections Detail, is incorrect because this Windows Vista and 7 GUI only shows a single network connection at a time. **B,** run **netstat,** is incorrect because this command displays information on the open connections by protocol and port number. **C, ipconfig /renew,** is incorrect because this command forces a DHCP client to send an IP address renewal request to a DHCP server.

9. ☑ **B.** A switch is the device that reduces network broadcasts in an Ethernet network.

☒ **A,** hub, is incorrect because a hub sends a packet to every port, which increases traffic, whereas a switch only sends packets to the destination port. **C,** router, is incorrect because a router connects LANs, whereas a switch is within a LAN. It is true that a router will keep broadcast traffic from traveling between LANs. **D,** NIC, is incorrect because this is a network adapter, which is not a device that reduces network traffic.

10. ☑ **A and C.** The indicator lights on the wireless NIC and the NIC's program available from the system tray are both correct as places where you look for the signal strength received by a wireless NIC.

☒ **B,** check indicator lights on the WAP, is incorrect because, since the WAP is the source of the signals, these do not indicate the strength of the signal received by a wireless NIC. **D,** run IPCONFIG, is incorrect because it is not how you check the signal strength received by a wireless NIC.

11. ☑ **D.** Network speed will be at the 802.11b level.

☒ **A,** network speed will be at the 802.11n level, and **B,** network speed will be mixed, are both incorrect because the presence of 802.11b devices will make the wireless LAN operate at the lower level. **C,** nothing—the two do not work together, is incorrect because they do work together, just at the speed of the slower devices.

12. ☑ **B.** The result of mixing Ethernet (10 Mbps) and Fast Ethernet (100 Mbps) is transmissions at 10 Mbps.

☒ **A,** transmissions at 100 Mbps, is incorrect because the presence of the slower Ethernet devices will cause communications between the slower and faster devices to run at the slower rate. **C,** transmissions at 1 Gbps, and **D,** transmissions at 10 Gbps, are both incorrect because neither Ethernet nor Fast Ethernet runs at these speeds.

13. ☑ **A.** The solution to the degraded signal due to distance is to install a signal booster.

☒ **B,** upgrade all the wireless devices to a faster speed, is incorrect because the question does not mention the standard of the device in use, and it may be at the highest level available.

C, install an Ethernet network, is incorrect because a wireless network is often installed where it is not possible or practical to install a wired network. **D,** install a router, is incorrect because this would not solve the problem of the weak signal within the wireless LAN.

14. ☑ **A.** DHCP is the type of server that automatically assigns IP addresses to hosts.
☒ **B,** WINS, is incorrect because a WINS server resolves NetBIOS names to IP addresses. **C,** DNS, is incorrect because the DNS server resolves Internet domain names to IP addresses. **D,** APIPA, is incorrect because this does not describe a server, but an IP address (beginning with 169.254) that a DHCP client can assign to itself if it does not get a response from a DHCP server.

15. ☑ **B.** You use the **ipconfig /renew** command to force a DHCP client to request an IP address assignment.
☒ **A, ping localhost,** is incorrect because this command is used to ping the local NIC. **C, ipconfig /all,** is incorrect because this command is used to look at the TCP/IP configuration. **D,** tracert, is incorrect because this command displays a trace of the route taken by packets to the destination.

16. ☑ **C.** TRACERT is the command to use to analyze the problem of a slow connection to a Website.
☒ **A,** NETSTAT, **B,** IPCONFIG, and **D,** NSLOOKUP, are all incorrect because none of these is the correct command to analyze the problem described.

17. ☑ **B** and **D.** PING and NSLOOKUP are the two programs you can use when troubleshooting a possible DNS problem.
☒ **A,** NETSTAT, and **C,** TRACERT, are not programs used to troubleshoot a DNS problem.

18. ☑ **B,** press the CTRL-C key combination, is correct, as this will stop the command and return you to the prompt.
☒ **A,** type **exit, C,** type **pause,** and **D,** press the CTRL-BREAK key combination, are all incorrect because none of these will not stop the command output.

Preventive Maintenance for Networks

19. ☑ **C.** A dedicated, climate-controlled room is the preferred environment for network equipment and servers in any organization.
☒ **A,** a broom closet, **B,** a reception desk, and **D,** a conference room, are all unsuitable locations because they do not restrict access to the equipment and do not provide the correct climate-controlled environment.

20. ☑ **D.** You should use cable trays to keep the wires organized within the ceiling area.
☒ **A,** an equipment rack, is incorrect because an equipment rack is not used within ceiling areas. **B,** a UPS, is incorrect because this is a power protection device, not something for organizing cables. **C,** cable wraps, is incorrect because, although you could use these to organize cables, they are not mentioned in the chapter and are not the best solution for organizing cables within the ceiling area.

16

Computer Security Fundamentals

CERTIFICATION OBJECTIVES

❑   **701:5.1**   Explain the basic principles of security concepts and technologies

❑   **701:5.2**   Summarize the following security features: wireless encryption, malicious software protection, BIOS Security, password management/password complexity, locking workstation, and biometrics

❑   **702:4.2**   Implement security and troubleshoot common issues

✓   Two-Minute Drill

Q&A   Self Test

W indows and other modern operating systems have a long list of security features. In addition, vendors update each OS as they discover new vulnerabilities. An entire multibillion-dollar industry has grown up to provide security products for home and business computers worldwide. It is a dangerous world out there, and today "out there" is everywhere.

No form of computing is safe from threats as long as a computer connects to any network; malicious code on flash drives, floppy disks, and even optical disks can still infect those few that do not connect to networks. In this chapter, learn what the threats to your data, to your identity, and even to your hardware are. Then explore the fundamentals for protecting yourself and your computer. In the following chapter, learn how to implement computer security.

CERTIFICATION OBJECTIVES

■ **701: 5.1** *Explain the basic principles of security concepts and technologies*

■ **701: 5.2** *Summarize the following security features: wireless encryption, malicious software protection, BIOS Security, password management/password complexity, locking workstation, and biometrics*

■ **702: 4.2** *Implement security and troubleshoot common issues*

The security domain of the CompTIA 701 exam requires that you have a good understanding of security basics, which includes the types of threats and the options for protecting computers from these threats. While Chapter 17 covers the security domain of the CompTIA 702 exam, one small part of objective 702: 4.2 is detailed in this chapter: understanding the role of local users and groups in implementing security.

Security Threats

Understanding security threats is necessary in order to put security concepts, technologies, and features into context. What are the threats? In this section, we will look at some that affect individuals and entire organizations, including hardware theft, identity theft, and a long list of others. New threats appear every day. Are you paranoid yet? Read on.

Computer Hardware Theft

People steal an astounding number of computers, especially laptops, each year from businesses, homes, and automobiles. The result is loss of important tools and valuable data files—and perhaps even a loss of identity. At one time, most computer equipment thieves simply wanted to sell the hardware quickly for cash—at a fraction of the value of your computer and data to you or your business. Today, thieves realize the value of the data itself so that may be their main objective in stealing hardware; they will go through your hard drive looking for bank account, credit card, and other financial data so they can steal your identity.

Identity Theft

Identity theft occurs when someone collects personal information belonging to another person and uses that information to fraudulently make purchases, open new credit accounts, and even obtain new driver's licenses and other forms of identification in the victim's name. All the thieves need is your social security number and other key personal information to steal your identity. They can do this by physically accessing your computer, by accessing it via the Internet, or by many other low-tech means. Several Websites maintained by the U.S. government offer valuable information for consumers who wish to protect themselves from identify theft.

Fraud

Fraud is the use of deceit and trickery to persuade someone to hand over money or valuables. Fraud is often associated with identity theft, because the perpetrator will falsely pose as the owner of the victim's credit cards and other personal and financial information.

Disasters, Big and Small

Accidents and mistakes happen. It seems as if everyone has at one time or another accidentally erased an important file, pressed the wrong button at the wrong instant, or created a file and thereafter forgotten its name and location. To the person who made the error, this is a disaster.

Disasters happen in many forms. Just to name a few, there are fires, earthquakes, and weather-induced disasters resulting from tornados, lightning strikes, and floods. There is, of course, the possibility of a disaster of an even greater magnitude, such as a nuclear explosion, with the obvious consequences of a bomb, but also the resulting electromagnetic pulse (EMP). This huge burst of electromagnetic energy has the potential to damage communications and power lines within a large geographic area, depending on the size of the pulse and the proximity to electrical lines and equipment. Predicting such events is imperfect at best. The principal protection against accidents, mistakes, and disasters is to make frequent, comprehensive backups.

Malicious Software Attacks

Malicious software, or *malware*, attacks are, sadly, now common on both private and public networks. The perpetrators of these malicious attacks, commonly called *hackers* or *crackers*, are people who make an avocation or vocation out of creating ways to invade computers and networks. At one time, this term "hacker" described a clever programmer, or anyone who enjoyed exploring the software innards of computers.

You probably have heard of many types of software threats against computers, such as viruses, worms, Trojan horses, or spam. But have you ever heard of pop-up downloads, drive-by downloads, war driving, Bluesnarfing, adware, spyware, rootkits, back doors, spim, phishing, or hoaxes? Read on to learn about these various forms of deliberate attacks.

Viruses

A *virus* is a program installed and activated on a computer without the knowledge or permission of the user. At the least, the intent is mischief, but most often, the intent is malicious. Like a living virus that infects humans, a computer virus can result in a wide range of symptoms and outcomes. Loss of data, damage to or complete failure of an operating system, or theft of personal and financial information are just a few of the results of viruses infecting an individual computer. If you extend the range of a virus to a corporate or government network or portions of the Internet, the results are devastating and costly in lost productivity, lost data, lost revenues, and more.

Password Crackers

A huge number of programs and techniques are available to people who want to discover passwords. One commonly used technique is to invade an unsecured Website to access information unwitting users provide to the site, such as user names and passwords. Another technique is to use a *password cracker*, a program used to discover a password. Some password crackers fall into the brute-force category, which simply means the program tries a huge number of permutations of possible passwords. Because most people tend to use simple passwords such as their initials, birthdates, addresses, pets' names, and so on, the brute-force method often works. Other password crackers use more sophisticated statistical or mathematical methods to discover passwords.

Worms

A *worm* is a self-replicating virus. Worms travel between machines in many different ways. In recent years, several worms have moved from one computer to another as compressed (zipped) attachments to e-mail, but they can also be executable files. The file might have an innocent-sounding or enticing name to tempt the user to open and execute the program. Some of these worms, upon execution, scan the local address book and replicate themselves to the addresses. Variants of such worms as Netsky and MyDoom slowed down entire networks just through the amount of network traffic they generated.

Trojan Horses

The purpose of the modern-day *Trojan horse* virus is to gain access to computers, much like the ancient Greek warriors who, in Homer's famous tale, *The Iliad,* gained access to the city of Troy by hiding in a large wooden horse presented as a gift to the city. A Trojan horse virus masquerades as a harmless program that a user innocently installs on a computer. The host program may actually work and provide some benefit. These programs are additionally attractive to users because they are often free. After installation, the virus activates itself and infects the computer.

Pop-Up Downloads

A *pop-up download* is a virus that downloads to a user's computer through a pop-up window that appears in a Web browser. It requires an action on the part of a user, such as clicking a button that implies acceptance of something like free information, although what that something may actually be is often not clear. The downloaded program may be, or contain, a virus or worm.

Drive-By Downloads

A *drive-by download* is a program downloaded to a computer without the user's consent. Any drive-by download can install a virus, a worm, adware, or spyware. The user unwittingly initiates the download by some simple act, such as browsing to a Website or opening an e-mail message written in HTML. Or a user may initiate a drive-by download by installing an application—one of several file-sharing programs that allow the sharing of music, data, or photo files over the Internet. Some drive-by downloads may alter your browser home page and/or redirect all your browser searches to one site—this is called "Web browser hijacking."

Keystroke Loggers

A *keystroke logger* is either a hardware device or a program that monitors and records a user's every keystroke, usually without their knowledge. In the case of a hardware logger, the person desiring the keystroke log must physically install it on the computer before recording keystrokes, and then remove it afterward in order to collect the stored log of keystrokes. A software keystroke logger program may not require physical access to the target computer, but simply a method for downloading and installing it on the computer. Any one of several methods—for instance, a pop-up downloader or drive-by downloader (see the preceding sections)—can be used to install a keystroke logger. A keystroke logger can send the collected information over a network to the person desiring the log.

Some parents install keystroke loggers to monitor children's Internet activity, but such programs have the potential for abuse by people with less benign motives, including stalking, identity theft, and more.

Denial of Service (DoS) Attacks

Hackers and others with malicious intent have many methods for attacking network servers, and most of these techniques are beyond the scope of the 2009 Edition of the CompTIA A+ Essentials Exams. However, two types of threats to servers are in the CompTIA A+ Acronyms list at the end of both the CompTIA A+ Essentials (2009 Edition) (Exam Number 220-701) Objectives and the CompTIA A+ Practical Application (2009 Edition) Objectives. They are DoS and DDoS. A *denial of service (DoS) attack* occurs when someone sends a large number of requests to a server, overwhelming the server so it stops functioning on the network. A *distributed denial of service (DDoS) attack* occurs when a massive number (as many as hundreds of thousands) of computers send DoS attacks to a server, making it unavailable to legitimate users.

Rootkits and Back Doors

A *rootkit* is malware that hides itself from detection by anti-malware programs. A rootkit is installed on a computer by someone who has privileged access to the computer. Once installed, any type of malware can then be installed to quietly carry out its mission. This includes the full range of malware described previously. A rootkit can also be used to install the infamous *back door,* described later in "Methods for Gaining Access and Obtaining Information."

Grayware

The term *grayware* describes threats that are not truly malicious code, but which have indirect negative effects, such as decreasing performance or using up bandwidth. They are still undesirable, and computers should have protection against grayware, which includes spyware, adware, spam, and spim.

Spyware

Spyware is a category of software that runs surreptitiously on a user's computer in order to gather information without his or her permission and then sends that information to the people who requested it. Internet-based spyware, sometimes called "tracking software" or "spybots," may be installed on a computer by one of many means of secretly installing software. A company may use spyware to trace users' surfing patterns in order to improve its marketing efforts. Some individuals use it for industrial espionage. With appropriate legal permissions, law enforcement officers use it to find sexual predators and other criminals. Governments use forms of spyware to investigate terrorism.

Adware

Adware, which also installs on a computer without permission, collects information about a user in order to display targeted advertisements, either in the form of inline banners or pop-ups. Inline banners are advertisements that run within the context of the current page, just taking up screen real estate. Pop-ups are a greater annoyance, because each ad runs in a separate browser window that you must close before you can continue with your task. Clicking on an offer presented on an inline banner or pop-up may trigger a pop-up download that can install a virus or worm.

Spam

Spam is unsolicited e-mail. Spam includes e-mail from a legitimate source selling a real service or product, as well as from sources with intent to do harm. If you did not give the sender permission to send such information to you, it is spam. Spam threatens you and your computer in a variety of ways, including the waste of network bandwidth and lost productivity as individuals and corporations deal with the volume of spam. Too often spam involves some form of scam—a bogus offer to sell a service or product that does not exist—or tries to include you in a questionable money-making deal, which often turns out to be outright fraud. If it sounds too good to be true, it is! The perpetrators of spam are called "spammers," and laws now make some spam illegal. The costs to the spammers are very low, and they will continue to spam as long as people reward them for their efforts. One estimate holds that 8 percent of users who receive spam make a purchase as a direct result of the spam.

Spim

Spim is an acronym for *Spam over Instant Messaging,* and the perpetrators are called "spimmers." Instant messaging screen names are often collected by small programs, called "bots" (short for robot, a program that runs automatically), that are sent out over the Internet to collect information. The spimbot then sends unsolicited instant messages to the screen names. A typical spim message may contain a link to a Website, where, as with spam, the recipient will find products or services for sale—legitimate or otherwise.

Dialers

A *dialer* is a program that causes a modem to dial phone numbers surreptitiously. These are often pay-per-call or international numbers charged to the user's phone bill and benefitting the entity originating the dialer program.

Prank Programs

A *prank program,* also called a joke program, produces strange behavior, such as screen distortions, erratic cursor behavior, or strange icons on the screen. Even though normally these programs do not directly harm data, they are costly in lost productivity and time to rid the computer of the problem.

Methods for Gaining Access and Obtaining Information

Malicious software and grayware gain access to computers and networks through a large variety of techniques. Here are just a few of these methods.

Back Door

In computing, a *back door* is program code that provides a way for someone to gain access to a computer while bypassing security. Only a person who knows how the back door works can use it, but once in, that individual has the same access as the host program to all the internal operating system code.

Sometimes a developer creates a back door into a program for easy access later for administering and/or troubleshooting the program after installing it on a client's computer. Or, an attacker may create a back door in an operating system or other program by taking advantage of a discovered weakness in the program's security. For example, using a rootkit, a cracker can install a secret authentication program that, when executed, accepts the cracker's authentication credentials and allows privileged (administrator) access to the system, ignoring the normal authentication mechanism and user accounts, and thus becoming a back door to the system that bypasses the operating system's security.

In one well-known situation, hackers used the Code Red worm, which took advantage of a vulnerability in Microsoft's Internet Information Server (its Web server software), to install a back door into Windows. Then, they infected PCs with the Nimda worm, which used that back door to invade each computer.

War Driving

War driving is the name given to the act of driving or walking through a neighborhood in a vehicle or on foot, using either a laptop equipped with Wi-Fi wireless network capability or a simple Wi-Fi sensor available for a few dollars from many sources. War drivers are searching for open hotspots, areas where a Wi-Fi network connects to the Internet without using security to keep out intruders. Using a practice called *war chalking*, a war driver may make a mark on a building where a hotspot exists. People "in the know" look for these marks to identify hotspots for their use.

People who use these hotspots without permission are trespassing, and, in addition to gaining Internet access, they can prey on other users of the wireless network who, if not protected from intrusions to their computers, are vulnerable. With this access to the network, the intruder can capture keystrokes, passwords, and user names. Further, if the wireless network connects to an organization's internal wired network, the intruder may gain access to the resources on that network.

Intentionally created hotspots are increasing in number as more and more are made available for free or for a small charge by various businesses, such as coffee shops, bookstores, restaurants, hotels, and even campgrounds and truck stops. In fact, city-sized areas are now hotspots made with overlapping Wi-Fi signals, as the City of Minneapolis did when it created its 57-square-mile hotspot available for $12 per month.

Bluesnarfing

Similar to war driving, *Bluesnarfing* is the act of covertly obtaining information broadcast from wireless devices using the Bluetooth standard. Using a cell phone, a Bluesnarfer can eavesdrop to acquire information, or even use the synchronizing feature of the device to pick up the user's information without being detected by the victim.

Exposure to Inappropriate or Distasteful Content

The Internet, and especially the World Wide Web, is a treasure trove of information. It is hard to imagine a subject that cannot be found somewhere on the Internet. However, some of this content is inappropriate or distasteful. What is inappropriate or distasteful content? To some extent, only an individual can judge, but there are many circumstances in which an individual or groups should be shielded from certain content.

Invasion of Privacy

Many of the threats we have described are also clearly invasions of privacy. Protecting against privacy invasion includes protecting your personal information at your bank, credit union, retail stores, and Websites, health clinics, and any organization in which you are a customer, member, patient, or employee. Every step you take to make your computer more secure contributes to the protection of your privacy.

Cookies—the Good and the Bad

Cookies are good—mostly. Under some circumstances people can use them for the wrong purposes, but for the most part, their benefits far outweigh the negatives. There is a great deal of misinformation about cookies, the small files a Web browser saves on the local hard drive at the request of a Website. The next time you connect to that same site, it will request the cookie saved on a previous visit. Cookies are text files, so they cannot contain viruses, which are executable code, but they may contain the following information:

- User preferences when visiting a specific site
- Information a user entered into a form at the Website, including personal information
- Browsing activity
- Shopping selections on a Website

The use of cookies is a convenience to users. Thanks to cookies, you do not have to reenter preferences and pertinent information on every visit to a favorite Website.

The cookies act as electronic notes about your preferences and activities within a Website, remembering selections you have made on each page so when you return to the page you do not have to reselect them. Just one example of this is when you are at a retail site and make selections that you add to your "shopping cart." In all likelihood, cookies save these selections, and when you decide to check out, the checkout page reads the cookie files to calculate your order.

Although users are not overtly aware when the Website saves or retrieves cookies on the local hard disk, most good Websites clearly detail whether they use cookies and what they use them for. Look for this information in the site's privacy policy statement.

Normally, only the Website that created the cookies can access them. However, some advertisers on Websites have the browser create cookies, and then other sites that include this advertiser can use them. These are "third-party cookies." Learn about browser settings for cookies in Chapter 17.

In Firefox, select Tools | Options | Privacy. On the Privacy page, click Show Cookies to open a window in which you can search for and view cookies listed in alphabetical order, as shown here.

Social Engineering

Social engineering encompasses a variety of persuasion techniques used for many purposes—both good and bad. People with malicious intent use social engineering to persuade someone to reveal confidential information, or give something else of value, to the perpetrator. The information sought may be confidential corporate data, personal identifying or financial information, user names and passwords, or anything you can imagine that could be of value to another person.

As social engineering is as old as Homo sapiens, there are countless techniques employed; everyone should learn to recognize these techniques. They all count on the natural trusting behavior of the targeted people. Once you understand the forms of social engineering threats, you are less likely to become a victim. We will now explore social engineering threats and appropriate responses. On the Internet, the most common vehicle for social engineering communications is e-mail.

The best response to any form of social engineering is to not respond and/or to not reveal any information. And you should never send money in response to a communication from a stranger, no matter how enticing the offer may be.

Phishing

Phishing is a fraudulent method of obtaining personal and financial information through pop-ups, e-mail, and even letters mailed via the U.S. Postal Service, that purport to be from a legitimate organization, such as a bank, credit card company, retailer, and so on. They often (falsely) appear to be from well-known organizations and Websites, such as various banks, eBay, PayPal, MSN, Yahoo, Best Buy, and America Online.

In a typical phishing scenario, the message will contain authentic-looking logos, and an e-mail may even link to the actual site, but the link specified for supplying personal financial information will take recipients to a "spoofed" Web page that asks them to enter their personal data. The Web page may look exactly like the company's real Web page, but it's not the legitimate site. A common practice is for a phisher to use the credit information to make purchases over the Internet, choosing items that are easy to resell, and having them delivered to an address unconnected to the phisher, such as a vacant house to which he has access.

Be very suspicious of e-mails requesting personal financial information, such as access codes, social security numbers, or passwords. Legitimate businesses will never ask you for personal financial information in an e-mail.

To learn more about phishing, and to see the latest examples, point your Web browser to www.antiphishing.org, the Website of the Anti-Phishing Working Group (APWG), which reports that every possible measurement of phishing activity shows huge increases. For instance, the number of unique phishing Websites detected in

June 2009 was 49,084, whereas "only" 27,300 were detected in January of that year. You can report phishing attacks at this site.

Would you recognize a phishing e-mail? There are Websites that work to educate people to recognize a phishing scam when they receive it in e-mail or other communications. Exercise 16-1 describes how to use just one of these sites.

EXERCISE 16-1

What Is Your Phishing IQ?

You can test your Phishing IQ and learn to identify phishing scams.

1. Use your Web browser to connect to the Phishing IQ test at www.sonicwall .com/phishing.

2. You will see ten e-mails. You must decide whether each is legitimate or phish.

3. When you finish, you can review the correct answers, along with a detailed explanation as to why each is either legitimate or phish.

If you completed Exercise 16-1, you will have noticed that phishing e-mails look very official, but in some cases, careful scrutiny reveals problems. Although the signs identified in these messages are not the full extent of the problems you can find in a phishing e-mail, this type of test helps to educate people so they do not become victims of phishing.

Although not all phishing e-mails have the same characteristics, the following lists just a few problems detected in phishing e-mails:

- The "To:" field is not your address, even though it appeared in your inbox.

- There is no greeting or one that omits your name.

- The message text shows bad grammar or punctuation.

- When you click a link, the URL you are directed to does not match what appears in the e-mail.

- A link does not use HTTPS.

- The title bar reveals that a foreign character set (e.g., Cyrillic) is used.

- What appears to be a protected account number (revealing only the last four digits) is not your number at all.

- What appears to be an account expiration date is not the correct expiration date for your account.

- A URL has a slightly misspelled domain name that resembles the legitimate domain name.
- There is no additional contact information, such as a toll-free phone number and a name and title of a contact person.

Now, to make things more confusing, some legitimate e-mails may show some of these problems or practices, and not all phishing e-mails have all of these negative characteristics.

A safer way to include a URL in a legitimate e-mail is not to make it a link, but to include it in the e-mail as unformatted text, with instructions to cut and paste it into a Web browser. This way, malware cannot redirect you to a bogus Website, but you must still be diligent and examine the URL before using it.

Phone Phishing

Phone phishing is another form of phishing. In order to gain the intended victim's confidence, a phishing e-mail will urge the reader to call a phone number to verify information, at which point the person on the phone will ask the victim to reveal the valuable information.

What makes this so compelling to the user is that phone phishing often involves a very authentic-sounding professional Interactive Voice Response (IVR) menu system, just like a legitimate financial institute would have. It may ask the user to enter his password or personal identifying number (PIN). To ensure that the system captures the correct password or PIN, the system may even ask the victim to repeat it. Some systems then have the victim talk to a "representative" who gathers more information.

on the Job

Keep yourself up-to-date on the latest threats. Microsoft, Symantec, Trend Micro, and other software vendors, particularly those who specialize in security products, offer a wealth of information on their Websites. You can also subscribe to newsletters from these same organizations.

Hoaxes

A *hoax* may take many forms. One is an e-mail message claiming to be from Microsoft, notifying the receiver of the availability of an update and providing a link to a Website for downloading the fix. When recipients click the link, rather than receiving the latest security update, they may be downloading a virus or other invasive program. Microsoft never sends out updates through e-mail!

SCENARIO & SOLUTION

What type of threat uses deceit and trickery to gain money or valuables?	Fraud is the use of deceit and trickery to persuade a person to give up money or valuables. Fraud is a crime.
What is the term used to describe a software attack that captures keystrokes, usually without the user's knowledge?	Keystroke logger
Phishing, phone phishing, hoaxes, and enticement to open attachments are all examples of techniques used to persuade someone to reveal confidential information or give something else of value to the perpetrator. What is the term used for this?	Social engineering

Enticements to Open Attachments

Social engineering is also involved in the enticements—called "gimmes" in e-mails, either in the subject line or the body of the e-mail—to open the attachments. Opening the attachment then executes and infects the local computer with some form of malware. There are a huge number of methods used. Sadly, enticements often appeal to basic characteristics in people, such as greed (an offer too good to be true), vanity (physical enhancements), or simple curiosity. Some bogus enticements appeal to people's sympathy and compassion by way of a nonexistent charity. Or the author of the e-mail will pose as a legitimate charity—anything to get you to open the attachment.

Defense Against Threats

Protection from threats begins with realistic security policies, which this section defines and describes. Most of the other topics in this section are included under the umbrella of tools to use to implement security policies. These include access control, data protection, firewalls, equipment disposal, and recovery.

Security Policies

A *security policy* is a rule that is usually part of an entire set of rules and practices describing how an organization protects and manages sensitive information.

Security policies define data sensitivity and data security practices, including security classifications of data and what job functions are allowed to have access to the various classes of data.

Policies in Practice

Most medium- to large-sized organizations have a set of written security policies defining appropriate behavior and the expected consequences of inappropriate behavior. Small organizations may have written policies, but more often only have implicit ones that are not formally defined and available to all employees or members. All organizations should have security policies and should require compliance by all employees. If you belong to an organization that does not, and you are not in a position to change that situation, at the very least protect yourself by behaving as if there were explicit security policies in place. Many of the basic concepts of a security policy are universal, and any computer professional with integrity should observe them.

Mandated Security Policies

Security policies have become critical for more organizations since the 1996 enactment of the Health Insurance Portability and Accountability Act (HIPAA) by the U.S. Congress. All healthcare companies are required to comply with the HIPAA requirements for storing patient information, and they must follow certain guidelines for risk analysis, awareness training, audit trails, disaster recovery plans, and information access control and encryption. HIPAA is one of the most compelling reasons you are required to study security for the A+ exams.

Controlling Access to Computers and Networks

Access control of resources on a local computer or over a network involves *authentication* (verifying a user's identity) and *authorization* (determining the level of access an authenticated user has to a resource). In the following sections, you will explore types of access control.

Physical Security

Locked doors and physically secured computers are the best protection from computer hardware theft. This is both possible and practical to do for special equipment like switches, routers, and servers, but the typical desktop computer or laptop cannot be physically secured. There are devices for physically securing computers, such as kiosk enclosures, but you rarely see them in use except in high-risk environments, such as schools and public buildings.

BIOS Security

Anyone who has physical access to a computer can also access the computer's BIOS Setup program and, intentionally or not, make changes that allow malicious attacks or that affect the computer's operation. For this reason, virtually all modern PCs have BIOS security settings such as drive lock, passwords, intrusion detection, and TPM, described shortly. Consider using BIOS security in an area where the computers are exposed to various users and minimally supervised. Just one such scenario is a school lab in which the computers are available most of the day for student's use to complete schoolwork. Let's look at how you might use various BIOS security options in such a scenario.

Passwords   The BIOS on most computers has an optional configuration setting that allows you to enable two entirely different passwords. One password controls access to the BIOS Setup program, requiring you to enter the password before you can access the BIOS Setup menus. If someone can access the BIOS Setup program, she could change the boot setting so it will boot from a disk or disc containing an alternative operating system, copy data from the computer, or install malicious code. The second type of BIOS password is the startup password, which, if enabled, must be entered before the system will start up.

TPM Drive lock   You might enable the features of *Trusted Platform Module (TPM)*, an embedded security chip that provides enhanced data, credential, and e-mail protection via enhanced encryption. For example, in one vendor's computers, their "TPM Enhanced DriveLock" uses the TPM chip to generate an extremely strong *drive lock password* that locks your hard drive. When you complement this with a setup password and a power-on password, the computer is virtually useless to a thief.

Intrusion detection   A less-common BIOS security feature found on some models is chassis intrusion detection. When turned on, and this feature detects that the case has been opened, then on the next reboot, it will display an alert message such as "Alert! Cover was previously removed." Combine the use of chassis intrusion detection with a BIOS Setup password for more security.

Authentication and Authorization

One of the first defenses against security threats is authentication and authorization by security systems built into the operating systems on your local computer and network servers. Authentication is the verification of who you are, and authorization determines your level of access to a computer or a resource. The most recent Windows desktop OSs support both of these and will display a logon screen before giving you access to the desktop. Figure 16-1 shows the Windows Vista logon screen on a desktop that is part of a Windows workgroup, meaning the user logs onto the desktop computer using a local account. This is in contrast to logging onto a Windows domain, in which a Windows server that authenticates the user before giving access to the desktop on the local computer maintains the account used.

Authentication Factors   The actual information or device used for authentication verification is an *authentication factor*. There are three categories of authentication factors: something you know, something you have, and something you are. An example of something you know is a user name and password or a personal identification number (PIN). Something you have may be a smart card, and something you are may be a measurement of a body part (a biometric), such as a fingerprint or retina scan. Authentication involves one or more of these factors, so you can have one-factor, two-factor, or three-factor authentication. We describe individual factors and their uses in the following sections.

FIGURE 16-1

The logon screen for Windows Vista

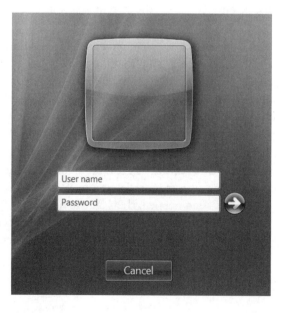

Passwords   We have used the term "password" many times in the previous chapters of this book, but until now, we have not stopped to define it. A *password* is a string of characters that a user enters, along with an identifier, such as a user name, in order for authentication to take place. This security tool is an important one for anyone who uses a computer, especially one connected to any network, including the Internet. Do not take your passwords for granted! You may have habits or practices that make you vulnerable to identity theft and other threats. Consider the following questions:

- Do you have too many passwords to remember?
- When you have an opportunity to create a new password, do you use your favorite password?
- Do you have your password written on sticky notes or your desk calendar at school or work?
- Have you used the same password for more than a few months?

If you answered "yes" to any of these questions, you are at risk, and you need to change your behavior.

Best Practices with User Names and Passwords

Here are some best practices to keep in mind when working with user names and passwords.

Don't Give Away Your User Name and Password   If you use the same user name and password at your bank as you do at an unrelated Website where you innocently provided personal information, you may have put your bank account and your other financial assets at risk. Perhaps someone created the Website just to gather personal information, or it may be harmless but has weak security. Either way, the outcome may be the same—someone has information that could enable them to access your bank account.

Someone can piece together information gathered from several Websites and other sources to figure out where you bank and to use the user name and password you provided elsewhere to access your account. Even if your bank uses the best security practices (which most do), if someone else knows and provides your user name and password, that person will have full access to your account.

Create Strong Passwords   A *strong password* is one that meets certain criteria in order to be difficult to crack. The criteria change over time as people with malicious intent (hackers) create more and more techniques and tools for discovering passwords.

One definition of a strong password is one that contains at least eight characters, includes a combination of letters, numbers, and other symbols (_, -, $, and so on), and is easy for you to remember but difficult for others to guess. For instance, some people take a song title or part of the lyrics from a favorite song, remove the spaces, and substitute numbers for some of the letters. For instance, the lyrics "Dance while the music goes on" (from the ABBA song "Dance") would turn into the password "dan2ewh1ilethem u3isg0es0n." The longer the better, and if nonalphanumeric characters are permitted, throw in a few of them, too, to make it even stronger.

Never Reuse Passwords   Every account should have a unique user name (if possible) and a unique password (always). Many Websites require your e-mail address as the user name, so these will not be unique.

Avoid Creating Unnecessary Online Accounts   Many Websites ask that you create an account and "join," but what are the benefits of joining? Why do they need information about you?

Don't Provide More Information than Necessary   Avoid creating accounts with Websites that request your social security number and other personal and financial information. Avoid having your credit card numbers and bank account information stored on a Website. Although it is not easy to do online, when a merchant asks you for your social security number, ask these four questions:

- Why do you need it?
- How will you protect it?
- How will you use it?
- What happens if I don't give it to you?

You may have to make a decision as to whether to do business with that merchant if he does not give you satisfactory answers.

Always Use Strong Passwords for Certain Types of Accounts   Use strong passwords for the following account types:

- Banks, investments, credit cards, and online payment providers
- E-mail
- Work-related

■ Online auction sites and retailers

■ Sites where you have provided personal information

Authentication Technologies

Authentication comes after a user presents credentials. In the vast majority of cases, you gain access to computers and networks with a standard interactive logon using a keyboard—most often the ubiquitous computer keyboard. Organizations requiring more stringent authentication practices will use specialized technologies, such as smart cards, key fobs, and even biometric scanners. All of these technologies provide more secure authentication at an additional cost, but the costs are decreasing, and the technologies are becoming more widespread. Learn more about just a few of them now.

Standard Interactive Logon   The type of authentication most commonly used on Windows PCs is a standard interactive logon in which the user enters a user name and password into a security dialog box. This type does not require any special hardware, as the user name and password can be entered using the keyboard or, in the case of someone with special needs, an adaptive input device.

Smart Card Logon   A *smart card* is a plastic card, often the size of a credit card, which contains a microchip. The microchip can store information and perform functions, depending on the type of smart card. Some smart cards only store data, whereas others may have a variety of functions, including security cards for logging on to facilities or computers. If configuration of the Windows domain controllers and local Windows computers allows acceptance of smart card logons, users may use this method of presenting credentials and logging on. The domain controllers require certain software security components, and the local computer must have a special piece of hardware called a *smart card reader* or card terminal. When the user inserts the card into the reader, the reader sends commands to the card in order to complete the authentication process. As is true of a bank cash card, the user may also need to enter a PIN into the keyboard in conjunction with the smart card. The two together comprise two-factor authentication.

Key Fob Logon   Much like a smart card, a *key fob* is a small device containing a microchip, and you can use it for logging on to a computer or a network. Also called a security token, it has a form factor that suggests something you might attach to a key chain, as its name implies. A common procedure for using a key fob is to enter the PIN, which identifies the user as the owner of the key fob. Then, the key fob displays a string of characters, and the user enters the string into the computer to gain access. This string is a *one-time password (OTP)*. The key fob generates a different password at a prespecified interval, and this guarantees that the user has a unique, strong password protected from the vulnerabilities of ordinary user-generated passwords, which may be too easy to guess, or which the user may write down somewhere to avoid having to memorize.

Biometric Logon   Users can easily forget passwords or PINs and lose smart cards. But each person can be uniquely identified by measurements of body parts—a biometric. A logon based on one of these measurements is a *biometric logon*. Commonly used biometrics includes fingerprints, handprints, and retinal scans. It uses a hardware device that can perform the scan, and through an interface with a local computer, the scanned information goes to the security components for processing. As with smart card logon, this requires specialized hardware attached to the local computer and specialized software on the domain controllers (in the case of a domain logon). The domain accounts database must contain the biometric information for each user account for which this type of logon is enabled. Anyone traveling with a laptop with sensitive data should look into purchasing a laptop with a built-in fingerprint scanner.

Windows User Accounts

Windows uses user-based access control, which requires authentication and authorization, and, therefore, requires that each user have an account. In a Windows network, the account can be a local account or a centralized domain account. Of course, whenever possible, use centralized accounts so each user only needs to log on to the centralized database for authentication, and, as the user attempts to access a resource on any computer on the network, the system performs authorization to verify the user's level of access to the resource. The user can use one user account to gain access to any network resources to which the user has permission.

Local Accounts   Beginning with Windows NT and continuing through Windows 7, each installation of Windows for desktop computers maintains a local security accounts database. Each installation contains local user accounts and local group accounts. A user account used for authentication is a record in the security accounts database that normally represents a single person. Authentication is validation of a user account and password that occurs before the security components of Windows will give the user access to the computer. At this point, you might envision the user account as standing on the threshold of the network or the remote computer to which it has connected, but it is the authorization process that allows the user in after assessing the permissions assigned to her for each requested resource (like a file share).

A local group account can contain one or more local user accounts, and when the computer is a member of a Windows domain, a local group may contain domain users or domain group accounts in order to give domain users and groups access to resources on the local computer. During installation, the local security accounts database is created with two user accounts: Administrator and Guest, but only the Administrator account is enabled by default. Administrator cannot be renamed or disabled.

Windows also has several built-in groups, including (but not limited to) Administrators, Backup Operators, Guests, Power Users, and Users. Installation of certain services and applications create some special groups automatically.

By default, Administrator is the only member of the Administrators group, and Guest is the only member of the Guests group. The other built-in groups are empty until an administrator creates additional local user accounts. At that point, all local user accounts are automatically members of the Users group. The administrator may make users members of any group, including new groups the administrator creates.

exam

ⓦatch *Local accounts always exist on Windows computers, whether they are in a workgroup or in a domain.*

Special Groups *Special groups* are groups created by the Windows' security system, and no user can create or modify these accounts. The membership of a special group is predefined, and the group is available to you only when you assign permissions or rights. Some Microsoft documentation for Windows calls special groups "built-in security principals." A few important special groups are Creator Owner (membership consists of the user who created a file or folder), System (the operating system), and the Everyone group, which includes all users on a network, even those who have not been authenticated.

Windows Logon

Windows 2000 and newer always require a logon, meaning you must provide a user name and password that are verified against a security database, either local or on a server on the network. Even your home computer that, perhaps, boots up right to the Windows desktop without asking for a user name or password is actually performing a logon. If your computer is not a member of a Windows domain, but rather a member of a workgroup, and you are only logging onto the local computer, then it is possible to configure it to start up right to the desktop. This scenario occurs when there is only one user account on a computer, and it does not have a password assigned to it—a very unsecure situation, but typical for a home computer. The system simply supplies the user name and blank password to the Windows security system during logon.

The next step up, security-wise, is the Welcome Screen, introduced with Windows XP and continuing in Windows Vista and Windows 7, which says "Welcome." This screen is only available if the computer is not a member of a Windows domain. The Welcome screen shows the names of all the local user accounts (except Administrator and Guest) and only requires that you select the user name and enter the password.

The last logon method is the Security dialog box. If a computer is a member of a domain, it uses the Security dialog box by default, and another level of security requires the user to press the CTRL-ALT-DELETE key combination before this dialog box will appear. To log on, you enter your user name, password, and (when appropriate) domain name into this box. Figure 16-2 shows the Windows XP Log On to Windows dialog including the Log On To box, in which you can select to log on locally to the computer or to use the down arrow to select a domain to log onto.

Lock Computer

Windows has the Lock Computer option that allows you to secure your desktop quickly, while leaving all your programs and files open. It is very simple to do. Before leaving your computer unattended, simply press CTRL-ALT-DELETE or the WINDOWS key/L.

FIGURE 16-2

This dialog box allows the user to log on to the local computer or to a domain.

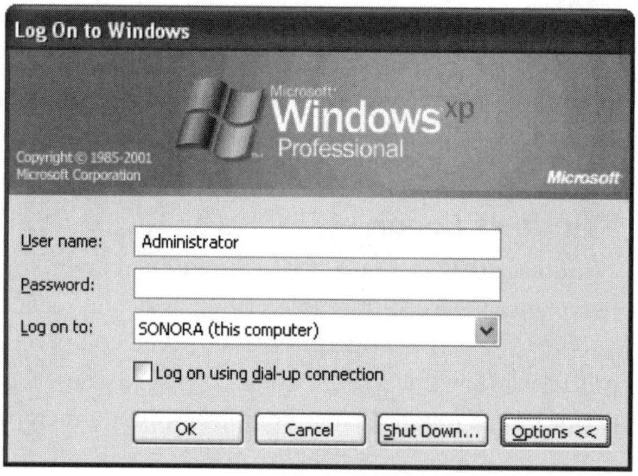

Log On to Windows
Microsoft Windows xp Professional
Copyright © 1985-2001 Microsoft Corporation
Microsoft
User name: Administrator
Password:
Log on to: SONORA (this computer)
☐ Log on using dial-up connection
OK   Cancel   Shut Down...   Options <<

The first key combination will only work if you normally log on using the Windows Security dialog box, whereas the WINDOWS key/L combination will lock the computer regardless of the logon method. The desktop will disappear, replaced by a screen with a message that the computer is locked, as shown in the center of Figure 16-3 where the word "Locked" appears below the user name and above the password box. When you return to your desk, simply enter your password and your desktop appears. Use this when you must leave your desk for a little while, like when you go to lunch. Do not use this when you leave for the day. Then, you should follow the security policy of your organization, which will most often require that you shut down your computer.

Protecting Data

While restricting access to computers serves as a first line of defense, there are other steps required to save data effectively. Learn about encrypting data on storage devices, as well as all data sent over wireless networks, and controlling access to files and folders in this next section. Finally, when taking a storage device out of service, be sure to remove all data before reusing or recycling it. Learn about all these data protection functions in the following sections.

FIGURE 16-3

This Windows 7 computer is locked until someone enters the correct password.

Encryption Technologies

Encryption is an important security tool for protecting data. As defined in Chapter 13, encryption is the transformation of data into a code that you can only decrypt by using a secret key or password. A secret key is a special code used to decrypt encrypted data, and the secret key may be held in a smart card or in a digital certificate, which is a special file stored on a computer. You can use encryption on data files that are stored on a local computer or on a network server. In addition, you can encrypt data sent over a network.

Windows NTFS Encryption   Encryption is very useful for data stored on a laptop or in a professional setting where data theft is a real concern. The NTFS file system on Windows 2000 or newer computers includes the ability to encrypt files and folders through a feature called *Encrypting File System (EFS)*. Learn how to implement NTFS encryption in Chapter 17.

BitLocker   BitLocker drive encryption is an encryption technology introduced in Windows Vista Enterprise and Ultimate editions, Windows Server 2008, and also in Windows 7 Ultimate and Enterprise editions. Rather than encrypting folders, as NTFS encryption does, BitLocker encrypts the entire boot volume, meaning the volume on which the Windows operating system is installed, which also, by default, contains installed programs and data. Learn when and how you can configure BitLocker in Chapter 17.

Encryption for Wi-Fi Networks   Wireless transmissions are vulnerable because they travel over radio waves, rather than physical cabling. Radio waves are easy to pick up, and anyone with the right equipment can read the data. Therefore, you should take steps to encrypt any data sent over a wireless network. There are three sets of standards for this: WEP, WPA, and WPA2.

Wired Equivalent Privacy (WEP) is the oldest of these standards, and you should consider it obsolete. Do not use it unless it is the only standard supported by your hardware, which would make it very old hardware. Although it uses a 64- or 128-bit encryption algorithm, it is easily broken and the data deencrypted. Its biggest drawback is that it does not encrypt the actual data in a packet, just the portion that contains the source and destination information. Another security issue with WEP is that it issues a single static key that is not changed from session to session and that all network clients share. Further, WEP has no way to perform user authentication on the packet, something added to later standards.

Wi-Fi Protected Access (WPA) is a data encryption standard based on the IEEE 802.11i security standard for wireless networks. It corrects many of the problems with WEP. It issues keys per-user and per-session and includes encryption key integrity checking. On top of the WPA data encryption, it uses a *Temporal Key Integrity Protocol (TKIP)* with a 128-bit encryption key. WPA was considered transitional because it supported most older NICs, and, once hackers broke the TKIP encryption key, it too became obsolete.

At this time, the latest wireless encryption standard is *Wi-Fi Protected Access 2 (WPA2)*, which complies with the 802.11i security standard in that it does not support older network cards and offers both secure authentication and encryption, thus providing true end-to-end data encryption with authentication. It uses Extensible Authentication Protocol (EAP), which defines a type of wrapper for a variety of authentication methods. Wireless devices usually use EAP with Personal Shared Key (EAP-PSK), which involves using a string of characters (a shared key) that both communicating devices know. WPA2 uses an encryption standard approved by the U.S. government—Advanced Encryption Standard (AES). Learn how to configure wireless security in Chapter 17.

Access Control to File Systems

File system security comes in the form of access control to file systems. It begins with an authentication and authorization system for restricting access to the computer itself. Next, the file system must allow application of *permissions* to restrict the level of access for each authenticated user or group in an accounts database. The NTFS file system in Windows supports file and folder permissions through use of an *access control list (ACL)* on each file and folder. This list is a table containing at least one *access control entry (ACE)*, which is a record containing just one user or group account name and the permissions assigned to that account. Administrators, or anyone with permission to create ACEs for the file or folder, can create ACEs. You manage permissions using the Security page in the Properties dialog box of a file or folder.

For sensitive files, consider adding encryption to the mix. NTFS permissions in the form of file and folder permissions and encryption are only available on NTFS volumes, which is one reason NTFS is your preferred file system.

When a user logs on to Windows for the first time, the operating system creates personal folders on the local hard drive for that user. If that local drive is an NTFS partition, Windows will assign a default set of permissions to those folders designed to keep other users out. The user has full control over his personal folders, as does the

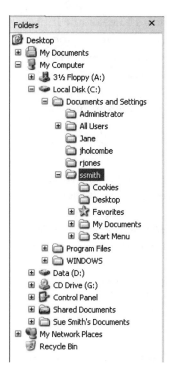

Administrators group and the System. No other user has permissions to these folders or can even view their contents.

The default location for these folders in Windows 2000/XP is in a folder that Windows assigns to the user's logon name and places in C:\Documents and Settings. See the Documents and Settings folder in Windows XP with personal folders for several users, shown on the right. We expanded the ssmith folder to show its contents.

The default location for personal folders in Windows Vista and Windows 7 is in a folder that Windows assigns to the user's logon name and places in C:\Users. As shown below, the Users folder in Windows Vista can contain personal folders for several users.

If you have a computer running Windows, and with an NTFS drive C:, use the steps in Exercise 16-2 to view permissions on your personal folders.

EXERCISE 16-2

Viewing Folder Permissions in Windows

View the permissions on your personal folders. In order to complete this exercise, you need to use the Security tab on the Properties dialog of a folder on an NTFS volume. If this tab is not available on an NTFS volume in Windows XP, turn off Simple File Sharing. If you do not know how to do this, search for it in Windows Help.

1. Open My Computer/Computer and browse to C:\Documents and Settings in Windows 2000/XP or C:\Users in Windows Vista/7. Notice the folders. There should be one for each user who has logged on, plus one titled All Users in Windows 2000/XP or Public in Windows Vista/7.

2. Open the folder with the user name that you used when you logged on. View the contents of this folder. These folders make up the user profile for your user account on this computer. Close the folder.

3. Right-click the folder with the user name that you used to log on. Select Properties, and then select the Security tab. Examine the list of users and groups that have permissions to the folder.

4. As shown in Figure 16-4, the only accounts given permissions to personal folders are the user's account, the Administrators group, and the SYSTEM (the Windows operating system). No other user has permission to access these folders. Close the window when you are finished.

Data Wiping

Permanent data removal is necessary in several scenarios. One involves moving computers from user to user in an organization; another is when an older computer is removed from service, perhaps donated to a charity or given to an employee to take home. Whatever happens, you should always take steps to remove the data from the storage devices on the computer. There are techniques for permanently destroying data from storage devices, called data wiping or shredding, that you will explore in Chapter 17.

What about those discarded computers? In this case, you should destroy the hard drives and other storage media and take it to a recycling and disposal company contracted to recycle all suitable components and safely and legally dispose of the other components.

The default
permissions
on personal
folders (shown in
Windows Vista)

Firewalls

A *firewall* protects you against the dangers of an unprotected connection to an untrusted network, such as the Internet. A firewall sits between a private network and the untrusted network and examines all traffic in and out of the network it is protecting. Using a variety of techniques, it will block any traffic it recognizes as a potential threat. A firewall can be a dedicated network device, part of a multifunction network device (as in most broadband routers), or software that is run on individual computers.

Firewall Technologies

A firewall may perform a large number of related tasks, but the most common and traditional tasks include IP packet filtering, proxy service, network address translation (NAT), encrypted authentication, and support for virtual private networks (VPNs).

IP Packet Filtering   *IP packet filtering* inspects (or filters) each packet that enters or leaves the network, applying a set of security rules defined by a network administrator. It does not allow packets that fail inspection to pass between the connected networks.

Proxy Server   A proxy server, described in Chapter 13, is often an important part of a firewall. The proxy server intercepts outbound connection requests from internal clients to certain types of external servers, and directs the resulting incoming traffic to the correct internal computer. While doing this, the proxy server hides the internal address of the client computer, acting as a stand-in (proxy) for the internal computers.

Port Security   Port security on a router involves blocking packets for all but the necessary incoming and outgoing port numbers. For instance, if you don't have an FTP server on your private network that needs access to the Internet, you should configure the router to block traffic to ports 20 and 21. A common term for an allowed port is *exception*.

Network Address Translation   Another method for hiding internal IP addresses is *network address translation (NAT)*. A TCP/IP protocol developed as a solution to the dwindling number of IP addresses on the Internet, NAT is available on most broadband routers, although you will rarely see the term "NAT" used and rarely need to configure NAT. The NAT component is often referred to as a NAT router. Although a NAT router does not examine the contents of packets as a proxy server does, it is a very valuable service.

To understand NAT, you need to first understand public and private IP addresses, which we described in Chapter 13. With a public address on the external NIC and a private address on the internal NIC, a typical NAT device translates the source address of each outgoing packet from hosts on the private network (NAT clients) into the NAT router's public address (sometimes using more than one public address). Along with changing the source IP address to the public address, the NAT device also identifies all traffic from each host with port numbers. We also described port numbers in Chapter 13, and they play a much larger role in networking than the numbers assigned by a NAT router. What NAT does during translation of outgoing packets is renumber source ports and maintain a port-mapping table that it uses to redirect the resulting incoming traffic to the correct host. This is called port address translation (PAT). Because the incoming packets are the result of requests from internal hosts, the redirection of these incoming packets to the requesting internal hosts is called *port triggering*.

NAT routing works faster than a proxy service, but it has some significant limits. It is only practical for a small private network in which there is only a single private IP network and no servers that must be accessible from the Internet, although you can use a method called port forwarding to allow outside access to a server behind a NAT router. In this case, the NAT router would forward any incoming packets with the port address of a specific service (e.g., port 80 for Web servers) to the internal address of the server. You would normally configure this as an exception in the NAT/firewall configuration.

Encrypted Authentication   *Encrypted authentication* is a security service that is not limited to firewalls. When a firewall receives connection requests originating from outside the private protected network, some of them require the external users to provide a user name and password before granting access. Because authentication information passes over the untrusted network, these firewalls often support and require encrypted authentication using one of several encryption protocols to encrypt the authentication credentials (user name and password) during transmission.

Virtual Private Network   Not truly a firewall technology, a virtual private network (VPN) is a virtual tunnel created between two endpoints over an untrusted network. You do this by encapsulating the packets within special packets for the tunnel. We also apply other security methods to a VPN, such as data encryption before encapsulating that data and encrypted authentication. When set up in combination with a properly configured firewall, a VPN is the safest way to connect two private networks over the Internet. Many SOHO broadband routers include support for VPN traffic through the router.

Content Filters   While not exactly a firewall technology, a content filter is a feature of popular Web browsers and security programs. Enable and configure a content filter when you wish to avoid exposing a certain group or individual to inappropriate or distasteful content. For instance, a company may choose to enable content filtering to avoid having employees or customers offended by certain content becoming visible on a computer. Parents can use content filters to protect children from exposure to content the parents believe would be harmful.

Hardware Firewalls

Your ISP and most corporations employ hardware firewalls, expensive and specialized devices manufactured by companies such as Cisco, NETGEAR, and others. These sophisticated firewalls require highly trained people to configure and manage them. At work or at school, such a firewall normally protects the internal network.

on the *Job*

Cisco offers certification in their router technologies. These certifications require experience and hands-on practice and are highly respected and valued by employers.

Based on its configuration, a firewall makes decisions about allowing traffic into a private network. The administrator determines the actual configuration to allow necessary traffic in and out of the private network. The type of computer on the private network, in turn, determines the necessary traffic.

If all the computers on a private network are desktop computers that connect to the Internet to browse Web pages and access FTP sites, the firewall protecting the network has a simple job. It blocks all inbound traffic that is not the result of a request from a computer on the internal network; matching incoming traffic with previous outgoing traffic that made requests that would result in incoming traffic. For instance, when you connect to a Website, outgoing traffic from your computer to the Website requests to see a page. That page comes to you in the form of incoming traffic. A firewall will allow it through because of your initial request.

If the private network includes servers that offer services on the Internet, then it must allow initiating traffic to come through the firewall, but it does not allow all incoming traffic through. In this case, the firewall configuration allows incoming traffic of the type that can communicate with the internally based servers. The various types of traffic include e-mail, HTTP (Web), FTP, and others. Each type of traffic has a certain port number recognized by the firewall. Figure 16-5 shows a firewall protecting a network containing both servers and desktop computers (shown as clients).

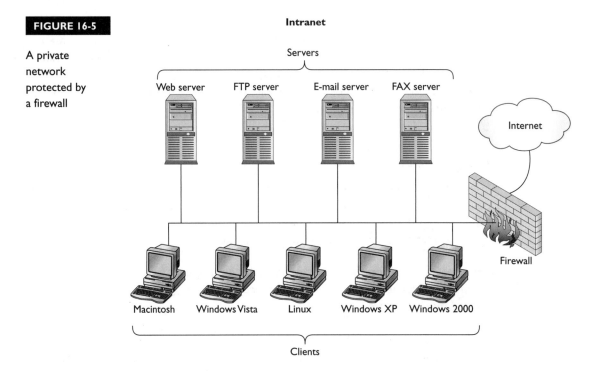

FIGURE 16-5

A private network protected by a firewall

A network professional would look at the simplified firewall example in Figure 16-5 and immediately recommend setting up a DMZ, a network between the internal network and the Internet with a firewall on both sides. The *DMZ*, named for a wartime *demilitarized zone*, would contain any servers an organization wishes to use to offer services to the Internet. The firewall between the DMZ and the private network would isolate the private network from the incoming traffic destined for the servers.

Software Firewalls

A *software firewall* is one that you can install on any computer, as opposed to the software built into a hardware firewall. Personal firewalls are the most common software firewalls because they are installed on individual desktop computers.

Windows XP, Vista, and 7 each come with a firewall, and there are many third-party firewalls to choose from as well, including Symantec's Norton Personal Firewall, Sunbelt/Kerio Personal Firewall, CheckPoint's ZoneAlarm Pro Personal Firewall, and many more. Before installing a third-party firewall in Windows, be sure to turn off the Windows Firewall, which you will find as an applet in the Control Panel.

Equipment Disposal

How does your organization dispose of old computer equipment? This is a topic we will pursue in Chapter 18 in regard to keeping discarded computer equipment out of the waste stream, recycling components, and disposing of hazardous waste contained in computers and related equipment. Whatever the policy on equipment disposal, it should include thorough removal of all data from hard drives and destruction of optical media containing data. The best practice is to destroy all the data on the hard drives before sending them to a recycler. Ordinary deletion of the files in Windows will not permanently delete these files, even if you reformat the hard drives. Therefore, use a program that will truly erase all the data from the hard drives, so it is not recoverable, even with very sophisticated tools.

Recovery

The ability to recover from an attack depends on your preparation work. For instance, have good backup procedures in place so you can restore destroyed data. Have all the protections in place against possible threats, including access control, antivirus, antispam, firewalls, and other procedures available for protecting systems and data. If these are in place, recovery will take a minimum of time.

SCENARIO & SOLUTION

I want to set a more restrictive level of permissions on a folder, but the user permissions are grayed out. What can I do?	If your account has permissions to modify the ACLs on the folder, turn off inheritance on the folder in the Advanced Security Settings page of the folder's Properties dialog box.
I plan to travel with a laptop running Windows Vista that contains very sensitive data. How can I protect the data in the event of theft of the laptop?	Encrypt any data stored on an NTFS volume. Purchase a laptop with a fingerprint scanner built-in, and if your laptop supports TPM, you can enable other security options, such as drive lock or BitLocker.
Our company disposes of old computer equipment through a service that recycles many of the components. How can we protect the sensitive data on the hard drives?	Take measures to delete the data permanently before sending the computers to the recycler.

CERTIFICATION SUMMARY

A computer professional must understand the threats to people, computers, and networks. To that end, this chapter begins with an overview of the various threats. Managers and technical staff implement access control to equipment as well as to computer, network, and file systems. Firewalls further protect networks and individual computers by examining and filtering traffic between a private network and an untrusted network like the Internet.

Also, according to good security policy, hardware is disposed of in a way that is both environmentally sound (more on this in Chapter 18), and that removes sensitive data previously stored on discarded hard drives. Further, security policy determines how recovery will occur, by defining a backup policy.

Both computer professionals and ordinary users should identify and report social engineering ploys.

✓ # TWO-MINUTE DRILL

Here are some of the key points covered in Chapter 16.

Threats

❑ Security begins with protecting hardware from theft. Although many thieves only want to sell the hardware quickly, physical theft also gives them an opportunity to steal data.

❑ Identity theft occurs when someone collects personal information belonging to another person and uses that information to fraudulently make purchases, open new credit accounts, and even obtain new driver's licenses and other forms of identification in the victim's name.

❑ Fraud is the use of deceit and trickery to persuade someone to hand over money or valuables.

❑ Disasters that affect computers, networks, and data come in many forms, including accidents, mistakes, and natural and unnatural disasters.

❑ Malicious software attacks are common on both private and public networks. Some forms include viruses, password crackers, worms, Trojan horses, keystroke loggers, pop-up downloads, and drive-by downloads.

❑ Grayware is a term for threats that are not truly malicious code but which can have indirect negative effects, such as decreasing performance or using up bandwidth. Grayware includes spyware, adware, spam, spim, dialers, and prank programs.

❑ Perpetrators use a variety of methods for gaining access and obtaining information. Some common methods include back doors, war driving, and Bluesnarfing.

❑ The wealth of information on the Internet also includes information that is generally distasteful or inappropriate for some individuals, such as children.

❑ Many of the threats described in this chapter are clearly invasions of privacy. Any steps you take to make your computer more secure contribute to protection of your privacy.

❑ Cookies are small files a Web browser saves on the local hard drive at the request of a Website. Most cookies are harmless first-party cookies that are not program code but small text files, and they can normally only be read by the Website that created them.

❑ Some advertisers on Websites create cookies that the program code from the same advertiser can read from other Websites. These are third-party cookies, and you can configure a Web browser to disable third-party cookie reading.

❑ Social engineering involves a variety of techniques used to persuade someone to reveal confidential information or give something else of value to the perpetrator. Phishing, phone phishing, hoaxes, and enticements to open attachments all employ persuasive social engineering tactics.

Defense Against Threats

❑ A set of security policies contains rules and practices describing how an organization protects and manages sensitive information. Applied to all employees, most medium to large organizations have explicit, written security policies.

❑ HIPAA and other government regulations have made security policies mandatory for many organizations in the healthcare or finance industries.

❑ Control access to restricted spaces, equipment, files, folders, and other resources of the organization.

❑ BIOS security includes enabling a password for accessing the BIOS setup and another password for booting up the computer.

❑ Control of access to computers and networks includes authentication. Access to resources then requires authorization and evaluation of the level of access granted to the user.

❑ Follow best practices for passwords, which include protecting the confidentiality of passwords, creating strong passwords, never reusing passwords, avoiding creating unnecessary online accounts, avoiding providing more information than necessary, and always using strong passwords.

❑ A variety of authentication technologies are available. Just a few include ordinary logons using the standard keyboard, smart card logons, key fob logons, and biometric logons.

❑ The NTFS file system in Windows supports file and folder permissions through use of an access control list (ACL) on each file and folder. This table contains at least one access control entry (ACE), which is a record containing just one user or group account name and the permissions assigned to that account.

❏ Administrators, or someone using an account with permission to create ACEs for the file or folder, can create ACEs. Manage permissions using the Security page in the properties dialog box of a file or folder.

❏ A newly created folder or file inherits the permission settings of the parent folder, unless you choose to block this inheritance through an option on the Security tab of the file's or folder's Properties dialog. Inherited permissions appear grayed out, and you cannot modify inherited permissions at the child level.

❏ Block inheritance on a folder or file to which you wish to assign different (usually more restrictive) permissions.

❏ When Windows creates personal folders for a user, it assigns a default set of permissions to the folders and their contents. The user, Administrators, and System all have full control, but no other user has any level of permissions to these folders.

❏ Encryption is the transformation of data into a code that only use of a secret key or password can decrypt. The NTFS file system in Windows 2000 and newer OSs supports file encryption, whereas BitLocker in Windows Vista, Windows 7, or Windows Server 2008 supports encryption of the boot volume.

❏ A firewall sits between a private network and an untrusted network and examines all traffic in and out of the network it is protecting. Firewalls use a variety of software technologies, including IP packet filtering, proxy servers, encrypted authentication, and virtual private networks.

❏ ISPs and most corporations use hardware firewalls, expensive and specialized devices manufactured by companies such as Cisco, NETGEAR, and others. They often require highly trained people to configure and manage them.

❏ A software firewall is one installable on almost any computer (allowing for minimum hardware and operating system requirements). The most common software firewalls are personal firewalls installed on desktop computers.

❏ Microsoft includes a firewall with Windows XP, Vista, and 7, and there are many third-party software firewalls as well.

❏ When disposing of old computer equipment, be sure to remove all data from hard drives and destroy optical media containing confidential data.

❏ Recovery from an attack depends on how well you prepared by making good backups and protecting against the threats outlined in this chapter.

SELF TEST

The following questions will help you measure your understanding of the material presented in this chapter. Read all of the choices carefully, because there might be more than one correct answer. Choose all correct answers for each question.

Threats

1. What is the term for the activity that results in someone using your personal information to obtain new credit or credentials?
   A. Virus
   B. Identity theft
   C. Trojan horse
   D. Social engineering

2. Netsky and MyDoom were this type of virus, which replicates itself, moving from computer to computer.
   A. Trojan horse
   B. Password cracker
   C. Worm
   D. Keystroke logger

3. What is the term used to describe the delivery of malicious code to a user's computer through a pop-up window in a Web browser?
   A. Worm
   B. Grayware
   C. Trojan horse
   D. Pop-up download

4. Which of the following is a category of software that runs surreptitiously on a user's computer to gather personal and financial information without the user's permission, and then sends that information to the people who requested it?
   A. Spam
   B. Spyware
   C. Adware
   D. Spim

5. Which of the following is a term for unsolicited e-mail?

A. Spyware

B. Spam

C. Back door

D. Worm

6. What type of program attempts to guess passwords on a computer?

A. Keystroke logger

B. Password cracker

C. Virus

D. Fraud

7. This program code gets its name from the way that it allows someone who knows how to use it to bypass security and have the privileges of the host program.

A. Back door

B. Bluesnarfing

C. Cookies

D. Phishing

8. Web browsers save these small text files at the direction of programs on a Website.

A. Back door

B. Spam

C. Cookies

D. Prank programs

Defense Against Threats

9. What term describes a set of rules and practices that applies to all employees in an organization, and describes how an organization protects and manages sensitive information?

A. Audit policy

B. Security policy

C. HIPAA

D. Remote access policy

10. This procedure informs security and technical personnel of actual violations of an organization's security policy.

A. Security policy

B. Phishing

C. Phone phishing

D. Incident reporting

11. What type of access control only requires that a resource have a password assigned to it? It does not require authentication to a user accounts database.
- **A.** User-based
- **B.** Password-based
- **C.** Three-factor
- **D.** Two-factor

12. What term describes a password meeting certain criteria in its construction that makes it very difficult to crack?
- **A.** User-based
- **B.** Healthy
- **C.** Strong
- **D.** Two-factor

13. Which encryption technology in Windows Vista/7 encrypts the entire boot volume?
- **A.** Intrusion detection
- **B.** UAC
- **C.** EFS
- **D.** TPM

14. This device uses a PIN and generates a new password every time a PIN is entered.
- **A.** Smart card
- **B.** Key fob
- **C.** Biometric logon
- **D.** Keyboard

15. What is the term for the table of users and/or groups and their permissions that is associated with a file or folder on an NTFS volume in Windows?
- **A.** Access control list (ACL)
- **B.** Security page
- **C.** Properties dialog
- **D.** Access control entry (ACE)

16. When a user logs on to Windows for the first time, what is the name of the set of folders Windows creates for that user on the local hard drive?
- **A.** My Documents
- **B.** My Computer
- **C.** Personal folders
- **D.** Logon folders

17. What term is used for the transformation of data into code that can only be decrypted using a secret key or password?

    A. Compression

    B. Encryption

    C. Deletion

    D. Programming

18. When a firewall inspects each incoming or outgoing packet and does not allow some to pass, it is performing this function.

    A. Proxy service

    B. VPN

    C. Encrypted authentication

    D. IP packet filtering

19. If a firewall allows packets with a certain port number to pass, this is called a/an _____.

    A. Trojan

    B. Exception

    C. Content filter

    D. Proxy server

20. Before walking away from your computer for lunch break, take this simple step to both save your open programs and files, and protect your computer from someone with physical access to your office from accessing your desktop unless he knows your password.

    A. Lock Computer

    B. Restart

    C. Log off

    D. Shut down

SELF TEST ANSWERS

Threats

1. ☑ **B.** Identity theft is the term for activity that results in someone using your personal information to obtain new credit or credentials.

☒ **A** and **C** are incorrect because they are both malicious code, not an activity. **D,** social engineering, is incorrect because it is the use of persuasion techniques for many purposes. Social engineering may be involved with identity theft, but the two terms do not identify the exact same behavior.

2. ☑ **C.** A worm is a type of virus that replicates itself, moving from computer to computer.

☒ **A,** Trojan horse, is incorrect because this is a type of virus that is hidden within an apparently harmless program. A worm, like any other virus, can transfer to a computer as a Trojan horse. **B,** password cracker, is incorrect because this program attempts to discover passwords. **D,** keystroke logger, is incorrect because this program logs the user's keystrokes.

3. ☑ **D.** Pop-up download describes the delivery of malicious code to a user's computer through a pop-up window in a Web browser.

☒ **A** and **C** are both incorrect because they are both types of viruses, not the method for delivering a virus. **B,** grayware, is incorrect because this describes threats that are not truly malicious code but that still have indirect negative effects.

4. ☑ **B.** Spyware is a category of software that runs surreptitiously on a user's computer to gather personal and financial information without the user's permission.

☒ **A** and **D** are both incorrect because they represent unwanted messages—spam being unwanted e-mail and spim being unwanted instant messaging messages. **C,** adware, is incorrect because, although it also installs on a computer without permission and collects information, its purpose is to collect information in order to display targeted advertisements.

5. ☑ **B.** Spam is a term for unsolicited e-mail.

☒ **A, C,** and **D** are all incorrect because they are examples of malicious program code and grayware, not e-mail. The e-mail could contain malicious code, but that is not part of the definition.

6. ☑ **B.** Password crackers attempt to guess passwords on a computer.

☒ **A** and **C** are both incorrect because, although both a keystroke logger and a virus are not malicious code, they do not attempt to guess passwords on a computer. **D,** fraud, is incorrect because this includes the use of deceit and trickery to persuade someone to hand over money or valuables. It does not match the narrow definition of a password cracker.

7. ☑ **A.** Back door is the name for code that allows someone to bypass security and access the operating system with the same privileges as the host program.

☒ **B,** Bluesnarfing, is incorrect because this is the act of covertly obtaining information broadcast from wireless devices using the Bluetooth standard. **C,** cookies, is incorrect because cookies are not program code, and they do not allow access to an operating system. **D,** phishing, is incorrect because phishing is a fraudulent method of obtaining personal and financial information through the use of pop-ups or e-mail messages that purport to be from a legitimate organization.

8. ☑ **C.** Cookies are small text files saved by a Web browser at the direction of programs on a Website.

☒ **A,** back door, is incorrect because this is program code and is used for an entirely different purpose. **B,** spam, is incorrect because spam is unsolicited e-mail. **D,** prank programs, is incorrect because these are programs, and they do not serve the same purpose as cookies.

Defense Against Threats

9. ☑ **B.** Security policy is a set of rules and practices that applies to all employees and describes how an organization protects and manages sensitive information.

☒ **A,** audit policy, is incorrect because it is just a small part of a security policy. **C,** HIPAA, the Health Insurance Portability and Accountability Act, is incorrect because this is an act of the U.S. Congress, not a set of rules and practices for an organization. HIPAA or other laws often influence security policy. **D,** remote access policy, is incorrect because this is just one small part of a security policy.

10. ☑ **D.** Incident reporting informs security and technical personnel of actual violations of an organization's security policy.

☒ **A,** security policy, is incorrect because, although security policy may define incident reporting procedures, incident reporting is just one of the actions taken within an organization in compliance with security policy. **B** and **C,** phishing and phone phishing, are both incorrect because neither is a procedure that informs security and technical personnel of actual violations of security policy. Both are violations of security policy.

11. ☑ **B.** Password-based access control only requires that a resource has a password assigned to it.

☒ **A,** user-based access control, is incorrect because this requires authentication and authorization. **C** and **D,** three-factor access control and two-factor access control, are both incorrect because they require more than just a password and require actual authentication and authorization.

12. ☑ **C.** A strong password is one that meets certain criteria in its construction that makes it very difficult to crack.

☒ **A, B,** and **D,** user-based, healthy, and two-factor, are all incorrect because they do not describe a password that meets certain criteria that makes a password difficult to crack.

13. ☑ **C.** EFS, or Encrypting File System, is the encryption technology in Windows Vista/7 that encrypts the entire boot volume.

    ☒ **A,** intrusion detection, is not an encryption technology. **B,** UAC, is User Access Control, also not an encryption technology, and **D,** TPM, is a special microchip, installed on a motherboard, that stores passwords, keys, and digital certificates. This is not an encryption technology.

14. ☑ **B.** A key fob is a device that uses a PIN and generates a new password every time a PIN is entered.

    ☒ **A,** smart card, is incorrect because, although it may be similar to a key fob, it is not generally used in the manner described in the question. **C,** biometric logon, is incorrect because it uses a body measurement for authentication. **D,** keyboard, is incorrect because you cannot use a keyboard in the manner described in the question.

15. ☑ **A.** Access control list (ACL) is the term for the table of users and/or groups and their permissions that is associated with a file or folder on an NTFS volume in Windows.

    ☒ **B** and **C** are both incorrect because both a Security tab and the Properties dialog are part of the user interface that allows you to administer the ACL to a file or folder object in Windows, not the ACL itself. **D,** access control entry (ACE), is incorrect because this is just a single entry in an ACL, not the entire table.

16. ☑ **C.** Windows creates personal folders the first time a user logs on to Windows.

    ☒ **A** and **B** are incorrect because both My Documents and My Computer are folders a user can access in Windows 2000 and XP, but neither entirely constitutes the personal folders of that user. **D,** logon folders, is incorrect because this is not a term used to describe the user's folders in Windows.

17. ☑ **B.** Encryption is the transformation of data into code that only use of a secret key or password can decrypt.

    ☒ **A,** compression, is incorrect because it is not the transformation of data into a code that only use of a secret key or password can decrypt. Compression is a method for reducing a file's size. **C,** deletion, is incorrect because this is the action of removing something, as in the deletion of a file from a hard drive. **D,** programming, is incorrect because this is not the transformation of data into a code that only use of a secret key or password can decrypt. Programming is the creating of executable code.

18. ☑ **D.** IP packet filtering is a firewall function that inspects each incoming or outgoing packet and does not allow some to pass.

    ☒ **A,** proxy service, is incorrect because this is a different function that intercepts outbound connection requests from internal clients to external servers and directs the resulting incoming traffic to the correct internal computer. **B,** VPN, is incorrect because this is a virtual tunnel created between two endpoints over an untrusted network. **C,** encrypted authentication, is incorrect because this is encryption of authentication credentials.

19. ☑ **B.** Exception is the term that describes packets with a certain port number that a firewall allows to pass.

    ☒ **A,** Trojan, is incorrect because this is a malware program that a user unwittingly runs because it appears to be benign. **C,** content filter, is incorrect because this is a function of an Internet browser that will filter out traffic based on content. **D,** proxy server, is also incorrect because this program intercepts outbound connection requests from internal clients to external servers and directs the resulting incoming traffic to the correct internal computer.

20. ☑ **A.** Lock Computer is a simple step to take to both save your open programs and files and keep your computer safe.

    ☒ **B,** restart, **C,** log off, and **D,** shut down, are all incorrect actions to take. None will preserve your open programs and files.

17

Implementing and Troubleshooting Security

CERTIFICATION OBJECTIVES

❏   **702: 4.1**   Given a scenario, prevent, troubleshoot, and remove viruses and malware

❏   **702: 4.2**   Implement security and troubleshoot common issues

✓   Two-Minute Drill

Q&A   Self Test

Making files and devices available to network users has led to the need for securing those resources, possibly the most important set of tasks on a network. Implementing security in this environment involves many different tasks, such as implementing authentication and data security, taking all necessary steps to prevent the invasion of malicious software, and discovering if malicious software is already on a system. Implementing security for a wireless network involves a specific set of skills, and you must be prepared to troubleshoot security problems.

CERTIFICATION OBJECTIVES

- **702: 4.1** *Given a scenario, prevent, troubleshoot, and remove viruses and malware*

- **702: 4.2** *Implement security and troubleshoot common issues*

    The security objectives for the CompTIA A+ Essentials Exams, include security subobjectives that involve both software and hardware security skills. The most important thing to understand about computer security is that there are no easy answers; you must continue to keep up-to-date on the latest identified security threats and know how to implement several security tasks to fully protect PCs.

Implementing Authentication and Data Security

In Chapter 16, you learned the options for authentication and data security. In this section, learn how to implement the various methods of authentication and data security.

Implementing Authentication Security

Windows most often performs authentication for access to a PC by authenticating a user using a local account or a domain account. However, you can set a password that must be entered before a PC will launch an operating system—a BIOS password. In this section, you will look at how these are set. In Chapter 16, you learned about authentication technologies that go beyond basic interactive logons, such as smart card readers, key fobs, and biometric logons, and in this chapter, you will see how to implement these authentication technologies. We also describe how to use the Lock Computer option in Windows to protect your computer.

BIOS Passwords/DriveLock/TPM

As described in Chapter 16, there are three types of BIOS passwords. One type restricts access to the computer itself; another type restricts access to the BIOS Setup; and a third, less common type restricts access to hard drives, a feature called "DriveLock" on HP computers. We will use this term to apply to all such implementations. As a further enhancement, an embedded TPM chip restricts access to hard drives, providing more advanced security.

BIOS Passwords for Setup and Startup   To set a BIOS password for setup or startup, check the manual for the motherboard, and then go into the BIOS Setup program and navigate to the correct setting. The example we discuss here is just one version from one BIOS maker. Figure 17-1 shows the screen in which you set the BIOS password. In this case, selecting this option will open a password dialog, in which you enter the new password. On another screen, you configure the password requirement for setup and/or startup.

DriveLock   Some manufacturers provide a BIOS DriveLock feature in which you set a password that you must provide at startup. This password is stored on the hard drive, which means that even if you move the drive to another computer, it will be

FIGURE 17-1

The highlighted setting will allow you to set a password on BIOS setup.

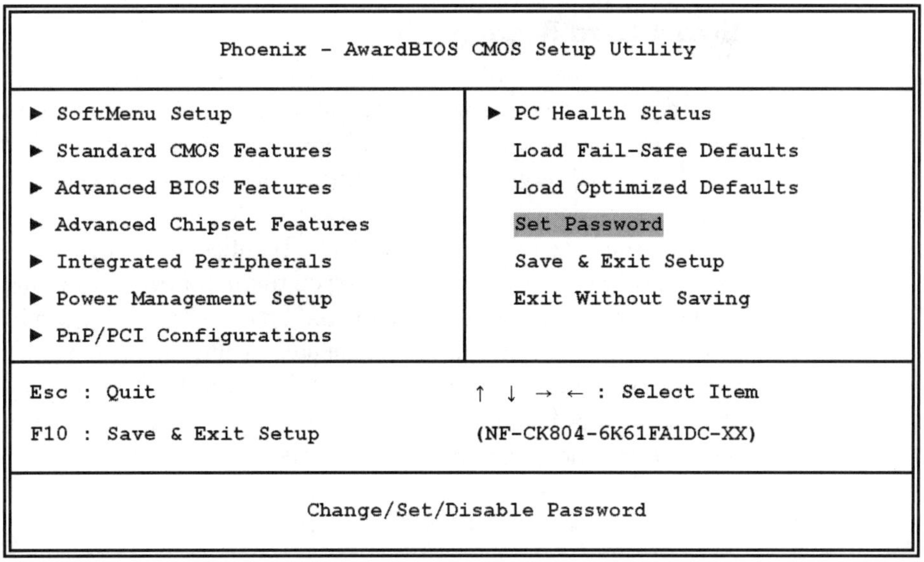

```
            Phoenix - AwardBIOS CMOS Setup Utility

 ▶ SoftMenu Setup              ▶ PC Health Status

 ▶ Standard CMOS Features        Load Fail-Safe Defaults

 ▶ Advanced BIOS Features        Load Optimized Defaults

 ▶ Advanced Chipset Features     Set Password

 ▶ Integrated Peripherals        Save & Exit Setup

 ▶ Power Management Setup         Exit Without Saving

 ▶ PnP/PCI Configurations

 Esc : Quit                    ↑  ↓  →  ←  : Select Item

 F10 : Save & Exit Setup       (NF-CK804-6K61FA1DC-XX)

                 Change/Set/Disable Password
```

inaccessible. With some implementations, if you use the same password for BIOS startup and DriveLock, you will only need to enter the password once to complete the start up; otherwise, you will need to enter two passwords.

DriveLock with TPM   A more sophisticated DriveLock method is to store the password in an embedded TPM chip. How TPM DriveLock works depends on the manufacturer, but it is usually separate from the other BIOS passwords. With TPM DriveLock enabled, the user must enter a password at bootup that the TPM chip authenticates against the stored encrypted password. If the passwords match, TPM allows the bootup to continue. Although TPM DriveLock is not impossible to break, it is very difficult. If the drive is removed from the computer and installed into another computer, it will not be accessible unless the encryption data was transferred from the original TPM chip to the new TPM-enabled computer.

Enabling TPM for any purpose is more complex than configuring the standard BIOS settings and can vary somewhat from manufacturer to manufacturer. In general, you must first establish ownership of the TPM chip by creating an owner password and a basic user password, and then you can enable TPM security. The opportunity to do this may occur the first time you log on to a new computer with Windows preinstalled. After you have established ownership of the TPM, restart the computer and enter BIOS Setup, providing a preconfigured administrator password to access the new menu for TPM embedded security.

Smart Card Readers

Before using smart cards, a special device called a *smart card reader* must be connected to the computer where the smart card will be used. Setup will require the device itself and the drivers and other software for the device. Further, you must install a special service called Certificate Services on the domain controllers for the Windows domain.

Once you have installed the reader and configured the domain controllers to support Certificate Services, users can log on to the computer. Inserting the card into the reader has the same effect as pressing the CTRL-ALT-DELETE key combination, which is normally required on a Windows computer logging onto a domain. Either action constitutes a *secure attention sequence (SAS)* that clears memory of certain types of viruses that may be lurking and waiting to capture a user name and password. Smart cards are a very secure and tamper-resistant method of authentication.

Key Fobs

Recall that to use the typical key fob, a user first enters a PIN into the key fob, and then the key fob generates a string of characters that the user must use to log on to the network. Installing support for a key fob involves installing an agent that runs on the local computer and a service on the active directory domain controllers. The agent acts as a front end to the authentication process, passing encrypted authentication information to the domain controller that responded to the authentication request.

On the domain controller, the service decrypts the password and provides the password and the user name to the Active Directory security components for authentication. If the password and user name match a domain user account, the user is allowed access to the resources that she has been granted permissions and rights to.

Biometrics

While in theory you can use many types of biometrics for computer login, the most popular and least expensive are fingerprint scanners (also called fingertip scanners). In fact, some laptops and Tablet PCs have a fingerprint scanner built in or packaged with the PC. These built-in devices are the size of a USB port, with a slender scanning slot. External fingerprint scanners are available as PC Card devices, in which the scanner protrudes from the PC Card slot. USB devices, available from several vendors, are approximately the size of a CompactFlash card and have a small, flat sensor pad you touch your finger to. Both the built-in and external devices require drivers and software to integrate with the computer's security system, including Windows domain controllers, if your computer is a member of a Windows domain.

Follow the manufacturer's instructions for installing the software and hardware. After installing the software, configure it to recognize your fingerprint and associate it with your user account. To do this, you will need to provide a user name and password. If your computer is a member of a workgroup, you will need to provide either the computer name or the workgroup name. If your computer is a member of a domain, you must provide the domain name and your user name and password in the domain. When the configuration utility is ready to scan your fingertip and associate it with your user account, it will prompt you. To do this, swipe your finger across the scanner's sensor. You can scan one or more fingers and use any one of them for login. In most cases, the scanner's associated software will also save passwords for applications and Websites and associate them with your profile.

Lock Computer

Before leaving your computer unattended, simply press CTRL-ALT-DELETE to open the Windows Security dialog box and click Lock Computer. That's it. Your desktop will disappear, and the Computer Locked dialog box will appear on the screen. Then, when you return, simply press CTRL-ALT-DELETE to open the Unlock Computer dialog box, shown here. Enter the password for your account, and you will return to the desktop exactly as you left it.

If you did not sign in to Windows through the Windows Security dialog box, pressing CTRL-ALT-DELETE brings up the Task Manager. Then, from the Task Manager menu bar, select Shut Down | Lock Computer. Finally, a keyboard shortcut works no matter how you logged on. If your keyboard has the WinKey (also called the Windows Key), a key with a Windows logo, located between the CTRL and ALT key, press and hold this key while pressing the "l" key (that is, the L key, but it only works in lowercase).

Implementing Data Security

In Chapter 16, you learned about the support built into NTFS for permissions and encryption, as well as BitLocker, a drive encryption feature built into the Ultimate or Enterprise versions of Windows Vista and Windows 7. Here, you will learn how to apply NTFS permissions and encryption and how to permanently remove data from hard drives.

NTFS and Share Permissions

The last line of defense for securing data on a Windows computer is NTFS file and folder permissions. NTFS permissions apply to both the local user sitting at the computer, as well as to someone accessing a file or folder over a network. Set NTFS permissions at the most restrictive level that will allow users to accomplish their work. When preparing to share a folder with network users, first create the folder, set the appropriate NTFS permissions, and then create the share. Finally, set the share permissions.

A shared folder is a folder that is available to network users. *Share permissions* only apply to network users. Therefore, a network user is affected by both share and NTFS permissions, but local users are only affected by NTFS permissions.

Applying NTFS Permissions　In Chapter 16, you learned how to open the Permissions dialog box for a folder, which is similar to opening the Permissions dialog box for a file. From this dialog box, you can assign permission to a file or folder. The standard folder permissions are

Full Control	List Folder Contents
Modify	Read
Read and Execute	Write

The standard file permissions are

Full Control	Read
Modify	Write
Read and Execute	

When folder permissions and the permissions on the files within the folder are combined, the least restrictive permissions apply. But we also need to address the issue of the permission propagation throughout the folder hierarchy, also called inheritance. When you create a new folder or file, it inherits the permissions of the parent folder, unless you choose to block propagation of permissions to child objects.

When you view permissions on a file or folder, the permissions inherited from the parent will be grayed out, and you will not be able to modify those permissions at the child (inherited) level. You can assign new permissions, but you cannot alter inherited permissions unless you modify them in the folder in which they originated. You can block inheritance on a folder or file to which you wish to assign different (usually more restrictive) permissions. Further, you can bypass inheritance with the Allow and Deny permissions for a file or folder. For instance, if you explicitly Allow one of the standard permissions, such as Full Control, the user will have full control to the file or folder, even if inheritance would have given the user a lesser permission. If you explicitly

Deny a permission, the user will be denied a permission, even if it was granted to the user at a higher level in the folder hierarchy or through membership in a group. When a conflict occurs, Deny overrides Allow, and Deny creates the one exception to the rule that when NTFS folder and file permissions, including all inherited permissions, are combined, the least restrictive permission applies.

Shares and Permissions   Although called file sharing, a file share must point to a file folder, not to a single file. To create a file share on your PC, browse to a folder you wish to share, right-click that folder, and select Properties. Click the Sharing tab in the folder's Properties dialog. In Windows 2000/XP, select Share This Folder and complete the rest of the settings. In Windows Vista/7, from the Sharing tab, click the Advanced Sharing button, and then select Share This folder, as shown in this example in which we share the SalesReports folder. A share has three permissions—Full Control, Change, and Read—and each permission has an explicit Allow or Deny permission level. The default permissions on a share give the Read permissions to the Everyone group. If you wish to change the default permission, click the Permissions button to access the Permissions dialog for the share, as shown in Figure 17-2.

FIGURE 17-2

The default
permission
on a shared
folder gives
the Everyone
group the Read
permission.

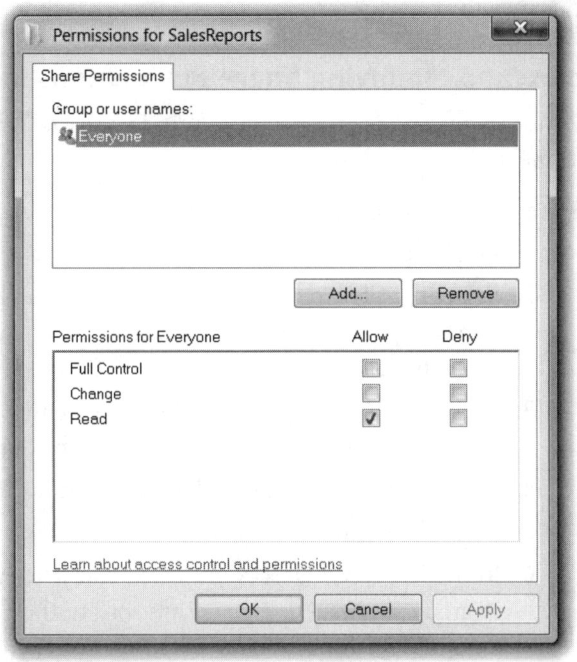

Permissions for SalesReports

Share Permissions

Group or user names:

    Everyone

                                        Add...   Remove

Permissions for Everyone   Allow   Deny

    Full Control   ☐   ☐
    Change   ☐   ☐
    Read   ☑   ☐

Learn about access control and permissions

                        OK   Cancel   Apply

Now, consider what happens when a user connects to files through a share. First, the NTFS file and folder permissions (inherited and otherwise) are combined with the resulting least-restrictive permission applying at the NTFS level, and then the resulting effective NTFS permission is combined with the share-level permission, and the most restrictive permission is applied.

Because you are depending on the NTFS permissions to provide file security to a shared folder, and you know that when NTFS and share permissions are combined, the most restrictive apply, it follows that the default Everyone Read Only permissions on a share will be both too permissive ("everyone" can read the contents) and yet too restrictive if you wish to allow network users to modify files in the shared folder. Exercise 17-1 walks through the steps to modify the share permissions in Windows Vista/7, so only the users or groups you wish to give access to have the Full Control permission, and the Everyone group is completely removed from the share. Modifying the permission actually simplifies your administrative tasks by allowing you to assign the specific permission at the NTFS level.

EXERCISE 17-1

Creating a Share and Modifying Share Permissions in Windows Vista/7

These instructions are specific for Windows Vista/7, but they are very similar to those in Windows 2000/XP:

1. From Windows Explorer, right-click on a folder you wish to share and select Properties.

2. Select the Sharing tab, and then click the Advanced Sharing button. This step is important because you wish to modify the permissions on the share you will create.

3. In the Advanced Sharing dialog, most of the options will be dimmed until you click to place a check in the check box labeled Share This Folder.

4. Once the share is created, the other options will be active.

5. Click the Permissions button.

6. In the Group Or User Names box, click the Add button and select the user or group you wish to give permissions to the share to. These should be users or groups to whom you have already assigned NTFS permissions to the folder. Click OK when you are done.

7. In the Group or User Names box, select each added user or group and give them Full Control. Then, select the Everyone group and click the Remove button.

Permissions and Moving and Copying   When a file or folder is created on an NTFS volume, it inherits permissions from its parent folder; this is also true when a file or folder is copied or moved to a folder on an NTFS volume. There is one important exception to this rule that occurs when you move a file or folder to a different folder on the same NTFS volume: in this case, the file or folder takes its permissions with it.

Administrative Shares

Windows has special hidden administrative shares that it creates automatically and uses when administrators, programs, and services connect to a computer over a network to perform special tasks that are mainly for use in a Microsoft domain network. Before Windows Vista, you could connect to an administrative share using a valid local account, but that feature is disabled in Windows Vista/7, only allowing access to users with domain accounts. You cannot modify the permissions on an administrative share.

An administrative share has a special name that ends in the $ character, which marks the share as being hidden as well as being administrative. You can create a hidden share by appending the dollar sign to its name, but only the operating system can create administrative shares. These are the administrative shares:

- **Root partitions or volumes** Only internal storage is shared, no removable drives (optical, USB flash drives, etc.). The administrative share for drive C: is C$. The complete network path to this share is \\*computername*\C$, which is a Universal Naming Convention (UNC) path.

- **System root folder** This share points to the folder in which Windows was installed, which usually is C:\Windows. The UNC path to this share is \\computername\admin$.

- **FAX$ share** This share points to a shared fax server.

- **IPC$ share** This share is used for temporary connections for remotely administering a computer.

- **PRINT$ share** This share is used for remote administration of shared printers.

Applying NTFS File and Folder Encryption

Encrypting a folder using the Encrypting Files System (EFS) on a Windows NTFS volume does not actually encrypt the folder itself, but all files in the folder are encrypted, and any new files saved in the folder are automatically encrypted. NTFS encryption only applies to files when they are saved in the encrypted folder and when they are moved or copied into unencrypted folders on NTFS volumes that support encryption. This is true, even if the folder to which the files are moved does not have encryption turned on. The files are not encrypted if they are copied to non-NTFS volumes or if they are e-mailed to someone.

Conversely, moving a nonencrypted file into an encrypted folder using drag-and-drop will not encrypt the file. Therefore, if you want a file to remain encrypted, be sure to only use cutting and pasting (or saving from within an application) to move the file into an encrypted folder.

It is simple to encrypt a folder. Simply open the properties dialog box of the folder and click Advanced. In the Advanced Attributes dialog box, click Encrypt Contents To Secure Data (see Figure 17-3), and then click OK.

FIGURE 17-3

Turn on the
Encrypt attribute.

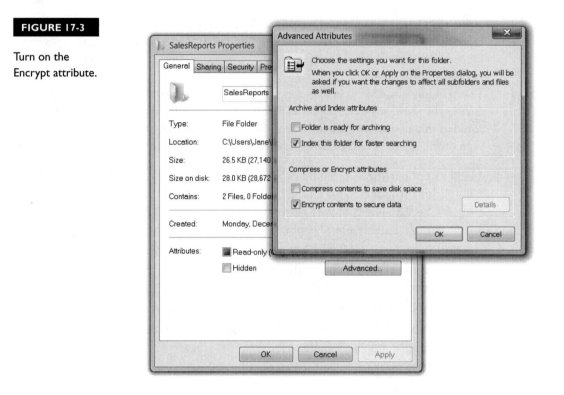

You can only decrypt a file when logged on with the account used to encrypt it. Knowing this is important. Then decryption is transparent; simply open the file using the usual application for that file type. Both normal permissions and a special authorization to decrypt are applied. Even when logged on with another account with Full Control permissions to the file, you will not be able to decrypt the file, and, therefore, you will not be able to use it in any way.

The Encrypting File System (EFS) in Windows XP/Vista/7 has the following features, which are not available in Windows 2000:

- A user can share encrypted files with other users.
- A user may encrypt offline files, which are files that are stored on a network server but cached in local memory when the local computer is disconnected from the server.

The only person who can decrypt a file or folder is the person who encrypted it, or a member of a special group called Recovery Agents. By default, only the local

Administrator account is a member of this group. Recovery is not the same as being able to directly access the data; it is an advanced task, described in the Windows Help utility in each version that supports NTFS encryption.

on the

on the ! *While the CompTIA A+ Essentials Exam objectives require that you understand*
(j)ob *NTFS encryption, this encryption has shortcomings that you will learn about later in this chapter in the section "Troubleshooting Security."*

Working with BitLocker

As described in Chapter 16, BitLocker will encrypt your entire boot volume. It requires that the boot volume be separate from the system volume, and when you install Windows Vista or Windows 7 on a blank hard disk, Windows Setup will create two volumes and will enable BitLocker. The system volume is the active primary partition containing the boot loader accessed by the BIOS during startup. Traditionally, the system and boot volumes are one and the same, but they must be separate because BitLocker cannot encrypt the system volume since it must be accessible by the BIOS startup, which cannot access an encrypted drive. Figure 17-4 shows the Disk Management snap-in on a Vista computer on which the system and

---

FIGURE 17-4   The system and boot partitions are combined on Drive 0.

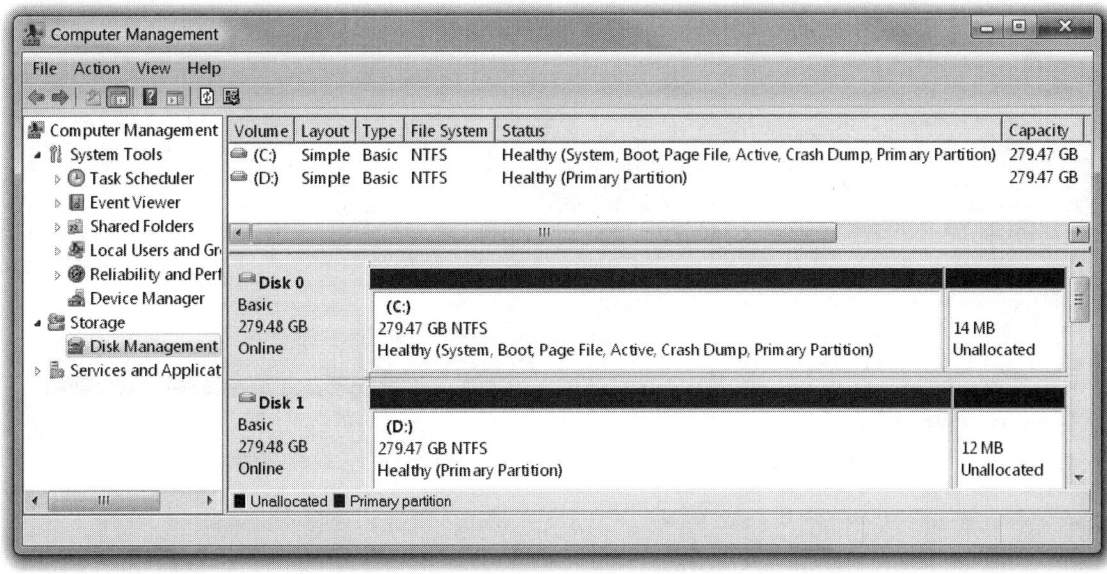

boot volumes (seen on Disk 0) are one and the same: Volume C:. Realizing that two volumes on the same physical disk are required, not two physical disks, is important. Further, beginning with Windows Vista Service Pack 1, drives other than the boot volume can be encrypted with BitLocker.

If you install Windows 7 on an unpartitioned hard drive, it will create a small (approximately 100 MB) system partition and a second partition containing the balance of the drive space as the boot partition, as shown in Figure 17-5, in which Disk 0 contains a 100 MB NTFS volume identified as System, Active, and Primary. The boot volume is drive C:. This configuration will allow BitLocker to store the encryption key on the hard drive.

You can configure BitLocker to install the encryption key in one of several locations, including a USB drive, a TPM chip, or on the system volume (Windows 7 only). The minimum requirements for using BitLocker in Windows Vista are

- Separate NTFS-formatted boot volume
- Separate NTFS-formatted system volume with a minimum of 1.5 GB

If you wish to store the encryption keys on a TPM chip, Vista requires

- TPM version 1.2
- System BIOS, with support to at least 1.2 Trusted Computer Group (TCG) standards

FIGURE 17-5   The system volume and boot volume are separate on Disk 0.

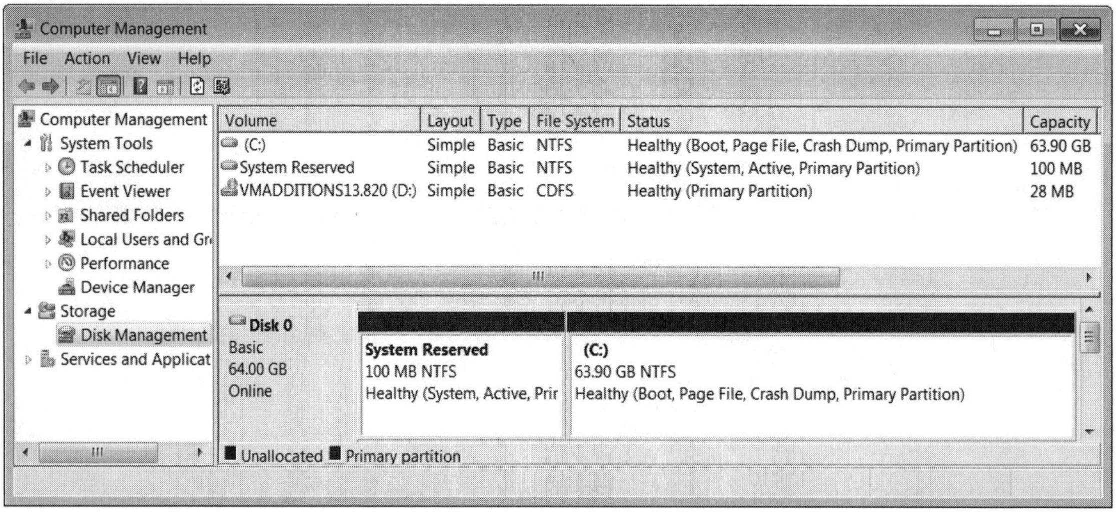

If you wish to store a personal ID number (PIN) on a USB drive, Vista requires

■ System BIOS with support for accessing USB storage devices

Table 17-1 compares the features of BitLocker with NTFS Encrypted File System (EFS).

When you install the Ultimate or Enterprise versions of Windows Vista or Windows 7 on a computer with a TPM 1.2 chip on the motherboard, Windows Setup will automatically enable BitLocker and install the BitLocker applet in Control Panel; otherwise, you will need to enable it yourself.

Data Wiping

In many organizations, the permanent removal of data is an important security function, but in too many organizations removing data from storage devices is overlooked. Further, the ordinary user deletes data every day that is not really deleted but saved in the Recycle Bin. Suppose you delete confidential files and then walk away from your computer without logging off. Someone with malicious intent could sit at your computer in your absence, open the Recycle Bin, and restore the deleted files.

In a scenario in which you remove computers from service, thoroughly removing the data from the hard drives is important because Windows' delete, format, and even partition programs do not truly destroy the data saved on hard drives. Therefore, a determined person can recover the data or even remnants of data files. So whether it

TABLE 17-1	BitLocker	NTFS Encrypted File System (EFS)
BitLocker vs. NTFS Encryption	Protects the entire boot volume.	Only protects specific files and folders; cannot protect operating system files.
	Protects system integrity during the boot process, looking for system changes.	Does not protect system integrity.
	Only administrators can enable or disable.	All users can encrypt files.
	Does not restrict file access to particular users.	Can restrict file access to specific users.
	Stores encryption keys in a TPM or USB drive.	Stores encryption keys in user profiles.
	Can prevent system startup without a PIN	Cannot prevent system startup.
	Requires two volumes.	Can be used when the system and boot volumes are combined.

is your personal financial data, or your employer's super-secret research and development information, start being smarter about removing data from hard drives before it falls into the wrong hands. In the extreme, you could remove a hard drive from a user's computer and physically destroy it. Most of us do not need this extreme measure, but can use one of the many inexpensive software tools for permanently removing data from hard drives.

To begin with, be smarter about deleting files from your hard drive in Windows. A simple delete from any menu in Windows will only move the file from its present folder into the special Recycle Bin folder. There are conditions under which normally deleted files do not go to the Recycle Bin. These include files stored on removable media, files stored on network drives, and files deleted from compressed folders. These files are said to be "permanently" deleted, but even they can be recovered, although not quite as easily as from the Recycle Bin. Undeleting these files takes special hardware.

Recovering a file from the Recycle Bin is easy. This is great for those times when you change your mind after deleting a file—or accidentally delete the wrong file. It is also a security hole. So, when you are absolutely sure that you want to permanently delete a file, you can avoid sending it to the Recycle Bin by selecting the file and holding down the SHIFT key while pressing the DELETE key.

This only protects you from the user who gains access to your computer and uses the Recycle Bin to recover deleted files. It does not protect you from someone who gains access to your computer or hard drive and uses specialized software (and hardware) to recover deleted files or files from a reformatted or repartitioned partition.

on the **Job**

Use the staying power of data on a hard drive to your advantage. If a hard drive with valuable data fails or somehow is damaged so you cannot access the data on the drive, you can send the drive to a company that will recover your data—at a price. If recovering the data is worth thousands of dollars, then this is an option to explore. You will find these services by searching on hard drive data recovery *in a search engine. Remember the bad guys can do this, too.*

To protect your data from malicious attempts to recover it, use a data-wiping program that removes the data from the hard drives and other writable storage devices. The most recent name for this class of program is "shredder." A shredder overwrites deleted files using random data, and it overwrites the same space multiple times. You can choose to shred an entire disk or just any one or more documents. Most of these programs will protect your data from all but the most aggressive attempts to recover data using very high-end software and equipment. Several free shredders and several commercial products are available. Use a shredder program to wipe out a hard drive before moving a computer to another user, donating it, or sending it to a recycler.

Consider using a shredder program on a regular basis to ensure that deleted files are truly deleted. Beginning with XP, Microsoft Windows comes with CIPHER, a command prompt utility for encrypting files and folders. However, one option of this command, the /w (wipe) switch, makes it work like a shredder, permanently removing all deleted files from a folder or an entire volume. When you enter the command

```
cipher /w:drive:\folder
```

all the empty space (which includes deleted files) in the folder specified will be overwritten. If you enter the command with this syntax and only specify a drive, it will overwrite all the "empty" space on the drive. Figure 17-6 shows the CIPHER command with the correct syntax to overwrite the deleted files in D:\SalaryReview. The line of dots acts as a progress bar, with more dots showing as the program works until it is finished. CIPHER makes three passes: in the first pass, it writes all zeros onto the empty space; on the second pass, it writes the hexadecimal value FF over the same space; and on the final pass, it writes random numbers. This technique is the same one used by shredder programs.

Neither the CIPHER command nor third-party shredder programs should be used without taking the precaution of first backing up any data on the same drive, because the way these programs manipulate data on the drives has the potential of damaging good files if anything goes wrong during the shredding process.

| FIGURE 17-6 | The CIPHER command is used to remove all deleted files in a single folder permanently. |

```
D:\>cipher /w:d:\salaryreview
To remove as much data as possible, please close all other applications while
running CIPHER /W.
Writing 0x00
.........................................................................................
.........................
Writing 0xFF
.........................................................................................
.........................
Writing Random Numbers
.........................................................................................
.........................

D:\>
```

Implementing a Defense Against Malicious Software

There are many small building blocks to an effective defense against malicious software. It begins with educating yourself about threats and defenses and setting up a foundation of secure authentication and data protection techniques, and continues with placing a firewall and related technologies at the junction between a private network and the Internet. Then, each computer in the private network must use a group of technologies, such as software firewalls and programs that detect and remove all types of malware, to protect it from attacks.

Self Education

Research malware types, symptoms, and solutions to keep yourself informed. Check out the many *virus encyclopedias* on the Internet sponsored by many different organizations, including security software manufacturers, such as Trend Micro, Kaspersky, and Symantec. Despite the use of the word "virus," these lists contain all types of known threats and are always up-to-date. Threat Encyclopedia is the title of the list maintained by Trend Micro, a security software manufacturer. Also look for antivirus support forums, which also include information about threats other than viruses.

Such resources categorize the malware by type and describe symptoms and solutions. The Web site www.av-comparatives.org contains lists of antivirus support forums and virus encyclopedias. The U.S. government maintains excellent general information on all types of threats to computers at the United States Computer Emergency Readiness Team (US-CERT) Website at www.us-cert.gov/cas/tips/.

Protecting Windows Files and Programs

As described in Chapter 11, Windows 2000/XP protects essential system files and programs using the Windows File Protection (WFP) service. Windows Vista/7 uses the Windows Resource Protection (WRP) service, which also protects critical registry keys.

User Account Control

We described User Account Control (UAC) in Chapter 8. This feature is new in Windows Vista and acts as a defense against all types of malware. With UAC enabled, all users are required to run in standard user mode, even if they log on as a member of the Administrators group. Both types of users can make changes to their own settings, but if either type of user attempts to run a program requiring administrator-level permissions, the screen grays out and a dialog box appears. A standard user will see the Credentials Prompt, requesting an administrator's user name and password. Supplying these credentials will allow the task to continue. An administrator will see a Consent Prompt, as shown here, and must click Continue. In both cases, only the identified task will run in the more privileged mode, while the user continues to work in standard mode.

UAC is turned on by default in both Windows Vista and Windows 7, although Microsoft made changes to Windows 7 that reduce the number of prompts you will see because they changed the number of Windows programs that require approval to run. Turn UAC off or on in Windows Vista by opening User Accounts in Control Panel and then selecting Turn User Account Control On Or Off and clearing the check box labeled Use User Account Control (UAC) To Help Protect Your Computer. Select OK and then click Restart Now or Restart Later. In Windows 7, access this dialog box quickly by typing **uac** in the Start Search box. This dialog is more complex in Windows 7 than in Windows Vista, allowing an administrator to further modify how UAC works. Figure 17-7 shows the Windows 7 User Account Control Settings with four options to control when the Consent Prompt appears when the administrator is logged on:

- **Always Notify** Notify when programs try to install software or make changes to the computer, or when the administrator user attempts to make changes to Windows settings. The desktop will dim when the prompt appears.
- **Notify Me Only When Programs Try To Make Changes To My Computer** The desktop will dim. This is the default setting.

FIGURE 17-7 The Windows 7 User Account Control Settings dialog box

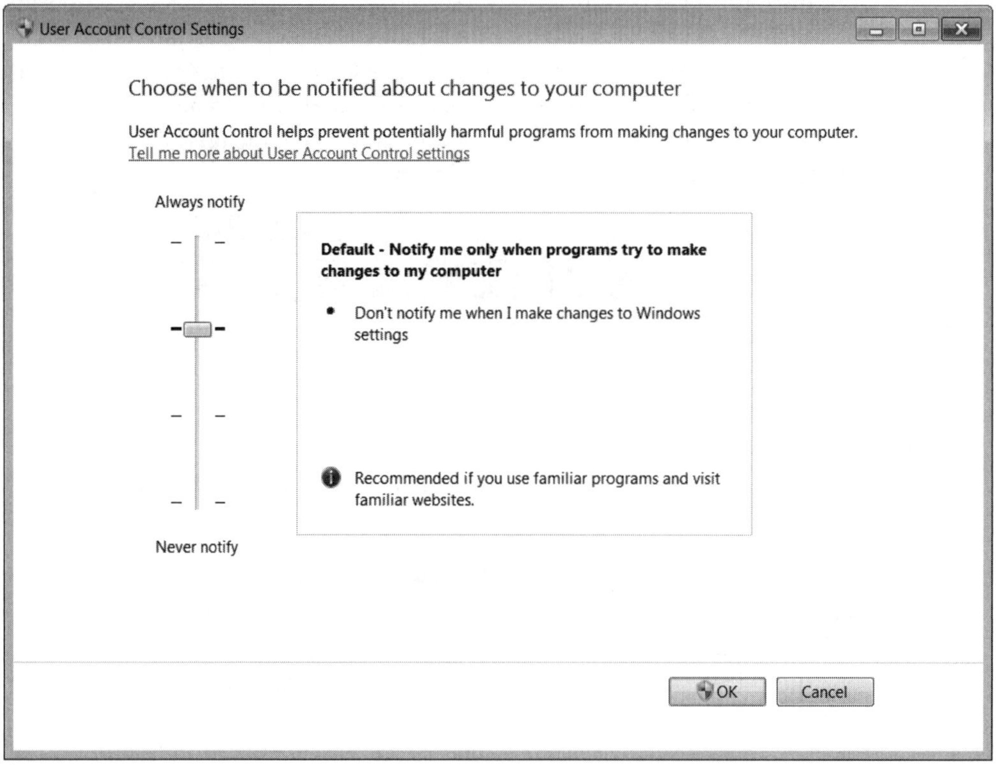

- **Notify Me Only When Programs Try To Make Changes To My Computer (Do Not Dim My Desktop)** Only choose this option if it takes a long time to dim the desktop.
- **Never Notify** Not recommended.

Software Firewalls

If your computer is behind a well-configured hardware firewall, that is all the firewall protection you should require for attacks coming from outside the private network. However, many attacks come from within a private network. Therefore, whether your computer is behind an expensive well-managed hardware firewall or an inexpensive SOHO broadband router, you still need to install and configure a software firewall on every Windows computer. The best strategy is to start with the most restrictive settings and then make exceptions to allow the required traffic to pass through the firewall. Since one of the main jobs of a firewall is to maintain port security, exceptions are in the form of port numbers and can even include specific IP addresses or domain names associated with port numbers. The Windows Firewall Exceptions page allows you to make an exception based on a program name or port. The program names work because Windows knows the port numbers of the listed programs.

Windows Firewall

Until Windows XP Service Pack 2, the Windows firewall was called Internet Connection Firewall (ICF) and was intended to be enabled on a Windows computer that was sharing its Internet connection with other computers on a LAN. When Windows XP installs, this firewall is not turned on. When Windows XP Service Pack 2 installs, it includes the Windows Firewall, which is more configurable than ICF. Windows Firewall is on by default, and you can open the Windows Firewall dialog box through its Control Panel applet. Here is the Windows Firewall dialog box with three tabbed pages as it appears in Windows XP Service Pack 2 or later.

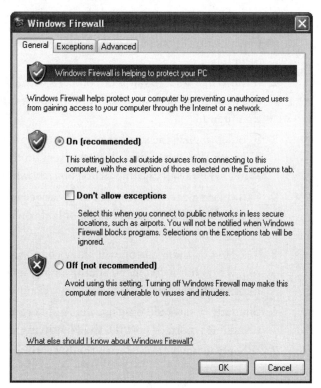

Windows Firewall is on by default in Windows Vista/7, and an easy way to access the Windows Firewall folder is to enter **windows firewall** in the Control Panel's Search box and then click Windows Firewall. Exercise 17-2 will help you learn more about the Windows Firewall. You must log on as the local administrator or a member of the local Administrators group to work with the Windows Firewall (and to complete this exercise). If you install a third-party firewall, you should turn off Windows Firewall, because multiple firewalls on the same computer do not cooperate. Therefore, when you do Exercise 17-2, if you find that it is turned off, do not turn it on unless you are sure that no other firewall is installed.

<hr>

EXERCISE 17-2

Configuring the Windows Firewall in Windows Vista

In this exercise, you may encounter UAC prompts. If you are logged on with an administrator account, simply choose to continue. If you are logged on with a standard account, you will need to enter credentials to continue, in which case, you should obtain these credentials before you begin.

1. Open Control Panel and enter **Windows Firewall** in the Control Panel Search box.

2. If the Windows Firewall is on, proceed with the next steps. If it is not on, find out why. If you have another firewall, you will need to look at the settings for that firewall.

3. In order to view the settings or create exceptions, select Allow A Program Through Windows Firewall (a task item on the left). This will open the Windows Firewall Settings dialog box, shown in Figure 17-8.

4. Only place a check in boxes next to services you need to use. For instance, turn on File And Printer Sharing only if you need to share folders or printers from your computer.

5. The Add Program button will allow you to add a program or service to the list. We do not recommend adding a program unless you have very reliable information that this is required and will not cause harm.

6. Similarly, you should only use the Add Port button if you have expert advice on adding a port, or port ID, the identifying information for an IP packet.

7. When you have finished with the Exceptions page, click the Advanced tab.

The Windows
Firewall Excep-
tions tab in
Windows Vista

8. The Network Connection Settings section of the Advanced page will allow you to enable or disable the firewall for network connections to this computer. If you only have a single network connection, you will see only one connection listed.

9. Finally, the Restore Defaults button at the bottom of this page allows you to restore Windows Firewall to the default settings.

10. When you are finished, close the Windows Firewall dialog box by clicking OK (to accept changes) or Cancel to quit without making changes.

Third-Party Software Firewalls

There are many inexpensive third-party software firewalls—some commercial and some free. Examples of personal firewalls are ZoneAlarm and ZoneAlarm Pro by CheckPoint, Norton Personal Firewall by Symantec, and Sunbelt Personal Firewall from Sunbelt (previously named Kerio Personal Firewall). Each of these is available as a separate product, or as part of a security software bundle. ZoneAlarm is a free program with fewer features than ZoneAlarm Pro.

Antivirus

An antivirus program can examine the contents of a disk and RAM looking for hidden viruses and files that may act as hosts for virus code. Effective antivirus products not only detect viruses in incoming files before they can infect your system, but also remove existing viruses and help you recover data that has been lost because of a virus.

To keep an antivirus program up-to-date, always enable the update option you will find in all popular antivirus programs. Configure it to connect automatically to the manufacturer's Website, check for updates, and install them. An antivirus program will update at least two components: the antivirus engine (the main program) and a set of patterns of recognized viruses, usually contained in files called definition files. Manufacturers of antivirus software commonly charge an annual fee for updates to the antivirus engine and to the definitions. Common commercial antivirus manufacturers with both home and business solutions include Symantec, TrendMicro, CA, McAfee, Kaspersky, and Grisoft. There are excellent free services for home users. One example is AVG Anti-Virus from Grisoft. Even the commercial vendors who do not offer a completely free product often allow you to try their product for a period, usually 30 days.

Phishing Filter

In Chapter 16, you learned about the dangers of phishing, a practice in which authentic-looking communications attempt to fool you into providing personal financial information. Phishing is often very difficult to detect for what it truly is. Along with educating yourself on what to look for, be sure to install or enable a phishing filter for your Web browser. You may already have an unenabled one. Keep in mind that even with a phishing filter, you must still be alert to possible phishing attacks. A phishing filter will check for suspicious behavior on the Websites you visit. It will also usually maintain a list of reported phishing sites. Here is how a phishing filter works:

- The filter manufacturer, such as Microsoft for Windows Internet Explorer 7 and 8, maintains a list of legitimate Websites, which it downloads to your computer on a regular basis. As you browse the Web, the phishing filter compares each site you visit with the list.

■ The phishing filter looks at the information posted on Websites and compares it to traits typical of phishing Websites on each site you visit. If it detects these traits, it will warn you and flag the Website as suspicious. If you receive a message that a site is suspicious, do not submit any personal information.

■ Depending on how you configure a phishing filter, it may automatically send addresses of Websites you visit to the manufacturer, which compares them to a list of reported phishing Websites. The information sent includes your IP address, which is encrypted using SSL, and only the domain and path of the Website. It sends no other information identifying your activities at the Website.

To configure Phishing Filter in Internet Explorer 7, open Internet Options. Internet Options is a Control Panel applet. You can open Internet Options from Control Panel or from within IE by selecting Tools | Phishing Filter | Phishing Filter Settings. In Internet Options, select the Advanced tab, and scroll down to Phishing Filter in the Settings list.

While browsing the Web, selecting the Tools | Phishing Filter option on the Tools menu in IE will allow you to check the current Website, turn off (or on) Automatic Website checking, report a site, or open the Internet Options menu to change Phishing Filter settings.

In Internet Explorer 8, the SmartScreen Filter, which also protects against fraudulent Websites and other threats, replaces Phishing Filter. It works much like Microsoft's Phishing filter, except it communicates with the Microsoft SmartScreen service while you are browsing the Internet, comparing sites you visit with known phishing and malware sites.

Keep one thing in mind: a phishing filter is only an aid. You must educate yourself, and the people whose computers you support, about the tactics phishers employ. Never provide your social security number or other financial information in response to an unsolicited message—no matter how official the message or the method of transmitting it appears to be. Phishing attacks can come to you via any means—through the mail (postal service) or via e-mail.

Antispyware/Anti-Adware/Pop-Up Blocker

As you learned in Chapter 16, spyware and adware are types of programs that install on your computer and perform functions on behalf of others. The intent of spyware can be very malicious, including identity theft, whereas the intent of adware is generally less malicious, even if the people responsible for the adware hope to profit by advertising their products.

How spyware and adware get installed on your computer is yet another issue. Users have a hard time believing that their actions invite malicious programs in, but that is how it happens. Perhaps you installed a wonderful free program. You may be very happy with the program itself, but you may have also installed spyware, adware, or worse along with the program.

The most insidious method used to install spyware and adware on your computer comes in the form of a pop-up window resembling a Windows alert. These bogus messages may warn you that spyware was installed on your computer, and you must take some action, such as clicking OK in the pop-up window. By clicking OK, you supposedly start downloading software from Microsoft or another credible source to install on your computer to rid you of the threat. In reality, it is only a disguised method for installing spyware or adware.

Do not fall for these tricks. Fighting these threats begins with being very careful about how you respond to messages in pop-up windows and what you install on your computer while browsing the Web. If you are unsure of a message, do not click any buttons or links within the window, but close it using the close button at the upper-right.

Many free and commercial programs are available that effectively block various forms of spyware and adware, especially pop-ups. These are the easiest to block, and the most annoying because a pop-up advertisement appears in its own window and must be closed or moved before you can see the content you were seeking. Such a blocking program is *a pop-up blocker*. Configure a pop-up blocker so it will block pop-ups quietly. You can also opt to configure it to make a sound, and/or display a message, allowing you to decide whether to block each pop-up.

Microsoft's Windows Defender protects your computer from spyware and some other types of malicious software packages. It installs with Windows Vista and Windows 7, and it is available as a free download for Windows XP, but it does not support Windows 2000.

We have found a few Websites where blocking all pop-ups has blocked much of the content we were seeking. If you find that to be the case, configure the pop-up blocker to allow pop-ups for that session or configure it to display a message. You can also configure it to always allow pop-ups from specified sites.

Pop-up blockers are now the norm in Web browsers, and third-party pop-up blockers are available. If your Web browser does not have a pop-up blocker option, you may simply need to update the browser to a newer version.

Antispyware software is now often part of an Internet security package that includes a software firewall, antivirus, antispam, as well as antispyware. Many vendors offer these packages, including Symantec, Trend, AVG, and others. You can also find free or inexpensive individual antispyware programs.

Implementing Security Programs

Today's security software is very different from a decade ago, because today's threats are more diverse than a decade ago. Therefore, you are not as likely to install a simple antivirus program, but rather an entire security suite, so we'll talk in terms of a multi-function security suite. Symantec, Trend Micro, and many other software manufacturers offer such suites, which normally offer a full range of security products including anti-virus, antispyware, phishing filters, and even firewalls. Like these third-party security suites, Microsoft's Windows Security Essentials protects against all known malicious software. It is available as a free download from Microsoft's Website at www.microsoft .com/security_essentials/.

Installing a security suite that includes a firewall will normally disable the Windows Firewall. Installing this into Windows Vista or Windows 7 automatically disables Windows Defender. Before installing a security suite in Windows XP, you must uninstall Windows Defender.

Part of the installation of a security suite is a thorough scan of your computer, including memory contents and all portions of all storage devices, examining all types of files, and the parts of the disk where viruses can hide, such as the boot sector or boot block. Also, as part of the installation, you can choose to turn on automatic scans (the normal default) and the frequency of those scans. Even when you configure automatic scans, you can choose to initiate a scan when you detect possible malware symptoms.

Identifying Malware Symptoms

Malware symptoms range from no symptoms to overt, but not too obvious, symptoms such as sudden slowness, unusual cursor movements, and unusual network activity (indicated by status lights or messages) when you are not actively accessing the network.

Removing Malware

When malware is detected, you must remediate the infected systems, removing the malware and repairing any damage it may have done. We will explore several techniques.

Quarantine

In the case of detected malware, your security program may quarantine the malware file or it may remove it entirely. It all depends on the security software configuration. A quarantined file is disabled, but not removed from the computer. Some security software talks about the malware being in a "vault," which is the same as quarantining. Since security software can make mistakes, identifying a critical and uninfected file as malware, configuring it to place detected malware into quarantine gives you an opportunity to review the file and decide what action to take. On a larger scale, some organizations, upon discovering that one or more computers are infected, will quarantine those computers, removing them from the network entirely until the malware is removed.

Scan and Removal Techniques

Some malware is not detectable under normal computer operation. These infections are often, but not always, ones that occurred before adequately protecting a system. They can also occur if you have not kept up-to-date with updates—both to the operating system and to the security programs. If you suspect that a computer is infected, but a normal scan from within Windows does not detect malware, then you should try a special technique for detecting and removing malware. For such a scenario, the top security programs have a special Safe Mode Scan that runs in Windows Safe Mode. To do this, restart Windows in Safe Mode, and then locate the security program and have it run a full scan. If it detects malware, have it quarantine or remove it, and then restart the computer and see if the symptoms have gone away.

Although the top security programs claim to protect against all types of malware, including boot sector viruses, these are rather difficult viruses to detect and remove once they have infected a computer. Therefore, security software will, by default, scan all removable media upon insertion, not allowing access to it or programs to run from it until the scan is complete. Never disable this option.

If you suspect a boot sector virus in Windows 2000 or Windows XP, repair the boot block with the Recovery Console. In Windows Vista or Windows 7, use the System Recovery Options menu described in Chapter 11.

Preventive Maintenance for Security

As all steps you take to implement security are preventive steps, we do not need to add a long description of preventive security maintenance. There are, however, certain tasks that we should add to those described so far in this chapter that fall under preventive maintenance, beginning with backing up data, keeping up-to-date on service packs and patches, training users, and recognizing social engineering.

Implementing Data Backup Procedures

An important part of data security is a backup policy that includes frequent backups of data to removable media. Storage of the media should also be part of the policy. Although backup media should be handy for quick restores, a full backup set should also be stored offsite in case something occurs to the building in which the computer is housed, as well as to the computer. The frequency of the backups, and of the full backup that is stored offsite, depends on the needs of the organization. It is not possible to overemphasize how important it is to back up data. We discussed backup in Chapter 10. We will talk about additional issues related to backup here.

Users can back up files they created on their local NTFS volume, including the My Documents or Documents folder in their own profile and its contents. Users can restore files and folders to which they have the Write permission on an NTFS volume. Members of the local Administrators and Backup Operators groups have the right to back up and restore all files. Individual users in these groups can back up and restore files that they do not normally have permissions to access. This ability does not give them any other access to these files and folders.

Installing Service Packs and Patches

Although this point was made previously in this book, it is important to the security of your computer and your confidential data that you keep your computer updated with the latest service packs and patches. If you have Internet access, turn on Automatic Updates in Windows. In addition, any security software you install will normally have an automatic update feature. Be sure to turn this on.

e**x**a m
ⓦatch   *Although every security measure you take is preventive against threats, the CompTIA A+ Essentials Exams stress the importance of keeping your operating system and security software up-to-date with service packs, patches,* *and user training. User training should include the use of the malware prevention technologies on users' systems and the social engineering situations they may encounter.*

SCENARIO & SOLUTION

I support computers in a large organization that uses Cisco routers and firewalls at all connections to the Internet. Why should we use personal firewalls on all our Windows computers?	A properly configured hardware firewall will protect against invasions to the network, but it will not protect each computer from invasion from within the private network.
Now that I have a phishing filter enabled in Windows, do I need to be on the watch for phishing?	Yes, you still must watch for phishing attempts. Educate yourself on the techniques phishers use to obtain your personal financial information.

Training Users

Knowledge of the danger of threats and ways to prevent malicious software from invading computers is important to both the computer professional and to each PC user. Do your part to keep yourself current on security technologies. Depending on your role in an organization, take all opportunities to educate users. Make them aware of the company's security policy and the role they need to play in preventing attacks.

Recognizing Social Engineering

In Chapter 16, you learned about social engineering and ways to recognize social engineering when you encounter it in e-mails and other messages. Do your part to inform other users about social engineering by sharing what you have learned and by directing them to look at a site that educates people about these threats. We gave an example in Exercise 15-1.

Securing a Wireless Network

In Chapter 14, you learned about creating a Wi-Fi network. The radio signals Wi-Fi uses make your Wi-Fi network vulnerable. Anyone with a computer with a Wi-Fi adapter can pick up these radio waves and access your network and your computers, unless you take steps to secure your wireless network.

Wireless Access Point/Wireless Router Configuration

The heart and soul of a wireless network is the wireless access point or wireless broadband router. This is the central point for implementing security, followed up by configuring the wireless NICs for each client. The important security tasks involve keeping the WAP updated, setting the administrator password, disabling the SSID broadcast, configuring MAC filtering, disabling DHCP, encrypting transmitted signals, and configuring firewall settings. You should implement as many of these changes as is practical, and be sure to document all the settings on your WAP and your wireless client computers. This will help you to restore the WLAN to the same level of protection if something should happen to the WAP, such as a complete failure or an invasion by someone who manages to lock you out. More on this last a bit later in the following discussion.

We assume that you have updated the firmware on your WAP and wireless NICs, as suggested in Chapter 14. Exercise 14-2 in Chapter 14 walked you through configuring a WAP, including basic security settings such as changing the default administrator user name and password and changing the SSID name. We will pick up where that exercise left off, describing other security tasks, such as disabling the SSID broadcast, and go into more detail here.

Disable SSID Broadcast

After you change the default SSID to a unique name, disable the SSID broadcast. Disabling the broadcast makes it difficult for the casual user to see your wireless network, since the wireless configuration software that comes with most wireless NICs only displays wireless networks detected from the access point's broadcast of the SSID name. Disabling this also reduces the volume of wireless traffic incrementally. As with the IP address, you will need to search for the SSID broadcast setting using the access point's Website. Once the SSID broadcast is disabled, you will need to manually configure each wireless client with the SSID. Remember you changed it from the default, and so you must use the new name.

Enable MAC Filtering

All wireless access points that we have worked with also allowed you to limit users of the wireless network based on the MAC address of each wireless NIC. Recall that all NICs have a universally unique physical address, called the MAC address. Filtering will require that you obtain the MAC address for each wireless computer. You can do this several ways, but we like using the IPCONFIG command on each computer.

Write down the MAC address and connect to the WAP using your browser. Search for the page where you can configure MAC filtering and enter the MAC address for each wireless NIC. If you cannot find a setting on the WAP that uses the term "MAC filtering," look for other terms, such as "Trusted Wireless Stations." Figure 17-9 shows the MAC filter page for a wireless broadband router with a single MAC address entered. Each address must be added separately to this list.

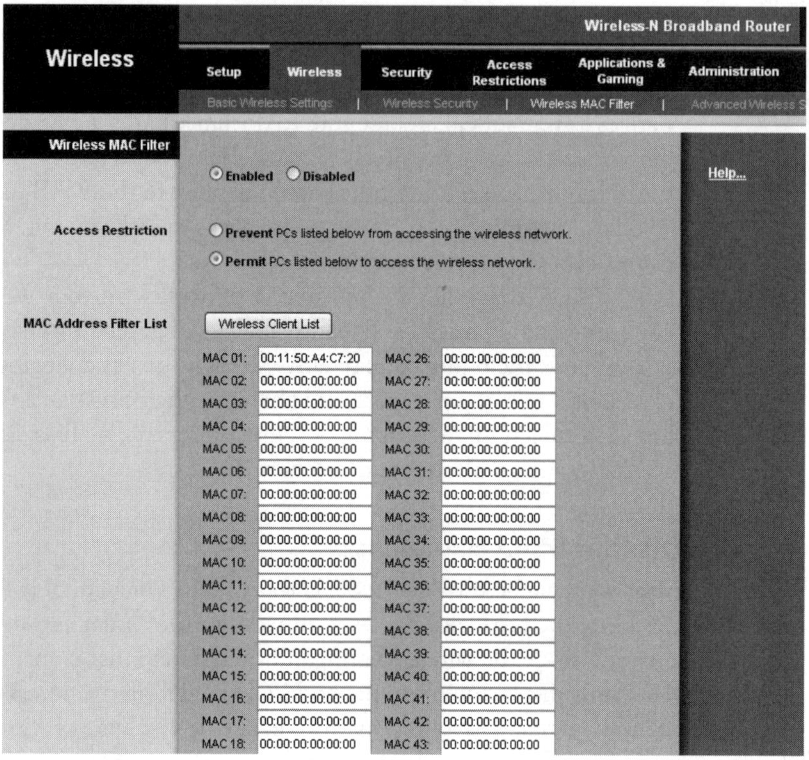

FIGURE 17-9

The Wireless
MAC filter page
on a wireless
broadband router

Disable DHCP

One task that will make your wireless network less vulnerable is to disable DHCP
on the wireless access point. Unwelcome wireless clients must have an IP address
to access your wireless network, and if, in the absence of other security, the DHCP
server gives out addresses indiscriminately it makes it easy for intruders.

To set up a wireless network without a DHCP server requires some knowledge of
IP addressing because, once you disable the DHCP server on the WAP, you will need
to give each wireless client on the network a unique IP address. You must make sure
the IP address for each wireless client is on the same logical network as the access
point. To do this, look at the IP address of the access point. This address is normally
the only one that is static because the access point includes the DHCP server, which
gives out addresses.

Using the Web-based administrative tool for your WAP, locate the DHCP settings
for the wireless network and turn off DHCP. Then assign appropriate static addresses
to each wireless NIC on your network. For instance, if the internal IP address for

the WAP is 192.168.1.1, with a network mask of 255.255.255.0, manually assign addresses in the 192.168.1/24 network to each wireless NIC, being careful not to duplicate addresses. See the instructions for manually configuring a client with an IP configuration later in this chapter in "Wireless Client Configuration."

If you do not wish to disable DHCP, then limit the number of IP addresses the DHCP server can give out to the number of wireless clients on your network. This will at least avoid unused wireless connections, but don't stop there.

Encrypt Wireless Signals

The most important setting you will find involves encrypting the wireless transmissions. On the wireless router's Website, this setting may simply be labeled "Security" or "Encryption." Once you locate it, look for the latest Wi-Fi encryption.

If you do not see a setting for WPA or WPA2, it may be labeled WPA-PSK or WPA-PSK for WPA pre-shared key, or simply PSK or PSK2. You will also need to choose the encryption method (TKIP or AES). Once you have done this, enter a passphrase from 8 to 64 characters. The more complicated and the longer the passphrase, the more secure it will be. Also, be sure you remember this passphrase, because you will need to enter it in the wireless configuration utility at each computer on the WLAN.

One big problem you could encounter is a mixture of old and new equipment. If your WAP supports WPA2, but your NICs do not, you need to make a choice. Use one of the weaker encryption standards that all the wireless devices support, or spend the time and money upgrading to newer NICs that support the same encryption standard as the WAP.

A wireless device manufactured before 2003 may only support an older encryption standard, Wired Equivalent Privacy (WEP). If wireless security is important to you, ensure that all of your wireless devices support WPA2, which may require upgrading the BIOS in the device, or even replacing it.

Enable the Firewall

Enable the firewall in your WAP. The firewall setting may be several menu layers down, but locate it and ensure it is turned on. Then, enable the options appropriate for your network. A wireless firewall may be minimal, because it assumes that you do not have servers on the wireless LAN. If available, enable the denial of service protection, perhaps labeled "DoS Firewall."

Wireless Client Configuration

Wireless client configuration follows the access point configuration and must be compatible with the settings on the access point.

DHCP Client Configuration

By default, when a new network interface card is installed on a computer that has the TCP/IP stack, Windows configures the card as a DHCP client. Therefore, you should not have to touch this if a DHCP server is enabled on the network.

Manual IP Configuration

If you have chosen to disable the DHCP server on the wireless access point and do not have another one on the network, you must manually configure the wireless NIC on each client computer with an appropriate IP configuration.

To do this, for each PC that has a wireless NIC, open the Network Connections applet from Control Panel. Right-click the connection for the wireless NIC and select Properties. On the General tab, scroll down, select Internet Protocol (TCP/IP), and click Properties. In the Internet Protocol (TCP/IP) Properties dialog box, enter a unique IP address that is on the same network as the WAP, enter the same subnet mask as that of the WAP, enter the WAP's IP address in the Default Gateway box, and enter the DNS service addresses provided by your ISP or network administrator. Figure 17-10 shows an example of a static IP address setting.

FIGURE 17-10

Manually enter the IP settings for each wireless NIC.

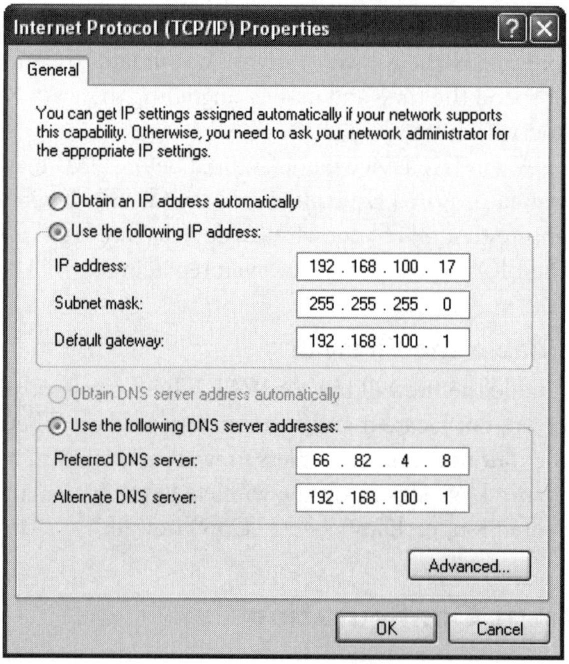

Manual SSID Configuration

If you have disabled the SSID broadcast on the WAP, then you will need to manually configure each wireless client with the SSID name, since the name cannot otherwise be easily discovered when SSID broadcast is turned off.

MAC Filtering

If you have configured the WAP to allow only specified MAC addresses, then every time you add a new client to the WLAN, you need to discover the MAC address of the wireless NIC on the new client and add it to the list on the WAP. You can usually find the MAC address on the wireless device itself or on the packaging, or else you can find it after installing the wireless NIC by running the IPCONFIG command using the following syntax: **ipconfig /all**.

Encryption

You will need to configure each wireless client to match the WAP's encryption setting. In most cases, you will need to enter the appropriate passphrase—the one you configured on the WAP. If the client is not at the same level of encryption as the WAP, determine if an upgrade is available from the manufacturer. If not, consider purchasing a new wireless NIC.

Troubleshooting Security

Troubleshooting security follows the same path as all computer troubleshooting. Gather information, perform an analysis, arrive at possible solutions, and apply the solution and test it. Once you are successful, document the process so you or your coworkers will not have to "solve" the same problem twice. There are certain problems that are specific to PC security, and you will explore some of these in the following sections.

BIOS Password Problems

Earlier in this chapter, we explored the issue of setting passwords in BIOS. As with all passwords, forgetting a BIOS password is easy. How this will affect the user depends on the type of BIOS password that was set.

If a BIOS password is set on the system at startup, no one will be able to get beyond the BIOS password prompt and boot up the computer until the password is provided. Forget the password, and you are locked out of using the computer.

If a BIOS password is set on the System Setup menu, and only on this menu, the computer will boot up normally without requiring a BIOS system startup password. Forget the password and you can start up the computer just fine, but you will not be able to access the System Setup menu and make changes. As we mentioned earlier, this password is necessary in situations in which people have physical access to computers, as in a computer lab.

In both cases, documenting the password or passwords is very important, and you should maintain and keep them in a safe place available to all authorized personnel. The password should not be something only the head techie knows but does not share with anyone else. There are better ways to gain job security.

If you set a password and later forget it, you will have to find out how to reset the BIOS in order to access BIOS Setup. Finding this in the motherboard manual can be difficult, as we have never seen one with an index. Fortunately, motherboard manuals are usually short and the instructions for resetting or cleaning the BIOS settings are usually near the back in a troubleshooting section. Alternatively, search the motherboard manufacturer's Website. What you must do after that depends on the system and can range from temporarily removing the battery that supports CMOS to changing a jumper setting and restarting the computer. Then, you can enter Setup without providing a password. Your work is not yet done, however, because you will have lost all custom settings and will need to reconfigure the BIOS settings. Recall Exercise 4-5 in Chapter 4, in which you learned how to back up CMOS settings. If you have access to a copy of the CMOS settings for the computer, the configuration process will be far easier than trying to guess what the settings were. If you do not know the previous BIOS settings, accept the default settings, but you may face more than one choice here, such as Fail-Safe Defaults and Optimized Defaults. If you have such a choice, select Optimized Defaults first and see if everything functions. If not, you will have to change to the Fail-Safe Defaults. The moral to this story is either don't set a BIOS password or, if you do, don't lose the password.

Anyone who knows how can remove a BIOS password from a physically unlocked computer case. This demonstrates the futility of setting BIOS passwords on physically unsecured computers.

Biometrics

Sometimes users cannot log on to a Windows XP computer using biometrics when the computer resumes from Standby or Hibernate. Microsoft solved this problem in a hotfix. A hotfix is program code that fixes a specific problem. A hotfix is normally only available from Microsoft Product Support Services to persons who identify the problem. In these cases, Microsoft usually waives the normal charges for Microsoft

Product Support Services. When we last checked, contacting Support Services was the only manner in which this fix was available. However, it is worth running Windows Update to see if this hotfix was added to the updates that are available free through this service. If you support one or more Windows computers that are using biometric authentication, check to see if they were updated, and update them before this becomes a problem.

When this problem occurs, the computer will still accept a basic interactive logon from the keyboard. Therefore, enter a user name and password from the keyboard. Then take steps to update the computer.

Forgotten Windows Password

If you have forgotten your password, there is help. For one thing, if you are part of a Windows domain, tell the network administrator about your problem. Lost passwords are at the top of the list of things administrators must fix, especially in an environment where people log on with a standard interactive logon—entering user names and passwords at their keyboard. The administrator can log on with the Domain Administrator account (or any account with appropriate rights), access the Domain User account, and reset the password. The administrator can assign a password and configure your account so you will sign on with the assigned password but then must change it during that logon.

Now, if you are not part of a Windows domain, there is still some hope if you can log on with the Administrator account. If you know the local Administrator password, or an account that is a member of the local Administrators group, simply log on with this user name and password modify the password setting for the user.

If you do not know the Administrator password, and you are working with Windows XP, your installation of Windows may possibly have a hidden Administrator account. To access this account, simply restart your computer in Safe Mode. Basic Safe Mode will do. If you need help with Safe Mode, flip back to Chapter 11 and read about Safe Mode. Log on in Safe Mode with the Administrator account. Unless the password was changed, you can leave the password blank when you log on. After logging on as the Administrator, run the User Accounts applet, and then reset the password on the user account.

No Permissions on FAT32

You would like to set permissions on a folder that you plan to share. You first notice that there is no Security tab in the Properties dialog box for the folder. Perhaps you don't have Simple File Sharing turned on. Then you notice that the volume is not

NTFS but FAT32. FAT32 does not support file- and folder-level permissions. The only permissions in this case will be at the share level, and you want to set NTFS permissions so you can assign permissions to each subfolder under the shared folder. What can you do?

If there is no compelling reason for using FAT32 on the volume, convert it to NTFS. Before doing this, back up the entire drive that you plan to convert, just in case something goes wrong during the process. Once the backup is completed, convert the volume using the Disk Management node of the Computer Management console, or by opening a Command Prompt window and running the CONVERT program. The syntax for running the convert program is

```
convert d: /fs:ntfs
```

where *d*: is the drive you wish to convert. Whether you use Disk Management or the CONVERT program, if the drive you are converting is not being used by the OS or any other program, the conversion will occur immediately. If the drive is in use, as is always the case with the system drive (normally drive C:), you will see a message that the conversion will occur the next time Windows is restarted.

This conversion is one-way. You cannot convert back from NTFS to FAT32 unless you reformat the drive, and then you lose all the data on the hard drive.

Once you have converted the file system from FAT32 to NTFS, you can assign permissions to files and folders and use other NTFS features not available in FAT32.

Encryption Issues

If you, or the users you support, encrypt files using NTFS encryption, you risk having the encryption defeated or being locked out of your own encrypted files. Sometimes we leave the worst news for last. After learning about NTFS encryption in Chapter 16, we will now explain its shortcomings, and why we do not use it.

NTFS Encryption Can Be Broken

One way in which someone can break NTFS encryption is by guessing your password. Once someone does that, that person can log on with your user name, which is often displayed in the logon dialog box as the last logged-on user. Once logged on, the invader has access to everything on your computer, including your encrypted files.

The key is to not allow any unauthorized person physical access to your computer. With physical access, someone can use a variety of tools to access your encrypted files. There are inexpensive software tools, classified as password recovery software, that can crack passwords on Windows accounts—both local and domain. If you need such a tool, use an Internet search engine to search on this category of software.

Encrypted Files Can Become Inaccessible

You have been careful to encrypt sensitive data files and to back up your computer. Then, one day your computer crashes. After trying many recovery options, you reformat the hard drive, reinstall Windows, and restore your data from the most recent backup set. Your new installation of Windows has an account with the same user name as your old one. You believe you did everything you were supposed to do, but you cannot access the encrypted files you restored to your computer. What can you do?

First, we will explain what went wrong in spite of your diligence. Your user account in the original installation of Windows had a unique security identifier (SID). The NTFS encryption associated this key with the encrypted file, and the only person who can open and use the encrypted files is someone who logs on with the account using this SID. Unfortunately, when Windows failed, it took your account and this identifier with it. After you reinstalled Windows and created a new account, even though you used the old name, the new account received an entirely different SID. Therefore, when logged on with this account, you cannot use the encrypted files.

Products such as ElcomSoft's Advanced EFS Recovery program may be able to decrypt NTFS files.

Software Firewall Issues

A firewall may prompt a pop-up message that a program running on your computer is trying to access the Internet; the firewall then requires that you make a decision to allow this action or not. When this happens, use a search engine to discover if the program is harmful. A wealth of information is on the Web about problem programs. If your firewall has blocked a program, you can be sure that others' firewalls have also. Your search will normally result in many hits, and some of the Websites it discovers may not be well monitored or the advice may not be from experienced and qualified people. Do not make a decision based on just one Website. Check out several. If you know and trust the company posting the information, such as one of the top security software companies, you may accept their answer as authoritative.

Some personal firewalls provide additional information on blocked files with a recommended action you may choose to take. Still, you often have to make a decision without being absolutely sure of the safety of the program, even when it appears to be one you are familiar with. Windows does protect certain operating system files with safeguards in the form of digital signatures. If Windows indicates that a program is digitally signed, you can usually trust the program.

Wireless Access Point Problems

You are the administrator of a wireless LAN and find that although you could once access the wireless access point's Web page, you no longer can do this from any computer on the WLAN. You also fear that someone has gotten into the WAP and made changes in the security settings. What can you do? You will need to reset the WAP, using the manufacturer's instructions. Then, because resetting the WAP erases all your settings, you will need to reconfigure it. Be sure to set a complex password on the Administrator account to keep intruders out, and set all the security settings on the WLAN.

SCENARIO & SOLUTION

I am preparing a new computer for a computer lab. How can I configure the computer so students will not be able to access the system setup and change the BIOS settings, making the computer unusable?	Check out the manufacturer's documentation on the computer's system settings and look for the password settings. Set the password to the BIOS Settings menu only. Do not set the password on system startup unless the security policy for the computer lab requires this.
We are getting ready to order ten laptops for traveling auditors who will have sensitive data on the hard drives. We are looking for a secure authentication method beyond a simple user name and password for basic interactive logon to a Windows domain. What do you recommend?	Since you are in the process of purchasing the laptops, check out biometric devices, such as fingerprint scanners. These are more secure than the basic interactive logon and work with a Windows domain.
Our employees' computers are in a public area where customers and others can easily wander in and out. Employees must frequently leave their computers unattended during the workday for brief periods. How can they keep their desktops secure without shutting down their applications and Windows?	We suggest you show the employees how to use Windows' Lock Computer option.

CERTIFICATION SUMMARY

There are no easy answers or quick fixes when it comes to computer security. Security threats go beyond simple computer invasions to inflict damage to threats against your very identity. Therefore, computer security must be multifaceted to protect computers, data, and users.

This multifaceted approach includes implementing a variety of security programs and features, including authentication, permissions at both the file system level and the share level, NTFS or BitLocker encryption, backing up data, and removing data from computers moved from one place to another or taken out of service with your organization.

Additionally, train users to protect their computers when they must temporarily walk away. One effective and simple solution is to use Windows' Lock Computer, which preserves the desktop and open files, while protecting them from intruders until the user enters a password to unlock the computer.

Take steps to secure wireless networks, beginning with the access point configuration and extending to the wireless clients, which must be compatible with the WAP. You will need to make decisions about the configuration based on what all the wireless devices in the WLAN support. Areas of concern are DHCP, SSID name and broadcasting, MAC filtering, the administrative password, firmware updates, encryption, and firewall settings.

Approach security troubleshooting as you would any PC troubleshooting. Some special security issues are BIOS passwords, biometric devices, forgotten Windows passwords, lack of permissions on FAT32 volumes, problems with NTFS encryption, software firewall messages, and preventive maintenance for security.

✓ TWO-MINUTE DRILL

Here are some of the key points covered in Chapter 17.

Implementing Authentication and Data Security

❑ Two types of BIOS passwords can be set—one that must be entered at startup before an operating system is loaded, and another that is required for access to the BIOS system settings (also known as CMOS settings).

❑ A smart card reader is a device for authenticating with a smart card. It requires software and drivers on the local computer and Certificate Services installed on the domain controllers for the Windows domain.

❑ A smart card cannot be used in three scenarios:

    ❑ When a user is required to join his or her computer to a domain.

    ❑ When a user needs to promote the logon computer to a domain controller.

    ❑ When a user is configuring a network connection for remote access.

❑ Installing support for a key fob involves installing an agent that runs on the local computer and a service on the active directory domain controllers.

❑ The most popular biometric devices are fingerprint scanners. Some are built into computers, such as Tablet PCs, and others can be added as external devices.

❑ Both the built-in and external biometric devices require drivers and software to integrate with the computer's security system.

❑ When a user needs to walk away from a PC for short periods, the Lock Computer option will hide the desktop until the user returns and enters his or her account password.

❑ In addition to authentication, take steps to protect data directly by using NTFS and share permissions.

❑ On any computer with Windows 2000 or greater, use NTFS encryption on the most sensitive data files. In the Ultimate and Enterprise editions of Windows Vista and Windows 7, enable BitLocker to encrypt the entire boot volume.

❑ Permanent data removal is an important security task, required when moving a computer from one user to another in an organization or when removing the computer from service within the organization.

❏ Data deleted by users is not truly deleted but saved in the Recycle Bin and easily recovered. Even after you remove data from the Recycle Bin and "permanently" delete it, it can be recovered.

❏ A class of programs called "shredders" removes data from hard drives. Run a shredder on your files as you delete them.

Implementing a Defense Against Malicious Software

❏ A properly configured hardware firewall will protect a network from certain types of invasions from the Internet or other untrusted network, but personal firewalls on each computer will protect from attacks that originate on the private network.

❏ Before Windows XP Service Pack 2, the Internet Connection Firewall (ICF) was available, but not turned on.

❏ The Windows Firewall that comes with Windows XP Service Pack 2 is an improvement on ICF, but does not stop traffic generated from your computer, including connections to the Internet that originate from locally installed malware.

❏ Antivirus programs examine the contents of a disk and RAM looking for hidden viruses and files that may act as hosts for virus code.

❏ Always enable the update option in an antivirus program and configure it to automatically connect to the manufacturer's Website, check for updates, and install them. These updates will include changes to the antivirus engine and definition files.

❏ Install or enable a phishing filter for your Web browser. This filter will check for suspicious behavior on the Websites you visit. You will still need to watch out for possible phishing attacks.

❏ Your response to an innocent-looking pop-up can result in spyware or adware being installed on your computer. A pop-up blocker can prevent unwanted windows from opening in your browser.

❏ Pop-up blockers are available in Web browsers or as add-ons to Web browsers. Because pop-ups are often necessary on some legitimate Websites, configure your pop-up blocker to allow certain sites, or just temporarily allow pop-ups for a single session at a site.

Securing a Wireless Network

❑ First configure the wireless access point (WAP), including DHCP (enable or disable). Then change the SSID name, disable SSID broadcast, enable MAC filtering, change the default Administrator password, update firmware, enable the strongest encryption available on the WAP, and enable the firewall.

❑ Configure each wireless client with settings compatible with the WAP.

Troubleshooting Security

❑ A BIOS password, depending on its function, will keep users from starting up the OS, or just keep everyone out of the Systems Settings menu.

❑ To remove a BIOS password, follow the manufacturer's instructions, which may require opening the computer and setting jumpers to erase the contents of CMOS where the BIOS password is saved.

❑ If you remove the BIOS password by erasing the contents of CMOS, you will need to run the system Setup program and enter the correct settings for the system.

❑ If users cannot log on to a Windows computer using biometrics as the computer resumes from Standby or Hibernate, check to see if the computer is up-to-date on updates. When this happens, the short-term fix is to log on with a basic interactive logon from the keyboard.

❑ A Windows hotfix that was not generally available solved the preceding problem, but by the time you read this, it may be. If not, contact Microsoft for the hotfix.

❑ You have several options if you forget your password, depending on the situation. If your logon account is in a Windows domain, ask the domain administrator to reset the password.

❑ If the forgotten password is for a local user account, you also have several options. Log on as the local Administrator if you know that password. Then reset the password for the user account.

❑ Or perhaps your installation of Windows has a hidden Administrator account. Access this account by restarting in Safe Mode and logging on with the Administrator account. Unless the password was changed, you can leave the field blank. Then reset the password for the user account.

❑ If the Security tab is missing from the Properties dialog of a file or folder on an NTFS volume, Simple File Sharing is probably on. Turn this off, and the Security tab will appear.

❑ FAT32 does not support file and folder permissions. Therefore, unless there is a special reason for having a FAT32 volume, convert FAT32 volumes to NTFS using the following syntax:

```
convert d: /fs:ntfs
```

where *d*: is the drive you wish to convert.

❑ Two major problems with NTFS file encryption are that it can be broken and that encrypted files can become inaccessible. Third-party programs may be able to recover the encrypted files.

❑ A message from the firewall may pop-up that a program running on your computer is trying to access the Internet. The firewall then requires that you decide to allow this action or not. You should research the filename displayed in the message to determine the action you should take. Use a search engine and/or information available from the firewall.

❑ If you cannot access a WAP's Web page and you previously could, reset the WAP using the manufacturer's instructions. This will erase the WAP's settings, so you will need to reconfigure it. Be sure to set a complex password on the administrative account to keep intruders out, and set all the security settings on the WLAN.

❑ Preventive maintenance for security includes installing service packs and patches, training users, recognizing social engineering, and performing all the security implementation steps described in this chapter.

SELF TEST

The following questions will help you measure your understanding of the material presented in this chapter. Read all of the choices carefully because there might be more than one correct answer. Choose all correct answers for each question.

Implementing Authentication and Data Security

1. On a computer that has DriveLock, or a similar feature, the password to access the hard drive at startup can either be stored on the hard drive itself or in this special type of chip, if present.
   A. Key Fob
   B. TPM
   C. CMOS
   D. Biometric

2. What service must be installed on domain controllers before users can log on to a client computer using a smart card?
   A. Smart Services
   B. Secure attention sequence (SAS)
   C. Remote access
   D. Certificate Services

3. What strategy should you use when setting NTFS permissions?
   A. Set the least restrictive level for all users.
   B. Set the most restrictive level that still allows users to accomplish their work.
   C. Give the Everyone group Read permissions.
   D. Use Allow or Deny on every permission.

4. What permission, applied directly to a file, defeats inheritance?
   A. Deny
   B. Allow
   C. Full Control
   D. Modify

5. What simple calculation rule does Windows apply to inherited NTFS permissions to determine effective permissions?
   A. Most restrictive applies.
   B. Least restrictive applies.
   C. Full Control is calculated first.
   D. Read is calculated first.

6. What is the recommended order of tasks for creating shares and applying permissions?

   A. Create the share, apply NTFS permissions, and apply share-level permissions.

   B. Give Everyone Read access, apply NTFS permissions, apply share-level permissions, and create the share.

   C. Apply NTFS permissions, create the share, and apply share-level permissions.

   D. Apply NTFS permissions, apply share-level permissions, and create the share.

7. When a user connects to a network file share, how are the effective NTFS permissions and the share permissions combined for that user?

   A. Most restrictive.

   B. Least restrictive applies.

   C. Full Control is calculated first.

   D. Read is calculated first.

8. If an encrypted file is moved or copied into an unencrypted folder on an NTFS volume, which of the following will occur?

   A. It will be decrypted.

   B. It will remain encrypted.

   C. It will be Read-Only.

   D. Encrypted files cannot be moved or copied.

9. Which type of encryption comes with the Ultimate and Enterprise versions of Windows Vista and Windows 7, as well as Windows Server 2008, and protects an entire boot volume?

   A. NTFS encryption

   B. WPA2

   C. DriveLock

   D. BitLocker

10. Which of the following identifies the administrative share that points to the system root folder?

   A. C$

   B. IPC$

   C. *computername*\admin$

   D. PRINT$

Implementing a Defense Against Malicious Software

11. What hardware device or software program uses several technologies to prevent unwanted traffic from entering a network?

A. Proxy server

B. Firewall

C. Router

D. Switch

12. What two antivirus components are frequently updated?

A. Antispyware

B. Engine and definitions

C. Engine and spam filter

D. Definition files and phishing filter

13. What type of security software examines Website content for certain social engineering traits and warns you if it detects one of these traits while you are browsing?

A. Antispyware

B. Spam filter

C. Phishing filter

D. Antivirus

14. What service do popular Web browsers, such as IE and Firefox, offer to prevent unwelcome browser windows from opening on your desktop?

A. Phishing filter

B. Spam filter

C. Pop-up blocker

D. Personal firewall

15. What security software examines the contents of a disk and RAM looking for hidden viruses and files that may act as hosts for virus code?

A. Phishing filter

B. Antivirus

C. Personal firewall

D. Pop-up blocker

16. What Control Panel applet allows you to manage temporary Internet files?

  A. Internet Options

  B. Computer Management

  C. Event Viewer

  D. Administrative Tools

Securing a Wireless Network

17 Where do you begin when configuring security for a wireless network?

  A. Wireless clients

  B. Windows

  C. WAP

  D. Ethernet router

18. When possible, which wireless encryption should you use to secure your wireless network?

  A. WEP

  B. WPA2

  C. WPA1

  D. NTFS

Troubleshooting Security

19. What are the direct consequences of forgetting the password on the Systems Settings menu?

  A. Inability to launch Windows.

  B. All systems settings will be reset.

  C. The Windows password will be reset.

  D. Inability to access the System Settings menu.

20. Because users frequently forget their passwords, administrators have the right to take this action.

  A. Reset the account.

  B. Restrict the account.

  C. Reset the password.

  D. Remove the password from the account.

SELF TEST ANSWERS

Implementing Authentication

1. ☑ **B.** TPM, or Trusted Platform Module, is a chip that can be used by DriveLock to store passwords or keys for accessing a computer's hard drive.

   ☒ **A,** key fob, is incorrect; although a key fob contains a microchip, DriveLock-type systems do not use one. **C,** CMOS, is incorrect; although this is a type of chip, DriveLock does not use it to store passwords. **D,** biometric, is incorrect because this is used to describe a type of device that uses a scan of (usually) a fingerprint for authentication.

2. ☑ **D.** Certificate Services must be installed on domain controllers before users can log on to a client computer using a smart card.

   ☒ **A,** Smart Services, is incorrect. **B,** secure attention sequence (SAS), is incorrect because this is a special key sequence used to access the logon dialog box in Windows. **C,** remote access, is incorrect because this service has nothing to do with using smart cards to log on to a domain.

3. ☑ **B.** Set the most restrictive level that still allows users to accomplish their work.

   ☒ **A,** set the least restrictive level for all users, is incorrect because this would expose data to unauthorized users. **C,** give the Everyone group Read permissions, is incorrect because this would often be too permissive. **D,** use Allow or Deny on every permission, is incorrect because this was not stated as a good strategy and it defeats inheritance, which is not always a good thing.

4. ☑ **A.** Deny explicitly defeats an inherited permission.

   ☒ **B,** Allow, is incorrect because this defeats all inherited permissions except Deny. **C,** Full Control, and **D,** Modify, are both defeated if they are explicitly set to Deny.

5. ☑ **B.** Least restrictive applies is the correct calculation rule for determining effective permissions on a file or folder on NTFS.

   ☒ **A,** most restrictive applies, is incorrect as this is not the rule used. **C,** Full Control is calculated first, and **D,** Read is calculated first, are both incorrect.

6. ☑ **C.** Apply NTFS permissions, create the share, and apply share-level permissions is correct.

   ☒ **A,** create the share, apply NTFS permissions, and apply share-level permissions, is incorrect because if you create the share before applying NTFS permissions, the share-level default permissions will leave the shared files and folder too vulnerable. **B,** give Everyone Read access, apply NTFS permissions, apply share-level permissions, and create the share, is incorrect for two reasons: Everyone Read is too open for most situations, and you cannot apply share-level permissions before you create a share. **D,** apply NTFS permissions, apply share-level permissions, and create the share, is also incorrect because you cannot apply share-level permissions before you create the share.

7. ☑ **A.** Most restrictive is how effective NTFS permissions and share permissions combine for a user.

☒ **B,** least restrictive, is incorrect, although this is how the effective NTFS permissions are applied. **C,** Full Control, is calculated first, and **D,** Read is calculated first, are both incorrect.

8. ☑ **B.** The file will remain encrypted if moved or copied into an unencrypted folder on an NTFS volume.

☒ **A,** it will be decrypted, is incorrect because as long as the move or copy is not performed as a drag-and-drop operation, an encrypted file will remain encrypted. **C,** it will be Read-Only, is incorrect because this is not the result of moving or copying an encrypted file into an unencrypted folder on an NTFS volume. **D,** encrypted files cannot be moved or copied, is incorrect because encrypted files can be moved or copied.

9. ☑ **D.** BitLocker is the encryption that comes with the OS and protects an entire boot volume on a Windows Vista or Windows 7 computer.

☒ **A,** NTFS encryption, is incorrect because it only encrypts at the folder level on an NTFS volume. **B,** WPA2, is incorrect because this is a Wi-Fi encryption standard. **C,** DriveLock, is incorrect because it is not an encryption technology, but a system for controlling access to an entire hard drive without data encryption.

10. ☑ **C.** *computername**admin$* identifies the system root folder administrative share.

☒ **A,** C$, **B,** IPC$, and **D,** PRINT$, although all administrative shares, do not point to the system root folder.

Implementing a Defense Against Malicious Software

11. ☑ **B.** A firewall is the hardware device or software program that uses several technologies to prevent unwanted traffic from entering a network.

☒ **A,** proxy server, is incorrect because, although this is one of the technologies used by a firewall, it does not fully describe a firewall. **C,** router, is incorrect because this is a separate device (or software), although it may use one or more of the technologies associated with a firewall. **D,** switch, is incorrect because this is not a device or software that prevents unwanted traffic from entering a network. A switch is a cable-connecting device used within a network.

12. ☑ **B.** The engine and definitions are the two antivirus components that are frequently updated.

☒ **A,** antispyware, is incorrect because this is not a component of antivirus, although antispyware and antivirus may both be part of a security bundle. **C,** engine and spam filter, is incorrect because, although the antivirus engine is one of the components that is updated, the spam filter is not part of antivirus, even though it may be bundled with antivirus software in a security package. **D,** definition files and phishing filter, is incorrect because, although definition file is part of the correct answer, phishing filter is not part of an antivirus program, but a Web browser add-on or feature.

13. ☑ **C.** Phishing filter is the type of security software that looks at Website contents for certain traits and warns you if it detects one of these traits while you are browsing.

    ☒ **A,** antispyware, is incorrect because antispyware looks for spyware on your computer, not social engineering traits. **B,** spam filter, is incorrect because this does not look for social engineering traits but for spam in your e-mail. **D,** antivirus, is incorrect because this does not look for social engineering traits, but for viruses.

14. ☑ **C.** A pop-up blocker is the service offered by Web browsers to prevent unwanted windows from opening on the desktop.

    ☒ **A,** phishing filter, is incorrect because, although this filter works within a browser, it scans Websites for certain social engineering traits. **B,** spam filter, is incorrect because this scans incoming e-mails for suspected spam messages. **D,** personal firewall, is incorrect because it does not work within a Web browser but blocks certain types of incoming messages based on information in the packet header.

15. ☑ **B.** Antivirus is security software that examines the contents of a disk and RAM looking for hidden viruses and files that may act as hosts for virus code.

    ☒ **A,** phishing filter, is incorrect because this filter works within a browser and scans Websites for certain social engineering traits. **C,** personal firewall, is incorrect because this firewall blocks certain types of incoming messages based on information in the packet header but does not look at the contents to determine if it is virus code. **D,** pop-up blocker, is incorrect because it only works within a browser to prevent unwanted browser windows from opening.

16. ☑ **A.** Internet Options is where you can manage temporary Internet files.

    ☒ **B,** Computer Management, **C,** Event Viewer, and **D,** Administrative Tools, are all incorrect because none of these administrative tools allows you to manage temporary Internet files.

Securing a Wireless Network

17. ☑ **C.** A WAP, or wireless access point, is the place to begin when configuring security for a wireless network.

    ☒ **A,** wireless clients, is incorrect because the access point must be configured before the wireless clients can be configured to connect. **B,** Windows, is incorrect because Windows is also on the client side of things and should not be configured until after configuring the access point. **D,** Ethernet router, is incorrect because, although a wireless network may be connected through the access point to an Ethernet router, this router has no other connection to the configuration of the wireless network.

18. ☑ **B.** WPA2 is the latest encryption method and the preferred one to use as of the writing of this book.

   ☒ **A,** WEP, is incorrect because this was replaced by WPA in 2003 and is no longer considered secure. **C,** WPA1, is incorrect because WPA2 is more secure. **D,** NTFS, is incorrect because NTFS encryption has nothing to do with wireless networks.

Troubleshooting Security

19. ☑ **D.** Inability to access the System Settings menu is the direct consequence of forgetting the password on the Systems Settings menu.

   ☒ **A,** inability to start up Windows, is incorrect because forgetting the password on the Systems Settings menu will have no effect on starting Windows. **B,** all systems settings will be reset, is incorrect because this will not happen just because you forget the Systems Settings menu password. **C,** the Windows password will be reset, is incorrect because the password on the Systems Settings menu will not affect the Windows password for any user account.

20. ☑ **C.** Resetting the password is something an administrator can do to help a user who forgot his password.

   ☒ **A,** reset the account, **B,** restrict the account, and **D,** remove the password from the account, are all incorrect actions when a user forgets her password.

18

Operational Procedures

CERTIFICATION OBJECTIVES

❑   **701: 6.1**   Outline the purpose of appropriate safety and environmental procedures and, given a scenario, apply them

❑   **701: 6.2**   Given a scenario, demonstrate the appropriate use of communications skills and professionalism in the workplace

✓   Two-Minute Drill

Q&A   Self Test

Operational procedures are an umbrella of professional behavior, covering the technical area of safety and environmental procedures, as well as the soft skills of communication and workplace professionalism. Your technical skills with computers, networks, and operating systems may be excellent, but if you do not follow proper operational procedures, you will put your job, and more, at risk.

CERTIFICATION OBJECTIVE

■ **701: 6.1** *Outline the purpose of appropriate safety and environmental procedures and, given a scenario, apply them*

The A+ candidate must prove she understands that everyone must take responsibility for a safe work environment and safe equipment handling to protect equipment, people, and the environment.

Workplace Safety and Safe Equipment Handling

Although your company may have specific people assigned direct responsibility for safety compliance and implementation, safety truly is everyone's job, regardless of job description. Everyone in an organization must play an active role in maintaining a safe work environment. A safe work environment includes developing an awareness of common safety hazards, such as spilled liquids, floor clutter, electrical dangers, and atmospheric hazards. Being aware of these hazards lets you take precautions against them. Be proactive to avoid accidents that can harm people and equipment. Safe equipment handling begins with using the appropriate tools, taking care when moving equipment, protecting yourself and equipment from electrostatic discharge, avoiding damage to transmissions and data from electromagnetic interference, and taking appropriate precautions when working with power supplies, displays, and printers.

Cable Management

One often-overlooked cause of an unsafe environment is the way that people just plug in the many cables connecting the various pieces of equipment and leave them piled in a jumble. This is not only hazardous to the user, but, depending on the physical layout, passersby can trip on the cables, damage the equipment, and injure themselves. Consider purchasing a simple cable manager product that eliminates such clutter and hazards. Search the Internet for **cable management**.

Using Appropriate Repair Tools

The typical computer technician's repair toolkit is not extensive. Recall the tools listed under "The Hardware Toolkit" in Chapter 5: various types and sizes of screwdrivers, a parts grabber, a flashlight, a small container for holding extra screws and jumpers, a multimeter, and antistatic equipment, such as a wrist strap and antistatic mat.

Be meticulous about using each tool only for its intended purposes. Attempting to use a flat-bladed screwdriver on a Phillips head screw can damage the screw and the screwdriver, and it does not work very well. Worse yet, using a tool that does not fit properly may cause it to slip and damage a component such as the motherboard, or even injure yourself.

on the
j o b
Do not carry loose objects like screwdrivers in shirt pockets, because they can fall into computers and other equipment when you lean over.

Moving Equipment

Power down all equipment and disconnect it from power outlets before moving it—even when moving it from one side of a desk to another. This includes laptops! Yes, they are portable devices, but moving any computer around while it is actively running can harm the hard drive.

Do not just flip the power switch. For instance, in Windows XP, you have three appropriate shutdown choices: Turn Off, Standby, or Hibernate (depending on the configuration), any of which will shut down the hard drive until you turn the computer back on or (in the case of Standby) select Resume. After the computer turns off, or goes into one of these other states, unplug the power cord.

You may question always unplugging a device before moving it—even from one side of a desk to another, but we have seen too many instances in which a connected power cord caused injury or damage to other things. You simply are not in complete control of a device when it is tethered to the wall.

Be very careful when moving displays—whether CRTs or flat panel displays. Both types are fragile, and you must take care not to drop a display or put any pressure on the front of the display.

Other devices require special handling when moving them. If you are unsure of the proper way to move a computer or peripheral, check out the documentation. For instance, some scanners have a transportation lock that you must engage before moving them, in order to protect fragile components.

Of course, consider your own safety when moving equipment. Protect your back when you lift equipment: wear a safety belt, keep your back straight, and use your knees. Do not try to carry heavy computer components farther than a few feet without the aid of a utility cart.

Whenever handling computer components, be very careful of the sharp edges on sheet metal in computer cases and in some peripherals. It is very easy to cut yourself on these. Similarly, the backs of many circuit boards contain very sharp wire ends that can cause puncture wounds. Work gloves offer protection, but most of us feel too awkward wearing gloves while handling delicate computer equipment. If you cannot wear gloves, be very cautious.

Hot Components

Some components remain hot enough to burn you after you shut down the equipment. For instance, CPU heat sinks can remain hot enough to burn. Be very careful around hot components to not either touch them or let anything else touch them.

Electrical Safety

Leave servicing high-voltage peripherals such as CRT monitors, laser printers, and power supplies to technicians trained in that area. Even after being unplugged for an extended period, such devices can store enough voltage to cause severe injury, or even death, from electrical shock. Never use an antistatic wristband or other antistatic equipment when working with high-voltage devices.

Although high voltage is the most dangerous, low voltage, under certain circumstances, can also cause serious injury or death. People have died from electrical injuries involving as little as 50 volts! Many variables determine the amount of damage to a victim of electric shock. These include (but are not limited to) the body's resistance or lack of resistance to the current, the path of the current through the body, and how long the body is in contact with the electrical current.

If the skin offers little resistance (if it is wet, for instance), it may appear undamaged, although internal organs might be damaged. If the skin, due to dryness or thickness or a combination of characteristics, offers greater resistance, the skin may burn badly but internal organs are not damaged.

e x a m

Both high voltage and low voltage can cause serious injuries and even death. Lack of external burns on a person *who has had an electric shock does not necessarily mean that the injury is minor.*

Electrostatic Discharge (ESD)

One of the most prevalent threats to a computer component is *electrostatic discharge (ESD)*, also known as static electricity, or simply, static. Static is all around us, especially when both the humidity and the temperature are low. When you put on a jacket that makes the hair on your arm stand up, you are encountering static electricity. When you slide your feet across a carpet and then touch someone else or a doorknob or a light switch and feel a jolt, you are experiencing a static discharge.

The Dangers of ESD

ESD happens when two objects of uneven electrical charge encounter one another. Electricity always travels from an area of higher charge to an area of lower charge, and the static shock that you feel is the result of electrons jumping from your skin to the other object. The same process can occur within a computer. If your body has a high electric potential, electrons will transfer to the first computer component that you touch.

Electrostatic discharge can cause irreparable damage to your computer components and peripherals. Typical ESD discharges range from 600 to 25,000 volts, although at minute amperages. Most computer components can safely withstand voltages of ±12 volts, so damage to computer components can occur at as little as 30 volts— a charge you will not even detect because, under the right conditions, your body can withstand 25,000 volts.

o n t h e
ⓘ o b
Do not count on the body's ability to withstand 25,000 volts. This ability depends on the right circumstances. Learn more about this in the next section.

People call these very low-voltage static charges "hidden ESD," and they can come from many sources, including dust buildup inside the computer. Dust and other foreign particles can hold an electric charge that slowly bleeds into nearby components. Hidden ESD can cause serious problems because you will have no hint of trouble until damage has occurred and the component malfunctions. This damage is very difficult to pinpoint.

ESD can cause the immediate, catastrophic malfunction of a device, or it can cause a gradually worsening problem in a device—a process called degradation. As unlikely as it might seem, degradation damage can be more costly in lost work time and in time spent to troubleshoot and repair than catastrophic damage. When a device suffers catastrophic damage, the result is immediate and typically obvious, so you will know to replace it right away. Degradation, on the other hand, can cause a component to malfunction sporadically, sometimes working and sometimes not. This makes pinpointing the cause harder, and the problem will persist for a longer period and be more disruptive to the user and to the support professional.

Additionally, a total failure of one component will typically not affect the usability of other components. However, degradation can cause a component to fail in ways that also result in the failure of other components.

Protection from ESD Damage and Injury

There are many ways to prevent ESD from damaging computer equipment. First, low humidity contributes to ESD; therefore, when possible, keep computer equipment in a room in which the humidity is between 50 and 80 percent. Do not allow the humidity to rise above 80 percent or condensation could form on the equipment and cause it to short out.

To prevent damage to the system, you must equalize the electrical charge between your body and the components inside your computer. Touching a grounded portion of your computer's chassis will work to some extent, but for complete safety, use an antistatic wristband with a ground wire attached to the computer frame. This gear will drain static charges from your body to ground. If a static charge has built up in the computer equipment, it will also bleed from the computer through your body to ground. This is true of any electrical flow; therefore, you must never use an antistatic strap attached to your body when working around high-voltage devices. Never use other antistatic devices in a manner that puts your body between a power source and ground.

Many computer assembly and repair shops use an antistatic floor mat that discharges static when you stand on it. Similarly, an antistatic mat on the bench table is often used. An antistatic mat looks like a vinyl placemat, but it has a wire lead and (usually) an alligator clip to connect it to ground. An antistatic mat is a safe place to put expansion cards or other internal components that you have removed from the computer.

Before you pick up a loose computer component, if you are not wearing or touching an antistatic device, discharge any static electricity on your body by touching something metal, such as a table leg or chair. Equipment placed on the mat will discharge static through the mat. All of these antistatic devices usually have cables that you must attach to a grounded metal object. Some have a single prong that you insert into the ground socket in a regular wall outlet. In the United States and Canada, the ground socket is the single round socket offset from the two slender blade sockets. Other cables on antistatic wrist or ankle straps or on antistatic mats may use alligator clips for making this attachment.

Another name for an antistatic device is an ESD device. You will find a wide array of these devices under either name. Searching on **ESD**, we found the expected ESD floor mats and wrist straps, plus gloves, finger cots, labels, bags, cleaners, bins, and meters.

Use antistatic spray to remove static from clothing and carpet. Never spray it directly on computer equipment or components. Exercise 18-1 will lead you through the process of protecting your workspace and computer from ESD damage.

EXERCISE 18-1

ESD-Proofing Your Workspace

Whether your workspace is a cubicle or desk at which you do minor repairs, or a computer workbench where you do more extensive service on computers and peripherals, follow these simple steps to ESD-proof your workspace:

1. Maintain the room's humidity between 50 percent and 80 percent.
2. Spray your clothing and the work area with antistatic spray. Never spray directly on the computer, its components, printers, or scanners.
3. Place an ESD mat on the workspace and attach its alligator clip to something stationary and metal, such as the leg of a table.
4. Remove all jewelry, including rings.
5. Put an ESD strap around your wrist or ankle, and attach the other end to a stationary metal object (if it has an alligator clip) or plug it into a wall outlet's ground socket (only if the grounding strap has an outlet prong).

Electromagnetic Interference (EMI)

Another problem related to electricity is *electromagnetic interference (EMI)*, which is the disruption of signal transmission caused by the radiation of electrical and magnetic fields. Electric motors are a common source of EMI. Be aware of nearby electrical devices. High-voltage transformers, electrical panels, fluorescent lights, and electric motors produce EMI, which can temporarily interfere with the functioning of computer equipment, such as monitors. For instance, a monitor experiencing EMI interference will have a jittery or distorted picture, but when you remove the source of the interference, or move the monitor, the picture will return to normal. The biggest problem with EMI is that it disturbs the transmission of data over copper wires, such as Ethernet cables.

We have actually seen people put a magnetic business card on a computer! That is highly risky. Remember, the read/write head in a hard drive actually functions like a tiny electromagnet, so erasing data by putting a magnet near it is easy. Keep magnets away from computers!

Power Supplies

The power found in a computer's high-voltage power supply is enough to cause injury or death. Always unplug the power supply from the wall outlet when you are working inside a computer or printer. Simply turning off the power switch is not enough. Even when turned off, the power supply in a computer can conduct electricity, and most motherboards continue to have power applied—a practice called soft power that we described in Chapter 3. To be safe, unplug the power supply. Some technicians prefer to leave the power supply plugged in while they work on the computer to allow static to bleed away from the computer into the wall outlet's ground wire. However, we do not recommend this; safer methods are available for removing static, such as placing the computer on an antistatic mat.

exam

ⓦatch *Do not be confused by the similarity in the names: ESD can damage or destroy hardware, whereas EMI usually causes temporary problems and is more dangerous to data than to hardware. Similarly, RFI (mentioned in Chapter 15), such as from cordless phones and microwave ovens, can disrupt network communications.*

Power supplies store electrical charges for a long time, even when unplugged. Never open the power supply's case, and never wear an antistatic wrist strap when replacing or handling a power supply. The high voltage from the power supply is sufficient to cause grave injury or death.

Matching power requirements for equipment with power distribution and UPSs is important. Therefore, ensure a power supply can handle the requirements of the components it supplies. Recall the discussion of power supplies, electrical terminology, and power requirements for PC components in Chapter 3, and power requirements for laptops in Chapter 6. Further, review the discussion in Chapter 5 about the devices for protecting computers and equipment from variations in power from the electricity source. The devices described were surge protectors for protection against surges and spikes and uninterruptible power supplies (UPSs) for complete online power protection, including power conditioning as well as protection from power outages and power sags.

Inverters

During the three years that we lived, traveled, and worked full time in a motorhome, we relied on an inverter to convert the DC power of our "house" batteries to the AC power required by our computers and communications equipment. With an array of solar panels on the roof that fed our batteries, we could sit in remote locations, enjoying an off-grid lifestyle while meeting writing deadlines. Similarly, many professionals, such as geologists, rescue workers, and others, use inverters to get appropriate power in remote locations. An inverter takes low-voltage DC power (usually 12 V, 24 V, 36 V, or 48 V from a battery pack) and transforms it to 110 V 60 cy output power. As with power supplies, ensure that an inverter has the appropriate capacity for the equipment to which it distributes power.

Although the input voltage is small, the amperage can be large for a 1000-watt or larger inverter, requiring heavy power cables from the battery pack. You must take care around such equipment to always disconnect the inverter from the battery pack when doing any work on it. Use the same care around an inverter that you do around household power circuits, because the inverter output is the same as household power.

on the **!** job *Recall that a laptop has an inboard inverter for supplying AC current to the LCD display and, as mentioned in Chapter 5, a flickering LCD display can indicate that either the inverter or the LCD's backlight is failing.*

Display Devices

Although, as we are writing this book, flat panel displays have largely replaced cathode ray tube (CRT) monitors, there are still many CRTs out in the real world and you may well have to work with them. *Remember*—like power supplies, CRT monitors are high-voltage equipment and can store a harmful electrical charge, even when unplugged. Never open a CRT case, and never wear a wrist strap when handling a CRT. You do not want to provide a path to ground through your body for this charge.

Printers

Printers have many moving parts, so you need to follow several basic safety procedures whenever you work with or around a printer. Do not allow long hair, clothing, jewelry, or other objects near the moving parts of a printer, because of the danger of their being entangled in the moving parts, including feed or exit rollers. In particular, a necktie or scarf itself may build up a static charge that it can pass to the component if it touches it. When wearing a tie or scarf, make sure you either tuck it into your shirt or use some kind of clip or tie tack. Figure 18-1 shows an open printer and the cartridge assembly, which rapidly moves back and forth when operating.

FIGURE 18-1

Keep loose clothing and jewelry away from open printers.

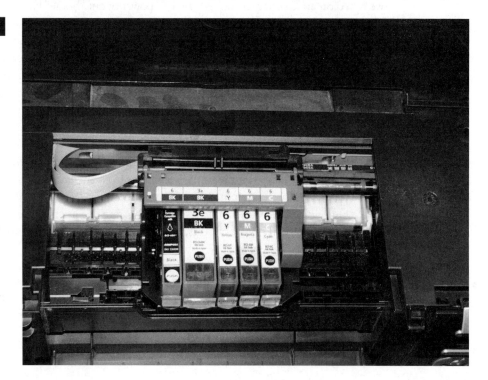

e x a m

ⓦ**a t c h**   *Power supplies and CRT monitors are high-voltage equipment. Never open them, and never wear an antistatic strap while working with either of these components.*

Furthermore, do not try to operate a printer with the cover off. The cartridge in an inkjet printer and the print head in a dot matrix printer move back and forth rapidly across the page, and getting your hands or other objects caught is possible, damaging both you and the printer. You must be especially careful when working around laser printers because the laser beam can cause eye damage. Fortunately, most printers do not work when their covers are open.

The two biggest dangers associated with working with a laser printer are the fusion assembly and the power supply. Avoid touching the fusing roller in a laser printer because it can be hot enough to burn. Power down a laser printer and allow it to cool off before opening it. Laser printers also use high-voltage and low-voltage/ high-current power supplies. Make sure you power off and unplug the laser printer before opening it. See Figure 18-2.

FIGURE 18-2

A laser printer with the toner cartridge removed, showing the fusion area deep in the back

Compressed Air

In Chapter 5, you learned about using canned compressed air to blow dust out of computers and peripherals. Recall that you should take care to keep the can upright while spraying; avoid tilting or turning the can upside down because the liquid gas that forces the air out may spill and cause freeze burns on your skin and/or damage components. Never use compressed air from an air compressor because the pressure is too high and it can damage delicate components.

Additionally, when you are using compressed air to clean anything, you should wear eye protection and even a simple mask to keep from inhaling dust and getting particles in your eyes.

Disposing of Computing Waste

Lead, mercury (including the mercury in laptop backlights), cadmium, chromium, brominated flame retardants, polychlorinated biphenyls (PCBs)—what do they all have in common? They are toxic to the environment and to humans, if mishandled, and they are widely used in electronics, including computers, printers, and monitors. You must dispose of or recycle these items in the proper manner. You should never discard them directly into the trash, where they will end up in landfills and potentially pollute the ground water.

In addition, electronics also contain plastic, steel, aluminum, and precious metals—all of which are recoverable and recyclable. Provide containers in which to collect these components for proper sorting and disposal.

Manufacturers' Recycling Programs

Computer companies, such as Dell and Hewlett-Packard (HP), and other electronics companies, such as Nokia, are using more environmentally friendly components and working to recycle components from discarded computers. In fact, there is a relationship between these two activities. The more a manufacturer is involved in recycling the wastes from its products, the more changes that company makes to use more eco-friendly material. If companies don't use environmentally hazardous materials in electronic components in the first place, then the environment is in less danger. Manufacturers are a long way from eliminating hazardous materials from electronics, however, so we will need to continue recycling for both hazardous materials and non-renewable materials, such as gold, copper, and aluminum. In spite of efforts by several manufacturers to help users recycle computer components, estimates are that only 10 to 15 percent of electronics are recycled.

Material Safety Data Sheets (MSDS)

If you are unsure of the proper handling or disposal procedures for a chemical, look for its *material safety data sheet (MSDS)*. A MSDS is a standardized document that contains general information, ingredients, and fire and explosion warnings as well as health, disposal, and safe transportation information about a particular product. Any manufacturer that sells a potentially hazardous product must issue a MSDS for it.

If a MSDS did not come with a particular chemical, contact the manufacturer or search for it on the Internet. A number of Websites contain large lists of MSDSs. There have been some major changes in these Websites. Therefore, if you wish to find a MSDS on a particular product or type of product, use a search engine with appropriate keywords, including **MSDS** and terms associated with the product.

Finally, when you purchase computer products, make a practice of asking the vendor for any applicable MSDS.

Batteries

Many batteries contain environmentally hazardous materials, such as lithium, mercury, or nickel-cadmium, so you cannot just put them in the trash where they will end up in a landfill. Many communities have special recycling depots that accept batteries so they do not introduce harmful elements into the environment. Many communities periodically conduct hazardous material pickups in which you can hand over toxic materials, such as batteries and paint, for proper disposal.

Never store computer batteries for extended periods, and never leave batteries in equipment that is being stored for extended periods because battery casings are notorious for corroding, allowing the chemicals inside to leak or explode out. Leaking or exploding chemicals can cause a large mess within the equipment, destroy nearby components, and cause skin burns if you touch it.

Toner Cartridges

Printer toner cartridges also provide a potential environmental hazard simply due to their large numbers and the space they can take up in a landfill. For this reason, you should not simply throw them away. Fortunately, most toner cartridges have reusable components. That is, many companies will buy back used toner cartridges, refill and recondition them (if necessary), and then resell them. Figure 18-3 shows a laser toner cartridge removed from a printer.

A laser printer
toner cartridge,
showing the drum

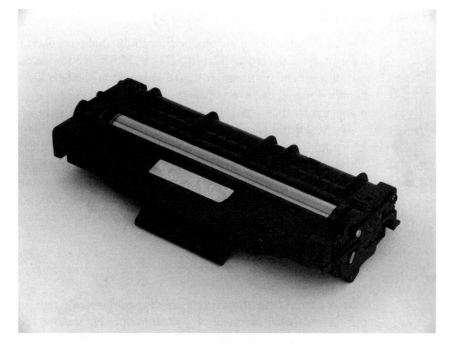

Display Devices

Cathode ray tube (CRT) displays contain lead, which is toxic to the environment
and is a useful metal that can be recycled. Therefore, never throw CRTs in trash
destined for a landfill. Always search for ways to recycle a CRT. Flat panel displays,
including those in laptop computers, use fluorescent lamps that contain toxic
material, so these displays too must be recycled. Call your local waste disposal
organization and arrange to have CRTs picked up or dropped off at its site. Many
communities advertise locations and hours for these recycling services.

Chemical Solvents and Cans

Chemical solvents designed for the computer are just as hazardous to the environment
as noncomputer-related chemical solvents. They must be disposed of in a similar
manner. Many communities collect chemical solvents and paints and make them
available for recycling. Residents can go to the recycling center and obtain the paints
for free or at a reduced cost. Those solvents and paints deemed unsafe for recycling
are disposed of properly. Look for a hazardous material pickup or depot in your area.

Similarly, the empty cans, including aerosol cans, should be disposed of in an appropriate manner. Contact your local waste disposal company for the proper handling and disposal of empty cans that once held solvents and other toxic materials. They may be as dangerous as the contents they once held.

EXERCISE 18-2

Researching Recycling Centers

Research the recycling options in your community.

1. First, use the local phone book and look under the local government listings for recycling. List the nearest center to your home here:_____.

2. Call the center and determine if it accepts the following items: computer monitors, chemicals, empty paint and solvent cans, circuit boards, old computers, or batteries.

3. Find out the days and times when the center accepts these items for recycling and list them here:_____.

4. Ask if the center has a private home pick-up service for recycling and how you can arrange this.

5. Ask if the center has a business pick-up service for recycling and how you can arrange this.

SCENARIO & SOLUTION

I need to remove a Phillips head screw from a computer case, but I do not have a Phillips head screwdriver that will fit. I would like to try a flat-bladed screwdriver. Should I do it?	Do not use a flat-bladed screwdriver in a Phillips head screw unless it is an emergency. To avoid damaging the screw or the computer, wait until you can obtain the correct tool.
Since a laptop is portable, is there any reason why I should not move it from desk to desk while it is operating?	A laptop's portability does not apply to when it is up and running with the hard drive spinning. Select one of these actions from within Windows before moving any PC, even a laptop: Turn Off, Standby, or Hibernate.
We have excellent climate control in our computer server room and equipment closet, but the manager prefers to keep the setting very cool and with a humidity level below 50 percent. Is this OK?	Such very low humidity levels create a perfect environment for ESD. At the very least, the manager should adjust the climate controls so that the humidity is above 50 percent, and raise the temperature to a comfortable level for employees.

CERTIFICATION OBJECTIVE

■ **701: 6.2** *Given a scenario, demonstrate the appropriate use of communications skills and professionalism in the workplace*

CompTIA requires that an A+ candidate demonstrates knowledge of good interpersonal communication skills and professionalism in the workplace. Real communication between people is the sum of the verbal and non-verbal behavior that results in exchanging thoughts, messages, or information. Not only must you say the right words, but your body language must convey the same message as your words. Professionalism includes your behavior in all interactions, as well as how you treat property belonging to your employer and customers.

Communicating with Customers and Colleagues

Communicating with customers and colleagues involves many important communication skills that are part of active communication. In other words, it isn't just what you say—it's how you say it and what you do while you are saying it.

Human Interaction Basics

People behave in certain basic ways that affect communication between them. We'll call them "paybacks" and getting "mentally stuck." These things happen to everyone (including you and me), and we are usually unaware we are participating in such behavior until we learn to watch for it. Once we understand the cause and effect of paybacks and getting mentally stuck, we improve all our interactions with others and learn to communicate more effectively. These two behaviors are the greatest inhibitors of effective communication. The "cure" is to learn to be aware of and to compensate for them.

The Golden Rule vs. Paybacks

The Golden Rule is "do unto others as you would have them do unto you." It assumes the best of human nature. This rule is critically important in all human interactions because human beings tend to reciprocate behavior and the dark side of the Golden Rule is "payback," meaning that negative behavior will be repaid in kind. It is automatic, immediate, and largely unrecognized by the party doing it.

If someone is polite, respectful, and interested in you, you will tend to behave the same way toward him (the Golden Rule at its best). If he is curt, abrupt, or uninterested in you, you will tend to treat him the same way—paying back the bad behavior. It's automatic—you almost can't help it. Therefore, carefully and intentionally choosing a positive way to behave when you are communicating with customers shows them you are interested in them and that you care that their problems are solved. If you do this, they will tend to be more cooperative in turn.

Getting Mentally Stuck

The second thing that happens to everyone is that when you are surprised, or threatened, or feel disconcerted or attacked, you tend to focus mentally on the thing that just happened to you. You go inside your own thoughts, which means that for that moment, you are effectively unaware of what is going on in front of you or what someone is saying to you. Getting mentally stuck is a gigantic communication killer. When you're focused within your own head, you cannot be paying attention to what the other person is saying or doing. Thus, if a customer is yelling at you because of a problem she has, you'll tend to shut down for a moment while you are mentally stuck, thus missing important information and providing payback for the negative behavior.

Communication Goals

On the job, there are several reasons for communicating effectively. First, you establish some rapport with the other person, which leads to building trust between you. You avoid misunderstandings. Respectful communication makes everything easier for everybody.

Establishing Rapport

What is rapport? It is when two people recognize that they share a commonality of perspective, of being in "sync," of sharing a bond, or having an affinity. When people interact, each person has an unconscious natural tendency to identify the similarities with the other person. Focusing some energy on this will improve communications between you. One effective strategy that most people do unconsciously is to mirror the other person to some degree. Mirroring the other person's speech cadence (whether they speak rapidly or slowly), for example, is a simple thing to do and actually makes the other person more comfortable.

During a phone conversation, you can only mirror the audible components, such as modulating your voice tone and tempo to match the caller. But be sure to exclude negative aspects of the caller's behavior. If the caller raises his voice, you can have your voice calm down, but adopt the same tempo. If the caller has a different accent than you, don't imitate it but simply match the cadence, or use some of the caller's expressions. For example, if the caller says a long, leisurely "Well," with a gentle rising inflection, you may want to use this word in the same way as you introduce a solution to her problem.

In a face-to-face conversation, mirror the other person's body posture and movements, but be careful to not make the person feel like you are mocking a behavior. When you mirror effectively, the other person feels more comfortable and, therefore, more likely to be open to what you are saying or doing.

Building Trust

Trust is confidence and faith in a person—a belief that the person will always deliver on promises and be reliable. You must earn trust. Although building trust in a single conversation is not easy, you can do it to a greater degree than most people realize. You should also treat each encounter with a customer or coworker as part of an ongoing relationship. Consider the following methods for building trust. Use these, plus the Keys to Effective Communication (described in the next section) in all your interactions with people.

- **Be consistent** Always behave in a consistent manner when dealing with other people.

- **Honor commitments** If you make any commitment to another person, be sure to follow through.

- **Model trustworthy behavior** As you practice the behaviors you learn here, and continue to do your work with integrity, you are showing that you are trustworthy. Your very behavior becomes a model for others to follow—whether they are customers or coworkers.

- **Avoid misunderstandings** A misunderstanding is a mix-up in communication between two or more people that leaves at least one person with a false impression of facts. Misunderstandings are very damaging to any type of relationship. Recovering from misunderstandings is difficult, and you need to work to avoid them. When a misunderstanding occurs, communication can completely break down.

■ **Communicate respectfully**   A little respect goes a long way, and using it in all your interactions will bring you rewards in better relationships with others and more efficient interactions that produce good results.

Keys to Effective Communications

The Keys to Effective Communications will help you to improve your interactions with others. They include providing context, using active communication, and gathering information.

Provide Context

When you say something to another person, you understand exactly how you mean it, but the odds are high that he won't understand it exactly the same way you mean it because his life experience, education, and attitudes are different from your own. Similarly, when you do something, he will interpret your action in ways that make sense to him, but that are not necessarily how you mean it. Context provides the framework surrounding what you are saying or doing and can throw light on its meaning. When you give context for your words or actions, it helps others to understand your intentions, which helps avoid a misunderstanding.

For instance, if you are at a customer's site, and you find you need to take a printer in for service, don't just unplug the printer and carry it out. Instead, tell the customer what you are about to do and why. Say something like, "I'm sorry, but I have to take this printer to the shop to fix it because I can do it much faster there. I'll get it back to you just as soon as I can." The customer deserves to know why you need to do this because it will be an inconvenience.

When you are gathering information about a computer problem, you will often need to ask questions that may seem unnecessary to the customer. Your experience will have taught you to gather information that goes beyond what the user believes you need to know to solve the problem. For example, nontechnical users may not see a connection between being unable to connect to the Internet and an overnight power failure, so you might not learn that upon arriving at work, her computer was off, although she had left it turned on the night before. To get this kind of information, give context for why you want to ask her certain questions. Say something like, "Many things can affect an Internet connection, and I'd like to ask you some questions that may seem odd. Would that be OK?" Then you might ask whether she had noticed anything unusual about her computer.

Use Active Communication

Active communication involves a set of behaviors that lets the other party know that you are engaged in the conversation and that enhances your effectiveness. We describe active communication in the next section.

Gather Information

A common job requirement for people who take the 701 exam is interacting with users to solve computer problems. This requires gathering information from the user. You can ask two kinds of questions: closed-end questions and open-end questions. You can also restate the issue and let the customer demonstrate the problem, while acting to relieve the customer's feelings of guilt about the problem.

Ask Closed-end Questions to Control the Process   A closed-end question is one that the user can answer with a simple fact or a yes or no. You ask closed-end questions to get data about the problem and to narrow the search for a solution. Closed-end questions could be, "When did you first notice the problem?" or "What did you do next?" or "How has this problem affected your work?" Closed-end questions tend to limit responses.

Ask Open-ended Questions to Narrow the Scope of the Problem   Open-ended questions are questions that require an answer beyond simply yes, no, or a fact. Open-end questions encourage the user to talk. Open-end questions are how you gain information about the problem beyond just the facts. They require that the person think through something, rather than just respond with a fact. Open-ended questions are great for getting at feelings or other more subtle things. The answers may reveal more about the problem that could be helpful, but if you ask an open-ended question and get a flood of irrelevant information, you can then ask a closed-end question to stop the flood.

Restate the Issue or Question to Verify Understanding   The purpose of communication is to share common understandings. One useful tool is to restate or rephrase the issue or the question, and then ask if you are correct in your understanding. If you are, then you can proceed. If you are not, you can ask the user to explain further and you can again restate your understanding. Restating the issue greatly enhances the chances of good, accurate communication.

Let the Customer Demonstrate   Users are often uncomfortable with the technology involved, and they may not have the vocabulary to describe the problem in terms that will allow you to resolve it quickly. So you need to couch the questions you must ask in language the user is comfortable with. Try to use words the user understands, and relate your questions to the user's job function and how she uses the computer and peripherals. Ask questions like, "When you tried to print the Daily Report, did you notice any messages on your screen?" Or ask the user to show you the exact steps that led up to the problem. Remember, users often do many tasks without knowing the vocabulary to describe what they are doing. Therefore, asking the user to demonstrate what she did in the few minutes before the problem appeared keeps her in her comfort zone of common activities, and does not require she find the words to describe her actions.

Relieve the Customer of Guilt   The customer may be worried about being held accountable for the problem and may withhold information that would help you solve the problem, but (in his mind, at least) reveal that he was responsible. You will need to deal with this type of situation more often than you think, and it may help to assure the customer that the more you know, the quicker you can solve the problem.

Active Communication

Remember that communication is a two-way street and involves much more than simply talking and hearing. The best communication is active communication, which involves a set of skills, behaviors, and positive attitudes called active listening and active speaking that show you are fully engaged in the conversation and that encourages the other person to also communicate in a positive manner. Active listening includes using a specific set of behaviors while you are listening to the other person, and active speaking covers the appropriate responses that you make during a conversation.

Active Listening

Active listening means that you give the speaker your complete attention. This must be apparent to them, even during a phone conversation. Do not interrupt; allow the speaker to complete statements. Do not jump to conclusions. If necessary, clarify customer statements by asking pertinent questions or restating your understanding. This shows that you are listening and helps you to avoid making incorrect assumptions. The following are several components of active listening.

e x a m
ⓦ a t c h   *Be sure to remember you should always allow a customer to explain a problem without interrupting him.*

Benefits of Active Listening   When you listen actively, you gather valuable information that you need, with the added benefit that you show the other person how to be an active listener. As with all good behavior you do, this serves as a model, and the other person will often respond by actively listening to you also.

Skills for Active Listening   Several active listening skills are very easy to acquire simply by practicing them. After awhile, you will find that these skills become second nature in your face-to-face interactions.

- Make good eye contact.
- Physically respond to what the other person is saying with a nod or by shifting your weight to lean toward them. This last action also shows interest in what she is saying.
- Repeat or rephrase the key points you heard to show that you are listening.
- Mentally check that you understand what the person means, not simply "hear" what the other person is saying.

on the

Job   *Resist the bad habits of communication that tell the other person that you are not interested in what he has to say. Do not interrupt to finish his sentences. Do not let your gaze turn into that of a daydreamer.*

Be Engaged   In a face-to-face conversation, engagement involves using eye contact and body language that tells the customer that she is important to you. Nod your head, and maintain a pleasant expression appropriate to the conversation. A big smile is not always the correct expression. If the customer is frustrated or angry, you don't want to be smiling at her. Instead, show concern with a serious and sympathetic expression. You can empathize with the customer by saying something like, "I don't blame you for being upset. If I were going through what you have gone through, I'd be upset, too."

In a phone conversation, when the customer pauses or takes a breath, use phrases such as "I understand" and "Please tell me more." Even a short "Yes" or "Okay" lets the customer know that you are listening and engaged in the conversation.

Allow the Customer to Fully Explain   The most important act a computer professional does is to allow the customer to fully explain the reason for the conversation: the problem as the customer perceives it. Listen without interruption; do not be distracted by the customer's misuse of, or total lack of, technical language.

Work toward gathering information without correcting the customer. Make a note if you determine that the customer could use appropriate training to make more effective use of his computer, but do not let the conversation get sidetracked from solving the problem.

Active Speaking

Active speaking involves speaking clearly, avoiding direct "you" statements, and using proper language. That means that you avoid using jargon, slang, and acronyms, and always make sure to confirm that the customer understands what you are saying.

Speak Clearly   Speak in clear, concise, and direct statements. Use language appropriate to the user without being condescending.

Do Not Start Sentences with "You"   Avoid beginning sentences with the word "you." This practice, sometimes called a direct "you" statement, tends to put the other party in a defensive position. It is also easy to fall into the trap of saying things like, "You didn't … ?" or "You should have…" Once this happens, communication can break down because the customer could get mentally stuck and no longer hear you.

Of course, don't completely eliminate the word "you," because it is a great word in sentences such as, "What can I do to help you?" or "What did you notice just before this occurred?" The first phrase lets the customer tell you what she wants, whereas the second one shows her that her input will be important in solving the problem. Repeat these two sentences out loud, and do the same with the next sentences and notice the difference in the emphasis on the word "you": "You must have changed something!" "You need to be careful when using [*insert name of component here*]."

Avoid Jargon and Slang   Jargon is not necessarily bad. *Jargon* is simply the use of words, often technical and uncommon, that both parties understand in the same way. The problems come when you use technical words that are familiar to you, but which are unknown to the other person.

Avoid using technical jargon, abbreviations, and acronyms with nontechnical customers and coworkers. Jargon confuses them because they don't know what you are talking about, and it can work against you by causing a communications breakdown. It clearly shows a lack of respect for the other person and for what you are trying to achieve and communicate. Sometimes people use jargon almost deliberately as a way to "one up" themselves over the other person—to subtly show their superiority. The problem is that tit-for-tat will come into play, and you will have unconsciously started a contest for control of the situation. That's not what you want!

In avoiding jargon, do not speak down to the other person. Here is an opportunity to be creative in describing things. If you have been a good listener, you will find ways to express yourself without overwhelming the customer with too much technical detail.

Get Acknowledgment   Frequently confirm that the customer understands what you are saying by asking questions like, "Does that make sense?" "Does that sound okay to you?" "Would you like to go through those steps while I am here?" Think of the conversation as a train, with you as the engineer. The customer is a passenger waiting on the platform; if you do not stop or slow down, the customer cannot get on the train, and you will find yourself at the destination, but the customer will still be back at the station. Slow down and confirm that he is on board before you race ahead with a technical explanation that would please your coworkers but bewilder the customer.

on the

ⓙob   *Every single profession in the world has its own jargon. Because professions tend to be separate cultures, the use of jargon, abbreviations, acronyms, and slang strictly among peers is generally acceptable, but do not let this spill over to your communications with people who are not part of your technical culture.*

Tact and Discretion

Tact and discretion are very important components of effective communication. *Tact* involves showing consideration for others. Tactful communication is more about what you do not say than what you do say. Take care to not offend no matter what you may think of the other person or what your own situation is. Being discreet includes not revealing information about someone that would be harmful to or embarrass her.

People often see *discretion* and tact as synonyms, but there is a subtle difference between them. For instance, a tactful person avoids embarrassing or distressing another. But discretion assumes a measure of good judgment based on the situation. It doesn't matter whether your encounters with customers are face-to-face, by phone, or purely via electronic messages (e-mail, newsgroups, or messaging)—you should still use tact and discretion.

Be culturally sensitive. In today's world, you may be dealing with people from across the globe. A smart-aleck comment that is amusing in your own culture may be offensive to a person from another culture who you are dealing with. Be cautious when dealing with people from other cultures, and be tactful.

Using Tact   We have seen it many times. A customer who does not seem to understand the connection between the power switch and the computer manages to figure out how to customize the Windows desktop with family photos on the background, customized pointers, and a desktop cluttered with dozens of files, folders, and shortcuts. Unless you are there to help the customer clean up the desktop, stick to the reason for the visit, and do not offer your opinion. This is using tact.

After you have solved the problem, you might inquire if he has had any end-user training on using the Windows desktop. If the answer is "Yes," then you should drop the subject, unless you find that his own desktop actually bewilders him, and he would like help cleaning it up and organizing his files.

Using Discretion   Being discrete requires that you deal appropriately with a customer's confidential materials located on her computer, desktop, printer, and so on. Whatever you see on her desk or in her computer is her property, and to be discrete, you don't reveal it to anyone. Further, don't reveal unnecessary information to customers or coworkers. Whether this information is about other people, unannounced company policies, or information about the company's research and development, just don't gossip about it because doing so is indiscrete. Especially if the information would hurt or offend a third party or harm your company, keep it to yourself.

If you do not follow this advice, and you divulge information you have no authority to share, you will find it difficult to build trust with other people. Even when someone seems to enjoy the information, your behavior tells her that you are not trustworthy.

Be Cautious   Be cautious with what you share with the customer. Sometimes technicians go too far in showing empathy for the customer's plight and speak negatively about the customer's working conditions, or the very equipment or software that the company pays you to support. The customer does not need to know that you think the printer the company bought for her is a poor one, or that you hate driving out to her office because of the terrible traffic conditions.

SCENARIO & SOLUTION

I get very bored with talking to customers at the front counter, and I find that I can pick up my e-mail while listening to a customer's description of a problem. My boss has told me not to do this. Why is that?	This behavior is inappropriate for many reasons. Just one reason is that you are not showing the customer respect by letting him know that you are listening. And you may miss important information if you do not use active listening techniques.
The company tells me not to begin sentences with "you" when speaking to customers. Why is this?	Starting a sentence with "you" tends to make the other party feel defensive.
I enjoy sharing information about office politics and unannounced changes in company policy. My boss has reprimanded me for this, but people seem to enjoy hearing this news. Why is doing this a problem?	Once again, this behavior is inappropriate for many reasons. At the very least, revealing this information shows a lack of discretion and does not engender trust in you, even though people may seem to enjoy hearing the information.

Professionalism

Professionalism involves using the set of behaviors that each of us should use whether we are being observed or not. You cannot fake professional behavior. People who do try to fake it will eventually fall into a trap of their own making, and they may well lose their job as a result. Many professions have a formal code of ethics that defines professionalism framed in the context of that profession. In this section, we will explore a general definition of professionalism as it applies to behavior in dealing with others and in the treatment of property.

Respectful Behavior Toward Others

Professional behavior is respectful. This includes being pleasant, reasonable, and positive in the face of the variety of events that can occur in the work environment, including dealing with difficult customers.

Maintain a Positive Attitude   Work to maintain a positive attitude and tone of voice. A positive attitude takes practice and discipline because everyone has personal problems and challenges in their lives, along with all the job issues such as politics, personalities, work goals, and more. You literally need to compartmentalize your life. Hold an image in your mind so that, when you are at work, the other parts of your life are behind doors. Try to keep the doors to these other parts of your life closed most of the time when you are at work, and only open one at an appropriate time. When you become successful at this, you will find that you are more effective in all the areas of your life, because you can give each the full attention it deserves at the appropriate time.

Avoid Confrontations   Avoid arguing with customers or coworkers, even if you feel the other person is being especially difficult. If you discover something that makes you angry, pause to calm yourself before engaging about the problem. When others approach you angrily, stay calm and avoid becoming defensive. Resist falling into the tit-for-tat trap. These measured responses can defuse a potentially volatile situation.

Do Not Minimize Others' Concerns   Never minimize another person's problems and concerns. You minimize when you interrupt an explanation and show through body language, such as a dismissive wave of the hand, that his concern is not important to you. Do not tell the customer about someone else who has a worse predicament. That is irrelevant to him. Imagine how you would feel if you could not get some work completed on time due to a computer problem, and while trying to explain your plight to a technician, she minimized or dismissed your concern as being of no importance.

However, you must strike a balance between not minimizing and assuring the customer that you have an easy fix for the problem. An easy fix just means that you can solve the problem soon; it does not mean the customer has no reason to mourn the lost time, lost deadline, or loss of productivity.

Avoid Judgmental Behavior   Avoid being judgmental and/or insulting to anyone. Never resort to name-calling, which is damaging to any relationship and is completely uncalled for in a professional environment. For instance, if the workings of computer hardware and software fascinate you, you may find it difficult to be patient with people who cannot seem to understand or even care how they work and frequently need help with hardware and software. If you believe that anyone can understand computers if he just takes the time to learn, you are judging another's decision to not study computers the way you have. From here, it is just a small baby step to behaving judgmentally toward the customer.

Be Attentive   Avoid distractions and/or interruptions when talking with customers or coworkers. You may have two standards for customers versus coworkers. Customers must have your complete attention, and only an emergency should distract you when talking with the customer. Even when you are talking on the phone with a customer, resist the urge to read e-mail or browse the Internet. You might relax these rules a bit with coworkers, depending on your working relationship, but be very careful not to be disrespectful of anyone.

Confidentiality and Respect for Privacy   In all human interactions, we learn things about one another, and some of what we learn is personal, and we should not share it with others. Part of professionalism is knowing when to keep your mouth shut. This includes knowledge about both company matters and someone's personal life. Being discrete shows respect for the privacy of others. When you keep such information to yourself, you will gain the trust of your coworkers and customers. Of course, being respectful of someone's privacy, you do not try to gain personal information, but sometimes you learn it inadvertently. However you learn such information, keep it to yourself.

Even if your organization does not formally provide a privacy policy, you should have one. This is your personal privacy policy that should be part of your personal standards of behavior.

Avoid Distractions

Distractions reduce your productivity and value as an employee. Some jobs are filled with distractions—ringing phones, conversations, music, construction noise, traffic noise, and more. Many distractions are unavoidable, but you can control many distractions, and how you control them is a measure of your professionalism. Just a few types of distractions are personal calls, talking to coworkers, and personal interruptions.

Personal Calls   You can only make some personal calls, such as calls to your doctor or child's school, during normal business hours when doctors have hours and schools are open. If these are permitted at work, don't abuse the privilege. Keep them to a very short duration. Unless your employer has a rule permitting personal long distance phone calls, do not spend company time and resources making them.

Talking to Coworkers   A productive work environment normally involves a community of people who treat each other professionally and work as a team. Therefore, in most jobs, you will have frequent conversations with coworkers—on both personal and professional topics. Personal discussion with coworkers should not occur within earshot of customers. When you are talking to a customer, she should have your full attention. The only excuse for a side conversation is if it concerns solving the customer's problem, and you should even do that outside the customer's hearing if possible. The best rule is not to talk to coworkers while interacting with customers.

Personal Interruptions   Personal interruptions come in many forms, such as personal calls (mentioned previously), leaving the office during working hours for personal business, a visit to the workplace by a family member or friend, and attending to personal business in any way during work hours—and especially while helping a customer. Avoid personal interruptions as much as possible, and when such an interruption is necessary, be sure to minimize its impact on the customer by keeping it very brief and not extending its effect by sharing details of the interruption with the customer.

Set and Meet Expectations   Many things, both actual and perceived, influence a customer's expectations. Your company may set expectations by describing your department and/or job function and the services it will provide to customers. This expectation exists even before you answer the customers call or walk into their office. One expectation you should always assume is the expectation that you will be on time. If you are delayed, be sure to contact the customer and provide a reliable estimate of when you will arrive.

Beyond that, you control the expectations—either consciously or unconsciously. Be aware of ways in which you do this. If a customer makes an unreasonable demand, do not simply smile without comment. This sets the expectation that you will deliver according to his demand. If you must disappoint, do it as soon as possible, so a simple disappointment doesn't turn into the perception that you broke a commitment—perceived or otherwise.

Control expectations. Once you have determined what a problem is, be sure to give the customer your best and most honest estimate of the timeline for solving the problem. When possible, offer different repair or replacements options. Options give the customer a sense of control of a situation.

At the conclusion of a service call or visit, provide the customer with proper documentation on the services you provided. Sit down with the customer and review all that you did. If appropriate, have her sign a receipt confirming the work you performed.

Follow up with each customer at a later date to verify satisfaction. This is important because people do not always inform you when they are not happy, and a quick phone call or e-mail might alert you to their dissatisfaction and give you a chance to rectify the situation.

SCENARIO & SOLUTION

How can I avoid a confrontation when someone else shows anger toward me?	Try to stay calm, avoid becoming defensive, and do not reciprocate the anger.
I try to put customers' concerns into perspective for them by telling them about others who are worse off. Is this a good practice?	No, this is not a good practice because the customers will believe (rightly so) that you are minimizing their concerns.
If the company gives me a laptop to take home, do I have the right to use it for personal purposes?	No. Unless you have an unusual arrangement, you are to use the laptop given to you by the company for business purposes only. Using it for personal purposes is unprofessional.

Respect for Property

Respect for property includes both the physical treatment of property and equipment belonging to others and the exact manner in which you use the property or equipment. Property includes the building, parking lot, and office space, as well as all the furniture and equipment within. Oddly enough, company policy manuals often define respect for property better than they do the interpersonal aspects of professional behavior. Use of company property is both a privilege and great responsibility. Whatever the equipment, treat it with respect because it is a tool of your trade.

You show respect for property in other ways than just proper physical handling. Never forget you should treat any equipment that belongs to the organization as its property. Do not let family members use it, unless you have specific permission to do so. Follow company guidelines for personal use of company equipment. Even if they allow it, be sure you are not abusing this privilege. This type of misuse includes using the company computer to shop online, play Internet games, or access Facebook or other social media—this is doubly unprofessional when you do it on company time.

Respect for property extends beyond company property to the property belonging to all persons with whom you have contact, including your customers and coworkers.

CERTIFICATION SUMMARY

This chapter explores operational procedures, first by examining appropriate safety and environmental procedures, and then by detailing the use of communication skills and professionalism in the workplace.

Safety in an organization is everyone's responsibility. Always be aware of potential safety hazards such as liquid spills, clutter in walkways and stairways, and exposure to high- and low-voltage devices. Practice safe equipment handling to protect both yourself and equipment. Use appropriate repair tools as they are meant to be used. Take precautions when moving computer equipment to protect both the equipment and yourself.

Protect yourself and computer equipment from electrostatic discharge (ESD) using appropriate antistatic devices. ESD can cause the immediate malfunction of a device or a gradual degradation, leading to eventual total failure. Maintain humidity between 50 percent and 80 percent to avoid ESD.

Electromagnetic interference (EMI) will not damage equipment, but it will disrupt usage and damage data. Removing the source of EMI (or moving equipment away from it) will eliminate the problem.

Improper handling of power supplies can cause injury or death. Always unplug the power supply from the wall outlet when you are working inside a computer or printer. A power supply stores electrical charges for long periods. Never open a power supply's or CRT monitor's case, and never wear an antistatic wrist strap when replacing or handling either as these are high-voltage pieces of equipment and can store a harmful electrical charge, even when unplugged.

Avoid the moving parts in printers. Keep long hair, clothing, jewelry, and other objects away from the moving parts in a printer.

Always dispose of computer components properly. You can check the component's MSDS for proper disposal instructions. You should also be wary of components that use high voltage or lasers, such as CRTs, power supplies, optical drives, and laser printers. Handle components carefully when you store them. Keep them out of hot or damp places, and keep magnetic storage devices away from EMI-emitting devices.

A+ candidates must understand the communication skills required for success on the job. This includes listening skills and communicating clearly while employing tact and discretion with all interpersonal contacts. Be conscious of your body language to ensure that your words and actions are not sending conflicting messages.

Good communication skills include what you say, the way you say it, and what you do while you are saying it. Communication goals include establishing rapport and building trust. Keys to effective communication include providing context, using active communication, and gathering information.

Active communication is a set of behaviors that include active listening and active speaking. These behaviors show that you are fully engaged in the conversation and encourage the other person to also communicate in a positive manner.

✓ TWO-MINUTE DRILL

Here are some of the key points covered in Chapter 18.

Workplace Safety and Safe Equipment Handling

❑ Safety is everyone's job. Be aware of common safety hazards and be proactive to avoid disasters.

❑ Liquids spilled on floors and stairways can cause falls and injuries.

❑ Avoid injury from tripping by keeping floors, stairways, and doorways clear of obstacles and clutter, including loose flooring and electrical wires.

❑ Do not try to service high-voltage peripherals, such as CRTs, laser printers, and power supplies, because there is a high danger of electrical shock.

❑ Do not use an antistatic wristband when working with high-voltage devices.

❑ Use appropriate repair tools, and use each tool only for its intended purposes.

❑ Turn off all equipment before moving it, even laptops. Moving any computer while powered up could damage the hard drive(s).

❑ Displays are very fragile, and you should move them with great care.

❑ Some devices require special handling when being moved. For instance, you should turn off computers (even laptops) or put them into Standby or Hibernate mode. Some scanners have a locking mechanism. Also disconnect power and equipment cords before moving computer equipment.

❑ Take care to protect your back when lifting equipment, and use a utility cart to move equipment more than a few feet.

❑ Low-voltage devices can cause serious injury or death under certain circumstances. As little as 50 volts can cause death, depending on many variables, including, but not limited to, the body's resistance to the current, the path of the current through the body, and how long the body is in contact with the current.

❑ Electrostatic discharge (ESD) occurs when two objects of uneven electrical charge contact each other. Electricity travels to areas with a lower charge.

❑ ESD can cause irreparable damage to your computer components and peripherals.

❑ Typical ESD discharges range from 600 to 25,000 volts. Computers can safely receive voltages of ±12 volts, but most static discharges are well above 600 volts, and a charge of only about 30 volts can destroy a computer component.

❑ Low-voltage ESD is "hidden ESD" and can be caused by dust buildup inside the computer.

❑ You may not have a hint of the presence of ESD until the component has sustained damage and it malfunctions.

❑ Low humidity contributes to ESD. Keep the humidity level between 50 percent and 80 percent. If humidity is too low, static will build up; if it's too high, condensation could form in the equipment and cause it to short out.

❑ Use antistatic devices (antistatic wrist straps, antistatic mats, and antistatic bags) when working with and storing computer equipment, especially internal components.

❑ If you are not wearing or touching an antistatic device when you need to handle computer components, first discharge any static electricity on your body by touching something metal, such as a table leg or chair.

❑ Attach the cable from an antistatic wristband or mat to a ground socket on an electrical outlet or onto a grounded metal object.

❑ Use antistatic spray to remove static from clothing and carpet. Never spray it directly on computer equipment.

❑ Electromagnetic interference (EMI) usually causes temporary problems and is more of a danger to data than to hardware.

❑ Once removed from a computer, a component is susceptible to damage unless it is properly stored to protect it from extremes of heat, cold, humidity, and high voltage, EMI, and other sources of magnetism.

❑ Store components in antistatic bags, but never place components on top of these bags. Leave components in the bags until ready to install them.

❑ Never open power supplies or CRTs for service. Even when turned off, they can continue to store electricity.

❑ Do not leave a computer plugged in while servicing it.

❑ Never wear a wrist strap when handling a power supply or a CRT.

❑ Take extra precautions when working with a printer because long hair, loose clothing, and jewelry can catch in the moving parts. In addition, any of these objects can pass ESD to the printer.

❑ Do not try to operate a printer with the cover off. Some printers will not operate in this state, but some, like inkjets, must be open when you change the print cartridges, and the cartridge assembly moves to allow access.

❑ Avoid touching the fusing roller in a laser printer because it can be hot enough to burn. Turn off a laser printer and allow it to cool off before opening it.

Disposing of Computing Waste

❑ Toxic metals and chemicals used in computers and peripherals include mercury, cadmium, chromium, brominated flame-retardants, and polychlorinated biphenyls (PCBs).

❑ When a computer or component reaches the end of its useful life, dispose of it appropriately, taking time to send all equipment that cannot be donated to a recycling center for proper handling of the toxic and reusable components.

Communicating with Customers and Colleagues

❑ Two predictable reactions that can interfere with communications are paybacks and getting mentally stuck.

❑ People automatically respond in kind to whatever another person says or does to her. The good side of this is the Golden Rule, and the bad side of this is payback.

❑ Learn to avoid responding in kind when the other person is negative, and you can turn the tone of a conversation to something more positive and productive.

❑ Getting mentally stuck is a reaction in which the person focuses internally and fails to pay attention to what is going on around him.

❑ Learn to recognize when something has triggered a mentally-stuck state in yourself, and resist the urge to go inside yourself so you can remain attentive to the other person.

❑ Learn to recognize the signs that another person is mentally stuck and try to draw him out of it.

❑ Communication goals include establishing rapport and trust.

❑ Keys to effective communication include providing context, using active communication, gathering information, noticing, and empathizing.

- ❑ Active communication involves behavior that shows you are fully engaged and encourages the other person to also communicate in a positive manner.
- ❑ An active listener makes good eye contact, uses body language to confirm that she is listening and interested, and mentally checks her understanding.
- ❑ Always allow the other person (especially a customer) to fully explain. An active speaker speaks clearly, does not start sentences with "you," avoids jargon, and confirms that the other person understands.
- ❑ Always practice tact and discretion in interactions with other people.
- ❑ Professionalism is a set of behaviors that everyone should do whether you are being observed or not.
- ❑ Professional behavior is respectful and includes a positive attitude, avoiding confrontation and a judgmental attitude, and never minimizing others' concerns.
- ❑ When you are respectful, you are attentive and respect confidentiality and privacy.
- ❑ Respect for property includes both the physical treatment of property and equipment belonging to others, and the exact manner in which you use the property or equipment.
- ❑ Most companies have a formal policy concerning the use of company property, and you should always be mindful of your use of company property, even when allowed to bring it into your own home.
- ❑ Be especially careful of equipment belonging to a customer. Showing respect and care in the way you handle his (often-expensive) property goes a long way toward establishing rapport and trust.

SELF TEST

The following questions will help you measure your understanding of the material presented in this chapter. Read all of the choices carefully because there might be more than one correct answer. Choose all correct answers for each question.

Workplace Safety and Safe Equipment Handling

1. Which statement is a true general comparison of the effects of EMI versus ESD?
   A. ESD can damage hardware; EMI harms data.
   B. EMI can harm hardware; ESD harms data.
   C. ESD and EMI are identical.
   D. EMI can cause injury or death; ESD is less harmful to people.

2. I plan to replace the power supply in a computer. What is the most important safety measure I should take?
   A. Wear an antistatic wristband.
   B. Do *not* ground yourself.
   C. Bend your knees when you lift it.
   D. Buy a name-brand power supply.

3. My CRT display is only a few years old and was quite expensive. It is now malfunctioning, and none of the external buttons on the monitor help, nor can I fix it using the Properties settings in Windows. What should I do?
   A. Open the CRT case and look for a loose connection.
   B. Take it to a qualified repair center.
   C. Immediately discard it.
   D. Recycle it.

4. What can I use to protect my PC from power sags?
   A. Surge protector
   B. Power supply
   C. UPS
   D. APS

5. What should you do before moving any computer equipment?
   A. Power down and disconnect the power cord.
   B. Select Standby.
   C. Select Hibernate.
   D. Remove the power supply.

6. What is the ideal environment for ESD to occur?
    A. Hot and humid
    B. Cold and humid
    C. Hot and dry
    D. Cold and dry

7. You are getting ready to install a new component, a memory stick that came in its own antistatic bag. What is the correct way to handle this component and the bag?
    A. Remove the component from the bag and place it on top of the bag until ready to install.
    B. Remove the component from the bag and immediately discard the bag.
    C. Leave the component in the bag until you are ready to install it.
    D. Remove the component from the bag and turn the bag inside out before placing the component on the bag.

8. My computer display is jittery; should I replace the display?
    A. Yes, this is a fatal defect.
    B. No, look for a source of EMI and increase the distance between that source and the display.
    C. Yes, and buy a display that resists ESD.
    D. No, look for a source of ESD and move it away from the display.

Disposing of Computing Waste

9. When a computer system is no longer functioning and is not repairable, how should you dispose of it?
    A. Put it in the trash.
    B. Donate it to a charity.
    C. Send it to a recycling center.
    D. Send it to a landfill.

10. We do not know the proper handling of an old solvent previously used in our company, but now we need to discard it. How can I find out more about it?
    A. Contact the manufacturer and ask for an MSDS.
    B. Send it to a recycling center.
    C. Transfer it to a glass jar for safe storage.
    D. Call 911.

11. What should we do with the large number of used batteries we accumulate in our office?

A. Dispose of them in the trash.

B. Find a recycling center that will accept them.

C. Send them back to the manufacturers.

D. Let them accumulate and dispose of them about once a year.

Communicating with Customers and Colleagues

12. What practices show that you are an active communicator? Select all that apply.

A. Making good eye contact

B. Interrupting the customer because you know the answer to his problem

C. Allowing the customer to explain the problem completely

D. Repeating points the customer makes to confirm that you understand

13. Which of the following are good ways to gather information when you are at the customer's desk? Select all that apply.

A. Letting the customer demonstrate what she was doing when the problem occurred

B. Asking the customer to leave the room so you can work on the computer

C. Noticing the surroundings

D. Noticing the customer's body language and tone of voice

14. Which technique tends to put the other party into a defensive position?

A. Empathizing

B. Using direct "you" statements

C. Allowing the other person to explain fully

D. Being engaged

15. When you are explaining something technical to a customer, which of the following is the best technique to use to confirm the customer understands your explanation?

A. Intersperse phrases to "check in" with the customer.

B. After the explanation, give the customer a quiz.

C. Give the customer a printed explanation to read as you speak.

D. Maintain eye contact.

16. When someone has explained something to you, how can you make sure you heard and understood what she said?

A. Focus.

B. Repeat it back in your own words.

C. Imagine how you sound and appear to the other person.

D. Nod your head frequently.

17. Which of the following is a technique used to show respect? Select all that apply.
   A. Be as clear as possible and correct any misunderstandings.
   B. Show the customer your privacy policy.
   C. Avoid disregarding what someone else tells you.
   D. Treat others the way you like to be treated.

18. Which phrase describes active listening in a face-to-face context?
   A. Words and actions that tell the speaker you are paying attention
   B. Closing your eyes to concentrate on what is being said
   C. Taking notes
   D. Helping the speaker by finishing her sentences

19. When a customer is explaining a problem, what is the most important thing an active listener must do?
   A. Nodding your head to show understanding
   B. Empathizing
   C. Allowing the customer to explain the problem without interruption
   D. Showing respect

20. What behavior shows a positive and professional attitude? Select all that apply.
   A. Avoiding confrontation
   B. Avoiding judgmental behavior
   C. Showing respect
   D. Minimizing another's concerns

SELF TEST ANSWERS

Workplace Safety and Safe Equipment Handling

1. ☑ **A.** ESD can damage hardware; EMI harms data. This general comparison is true concerning the effects of EMI versus ESD.

   ☒ **B** is incorrect because the opposite is true. **C,** ESD and EMI are identical, is incorrect. There is a difference. **D,** EMI can cause injury or death; ESD is less harmful to people, is incorrect because ESD is potentially more harmful.

2. ☑ **B.** To not ground yourself is the most important safety measure. You do not want to make your body a path to ground. Wearing an antistatic wristband, standing on a grounding mat, or touching something already grounded would do this and put you in danger.

   ☒ **A,** wear an antistatic wristband, is incorrect because this would expose you to possible electrical shock. **C,** bend your knees when you lift it, is incorrect because replacing a power supply should not require heavy lifting. **D,** buy a name-brand power supply, is incorrect because this is not a safety measure.

3. ☑ **B.** Take it to a qualified repair center. Never open a CRT case.

   ☒ **A,** open the CRT case and look for a loose connection, is incorrect because only highly trained technicians should open a CRT case. **C,** immediately discard it, is incorrect because this is an extreme reaction until you know more about the nature of the problem and whether the CRT can be repaired. If it cannot, then recycle it, rather than "discard" it. **D,** recycle it, is also incorrect until you have more information about the problem and whether the CRT can be repaired. If you cannot get it repaired, then you will need to recycle it.

4. ☑ **C.** A UPS will protect a PC from power sags because it provides conditioned power, free from the surges, spikes, and sags coming from the power company.

   ☒ **A,** a surge protector, is incorrect because this only protects from power surges, not from power sags. **B,** power supply, is incorrect because a power supply does not protect a PC from power sags. **D,** an APS, is incorrect because this is not a standard acronym for a power protection device.

5. ☑ **A.** Power down and disconnect the power cord before moving any computer component.

   ☒ **B** and **C,** select Standby and select Hibernate, are both incorrect because they do not apply to all computer equipment; they only apply to Windows PCs, and these answers do not include the need to disconnect the power cord. **D,** remove the power supply, is incorrect because this is a very extreme and unnecessary action to take before moving computer equipment.

6. ☑ **D.** Cold and dry is the ideal environment for ESD to occur.

   ☒ **A, B,** and **C** are all incorrect because none of these is an ideal environment for ESD.

7. ☑ **C.** Leave the component in the bag until you are ready to install it.

☒ **A,** remove the component and place on top of the bag until ready to install, is incorrect because the outside of the bag may hold a static charge. **B,** remove the component from the bag and immediately discard the bag, is incorrect because you may want to reuse the bag if you need to store this or another component at some time. **D,** remove the component from the bag and turn the bag inside out before placing the component on the bag, is incorrect because this procedure is not recommended and could expose the component to ESD.

8. ☑ **B.** Look for a source of EMI and increase the distance between that source and the display because you should not replace the display until you know more about the problem, and it sounds like an EMI problem.

☒ **A,** yes, this is a fatal defect, is incorrect because you do not know that it is a defect at all, and it sounds like a possible EMI problem. **C,** yes, and buy a display that resists ESD, is incorrect because you do not yet know that the display should be replaced, and you have no reason to believe the problem has anything to do with ESD. **D,** no, look for a source of ESD and move it away from the display, is incorrect because the symptom is more likely to be caused by EMI.

Disposing of Computing Waste

9. ☑ **C.** Send it to a recycling center. Even a nonfunctioning computer has material in it that can and should be recycled.

☒ **A** and **B** are both incorrect for the same reason. Something put into the trash will end up in a landfill and so will donating something that is beyond repair. **D,** send it to a landfill, is incorrect because computers contain components that can contaminate the environment and they also contain components that should be recycled.

10. ☑ **A.** Contact the manufacturer and ask for an MSDS because this document will contain instructions on safe handling and safe disposal of the chemical.

☒ **B,** send it to a recycling center, is incorrect, although this is what you may ultimately do. You first need to know how to safely handle the chemical. **C,** transfer it to a glass jar for safe storage, is incorrect because no information is available to lead us to believe the original container is not adequate. **D,** call 911, is incorrect because there is no emergency.

11. ☑ **B.** Find a recycling center that will accept batteries is correct.

☒ **A,** dispose of them in the trash, is incorrect because batteries should never be thrown in the trash. They contain environmentally dangerous components and chemicals. **C,** send them back to the manufacturer, is incorrect in general. Some manufacturers may have a program for used batteries, but first locate a recycling center. **D,** let them accumulate and dispose of them about once a year, is incorrect because batteries stored for long periods can leak toxic chemicals.

Communicating with Customers and Colleagues

12. ☑ **A, C,** and **D.** These are all correct because these are all practices of an active communicator.
    ☒ **B,** interrupting the customer because you believe you know the answer to his problem, is incorrect because interrupting is not a practice of an active communicator and is disrespectful.

13. ☑ **A, C,** and **D.** These are all correct because they are all good ways to gather information when you are at the customer's desk.
    ☒ **B,** asking the customer to leave the room so you can work on the computer, is incorrect because this is not a way to gather information.

14. ☑ **B.** Using direct "you" statements tends to put the other party into a defensive position.
    ☒ **A, C,** and **D** are all incorrect because they are all good behaviors that are part of active communication and would not put the other party into a defensive position.

15. ☑ **A.** Intersperse phrases to "check in" with the customer confirms the customer's understanding.
    ☒ **B,** after the explanation, give the customer a quiz, is incorrect because giving a quiz is certainly not the best technique and would probably make the customer angry. **C,** give the customer a printed explanation to read as you speak, is incorrect because this is not the best way to treat a customer. **D,** maintain eye contact, is incorrect because, although this should always be part of face-to-face interactions, eye contact is not the best technique to use to confirm understanding.

16. ☑ **B.** Repeat it back in your own words. This confirms that you heard and understand.
    ☒ **A,** focus, is incorrect although focusing on the customer and the problem is an important thing to do. **C,** imagine how you sound and appear to the other person, is incorrect, although this is a good habit when you are the one doing the speaking. **D,** nod your head frequently, is incorrect because, although this tells the speaker that you are listening, nodding does not confirm that you heard and understand what she said.

17. ☑ **A, C,** and **D** are all correct techniques for showing respect.
    ☒ **B,** show the customer your privacy policy, is incorrect because, although this is an important policy for an organization, and you should practice respect for privacy, this does not directly show respect at the personal level.

18. ☑ **A.** Words and actions that tell the speaker you are paying attention describe active listening.
    ☒ **B,** closing your eyes to concentrate on what is being said, is incorrect because closing your eyes does not give the other person any clue that you are an active listener who is engaged in the conversation. **C,** taking notes, is incorrect because, although you may want to do this, it is not part of active listening. **D,** helping the speaker by finishing her sentences, is incorrect because this is not active listening, and it is certainly not respectful.

19. ☑ **C.** Allowing the customer to explain the problem without interruption is the most important thing an active listener must do when a customer is explaining a problem.

☒ **A, B,** and **D** are all incorrect because, although all of these should be used in your interactions with the customer, the most important thing to do in this case is to allow the customer to explain without interruption.

20. ☑ **A, B,** and **C.** These are all correct behaviors that show a positive and professional attitude.

☒ **D,** minimizing another's concerns, is incorrect because this is negative and unprofessional behavior.

Appendix

About the CD

The CD-ROM included with this book comes complete with MasterExam practice exam software, MasterSim task simulations, CertCam movie clips, the electronic version of the book, and Session #1 of LearnKey's online training. The software is easy to install on any Windows 2000/XP/Vista computer and must be installed to access the MasterExam and MasterSim features. You may, however, browse the electronic book and CertCams directly from the CD without installation. To register for LearnKey's Online Training and the bonus MasterExam, simply click the Bonus MasterExam link or the LearnKey Online Training link on the main launch page and follow the directions to the free online registration.

System Requirements

The software requires Windows 2000 or higher and Internet Explorer 6.0 or above and 20 MB of hard disk space for full installation. The electronic book requires Adobe Reader. To access the Online Training from LearnKey, you must have Windows Media Player 9 or higher and Adobe Flash Player 9 or higher.

LearnKey Online Training

The LearnKey Online Training link will allow you to access online training from Osborne.OnlineExpert.com. The first session of this course is provided at no charge. Additional sessions for this course and other courses may be purchased directly from www.LearnKey.com or by calling 800-865-0165.

The first time that you click the LearnKey Online Training link, you will be required to complete a free online registration. Follow the instructions for a first-time user. Please make sure to use a valid e-mail address.

Installing and Running MasterExam and MasterSim

If your computer CD-ROM drive is configured to autorun, the CD-ROM will automatically start up upon inserting the disk. From the opening screen, you may install MasterExam or MasterSim by clicking the MasterExam or MasterSim links. This will begin the installation process and create a program group named LearnKey. To run MasterExam or MasterSim, use Start | All Programs | LearnKey. If the autorun feature did not launch your CD, browse to the CD and click on the LaunchTraining .exe icon.

MasterExam

MasterExam provides you with a simulation of the actual exam. The number of questions, the type of questions, and the time allowed are intended to be an accurate representation of the exam environment. You have the option to take an open-book exam; including hints, references, and answers; a closed-book exam; or the timed MasterExam simulation.

When you launch MasterExam, a digital clock display will appear in the upper-left corner of your screen. The clock will continue to count down to zero unless you choose to end the exam before the time expires.

MasterSim

The MasterSim is a set of interactive labs that will provide you with a wide variety of tasks to allow the user to experience the software environment even if the software is not installed. Once you have installed the MasterSim, you may access it quickly through the CD launch page, or you may also access it through the Start | All Programs | LearnKey | MasterSim option.

Electronic Book

The entire contents of the Study Guide are provided in PDF. Adobe Reader has been included on the CD.

CertCam Video Training

CertCam .AVI clips walk you through the steps of a selection of the exercises in the book. These videos show exactly what occurs on the screen in Windows, while a voice-over provides helpful commentary. You can access the clips directly from the CertCam table of the contents by clicking the CertCam link on the main launch page.

The CertCam .avi clips are recorded and produced using TechSmith's Camtasia Producer. Since .avi clips can be very large, ExamSim uses TechSmith's special .avi codec to compress the clips. The file named tsccvid.dll is copied to your Windows\ System folder during the first autorun. If the .avi clip runs with audio but no video, you may need to reinstall the file from the CD-ROM. Browse to the Programs\ CertCams folder, and double-click on the tscc.exe file.

Help

A help file is provided through the help button on the main page in the lower-left corner. Individual help features are also available through MasterExam, MasterSim, and LearnKey's Online Training.

Removing Installation(s)

MasterExam and MasterSim are installed to your hard drive. For best results removing LearnKey programs, use the Start | All Programs | LearnKey Uninstall options to remove MasterExam or MasterSim.

Technical Support

For questions regarding the content of the electronic book, MasterExam, or CertCams, please visit http://www.mhprofessional.com/techsupport/. For customers outside the 50 United States, email international_cs@mcgraw-hill.com.

LearnKey Technical Support

For technical problems with the software (installation, operation, removing installations), and for questions regarding LearnKey Online Training and MasterSim content, please visit www.learnkey.com, email techsupport@learnkey.com, or call toll free at 1-800-482-8244.

Glossary

P lease refer to the chapter whose number is given in parentheses after each definition to learn more about that topic.

10Base-T   See *Ethernet*.

100Base-T   See *Fast Ethernet*.

1000Base-T   See *Gigabit Ethernet*.

32-bit   In reference to the Windows operating systems, one that can utilize up to 4 GB of address space. (5)

64-bit   In reference to the Windows operating systems, one that can utilize more than 4 GB of address space. Depending on the version, 64-bit Windows can address a maximum of from 8 to 192 GB. (5)

8-bit high color   Describes the VGA mode color setting that, although it can produce around 16 million different colors, can only display up to 256 different colors at a time. (3)

802.11a   A wireless network standard that uses the 5 GHz band. (13)

802.11b   A wireless network standard that uses the 2.4 GHz band at a speed of up to 10 Mbps. (13)

802.11g   A wireless network standard that uses the 2.4 GHz band at a speed of up to 54 Mbps. It is downward-compatible with 802.11b. (13)

802.11n   A wireless network standard that defines speeds of up to 600 Mbps. It is downward-compatible with 802.11a, 802.11b, and 802.11g. (13)

AC   See *alternating current*.

AC adapter   A type of power supply that converts AC power to voltages needed for a device. AC adapters are generally used for portable PC systems and other devices. (6)

accelerated graphics port (AGP)   A local bus designed for video only, it provides a direct link between the processor and the video card, giving the video card direct access to main memory. (1)

access control   Managing access to resources. Access control to computers and network resources involves authentication and authorization. (16)

access control entry (ACE)   In an access control list, a record containing just one user or group account name and the permissions assigned to that account. (16)

access control list (ACL)   A table on each file and folder in the NTFS file system that contains one or more access control entries. (16)

accessory bay   In a laptop, a compartment that holds a single media device that is switchable with another. (6)

ACE   See *access control entry*.

ACL   See *access control list*.

ACPI   See *Advanced Configuration and Power Interface*.

ACR   See *Advanced Communications Riser*.

ACT   The "activity" status light on a NIC that indicates data is being transmitted. (5)

activation   A method used by several software manufacturers to combat software piracy. The formal name for Microsoft's activation is Microsoft Product Activation (MPA). (9)

active communication   A set of behaviors including active listening and active speaking that shows you are fully engaged in the conversation and encourages the other person to also communicate in a positive manner. (18)

active KVM switch   See *electronic KVM switch*.

active listening   A set of skills, behaviors, and attitudes to use when listening to another person. (18)

active matrix display   An LCD technology based on thin-film transistor (TFT) technology. An active matrix display has a transistor at every pixel, which enables much quicker display changes than passive matrix displays and produces a display quality comparable to a CRT. (3)

active partition   A primary partition that is marked for use by the system during startup. Windows operating systems can only be booted from an active partition. (10)

active speaking   The appropriate responses that you make during a conversation. (18)

ad hoc mode   In a Wi-Fi network, the networking mode that allows peer-to-peer communications without the use of a centralized wireless hub, called a wireless access point (WAP). (14)

adapter card   A printed circuit card that you add to the motherboard to enhance functionality. Also called an *expansion card*. Video adapters and network interface cards (NICs) are examples of adapter cards. (2)

address bus   A group of wires used to identify addresses in main system memory in a computer. The number of wires in an address bus is called the width of the bus and determines the number of unique memory locations that can be addressed using binary math with the two raised to the power of the number of wires in the bus. A 32-bit bus can address up to 4 GB of memory, whereas a 36-bit address bus can address up to 64 GB of memory. (1)

Address Resolution Protocol (ARP)   A protocol used to resolve an IP address to a MAC address. (13)

Advanced Communications Riser (ACR)   A riser card standard that AMD, 3Com, and others introduced in 2000 to supersede AMR. It uses one PCI slot, provides accelerated audio and modem functions as well as networking, and supports multiple Ethernet NICs. (2)

Advanced Configuration and Power Interface (ACPI) A power management standard that includes all the power states of APM, plus two more. It also supports soft power. (6)

Advanced Micro Devices (AMD) AMD manufactures CPUs and other products, and its chief rival is Intel Corporation. (1)

Advanced Power Management (APM) A power management standard, introduced by Intel in 1992, that defines four power-usage operating levels. (6)

Advanced Technology (AT) A type of motherboard used in older PC systems; also refers to the 1984 IBM PC AT model. (1)

Advanced Technology Attachment (ATA) The former name of the Parallel AT Attachment (PATA) interface standard. (1)

Advanced Technology eXtended (ATX) A type of motherboard and its variants most commonly used in recent PC systems. (1)

adware Software installed on a computer without permission that collects information about a user in order to display targeted advertisements, in the form of either inline banners or pop-ups. Inline banners are advertisements that run within the context of the current page, taking up screen real estate. (16)

AGP See *accelerated graphics port*.

alternating current The delivery of electricity (as from a wall outlet) in which the flow of electrons reverses periodically and has alternating positive and negative values. (3)

ALU See *arithmetic logic unit*.

AMD See *Advanced Micro Devices*.

American National Standards Institute (ANSI) A technical standards organization. (3)

amperes (amps) A measurement of the volume of electrons, also called *current*. It is calculated with the formula amps = watts / volts. (3)

AMR See *audio modem riser*.

analog LCD display An LCD display that uses a DB-15 connector, which means that it accepts analog signals that it converts to digital. (3)

analog modem A modulator/demodulator device that allows computers to communicate with one another over existing phone lines. (2)

ANSI See *American National Standards Institute*.

answer file A file used during an unattended installation of Windows. It provides a script of responses to the questions Setup asks so the user does not have to answer them manually. (9)

antistatic mat A mat that provides a path to ground for a static charge and is designed for the desktop or floor of a workspace. One placed on the workbench reduces the risk of electrostatic discharge for components placed on it, while one placed on the floor provides the same protection for anyone standing on the mat. (5)

antistatic wrist strap A strap designed to discharge static electricity from your body. One end attaches to the wrist, whereas the other end attaches to a grounded object. (5)

APIPA See *Automatic Private IP Address.*

APM See *Advanced Power Management.*

archive attribute A file attribute set by the OS when a file is created or modified. Backup software often removes this attribute when backing up a file in order to mark it as a backed-up file. (10)

arithmetic logic unit (ALU) A component of a CPU that is responsible for all logical and mathematical operations in the system. (1)

ARP See *Address Resolution Protocol.*

aspect ratio The proportion between an image's width and height. Traditional CRT monitors have an aspect ratio of 4:3. Widescreen displays have an aspect ratio of 16:9. (3)

ASR See *automated system recovery.*

asymmetrical digital subscriber line (ADSL) A type of DSL service in which the download speed is higher than the upload speed. (13)

asynchronous transfer mode (ATM) A type of switched network used by phone companies. (13)

AT See *Advanced Technology.*

ATA See *Advanced Technology Attachment.*

ATA Packet Interface (ATAPI) The protocol for connecting optical drives and tape drives to an ATA channel. (1)

ATAPI See *ATA Packet Interface.*

ATM See *asynchronous transfer mode.*

attended installation An installation of Windows that is not automated, where the user is required to pay attention throughout the entire process to provide information and to respond to messages. Also called *a manual installation.* (9)

ATV12V A power supply standard that has both the 20-pin connector for the motherboard and a 4-pin 12 V connector. (3)

ATX   See *Advanced Technology eXtended.*

ATX power supply   A power supply form factor that pairs with an ATX motherboard and case. (3)

audio modem riser (AMR)   A small expansion card introduced in the late 1990s that plugs into a special slot on a motherboard and uses the CPU to perform modem functions and sound functions. It is not plug and play compatible. (2)

auditing   See *security auditing.*

Audit Policy   In Windows, one or more settings found in the Local Security Settings console. (16)

auto-switching power supply   A power supply that detects the incoming voltage and switches to accept either 120 or 240 VAC. (6)

Automated System Recovery (ASR)   An option available in the Windows XP Backup program for recovering from damage that prevents the operating system from starting. It replaced the Emergency Repair Disk (ERD) process in Windows 2000. (11)

authentication   Authentication is validation of a user account and password that occurs before the security components of Windows will give the user access to the computer. (16)

authentication factor   Things used for authentication, such as something you know, something you have, or something you are. Authentication involves one or more of these factors and can, therefore, be one-factor, two-factor, or three-factor authentication. (16)

authorization   The process that authenticates a user and verifies the user account's level of access to a resource. (16)

Automated System Recovery (ASR)   In Windows XP, this replaces the Emergency Repair process of Windows NT and Windows 2000. ASR is available from the Windows Backup program (NTBACKUP.EXE). (11)

Automatic Private IP Address (APIPA)   An address that a DHCP client will assign to itself after requesting an address and failing to receive one from a DHCP server. The address it will assign is in the 169.254 /16 network, which is the range of addresses from 169.254.0.1 to 169.254.255.254. (13)

back door   Program code that provides a way for someone to gain access to a computer while bypassing security. Only a person who knows how the back door works can use it, but once in, that individual has the same access as the host program to all the internal operating system code. (16)

background process   A process that runs "behind the scenes" with a low priority, does not require input, and rarely creates output. (11)

backup media   Any writable mass storage device, removable or fixed in place. (2)

Balanced Technology eXtended   A motherboard form factor introduced in 2003 by Intel as the successor to ATX. (1)

bandwidth   The amount of data that can travel over a network at a given time. (13)

bar code reader   A specialized type of scanner that reads bar codes, which are patterns of bars of varying widths printed on labels or directly on items. The bar pattern is converted into a numeric code that is transmitted to a computer as data. (3)

base priority level   See *process priority level.*

basic disk   A disk that uses basic storage, which means that it uses the partition table in the master boot record (MBR) to define disk partitions. (10)

Basic Service Set (BSS)   The wireless nodes (including the WAP) communicating together in infrastructure mode. (14)

basic storage   A storage type in Windows that uses the partition table in the master boot record (MBR) to define disk partitions. (10)

basic input/output system (BIOS)   A type of computer firmware that is responsible for informing the CPU of installed devices and how to communicate with them. (1)

BDD Workbench   A tool used to create and manage a distribution share and various installation images. (9)

beam-on-blade connector   The type of connector used in the ExpressCard interface. (6)

bidirectional mode   A parallel port mode in which the signals can be transmitted in both directions between the PC and parallel devices connected to the computer. (4)

biometric   A measurement of a body part, such as a fingerprint or retina scan. (16)

biometric device   A device that uses a measurement of a body part, such as a fingerprint or retina scan. (3)

biometric logon   The use of a biometric for authentication. (16)

BIOS   See *basic input/output system.*

BIOS settings   The BIOS configuration settings, also called system settings, accessed via a special BIOS-based menu during system startup. (4)

bit width   In reference to a memory module, how much information the processor can access from or write to memory in a single cycle. (2)

BitLocker drive encryption   An encryption technology introduced in Windows Vista Enterprise and Ultimate editions, Windows Server 2008, and also in Windows 7 Ultimate and Enterprise editions. It encrypts the entire boot volume. (16)

Blu-ray disc   The high-definition optical disc formatting standard developed by the Blu-ray Disc Association whose members include Sony, 20th Century Fox, Dell, Hewlett-Packard, and many other industry leaders. (2)

bluesnarfing The act of covertly obtaining information broadcast from wireless devices using the Bluetooth standard. (16)

Bluetooth A wireless standard for using radio waves to communicate between devices. Class 3 Bluetooth devices (the most common) communicate at distances up to one meter. (6)

BNC A connector used to attach coaxial cables to computers and network equipment. Origin of the term may be "Bayonet-Neill-Concelman" or "British Naval Connector." (2)

boot record The first physical sector on a floppy disk or the first sector on a hard drive partition. The boot record contains information about the OS. The boot record on a primary active partition is used to start the operating system. Also called the *boot sector*. Do not confuse this with the master boot record. (10)

boot sector See *boot record*.

boot sequence The order in which the BIOS will search devices for an operating system to start. (4)

bridge A network connection device that passes traffic between two networks, using the physical address (MAC address) of the destination device. (13)

broadband WAN A wide area network (WAN) connection that allows a large amount of data to be transmitted. Broadband WANs includes cellular, ISDN, DSL, cable, T-carrier, satellite, and fiber. (13)

BTX See *Balanced Technology eXtended*.

Bubble Jet A popular inkjet printer developed by Canon. (12)

bus In a computer, pathways that power, data, and control signals travel from one component to another within the system. (2)

C Used to represent the chrominance signal in S-Video. (3)

cable select An EIDE drive setting that has the system select the drive's role (master or slave) based on the drive's position on the cable. If the drive is on the end of the cable, it is the master drive, and if it is in the middle of the cable, it is the slave drive. (4)

cable tester A tool for testing if a cable can connect properly end-to-end and to determine if a cable has a short. These tools are available for a variety of cable types. (5)

cache controller A CPU component that manages the CPU cache. (1)

capacity In power supplies, the amount of wattage the power supply can handle. (3)

capture card A category of adapter card that accepts and records video signals to a PC's hard drive. A TV tuner card is a type of capture card. (2)

CardBus The PCMCIA standard that succeeds the PC Card. (6)

card services   A service on a laptop that configures a card after socket services has recognized it. (6)

case   The box that houses the main computer system. (1)

case fan   A cooling fan mounted directly on the case, as opposed to a power supply fan, which is inside the power supply. (3)

cathode ray tube (CRT) monitor   A display device that contains a cathode ray tube and uses an electron gun to activate phosphors behind the screen at the front of the tub. (3)

CD   See *compact disc*.

CD-R (CD-Record)   A drive that can write once to a special CD-R disc. (1)

CD-ROM   See *Compact Disc-Read-Only Memory*.

CD-ROM drive   A drive on a computer that can play music CDs and read data CDs, but cannot write to CDs. (1)

CD-RW (CD-rewritable)   A drive that can write either to CD-R discs or to specially designed CD-RW discs. In the case of the CD-RW discs, the drive can write more than once to the same portion of disc, overwriting old data. (1)

cellular WAN   Data communications over the cellular telecommunications networks. (6)

central processing unit (CPU)   The primary control device for a computer system. The CPU is simply a chip containing a set of components that manages all the activities. Also called a *processor*. (1)

Centronics   A 36-pin connector mounted to a device's parallel interface. (3)

channel service unit (CSU)   A device required at both ends of a T-carrier system connection. (13)

charging   In the laser printing process, the stage in which the printer's high-voltage power supply (HVPS) conducts electricity to the primary corona wire so it can pass the voltage on to the printer's electro-photosensitive drum. (12)

chipset   One or more chips designed to work closely with the CPU. Two parts of this chipset are the *Northbridge* and the *Southbridge*. (1)

chrominance   The signal in a television transmission that contains the color of the image. (3)

cleaning   In the laser printing process, the stage in which the image is removed from the photosensitive drum so it can accept the next image. (12)

cleaning blade   In the laser printing process, a blade that removes residual toner from the drum. (12)

client/server-based network A network in which dedicated computers called *servers* store data and provide print services or other capabilities to computers running the appropriate client service or services. (13)

clock speed In a CPU, the speed at which it can potentially execute instructions, measured in millions of cycles per second—megahertz (MHz)—or billions of cycles per second—gigahertz (GHz). (1)

cluster The minimum disk space that a file can use, allocated in the file system. (10)

CMOS See *complementary metal-oxide semiconductor.*

CMOS settings A misnomer, referring to the BIOS settings that are stored in a CMOS chip. (1)

CNR See *communication network riser.*

coaxial cable Cabling that contains a single copper wire surrounded by several layers of insulating plastic and a woven wire sheath that provides protection. (3)

Code Division Multiple Access (CDMA) The cellular network standards used by Verizon and Sprint-Nextel. (13)

code signing A practice begun in Windows 2000 in which all of the operating system code is digitally signed to show that it has not been tampered with. (9)

color depth The number of colors used by a display. (3)

Color Quality A Windows display setting that allows you to adjust the number of colors, or *color depth*, used by the display. (3)

communication network riser (CNR) A riser card that is similar to *audio modem riser (AMR)* except that it is plug and play–compatible and supports LANs in addition to audio, modem, and sound. (2)

compact disc (CD) An optical disc created and read by a mechanism using a laser. (2)

Compact Disc File System (CDFS) A file system used by operating systems for organizing, reading, and writing optical discs. (10)

Compact Disc–Read-Only Memory (CD-ROM) Laser discs sold at retail stores that contain music (audio CDs) or software (data CDs). (1)

CompactFlash A type of solid-state storage that is commonly used in a variety of devices, such as digital cameras. (2)

complementary metal-oxide semiconductor (CMOS) A chip that retains system settings such as the time, keyboard settings, and boot sequence. (1)

component video A video signaling method in which analog video information is transmitted as two or more discrete signals. Two general types of component video are RGB Video and S-Video. (3)

composite video   The traditional transmission system for television video signals, which combines the color and brightness information with the synchronization data into one signal. The TV circuitry then separates the two signals from the composite signal. (3)

computer platform   The hardware architecture, including the CPU, BIOS, and chipset. (8)

COMx   A generic reference to a PC's serial communications port, in which the *x* represents the port number. (5)

connector   The plug at the end of a cable or the port or connection point on a computer or device. (3)

continuity RIMM (CRIMM)   A special terminating stick that must be inserted into the open RIMM sockets. (4)

contrast ratio   The difference in value between a display's brightest white and darkest black. Modern LCD displays have a contrast ratio of 500:1 or greater. (3)

Control Panel   A Windows folder that contains numerous applets you can use to adjust the configuration of many different aspects of the OS. (8)

control unit   In a CPU, the component that is primarily responsible for directing all the activities of the computer and the interactions of its components. (1)

cookies   Small text files a Web browser saves on the local hard drive at the request of a Website. Cookies can contain information that will be used the next time the user connects to the Website. (16)

copy   A file operation in which the file or folder remains in the source location, and a duplicate is created in the target (destination) location. (10)

CPE   See *customer premises equipment.*

CPU   See *central processing unit.*

CPU fan   A cooling fan located on a CPU. (3)

CRIMM   See *continuity RIMM.*

cracker   See *hacker.*

CrossFire   A multi-GPU solution developed by ATI. (3)

CRT   See *cathode ray tube (CRT) monitor.*

CSU   See *channel service unit.*

customer premises equipment (CPE)   A T-1 multiplexer or a special LAN bridge that connects to the telephone company's channel service unit (CSU), which encodes data for transmission over a T-carrier circuit. (13)

data migration   The moving of data from one storage device to another. (9)

datagram The chunks into which the TCP protocol packages data. In addition to the data, each datagram contains information, stored in a header, which is used by the TCP protocol on the receiving end to reassemble the chunks of data into the original message. (13)

daughter card A type of riser card that connects directly into a motherboard and adds no additional functionality of its own, but extends the expansion bus and allows expansion cards to be added in a different physical orientation. (2)

DB-9 A 9-pin D-shell connector. (3)

DB-25 A 25-pin D-shell connector. (3)

DC See *direct current.*

DC Controller A device found in laptops that monitors and regulates power usage. The features vary by manufacturer, but typically, they provide short-circuit protection, give "low battery" warnings, and can be configured to shut down the computer automatically when the power is low. (6)

DDoS Attack See *distributed denial of service attack.*

DDR See *double-data rate (DDR) SDRAM.*

DDR RAM See *double-data rate (DDR) SDRAM.*

DDR SDRAM See *double-data rate (DDR) SDRAM.*

DDR1 See *double-data rate (DDR) SDRAM.*

DDR2 See *DDR2 SDRAM.*

DDR2 SDRAM A RAM standard that replaces the original DDR standard. Using far less power than DDR1, a stick of DDR2 SDRAM has 240 pins. (2)

DDR3 See *DDR3 SDRAM.*

DDR3 SDRAM A RAM standard that replaces the original DDR2 standard and requires far less power, while providing almost twice the bandwidth. A stick of DDR3 SDRAM has 240 pins, but is keyed so it will not fit into a socket designed for DDR2. DDR3 SO-DIMMs have 204 pins. (2)

dead pixel A dark spot on an LCD screen caused when a transistor is permanently off. (7)

Debugging Mode A Windows Advanced Options menu choice used to send debugging information about the Windows startup over a serial cable to another computer running a special program called a debugger. (11)

default gateway In an IP configuration, the address of the local router that acts as a gateway from the local network to other IP networks. (13)

degaussing The process of using an oscillating magnetic field to reduce and randomize the magnetic field that builds up on the shadow mask of a CRT monitor. (3)

demilitarized zone (DMZ)   In computer networking, a network located between a private network and the Internet with a firewall on both sides. A DMZ contains servers offering services to users on the Internet and inside the protected private network. (16)

denial of service (DoS) attack   This attack occurs when someone sends a large number of requests to a server, overwhelming the server so it stops functioning on the network. (16)

developing   In the laser printing process, this is the step in which the cover on the printer's toner cartridge is opened and the toner particles are attracted to the relatively less negatively charged areas of the drum. (12)

device driver   Program code that allows an operating system to control the use of a physical device. (9)

Device Manager   A Windows GUI utility that allows an administrator to view the status of devices and install, remove, and update device drivers. (8)

DHCP   See *Dynamic Host Configuration Protocol*.

DHCP Server   A server running the Dynamic Host Configuration Protocol (DHCP) service. This server allocates IP addresses to DHCP client computers. (13)

dial-up   A WAN connection that uses an analog modem rather than a network card and uses standard phone cables rather than network cables. (13)

dial-up modem   See *analog modem*.

dialer   A program that causes a modem to dial phone numbers surreptitiously. (16)

digital LCD display   An LCD display that accepts a digital signal. Early LCD displays accepted an analog signal and converted it to digital internally. (3)

Digital Light Processing (DLP)   An optical semiconductor used in small projectors and in rear-projection televisions. (3)

digital linear tape (DLT)   A technology developed in the 1980s for storing data. Variations of this format are in use today. (2)

digital signature   Encrypted data placed in a file to guard against tampering. (9)

digital subscriber line (DSL)   A WAN connection that uses existing copper telephone wire for the communication circuit. To accomplish this, a DSL modem splits the existing phone line into two bands; voice transmission uses the frequencies below 4000 Hz, whereas data transmission uses everything else. (13)

digital versatile disc (DVD)   A disc designed to store all types of data usable by a computer. This term also refers to the drives that read and write to these discs. There are various types of DVD drives and media. (1)

digital video discs   The original digital discs created in 1995 for storing video. (1)

digital video interface (DVI) A digital video interface that has several modes, including one that offers downward compatibility with analog displays. It requires a special connector, which comes in several variations to support the DVI modes. (3)

digital video recorder (DVR) A device that records video content to disk. (4)

digitizer See *digitizing tablet*.

digitizing tablet An input device that uses a stylus. Available as an external device, it uses touch screen technology and is usually at least the size of a sheet of paper. Also called a *digitizer*. (6)

DIMM See *dual inline memory module (DIMM)*.

DIN connector A round connector that gets its name from Deutsche Industrie Norm, a German standards organization. Normally a round connector with a circular or semicircle of pins. (3)

DIP switch Dual inline package. A very tiny slide that indicates two states. Motherboard and other circuit cards often have one or more groupings of DIP switches for configuring options. (4)

direct current (DC) The type of electrical current delivered by a battery in which the electrons flow in only one direction. (3)

direct memory access (DMA) channel A system resource that certain devices, such as sound cards and hard drives, can use to move data between the device and system RAM without involving the processor. (5)

direct thermal printer A type of thermal printer in which a heated print head burns dots into the surface of heat-sensitive paper. (12)

Directory Services Restore Mode In Windows, an Advanced Option that is only available in Windows Servers in the role of domain controllers, although it appears on the menu in non–domain controllers. (11)

Disable Automatic Restart An Advanced Options choice that will temporarily disable the Automatically Restart option on the Advanced page of System Properties. (11)

discretion Not revealing information about someone that would be harmful to or embarrass him or her. (18)

display A screen device for video output. Also called a *monitor*. (3)

Display Brightness Key A key on a laptop that, when pressed along with the FN key, changes the laptop display brightness at the hardware level. On some laptops, when this key combination is pressed, a small brightness control panel will display on the screen. Use the up (↑) or right (→) arrow key to increase the brightness, and use the left (←) or down (↓) arrow key to decrease the brightness. The DISPLAY BRIGHTNESS key is normally a function key, such as F5, that displays a sun-like symbol. (6)

Display Mode Key   A key on a laptop that is pressed along with the FN key to change display modes so the output will be only to the laptop's display, only to an external display, or simultaneously to both displays. The DISPLAY MODE key is normally a function key, such as F7, that displays a display symbol. (6)

display power-management signaling (DPMS)   A VESA standard for power management in display devices. (3)

display resolution   The displayable number of pixels, expressed as *x* and *y* numbers, such as 1024 × 768, 1152 × 864, and 1280 × 1024. (3)

DisplayPort   A digital display interface standard developed by the Video Electronics Standards Association that supports both video and audio signals, contains HDCP copy protection, and is unique because it is royalty-free to manufacturers. (3)

distributed denial of service (DDoS) attack   This attack occurs when a massive number (up to hundreds of thousands) of computers send DoS attacks to a server, making it unavailable. (16)

Distributed File System (DFS)   A service implemented on Windows Servers that hides the complexity of the network from end users in that it makes files that are distributed across multiple servers appear as if they are in one place. (10)

distribution server   A server containing source files for installing software onto client computers. The shared folder containing these files is a software distribution point. (9)

distribution share   A shared folder on a distribution server containing the source files for a remote installation. (9)

DLP   See *Digital Light Processing*.

DLT   See *digital linear tape*.

DMA controller   A specialized chip that controls DMA channels. (5)

DMZ   See *demilitarized zone*.

DNS   See *Domain Name Service*.

DNS Server   A server that manages DNS names. (13)

docking station   A more advanced and more expensive alternative to a port replicator. In addition to the ports normally found on a port replicator, a docking station may include full-size expansion slots and drives. (6)

domain   In a Microsoft Windows network, an administrative organization with a centralized security accounts database maintained on one or more special servers called domain controllers. This centralized database contains accounts for users, groups, and computers participating in the domain, and it is used to authenticate a user for access to any resource in the domain. (13)

Domain Name Service (DNS)   The Internet service that manages access to Internet domain names and the naming system it uses for computers and resources connected to the Internet or in a private network. (13)

DoS Attack   See *denial of service (DoS) attack*.

dot matrix printer   A type of printer that uses a matrix of pins striking paper through an ink ribbon to create dots on the paper, forming alphanumeric characters and graphic images. (12)

dotted decimal notation   The format in which IP addresses are usually shown, with decimal numbers separated by "dots" as in 192.168.100.2. (13)

double-data rate (DDR) SDRAM   RAM that doubles the rate of speed at which a standard SDRAM can process data. Also called *DDR* and *DDR1*. A stick of DDR1 SDRAM has 184 pins. (2)

double-sided (DS) DVD   A DVD of any type that can store data on both sides of the disc. (1)

DPMS   See *display power-management signaling*.

DRAM   See *dynamic RAM*.

drive-by download   A program downloaded to a computer without the user's consent. The user unwittingly initiates the download by some simple act, such as browsing to a Website or opening an e-mail message written in HTML. Or a user may initiate a drive-by download by installing an application. (16)

drive image   An exact duplicate of an entire hard drive's contents, including the OS and all installed software. (9)

drive lock password   A password that locks your hard drive and is often stored in a TPM chip. (16)

drive path   When a mount point exists between a partition or volume to a folder on another volume, the drive path is the path (including a drive letter) to that partition or volume. (10)

driver signing   The practice of applying a digital signature to device driver code. (9)

DSL   See *digital subscriber line*.

dual-core CPU   A CPU containing two CPU cores. (1)

dual inline memory module (DIMM)   A memory module (stick) that installs into matching DIMM sockets found on many motherboards. The word "dual" refers to the separate pins or connections on both sides of the module and socket. (1)

dual layer (DL)   Pertaining to a DVD drive and disc that can store data in two pitted layers on each data side, with each layer having a different reflectivity index. (1)

DVD   See *digital versatile disc (DVD)*.

DVD-5   A single-sided, single-layer digital versatile disc (DVD) that stores 4.7 GB of data, or over two hours of video. (2)

DVD-9   A single-sided, double-layer digital versatile disc (DVD) that stores 8.54 GB of data, or over four hours of video. (2)

DVD-10   A double-sided, single-layer digital versatile disc (DVD) that stores 9.4 GB of data, or over four hours of video. (2)

DVD-18   A double-sided, double-layer digital versatile disc (DVD) that stores 17.08 GB of data, or over eight hours of video. (2)

DVD-Data discs   A blanket term used for DVD discs regardless of the type of data they contain. (2)

DVD-R   Digital versatile disc (DVD) discs that can be written to once, but data cannot be overwritten. This term also refers to the drives that can write to these discs. (2)

DVD-RAM   The digital versatile disc (DVD) encoding format used for data storage. (2)

DVD+R   Digital versatile disc (DVD) discs that can be written to, but data cannot be overwritten. This standard is newer than DVD-R. This term also refers to the drives that can write to these discs. (2)

DVD-ROM   The read-only DVD discs sold at retail stores, containing video or software and having a maximum capacity of 15.9 GB of data. This term also applies to the drives that can only read DVDs. (2)

DVD-ROM drive   A DVD drive that cannot write to but can read DVD discs. (2)

DVD-RW   Digital versatile disc (DVD) discs that can be written to, and data can also be overwritten. This term also refers to the drives that can write to these discs. (2)

DVD+RW   Digital versatile disc (DVD) discs that can be rewritten to, and data can also be overwritten. This standard is newer than DVD-RW. This term also refers to the drives that can write to these discs. (2)

DVD-Video   The original digital versatile disc (DVD) encoding format used for movies sold at retail. (2)

DVI   See *digital video interface*.

DVI-A   A DVI mode that supports downward compatibility with analog displays. (3)

DVI-D   A DVI mode that supports digital video signals and is partially compatible with HDMI. See also *digital video interface* and *High-Definition Multimedia Interface*. (3)

DVI-I   A DVI mode that supports both analog and digital video signals. (3)

DXDIAG   Windows run-line utility for testing the DirectX support. Launch this program when experiencing video problems and/or audio problems when running DirectX applications. (11)

dynamic disk   A disk type introduced with Windows 2000 that contains space allocated in volumes without the limits imposed on basic disks. On a dynamic disk, the number of volumes are unlimited, and a volume can extend to include available space on any hard disk in the computer. (10)

Dynamic Host Configuration Protocol (DHCP)   The protocol used by DHCP servers and clients. A DHCP server allocates IP addresses within the scope of addresses configured on the server by an administrator. DHCP clients request IP addresses and other IP configuration settings from DHCP Servers. (13)

dynamic RAM (DRAM)   Memory chips that provide much slower access than SRAM chips but that can store several megabytes of data on a single chip (or hundreds of megabytes, or even gigabytes, when they are packaged together on a "stick"). (2)

dynamic storage   A method for allocating disk space on hard disks in which configuration information for each dynamic disk is located on the disk space beyond the first physical sector. This configuration information is stored outside of any volume on the hard disk. (10)

ECC   See *error-correcting code*.

ECP   See *enhanced capabilities port (ECP) mode*.

edition   A subpackaging of a Windows revision that contains the core OS plus a special set of features that is offered as a separate product targeted to a certain type of end user. (8)

EEPROM   Electrically erasable programmable ROM. A ROM chip that is erasable using an electrical charge. (2)

EFS   See *Encrypting File System (EFS)*.

EIDE   See *Enhanced IDE*.

electromagnetic interference (EMI)   The disruption of signal transmission caused by the radiation of electrical and magnetic fields. Electric motors are a common source of EMI. (18)

electromagnetic pulse (EMP)   A large burst of electromagnetic energy, as from a nuclear explosion, that has the potential to damage communications and power lines within a large geographic area, depending on the size and location of the pulse. (16)

electronic KVM switch   A KVM switch that uses software and special keyboard commands to switch among controlled computers. Also called an *active KVM switch*. (3)

electro-photosensitive drum   In a laser printer, a metal drum with an electro-photosensitive coating to which a charge can be applied by a laser beam. (12)

electrostatic discharge (ESD)   The sudden and uncontrolled movement of electricity from an object with a greater charge to one with a lesser charge. Also called *static electricity*. (18)

embedded systems   A special-purpose computer designed for a certain task and installed within a device. (2)

emergency repair disk (ERD)   A special disk used for recovering an OS failure in Windows 2000. It requires that you create the ERD while the system is healthy, and then use it, along with the Windows Setup CD, to repair Windows. (11)

Emergency Repair Process   A Windows 2000 recovery tool requiring an up-to-date emergency repair disk (ERD) or recent emergency repair information stored on the local hard disk. (11)

EMP   See *electromagnetic pulse*.

Enable Boot Logging   An Advanced Options menu choice that creates a log of the Windows startup in a file named NTBTLOG.TXT and saved in the *systemroot* folder (normally C:\Windows). (11)

Enable Low Resolution Video   In Windows Vista and Windows 7, an Advanced Options menu choice that starts Windows normally, except that the video mode is changed to the lowest resolution, using the currently installed video driver. This option does not switch to the basic Windows video driver. (11)

Enable VGA Mode   In Windows 2000 and Windows XP, an Advanced Options menu choice that starts Windows normally, except that video mode is changed to the lowest resolution, using the currently installed video driver. This option does not switch to the basic Windows video driver. (11)

encrypted authentication   A security service in which authentication credentials are encrypted (user name and password) before transmission over a network. (16)

Encrypting File System (EFS)   A security feature of many Windows versions that allows it to encrypt files on an NTFS volume. (16)

encryption   The conversion of data into a special format that cannot be read by anyone unless they have a software key to convert it back into its usable form. (13)

enhanced capability port (ECP) mode   A mode for parallel ports that allows access to special features in the PC called DMA channels. This mode is approximately ten times faster than regular bidirectional mode and is designed for printers and scanners. (4)

Enhanced IDE (EIDE)   A standard for hard drives that attach to the *Parallel AT Attachment (PATA)* interface. (1)

enhanced parallel port (EPP) mode   A parallel port mode that has the same performance as ECP but is used with parallel devices other than printers and scanners. (4)

EPP   See *enhanced parallel port (EPP) mode*.

EPROM   Erasable programmable read-only memory. A ROM chip that is erasable and reprogrammable through the use of specialized software. (2)

ERD   See *emergency repair disk*.

erasure lamp   In a laser printer, a high-intensity lamp that, when shone on a portion of the electro-photosensitive drum, removes any remaining charge on that portion of the drum. (12)

error-correcting code (ECC)   A method of memory error-checking that is more sophisticated than parity checking. Like parity checking, it adds an extra bit per byte. In addition, software in the system memory controller uses an algorithm to both detect and correct errors. (2)

eSATA   See *External Serial ATA*.

Ethernet   A group of networking standards created by the IEEE 802.3 subcommittee. (13)

even parity   A memory error-checking method in which the parity bit is used to ensure that the total number of 1s in the data stream is even. (2)

EVGA   See *Extended Video Graphics Array*.

exception   In router configuration, a term that is used to describe traffic that is allowed, as in allowing traffic using a certain port number through the router. (16)

expansion bus   A grouping of wires built into a PC that, based on certain protocols, transfers data, control signals, and power to printed circuit boards (adapter cards) that are plugged into connectors in the expansion bus. Technicians often use the terms *expansion bus*, *bus*, and *system bus* interchangeably. (1)

expansion card   See *adapter card*.

ExpressCard   A PCMCIA card standard that comes in two interfaces: PCIe and USB 2.0. (6)

extended partition   A partition type that can exist on a basic disk and have one or more logical drive letters assigned to it. A Windows operating system cannot boot from an extended partition. (10)

Extended Video Graphics Array (EVGA)   A VESA standard for graphics adapters with a maximum graphics resolution of 1024 × 768 pixels. (3)

extending extractor   See *parts grabber*.

extension magnet   A long-handled tool with a magnet on one end, used to pick up small objects containing iron. (5)

external cache   In a CPU, special memory that resides outside the CPU's core and is used to temporarily store instructions and data in order to increase the processing speed. Also called *Level 2 (L2) cache* and *Level 3 (L3) cache*, depending on the design of the CPU and motherboard. (1)

External Serial ATA (eSATA)   An extension of the SATA standard for external SATA devices, with speeds triple that of USB 2.0. (1)

Fast Ethernet   Using the same cabling as *10BaseT, Fast Ethernet,* or *100Base-T,* operates at 100 Mbps and uses different network interface cards. (13)

fast page mode (FPM)   An early technology for increasing the performance of DRAM. (2)

FAT   See *FAT file system.*

FAT file system   A file system in which one of the basic structures is a table used for allocating space. This table is called the *file allocation table (FAT).* (10)

FAT table   See *file allocation table.*

FAT12   A version of the FAT file system for very small drives—mainly for floppy drives, using a 12-bit file allocation table. (10)

FAT16   A version of the FAT file system used by MS-DOS for hard drives, using a 16-bit file allocation table. (10)

FAT32   A version of the FAT file system used by hard drives and some flash drives (thumb drives, etc.), using a 32-bit file allocation table. (10)

FDD   See *floppy disk drive.*

fiber-optic cable   A cable medium that transmits light pulses rather than electrical signals, so it is not susceptible to electromagnetic interference (EMI). (13)

field replaceable unit (FRU)   A component that you can install into a system onsite, such as memory modules, heat sinks, and CMOS batteries. (5)

file   Information organized as a unit into a container. The author (creator) of a file controls how much information the file contains. (10)

file allocation table (FAT)   The file system component in the FAT file system in which the OS creates a table that serves as a map of where files reside on disk. Also called the *FAT table.* (10)

file signature verification   A process applied to digitally signed code to unencrypt the signature data and use the information to verify the program code was not modified since the signature was added. (9)

file system   The logical structure on disk that allows the operating system to save and retrieve files. Examples of file systems are FAT and NTFS. Both of these file system have different versions, such as FAT12, FAT16, FAT32, and NTFS 4.0 and NTFS 5.0. (10)

File Transfer Protocol (FTP)   A protocol for computer-to-computer (host-to-host) transfer of files over a TCP/IP network, regardless of the operating system in use. (13)

firewall   A computer (or dedicated device) that sits between a private network and an untrusted network and examines all traffic in and out of the network it is protecting. It will block any traffic it recognizes as a potential threat, using a variety of techniques. (16)

FireWire   See *IEEE 1394*.

firmware   Software instructions stored in ROM chips. It exists on most PC components and on the motherboard. (1)

fixed input power supply   A power supply that only accepts one input power voltage. (6)

flash BIOS   BIOS that can be electronically upgraded. (1)

flash drive   See *thumb drive*.

flash memory   A type of solid-state storage that is commonly used in a variety of devices, such as digital cameras, which often use CompactFlash. (2)

flash ROM   A technology for ROM that can be reprogrammed using special software. (2)

flashing   The act of electronically upgrading BIOS. (5)

flat panel display (FPD)   A computer display that uses liquid crystal or plasma technology and does not require the bulk of a large picture tube. The screen enclosure can be as thin as one to two inches. (3)

floating-point unit (FPU)   A type of *arithmetic logic unit (ALU)* that is used to perform specialized functions, such as division and large decimal number operations. Also called a *math coprocessor*. (1)

floppy disk   A magnetic storage device that contains a thin internal plastic disk, capable of receiving magnetic charges contained in the thin magnetic coating on the disk. (1)

floppy disk drive   A drive used for reading from and writing to removable floppy disks. Also called *FDD*. (1)

Fn key   A special modifier key on a laptop keyboard that when pressed together with certain alphanumeric keys, changes the output of the pressed key. It is often called the *function key*. (6)

Foreign   In Disk Management, the status given to a dynamic disk that has not had its configuration information (stored on the disk) imported into Windows. This status occurs when a dynamic disk is moved to a different Windows computer or when a dynamic disk fails. (10)

form factor   On a motherboard, the type and location of components, as well as the size of the board itself. (1)

format   A process that places the logical structure of a file system on a partitioned volume. (4)

frame relay   A type of switched network used by phone companies. (13)

FPM   See *fast page mode*.

FPU   See *floating-point unit*.

front side bus (FSB)   An internal bus in a CPU that connects it to memory and video. (1)

FSB   See *front side bus*.

FTP   See *File Transfer Protocol (FTP)*.

fraud   The use of deceit and trickery to persuade someone to hand over money or valuables. (16)

full-duplex   In reference to networks, communications in both directions at the same time. (13)

fusing   In the laser printing process, the step at which the heat-sensitive toner is fused to the paper by heated fusing rollers. (12)

fusing lamp   In a laser printer, the lamp that heats the fusing rollers. (12)

fusing rollers   In the laser printer, the heated rollers that fuse the toner to the paper. (12)

gadget   A small program, such as those that can be run from the Windows Sidebar. (8)

Gigabit Ethernet   Also called *1000Base-T*, this networking standard supports speeds up to 1 Gbps. (13)

Global System for Mobile communications (GSM)   The cellular network standards used by AT&T and T-Mobile. (13)

graphical processing unit (GPU)   A processor on a graphics adapter used to render graphics images for the display, saving the CPU for other functions. (1)

graphical user interface (GUI)   A user interface that takes advantage of the video system's graphics capabilities for manipulated graphic elements that represent objects and tasks. (8)

graphics tablet   See *digitizing tablet*.

grayware   Threats that are not truly malicious code, but can have indirect negative effects, such as decreasing performance or using up bandwidth. Grayware includes spyware, adware, spam, and spim. (16)

grounding mat   See *antistatic mat*.

h-hold   A CRT video setting, also known at *horizontal hold*, that holds the image horizontally on the screen. (3)

hacker   A perpetrator of malicious software attacks against computers and networks. Also called a *cracker*. (16)

half-duplex   In networks, when data can travel in either direction, but only in one direction at a time. (13)

hard disk drive   A magnetic storage device that stores data on metal platters that have a coating that holds data in the form of changes to small magnetic particles in the coating. Also called *HDD*. (1)

hardware abstraction layer (HAL)   A component of the Windows operating system that resides in a file and is loaded into memory during the kernel loading phase of the Windows startup. (10)

HD-DVD   The high-definition optical disc formatting standard, promoted by Toshiba, that was defeated by the Blu-ray Disc standard as the widely accepted high-definition standard. (2)

HDD   See *hard disk drive*.

HDMI   See *High-Definition Multimedia Interface*.

heat sink   A heat dissipation device, usually a passive metal object with a flat surface attached to a component, such as a chip. (3)

heat sink compound   See *thermal compound*.

hibernate   A Windows sleep mode that uses hard drive space to save all the programs and data that are in memory at the time you choose this mode. The computer then completely shuts down and requires no power while it is hibernating. (6)

hidden attribute   A file attribute that is given to a file to indicate it should not be visible in Windows Explorer unless View settings override the attribute and allow the file to be shown.

High-Bandwidth Digital Content Protection (HDCP)   A feature of HDMI that prevents people from illegally copying HD DVDs. See also *High-Definition Multimedia Interface (HDMI)*. (3)

High-Definition Multimedia Interface (HDMI)   An interface standard for use with DVD players, digital television (DTV) players, set-top cable or satellite service boxes, and other devices. It combines audio and video signals into an uncompressed signal and has a bandwidth of up to 5 GB/second. Only one specially designed cable is required where previously several were required. (3)

high-voltage power supply (HVPS)   Any power supply that provides high voltage, such as those in laser printers and CRTs. (3)

horizontal position   A setting on an LCD display that adjusts the viewable area of the display horizontally. (3)

hot spot   A physical area where a Wi-Fi network connects to the Internet. (13)

hot-swappable drive   A drive that can be safely installed and removed while a computer is up and running without damaging the data stored on the drive. (2)

hot swapping   The act of safely installing/uninstalling or attaching/removing a device while a computer is up and running. (3)

HTML   See *Hypertext Markup Language (HTML)*.

HTTP   See *Hypertext Transfer Protocol (HTTP)*.

hub   [1] A device that is the central connecting point of a LAN. A hub is little more than a multiport repeater taking incoming signals on one port and repeating them to all other ports. Ethernet hubs have been largely replaced by Ethernet switches. (13). [2] A multiport connecting device for USB devices. (4)

hyper threading   A CPU technology that allows two threads to execute at the same time within a single execution core. This technology is considered to be partially parallel execution. Intel introduced it in the Pentium 4 Xeon CPU. Also known as *simultaneous multithreading (SMT)*. (1)

Hypertext Markup Language (HTML)   The language of Web pages. Web designers use the HTML language to create Web page code, which your Web browser converts into the pages you view on your screen. (13)

Hypertext Transfer Protocol (HTTP)   The information transfer protocol of the World Wide Web (WWW). Included in HTTP are the commands Web browsers use to request Web pages from Web servers and then display them on the screen of the local computer. (13)

Hypertext Transfer Protocol over Secure Sockets Layer (HTTPS)   A protocol for securing data for transmission by encrypting it. (13)

I/O   See *input/output*.

I/O address   An assigned address or range of addresses on a system's address bus that, together with an interrupt request line (IRQ), allows a device to be recognized by the processor. (5)

ICMP   See *Internet Control Message Protocol*.

icon   In an operating system GUI, a tiny graphic representing an application, folder, disk, menu item, or other entity. (8)

IDE   See *Integrated Drive Electronics*.

identity theft   This occurs when someone collects personal information belonging to another person and uses that information to fraudulently make purchases, open new credit accounts, and even obtain new driver's licenses and other forms of identification in the victim's name. (16)

IEC-320 connector   A slide switch on the exterior of a PC power supply used to switch between two input voltages.

IEEE   The Institute of Electrical and Electronics Engineers, an international nonprofit organization that sets standards as part of its charter. (3)

IEEE 1284   A parallel interface standard that supports bidirectional communication and transfer rates of up to 2 MBps. (3)

IEEE 1394   An external serial bus standardized by the IEEE. Apple first developed it as FireWire. Other manufacturers call it *i.link* or *Lynx*. It can support up to 63 daisy-chained devices. Since the introduction of the faster update, IEEE 1394b, the original standard is called IEEE 1394a. (3)

IEEE 1394a   The original version of the IEEE 1394 standard that supports speeds up to 400 Mbps. (3)

IEEE 1394b   The second version of the IEEE 1394 standard; it supports speeds up to 3.2 Gbps and distances of up to 100 meters. (3)

IEEE 1394c-2006   The third version of the IEEE 1394 standard; it is a departure from the old standards in that it uses Category 5e twisted pair cable with RJ-45 connectors, combining Ethernet and FireWire. (3)

IMAP   See *Internet Message Access Protocol (IMAP)*.

impact printer   A type of printer that transfers ink to paper by causing a print head to strike a printer ribbon containing ink against the paper. (12)

inactive KVM switch   A type of KVM switch that is controlled through a mechanical switch on the box. (3)

Independent Basic Service Set (IBSS)   A small group of computers communicating wirelessly with one another without the use of a centralized wireless access point (WAP). (14)

industry standard architecture (ISA)   A very old expansion bus standard, seen in the early IBM PC. (1)

Infrared (IR)   Light waves in the infrared spectrum. (6)

Infrared Data Association (IrDA)   An organization that creates specifications for infrared wireless communication. (6)

infrastructure mode   A wireless mode requiring a wireless access point (WAP). (14)

ink cartridge   A small cassette containing an ink reservoir used to provide the medium for certain printers. An ink cartridge will only fit a certain model printer. (12)

inkjet   A type of printer that uses one of several technologies to apply wet ink to paper to create text or graphic printouts. The two most popular inkjet printer models are the *InkJet,* developed by Hewlett-Packard, and the *Bubble Jet,* developed by Canon. Epson uses the term "ink jet" (with a space), but it does not appear in the model names of their printers. (12)

input/out (I/O)   In reference to computers, the pathways or methods for what goes into a computer in the form of data and instructions and similarly what comes out of the computer in many forms, including an onscreen display, a printout sent to a printer, or data sent to another device or computer. (1)

Integrated Access Device (IAD)   A device that converts digital signals from the broadband connection to voice for the analog phone and the analog voice signals to digital signals for the digital network. (14)

Integrated Drive Electronics (IDE)   An early PC hard drive interface. (1)

Integrated Service Digital Network (ISDN)   An early international standard for sending voice and data over digital telephone wires. ISDN uses existing telephone circuits or higher-speed conditioned lines to get speeds of either 64 Kbps or 128 Kbps. ISDN lines also have the ability to carry voice and data simultaneously over the circuit. (13)

Intel Corporation   One of the two prevailing CPU manufacturers. (1)

Intel x86 Specification   An Intel specification for the PC 32-bit architecture defining CPUs, motherboards, and other components. (5)

internal bus   The bus within a CPU that connects the CPU to external components. (1)

internal cache memory   In a CPU, special memory that resides within the CPU's core and is used to temporarily store instructions and data in order to increase the processing speed. Also called *L1 cache*. (1)

InterNational Committee on Information Technology Standards (INCITS)   A standards organization, of which the T10 SCSI committee maintains the SCSI standard. (4)

Internet   The worldwide interconnection of networks that can be accessed with various Internet-based software. The World Wide Web is one of the many services of the Internet. (13)

Internet Control Message Protocol (ICMP)   A subprotocol of IP that detects and reports problems that can cause errors. (15)

Internet Explorer (IE)   A Web browser created by Microsoft. (14)

Internet Message Access Protocol (IMAP)   A protocol used by e-mail clients for communicating with e-mail servers. This protocol is replacing the POP protocol. IMAP allows users to connect to e-mail servers and not only retrieve e-mail, which removes the messages from the server, as they can do with the POP protocol, but also manage their stored messages without removing them from the server. (13)

Internet Protocol (IP)   One of the main protocols of the TCP/IP protocol suite, IP manages logical addressing of network packets so routing protocols can route the packets over the network. (13)

Internet service provider (ISP)   A company in the business of providing Internet access to users. (13)

internetwork   An interconnected network. The Internet is the largest example. (13)

interrupt request line (IRQ)   An assigned channel over which a device can send a signal to the processor to get its attention. (5)

intranet   A private internetwork. (13)

inverter   A device that converts DC current to AC. An inverter is required in a laptop to provide the AC current required by the display. (6)

IP packet filtering   A firewall service that inspects (or filters) each packet that enters or leaves the network, applying a set of security rules defined by a network administrator, and not allowing packets that fail inspection to pass between networks. (16)

IPCONFIG   A command-line utility installed on a Windows computer with the TCP/IP protocol suite; it's used to view the IP configuration of a network connection and to perform certain administrative tasks. (15)

IRQ   See *interrupt request line*.

ISDN   See *Integrated Service Digital Network*.

IP router   A network connection device that routes IP packets between networks. (13)

ISP   See *Internet service provider*.

jargon   The use of words, often technical and uncommon, that both parties understand in the same way. (18)

jump drive   See *thumb drive*.

jumper   On a circuit board, a small connector that slides down on a pair of pins jutting up from the board. Multiple pins are often side-by-side, and a jumper joins a pair of them. (4)

key fob   A small device containing a microchip used to generate unique passwords for logging on to a computer or a network. (16)

keystroke logger   A hardware device or a program that monitors and records a user's every keystroke, usually without the user's knowledge. (16)

KVM over IP   A *remote KVM switch* that captures the keyboard, video, and mouse signals, encodes them into IP packets, and sends them over an IP network. (3)

KVM switch   A device that in its traditional configuration as a local KVM switch connects a single keyboard, video display, and mouse to two or more computer systems, allowing the user to switch control from one computer to another. (3)

L1 cache   See *internal cache memory*.

LAN   See *local area network*.

land   A raised area on an optical disc that is alternated with depressed areas to be interpreted as data. (2)

land-grid array (LGA)   A processor packaging that uses pads on the processor that come in contact with pins in the socket on the motherboard, permitting a higher density than possible with PGA. (4)

laptop   A laptop is a small, easily transported computer, generally weighing less than 7 pounds and with roughly the same dimensions as a 1- to 2-inch-thick stack of magazines. Laptops computers have an all-in-one layout in which the keyboard, and often the pointing device, is integrated into the computer chassis and an LCD display is in a hinged lid. (6)

laser beam   A coherent and concentrated light beam, also simply called a *laser*. (12)

laser printer   A printer that uses a light beam (laser) in the printing process. (12)

Last Known Good Configuration   A Windows Advanced Options menu choice that restores a group of registry keys containing system settings such as services and drivers. These are the last settings that worked, and you have only a narrow window of opportunity to use Last Known Good—on the *first* reboot after making a configuration change and *before* logging on. Also called *Last Known Good (LKG)*. (11)

latency   The amount of time it takes a packet to travel from one point to another. (13)

LBA   See *logical block address*.

LCD   See *liquid crystal display*.

LED   Light emitting diode, a tiny bulb light found on many devices, often used to indicate operational status. (5)

letterbox   The black box that appears around an image, such as a widescreen video when it is displayed on a screen with a 4:3 aspect ratio. (3)

Level 1 (L1) cache   See *internal cache memory*.

Level 2 (L2) cache   See *external cache*.

Level 3 (L3) cache   See *external cache*.

Li-ion   See *lithium-ion (Li-ion) battery*.

line printer   A printer that creates printed output line by line. (12)

liquid cooling system   A cooling system that uses liquid to transfer heat away from components. (3)

liquid crystal display (LCD)   A display device that uses liquid crystals to display images. (3)

lithium-ion (Li-ion) battery   A type of rechargeable battery used in laptops and other portable devices. (6)

lit pixel   A pixel that is permanently turned on, causing the pixel to show constantly as red, green, or blue. Also called a *stuck pixel*. (7)

local area network (LAN)   A network that covers a relatively small area, such as a building, home, office, or campus. The typical distances are measured in hundreds of meters. (13)

local group account   In Windows, a security account that contains one or more local user accounts, and when a computer is a member of a Windows domain, may also contain domain user or group accounts. (16)

local KVM switch   See *KVM switch*.

local remote KVM switch   A remote KVM switch that uses either Cat 5 or USB cabling. The distance it can be from the computers it controls is a function of the length limits of the cabling; it normally uses a proprietary protocol and special hardware.

local user account   A security account that exists in a local security accounts database. (16)

logical block address (LBA)   A method for supporting up to 8.3 GB capacity hard drives. Both the BIOS and hard drive system must use LBA. (1)

long filename (LFN)   A file or folder name that breaks the 8.3 file-naming convention used in the FAT file system. This term continues to be used on newer file systems. (10)

loopback plug   A plug designed for testing a specific port type (e.g., serial, parallel, or USB). The plug does not connect to a cable but reroutes the sending pins to the receiving pins. Using special software on the computer, a loopback test is performed in which signals are both sent and received. (5)

low-voltage differential (LVD)   A technology for transferring serial data at high speeds. Also known as *low-voltage differential signaling (LVDS)*. (3)

low-voltage differential signaling (LVDS)   See *low-voltage differential*.

LPT   A name used by the Windows operating systems to identify any parallel port. (5)

LPT1   The name used by the Windows operating systems to identify the first parallel port. (5)

LPT2   The name used by the Windows operating systems to identify the second parallel port. (5)

Lucent connector (LC)   A fiber-optic connector that has a snap coupling and, at 1.25 mm, is half the size of the SC connector. Also called a *local connector*. (13)

luminance   The signal in a television transmission that contains the brightness of the image. (3)

LVD   See *low-voltage differential (LVD)*.

LVDS   See *low-voltage differential signaling (LVDS)*.

MAC   See *Media Access Control (MAC) address*.

MBR   See *master boot record*.

magnetic mass storage   Device that stores digital data on magnetized media, such as floppy disks, the metal platters in hard disk drives, and magnetic tape media used in tape drives. (1)

mainboard   See *motherboard*.

malware   Software created to perform malicious acts. Also called *malicious software*. (16)

master boot record (MBR)   The first physical sector on a hard disk, which contains the initial boot program that the BIOS loads into memory during bootup. It also contains the partition table. (10)

mass storage device   A device that stores a large amount of information, even when it is powered off. (1)

master drive   The role of the first EIDE drive on a PATA channel. (4)

master file table (MFT)   A part of the NTFS file system used to store a transaction-based database, with all file accesses treated as transactions, and if a transaction is not complete, NTFS will roll back to the last successful transaction.

material safety data sheet (MSDS)   A standardized document that contains general information, ingredients, and fire and explosion warnings as well as health, disposal, and safe transportation information about a particular product. Any manufacturer that sells a potentially hazardous product must issue an MSDS for it. (18)

math coprocessor   See *floating-point unit*.

Mechanical Transfer Registered Jack (MT-RJ) connector   A fiber-optic connector that resembles an RJ-45 network connector and is less expensive and easier to work with than ST or SC connectors. (13)

Media Access Control (MAC) address   The hardware address of a network device, also called the *Ethernet address* (on Ethernet devices) or *NIC address*. (13)

media bay   A compartment in a portable computer's case that holds a single media device that can be swapped with another. For instance, you may swap an optical drive, a secondary hard drive, or a floppy drive into and out of a single bay. (6)

memory   A computer's temporary working space, usually in DRAM chips. (2)

memory address   A logical memory address defined in a processor's address bus that allows the system to access physical RAM or ROM memory locations. (3)

memory bank   In reference to a memory module, the number of memory modules required to match the data bus width of the processor. (2)

memory controller chip (MCC)   The portion of the chipset that controls communications between the CPU and system RAM. (1)

metropolitan area network (MAN)   A network that covers a metropolitan area, usually using high-speed fiber-optic cable (operating in the gigabits-per-second range). (13)

microcode   One of many low-level instructions built into the control unit of a CPU. Also called a *microprogram*. (1)

MicroDIMM   A RAM module designed for subcompact and laptop computers. It is half the size of a SoDIMM module. (6)

microprogram   See *microcode*.

Microsoft Management Console (MMC)   Introduced in Windows 2000, a user interface for Windows administration tools that is flexible and configurable. (8)

Microsoft Product Activation (MPA)   Microsoft's product activation program. (9)

Microsoft Windows Vista Home Premium   A version of Windows Vista that includes Windows Media Center, which supports advanced multimedia functions. (2)

Microsoft Windows XP Media Center   A version of Windows XP that includes Windows Media Center, which supports advanced multimedia functions. (2)

MIDI   See *musical instrument digital interface*.

MIMO (multiple input/multiple output)   A technology that makes 802.11n speeds possible, using multiple antennas to send and receive digital data in simultaneous radio streams that increases performance. (13)

Mini PCI   A standard used in laptops that is based on PCI. The biggest difference is that Mini PCI is much smaller than PCI—both the card and the slot. Mini PCI has a 32-bit data bus. (6)

mini-audio connector   Audio connectors that use a 1/8" single pin plug. (3)

miniconnector   A common connector used to connect a power supply to floppy drives. (3)

mini-DIN-6   A connector commonly used for PC keyboards. It is much smaller than the original DIN connector. (3)

mini-notebook   The smallest laptop type, weighing less than 3 pounds. See also *netbook* and *mini-notebook*. (6)

mirrored set   Two disk drives used for RAID 1, in which data is written to both drives at the same time, a practice called mirroring. (2)

mirroring   The act of writing to two disk drives at the same time, creating identical drives. (2)

MMC   See *Microsoft Management Console*.

mobo   Slang for motherboard. (1)

modem   Traditionally, this term only applied to the type of device described in the definition for *analog modem*. Now, it is also used for the digital devices in DSL and cable data communications. (2)

modding   The practice, mostly among gamers, of modifying a computer case. (1)

mode   In fiber-optics, a single light wave passing down a cable. (13)

molex connector   A common connector used to connect a power supply to internal peripherals. (3)

monitor   See *display.*

motherboard   The circuit board in a computer to which all other components directly or indirectly connect. Also called a *mainboard, system board, mobo, or planar board.* (1)

mount point   The connecting point of a mounted drive to a folder on an NTFS volume. (10)

mounted drive   A drive that is mapped to an empty folder on an NTFS volume and is assigned a drive path rather than drive letters. (10)

MSCONFIG   The filename for the System Configuration Utility, which allows you to test various scenarios for Windows startup for troubleshooting purposes. (11)

MSINFO32.EXE   See *System Information.*

multifunction device (MFD)   A device that combines two or more devices, such as a printer, scanner, and fax machine. (12)

multifunction printers (MFDs)   A printer that includes one or more other functions, such as a scanner and fax machine. (12)

multi-GPU solution   The use of two or more video adapters (hence the term "GPU") to drive a single display for the purpose of increasing performance. (3)

multimode fiber (MMF)   Fiber-optic cable in which multiple light waves can pass simultaneously. Usually larger in diameter than single-mode fiber; and each wave uses a certain portion of the fiber cable for transmission. (13)

multi-monitor   The use of more than one monitor on a single computer. (3)

Multilingual User Interface (MUI)   The code used to provide multiple language support to Windows. (9)

Multimedia Terminal Adapter (MTA)   On a cable network, the device used at the customer site for the analog/digital conversion. (14)

multimeter   A handheld device used to measure electrical resistance, voltage, and/or current. (5)

multiplexing   In telecommunications, a technique that combines multiple messages or signals onto a single transmission channel. (13)

musical instrument digital interface (MIDI)   A standard for interconnecting electronic musical instruments to communicate with computers and among themselves. (3)

NAT   See *network address translation.*

NetBEUI   A non-routable network protocol suite for use only in small networks. (13)

NetBIOS   A protocol developed in the 1980s by IBM for managing names on a network. Also used by Microsoft in early networking. Replaced by DNS on TCP/IP networks. (13)

netbook   A scaled-down laptop in the ultra-portable category, designed for Internet access. See also *ultra-portable* and *mini-notebook*. (6)

NETSTAT   A command-line command, installed with the TCP/IP protocol suite, which provides statistical information about the TCP/IP protocols and network connections involving your computer, depending on the switches you use when you enter the command. (15)

network address translation (NAT)   A TCP/IP protocol developed as a solution to the dwindling number of IP addresses on the Internet and that also serves to hide IP addresses on a private network from the Internet. (16)

network client   Software that runs on the computers in a network and that receives services from servers. (13)

network interface card (NIC)   An adapter used to connect a computer or other device to a network medium. (13)

network operating system (NOS)   An operating system that runs on a network server and provides file sharing and access to other resources, account management, authentication, and authorization services. (13)

New Low-profile eXtended (NLX)   An Intel standard for motherboards targeted to the low-end consumer market that includes built-in components, while saving space and fitting into a smaller case. (1)

NIC   See *network interface card*.

NiCD   See *nickel-cadmium*.

nickel-cadmium (NiCD)   The type of battery used in the first portable PCs, which was heavy and inefficient. (6)

nickel metal hydride (NiMH) batteries   A now-obsolete type of rechargeable battery used in laptops and other portable devices, replaced by lithium-ion batteries. (6)

NiMH   See *nickel metal hydride*.

NLX   See *New Low-profile eXtended*.

nonvolatile memory   Memory that does not require power to keep stored data intact. Also called *flash memory*. (2)

Northbridge   One or more chips in a computer's chipset that controls communications between the CPU and RAM on the motherboard. (1)

notification area   See *systray*.

NSLOOKUP   A command-line utility, installed with the TCP/IP protocol suite, that is used to troubleshoot DNS problems by querying DNS name servers and displaying the results of the queries. (15)

NTFS   The default Windows file system that includes many important features, including encryption and permissions. (10)

NTFS permissions   In Microsoft Windows, NTFS permissions are used to specify and control which users and groups can access certain files and folders and what each user or group can do with them. (10)

NTLDR   The boot loader file in Windows 2000 and Windows XP. During the boot loader phase, NTLDR takes control of the system, switches the CPU to protected mode, starts the file system, and reads the BOOT.INI file. (10)

OCR   See *optical character recognition*.

odd parity   A memory error-checking method in which the parity bit is used to ensure that the total number of 1s in the data stream is odd. (2)

optical character recognition (OCR)   Software that takes a scanned image and interprets the patterns in the image into alphanumeric characters. (12)

optical drive   A disc drive that uses laser technology to read and/or write to special discs. (2)

original equipment manufacturer (OEM)   In regard to Windows operating systems, a version of Windows that is designed to work with a certain manufacturer's equipment. (9)

overclocking   The practice of forcing a CPU or other computer component to run at a higher clock rate than the manufacturer intended. (1)

P1 power connector   A 20- or 24- pin connector that supplies power from a PC's power supply to the motherboard. (3)

P4 12V   A 4-pin connector that, in addition to a 20-pin connector, is part of motherboard power connector that follows the ATX 12V standard. (3)

PAGEFILE.SYS   See *paging file*.

paging file   A file used by Windows for virtual memory. Also called the *swap file*. The actual filename in Windows is *PAGEFILE.SYS*. (9)

Parallel AT Attachment (PATA)   A hard drive interface that transfers data in parallel. EIDE and ATAPI drives attach to the PATA interface. (1)

parallel port   An interface on a PC that originally was unidirectional and operated at a speed of 150 KBps, but now has several operation modes. (2)

parity   A type of memory checking in which every eight-bit byte of data is accompanied by a ninth bit (the parity bit), which is used to determine the presence of errors in the data. The two types of parity are *odd* and *even*. (2)

partition   (n.) An area of a physical hard disk that defines space that will be used for logical drives. (4). (v.) To define the space to be used for logical drives using a special program, such as the Windows Setup program. (9)

partition type   The style of partition on a basic disk, which includes primary and extended. (10)

parts grabber   A pen-sized tool that has a plunger at one end. When pressed, the plunger causes small, hooked prongs to extend from the other end of the tool for retrieving dropped objects from inside a computer. (5)

passive matrix display   An LCD display using an old technology that has a grid of horizontal and vertical wires with a transistor at the end of each wire. When two transistors (one at the x-axis and one at the y-axis) send voltage along their wires, the pixel at the intersection of the two wires lights up. (3)

password   A string of characters that a user enters, along with an identifier, such as a user name, in order to be authenticated. (16)

password cracker   A program used to discover a password. (16)

patch   A software fix for a single problem. (8)

PC Card   The early standard developed by PCMCIA for credit-card-sized devices used in laptops. (6)

PCI   See *peripheral component interconnect.*

PCI Express   See *PCIe.*

PCI-E   See *PCIe.*

PCIe (peripheral component interconnect express)   An expansion bus architecture that uses serial communications rather than the parallel communications of PCI. Also called *PCI Express* and *PCI-E.* (1)

PCIe Mini Card   The successor to the Mini PCI. It has a 64-bit data bus and is half the size of a Mini PCI Card. (6)

peer-to-peer network   A network in which all of the computers essentially operate as both servers (providing access to shared resources) and clients (accessing those shared resources). (13)

Performance Monitor   A utility in Windows NT for gathering and viewing performance data involving memory, disks, processors, network, and other objectives. (11)

peripheral component interconnect (PCI)   Introduced in 1993, the most common expansion bus architecture in PCs in the mid 1990s. It transfers data in parallel over a data bus that is either 32- or 64-bits wide. (1)

permanent virtual circuit (PVC)   A virtual communication circuit that is created and remains available between two endpoints, which are normally some form of data terminal equipment (DTE). Telecommunications companies provide PVC service to companies requiring a dedicated circuit between two sites that require communications that are always on. (13)

permission   In networking, the authorization to access a computer or resource on a computer. Specific permission levels include read, change, modify, etc. (16)

personal area network (PAN)   A communications network made up of personal computing devices, such as computers, telephones, and personal digital assistants. (13)

Personal Computer Memory Card International Association (PCMCIA)   An organization that creates standards for laptop computer peripheral devices. (6)

Personal Digital Assistant (PDA)   A portable computer small enough to fit in your hand, also referred to as a "palmtop" computer. Because it is so small, a PDA does not have the functionality of a laptop or desktop computer. In other words, a typical PDA allows you to perform only a small number of functions. (6)

personal firewall   See *software firewall*.

PGA   See *pin grid array*.

PGA2   A variation of the PGA CPU packaging that was used with Pentium CPUs. (4)

phishing   A fraudulent method of obtaining personal and financial information through the use of pop-ups or e-mail messages that purport to be from a legitimate organization, such as a bank, credit card company, or retailer. (16)

pin grid array (PGA)   A term used for CPU packaging that indicates that a chip has columns and rows of pins. (1)

PING   A command-line tool installed with the TCP/IP protocol suite that is used for testing communications between two hosts. (15)

pinned items list   An area on the top left of the Windows XP Start menu containing shortcuts to Windows Update and programs for browsing the Internet and using e-mail. (8)

pin-out   A diagram showing the purpose of each wire in a connector. (4)

pit   A depressed area on an optical disc that is alternated with raised areas to be interpreted as data. (2)

pixel   A single dot on a display screen. A contraction of "Picture Element." (3)

plain-old telephone service (POTS)   The traditional wired telephone network. (13)

planar board   See *motherboard*.

plug and play (PnP)   A system by which the computer BIOS and operating system recognizes a device and the operating system automatically installs and configures a device driver. (3)

point stick   See *pointing stick*.

point-to-point protocol (PPP)   A protocol that allows two devices to connect, authenticate, and negotiate what protocols they will use (almost always TCP/IP). (16)

Point-to-Point Tunneling Protocol (PPTP)   An enhanced version of PPP, which adds the ability to secure the point-to-point connection with encryption. (16)

pointing stick   A pointing device built into some laptop keyboards. It appears to be a very tiny joystick-type button that barely protrudes above the level of the keys. (6)

POP   See *Post Office Protocol.*

pop-up download   A virus that downloads to a user's computer through a pop-up window that appears in a Web browser. It requires an action on the part of a user, such as clicking a button that implies acceptance of something like free information. (16)

pop-up blocker   A program that blocks browser pop-ups. (17)

port   A connection point on a device or computer, sometimes called a socket. (3)

portable computer   Any type of computer that you can easily transport and that contains an all-in-one component layout. (6)

port replicator   A device used with a laptop. The port replicator remains on the desktop with external devices connected to ports on it. A laptop then needs only one connection to the port replicator to have access to the peripherals. (6)

port triggering   The redirection of incoming traffic to the requesting internal hosts that initiated the communication with an external host. (16)

POST   See *power-on self-test.*

POST card   An adapter card used to run a special diagnostic test on a computer as it is powering up. These tests usually go beyond those performed by the system BIOS-based POST. (5)

Post Office Protocol (POP)   The protocol used to allow client computers to pick up e-mail from mail servers. The current version is POP3. (13)

POTS   See *plain-old telephone service.*

power-on self-test (POST)   A group of tests, stored in the BIOS and performed as a PC boots up, to check for the presence and function of system components. (1)

power management   A group of features in the system BIOS, the chipset, the operating system, device drivers, and the individual components that enable efficient use of power in a computer. (6)

power state   A power-usage level. (6)

power supply   The component that provides power for all components on the motherboard and internal to the PC case. Also called a *power supply unit (PSU)*. (3)

power supply tester A specialized device for testing a power supply unit that comes with connectors compatible with the output connectors on a standard power supply. (5)

power supply unit (PSU) See *power supply*.

PPP See *point-to-point protocol*.

PPTP See *Point-to-Point Tunneling Protocol*.

prank program A joke program that produces strange behavior, such as screen distortions, erratic cursor behavior, or strange icons to appear on the screen. (16)

Preboot eXecution Environment An Intel standard for starting up a computer over the network, without relying on a disk-based operating system. Used to install a new operating system or run diagnostics software. (13)

primary corona wire In a laser printer, a wire that stretches across the printer's drum, not touching it, but positioned very close to the drum's surface so it can pass high voltage to the drum. (12)

primary master In reference to IDE PATA drives, the master drive on the first channel. (4)

primary partition A partition type on a basic disk that can have only one logical drive assigned to it encompassing the entire partition. This partition type is also the only type of partition on a basic disk that can be marked as active for booting up an operating system. (10)

primary slave In reference to IDE PATA drives, the slave drive on the first channel. (4)

process The memory space, program code, data, and system resources required by a running program. (11)

process ID An identifier assigned to a process when it starts. (11)

process priority level A value assigned to a process that controls the order in which the program code is executed in relation to other code. (11)

processor See *central processing unit*.

processor board Another name for a motherboard in a laptop. (6)

processor bus A set of wires used by data traveling into and out of a processor. (1)

professionalism A set of behaviors for the workplace that includes how you interact with people and how you treat property. (18)

projector A device that takes video output and projects it onto a screen for viewing by a larger audience. (3)

Program Compatibility Wizard A Windows wizard that sets options for starting and running a specific old program that will not otherwise run properly in Windows. (8)

PROM   Programmable ROM. A ROM chip that can have programs added to it. (2)

protocol   In networking, this is a set of rules for using network hardware and software. In most discussions about networks, this term is assigned to certain network software components. (13)

proxy server   A network service that handles the requests for Internet services, such as Web pages, files on an FTP server, and mail for a proxy client without exposing that client's IP address to the Internet. There is specific proxy server and client software for each type of service. (13)

PS/2   Personal System/2, as in PS/2-style mice and keyboards and connectors. Also called *mini-DIN connectors*. (3)

public switched telephone network (PSTN)   The worldwide network that carries traditional voice traffic. (13)

PVC   See *permanent virtual circuit*.

quad-core CPU   A CPU containing four CPU cores. (1)

Quick Launch bar   An optional toolbar you can add to the taskbar just to the right of the Start button. Shortcuts on this bar launch with a single-click. (8)

radio frequency (RF)   Signals broadcast through the air. (4)

RAID 0   A RAID array in which every time data is written to disk, a portion (block) is written to each disk in turn, creating a "stripe" of data across the member disks. RAID 0 uses the total disk space in the array for storage, without protecting the data from drive failure. (2)

RAID 1   Also called *mirroring*, this RAID array type provides fault tolerance because all the data is written identically to the two drives in the mirrored set. (2)

RAID 5   Also called *striping with distributed parity* or *striping with interleave parity*, this RAID method involves a set of disks in which every time data is written to disk, a portion is written to each disk in turn, creating a "stripe" of data across the member disks. However, in each stripe, the portion on one disk is not the actual data, but the result of an algorithm performed on the data contained in the other blocks in the stripe. This block is called the parity block, and because of the space required, the total disk space in the array available for data storage is equal to the total disk space less one entire disk. (2)

RAID array   Two or more disks working together in one of the several RAID schemes. (2)

RAID controller   Specialized hardware used to create and manage a RAID array. (2)

RAM   See *random access memory*.

Rambus Dynamic RAM (RDRAM)   Memory chips that use a special Rambus channel that has a data transfer rate of 800 MHz. A double channel width results in a 1.6 GHz data transfer. RDRAM sticks use special RIMM slots. (2)

RAMBUS Inline Memory Module (RIMM) Both the connectors on the RDRAM memory modules and the motherboard sockets (or slots) that match them. (1)

random access memory (RAM) Memory that is accessible in any (random) order. Most of the memory in a PC is RAM. (2)

RDRAM See *Rambus Dynamic RAM.*

reactivate To renew a product activation, required when the activation program discovers significant changes in a computer or the activated product has been installed on a second computer. (9)

real-time clock (RTC) A chip that keeps track of the date and time on a PC. Set the date and time through your operating system or in the BIOS Setup program. (4)

read-only memory (ROM) Memory that can only be read and that contains program code. ROM is also called *firmware.* (2)

read/write head A reading and writing device in a floppy or hard drive that is mounted on an articulated arm that moves back and forth over the floppy disk or metal platter. (1)

recently used programs list An area under the pinned items list on the Windows XP Start menu that contains shortcuts to recently run programs. (8)

redundant array of independent disks (RAID) A group of schemes designed to provide either better performance or improved data reliability through redundancy. (2)

refresh rate A CRT video setting, also known as the *vertical refresh rate*, that controls the rate per second at which an image appears on the tube. (3)

regional settings Operating system interface settings, such as the language used and the date, time, and currency formats. (9)

register Memory locations within a CPU that is used as a scratch pad for calculations. Modern CPUs have dedicated registers for specific functions and general-purpose registers for multiple purposes. (1)

registered jack (RJ) A rectangular connector with a locking clip on one side and a number designation that refers to the size rather than the number of wires. (3)

registration The process of informing the software manufacturer who the official owner or user of the product is, and providing contact information such as name, address, company, phone number, e-mail address, and so on, about them. Registration is usually a voluntary action. (9)

registry A database of all configuration settings in Windows. (8)

registry key In the Windows registry, a folder that may contain one or more sets of settings as well as other keys. (8)

Reliability and Performance Monitor   The Windows Vista and Windows 7 tool for gathering and viewing performance data involving memory, disks, processors, network, and other objectives. (11)

Remote Assistance   A Windows service designed to allow a user to invite someone to help troubleshoot a problem. (11)

Remote Desktop   A Windows service that allows a user to connect remotely to a computer and run the Windows desktop on the remote computer, but have the same access as if logged on to the computer and its local network. (11)

Remote Desktop Protocol (RDP)   An underlying protocol that supports Microsoft Remote Desktop. (11)

remote KVM switch   A type of KVM switch that controls computers over a distance that is a function of the cabling and protocols it uses. The two types of switches are local remote KVM switch and KVM over IP. (3)

removable storage   Storage media that is removable, meaning the drive stays in place, while the media (disk, disc, or tape) is removed and replaced with another disk, disc, or tape. (2)

repeater   A network device that is used to extend the range of a network by taking the signals received on a port from one network and regenerating (repeating) those signals to another port to transmit them on a second network. (13)

response time   An LCD display characteristic that indicates the amount of time in milliseconds (ms) it takes for a single pixel to go from the active to the inactive state and back again. (3)

Return To OS Choices menu   An Advanced Options menu choice that appears under certain circumstances. When available, selecting this option will return to the OS Choices menu (OS Loader menu). (11)

RF   See *radio frequency*.

RFI   Radio frequency interference. Radio signals that occur in proximity to equipment that is sensitive to these types of signals. (15)

RGB video   A simple type of component video signal that sends three separate signals—red, green, and blue—using three coaxial cables. (3)

RIMM   See *RAMBUS Inline Memory Module*.

RIP   See *routing information protocol*.

riser card   In a low-profile PC case, a card that plugs into a motherboard to allow other cards to be inserted at a right angle to the riser card and parallel to the motherboard. Also, a single expansion card containing multiple functions, such as modem, sound, and network. (1)

RJ-11   A connector that contains two to four wires and usually attaches phone cables to modems and to wall-mounted phone jacks. (3)

RJ-45   A connector that is slightly larger than an RJ-11 connector and contains eight wires. RJ-45 connectors most commonly attach twisted-pair cables to Ethernet network cards. (3)

ROM   See *read-only memory.*

root directory   In the *FAT file system,* the top-level directory in which the operating system stores information about files, including a reference to the FAT table so it knows where to find the file's contents on disk. The NTFS file system also has a root, or top-level directory, but NTFS does not rely on this structure in the same way that FAT does. (10)

root folder   The top-level folder or directory in the file structure. This appears the same, regardless of the underlying file system. (10)

root key   In the Windows registry, the top five folders, each of which is the top of a hierarchical structure. Also called *subtrees.* (8)

rootkit   Malware that hides itself from detection by antimalware programs; it is installed on a computer by someone who has privileged access to the computer. (16)

router   A device that sits at the connection between networks and routes packets based on their logical destination addresses. (13)

routing information protocol (RIP)   A protocol that allows routers to update their list of routes dynamically. RIP dates to the 1980s and is considered obsolete; even though, it has been updated a few times and is still supported by most routers. (13)

RS-232 port   The classic PC serial port that complies with the Recommended Standard-232 (RS-232) in its circuitry, cabling, and connector design, and transfers data one bit at a time. (3)

S/PDIF   Sony-Philips digital interface format—a single-pin RCA phone jack used for transferring digital audio from CD and DVD players to amplifiers and speakers. (3)

S-Video   A video interface, also called *Super Video,* that transmits video using two signals—luminance, represented by a Y, and chrominance, represented by a C. S-video ports are round to accommodate a round plug with four pins. (3)

Safe Mode   In Windows, an Advanced Options menu choice that starts Windows without several drivers and components and loads only very basic, non-vendor-specific drivers for mouse, video, keyboard, mass storage, and system services. Safe Mode also displays in low resolution. (11)

Safe Mode With Command Prompt   In Windows, an Advanced Options menu choice that will start Windows without the Windows GUI (EXPLORER.EXE) and with only a simple Command Prompt window from which you can launch Windows administrative utilities. (11)

Safe Mode With Networking In Windows, an Advanced Options menu choice that starts Windows without several drivers and components and loads only very basic, non-vendor-specific drivers for mouse, video, keyboard, mass storage, and system services. It also displays in low resolution. The difference between *Safe Mode* and *Safe Mode With Networking* is that the latter will launch networking components. (11)

SAS See *Serial Attached SCSI*.

SATA See *serial ATA*.

satellite communications A communications system now used for data communications via satellite that usually uses microwave radio frequencies and requires a dish antenna, receiver, and transmitter. (13)

Scalable Link Interface (SLI) A multi-GPU solution developed by NVIDIA. (3)

SCSI See *Small Computer System Interface*.

SCSI controller See *SCSI host adapter*.

SCSI host adapter A computer circuit board that attaches to and controls SCSI devices. (4)

SCSI ID A number that identifies a device on a SCSI chain. (4)

SD Card See *Secure Digital (SD) Card*.

SDRAM See *synchronous dynamic RAM*.

secondary master In reference to IDE PATA drives, the master drive on the second channel. (4)

secondary slave In reference to IDE PATA drives, the slave drive on the second channel. (4)

second-level domain (SLD) In the domain name system, a name that is registered under a top-level domain, such as mcgraw-hill.com or microsoft.com. (15)

sector translation An early method for addressing the disparity between the drive geometry supported by PC BIOSs and the physical geometry of drives. (1)

secure attention sequence (SAS) An action, such as the CTRL-ALT-DELETE key combination or the insertion of a smart card, that clears memory of certain types of viruses before a user logs on. (17)

Secure Digital (SD) Card A solid-state storage standard for high-capacity (2, 4, and 8 GB) memory cards that are tiny—32 mm × 24 mm × 2.1 mm—and support high-speed data transfer. SD cards are in portable devices, such as digital video recorders, digital cameras, handheld computers, audio players, and cell phones. (2)

security auditing A way to monitor security-related events. (16)

security policy   A set of rules and practices describing how an organization protects and manages sensitive information. A security policy applies to all employees. (16)

secure socket layer (SSL)   A data encryption technology used for securing data transmitted over the Internet. (13)

serial ATA (SATA)   A drive interface for EIDE drives that transfers data serially at speeds between 150 MBps and 300 MBps and 6 Gbps, depending on the version of the standard. (1)

Serial Attached SCSI (SAS)   A marriage of SCSI and Serial ATA, this uses a serial interface to a SCSI bus. (3)

server   A dedicated computer that stores data and provides print services or other capabilities to network clients. (13)

service pack   A bundle of patches or updates released periodically by a software publisher. (8)

Service Set ID (SSID)   A network name used to identify a wireless network. Consisting of up to 32 characters, the SSID travels with the messages on the wireless network. All of the wireless devices on a WLAN must use the same SSID in order to communicate. (14)

SGRAM   Synchronous graphics random access memory is a type of RAM used on video adapters. (2)

shadow mask   A metal plate behind the front of a CRT monitor that focuses the electron beams from the gun. (3)

share   On a Microsoft Windows network, a resource, such as a file folder or printer, that is available on the network. (15)

shared video memory   A portion of system memory used by a video adapter built into a motherboard. (6)

shortcut   An icon that represents a link to any object that an icon can represent. Activating a shortcut (by double-clicking it) is a quick way to access an object or to launch a program from the desktop without having to find the actual location of the object on your computer. (8)

sidebar   In Windows Vista, a vertical bar found by default on the right side of the desktop. Here, you will find gadgets and mini-programs. (8)

SIMM   See *single inline memory module*.

Simple Mail Transfer Protocol (SMTP)   A protocol that transfers e-mail messages between mail servers. Clients also use this protocol to send e-mail to mail servers. (13)

simultaneous multithreading (SMT)   See *hyper threading*.

single inline memory module (SIMM)   An obsolete memory module standard that was produced in 30-pin and 72-pin sizes. Thirty-pin SIMMs are 8-bit, and 72-pin SIMMs are 32-bit. (1)

single-layer (SL)   Pertaining to a DVD drive or disc that can store data in a single layer of pits on each data side. (1)

single-mode fiber (SMF)   Fiber-optic cable that allows only a single light wave to pass down the cable. (13)

single-sided (SS) DVD   A DVD of any type that can contain data on only one side. (1)

slave drive   The role of the second EIDE drive on a PATA channel. (4)

SLD   See *second-level domain.*

SLI   See *Scalable Link Interface.*

slot cover   A metal strip used to cover an empty slot in order to preserve the correct air flow and keep dust out. (3)

Small Computer System Interface (SCSI)   An interface standard developed by the American National Standards Institute (ANSI), it is used for both internal and external hard drives and optical drives as well as devices such as printers, modems, scanners, and many other peripherals. (3)

Small Outline DIMM (SODIMM)   A type of DIMM memory module used in laptops. (6)

Small Outline RIMM (SORIMM)   A type of RIMM memory module used in laptops. (6)

smart card   A plastic card, often the size of a credit card, that contains a microchip. The microchip can store information and perform functions, depending on the type of smart card. Some smart cards only store data, whereas others may have a variety of functions, including security cards for facilities or logging on to computers. (16)

smart card reader   A device used to scan smart cards. (16)

smart phone   A cell phone with Personal Digital Assistant (PDA) functions built in. (6)

SMTP   See *Simple Mail Transfer Protocol.*

social engineering   A variety of persuasion techniques used for many purposes—good and bad. People with malicious intent use social engineering to persuade someone to reveal confidential information or give something else of value to the perpetrator. (16)

socket   The location where a cable attaches to a computer. Alternatively, a connector on a motherboard for memory, CPUs, power, or other circuitry. (3)

socket services   A service of the operating system on a laptop that detects when a card has been inserted. (6)

SODIMM   See *Small Outline DIMM.*

soft power A power supply and motherboard feature that allows software to turn off a computer rather than only using a physical switch. (3)

software firewall A firewall consisting of software that you can install on any computer, as opposed to the software built into a hardware firewall. Also called *personal firewalls* because they are designed to be installed on individual desktop computers. (16)

solid ink A type of printer that uses solid, rather than liquid, ink. (12)

solid-state drive (SSD) See *solid-state storage*.

solid-state storage Data storage technology with no moving mechanical parts that uses large-capacity, nonvolatile memory, commonly called *flash memory* or *solid-state drives*. (2)

Sony/Philips Digital Interface (S/PDIF) A single-pin RCA phone jack for transferring digital audio from CD and DVD players to amplifiers and speakers. (3)

SONET A long-established fiber-optic WAN technology. (13)

SORIMM See *Small Outline RIMM*.

Southbridge A portion of a computer's chipset that controls communications between the CPU and such I/O busses as USB, IDE, PS2, SATA, and others. (1)

S/PDIF See *Sony/Philips Digital Interface*.

spam Unsolicited e-mail. (16)

Spam over Instant Messaging (spim) Unsolicited messages sent over an instant messaging service, such as Windows Messenger. (16)

Speaker On/Off key A key on a laptop that is combined with the FN key to toggle the laptop's speaker on and off. The SPEAKER ON/OFF key is usually one of the standard function keys, such as F3, that displays a speaker symbol. (7)

Speaker Volume Key A key on a laptop that is combined with the FN key to bring up a small volume control panel on the display. Using the up ($\uparrow$) or right ($\rightarrow$) arrow key, the volume will increase. To decrease the volume, press the FN key and the SPEAKER VOLUME key along with either the left ($\leftarrow$) or down ($\downarrow$) arrow key. This changes the speaker volume at the hardware level, bypassing Windows' volume control. (7)

special group One of several groups that no user can create or modify. The membership of a special group is predefined, and it is available to you only when you assign permissions or rights. A few important special groups are Creator Owner, System, and Everyone. (16)

spim See *Spam over Instant Messaging*.

spindle In a disk drive, the rotating shaft used to spin the disks. (1)

spyware A category of software that runs surreptitiously on a user's computer in order to gather information without the user's permission and then sends that information to the people who requested it. (16)

SRAM   See *Static RAM*.

SSL   See *secure socket layer*.

SPGA (staggered pin grid array)   An arrangement of pins on a processor in which the pins are offset in a way that allows for a higher pin density than PGA. (4)

Static RAM (SRAM)   The first type of RAM available. It is very fast, compared to DRAM, but also very expensive. (2)

stand-alone computer   A computer that is not connected to a network of any kind. (13)

Standby   A sleep mode that is available on any computer that supports ACPI power management. It conserves power while saving the desktop in RAM memory in a work state. To resume, you simply press the power button, and the desktop is quickly displayed. (6)

Start Bar   See *taskbar*.

Start menu   A menu that opens from the Start button on the taskbar. (8)

Start Windows Normally   An Advanced Options menu choice that simply causes Windows to restart normally (if it can). (11)

status light indicator   One or more lights (usually LEDs) on a device that indicate the device's operational status through the color of the light, by blinking or remaining steady or both. (5)

straight-tip (ST) connector   A straight, round connector used to connect fiber-optic cabling to a network device. It has a twist-type coupling. (13)

striping with distributed parity   See *RAID 5*.

striping with interleave parity   See *RAID 5*.

strong password   A password that meets certain criteria in order to be difficult to crack. One definition of a strong password is one that contains at least eight characters, includes a combination of letters, numbers, and other symbols (_, –, $, and so on) and is easy for you to remember but difficult for others to guess. (16)

stuck pixel   See *lit pixel*.

stylus   The primary input device for a PDA, shaped like a pen and used to press small keys on a keypad, tap the screen to select items, or write data on the screen. (6)

sub-mini audio connector   A 3/32" audio connector. (3)

subkey   A registry key that exists within another key. (8)

subscriber connector (SC)   A square snap coupling for fiber-optic cable, about 2.5 mm wide, used for cable-to-cable connections or to connect cables to network devices. It latches with a push-pull action similar to audio and video jacks. (13)

subscription channel (SC)   A paid television subscription service offered by cable television providers. (13)

subtree   See *root key.*

Super Video   See *S-Video.*

super video graphics array (SVGA)   Any video adapter or monitor that exceeds the VGA standard in resolution and color depth with a maximum resolution of 1600 × 1200. (3)

surge protector   A device, usually resembling a power strip, that protects equipment from power surges. (5)

surge suppressor   See *surge protector.*

SVGA   See *super video graphics array.*

swap file   See *paging file.*

switch   [1] On computer circuit boards, a very tiny slide that indicates two states. (4). [2] In a network, a network device, much like a *hub*, except that a switch takes an incoming signal and sends it to only the destination port, avoiding collisions and making it more efficient than a hub. (13)

switching mode power supply   A power supply that converts between alternating current and direct current. (3)

SXGA   Super XGA, a video graphics mode with a maximum resolution of 1280 × 1024. (3)

synchronous dynamic RAM   DRAM that runs at the speed of the system bus (up to 100–133 MHz). (2)

system area   The area at the beginning of a disk formatted with the FAT file system. This area contains the boot record, FAT table, and root directory. (10)

system attribute   A file attribute assigned to a file by the operating system to identify it as a system file. (10)

system board   See *motherboard.*

system bus   See *expansion bus.*

System Configuration Utility   See MSCONFIG.

system file   A program file or some special data file that is part of the operating system and is very important to proper operation of the OS. (10)

System File Checker (SFC)   A Windows command prompt utility that uses the WFP (Windows 2000 and Windows XP) or WRP (Windows Vista and Windows 7) service to scan and verify the versions of all protected system files after you restart your computer. (11)

System Information (MSINFO32.EXE) This GUI utility will display a system summary of the hardware, operating system, and other software. (11)

System Management Mode (SMM) A CPU power-saving mode that allows a CPU to reduce its speed without losing its place so it does not stop working altogether. SMM also allows the CPU to trigger power saving in other components. (6)

System Monitor A utility in Windows XP and Windows 2000 for gathering and viewing performance data involving memory, disks, processors, networks, and other objectives. (11)

system resources A finite set of resources controlled by the operating system and critical to the use of all computer components. (5)

system tray See *systray*.

system requirements The specific requirements for the level of CPU, amount of memory, and size of the hard disk for the computer on which an operating system can be installed. (8)

System Restore An operating system recovery tool introduced in Windows Me and improved in later versions of Windows. System Restore creates restore points, which are snapshots of Windows, its configuration, and all installed programs. If your computer has nonfatal problems after you have made a change, you can use System Restore to roll it back to a restore point. (11)

systray An area of the Windows taskbar used by programs and some hardware devices to display status icons. Also called the *notification area* or *system tray*. (8)

T1 A level of service offered by the telephone companies over a T-carrier circuit that provides full-duplex transmissions at 1.544 Mbps, carrying digital voice, data, or video signals. (13)

T-carrier system A communications system, owned and operated by the telephone companies, that multiplexes voice and data signals onto digital transmission line. (13)

Tablet PC A laptop in which the display is an integrated digitizer. (6)

tact Showing consideration for others. (18)

tape drive A magnetic mass storage device primarily used for backing up data from computers. (1)

taskbar In the Windows GUI, a horizontal bar normally positioned across the bottom of the desktop containing a Start button, the Quick Launch toolbar, buttons for running programs, and at the far right, the *notification area*. Sometimes called the *Start Bar*. (8)

Task Scheduler A Windows utility that allows you to create tasks that run automatically at the times you select. (11)

TCP/IP A network protocol suite originally developed for the Internet; it has been mostly adopted on private networks. (13)

Telnet A utility that provides remote terminal emulation for connecting to computers and network devices running server software that can respond, without needing to be concerned with the actual operating system running on either system. (13)

Temporal Key Integrity Protocol (TKIP) A protocol used with WPA wireless encryption that was broken by hackers. (16)

terminal At first, a terminal was not much more than a display, a keyboard, and the minimal circuitry for connecting to the mainframe. Now, a terminal can be a computer running Windows or other operating system, plus terminal client emulation software that allows it to connect to a server in which a separate session is run for the client computer. (13)

terminating resistor A device installed at the end of a SCSI chain to absorb signals so they do not bounce back along the cable. (4)

thermal compound A special substance, also called *thermal paste* or *heat sink compound*, that increases the heat conductivity between a fan or heat sink and a chip. (3)

thermal paste See *thermal compound*.

thermal printer A type of printer that uses heat in the image transfer process. (12)

thermal wax transfer printer A type of printer that uses a film coated with colored wax that melts onto paper. These printers are similar to *dye-sublimation* printers but differ in two major ways: the film contains wax rather than dye, and these printers do not require special paper. (12)

thin-film transistor (TFT) A technology for LCD displays in which transistors are positioned at each pixel. (3)

thread A portion of a program that can run separately from and concurrently with other portions of the program. Also called *thread of execution*. (1)

thread of execution See *thread*.

thumb drive A type of solid-state storage that is portable, about the size of a flattened thumb, and usually has a USB interface. Also called a *flash drive* or *jump drive*. (2)

time to live (TTL) In an IP packet, a value field that shows how many routers the packet can cross before being discarded. (15)

TLD See *top-level domain*.

toner The medium for a laser printer, which is normally packaged within a toner cartridge. (12)

toner cartridge The cartridge for a laser printer that contains both the medium (toner) and other printing components. (12)

top-level domain (TLD) In the domain name system, a first-level domain, which is a suffix added to a registered domain name and separated from the domain name with a "dot" (.). Among the TLDs are .com, .gov, .edu, .org, .mil, .net, .biz, many two-lettered country codes, and several others. (15)

touchpad   A pointing device, often built into a laptop, which is a smooth rectangular panel over which you move your finger to move the pointer on the display. (6)

touch screen   A type of display device that includes a touch-sensitive face to accept input from the user. (3)

traces   The fine copper lines that are the electronic circuits through which power, data, and control signals travel on a circuit board. (1)

TRACERT   A command-line utility, installed with the TCP/IP protocol suite, that traces the route taken by packets to a destination. (15)

track point   The generic term for a pointing stick. (6)

TrackPoint   The IBM branded name for a pointing stick or track point. (6)

transfer corona wire   In the laser printing process, a wire that passes a small positive charge to paper as it travels through the printer. This positive charge attracts the negatively charged toner particles on the drum to the paper. (12)

transferring   In the laser printing process, the step in which the toner on the drum is transferred to the paper. (12)

Transmission Control Protocol (TCP)   One of the two main protocols of the TCP/IP protocol suite, TCP breaks the data into chunks, called datagrams. Each datagram also contains information, stored in a header, which is used by the TCP protocol on the receiving end to reassemble the chunks of data into the original message. (13)

transport layer security (TLS)   A data encryption technology used for securing data transmitted over the Internet. TLS succeeded SSL. (13)

Trojan horse   A virus that gains access to a computer by masquerading as a harmless program that a user innocently installs on the computer. (16)

troubleshooting   The act of discovering the cause of a problem and correcting it. (5)

trusted platform module (TPM)   A TPM is a special microchip, installed on a motherboard, that stores passwords, keys, and digital certificates. Various services, such as BitLocker can store such security data in this chip. (16)

TTL   See *time to live*.

TV tuner card   See *capture card*.

TWAIN   A set of standards for imaging devices, such as scanners and cameras, that is used in drivers and other software for these devices. (12)

twisted-pair cable   Cable that consists of pairs of wires twisted around each other. The twists help to boost each wire's signals and make them less susceptible to electromagnetic interference (EMI). (3)

Type I   A card that fits into the PC Card interface, including both PC Card and CardBus cards. This type measures 85.6 millimeters long by 54 millimeters wide and 3.3 millimeters thick. (6)

Type II   A card that fits into the PC Card interface, including both PC Card and CardBus cards. This type measures 85.6 millimeters long by 54 millimeters wide and 5.0 millimeters thick. (6)

Type III   A card that fits into the PC Card interface, including both PC Card and CardBus cards. This type measures 85.6 millimeters long by 54 millimeters wide and measures 10.5 mm thick. (6)

UDF   See *uniqueness database file*.

Ultra DMA (UDMA)   A technology used by hard drives to speed up data transfers by using DMA channels. (1)

ultra-portable   The smallest laptop type, weighing less than 3 pounds. See also *netbook* and *mini-notebook*. (6)

unattended installation   An automated software installation that does not require a person be present to respond to prompts for information. (9)

unidirectional mode   In reference to parallel ports, a mode in which the parallel device connected to the parallel port can receive data but cannot send data. CMOS settings (system settings) may refer to this mode as "Transfer only." (4)

uninterruptible power supply (UPS)   An online power protection device that isolates a computer or other device plugged into it. During normal operation, the devices run directly off the battery through an inverter, rather than switching to the battery only after a loss of power. (5)

uniqueness database file (UDF)   A file used with a scripted unattended installation along with an answer file. The UDF file provides settings that are unique for each computer. (9)

universal asynchronous receiver/transmitter (UART)   A chip that works with a serial port, converting outgoing data from parallel to serial and incoming data from serial to parallel. (3)

universal data format (UDF)   A file format for movie DVDs. (10)

Universal Serial Bus (USB)   An external bus that connects into the PC's PCI bus. With USB, you can theoretically connect up to 127 devices to your computer. (3)

update   In Microsoft terminology, software that contains one or more software fixes or changes to the operating system. (8)

UPS   See *uninterruptible power supply*.

USB   See *Universal Serial Bus*.

User Account Control (UAC)   A security feature introduced in Windows Vista to prevent unauthorized changes to Windows. (8)

User Datagram Protocol (UDP)   A subprotocol of TCP/IP used for connectionless communications in which each packet is sent without establishing a connection. (13)

User State Migration Tool (USMT)   A utility for migrating data from many computers, or if you need to perform what Microsoft calls a "wipe-and-load migration" from and to the same computer. Available in Windows XP, Vista, and Windows 7. (9)

UXGA   Ultra extended graphics array, a video graphics mode with a maximum resolution of 1600 × 1200. (3)

v-hold   A CRT video setting, also known as *vertical hold*, that holds the image vertically on the screen. (3)

value entry   The settings within a registry key. (8)

VC   See *virtual circuit*.

version   A new level of an operating system with major changes to the core components. (8)

vertical hold   See *v-hold*.

vertical position   An LCD display setting that adjusts the viewable area of the display vertically. (3)

vertical refresh rate   See *refresh rate*.

VESA   See *Video Electronics Standards Organization*.

VFAT   See *virtual file allocation table*.

VGA   See *video graphics array*.

VGA Mode   A video mode that most often consists of a combination of 640 × 480 pixels display resolution and 16 colors. VGA can produce around 16 million different colors, but can display only up to 256 different colors at a time. (3)

video adapter   Circuitry in a PC on an adapter card, or directly on the motherboard, that controls the output from the PC to the display device. (3)

video adapter card   A circuit card in a PC that controls the output to the display device(s). (2)

Video Electronics Standards Organization (VESA)   An organization that created several PC standards, including the VGA connector. (3)

video graphics array (VGA)   An obsolete video standard introduced with IBM PS/2 computers in the late 1980s. VGA had a maximum resolution of 720 × 400 in text mode and 640 × 480 in graphics mode. (3)

video RAM (VRAM)   A specialized type of memory used only with video adapters. (2)

virtual circuit (VC)   A communication service provided over a telecommunications network or computer network. A VC logically resembles a circuit while passing over a complex routed or switched network, such as the phone company's frame relay network. (13)

virtual file allocation table (VFAT)   A modified version of FAT12 and FAT16 used in Windows since Windows 95. (10)

virtual private network (VPN)   A virtual tunnel created between two endpoints over an untrusted network. The tunnel is created by encapsulating the packets within special packets for the tunnel. Other security methods are also usually applied to a VPN, such as encrypting the data before encapsulating it, along with encrypted authentication. (13)

virtual memory   The use by the operating system of a portion of hard disk as memory. (9)

virus   A program installed and activated on a computer without the user's knowledge or permission. At the least, the intent is mischief, but most often the intent is to cause damage. (16)

virus encyclopedia   A generic term for a collection of information on known malware (not just viruses). (17)

Voice over IP (VoIP)   A set of technologies that allow voice transmission over an IP network—specifically used for placing phone calls over the Internet—rather than the public switched telephone network (PSTN), the worldwide network that carries traditional voice traffic. (13)

VoIP   See *Voice over IP (VoIP)*.

volatile   A word used to describe memory that cannot work without a steady supply of power. (2)

voltage regulator module (VRM)   A circuit on a motherboard through which incoming power passes. Several voltage regulators maintain a steady voltage as demand goes up and down, with one or more voltage regulators for the various voltages required (5 volts, 12 volts, 3.3 volts, etc.). (1)

volts   A measurement of the pressure of electrons, the electromotive force. It is calculated by the formula volts = watts / amps. (3)

volume   The term used for dynamic space allocation that can be formatted with a file system. (10)

VRAM   See *video RAM*.

WAN connection   A connection over a wide area network. (13)

WAP   See *wireless access point*.

war chalking   A mark on a building created by a war driver to specify where a hotspot exists. People "in the know" look for these marks to identify hotspots for their use. (16)

war driving   The act of moving through a neighborhood in a vehicle or on foot, using either a laptop equipped with Wi-Fi wireless network capability or a simple Wi-Fi sensor available for a few dollars from many sources. War drivers are searching for open hotspots—areas where a Wi-Fi network connects to the Internet without using security to keep out intruders. (16)

watts   A unit of measurement of actual delivered power, calculated by the formula watts = volts × amps. (3)

Web browser   Client software for browsing and accessing the content on the World Wide Web. Examples include Internet Explorer and Firefox. (14)

WEP   See *Wired Equivalent Privacy*.

Wi-Fi   See *Wireless Fidelity*.

Wi-Fi Protected Access (WPA)   A wireless data encryption standard based on the IEEE 802.11i security standard. It issues keys per-user and per-session and includes encryption key integrity checking. It uses Temporal Key Integrity Protocol (TKIP). (16)

Wi-Fi Protected Access 2 (WPA2)   An improved version of WPA that does not support older network cards and offers both secure authentication and data encryption. It uses EAP for a variety of authentication methods—most often EAP-PSK. (16)

wide area network (WAN)   A network connection over long distances, traditionally using phone lines or satellite communications. (13)

Windows Easy Transfer (WET)   The utility to use when doing a single data and settings transfer to a new Windows Vista computer from one running Windows XP or Windows Vista. (9)

Windows Explorer   The EXPLORER.EXE program. This program supports the entire Windows GUI. If EXPLORER.EXE is called up from inside the GUI, it opens a window for browsing your local disks and files. (8)

Windows Internet Naming Service (WINS)   A service that manages Microsoft NetBIOS names for a Windows network. This service is becoming obsolete, as Windows has moved to DNS for naming and name service. (13)

Windows Update   A Windows program that launches Internet Explorer and connects to the Windows Update Website. (9)

Windows Update Website   The Microsoft Website from which you can download updates to Windows. (9)

Windows XP Files and Settings Transfer Wizard   A tool for migrating user data and settings from one Windows computer to a computer running Windows XP. (9)

WINS   See *Windows Internet Naming Service*.

WINS Server A Windows server running the WINS service to maintain and resolve NetBIOS names. (13)

Wired Equivalent Privacy (WEP) The oldest of the Wi-Fi encryption standards. It uses 64- or 128-bit encryption that is easily broken. It does not encrypt the actual data in a packet, and it does not perform user authentication on a packet. (16)

wireless access point (WAP) A network connection device at the core of a wireless network. (13)

Wireless Fidelity (Wi-Fi) Local area networking using radio waves that includes several implementations based on the IEEE 802.11 group of standards. (13)

Wireless LAN (WLAN) Local area networking using radio waves, with the most common based on the IEEE 802.11 group of standards (802.11a, 802.11b, 802.11g, and 802.11n). (13)

workgroup A term used by Microsoft for a peer-to-peer network in which each computer can be either a client or a server or both. (13)

World Wide Web The graphical Internet consisting of a vast array of documents located on millions of specialized servers worldwide. The documents are created using HTML and other specialized languages, and transferred from servers to client computers using HTTP and related transport protocols. Client software for the World Wide Web is called a Web browser. (13)

worm A virus that is self-replicating. (16)

WPA See *Wi-Fi Protected Access (WPA)*.

WPA2 See *Wi-Fi Protected Access 2*.

WRAM Video RAM memory that uses a technique for using video RAM to perform Windows-specific functions to speed up the OS. (2)

writing In the laser printing process, the step in which the laser beam creates a negative of the image that will eventually appear on the printout. Each place that the laser beam touches loses most of its charge, creating an image, whereas the rest of the drum remains highly negatively charged. (12)

WUXGA Wide-ultra-extended graphics array—a widescreen video graphics mode with a maximum resolution of 1920 × 1200. (3)

WWW See *World Wide Web*.

x86 A term applied to a CPU, motherboard, or other components that conform to the Intel 32-bit x86 specification. Also referred to as *32-bit*. (5)

x86-64 A term applied to a CPU, motherboard, or other components that conform to the newer 64-bit architecture. Also referred to as *64-bit*. (5)

XGA   A video mode with a maximum graphics resolution of 1024 × 768. (3)

Y   Used to represent the luminance signal in S-Video. (3)

zero insertion force (ZIF) socket   A socket for a PGA CPU that has a retention lever as well as contacts to match the number of pins on the CPU. The lever is used to attach the CPU to the socket in a manner that does not require force to insert or to remove the CPU. (1)

ZIF   See *zero insertion force (ZIF) socket*.

INDEX

* (asterisk), 450
$ (dollar sign), 759
.. command, 449–450
16-bit drivers, 18
17xx error, 227
32-bit addressing, 21
32-bit drivers, 18
32-bit operating systems, 333–335, 373
32-bit PCI bus, 9
32-bit registers, 333–335
32-bit SCSI systems, 166
36-bit address bus, 21
64-bit address bus, 21
64-bit data bus, 9, 64–65
64-bit drivers, 18
64-bit operating systems, 333–335, 373
64-bit registers, 333–335
802.11 standards, 579–580, 631, 632
802.11a standard, 579, 632
802.11b standard, 579, 631, 632
802.11g standard, 579, 631, 632
802.11i security standard, 727
802.11n standard, 579–580, 631, 632

About Windows dialog box, 333
AC adapters
    described, 87, 277
    laptop computers, 277–278,
        297–298, 300–303
    testing with multimeter, 299
    troubleshooting, 297–298, 300–303
AC (alternating current) voltage, 85
ACCDB extension, 442
accelerated graphics port. See AGP
access control
    computers/networks, 716–725
    file systems, 727–729
    Media Access Control, 592–593
    password-based, 717
    restricted spaces, 725, 727
    user-based, 722–723
access control entries (ACEs), 727
access control lists (ACLs), 727
ACEs (access control entries), 727
ACK messages, 592
ACLs (access control lists), 727

ACPI (Advanced Configuration and
    Power Interface) standard, 282
ACR (Advanced Communications
    Riser), 71
activation, 393–394
active matrix displays, 97
ActiveX language, 651
ad hoc mode, 634
adapter cards, 67–72. See also cards
    capture cards, 68
    configuring, 154–155
    considerations, 153–154
    daughter cards, 70–72
    described, 67–68
    examples of, 67
    installing, 154–155
    I/O, 68–69
    multimedia, 67–68
    network interface card. See NIC
    removing, 155
    riser cards, 4, 70–72
    selecting, 154
    sound cards, 68
    troubleshooting, 200, 215,
        217–219, 224–225
    TV tuner cards, 68, 70, 219–220
    upgrading, 153–155
    USB, 153
    viewing, 72
adapters
    AC. See AC adapters
    Bluetooth, 274
    communications, 69–70
    Ethernet, 69
    MTA, 648
    network, 69, 391, 602
    video. See video adapters
    wireless, 69
Add Hardware Wizard, 398
Add Or Remove Programs utility, 387
Add Printer Wizard, 541–543
Add/Remove Programs utility, 387
Add/Remove Windows Components
    button, 388
address bus, 21
Address Resolution Protocol
    (ARP), 591
address space, 334, 336, 342
administrative alert message, 485
administrative shares, 758–759
Administrative Tools shortcut, 352

administrator
    hardware installation, 398
    hidden, 785
    network, 589, 598
    password, 379, 779, 785
    permissions, 767
    restores/recoveries, 479–483
    Run As Administrator option, 354
    security and, 723, 727–728, 733
Adobe Acrobat, 650
ADSL (asymmetrical digital subscriber
    line), 583, 584
Advanced Communications Riser
    (ACR), 71
Advanced Configuration and Power
    Interface (ACPI) standard, 282
Advanced Encryption Standard (AES),
    727, 781
Advanced Micro Devices. See AMD
Advanced Options menu, 469–478
Advanced Power Management (APM)
    standard, 282
Advanced RISC Computing (ARC), 430
Advanced Technology Attachment.
    See ATA
Advanced Technology Extended (ATX)
    motherboard, 4–6
adware, 707, 773–775
Aero Wizards, 344
AES (Advanced Encryption Standard),
    727, 781
AGP (accelerated graphics port), 11
AGP cards, 218
AGP connectors, 11, 12
AGP controller, 11
AGP slots, 11
alerts, 500
All Programs menu item, 344, 348
alligator clip, 228, 809
all-in-one devices, 532, 544
alternating current. See AC
ALU (arithmetic logic unit), 21–22
AMD (Advanced Micro Devices), 25, 26
AMD processors, 25, 26
American National Standards Institute
    (ANSI), 114, 164
amperage, 297
amperes (amps), 85
AMR (Audio Modem Riser), 71
analog modems, 209, 627
analog signals, 93

ANSI (American National Standards Institute), 114, 164
answer files, 383
antennas, wireless, 311–312, 635–636
antistatic bags, 137, 139, 155, 263
antistatic mat, 228, 808–809
antistatic spray, 237, 809
antistatic wrist strap, 136, 149, 228, 229, 808, 811
antivirus programs, 766, 772, 775. See also viruses
APIPA (Automatic Private IP Address), 601, 676
APM (Advanced Power Management) standard, 282
Apple iPhone, 99
Apple Mac systems. See Mac OS–based systems
application events, 491
application files, 196–197
application log, 491
applications. See also software; *specific applications*
    antivirus programs, 766, 772, 775
    automatic startup, 430
    back door programs, 707, 708–709
    compatibility issues, 196, 336–340, 386, 486, 493
    installing, 397
    minimum requirements for, 196
    not found, 490
    older versions of, 339–341
    prank (joke) programs, 708
    recently used, 348
    reinstalling, 196
    removing unwanted, 387
    security, 767–768
    troubleshooting, 196–197, 486–487
    updates, 197
    Windows utilities, 452–455
ARC (Advanced RISC Computing), 430
archive attribute, 440
arithmetic logic unit (ALU), 21–22
ARP (Address Resolution Protocol), 591
aspect ratio, 98
ASR (Automated System Recovery), 481–482
asterisk (*), 450
asymmetrical digital subscriber line (ADSL), 583, 584
asynchronous transfer mode (ATM), 585–586
ATA Packet Interface (ATAPI) standard, 13, 156
ATA (Advanced Technology Attachment) standards, 11–16
ATAPI drives, 156
ATAPI (ATA Packet Interface) standard, 13, 156
Athlon CPU model, 26
ATI solution, 96
ATM (asynchronous transfer mode), 585–586

Atom CPU models, 25
ATTRIB command, 455
attributes, file, 439–441
ATV12V standard, 88
ATX (Advanced Technology Extended) motherboard, 4–6
ATX power supply, 87, 88–89, 149
ATX12V 2.0 connectors, 149
audio. See sound
audio connectors, 111, 119
audio error codes, 198–199
audio inspection, 234
Audio Modem Riser (AMR), 71
authentication, 721–722. See also passwords; security
    biometric logon, 722, 753, 784–785
    BIOS password, 750, 783–784
    described, 716, 718, 721
    encrypted, 732
    implementing, 750–754
    key fobs, 721–722, 753
    Lock Computer option, 754
    smart card logons, 721, 752
    smart card readers, 752
    standard interactive logon, 721
    user accounts, 722–723
authentication verification, 718
authorization, 273, 716, 718, 722, 727
Autodetect feature, 146
Automated System Recovery (ASR), 481–482
Automatic Private IP Address (APIPA), 601, 676
Automatic Updates, 395–396, 511, 777
auto-restart errors, 474–475

B

back door programs, 707, 708–709
backlight problems, 306
Backup And Restore Center, 456–457
backup media, 56–57
Backup Or Restore Wizard, 456
Backup Utility, 387, 456, 481–482
backups. See also recovery options
    archive attribute, 440
    ASR backup set, 481–482
    automatic, 456
    BIOS settings, 143
    complete, 457
    hard drive data, 456–457
    before installs/upgrades, 387
    media for, 56–57
    NTBACKUP utility, 456, 481–482
    procedures for, 777
    scheduled, 512
    security and, 777
    strategies for, 456
    to tape, 46, 456
    test restores of, 512
Balanced Technology Extended (BTX) motherboard, 6, 7

bandwidth, 61–62, 587, 669–671
bar code readers, 109, 171
bar codes, 109, 171
base priority level, 498
basic disks, 417–424
basic input/output system. See BIOS
Basic Rate Interface (BRI), 582
Basic Service Set (BSS), 634
batteries
    CMOS, 148
    disposal of, 815
    laptop computers, 261, 276–277, 284, 285, 299
    life of, 257, 261, 276, 285
    motherboard, 148
    problems with, 299
    rechargeable, 276–277, 299
    replacing CMOS battery, 200–201
BCD (Boot Configuration Database), 431–432
BCDEDIT program, 431–432
BDD (Business Desktop Deployment), 385
BDD Workbench, 385
beep sounds, 198–199, 217, 218
Belarc Advisor, 226
BHO (browser helper objects), 650
bidirectional mode, 144, 538
biometric devices, 111, 171, 753
biometric logon, 722, 753, 784–785
biometrics, 753, 784–785
BIOS (basic input/output system)
    BIOS password, 146–147
    drive capacity and, 15
    firmware update, 201
    flash, 17, 148, 201
    hardware compatibility and, 337
    installation considerations, 376
    overview, 16–17
    partition size limit, 422
    password, 146–147, 750, 751, 783–784
    plug and play, 147
    read-only, 16–17
    replacing, 147–148
    role in boot process, 18–19
    security, 717
    self-tests, 226–227
    setup configuration, 142–147
    upgrading, 147–148, 227, 337
BIOS, flashing, 17, 148, 201
BIOS DriveLock, 751–752
BIOS error codes, 198–199
BIOS parity option, 146
BIOS settings
    accessing, 142
    advanced, 201
    backing up, 143
    boot process, 18–19
    described, 17, 18
    hard disk drives, 145–146, 227
    incorrect, 200, 201
    jumper-free, 200
    modifying, 17
    printing, 142, 143

updates and, 201
viewing, 19
BIOS setup menus/configuration,
142–147, 201. *See also* CMOS settings
BIOS Setup program, 144, 145, 205, 717
bit width, 64, 65
BitLocker, 726, 761–763
Blackberry devices, 99
Bluesnarfing, 709–710
Bluetooth adapter, 274
Bluetooth devices, 170–171, 646–647
Bluetooth drivers, 646
Bluetooth keyboard/mouse, 274
Bluetooth technology
    Bluesnarfing, 709–710
    configuring, 646–647
    considerations, 170–171, 577
    keyboards, 170
    laptop computers, 274–275
    mice, 170
    overview, 274–275
    printers, 539
    version issues, 647
Bluetooth transceiver, 170–171, 646
Blu-ray discs/drives, 50–51, 57, 94, 160, 214
Blu-ray recorders, 160
Blu-ray standard, 50
BMP extension, 442
BNC connectors, 121
boot code, 426
Boot Configuration Database. *See* BCD
boot devices, 144–145, 377, 488–489
boot disks, 144–145, 225, 230, 376–377
boot loader, 426–427
boot logging, 473
boot media, 376–377
boot partition, 761–762
boot record, 435
boot sector, 426, 435
boot sector file, 426–427
boot sector viruses, 144–145,
    488–489, 776
boot sequence settings, 144–145
boot volume, 489, 726, 761–763
BOOT.INI file, 428, 430–434, 445
BOOT.INI switches, 431
BOOTMGR file, 428
BOOTP protocol, 598
bootup. *See also* Windows startup
    BIOS/CMOS roles in, 18–19
    problems during, 210–211,
        217–218, 221
bots (robots), 708
BRI (Basic Rate Interface), 582
bridges, 606
broadband connections, 582–587
broadband router, 627–628, 645, 731,
    778–780
broadcast traffic, 669–670
browser helper objects (BHO), 650
browsers. *See* Web browsers
BSS (Basic Service Set), 634
BTX (Balanced Technology Extended)
    motherboard, 6, 7

bubblejet printers. *See* inkjet printers
built-in security principals, 723
bus architecture, 8–9, 8–11
bus cards, 172
bus NICs, 627, 632
Business Desktop Deployment (BDD), 385
busses
    32-bit, 9
    64-bit, 64–65
    address, 21
    CPU, 20–21
    data, 8, 9, 64–65
    described, 3, 20
    external, 20
    front side, 20, 21
    internal, 20
    ISA, 4
    PCI, 9–11, 172
    PCIe, 9–11, 172
    USB. *See* USB *entries*
byte mode, 538

cable modem networks, 584, 609, 645
cable select setting, 158, 210
cables
    categories, 603–604, 673–674
    coaxial, 122, 604
    Ethernet, 629–630
    fiber-optic, 604–605
    in networks, 668–669, 673–674, 690
    overview, 122
    PATA, 158
    patch, 690
    P-cables, 166
    Plenum vs. PVC, 603
    power splitter, 87
    Q-cables, 166
    SATA, 161–162
    SCSI, 166
    securing/protecting, 690, 804–805
    testing, 230, 668–669, 673–674
    troubleshooting, 190, 668–669,
        673–674
    twisted-pair, 122, 603–604
    USB devices and, 208
cache controller, 22
cache memory, 8, 22–23, 59, 64, 139
cameras
    digital, 52–53, 110, 172, 230
    still, 110
    video, 110
    Webcam, 110, 172, 648
capture cards, 68
card readers, 52, 216
CardBus cards, 270–272, 273
cards. *See also* adapter cards
    sound, 206–207
    troubleshooting, 203–209
case
    categories, 29
    cleaning, 237

computer, 27–29, 90, 91
cooling system and, 91
design of, 91
fans, 90, 151
form factors, 28–29
laptop, 260, 313, 314
overview, 27–28
precautions when opening, 136
sizes, 29
case modding, 28
Category view, 352–353
cathode ray tube. *See* CRT
CCFL (Cold Cathode Fluorescent
    Lighting) tubes, 306
CD command, 449
CD drive speeds, 48, 49–50
CD media, 47–48
CD players, 47
CDFS (Compact Disc File System), 438
CDMA (Code Division Multiple
    Access), 582
CD-R discs/drives, 47–48
CD-ROM discs
    booting from, 144, 145, 225,
        230, 376
    cleaning, 239
    data CDs, 47
    described, 47
    dust/scratches on, 49
    installing from, 377–378
    problems with, 214
    recovery, 377–378
    troubleshooting, 214
CD-ROM drives, 47–48, 156, 158, 214.
    See also optical drives
CD-RW discs/drives, 47–48
CDSL (consumer DSL), 583, 584
Celeron CPU models, 25
cell phones, 99, 577, 647
cellular connections, 644
Cellular Internet data connections, 582
cellular networks, 275, 582, 609. *See also*
    wireless networks
cellular WAN communications, 275
central processing unit. *See* CPU
Centrino brand, 25
Centronics mode, 537, 538
Certificate Services, 752
CF (CompactFlash) technology, 52–53
channel service unit (CSU), 585
character mode screen, 380
chemical solvents, 816–817
chipsets, 16
CHKDSK command, 454–455, 489
Chrome browser, 649
chrominance, 103
chrominance signal, 104
CIDR (Classless Inter-Domain
    Routing), 595
CIPHER command, 765
circuit breaker, 297, 301
Class IDs, 595
Classic View, 353
Classless Inter-Domain Routing (CIDR), 595

cleaning. *See also* dust/debris; maintenance
  compressed air for, 233, 236, 239, 562, 814
  external components, 237
  importance of, 234
  internal components, 236–237
  laptop computers, 314
  lint-free cloths, 237
  liquid cleaning compounds, 237
  mouse, 224, 238
  printer, 237, 561–563
  products for, 233
  removing dust/debris, 236–237
  vacuuming, 236–237
client computers, 581, 598, 609
clients
  DHCP, 598, 601, 675–677, 782
  DNS, 597
  network, 590
  wireless, 781–783
client/server-based networks, 588–589
clock speed, 24
CLS command, 450
clusters, 436–437
CMOS (complementary metal-oxide semiconductor), 17–19
CMOS battery, 148, 200–201
CMOS chips, 17–19, 200–201
CMOS settings, 751, 784
CNR (Communication Network Riser) card, 71
coaxial cables, 122, 604
Code Division Multiple Access (CDMA), 582
code signing, 398
Cold Cathode Fluorescent Lighting (CCFL) tubes, 306
collisions, 673
color density, 94–95
color depth, 106
Color Quality setting, 106
COM extension, 441
COM port, 144, 204–205
command prompt
  file management at, 449–452
  opening, 354
  overview, 353–354
  running as administrator, 354
  Safe Mode option, 472–473, 476, 477, 776, 786
  security, 354
Command Prompt tool, 481
command-line utilities, 354, 453–455, 667–668
communication
  active, 823–828
  body language, 818, 824, 829, 833
  context, 821
  goals of, 819–821
  Golden Rule vs. paybacks, 818–819
  human interactions, 818–819
  information gathering, 189–191, 822–823

jargon, 825–826
keys to effective communications, 821–823
obtaining acknowledgment, 826
questioning customers about problems, 822–823
rapport, establishing, 819–820, 833
reciprocity, 818–819
tact/discretion, 286–288
trust, building, 820–821
Communication Network Riser (CNR) card, 71
communications adapters, 69–70
Compact Disc File System (CDFS), 438
Compact Disc–Read-Only Memory. *See* CD-ROM
Compact Flash card, 52–53
CompactFlash (CF) technology, 52–53
compatibility mode, 340, 537
complementary metal-oxide semiconductor. *See* CMOS
COMPMGMT.MSC (Computer Management Console), 473
component video, 103–104
components. *See also* devices; equipment; hardware; *specific components*
  hot, 806
  installing, 397
  laptop computers, 258–281
  maintenance of, 236–239
  motherboard, 3–19
  printer, 533–536
  problems with, 197–225
  recycling, 814, 817
  removing unwanted, 388
  self-tests, 226–227
  troubleshooting, 190, 197–225
  Windows Components Wizard, 388
  Windows operating system, 343–360
composite video, 103
compressed air, 233, 236, 239, 562, 814
compressed files, 442
CompTIA A+ 2009 Exams, 2, 26, 329
CompTIA A+ terminology, 851–908
computer case. *See* case
Computer folder, 349, 351
computer platform, 335
Computer shortcut, 351
computers. *See also* laptop computers; PCs
  disposal of, 729, 735, 814–815
  handheld, 258
  computing waste, 814–818
CONFIG folder, 359
confrontations, 829
connectors. *See also* ports
  AGP, 11, 12
  ATX12V, 149
  audio, 111, 119
  BNC, 121
  classic, 119–122
  DB-15, 99–100, 113–114, 206
  display, 99–104
  D-Shell, 112–113, 114

DVI, 100–102
EPS12V, 149
fiber-optic cables, 604–605
IEC-320, 85
miniconnectors, 87
mini-DIN, 121–122, 170, 224
Mini-DVI, 102
Molex, 87–88
multimedia, 119–120
PS/2, 121–122, 206
RJ, 120–121, 604, 647
SATA, 14
sound, 206–207
troubleshooting, 190, 206–207
USB, 115–118, 222
vs. ports, 112
consoles. *See* MMC
consumer DSL (CDSL), 583, 584
context, 821
continuity RIMM (CRIMM), 140
contrast ratio, 98
Control Panel, 352–353
Control Panel applets, 353–354
Control Panel folder, 352–353
control unit, 20
controllers, 20, 22
CONVERT program, 786
cookies, 710–711
cooling systems, 89–91. *See also* fans
  case design, 91
  configuring, 152
  considerations, 150
  CPU fans, 90, 152
  described, 90
  excess dust, 150
  heat sinks, 90, 152
  inspecting, 91
  installing, 152
  liquid, 91, 152
  problems with, 222
  removing, 152
  selecting, 151–152
  upgrading, 152–153
copier devices, 532
COPY command, 450
CPE (customer premises equipment), 585
CPU (central processing unit), 19–27
  32-bit, 334
  64-bit, 334
  AMD processors, 25, 26
  clock speed, 24
  considerations, 135
  controllers, 20, 22
  dual-core, 23–24
  fans, 90, 152
  heat sink, 152
  illustrated, 21
  installing, 139
  Intel processors, 25–26
  laptop computers, 261–262
  manufacturers/models of, 25–27
  memory, 21, 22–23
  microcode, 24–25

motherboard compatibility, 4
multi-core, 23–24, 26
operating systems and, 333–335
overclocking, 24
overheating, 202
overview, 19
performance and, 138
PGA, 138–139
precautions, 138–139
programs, 22
real mode, 426
removing, 138–139
system minimums, 335, 336
technologies used by, 20–25
thermal throttling, 202
triple-core, 24
troubleshooting, 202–203
upgrading, 138–139
voltage, 24
CPU sockets, 8
Creator Owner group, 723
CRIMM (continuity RIMM), 140
CrossFire product, 96
CRT displays. *See also* displays
aspect ratio, 98
described, 97
disposal of, 816
precautions, 805, 812, 816
refresh rate, 104–105, 218–219
settings, 104–106
CSRSS.EXE file, 429
CSU (channel service unit), 585
CTRL-ALT-DELETE key
combination, 724
current, 298
customer premises equipment (CPE), 585
customers. *See also* users
bad behavior of, 817
being attentive toward, 829–831
body language and, 818, 824,
829, 833
communicating with. *See*
communication
confidentiality/privacy issues, 830
confrontations with, 829
judgmental behavior toward, 829
misunderstandings with, 820, 821
questioning about problems,
190–191, 822–823
reassuring, 829
respect for property, 832
respectful behavior towards, 819,
821, 828
setting/meeting expectations, 831
training, 195, 777
trust, building, 820–821

D

daisy chain, 114, 116, 118, 153, 164
data. *See also* data files
migration of, 374–376
permanent removal of, 729, 763–766

protecting, 725–730
security. *See* data security
user, 374–376
data busses, 8, 9, 64–65. *See also* busses
data CDs, 47
data files, 441–442
data security, 754–765. *See also* security
backup procedures. *See* backups
data wiping, 729, 763–766
encryption. *See* encryption
migration of data, 374–376
permissions. *See* permissions
data wiping, 729, 763–766
database files, 442
datagrams, 591–592
date/time settings, 146, 200, 201, 380
daughter cards, 70–72
DB-9 connectors, 113
DB-15 connectors, 99–100, 206
DB-25 connectors, 113, 114
DC controllers, 277
DC (direct current) voltage, 85, 297
DDoS (distributed denial of service)
attacks, 706
DDR1 (double-data rate), 60–61, 140
DDR2 (double-data-rate two), 61–62, 140
DDR3 (double-data-rate three), 62–63, 140
debugging information, 485
debugging mode, 474
decision tree, 22
DEFAULT file, 359
Default Gateway, 597, 598
DEFAULT USER folder, 359
DEFRAG command, 453–454
DEFRAG.EXE program, 508
defragmenting hard drives, 239, 389,
507–508
degaussing, 106
Dell recycling program, 814
denial of service (DoS) attacks, 706
desktop
Business Desktop Deployment, 385
preferences, 508–509
Remote Desktop, 501–504
Windows, 343–355
desktop-tower case, 29
Deutsche Industrie Norm. *See* DIN
device drivers. *See* drivers
"Device has failed to start" error
message, 489
Device Manager
COM port assignments, 204–205
overview, 495–496
troubleshooting with, 192, 193
verifying driver installation, 400
viewing adapter cards in, 72
viewing CardBus adapters, 271
viewing parallel ports, 205
"Device referenced in registry not found"
message, 489
devices. *See also* components; equipment;
specific devices
all-in-one, 532, 544
attaching, 398

biometric, 111, 171, 753
Blackberry, 99
Bluetooth, 170–171, 646–647
boot, 144–145, 377, 488–489
conflicts, 192
drivers for. *See* drivers
ESD, 149, 228, 808–809, 833
external storage, 156, 166,
167–168, 216
failure to start, 489
fax, 532
FireWire, 209, 216
hot-swappable, 54, 116, 267–268
input. *See* input devices
installing, 397–400
I/O. *See* I/O devices
IrDA, 274, 577
MIDI, 109, 110
multifunction-, 532, 544
multimedia input, 109–111,
172–173
non-plug and play, 541–543
plug and play, 397–400, 430, 540
SATA, 14–15, 115, 156, 161–162
scanner-printer-fax-copier, 532
SCSI. *See* SCSI devices
storage. *See* storage devices
thermal sensitive, 239–240
unknown, 192
USB. *See* USB devices
DFS (Distributed File System), 439
DHCP (Dynamic Host Configuration
Protocol), 780–781, 782
DHCP clients, 598, 601, 675–677, 782
DHCP servers, 598–601
disabling, 780–781, 782
IP addresses, 599–601
IP configuration, 645, 676–677
overview, 598
diagnostic tests, 227
diagnostic toolkits, 230–232
diagnostics hardware, 231–232
diagnostics software, 230–231
dialers, 708
dial-up networks, 276, 581, 644
DIB extension, 442
digital cameras, 52–53, 110, 172, 230
Digital Light Processing (DLP) chips, 99
Digital Linear Tape (DLT) technology, 46
digital projectors, 99
digital signals, 100–101
digital signature, 398–399
digital subscriber line (DSL), 583–584,
609, 645
digital versatile discs. *See* DVD discs
digital video camera, 110
digital video interface (DVI) connectors,
100–102
digital video recorders (DVRs), 68,
172–173
Digital Visual Interface (DVI), 93, 94, 160
digitizing tablet, 267, 307, 310–311
DIMM (Dual Inline Memory Module), 7,
64, 65, 77, 140–141

DIN connectors, 121–122
DIP (dual inline package), 142
DIP switch, 142
DIR command, 449, 451
direct current. *See* DC
direct memory access. *See* DMA
directories
    changing, 450–451
    creating, 449, 451, 452
    deleting, 449, 452
    described, 438
    managing at command prompt,
      449–452
    root, 435
    subdirectories, 435, 436
    viewing, 450, 451
    vs. folders, 438
Directory Services Restore mode, 474
DirectX Diagnostic Tool (DXDIAG),
    506–507
Disable Automatic Restart on System
    Failure mode, 474–475
disasters, 236, 703–704, 716
discs. *See* disks/discs
Disk Cleanup utility, 388–389
Disk Defragmenter, 389, 507–508
disk drives. *See* hard disk drives
Disk Fragmenter utility, 389
disk type, 435
DISKPART command, 480
disks/discs
    basic disks, 417–424
    Blu-ray, 50–51, 57, 94, 160, 214
    boot disks, 144–145, 225, 230,
      376–377
    CD-R discs, 47
    CD-ROM. *See* CD-ROM discs
    CD-RW discs, 47
    DVDs. *See* DVD discs
    Emergency Repair Disk, 482–483
    floppy. *See* floppy disks
    hard disks. *See* hard disk drives
    RAID. *See* RAID *entries*
    recovery, 377–378
    startup, 144–145, 225, 230
display connectors, 99–104
display mode key, 309–310
display power-management signaling
    (DPMS) standard, 98
DisplayPort, 94, 103
displays, 96–99
    aspect ratio, 98
    clearing screen, 450, 451
    color quality, 106
    configuring, 173–175
    considerations, 96–97, 173
    CRT. *See* CRT displays
    disposal of, 816
    flat panel, 97
    installing, 173–175
    laptop computers, 257, 266–267,
      304–307, 309
    LCD. *See* LCD displays

maintenance of, 237
moving, 805
multiple, 95–96, 173–174
multiple video adapters for, 96
problems with, 217–220
refresh rate, 104–105
removing, 175
repeated screen elements, 219
resolution, 94–95, 97, 98, 106, 219
safety precautions, 805,
    812–813, 816
settings, 104–106, 509
touch screen, 99, 174–175, 267
wide-screen, 94
distributed denial of service (DDoS)
    attacks, 706
Distributed File System (DFS), 439
distribution server, 384
distribution share, 384
DL (dual-layer) format, 48
DLL extension, 441
DLP (Digital Light Processing) chips, 99
DLT (Digital Linear Tape) technology, 46
DMA (direct memory access), 15
DMA channels, 144, 203
DMA controller, 203
DNS (Domain Name Service), 597,
    683–686
DNS clients, 597
DNS problems, 683–686
DNS servers, 597, 598, 643, 645, 684–686
DOC extension, 442
docking stations, 268
document files, 442
documentation resources, 494–495
Documents and Settings folder, 444
Documents folder, 349
Documents icon, 349
DOCX extension, 442
dollar sign ($), 759
domain controllers, 752–753
Domain Name Service. *See* DNS
domains, 589, 785
DoS (denial of service) attacks, 706
DOS program, 453
dot matrix printers, 527, 533, 552,
    554, 555
dotted decimal format, 594
double-data-rate one (DDR1), 60–61, 140
double-data-rate three (DDR3),
    62–63, 140
double-data-rate two (DDR2), 61–62, 140
DPMS (display power-management
    signaling) standard, 98
drag/drop operations, 447–449
DRAM (Dynamic RAM), 7, 22, 59–60,
    63–64
drive imaging, 384–385
drive interface standards, 11–16
drive letters, 373, 420, 422–423, 479, 482
drive paths, 422
drive-by downloads, 705–706
DriveLock, 717, 751–752

driver signing, 398
drivers
    16-bit, 18
    32-bit, 18
    64-bit, 18
    biometric devices, 171
    Bluetooth, 646
    corrupted, 489
    described, 398
    digitizer, 310–311
    incompatibility issues, 386, 471, 555
    information about, 379
    installing, 397–400
    motherboards, 147
    mouse, 224
    network adapters, 69, 391, 602
    optical drives, 160, 214
    permissions, 398
    printer, 534, 540–542, 548, 555–559
    Roll Back Driver option, 472
    scanner, 544
    SCSI devices, 165
    signed, 398–399
    TWAIN, 544
    unsigned, 399
    updates, 234
    USB devices, 170, 207–209
drives. *See also* storage devices
    ATAPI, 156
    Blu-ray, 214
    cable select setting, 158, 210
    EIDE, 13, 14, 156–158
    eSATA, 211
    external, 44, 45
    flash memory, 167
    floppy. *See* floppy disk drives
    hard. *See* hard disk drives
    hot-swappable, 54, 156
    IDE, 14
    installing/removing, 167–168
    internal, 44, 45
    master/slave configuration, 156–159
    optical. *See* optical drives
    PATA, 156–158, 212
    SATA, 14–15, 156, 161–162, 211
    SCSI, 164–166
    solid-state, 51–52, 160–161
    tape, 46, 215
    thumb, 52, 160, 167, 168, 213–214
    USB, 167–168
D-Shell connectors, 112–113, 114
DSL (digital subscriber line), 583–584,
    609, 645
Dual Inline Memory Module (DIMM), 7,
    64, 65, 77, 140–141
dual inline package (DIP), 142
dual-boot computer, 426–427
dual-core CPUs, 23–24
dual-layer (DL) format, 48
dump files, 485
dust/debris. *See also* cleaning
    CDs/DVDs, 49
    computer, 234, 236–237

mouse, 223–224
storage devices, 213–214
DVD discs, 48–51
Blu-ray, 50–51, 94, 214, 239
booting from, 144, 145, 376
cleaning, 239
copy protection for, 94
drive speeds, 49–50
high-definition, 50–51
installing from, 377–378
overview, 48–50
recovery, 377–378
troubleshooting, 214
DVD drive speeds, 49–50
DVD drives, 48–51, 214. *See also*
optical drives
DVD media, 48–49
DVD-Audio discs, 49
DVD+R discs, 49
DVD-R discs, 49
DVD-RAM format, 49
DVD-ROM discs, 49
DVD-RW discs, 49
DVD-Video discs, 49
DVI (Digital Visual Interface), 93, 94, 160
DVI (digital video interface) connectors,
100–102
Dvorak keyboard, 108, 109
DVRs (digital video recorders), 68,
172–173
DXDIAG (DirectX Diagnostic Tool),
506–507
dye-sublimation printers, 531
dynamic disks, 417
Dynamic Host Configuration Protocol.
See DHCP
Dynamic RAM (DRAM), 7, 22, 59–60,
63–64

E

EAP (Extensible Authentication
Protocol), 727
EAP with Personal Shared Key
(EAP-PSK), 727
EAP-PSK (EAP with Personal Shared
Key), 727
ECC (error checking code), 65, 66
ECP (enhanced capability port) mode,
144, 206, 538
Edit text editor, 446
editions, Windows, 329–331
EEPROM (electrically erasable
programmable ROM), 59
EFS (Encrypting File System), 726,
759–761
EIDE (Enhanced IDE), 13, 14
EIDE drives, 13, 14, 156–158
EIDE systems, 164
electrical dangers, 2, 149, 806–807, 812
electrical safety, 806–807
electrical shock, 147, 806–807
electrical terminology, 85

electrically erasable programmable ROM
(EEPROM), 59
electromagnetic interference (EMI),
674, 810
electromagnetic pulse (EMP), 704
electrostatic discharge. *See* ESD
e-mail
hoaxes, 714–715
IMAP, 609
infected attachments, 715
phishing, 712–714, 772–773
POP, 609
SMTP, 609
spam, 707–708
Emergency Repair Disk (ERD), 482–483
Emergency Repair Process, 482–483
EMF (Enhanced Metafile Format), 546
EMI (electromagnetic interference),
674, 810
EMP (electromagnetic pulse), 704
Enable Boot Logging option, 473
Enable Low Resolution Video option, 473
Enable VGA Mode option, 473
encrypted authentication, 732
Encrypting File System (EFS), 726,
759–761
encryption, 726–727. *See also* security
BitLocker, 726, 761–763
boot volume, 726, 761–763
described, 726
file systems and, 726, 727–729,
759–761
files, 759–761, 765
folders, 759–761, 765
HTTPS, 601
NTFS, 438, 726–727, 759–761, 763
problems with, 786–787
SSL, 610
for wireless networks, 726–727
wireless signals, 781
wireless transmissions, 783
End User License Agreement
(EULA), 381
energy efficiency, 89, 98
enhanced capability port (ECP) mode,
144, 206, 538
Enhanced IDE. *See* EIDE
Enhanced Metafile Format (EMF), 546
enhanced parallel port (EPP) mode, 144,
206, 538
environment
computer, 189–190, 234
laptop, 314
printers, 563
EPP (enhanced parallel port) mode, 144,
206, 538
EPROM (erasable programmable
ROM), 59
EPS12V connectors, 149
equipment. *See also* components; devices
disposal of, 729, 735, 814–817
moving, 805–806
powering down, 805
safe handling of, 804–814

erasable programmable ROM
(EPROM), 59
ERD (Emergency Repair Disk), 482–483
error checking code (ECC), 65, 66
error messages, 487–494. *See also* errors;
troubleshooting
audio error codes, 198–199
BIOS error codes, 198–199
common, 487–494
"Device has failed to start," 489
"Inaccessible boot drive," 488–489
memory, 223
"NTDETECT.COM is missing," 487
"NTLDR is missing," 487
"NTOSKRNL is invalid or missing,"
487–488
power-on self-test (POST), 198–199,
304, 305
"Program referenced in registry not
found," 490
questioning users about, 190
"Service has failed to start," 489
startup, 487
text, 198, 199
"USB device is unknown," 208
viewing in Event Viewer, 473,
490–493
Error-Checking program, 454–455
errors. *See also* error messages
17*xx*, 227
audio, 198–199
auto-restart, 474–475
fatal, 202, 223
printer, 550–552
eSATA (External Serial ATA),
15, 57, 167
eSATA channel, 211
eSATA drives, 211
eSATA interface, 211
ESD (electrostatic discharge), 2, 152, 236,
807–809, 807–810
ESD devices, 149, 228, 808–809, 833
Ethernet adapters, 69
Ethernet cables, 629–630
Ethernet connections, 276, 277
Ethernet frames, 577–578
Ethernet hubs, 606, 670
Ethernet networks, 577–578, 670–671
Ethernet NICs, 577–578, 627–630
Ethernet switches, 607, 627–628, 634, 673
EULA (End User License Agreement), 381
EVDO (Evolution Data Optimized), 582
event logs, 190, 490–493
Event Viewer, 473, 490–493
events
application, 491
clearing from log, 492
refreshing, 492
security, 491–492
system, 490–491
viewing in Event Viewer, 473,
490–493
writing to systemlog, 485
Everyone group, 723

EVGA (Extended Video Graphics Array), 95
Evolution Data Optimized (EVDO), 582
EXE extension, 441
EXIT command, 480
expansion boards. *See* adapter cards
expansion bus types/slots, 9–11
expansion busses, 9–11. *See also* busses
expansion slots, 269–273
EXPLORER.EXE program, 344, 472–473
ExpressCard modules, 272
eXtended Graphics Array (XGA) standard, 95
Extended Video Graphics Array (EVGA), 95
extending extractor, 228, 809
Extensible Authentication Protocol. *See* EAP
extensions, 441–442
external bus, 20
external cache memory, 8, 23
External Serial ATA. *See* eSATA
external storage devices, 156, 166, 167–168, 216

F

factory recovery partition, 378
fans. *See also* cooling systems
    case, 90, 151
    CPU, 90, 152
    laptop computers, 264–265
    noisy, 222
    power supplies, 87, 90, 221
    problems with, 221, 222
Fast Ethernet, 578
FAT (file allocation table), 435–437
FAT clusters, 436–437
FAT file system, 381, 435–437
FAT partitions, 381
FAT12 file system, 435
FAT16 file system, 373–374, 421–422, 435–437
FAT32 file system
    converting to NTFS, 786
    file/folder-level permissions and, 785–786
    overview, 374, 436
    partition size limit, 422
FAT32 partitions, 436, 437
fatal errors, 202, 223
fax devices, 532
fax server, 759
FAX$ share, 759
FDDs. *See* floppy disk drives
fiber installations, 578, 585
fiber-optic cables/connectors, 604–605
field replaceable units (FRUs), 229
file allocation table. *See* FAT
file attributes, 439–441, 455
file extensions, 441–442
file formats, 546

file management, 434–452. *See also* files
file signature verification, 399
file systems, 434–439
    CDFS, 438
    controlling access to, 727–729
    DFS, 439
    drive formatting and, 169
    encryption, 726, 727–729, 759–761
    FAT, 381, 435–437
    FAT12, 435
    FAT16, 373–374, 421–422, 435–437
    FAT32. *See* FAT32 file system
    NT File System. *See* NTFS
    permissions, 438
    selecting, 373–374
    UDF, 438
    VFAT, 435
    vs. disk types, 435
file types, 441–445
files. *See also* data; data files; *specific file names*
    answer, 383
    application, 196–197
    basic tasks, 447–449
    compressed, 442
    copying, 450, 451, 452, 758
    damaged, 500–501
    data, 441–442
    database, 442
    deleting, 451, 764
    document, 442
    dragging/dropping, 447–449
    dump, 485
    editing, 445–446
    encryption, 759–761, 765
    folders for. *See* folders
    fragmented, 389, 507–508
    graphic, 442
    hidden, 440, 442, 443
    inaccessible, 787
    log. *See* log files
    management tasks, 447–449
    managing at command prompt, 449–452
    moving, 758
    naming, 439, 448
    offline, 445
    organizing in folders, 446–452
    overview, 439
    PDF, 650
    permissions, 438, 727, 754–758, 785–786
    presentation, 442
    program, 442
    protected, 500–501
    quarantined, 776
    recovering from Recycle Bin, 764
    registry, 359
    removing unnecessary, 388–389
    searching for, 438, 450
    showing, 442
    spreadsheet, 442
    swap, 401
    system, 442–443, 444, 481

    temporary, 444, 445
    text, 442, 445–446
    UDFs, 383, 438
    video, 442
    viewing, 450, 451
    viewing contents of, 451
    Windows File Protection, 500–501, 766
Files and Settings Transfer Wizard, 374–375
fingerprint scanners, 171, 718, 722, 753
Firefox web browser, 650, 651–652
FireFTP add-on, 650
firewalls, 730–734
    hardware, 733–734, 768, 778
    overview, 730–733
    Remote Desktop and, 503
    routers as, 768
    software, 734, 768–772, 787–788
    third-party, 771–772
    Windows Firewall, 769–771, 775
    wireless access point, 779, 781
FireWire devices, 209, 216
FireWire interface, 113, 118–119
FireWire NICs, 627
FireWire standard, 113, 118–119, 539
firmware
    described, 16
    motherboards, 16–19
    NICs, 634–635
    printers, 534, 548
    updates to, 234, 634–635
    WAP, 634–635, 779
FIXBOOT command, 480
FIXMBR command, 480
flash drives, 52, 437
flash memory, 51, 52–53, 167
flash memory drives, 167
flash ROM, 59
flashing BIOS, 17, 148, 201
flashlight, 228
flat panel displays (FPDs), 97
Flex ATX motherboard, 6
floating-point unit (FPU), 21
floppy disk drives (FDDs)
    configuring, 144–145
    installing, 163
    internal, 163–164
    maintenance of, 239
    overview, 43
    removing, 164
    settings, 144–145
    troubleshooting, 215
floppy disks
    booting from, 144–145, 225, 230, 376–377
    cleaning, 239
    formatting, 455
    overview, 43
    problems with, 215
folders. *See also* shares; *specific folder names*
    basic tasks, 447–449
    Control Panel, 352–353

copying, 758
creating, 447, 451
default, 439
deleting, 451
described, 343, 438
dragging/dropping, 447–449
encryption, 759–761, 765
GUI techniques, 447–449
hiding contents of, 442, 443
hierarchy, 351
management tasks, 447–449
moving, 758
naming, 439, 447
offline, 445
opening, 448
organizing files in, 446–452
permissions, 438, 727–729, 754–758, 785–786
personal, 349, 727–729
program files, 397
programs, 348
root, 397, 442–445, 447
showing contents of, 442
subfolders, 447
views, 351
vs. directories, 438
Folders button, 351
fonts, 444
Fonts folder, 444
form factors
computer case, 28–29
memory cards, 52–53
motherboards, 4–6, 135
power supplies, 87–89
FORMAT command, 455
formatting hard disks, 168–169, 455
Found New Hardware Wizard, 398, 540, 634, 640
FPDs (flat panel displays), 97
FPU (floating-point unit), 21
fragmentation, 239, 389, 507–508
fragmented files, 389, 507–508
frame relay, 585–586
fraud, 703
front side bus, 20, 21
FRUs (field replaceable units), 229
FTP file transfers, 650
full-tower case, 29

G

gadgets, 355
gameport, 110
generators, 236
GIF extension, 442
Gigabit Ethernet, 578
Global System for Mobile communications (GSM), 582
glossary, 851–908
Google Chrome, 649
GPU (graphics processing unit), 19, 21, 63, 96
graphic files, 442

graphical user interface. See GUI
graphics processing unit (GPU), 19, 21, 63, 96
graphics tablet, 267
grayware, 707–708
grounding mat, 136, 228
group accounts, 723, 727
groups
built-in, 723
local, 723
names, 592, 753
permissions, 756–758
special, 723
GSM (Global System for Mobile communications), 582
GUI (graphical user interface)
folders, 447–449
Windows GUI, 343–355

H

hackers, 704
HAL (hardware abstraction layer) file, 428
handheld computers, 258
hard disk drives (HDDs), 44–46. See also drives
analyzing with DEFRAG command, 453–454
backing up data on. See backups
basic storage, 417–424
BIOS settings, 145–146, 227
booting from, 144–145, 377
capacity, 15
cleaning up, 387–389
defragmenting, 239, 389, 507–508
disk management, 416–424
disk storage types, 416–419
drive imaging, 384–385
drive letters, 373, 420, 422–423, 479, 482
dynamic storage, 417
external, 44, 45, 57, 156
formatting, 168–169, 455
identifying, 146, 148
installing/removing, 167–168
internal, 44, 45, 156–159
laptop computers, 265, 266
maintenance of, 239
master/slave configuration, 156–159
minimum free disk space, 335, 336
partitioning. See partitioning; partitions
preparing for use, 168–169, 373
RAID. See RAID entries
removing data on, 763–766
size, 148
software diagnostic tests, 227
space on, 57–58
status information, 418–419
troubleshooting, 209–213, 227

hardware. See also components; devices; equipment
Add Hardware Wizard, 398
cleaning products, 233
compatibility issues, 336–339, 373, 386–387
laptop computers, 261–273
network, 602–608, 666, 670–675
requirements, 337, 386–387
Safely Remove Hardware icon, 168, 216, 217
status indicators, 666–667
troubleshooting, 191–192, 197–225, 231–232
hardware abstraction layer (HAL) file, 428
hardware addressing, 592–593
hardware firewalls, 733–734, 768, 778
hardware hash, 394
hardware identifier, 394
hardware power switch, 298–299
hardware profile, 359
hardware toolkit, 227–233
HDCP (High-Definition Content Protection), 94, 160
HDDs. See hard disk drives
HD-DVD standard, 50
HDMI (High-Definition Multimedia Interface), 93–94, 102–103, 160
HDSL (high-data-rate DSL), 584
HDTV (high-definition television), 50–51
headphones, 110
Health Insurance Portability and Accountability Act (HIPAA), 716
heat buildup, 87, 202, 234, 314. See also cooling systems; fans
heat pipe, 265
heat sinks, 90, 152
HELP command, 453, 480
Help screen, 480
Hewlett-Packard recycling program, 814
Hibernate mode, 283, 285, 346
hidden administrator, 785
hidden attribute, 440, 443
hidden files, 440, 442, 443
high-data-rate DSL (HDSL), 584
High-Definition Content Protection (HDCP), 90, 160
high-definition DVDs, 50–51
High-Definition Multimedia Interface (HDMI), 93–94, 102–103, 160
high-definition television (HDTV), 50–51
high-voltage power supply (HVPS), 85
HIPAA (Health Insurance Portability and Accountability Act), 716
HKEY_CLASSES_ROOT subtree, 358
HKEY_CURRENT_CONFIG subtree, 359
HKEY_CURRENT_USER subtree, 359
HKEY_LOCAL_MACHINE subtree, 358
HKEY_USERS subtree, 359
hoaxes, 714–715
Home Theater PCs (HTPCs), 94
horizontal hold (h-hold) setting, 104

horizontal position setting, 104
host ID, 594, 595, 598, 676
hot components, 806
hot spots, 579
hot swapping, 116, 156
hot-swappable devices, 54, 116, 267–268
hot-swappable drives, 54, 156
HTML (Hypertext Markup
    Language), 610
HTPCs (Home Theater PCs), 94
HTTP (Hypertext Transfer Protocol),
    601, 610
HTTPS (Hypertext Transfer Protocol over
    Secure Sockets Layer), 601
hubs
    Ethernet, 606, 670
    USB, 116–117, 153, 207–209
    vs. switches, 670
human interactions, 818–819
humidity, 222, 234, 808, 809
HVPS (high-voltage power supply), 85
hyper threading, 23
Hypertext Markup Language
    (HTML), 610
Hypertext Transfer Protocol (HTTP),
    601, 610
Hypertext Transfer Protocol over Secure
    Sockets Layer (HTTPS), 601

I

IAD (Integrated Access Device),
    647–648
IANA (Internet Assigned Numbers
    Authority), 595
IBSS (Independent Basic Service Set), 634
ICF (Internet Connection Firewall). See
    Windows Firewall
ICMP (Internet Control Message
    Protocol), 679
icons, 344, 345
IDE (Integrated Drive Electronics), 13
IDE drives, 14
identity theft, 703
IE. See Internet Explorer
IEC-320 connector, 85
IEEE (Institute of Electrical and Electron-
    ics Engineers), 118–119
IEEE 203.3 standard. See Ethernet
IEEE 1284 (parallel) standard, 113,
    538, 539
IEEE 1394. See FireWire standard
IEEE 1394a standard, 118, 209
IEEE 1394b standard, 118, 209
IEEE-1394 ports, 153
i.link technology. See FireWire standard
ImageX, 385
imaging program, 384–385
IMAP (Internet Message Access
    Protocol), 609
"Inaccessible boot drive" error message,
    488–489

INCITS (InterNational Committee on In-
    formation Technology Standards), 164
indexing settings, 509–510
industry standard architecture
    (ISA) bus, 4
Infrared Data Association. See IrDA
infrared wireless communication, 274
infrastructure mode, 634
inheritance, 735
inkjet cartridges, 534–535, 552, 559
inkjet printers, 530–535, 552, 554,
    559, 562
in-place installations. See upgrades
input devices, 107–109
    bar code readers, 109
    biometric, 753
    keyboard. See keyboards
    laptop computers, 278–281, 307–311
    maintenance of, 237–238
    microphones, 111, 172
    MIDI devices, 110
    mouse. See mouse
    multimedia, 109–111, 172–173
    pointing devices, 108–109
    stylus pen, 267, 311
    touch screen display, 99, 267
    touchpads, 280, 308, 312
    trackball, 109, 223–224, 237, 280
    troubleshooting, 223–224, 307–311
installation ID code, 393
installation manuals, 494
installations. See also upgrades
    activation, 393–394
    adapter cards, 154–155
    all-in-one devices, 544
    attended (manual) installation,
        378–383
    clean, 342, 374, 379
    CPU, 139
    devices, 395–396
    from factory recovery partition, 378
    flawed, 196–197
    gathering information for, 379
    motherboards, 136–138
    networks, 377
    power supplies, 149–150
    printers, 540–544
    problems with, 196–197
    product key, 334, 380–381, 390, 393
    RAM, 139–141
    reactivation, 394
    from recovery CD/DVD, 377–378
    regional/language options, 380, 381
    registration, 393–394
    safety precautions. See safety pre-
        cautions
    scripted, 383–384
    service packs/patches, 332–333, 777
    startup/source locations, 376–378
    unattended installation, 383–384
    Windows operating system, 372–390
instant messaging, 708
Institute of Electrical and Electronics
    Engineers. See IEEE

Integrated Access Device (IAD), 647–648
Integrated Drive Electronics. See IDE
Integrated Service Digital Network
    (ISDN), 582–583
Intel Celeron CPUs, 25
Intel motherboards, 4
Intel Pentium processors, 25
Intel processors, 25–26
Intel Xeon CPUs, 25
interference, 312, 630–631
internal bus, 20
internal cache memory, 23
InterNational Committee on Information
    Technology Standards (INCITS), 164
Internet. See also networks; Web browsers
    basic concepts, 581, 608–612
    Bluesnarfing, 709–710
    bots (robots), 708
    dial-up access, 276
    e-mail. See e-mail
    firewalls. See firewalls
    grayware, 707–708
    inappropriate/distasteful
        content, 710
    instant messaging, 708
    phishing, 712–714, 772–773
    pop-ups, 705, 712, 773–775
    proxy settings, 652–653
    services/protocols, 609–612
    temporary files, 388–389
    war driving, 709
    wireless access. See wireless networks
Internet Assigned Numbers Authority
    (IANA), 595
Internet Connection Firewall (ICF). See
    Windows Firewall
Internet Control Message Protocol
    (ICMP), 679
Internet Explorer. See also Web browsers
    add-ons, 650
    configuring, 651
    described, 650
    installing, 651
    pop-up blocker, 773–775
    problems with, 651
    removal of, 651
    temporary Internet files, 388–389
    upgrading, 651
Internet Message Access Protocol
    (IMAP), 609
Internet Packet Exchange/Sequenced
    Exchange. See IPX/SPX
Internet Printing Client, 543
Internet Protocol. See IP
Internet service provider (ISP), 595,
    608–609
Internet services, 601–602
Internet/Web-based documentation, 495
internetworks, 581
interpersonal skills. See communication;
    professionalism
interrupt request line (IRQ), 17, 203
intranets, 581

intrusion detection, 717
inventory tools, 226
inverters, 811
I/O adapter cards, 68–69
I/O addresses, 203
I/O devices, 170–175
    installing/removing, 170–173
    interfaces for, 112–119
    laptop computers, 278–281
    selecting, 170
I/O interfaces, 112–119
I/O ports, 203–209
IP (Internet Protocol), 591, 953
IP addresses
    assigning, 598–599
    configuration, 640–643, 675–683, 782
    hiding with NAT, 731
    leased, 598
    logical addressing and, 593–601
    loopback, 600
    packets and, 591
    pinging, 677–679
    printing via, 543, 547
    private, 601
    public vs. private, 731
    viewing, 599–600
    wireless access point, 780–781, 782
IP packet filtering, 730
IP printing support, 543
IP router, 607
IPC$ share, 759
IPCONFIG utility, 596, 667–668, 675–677, 779
iPhone, 99
IPv4 addresses, 594–595, 600–601
IPv4 protocol, 593, 594–595
IPv6 addresses, 595–596
IPv6 protocol, 593, 595–596
IPX/SPX (Internet Packet Exchange/ Sequenced Exchange), 591, 670
IrDA devices, 274, 540, 577
IrDA (Infrared Data Association) standard, 274
IRQ (interrupt request line), 17, 203
ISA (industry standard architecture) bus, 4
ISDN (Integrated Service Digital Network), 582–583
ISP (Internet service provider), 595, 608–609
Itanium CPU models, 25, 202

jargon, 825–826
JavaScript, 651
JEDEC Solid State Technology Association, 60
JEDEC Speed Standards, 61–62, 63
Joint Electron Device Engineering Council. *See* JEDEC
joystick, 206

JPG extension, 442
jump drives, 52
jumpers, 142, 157, 199–200

K

Kazaa file-sharing system, 611
kernel loading, 427–429
key fob logon, 721–722, 753
key fobs, 721–722, 753
keyboards. *See also* input devices
    Bluetooth, 170, 274
    cleaning, 237
    drivers, 170
    Dvorak, 108, 109
    ergonomic, 108
    installing/removing, 170–171
    laptop computers, 274, 279–280, 283, 309–310
    layouts, 109
    maintenance of, 237
    overview, 108
    problems with, 206
    QWERTY, 108, 109
    USB, 207–208, 280
keystroke loggers, 706
KVM switches, 111–112, 171–172

L

L1 (Level 1 cache), 23
L2 (Level 2 cache), 23
L3 (Level 3 cache), 23
lands, 47
language options, 380, 381
LANs (local area networks), 69, 577–578, 606–608
LANshack, 669
laptop computers, 255–325
    AC adapter, 277–278, 297–298, 300–303
    batteries, 261, 276–277, 284, 285, 299
    CardBus, 270–272, 273
    case for, 260, 313, 314
    cleaning, 314
    communications connections, 274–276
    cooling issues, 314
    CPU, 261–262
    DC controller, 277
    display, 257, 266–267, 304–307, 309
    docking stations, 268
    expansion slots, 269–273
    ExpressCards, 272
    fans, 264–265
    hard drives, 265, 266
    hardware, 261–273
    hardware power switch, 298–299
    hot-swappable devices, 267–268
    input devices, 278–281, 307–311

    introduction, 256–258
    inverters and, 811
    keyboard, 274, 279–280, 283, 309–310
    maintenance, 313–314
    manufacturer's documentation, 259–260
    media/accessory bay, 268–269
    memory, 262–264
    memory card reader, 269
    motherboard, 261
    mouse, 274, 280, 283
    non-hot-swappable devices, 268
    opening up, 258–259
    optical drives, 265
    PC Card, 270–272
    peripherals, 265–269, 274, 275
    pointing devices, 280
    port replicators, 268
    power devices, 276–278
    power management, 281–285
    power problems, 297–303
    replacement parts, 260
    replacing components, 258–281
    safety procedures, 259, 805
    security issues, 735
    shutdown options, 298–299
    speakers, 281, 309–310
    startup problems, 303–304
    storage devices, 265
    system instability, 398–399
    touchpads, 280, 308, 312
    transporting/shipping, 313
    troubleshooting, 295–325
    upgrading, 258–281
    video adapter, 266, 307
    wired communications, 275–276
    wireless communications, 69, 274–275, 311–312, 579–580
    work environment for, 314
laser printers. *See also* toner cartridges
    cleaning, 561, 562
    maintenance counts, 561
    overview, 528–530
    problems with, 551–555, 557, 559
    upgrades, 548
Last Known Good (LKG) configuration, 474
latency, 587
LBA (logical block address), 15
LCD displays. *See also* displays
    connections, 100
    laptop computers, 257, 266–267, 304–307, 309
    overview, 97–98
    problems with, 217, 219, 304–307
    settings, 104–106
LEDs (light-emitting diodes), 99, 198, 231–232, 666, 668
Level 1 cache (L1), 23
Level 2 cache (L2), 23
Level 3 cache (L3), 23
LFN (long filename), 439

light-emitting diodes (LEDs), 99, 198, 231–232, 666, 668
line in port, 207
line out port, 207
Line Printer Daemon (LPD) software, 543
Line Printer Remote (LPR) software, 543
Linux-based systems, 257, 590
liquid cooling systems, 91, 152
liquid crystal displays. *See* LCD displays
LKG (Last Known Good) configuration, 474
local area networks. *See* LANs
local groups, 723
local user accounts, 722–723
local users, 754–755
lock button, 347
Lock Computer option, 347, 724–725, 754
Lock option, 347
locking computer, 347
log files
    application log, 491
    creating, 500
    event logs, 190, 490–493
    security log, 491–492
    system log, 485, 490–493
Log Off option, 346, 347
Log On To dialog box, 724
logging on/off. *See also* Windows startup
    biometric logon, 722, 753, 784–785
    Interactive Logon, 721
    key fob logon, 721–722, 753
    Log Off option, 346, 347
    Log On To dialog box, 724
    smart card logons, 721, 752
    Windows Logon service, 429–430
logical addressing, 593–601
logical block address (LBA), 15
LOGON command, 480
logon security features, 723–724
long filename (LFN), 439
loopback addresses, 600
loopback plugs, 204, 207, 231–232
low-profile case, 29
low-profile tower case, 29
low-voltage differential (LVD) data transfer method, 115
low-voltage differential signaling (LVDS), 115
LPD Print Service, 543
LPD (Line Printer Daemon) software, 543
LPR Port Monitor, 543
LPR (Line Printer Remote) software, 543
LSASS.EXE file, 429
luminance, 103
luminance signal, 103–104
LVD (low-voltage differential) data transfer method, 115
LVDS (low-voltage differential signaling), 115
Lynx technology. *See* FireWire standard

M

MAC addresses, 592–593, 779–780, 783
MAC filtering, 779–780, 783
Mac OS–based systems, 211, 590, 650
mainboard. *See* motherboards
maintenance, 233–240. *See also* cleaning
    audio inspection, 234
    backups. *See* backups
    components, 236–239
    defragmenting hard drives, 239, 389, 507–508
    display devices, 237
    driver/firmware updates, 234
    input devices, 237–239
    laptop computers, 313–314
    networks, 688–690
    power devices, 234–236
    printers, 560–564
    security, 776–778
    storage devices, 238–239
    surge protectors, 235
    thermal sensitive devices, 239–240
    uninterruptible power supply, 689, 811
    visual inspection, 233–234
    Windows operating system, 507–513
malicious software, 704–707
    denial of service attacks, 706
    drive-by downloads, 705–706
    keystroke loggers, 706
    overview, 704
    password crackers, 704–705
    pop-ups, 705, 712, 773–775
    protecting against, 766–778
    removing malware, 775–776
    rootkits/back doors, 706–707
    symptoms of, 775
    Trojan horses, 705
    viruses. *See* viruses
    worms, 705
MAN (metropolitan area network), 580–581
mapped drive, 482
mass storage devices. *See* storage devices
master boot record (MBR), 168, 418, 426, 480
master drive, 156–159
master file table (MFT), 437
master/slave configuration, 156–159
material safety data sheet (MSDS), 815
math coprocessor, 21
MBR (master boot record), 168, 418, 426, 480
MCCs (memory controller chips), 16, 61, 202
MD command, 449
MDB extension, 442
Media Access Control. *See* MAC
media readers, 216
memory, 57–66. *See also* RAM
    address bus and, 21
    amount of, 139

bandwidth of, 61–62
cache, 8, 22–23, 59, 64, 139
considerations, 135
CPU, 21, 22–23
CRIMM, 140
DIMM, 7, 64, 65, 77, 140–141
flash, 51, 52–53, 167
installing, 139–141
laptop computers, 262–264
nonvolatile, 51
overview, 57–58
parity error checking, 146
performance and, 139
printers, 533–534, 545, 548, 556
problems with, 223, 481
removing, 139–141
RIMM, 7, 64, 140–141
ROM, 58–59, 64, 203, 334
settings, 146
SIMM, 7, 139–140
single-sided vs. double-sided, 66
SORIMM, 7, 140
virtual, 400–402
volatile, 58
vs. hard drive space, 57–58
vs. magnetic mass storage, 42
memory address, 203
memory address space, 334, 336, 342
memory banks, 64–65
memory card readers, 52, 269
memory cards, 52–53
memory controller chips (MCCs), 16, 62, 202
memory dumps, 485
memory error checking, 65
memory errors, 220, 223
memory limits, Windows, 334
memory modules
    bit width of, 64, 65
    CRIMM, 140
    DIMM, 7, 64, 65, 77, 140–141
    failure of, 223
    installing/removing, 139–141
    laptop, 262–264
    MicroDIMM, 262
    parity and, 65–66
    replacement of, 223
    RIMM, 7, 64, 140–141
    SIMM, 7, 139–140
    SORIMM, 7, 140
memory parity, 65–66
memory slots, 7
Memory Stick, 52
message balloon, 345, 395
metropolitan area network (MAN), 580–581
MFDs (multifunction devices), 532, 544
MFT (master file table), 437
MicroATX motherboard, 4–6
MicroBTX motherboard, 6
microcode, 20, 24–25
MicroDIMM modules, 272

microphones, 111, 172, 207
microprogram, 24–25
Microsoft Management Console
(MMC), 355
Microsoft Office, 395, 511
Microsoft Product Activation (MPA),
393–394
Microsoft Update site, 395
Microsoft Virtual PC, 340–341
Microsoft Windows. *See* Windows
MIDI (Musical Instrument Digital Interface), 68, 70, 110, 172
MIDI devices, 109, 110
MIDI ports, 110
mid-tower case, 29
migration, data, 374–376
MIMO (multiple input/multiple
output), 580
mini PCI standard, 273
miniconnectors, 87
mini-DIN connectors, 121–122, 170, 224
Mini-DVI connectors, 102
mini-expansion slots, 272–273
mini-tower case, 29
mirrored sets, 54–55
mirroring, 54–55
MMC (Microsoft Management
Console), 355
mobo. *See* motherboards
modem communication adapters, 69–70
modems
analog, 209, 627
laptop computers, 276
overview, 69–70
troubleshooting, 671–672
modes, 15
Molex connectors, 87–88, 151
monitors. *See* displays
MORE filter, 453
motherboards, 3–19
ATX, 4–6
battery, 148
BIOS settings, 16–17, 142–147
BTX, 6, 7
bus architecture, 8–9
chipsets, 16
CMOS, 17–19
components, 6–16
configuring, 142–147
CPU compatibility, 4
CPU voltage, 25
CPU/memory combinations, 135
drive interface standards, 11–16
drivers, 147
expansion bus types/slots, 9–11
external cache memory, 8
failures, 135–136, 202
firmware, 16–19
form factors, 4–6, 135
handling, 137–138
installing, 136–138
Intel, 4
laptop computers, 261

memory slots, 7
MicroATX, 6
NLX, 4
onboard components, 134–148
optimizing, 142–147
overview, 3
power supplies, 88–89
processor/CPU sockets, 8
removing, 137
replacing, 135–136
soft power and, 88–89, 810
troubleshooting, 135–136,
196–201, 202
mount points, 422–423
mounted volumes, 422–423
mouse
Bluetooth, 170, 274
cleaning, 224, 237–238
drag/drop actions, 447–449
drivers, 170, 224
installing/removing, 170–171
laptop computers, 274, 280, 283
troubleshooting, 206, 223–224
USB, 280
using, 108–109
MP3 extension, 442
MP4 extension, 442
MPA (Microsoft Product Activation),
393–394
MPEG extension, 442
MPG extension, 442
.msc extension, 355
MSCONFIG.EXE program, 498–499
MS-DOS prompt, 453
MSDS (material safety data sheet), 815
MSINFO32.EXE, 495
MTA (Multimedia Terminal
Adapter), 648
MUI (Multilingual User Interface), 380
multi-core CPUs, 23–24, 26
multifunction devices (MFDs), 532, 544
Multilingual User Interface (MUI), 380
multimedia adapter cards, 67–68
multimedia connectors, 119–120
multimedia input devices, 109–111,
172–173
multimedia PC, 67–68
Multimedia Terminal Adapter
(MTA), 648
multimeter, 229–230, 299
multi-monitor configuration, 95–96
multiple input/multiple output
(MIMO), 580
multitasking, 400
Music folder, 349
Musical Instrument Digital Interface. *See*
MIDI
My Computer folder, 349, 351, 352
My Computer shortcut, 351
My Documents folder, 349
My Music folder, 349
My Network Places folder, 349, 351
My Network Places shortcut, 351

My Network Places utility, 391
My Pictures folder, 349
My Recent Documents folder, 349
My Videos folder, 349

NAK messages, 592
naming conventions, 439, 759
NAT (network address translation),
731–733
NET command, 682–683
NetBEUI (NetBIOS Extended User Interface), 591, 592, 670
NetBIOS, 592, 597, 686–687
NetBIOS Extended User Interface
(NetBEUI), 591, 592, 670
NetID, 645
NETSTAT command, 681–682
network adapters, 69, 391, 602. *See also*
NIC (network interface card)
network address translation (NAT),
731–733
network addressing, 592–601
network broadcasts, 669–670
network client, 590
network configuration, 391–392
Network folder, 349, 351
network hardware, 602–608, 666, 670–675
network ID, 594, 598
network interface card. *See* NIC
Network Neighborhood, 686
network operating system (NOS),
589–590
network printers, 539–540, 547
network services, 682–683
Network shortcut, 351
network software, 588–602
network troubleshooting, 655–691
cable testing, 668–669, 673–674
command prompt utilities, 667–668
common problems, 669–688
connectivity problems, 672–688
DNS problems, 683–686
hardware issues, 666, 670–675
insufficient bandwidth, 669–671
IP configuration/connectivity,
675–683
IPCONFIG utility, 667–668,
675–677, 779, 783
modem problems, 209, 671–672
NET command, 682–683
NETSTAT command, 681–682
NICs, 209
NSLOOKUP command, 685–686
PING command, 677–679, 684
Remote Desktop, 501–504
status indicators, 666–667
tools for, 666–669
TRACERT utility, 679–681
WINS problems, 686–687

networks, 575–691. *See also* Internet
 bandwidth, 61–62, 587, 669–671
 basics, 575–612
 broadband connections, 582–587
 cable modem, 584, 609, 645
 cables/connections, 668–669,
  673–674, 690
 cellular, 609, 644
 checking connectivity, 391
 classful, 595
 client/server-based, 588–589
 configuring, 379, 382, 391–392
 connecting NIC to, 627–630
 controlling access to, 716–725
 dial-up connections, 276, 581, 644
 DSL, 583–584, 609, 645
 Ethernet, 577–578, 670–671
 geographic classifications, 577–587
 hubs. *See* hubs
 installation of, 377
 intranets, 581
 IPX/SPX, 591, 670
 ISDN, 582–583
 LAN. *See* LANs
 MAN, 580–581
 NetBEUI, 591
 network interface card. *See* NIC
 Novell, 591
 NWLink, 670
 overview, 602
 PAN, 274, 577
 patch panels, 690
 peer-to-peer, 588
 power management, 689
 preventive maintenance, 688–690
 protocol suites, 569–570, 591, 670
 roles, 588
 routers. *See* routers
 Safe Mode option, 471
 SOHO. *See* SOHO networks
 speed tests, 586–587
 switches, 606–607, 670
 TCP/IP, 590–592, 607, 782
 technologies, 577–587
 transmission medium, 603–606
 troubleshooting. *See* network
  troubleshooting
 upgrading hardware, 670–671
 VPN, 586, 645–646, 732
 WAN, 581–587, 644–646
 wireless. *See* wireless networks
New Low-Profile Extended (NLX)
 motherboard, 4
nibble mode, 537
NIC (network interface card). *See also*
 network adapters
 bus, 627, 632
 connecting to networks, 627–630
 Ethernet, 577–578, 627–630
 FireWire, 627
 installing, 626–627
 IP addresses of, 599–600
 overview, 602

 PC Card, 627
 physical addresses of, 599–600
 printer access, 539
 troubleshooting, 209, 673–675
 updating firmware, 631–633
 USB, 627, 631–632, 633
 wired, 627–630
 wireless, 630–635, 639–640,
  673–675
NLX (New Low-Profile Extended)
 motherboard, 4
nodes, 630, 634
noisy fan, 222
nonvolatile memory, 51, 58
Northbridge chips, 16
NOS (network operating system),
 589–590
notebook computers. *See* laptop computers
Notepad text editor, 433, 445
notification area, 345
Novell networks, 591
Novell servers, 590
NSLOOKUP command, 685–686
NTBACKUP utility, 387, 456, 481–482
NTBTLOG.TXT file, 473
NTDETECT.COM file, 428, 431, 487
"NTDETECT.COM is missing" error, 487
NTFS (NT File System). *See also* file
 systems
  access control, 727–729
  ACLs/ACEs, 727
  considerations, 373–374
  converting to from FAT32, 786
  encryption, 438, 726–727
  file attributes, 440–441
  file encryption, 759–761, 763
  folder encryption, 759–761
  overview, 437–438
  partitions, 381, 422, 438, 727
  permissions, 438, 727–729, 757–758
NTLDR file, 426–427, 428, 487
"NTLDR is missing" error, 487
NTORKRNL.EXE file, 428
"NTOSKRNL is invalid or missing" error,
 487–488
NTOSKRNL.EXE file, 427–428, 487–488
NTUSER.DAT file, 359
nvidia product, 96
NWLink protocol, 670

OCR (optical character recognition), 544
OEM (original equipment
 manufacturer), 331
OEM Windows, 331, 377–378
Office. *See* Microsoft Office
offline files/folders, 445
Ohms Law, 85
Online Help utilities, 494
online power protection device. *See* UPS

Opera browser, 649
operating environment, 189–190, 234,
 804–814
operating system (OS). *See also* Windows
 operating system
  32-bit vs. 64-bit, 333–335, 373
  alternate startup options, 225
  compatibility issues, 336–339
  differences between, 329–333
  file systems. *See* file systems
  fundamental principles of, 327–360
  Linux-based, 257, 590
  Mac OS–based, 211, 590, 650
  patches, 197, 332, 777
  purpose of, 329
  revision levels, 335
  service packs, 332–333, 777
  system requirements, 335–336,
   386–387
operational procedures, 803–832
  computing waste disposal, 814–818
  moving equipment, 805–806
  repair tools, 805
  workplace safety, 804–814
Opteron CPU model, 26
optical character recognition (OCR), 544
optical drives, 46–51
  BIOS settings, 160
  as boot media, 376
  drive letters, 423–424
  drivers, 160, 214
  installing, 159–160, 265
  maintenance of, 239
  master/slave configuration, 158
  overview, 46–47
  removing, 159–160
  troubleshooting, 214
optical media, 239
optimization
  defragmenting hard drives, 507–508
  motherboards, 142–147
  with RAM, 139
original equipment manufacturer. *See*
 OEM
OS. *See* operating system
overclocking, 24
overheating, 24, 202, 222, 314

P1 connector, 88
P4 connector, 88
packet filtering, 730
Packet Internet Groper. *See* PING
packets, 591, 594, 597
PAGEFILE.SYS file, 401, 429
paging file, 401
PAN (personal area network), 274, 577
paper, printer, 536, 549, 551–552,
 556–557
paper jams, 562, 563

paper-feed problems, 550–552
Parallel AT Attachment. *See* PATA
parallel interface, 113–114
parallel port settings, 144
parallel ports, 113–114, 144, 205–206,
    537–538
parity, 65–66
parity error checking, 146
partitioning hard disks, 168–169, 373,
    419–424
partitions
    active, 421
    basic disks, 419–424
    boot, 761–762
    creating, 168–169, 381
    drive letters, 373, 420, 423
    extended, 420–421
    factory recovery, 378
    FAT, 381
    FAT32, 436, 437
    mounted volumes, 422–423
    NTFS, 381, 422, 438, 727
    overview, 168–169, 373
    primary, 420
    root, 759
    size limits, 421–422
    strategies for, 423–424
    system, 761–762
    viewing, 381
parts grabber, 227
passive matrix displays, 97
passphrase, 781, 783
password crackers, 704–705
password recovery software, 787
password-based access control, 717
passwords, 719–721. *See also*
    authentication
    administrator, 379, 779, 785
    best practices, 719–721
    BIOS, 717, 751, 783–784
    clear password jumper, 146
    forgotten (lost), 785
    guidelines for, 719–721
    locked computer and, 724–725
    logon, 429
    one-time, 722
    overview, 719
    Remote Desktop, 503
    reusing, 720
    supervisor, 146
    user, 146
PATA channels, 156–158, 210
PATA drives, 156–158, 212
PATA interface, 212
PATA (Parallel AT Attachment) inter-
    face, 12, 13–14, 156, 160, 212
patch cables, 690
patch panels, 690
patch Tuesday, 332
patches, 197, 332, 777
PBX (Private Branch Exchange), 648
PC Card, 270–272
PC Card NICs, 627

P-cables, 166
PCI (peripheral component interconnect)
    bus, 9–11, 172
PCIe (peripheral component interconnect
    express) bus, 9–11, 172
PCIe Mini Card, 273
PCMCIA (Personal Computer Memory
    Card International Association), 269,
    270, 272
PCs (personal computers)
    case for. *See* case
    cleaning. *See* cleaning
    client computers, 581, 598, 609
    controlling access to, 716–725
    disposal of, 729, 735, 814–817
    dual-boot, 426–427
    laptop. *See* laptop computers
    Lock Computer option, 724–725
    locking, 347, 754
    maintaining. *See* maintenance
    multimedia, 67–68
    operating environment for,
        189–190, 234
    photo of typical PC, 3
    powering down, 805
    recycling programs, 187, 814
    remote assistance for, 504–506
    remote connections to, 501–504
    restarting. *See* restarting computer
    stand-alone, 576
    starting. *See* Windows startup
    tablet PCs, 267, 305, 310, 311
    theft of, 703
    waking over LAN, 391–392
PDAs (personal digital assistants), 99,
    258, 577
PDF files, 650
peer-to-peer networks, 588
Pentium processors, 25
performance
    CPU and, 138
    memory and, 139
    monitoring, 499–500
    solid-state drives, 213
peripheral component interconnect
    (PCI) bus, 9–11
peripheral component interconnect
    express (PCIe) bus, 9–11
peripherals, 265–269, 274, 275. *See also*
    components; devices
permanent virtual circuit. *See* PVC
permissions
    administrators, 767
    default, 756, 757
    device drivers, 398
    FAT32, 785–786
    file systems, 438
    files, 438, 727, 754–758, 785–786
    folders, 438, 727–729, 754–758,
        785–786
    groups, 756–758
    inheritance, 735
    NTFS, 438, 727–729, 757–758

    shares, 754–758
    users, 767
personal area network (PAN), 274, 577
Personal Computer Memory Card
    International Association (PCMCIA),
    269, 270, 272
personal computers. *See* PCs
personal digital assistants (PDAs), 99,
    258, 577
personal folders, 349
PGA (pin grid array), 8
PGA processor, 138–139
phishing, 712–714, 772–773
Phishing Filter, 772–773
phone phishing, 714
phones, 99, 577, 647
physical addressing, 592–593, 599–600
PicoBTX motherboard, 6
Pictures folder, 349
PID (Process ID), 498
pin grid array. *See* PGA
Pin To Start Menu option, 347
PING command, 667, 677–679, 684
pinging DNS names, 684
pinging IP addresses, 677–679
pinned items list, 347
pin-outs, 149
pits, 47
pixels, 97, 98, 306–307
pixilation problems, 306–307
plain-old telephone service (POTS), 611
planar board. *See* motherboards
Plenum cables, 603
plug and play BIOS, 147
plug and play capability, 71, 116
plug and play detection, 430
plug and play devices, 397–400, 430, 540
pointer, problems with, 223–224
pointing devices, 108–109, 280
pointing stick, 280
Point-to-Point Protocol (PPP), 732
Point-to-Point Tunneling Protocol
    (PPTP), 732
POP (Post Office Protocol), 609
pop-up blocker, 773–775
pop-up downloads, 705, 773–775
pop-ups, fraudulent, 712
port replicators, 268
port triggering, 731
portable computers
    handhelds, 258
    introduction, 256–258
    laptops. *See* laptop computers
ports. *See also* connectors; *specific ports*
    COM, 144, 204–205
    common, 601–602
    IEEE-1394, 153
    I/O, 203–209
    MIDI, 110
    parallel, 113–114, 144, 205–206,
        537–538
    problems with, 203–209
    RS-232, 112–113

ports (*cont.*)
  serial, 144, 204–205, 538
  TCP/IP services, 601–602
  USB, 115–118, 153
  vs. connectors, 112
POST cards, 199, 232
POST (power-on self-test) errors,
  198–199, 304, 305
Post Office Protocol (POP), 609
POST (power-on self-test) process, 18,
  232, 425
POTS (plain-old telephone service), 611
power cords, 298, 301, 805
power devices
  laptop computers, 276–278
  maintenance of, 234–236
  UPS (uninterruptible power supply),
    235–236, 689, 811
power management/issues. *See also*
  electrical entries
  considerations, 234–235
  described, 282
  electrical dangers, 2, 149, 806–807
  generators, 236
  hardware power switch, 298–299
  inverters, 811
  laptops, 281–285, 297–303
  networks, 689
  Power Options applet, 283, 284, 299,
    403, 508–509
  power outages, 235–236
  power-down guidelines, 805
  settings, 402–403, 508–509
  soft power, 88–89, 810
  stand by vs. hibernate,
    283–284, 285
  voltage, 25, 85–86, 297–298
power mode setting, 218
Power Options applet, 283, 284, 299, 403,
  508–509
power outages, 235–236
Power Saver plan, 509
power splitter cable, 87
power states, 282
power supplies, 84–89
  AC adapters, 87
  ATX, 87, 88–89, 149
  energy efficiency, 88, 89, 98
  fans, 87, 90, 221
  form factors, 87–89
  installing, 149–150
  precautions, 149, 220, 810–811
  proprietary, 89
  protecting, 689
  removing, 149–150
  replacing, 149–150
  safety considerations, 2, 220,
    810–811
  selecting, 149
  testing, 230
  troubleshooting, 220–221
  upgrading, 149–150

  voltage, 85–86
  wattage, 86–87
power supply tester, 230
power supply unit (PSU), 84
power-on self-test. *See* POST
power-saving modes, 282–284
PPP (Point-to-Point Protocol), 732
PPT extension, 442
PPTP (Point-to-Point Tunneling
  Protocol), 732
Preboot Execution Environment
  (PXE), 600
preferences, 508–509
presentation files, 442
preventive maintenance. *See* maintenance
PRINT$ share, 759
print spooler, 545–546, 559–560
printer language, 534
printer properties, 544–546
printers, 525–564
  all-in-one, 532, 544
  basics, 526–540
  blank pages, 552–553
  cleaning, 237, 561–563
  color issues, 555
  compatibility testing, 543
  components, 533–536
  configuring, 544–547
  consumables, 534–536, 563–564
  default, 542, 558–559
  deleting, 549, 561
  dot matrix, 527, 533, 552, 554, 555
  drivers, 534, 540–542, 548,
    555–559
  dye-sublimation, 531
  environmental considerations, 563
  error messages, 556–559
  FireWire interface, 539
  firmware, 534, 548
  impact, 526–527
  ink for, 535, 559
  inkjet, 530–535, 552, 554, 559, 562
  installing, 540–544
  interfaces, 537–540
  Internet Printing Client, 543
  IP printing support, 543, 547
  laser, 528–530, 548, 551–555,
    561–562
  memory, 533–534, 545, 548, 556
  multifunction, 532, 544
  network, 539–540, 547
  non–plug and play, 541–543
  optimizing performance, 548–549
  page counts, 561
  paper for, 536, 549, 551–552,
    556–557
  paper jams, 550–552, 562, 563
  paper out, 556–557
  paper-feed problems, 550–552
  paper-feed technologies, 533
  parallel interface, 537–538
  preventive maintenance, 560–564

  print quality, 552–556
  print spooler problems, 559–560
  resolution, 527, 530, 545
  restarting print service, 559–560
  safety precautions, 812–813
  serial interface, 538
  shared, 759
  solid ink, 531
  system board, 533–534
  thermal, 532
  thermal wax, 532
  toner. *See* toner cartridges
  trays, 548, 549, 550–551, 556–557
  troubleshooting, 550–560
  types of, 526–533
  upgrades, 548
  USB, 208, 539
  wireless, 539
Printing Preferences, 546
privacy invasion, 710
privacy policy, 830
Private Branch Exchange (PBX), 648
problems. *See* troubleshooting
Process ID (PID), 498
process priority level, 498
processes, 497–498
processor. *See* CPU
processor/CPU sockets, 8
product ID, 379
product key, 334, 380–381, 390, 393
professionalism, 828–832
Program Compatibility Wizard,
  340, 486, 493
program files, 397
Program Files folder, 397
"Program referenced in registry not found"
  message, 490
ProgramData folder, 444
programmable ROM (PROM), 59
programs. *See* applications
Programs And Features utility, 387
Programs menu item, 348
projectors, 99
PROM (programmable ROM), 59
protocol suites, 569–570, 591, 670
protocols, 590–592. *See also specific*
  protocols
proxy server, 611–612, 652–653, 731
proxy settings, 652–653
PS/2 connectors, 121–122, 170, 206
PSTN (public-switched telephone
  network), 611
PSU (power supply unit), 84
public-switched telephone network
  (PSTN), 611
PVC (permanent virtual circuit),
  585–586
PVC cables, 603
PXE (Preboot Execution
  Environment), 600

Q-cables, 166
QUERTY keyboard, 108, 109
Quick Launch bar, 345
Quick Search, 350–351

radio frequency (RF), 170
radio frequency interference (RFI), 674
RAID 5 drive arrays, 66
RAID arrays, 54–56, 162–163, 212–213
RAID controllers, 54, 55–56, 163, 213
RAID sets, 18
RAM (random access memory), 58–64.
    See also memory; ROM
        address space, 334
        installing, 139–141
        memory addresses and, 203
        memory limits, 334
        overview, 58–59
        physical location, 203
        printer, 534
        settings, 146
        system minimums, 335, 336
        testing, 481
        video adapters and, 217
        vs. cache memory, 22
Rambus Dynamic RAM (RDRAM), 7,
    60, 64
Rambus Inline Memory (RIMM), 7, 64,
    140–141
random access memory. See RAM
RAW data type, 546
RD command, 449
RDP (Remote Desktop Protocol),
    501–504
RDRAM (Rambus Dynamic RAM), 7,
    60, 64
RDRAM RIMMs, 7, 60, 64
reactivation, 394
Readiness Analyzer, 337
read-only attribute, 440
read-only memory. See ROM
real-time clock (RTC), 146
Reboot mode, 475
reboot problems, 221
Recent Items folder, 349
Recently Used Programs list, 348
Recovery Agents, 760–761
recovery CD/DVD, 377–378
Recovery Console, 479–480
recovery options, 479–483. See also
    backups
Recycle Bin, 346, 763, 764
recycling programs, 814, 817
redundant array of independent disks. See
    RAID

refresh rate, 104–105, 218–219
REGEDIT command, 357
Regional Internet Registries (RIRs), 595
regional options, 380
registered jack. See RJ
registers, 22
registration, 393–394
registry, 357–359
Registry Editor, 357–358
registry files, 359
registry keys, 357–358, 766
Remote Assistance, 504–506
Remote Desktop, 501–504
Remote Desktop Protocol (RDP),
    501–504
removable storage, 56
repair tools, 805
repeaters, 606. See also signal boosters
resolution
    display, 94–95, 97, 98, 106, 219
    printer, 527, 530, 545
    video, 473
resolvers, 597
response time, 105
Restart option, 346, 347
restarting computer
    auto-restart errors, 474–475
    as solution for problems, 194, 196,
        469, 485
restore operations
    Directory Services Restore
        mode, 474
    System Restore utility, 399, 476–478,
        481, 512–513
    test restores of backups, 512
restore points, 399, 476–478, 481
Return to OS Choices Menu mode,
    475–476
RF (radio frequency), 170
RFI (radio frequency interference), 674
RIMM (Rambus Inline Memory), 7, 64,
    140–141
RIRs (Regional Internet Registries), 595
riser cards, 4, 70–72
RJ (registered jack) connector, 120–121
RJ-11 connectors, 120, 604, 647
RJ-45 connectors, 120–121, 604
Roll Back Driver option, 472
ROM (read-only memory), 58–59, 64,
    203, 334. See also memory; RAM
ROM BIOS, 59, 548, 590
root directory, 435
root folder, 397, 442–445, 447
root keys, 358
root partitions, 759
rootkits, 706–707
routers
    broadband, 627–628, 645, 731,
        778–780
    displaying address of, 680
    as firewalls, 768
    IP addresses, 607

network address translation,
    731–732
network problems and, 677–680, 684
overview, 607
wireless, 547, 579, 634, 637,
    778–780
RS-232 port, 112–113, 204, 538
RTC (real-time clock), 146
Run As Administrator option, 354
Run line, 350, 351, 355, 357
run line utilities, 343, 350, 506

Safe Mode option, 470–473, 476, 477,
    776, 786
Safe Mode With Command Prompt
    option, 472–473
Safe Mode With Networking option, 471
Safely Remove Hardware icon, 168, 216,
    217, 268
safety precautions
    antistatic bags, 137, 139, 155, 263
    antistatic mat, 228, 808–809
    antistatic spray, 237, 809
    antistatic wrist strap, 136, 149, 228,
        229, 808, 811
    batteries, 815
    cable protection, 804–805
    chemical solvents, 816–817
    compressed air, 236–237, 814
    computing waste disposal, 814–818
    CPU, 138–139
    displays, 805, 812–813, 816
    electrical dangers, 2, 149, 806–807
    electrical shock, 806–807
    electromagnetic interference,
        674, 810
    electrostatic discharge, 2, 807–810
    equipment handling, 804–814
    ESD, 2, 152, 236, 807–809
    grounding mat, 136, 228
    hot components, 806
    inverters, 811
    laptop computers, 259
    material safety data sheet, 815
    opening computer case, 136
    power supplies, 2, 220, 810–811
    printers, 812–813
    repair tools, 805
SAM (Security Accounts Manager)
    file, 359
SAS (secure attention sequence), 752
SAS (Serial Attached SCSI) systems,
    115, 166
SATA cables, 161–162
SATA channels, 161–162, 210
SATA connectors, 14, 115
SATA devices/drives, 14–15, 115, 156,
    161–162

SATA drives, 211
SATA interface, 211
SATA (Serial ATA) standard, 12, 14–15
satellite communications systems, 585
satellite connections, 645
Scalable Link Interface (SLI), 96
scanner software, 544
scanner-printer-fax-copier devices, 532
scanners, 171, 208, 544
screen. *See* display
screensaver, 218
screwdriver, 227–228
scripted installation, 383–384
SCSI cabling, 166
SCSI chain, 114, 164–165, 166, 216
SCSI controllers, 114, 164, 165, 210
SCSI devices, 164–166
    addressing, 165
    configuring, 164–166
    drivers, 165
    external, 166
    installing, 164
    overview, 114–115, 164
    termination, 164–165, 166, 216
    troubleshooting, 216
    types of, 164
SCSI drives, 164–166
SCSI host adapter, 114–115, 164
SCSI ID, 164–165, 216
SCSI standards, 164
SCSI (Small Computer System Interface)
    systems, 114–115, 164–166
SCSI tape drives, 215
SD (Secure Digital) card, 53
SDHC (Secure Digital High Capacity)
    cards, 265
SDLT (Super DLT) technology, 46
SDRAM (Synchronous Dynamic RAM),
    60–64
SDRAM DIMMs, 64
SDSL (symmetric DSL), 584
Search box, 344, 351
Search toolbar button, 344
search tools, 344, 350–351
searches, files, 450
secret key, 726. *See also* passwords
sector translation, 15
secure attention sequence (SAS), 752
Secure Digital (SD) card, 53
Secure Digital High Capacity (SDHC)
    cards, 265
Secure Sockets Layer (SSL), 610
security, 701–789. *See also* authentication
    access control, 716–725
    accidents/mistakes, 703–704
    administrator and, 723,
        727–728, 733
    adware, 707, 773–775
    applications, 767–768
    authorization, 273, 716, 718,
        722, 727
    back door programs, 707, 708–709

backups and, 777
biometric devices, 111, 171
BIOS, 717
Bluesnarfing, 709–710
built-in security principals, 723
cable protection, 690, 804–805
command prompts, 354
computer access, 716–725
computer hardware theft, 703
cookies, 710–711
CTRL-ALT-DELETE key
    combination, 724
data. *See* data security
data wiping, 729, 763–766
dialers, 708
disasters, 703–704
drive-by downloads, 705–706
encryption. *See* encryption
equipment disposal, 729, 735,
    814–817
file system access, 727–729
firewalls. *See* firewalls
fraud, 703
gaining access, 708–710
grayware, 707–708
hoaxes, 714–715
identity theft, 703
inappropriate/distasteful
    content, 710
infected e-mail attachments, 715
Internet transactions, 610
intrusion detection, 717
keystroke loggers, 706
laptop computers, 735
Lock Computer option, 724–725
malicious software attacks. *See*
    malicious software
missing Security tab, 785–786
network access, 716–725
network devices, 689–690
notification of changes to computer,
    767–768
overview, 702
passwords. *See* passwords
phishing, 712–714, 772–773
physical, 716–717
pop-ups, 705, 712, 773–775
prank (joke) programs, 708
preventive maintenance, 776–778
privacy invasion, 710
protecting data, 725–730
protection from threats, 715–735
recovery from attacks, 735
secret key, 730
servers, 689–690
social engineering, 712–715, 778
spam, 707–708
special groups, 723
Spim (Spam over Instant
    Messaging), 708
spyware, 707, 773–775
threats to, 702–715

Trojan horses, 705
troubleshooting, 783–788
Trusted Platform Module, 717
User Account Control, 349–350,
    510–511, 766–768
user accounts, 766–768
viruses. *See* viruses
war driving, 709
Windows File Protection,
    500–501, 766
wireless networks, 726–727,
    778–783
worms, 705
Security dialog box, 724
security events, 491–492
SECURITY file, 359
security identifier (SID), 787
security log, 491–492
security policies, 715–716
Security tab, 785–786
Serial ATA. *See* SATA
Serial Attached SCSI (SAS) systems,
    115, 166
serial interfaces, 112–113
serial ports, 144, 204–205, 538
servers
    client-server networks, 588–589
    DHCP. *See* DHCP servers
    distribution, 384
    DNS, 597, 598, 643, 645, 684–686
    fax, 759
    housing, 689–690
    Novell, 590
    proxy, 611–612, 652–653, 731
    WINS Server, 597, 598, 643,
        686–687
"Service has failed to start"
    message, 489
service packs, 332–333, 777
service patches, 197, 332, 777
service set ID (SSID), 633, 779, 783
SERVICES.EXE file, 429
Settings menu, 352
Settings shortcut, 352
SFC (System File Checker), 500–501
SGRAM (synchronous graphics
    RAM), 63
shadow mask, 106
shares. *See also* folders
    administrative, 758–759
    permissions, 754–758
shielded twisted pair (STP), 603
shortcuts, 344–354
shredder programs, 764–765
Shut Down option, 346, 347
SID (security identifier), 787
sidebar, 355
signal boosters, 606, 635–636, 671
SIMM (Single Inline Memory Module),
    7, 139–140
Simple Mail Transfer Protocol
    (SMTP), 609

simultaneous multithreading (SMT), 23
Single Inline Memory Module (SIMM), 7, 139–140
single-layer (SL) format, 48
site survey, 630
Skype, 611, 648, 649
SL (single-layer) format, 48
slave drive, 156–159
sleep mode, 284, 299
Sleep option, 347
SLI (Scalable Link Interface), 96
slot covers, 91, 222
Small Computer System Interface. *See* SCSI
small office/home office. *See* SOHO
Small Outline DIMM (SODIMM) modules, 7, 62, 262–264
Small Outline RIMM (SORIMM) modules, 7, 140
smart card logons, 721, 752
smart card readers, 752
smart cards, 721, 752
smart phones, 99, 258, 647
SmartMedia, 52
SMB IP PBX, 648
SMM (System Management Mode), 282
SMS (Systems Management Server), 384
SMT (simultaneous multithreading), 23
SMTP (Simple Mail Transfer Protocol), 609
snap-ins. *See* MMC
social engineering, 712–715, 778
socket services, 269–270
sockets, 7, 8, 112. *See also* connectors
Socks protocol, 653
SODIMM (Small Outline DIMM) modules, 7, 62, 262–264
soft power, 88–89, 810
software. *See also* applications
    compatibility issues, 196, 337, 373, 386
    malicious. *See* malicious software
    network, 588–602
    reinstalling, 196
    requirements, 196, 386
    troubleshooting, 191–192, 196–197, 230–231
    updates to. *See* updates
SOFTWARE file, 359
software firewalls, 734, 768–772, 787–788
software troubleshooting tools, 225–227, 230–231
SOHO (small office/home office) network, 625–654
    cellular connections, 644
    connecting wired NICs, 627–630
    creating Wi-Fi networks, 630–640
    dial-up connections, 644
    installing NICs, 626–627
    IP configuration, 640–643
    WAN connections, 644–646

solid-state drives (SSDs)
    considerations, 51–52
    in laptops, 265
    overview, 51, 160–161
    problems with, 213–214
solid-state storage, 51–53, 160–161
SONET, 580
Sony/Philips Digital Interface (S/PDIF) format, 119, 120
SORIMM (Small Outline RIMM) modules, 7, 140
sound. *See also audio entries*
    beep sounds, 198–199, 217, 218
    checking, 234
    headphones, 110
    microphones, 111, 172, 207
    speakers, 110, 206, 281, 309–310
sound cards, 68, 110, 206–207
sound connectors, 206–207
sound output, 110, 206
Southbridge chips, 16
spam, 707–708
Spam over Instant Messaging (Spim), 708
S/PDIF (Sony/Philips Digital Interface) format, 119, 120
speakers, 110, 206, 281, 309–310
special groups, 723
spim (Spam over Instant Messaging), 708
spindle, 44
spreadsheet files, 442
spyware, 707, 773–775
SRAM (Static RAM), 22, 59
SSDs. *See* solid-state drives (SSDs)
SSID (service set ID), 633, 779, 783
SSL (Secure Sockets Layer), 610
Stand By mode, 284, 285
stand-alone computer, 576
standards, 569–570. *See also specific standards*
Standby option, 346
Start Bar, 345
Start button, 345, 346
Start menu, 346–347
Start Search box, 350–351
Start Windows Normally mode, 475
Startup And Recovery settings, 432, 474, 484–485
startup disks, 144–145, 225, 230
startup modes, 469–478
startup process. *See* Windows startup
Startup Repair tool, 481
startup/source locations, 376–378
static addresses, 598
static electricity. *See* ESD
Static RAM (SRAM), 22, 59
status box, 345
status icons, 345
status light indicators, 198
storage controllers, 213
storage devices, 42–57. *See also* drives
    backup media, 56–57
    considerations, 155

external, 156, 166, 167–168, 216
floppy drives. *See* floppy disk drives
hard disks. *See* hard disk drives
hot-swappable drives, 54, 156
identifying, 53
internal, 156–159, 166–167
laptop computers, 265
magnetic mass storage, 42–46
maintenance of, 238–239
optical drives. *See* optical drives
overview, 42–43
on PATA channels, 156–158
RAID arrays. *See* RAID entries
removable storage, 56
removing, 166–168
replacing, 155–169
on SATA channels, 161–162
selecting, 156
solid-state storage, 51–53, 160–161
tape drives, 46, 215
upgrading, 155–169
STP (shielded twisted pair), 603
striped sets, 54–55
stylus pen, 267, 311
subkey, 357–358
subnet mask, 594–595, 598
subscription support, 495
subtrees, 358–359
Super DLT (SDLT) technology, 46
super video graphics array (SVGA) standard, 93, 95
Super XGA Plus (SXGA+) standard, 95
Super XGA (SXGA) standard, 95
supervisor passwords, 146
surge protectors, 235, 811
SVGA (super video graphics array) standard, 93, 95
S-video (Super-Video), 103–104
swap file, 401
swapping, 401
Switch User option, 347
switches
    BOOT.INI, 431
    DIP, 142
    Ethernet, 607, 627–628, 634, 673
    hardware power, 298–299
    KVM, 111–112, 171–172
    motherboard, 142, 199–200
    network, 606–607, 670
switching mode power supply, 85
SXGA (Super XGA) standard, 95
SXGA+ (Super XGA Plus) standard, 95
symmetric DSL (SDSL), 584
Synchronous Dynamic RAM (SDRAM), 60–64
synchronous graphics RAM (SGRAM), 63
system area, 435
system attribute, 440
system board. *See* motherboards
system busses. *See* busses

system clock problems, 200, 201
System Configuration Utility (MSCON-FIG.EXE), 498–499
system events, 490–491
SYSTEM file, 359
System File Checker (SFC), 500–501
system files, 442–443, 444, 481
System group, 723
system information, 495
system instability, 398–399
system limits, 336
system log, 485, 490–493
System Management Mode (SMM), 282
System Monitor, 500
system partition, 761–762
System Recovery Options menu, 481
system requirements, 335–336, 337, 386–387
system resources, 203
System Restore utility, 399, 476–478, 481, 512–513
system ROM, 58, 64
system root folder, 759
system tray, 345
System32 folder, 444
SYSTEMROOT command, 480
systemroot folder, 473
Systems Management Server (SMS), 384
systray, 345
SysWOW64 folder, 444

tablet PCs, 267, 305, 310, 311
tape backup system, 46, 456
tape drives, 46, 215
Task Manager, 356–357, 496–498, 754
Task Scheduler, 498
taskbar, 345–346
T-carrier system, 584–585
TCP (Transmission Control Protocol), 591–592
TCP/IP networks, 590–592, 607, 782
TCP/IP services, 601–602
Temp folder, 444, 445
temperature, 234, 240, 304, 306, 313. *See also* overheating
Temporal Key Integrity Protocol (TKIP), 727
terminals, 610–611
terminating resistors, 166
terms, glossary of, 851–908
test restores, 512
text editors, 445–446
text files, 442, 445–446
TFT (thin-film transistor) technology, 97
thermal compounds, 90–91, 152, 222
thermal paste, 90–91
thermal printers, 532
thermal sensitive devices, 239–240

thermal throttling, 202
thermal wax printers, 532
thin-film transistor (TFT) technology, 97
thread of execution, 23
Threat Encyclopedia, 766
throttling, 202
thumb drives, 52, 160, 167, 168, 213–214
TIF extension, 442
time to live (TTL), 679–680
time/date settings, 146, 200, 201, 380
TKIP (Temporal Key Integrity Protocol), 727
toner cartridges. *See also* laser printers
    disposal of, 815–816
    low toner message, 559
    overview, 536
    shelf life, 534, 536
touch screen display, 99, 174–175, 267
touchpads, 280, 308, 312
tower cases, 29
TPM (Trusted Platform Module), 717, 752, 762–763
TPM DriveLock, 717, 751–752
TRACERT utility, 679–681
traces, 3
trackball, 109, 223–224, 237, 280. *See also* input devices
TrackPoint, 280
training materials, 495
training users, 195, 495, 778
Transmission Control Protocol (TCP), 591–592
triple-core CPUs, 24
Trojan horses, 705
troubleshooting, 188–233. *See also* error messages; errors
    AC adapters, 297–298, 300–303
    adapter cards, 200, 215, 217–219, 224–225
    Advanced Options menu, 469–478
    applications, 196–197, 486–487
    Automated System Recovery, 481–482
    battery problems, 299
    beep sounds, 198–199, 217, 218
    Belarc Advisor, 226
    cables/connectors, 190, 206–207
    CMOS problems, 200–201
    compatibility issues, 196
    component problems, 190, 197–225
    considerations, 188
    cooling systems, 222
    CPU problems, 202–203
    damaged wiring, 305
    determining actual cause, 192–193
    with Device Manager, 192, 193
    diagnostic tests/procedures, 189–191, 227
    diagnostic toolkits, 230–232
    DirectX Diagnostic Tool, 506–507
    display problems, 217–220, 304–307, 309

documentation resources, 494–495
documenting activities/outcomes, 195
Emergency Repair Disk, 482–483
Emergency Repair Process, 482–483
establishing probable cause, 191–192
examining environment, 189–190
fan problems, 221, 222
FireWire devices, 209
flawed installations, 190
floppy drives/disks, 215
general procedures for, 189–195
hard drives, 209–213, 227
hardware problems, 191–192, 197–225, 231–232
hardware tools, 227–233
hardware vs. software problems, 191–192
implementing preventative measures, 194
input devices, 223–224, 307–311
Internet Explorer, 651
I/O ports/cards, 203–209
keyboard, 206
laptop computers, 295–325
memory problems, 223, 481
motherboards, 135–136, 196–201, 202
mouse problems, 206, 223–224
MSCONFIG.EXE program, 498–499
networks. *See* network troubleshooting
no operating system, 211
noisy fan, 222
optical drives, 214
OS failures, 469–483
overclocking, 24
overheating, 24, 202, 222, 314
physical symptoms, 198
pointer problems, 223–224
ports, 203–209
POST errors, 198–199, 304, 305
power problems, laptops, 297–303
power supplies, 219–220
preliminary steps, 188–189
printer problems, 550–560
problem identification, 189–191
questioning users about problems, 190–191
RAID arrays, 212–213
reboot problems, 221
Recovery Console, 479–480
Remote Assistance, 504–506
restarting computer as solution, 194, 196, 469, 485
Safe Mode option, 470–473, 476, 477
SCSI devices, 216
security, 783–788
software problems, 191–192, 196–197, 230–231

software tools, 225–227, 230–231
startup problems, 202, 210–211, 217–218, 221
system clock problems, 200, 201
System File Checker, 500–501
system instability, 398–399
system resources, 203
System Restore utility, 399, 476–478, 481, 512–513
tape drives, 215
Task Manager, 356–357, 496–498, 754
techniques for, 188–195
theory, 187–195
training users and, 195
updates and, 197, 397
USB devices, 153, 207–209
vendor documentation and, 191
verifying system functionality, 194
video system, 217–220
visual inspection, 190, 198
Windows File Protection, 500–501
WINS problems, 686–687
wireless problems, 311–312, 788
trust, building, 820–821
Trusted Platform Module. See TPM
TTL (time to live), 679–680
Turn Off Computer option, 346
Turn Off option, 346, 347
Turn Windows Features On Or Off task, 388
TV input, 172–173
TV tuner cards, 68, 70, 219–220
TWAIN drivers, 544
twisted-pair cables, 122, 603–604
TXT extension, 442, 445

UAC (User Account Control), 349–350, 510–511, 766–768
UART (universal asynchronous receiver/transmitter) chip, 112
UDF (Universal Data Format), 438
UDFs (Uniqueness Database Files), 383
UDMA (Ultra DMA), 15
UDP (Universal Datagram Protocol), 601
Ultra DMA (UDMA), 15
Ultra XGA (UXGA) standard, 95
unidirectional mode, 144
uninterruptible power supply (UPS), 235–236, 689, 811
Uniqueness Database Files (UDFs), 383
United States Computer Emergency Readiness Team (US-CERT), 766
universal asynchronous receiver/transmitter (UART) chip, 112
Universal Data Format (UDF), 438
Universal Datagram Protocol (UDP), 601
Universal Serial Bus. See USB
Unpin From Start Menu option, 347

unshielded twisted pair (UTP), 603
UPC codes. See bar codes
updates
    automatic, 395–396, 511, 777
    BIOS firmware, 201
    computer shutdown and, 347
    driver, 234
    firmware, 234
    problems with, 197, 397
    software, 196, 511
    Windows operating system, 332, 395–397
Upgrade Advisor, 337–339, 373, 386
upgrade paths, 341–343
upgrades. See also installations
    adapter cards, 153–155
    advantages of, 341
    BIOS, 147–148, 227, 337
    considerations, 386–387
    cooling systems, 150–153
    CPU, 138–139
    laptops, 258–281
    network hardware, 670–671
    power supplies, 149–150
    preliminary tasks, 386–387
    printers, 548
    reasons for, 385–386
    safety precautions. See safety precautions
    storage devices, 155–169
    Windows 7 upgrade path, 342
    Windows operating system, 385–390
    Windows Vista upgrade path, 341
UPS (uninterruptible power supply), 235–236, 689, 811
USB 2.0 standard, 116
USB adapter card, 153
USB cables, 216
USB connectors, 115–118, 224
"USB device is unknown" error, 208
USB devices
    booting from, 144–145, 377, 488–489
    drivers, 170, 207–209
    overview, 116–117
    troubleshooting, 153, 207–209
USB drives, 52, 167–168, 437, 763
USB flash drive, 52, 437
USB floppy drive, 43
USB hubs, 116–117, 153, 207–209
USB (Universal Serial Bus) interface, 115–118
USB keyboards, 207–208, 280
USB loopback plug, 204, 207, 231–232
USB mouse, 280
USB NICs, 627, 631–632, 633
USB ports, 115–118, 153
USB printers, 208, 539
USB scanners/printers, 208
USB3 standard, 116
US-CERT (United States Computer Emergency Readiness Team), 766

User Account Control (UAC), 349–350, 510–511, 766–768
user accounts. See also users
    authentication, 722–723
    local, 722–723
    passwords. See passwords
    permissions. See permissions
    security issues, 722–723
    User Account Control, 349–350, 510–511, 766–768
user data, 374–376
user interface, 343–355. See also GUI (graphical user interface)
user manuals, 494
User State Migration Tool (USMT), 376, 385
user-based access control, 722–723
users. See also customers; user accounts
    best practices, 719, 720
    local, 754–755
    names, 382, 383, 429, 732
    passwords. See passwords
    permissions. See permissions
    picture, 382, 383
    questioning about problems, 190–191
    security, 766–768
    training, 195, 495, 778
Users folder, 444
USMT (User State Migration Tool), 376, 385
utilities. See Windows utilities
utility software, 225–226
UTP (unshielded twisted pair), 603
UXGA (Ultra XGA) standard, 95

vacuuming computer/devices, 150, 236–237
value entries, 358
VC (virtual circuit), 585–586
VDSL (very high-data-rate DSL), 584
vendor documentation, 191
vertical hold (v-hold) setting, 104
vertical position setting, 104
vertical refresh rate, 104
very high-data-rate DSL (VDSL), 584
VESA (Video Electronics Standards Association), 98, 100
VFAT (virtual file allocation table) file system, 435
VGA (video graphics array), 93, 95, 473
video
    blank screen, 218
    component, 103–104
    composite, 103
    DisplayPort, 94, 103
    DVI, 93–94
    HDMI, 93–94, 102–103
    laptop computers, 304–307, 309

video (*cont.*)
   projectors, 99
   repeated screen elements, 219
   resolution, 473
   RGB, 103
   slow screen movement, 217
   S-video, 103–104
   troubleshooting, 217–220
video adapters, 92–96. *See also* adapter
  cards
   considerations, 173–174
   faulty, 217–219
   interfaces, 95
   laptop computers, 266, 307
   multiple, 96
   overview, 67, 92
   problems with, 217–219, 224–225
   replacing, 153
   SVGA, 95
   system minimums, 335, 336
   VGA, 93, 473
   video modes, 92–94, 473
video camera, 110
video capture cards, 172, 219–220
video cards. *See* video adapters
Video Electronics Standards Association
  (VESA), 98, 100
video files, 442
video graphics array (VGA), 93, 95, 473
video instructions, 22
video modes, 92–94, 473
Video RAM (VRAM), 63
Videos folder, 349
View settings, 440
virtual circuit (VC), 585–586
virtual file allocation table (VFAT) file
  system, 435
virtual memory, 400–402
Virtual PC, 340–341
virtual private networks (VPNs), 586,
  645–646, 732
Virtual XP Mode, 340
virus encyclopedia, 766
viruses
   adware, 707
   antivirus programs, 766, 772, 775
   boot sector, 144–145, 488–489, 776
   detecting/removing, 766, 772, 775
   overview, 704
   resources for, 766
   security update hoax, 714
   smart cards and, 752
   System Restore and, 478
   Trojan horse, 705
visual inspection, 190, 198, 233–234
Voice over IP (VoIP), 611, 647–649
VoIP (Voice over IP), 611, 647–649
voltage, 25, 85–86, 297–298
voltage regulator module (VRM), 25
volts, 85

volumes. *See* partitions
VPNs (virtual private networks), 586,
  645–646, 732
VRAM (Video RAM), 63
VRM (voltage regulator module), 25

Wake On LAN feature, 391–392
WANs (wide area networks)
   configuring, 644–646
   overview, 581–587
WAP. *See* wireless access point
war driving, 709
wattage (W), 86–87
watts, 85
Web browsers, 649–654. *See also* Internet
  Explorer
   add-ons, 650
   browser helper objects, 650
   configuring, 650–654
   cookies, 710–711
   Firefox web browser, 650, 651–652
   installing, 650–653
   overview, 649–650
   pop-ups, 705, 712, 773–775
Web camera (Webcam), 110, 172, 648
Webcam (Web camera), 110, 172, 648
WEP (Wired Equivalent Privacy),
  726, 781
WET (Windows Easy Transfer) utility,
  375–376
WFP (Windows File Protection),
  500–501, 766
wide area networks. *See* WANs
Wide Quad UXGA (WQUXGA), 95
Wide Quad XGA (WQXGA), 95
Wide UXGA (WUXGA) standard, 95
Wi-Fi Protected Access (WPA), 727
Wi-Fi Protected Access 2 (WPA2),
  727, 781
Wi-Fi technology, 275, 579–580. *See also*
  wireless networks
wildcards, 450
WiMax (Worldwide Interoperability for
  Microwave Access), 582
Windows 7 systems, 330, 335, 336, 342
Windows 2000 Professional, 335, 336
Windows 2000 systems, 329, 330
Windows Aero, 344–345
Windows Backup, 387, 456, 481–482
Windows Complete PC Restore tool, 481
Windows components. *See* components
Windows Components Wizard, 388
Windows Defender, 774, 775
Windows desktop. *See* desktop
Windows Device Manager. *See* Device
  Manager
Windows Domain, 382

Windows Easy Transfer (WET) utility,
  375–376
Windows editions, 329–331
Windows Explorer, 344
Windows File Protection (WFP),
  500–501, 766
Windows Firewall, 769–771, 775. *See also*
  firewalls
Windows folder, 442, 444
Windows GUI, 343–355. *See also* GUI
Windows Indexing Service, 509–510
Windows Internet Naming Service.
  See WINS
Windows kernel, 427–429
Windows Key (WinKey), 754
Windows Logon service, 429–430
Windows Marketplace, 373
Windows Media Center, 336
Windows Memory Diagnostic Tool, 481
Windows operating system, 327–360. *See*
  also operating system
   activation, 393–394
   Advanced Options menu, 469–478
   components of, 343–360
   configuring, 390–403
   editions, 329–331
   Emergency Repair Process, 482–483
   Enterprise Edition, 330, 331
   installing, 372–390
   introduction to, 328–343
   OEM Windows, 331
   overview, 333–335
   preventive maintenance, 507–513
   product ID, 379
   product key, 380–381, 390, 393
   reactivation, 393–394
   Recovery Console, 479–480
   registration, 393–394
   Safe Mode option, 470–473, 476,
     477, 776, 786
   startup process. *See* Windows startup
   system requirements, 335–336
   System Restore utility, 399, 476–478,
     481, 512–513
   troubleshooting. *See* troubleshooting
   updates. *See* updates
   upgrades. *See* upgrades
   user interface, 343–355
   versions, 329, 333
   viewing information about, 333
   workgroups, 379, 503, 588, 718,
     724, 753
Windows PE (Windows Preinstallation
  Environment), 385
Windows Preinstallation Environment
  (Windows PE), 385
Windows registry. *See* registry
Windows Resource Protection (WRP),
  501, 766
Windows Safe Mode, 776

Windows Security dialog box, 754
Windows Security Essentials, 775
Windows Server edition, 330
Windows Setup program, 376–391
Windows Setup Wizard, 378–383
Windows startup, 425–433. *See also*
    bootup; logging on/off
    applications, 430
    BIOS password for, 751
    BIOS/CMOS roles in, 18–19
    boot disks, 144–145, 225, 230,
        376–377
    boot media, 376–377
    BOOT.INI file, 428, 430–434
    error messages, 487
    initial startup phase, 425–426
    modifying system startup, 432–433
    options for, 225
    phases, 425–430
    power-on self-test (POST)
        phase, 425
    problems, desktops, 202, 210–211,
        217–218, 221
    problems, laptops, 303–304
    security features, 723–724
    Start Windows Normally mode, 475
    startup disks, 225, 230
    startup modes, 469–478
    startup/source locations, 376–378
    system settings, 430–434
    Windows Logon service, 429–430
Windows System Image Manager, 385
Windows Update site, 395
Windows user accounts, 722–723
Windows utilities, 452–455, 667–668
Windows Virtual PC, 340–341
Windows Vista Home Premium/Business/
    Ultimate, 335, 336
Windows Vista Starter Edition, 330
Windows Vista systems
    configuring IP settings, 642–643
    desktop, 332
    general information, 329
    migrating user data, 375–376
    upgrade paths to, 341
    Windows Easy Transfer utility,
        375–376
Windows Vista Ultimate, 334
Windows XP Files and Settings Transfer
    Wizard, 374–375
Windows XP Mode, 340
Windows XP Professional, 335, 336
Windows XP systems
    configuring IP settings, 641–642
    desktop, 331
    general information, 329
    migrating user data, 374–375
    transferring files/settings, 374–375

Windows-based systems. *See also* Windows
    operating system; *specific OS versions*
    command prompt usage in, 449–452
    compatibility issues, 336–339, 373,
        386–387
    memory limits, 334
    OEM Windows, 377–378
    service packs, 332–333, 777
    service patches, 197, 332, 777
    system information, 495
    system limits, 336
    system requirements, 335–336
    Upgrade Adviser, 337–339, 373, 386
    upgrades. *See* upgrades
WinKey (Windows Key), 754
WINLOGON.EXE file, 428, 429
WINLOGON.EXE service, 429–430
WINNT folder, 442
WINS (Windows Internet Naming
    Service), 597, 686–687
WINS Server, 597, 598, 643, 686–687
Wintel platforms, 335
wipe-and-load migration, 376
wired communications, 275–276
Wired Equivalent Privacy (WEP),
    726, 781
wireless access point (WAP)
    administrator password, 779
    channel selection, 630, 631
    configuring, 633, 637–639, 778–781
    described, 607
    disabling DHCP, 780–781
    encryption, 781, 783
    firewall, 779, 781
    firmware updates, 631–633, 779
    infrastructure setup, 635–639
    IP addresses, 780–781, 782
    MAC filtering, 779–780, 783
    setting up, 633, 637–639
    SSID issues, 633, 779, 782
    wireless client configuration,
        781–783
    wireless modes and, 633–634
wireless adapters, 69
Wireless Fidelity. *See* Wi-Fi technology
wireless local area network (WLAN), 274,
    579–580
wireless modes, 633–634
wireless networks. *See also* cellular
    networks
    ad hoc setup, 634
    Bluesnarfing, 709–710
    creating, 630–640
    distances/speeds, 631–633
    encryption for, 726–727
    hot spots, 579
    infrastructure mode, 634

interference, 312, 630–631
laptops, 274–275, 311–312,
    579–580
range extenders, 632
security, 726–727, 778–783
standards, 631, 632
troubleshooting, 311–312, 788
war driving, 709
wireless access point. *See* wireless
    access point
WLANs, 274, 579–580
wireless NICs, 630–635, 639–640,
    673–675
wireless printers, 539
wireless routers, 547, 579, 634, 637,
    778–780
wireless signal boosters, 606, 635–636, 671
wireless WAN (WWAN), 582
wiring, damaged, 305
WLAN (wireless local area network), 274,
    579–580
word processors, 442
workgroups, 379, 503, 588, 718, 724, 753
workplace safety, 804–814
World Wide Web, 649. *See also* Internet
Worldwide Interoperability for Microwave
    Access (WiMax), 582
worms, 705
WPA (Wi-Fi Protected Access), 727
WPA2 (Wi-Fi Protected Access 2),
    727, 781
WPA2 encryption, 727
WQUXGA (Wide Quad UXGA), 95
WQXGA (Wide Quad XGA), 95
WRP (Windows Resource Protection),
    501, 766
WUXGA (Wide UXGA) standard, 95
WWAN (wireless WAN), 582

XCOPY command, 450, 451
Xeon CPU models, 25
XGA (eXtended Graphics Array)
    standard, 95
XLS extension, 442

zero insertion force (ZIF) socket, 8
ZIF sockets, 138–139
ZIP extension, 442